Business-to-Business Marketing

We work with leading authors to develop the
strongest educational materials in marketing,
bringing cutting-edge thinking and best learning
practice to a global market.

Under a range of well-known imprints, including
Financial Times Prentice Hall, we craft high quality
print and electronic publications which help readers
to understand and apply their content, whether
studying or at work.

To find out more about the complete range of our
publishing, please visit us on the World Wide Web at
www.pearsoneduc.com

Business-to-Business Marketing

A Step-by-Step Guide

Ray Wright

FT Prentice Hall
FINANCIAL TIMES

An imprint of **Pearson Education**
Harlow, England • London • New York • Boston • San Francisco • Toronto • Sydney • Singapore • Hong Kong
Tokyo • Seoul • Taipei • New Delhi • Cape Town • Madrid • Mexico City • Amsterdam • Munich • Paris • Milan

Pearson Education Limited

Edinburgh Gate
Harlow
Essex CM20 2JE
England

and Associated Companies throughout the world

Visit us on the World Wide Web at
www.pearsoneduc.com

First edition 2004

© Pearson Education Limited 2004

ISBN 0 273 64647 8

British Library Cataloguing-in-Publication Data
A catalogue record for this book is available from the British Library

Library of Congress Cataloging-in-Publication Data
Wright, Ray, 1942–
    Business-to-business marketing / Ray Wright. – 1st ed.
        p. cm.
    Includes bibliographical references and index.
    ISBN 0-273-64647-8
    1. Industrial marketing.   I. Title: B2B marketing.   II. Title.
    HF5415.1263.W75 2004
    658.8'04–dc21

                                2003048260

10 9 8 7 6 5 4 3 2 1
08 07 06 05 04

Typeset in 9.25/12pt Stone Serif by 35
Printed and bound by Bell & Bain Ltd, Glasgow

The publisher's policy is to use paper manufactured from sustainable forests.

I would like to dedicate this book to my wife Barbara for showing, despite little understanding, intermittent tolerance and patience for the many hours I spent working alone on the word processor. Anything else would have been de-stabilising.

Contents

Chapter 5   Managing business products/services for strategic advantage in business-to-business markets   204

Chapter 6   Managing business marketing channels   253

Chapter 7   Pricing strategies for business markets   316

Business-to-business marketing involves one business marketing products and services to another for its own use. Abbreviated to B2B marketing, this newly emerging market and discipline has not received as much attention as business marketing to end consumers, known as B2C marketing. The appeal of everyday consumer goods such as cars, perfumes, chocolate, and fashion clothes plays a more integral role in our everyday lives; whereas we, as consumers, don't tend to think about products such as chemicals, component parts, aggregates and capital equipment in quite the same way.

Business marketing, however, has enormous hidden depths covering many more industrial and commercial transactions along the supply chain than many students and practitioners might imagine. If all interactions were considered – from raw material suppliers, agents, distributors, manufacturers, wholesalers and business buyers – then we would see that B2B markets are substantially larger and often more valuable than B2C markets and, surprisingly enough, they can be just as interesting. Since a large percentage of business and marketing students will land careers in the industrial and commercial sector, this book was written with them in mind.

☐ A book with a global approach

While books on B2B marketing have started to emerge, most texts provide a US-centric approach. This book is structured so that it appeals to the global audience, with special emphasis on the UK and Europe. The book is presented in a straight-forward, step-by-step manner that is suited to the needs of both marketing students and business and marketing practitioners. The book gives examples that constantly compare B2B and B2C marketing.

☐ Structure of the book

The book is divided into 10 chapters. Each chapter opens with Aims and Object-ives and then launches into core content. Within each chapter the reader will find real-world examples, definitions and B2B and B2C comparisons. Each time the reader encounters the icon shown on the left, go to http://booksites.net/wright for further discussion and valuable supplementary resources.

Supplement download site

As an added bonus available to both lecturers and students, access http://booksites.net/wright to find rich and diverse case studies, questions on the case studies, Internet exercises and a full hyperlinked list of the Internet sites listed in each chapter. In addition, five key points of the text will refer the reader to the website to explore in detail key aspects of B2B marketing.

Chapter 11 (Understanding Organisational Behaviour – the theory) can be downloaded from this site. This is a comprehensive and invaluable theoretical discussion of this complex and challenging area.

In addition, the supplement download site offers an Instructor's Manual, written by the author, to help facilitate learning. The guide offers teaching tips and suggestions.

☐ Acknowledgements

We are grateful to the following for permission to reproduce copyright material:

Figure 2.1, Porter's Five Forces, adapted with permission of The Free Press, a division of Simon & Schuster Adult Publishing Group, from *Competitive Advantage: Creating and Sustaining Superior Performance* (Porter, M.E.), copyright © 1985, 1998 by Michael E. Porter; Fig. 9.14, Ansoff's Matrix, reprinted by permission of *Harvard Business Review* from 'Strategies for diversification' (Ansoff, H.I.), September–October 1957, copyright © 1957 by the Harvard Business School Corporation, all rights reserved; Fig. 10.1, adapted from 'The world's most admired companies', *Fortune*, 3 March 2003, © 2003 by Time, Inc., all rights reserved; Fig. 11.4, Herzberg's Theory of Motivation, adapted from *Work and the Nature of Man*, World Publishing (Herzberg, F., 1966); Fig. 11.5, Maslow's hierarchy of Needs, adapted from *Motivation and Personality*, Addison-Wesley (Maslow, A.H., 1954); Fig. 11.9, Blake and Mouton's Managerial Grid, adapted from *The Managerial Grid*, Gulf Publishing (Blake, R.R. and Mouton, J.S., 1964). Harvard Business School Publishing for extracts adapted from "What is strategy?" by Michael E. Porter published in *Harvard Business Review*, November–December 1996, and *The Balanced Scorecard* by R. Kaplan and D. Norton, 1996; Pearson Education Limited for an extract adapted from *Human Resource Management: Issues and Strategies* by Roger Harrison published by Addison-Wesley Publishing Company, 1993; and Telegraph Group Limited for an extract adapted from "Proposals to stop ice cream giant freezing out rivals" by Robert Shrimsley published in the *Daily Telegraph* 29 January 2000 © Telegraph Group Limited 2000.

In some instances, we have been unable to trace the owners of copyright material, and we would appreciate any information that would enable us to do so.

The business marketing environment in the modern world

If you ask managers what they do, they will most likely tell you that they plan, organize, coordinate and control. Then watch what they do. Don't be surprised if you can't relate what you see to those four words.

(Henry Mintzberg)

Aims and objectives

By the end of this chapter the student should be able to:

1. Identify the meaning of business-to-business marketing and demonstrate the part it plays in both national and global markets.

2. Outline the factors that have contributed to the growth and development of these markets.

3. Identify the different types of markets and the different types of organisations that have played a part in the process.

Part 1 What is the business market?

□ Introduction

Marketing theory and concepts were originally developed in the USA before World War II and did not enter into business thinking as a compact and consistent approach in the UK and the rest of the modern world until much later. This marketing approach, however, was in the context of individuals and groups within end consumer markets and, though highly successful and widespread, did not apply to one company buying and selling to another. With the study of organisations and organisational behaviour in the 1950s and 1960s came the realisation that companies operate in significantly different ways when buying products and services than do end consumers and thus demand different marketing strategies. Of course many sales people, being at company buying level, had seen that organisational purchase and supply methods demanded a different approach and the more successful had quickly adapted, knowing that the right approach to customer satisfaction would lead to more sales and more commission. However, a consistent and integrated approach based on sound marketing principles did not surface until much later. Even now, in the new millennium decade, despite its size and importance, business-to-business marketing could still be described as the poor neighbour of consumer marketing, although this is now changing.

☐ What is the business-to-business market?

Business-to-business (B2B) markets operate at both a national and a global level. They can best be described as markets where one business markets and sells products and services for an organisation's own use or to sell on to other businesses for their own use. They exist in the commercial, not-for-profit (NFP) and government sectors. They are different from consumer markets in that the end customer is either the owner or the employee of some type of organisation buying products and services for their company rather than for individual or private use. Depending on how the market is measured, it can account for over 40 per cent of all national, international and global transactions. In terms of the amount of revenue collected, the end consumer price will be higher than intervening prices between B2B companies but if value added is taken into account then it could be three or four times larger in consumer markets. This is because for every business-to-consumer (B2C) purchase there could be many more transactions between raw material suppliers, producers, manufacturers, agents and wholesalers back 'upstream' along the supply chain (Figure 1.1).

Business-to-business compared with business-to-consumer

There are slightly different definitions of B2B or industrial marketing (as it has sometimes been known) depending on the approach taken. To save confusion we intend to compare B2B marketing with business-to-consumer marketing and use this as our definition.

Business-to-consumer

Business-to-consumer marketing can be defined as a market where organisations market and sell already finished consumer products to the end consumer. This might be direct, through a wholesaler, or as is much more likely through the retail sector. It might involve products and services sold direct to the end consumer through direct mail, door-to-door or through the internet or goods and services sold through the huge retail sector. Building services such as double glazing, clothing, financial services, farm produce and so on are all examples of products

Figure 1.1
Transactions along the supply chain

	B2B	B2B	B2B		B2C		
Raw materials →	Agent →	Supplier →	Manufacturer →	Wholesaler →	→ Retailer →	Customer	

Value added and prices increased →

and services that are purchased direct. Much more likely, however, is for the end consumers to purchase goods and services from an intermediary. The choice is monumental. It might be from a department store, a supermarket, a chain store, a convenience store or one of the many tens of thousands of independent stores. It can be purchased from the high street, a shopping arcade, a retail park, a factory village or a regional shopping centre.

So we can take as an obvious and simple example branded and packaged fast-moving consumer goods (FMCG) sold by the big supermarkets such as Tesco, Sainsbury's and Wal-Mart. These will be manufactured by a company such as Sara Lee or P&G and sold to the intermediary who will then merchandise, display and sell to the end consumer. The big brand manufacturers will in a sense thus have two target markets, the retail buyer and the end consumer. Both will be the target of an integrated marketing and promotional campaign often known as a 'push' and 'pull' approach, for the retailer, to stock and merchandise the product, and for the end consumer to purchase and repurchase the product. The important point to remember is that the marketing approaches used will be different for the two markets, a business approach to the retailer and an individual approach to the end consumer, but both will be seen in the context of a B2C market. This is because the end objective for both organisations is the sale of the product for consumer use.

Example 1.1 **Marketing in B2C markets**

Sara Lee Corporation is a global manufacturer and marketer of high-quality, brand-name products for consumers throughout the world. With headquarters in Chicago, Sara Lee has operations in 55 countries and markets products in nearly 200 nations. The corporation employs 154,900 people worldwide.

Business-to-consumer marketing, B2C definition

Business-to-consumer marketing is where one business markets products and services either to another business, i.e. a wholesaler or a retailer to sell on to the end consumer, or to the end consumer direct.

Business-to-business market defined

Business-to-business products and services can be seen as quite different. These are goods and services marketed and sold by one organisation to another organisation for its own use in some way or to be sold on to another organisation for its own use. A component part, for example a stainless steel washing drum, may go into a consumer product but it will be bought by the domestic appliance manufacturer, perhaps Whirlpool, for its own use. Similarly P&G will want to buy such things as packaging, food flavouring, vegetables, tea and coffee for its own use to go into its branded FMCG product. All can be identified as B2B products and services. In some markets suppliers sell these B2B products to other intermediaries such as agents or wholesalers before they are bought by companies such as P&G and Whirlpool. In these cases they are still seen as B2B products.

Business-to-business marketing, B2B definition

Business-to-business marketing is where one business markets products or services to another business for use in that business or to sell on to other businesses for their own use.

Throughout the book we will be comparing B2B marketing with B2C marketing. In this way we feel that the student will be better able to understand many of the differences inherent in producing goods and services and marketing to a business customer rather than the end consumer.

Example 1.2 ### Marketing in B2B

Suppliers closely connected to the Jeep markets factory will not make a vehicle's parts until it starts to move down the assembly line. Eight suppliers, including seven with plants newly built or leased for this purpose near Toledo, are delivering parts and subassemblies not only just in time but also exactly in production line sequence, with each item bearing the vehicle identification number (VIN) of the Jeep for which it was built. Half of those suppliers don't start building parts until they get electronic notification that the painted body of the Jeep for which they're intended is heading into the first assembly line workstation.

Business-to-business and business-to-consumer markets

The differences between B2B and B2C marketing will be highlighted throughout the book but it is important at this stage to clearly identify the basic differences for the sake of a clear B2B definition. As we saw earlier, our definition of B2B marketing was one organisation selling to another organisation products and/or services for own use or to sell on to other organisations for own use. So this definition will exclude selling products into retailers for onward sales to the end consumer but it will include selling products or services into the retailer for the running of that business. So selling soups into Tesco for onward sale to the end consumer is B2C but selling shelving is B2B. Selling cars into the showroom for the end consumer is B2C and selling fleet cars is B2B.

Example 1.3 ### B2B and B2C in retail markets

B2B marketing	B2C marketing
Electronic tills to Curry's	Refrigerators to Curry's
Shelving to Tesco	Confectionery to Tesco
Computer systems for own use to PC World	Computers to PC World to sell on to consumers
Display racks to Next	Fashion clothes to Next

Marketing to retail

Although a business selling finished products into the retailer to sell on to the end consumer is not classified as B2B under our definition, it should be recognised that in B2C marketing benefits wanted by the retail buyer will not necessarily be those wanted by the end consumer. For example, the retailer wants bottles of orange juice to stack onto pallets, sell well and make a decent profit, whereas the end consumer wants a bottle of orange juice to taste like oranges, be energising and contribute to a healthy lifestyle. The retailer will want to know that if a seller's products are to be stocked they will sell out within a reasonable time to the end customer. Similarly the retail buyer will want to know that products will be delivered promptly when wanted, stock taken back if found to be faulty in some way, and after-sales service undertaken efficiently if this is part of the agreement. Other factors will be different and will more readily mirror B2B than B2C. Marketing mix concerns covering price and promotion will be more like marketing mix concerns in B2B.

☐ Why business-to-business marketing?

B2B markets are clearly identified because it is important for students and practitioners to understand that the markets and customers are very different from those of B2C markets in very many ways and marketing strategies and tactics to be used will have to be different. If this fact is not realised the wrong methods might be taken and so customers and markets lost. For example, B2B markets could be said to be more complex, the buying process more intricate, the products and services offered often of a strategic nature and the sales value of each order much larger than in consumer markets. This means that an alternative approach will more often than not be needed.

Having said this there are still basic concepts that remain the same in both B2B and B2C markets. Concern for ultimate customer satisfaction, knowing the market, understanding the customer needs, realising that customers will want differing benefits, and monitoring and controlling buyer concerns will not be altered. The imperative to have a knowledge of the market and the marketing tools and techniques employed will still be used but in ways that reflect the special needs of B2B markets.

So B2B marketers will still use both primary and secondary marketing research, still need an understanding of customer behaviour and still need to develop innovative product and services, to price in an attractive manner, to match customer wants, and so on. They will still need to identify channels of distribution and to communicate and promote using realistic techniques that reach identified audiences. Similarly planning and control processes must be discussed, strategic choices made, resources garnered and programmes implemented. The whole strategic approach taken and the programmes selected and managed, however, will be different in that they must match the clearly identified needs, wants and demands of buyers and buying organisations in B2B industries.

As with B2C markets, but at a much higher level, the more demanding the customer becomes, the more sophisticated must be the marketing response if sustainable competitive advantage is to be maintained. Markets in B2B are now more likely to be international and global with suppliers expected to market and sell products and services around the world if they are to keep pace with market developments. This all calls for a detailed understanding by marketers of both the importance and the workings of B2B markets and the clear differences from B2C markets.

□ Marketing definitions

It is felt to be important at this early stage to establish clearly what we mean by marketing as there still tends to be some confusion among both students and practitioners (more enlightened readers can skip this part if they wish). In terms of fundamentals marketing is more or less the same in both consumer and business markets. This is working on the concept that making the customer continuously happy with the value and benefits offered by the company's products and services will lead to healthy business and through this to satisfactory profits. How these benefit satisfactions are achieved will differ according to the type of customer, the type of organisation and the type of market. In some markets after-sales service is important, in others innovative products, in others the use of technology, and so on. What is crucial is that the supplier keeps pace with environmental and market changes, matches or beats the competition and always keeps close to and listens to the customers' needs and wants.

Marketing is now used in every conceivable B2B and B2C market and market sector across commercial, industrial, not-for-profit and governmental markets. Charities buy B2B computer services to help organise their revenue gathering activities and they have set up charity shops to sell in B2C markets. Government departments such as social services have B2C marketing training courses on how to treat unemployment claimants and purchase office equipment from a B2B organisation. Banking corporations buy in advice from B2B consultants and sell financial retail services to the end consumer.

Of course across all these examples there are many important differences and these will be discussed again and again throughout the book. Below are some basic definitions that will be at the heart of marketing whatever the type and will be used to underpin the discussion on B2B marketing as we move from chapter to chapter.

Management definition of marketing

We can start by looking at a common definition used by, amongst others, the Chartered Institute of Marketing (www.cim.co.uk). Here marketing is seen as a management process:

Identifying, anticipating, satisfying (exceeding), customer needs and wants at a profit (or cost effectively) on both a short and long term basis.

Marketing as a philosophy

There is, however, a broader way in which the concept of marketing can be viewed and this is as an underlying business philosophy. Ultimately the enlightened and dedicated marketer would want to see marketing, that is concern for ultimate customer satisfaction, expressed throughout the organisation as a philosophy of the heart as well as the mind. Much easier said than done, an obsessive concern for the welfare of the customer should be imbued in all employees so that they truly believe this to be the correct approach and not just a mantra to be forgotten as soon as interactive customer contact begins.

> Marketing, an obsessive concern for the welfare of the customer, should permeate every action of all within the organisation.
> *Ray Wright*

Strategic definition of marketing

There is yet another way that we can understand and use the marketing concept. We can take the basic idea of achieving customer satisfaction and translate it into a higher level management concept. It is now realised by successful companies that if marketing is to be successful and concern for the customer is to permeate all organisational functions it must be adopted, given support and driven by senior management at the strategic level. Long-term customer satisfaction is too important to be left solely to salespeople on the shop floor or the sales representative in the buyer's office. Yes, it is important to smile at customers, to be pleasant, helpful and friendly. For a sales manager to follow up complaints and do what he or she says they will do is crucial to achieving buyer satisfaction, but these tactical marketing issues alone are not enough. There must be strategic support coming from the top of the organisation and this must be inherent in the strategic planning process. Organisational strategies, systems and structures, new product development, supply chain alliances, marketing research and so on should all be driven by ultimate customer demand. Only if a thorough market examination, looking at competition, markets, suppliers, publics, etc., is taken at the strategic level when developing internal resources – the marketing mix – will ultimate and lasting customer happiness be achieved. To this end we can now identify marketing as a strategic 'matching' process.

> A strategic definition sees marketing as a 'matching' process:
> Matching the resources of the organisation to the demands of the market place.
> *Ray Wright*

The internal and external environmental model

We can take the idea of strategic marketing being a 'matching' process by developing a simple model shown in Figure 1.2. The external environment can be identified under the macro (PEST) environment and the micro (SPICC) environment. The internal resources can be identified under the eight Ss and the eight Ps. The 'matching' process can then be shown in Figure 1.3.

Figure 1.2
The external environment can be defined as PEST and SPICC

☐ The macro-environment: Political/legal, Economic/demographic, Social/cultural, Technical/physical (PEST)

☐ The micro-environment: Suppliers, Publics, Intermediaries, Customers and markets, Competition (SPICC)

The resources of the organisation can be defined as the eight Ss and the eight Ps

☐ Strategy, Structure, Systems, Skills, Shared values (culture), Staffing, Style (corporate image), Sustainable competitive advantage – the eight Ss.

The eight Ss back up the marketing mix:

☐ Product, Price, Place, Promotion, People, Processes, Profit, Physical evidence – the eight Ps.

Figure 1.3
Model of business-to-business marketing as a matching process

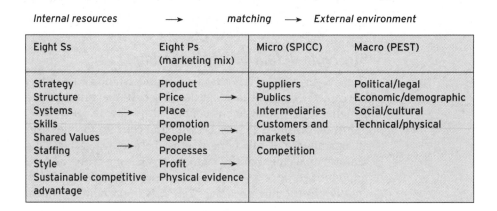

Internal resources → matching → External environment

Eight Ss	Eight Ps (marketing mix)	Micro (SPICC)	Macro (PEST)
Strategy	Product	Suppliers	Political/legal
Structure	Price →	Publics	Economic/demographic
Systems →	Place	Intermediaries	Social/cultural
Skills	Promotion →	Customers and	Technical/physical
Shared Values	People	markets	
Staffing →	Processes	Competition	
Style	Profit →		
Sustainable competitive advantage	Physical evidence		

The use of models

All models are wrong but some are useful.

(Anon.)

It should be remembered that models are not a direct reflection of reality. They are used to simplify very complex processes. They allow acronyms to be used for both memory purposes (mnemonics) and to make as certain as possible that important areas of concern are not overlooked. In the case of the model used in Figure 1.2, each area and category identified has an important part to play in the marketing process, internal resources being the eight Ss and the marketing mix and the external resources being the micro and the macro environment. In Figure 1.3 we see the model taken a step further in identifying the concept. Of course these are not arbitrary, nor are they mutually exclusive. Students and practitioners may want to develop their own acronyms and this is not a problem. We will revisit this model when we look at the planning and control process in a later chapter.

The role of the business marketing manager

Using the same type of model discussed above, we can identify the role of the B2B marketing manager under the acronym PODC. This stands for:

- ☐ **Planning and forecasting** – forecasting demand and planning the marketing effort

- ☐ **Organising and controlling** – bringing together resources, material, people, information, finance, etc. both within the marketing department and across the whole organisation for optimal customer satisfaction

- ☐ **Directing** – leadership skills, motivating, empowering, communicating, decision making; all those activities involving people

- ☐ **Controlling and evaluating** – making certain that what should happen does happen.

All these factors will surface time and again as we move through the book. It is a simple but nevertheless excellent way to remember the major responsibilities of the manager and the B2B marketer (other theoretical ways of viewing an organisation are discussed in detail in Chapter 11 on the website at http://booksites.net/wright – understanding organisation behaviour).

Example 1.4   **Brand management**

Brand management is about motivating a team of individuals to see the product almost as a close member of the family. It's the need to understand business and market trends and making sure that the brand remains relevant to the needs of organisations today and into the foreseeable future. It is about organising and coordinating everybody concerned so as to keep ahead of the game, benchmarking themselves against the competition, developing the product and creating new ones. All products have different market segments and needs and wants will change. The brand manager must control and evaluate all strategic approaches, making certain that what needs to happen happens.

☐ Growth of business-to-business markets

Most countries operating in modern developed markets (USA, Japan, Germany, UK, France, Italy, Canada) have seen their gross national product (GNP) grow at a steady rate year upon year since the turn of the century, fluctuating between 1 per cent and 10 per cent a year, giving a rough average of 2–3 per cent a year. In this way these national economies are doubling their input and output every 30–40 years. We have also seen the growth of later developing nations such as Malaysia, Thailand, Singapore, Korea and Taiwan. China is a sleeping giant with a population of 1.3 billion still waiting in the wings ready to leap onto the world stage at any time. As we embark on the new millennium, the world is increasingly interconnected by trade and financial flows. Evidence can be seen as more than US$1.5 trillion (more than the total GDP of the UK) is now exchanged in the global currency markets each day, and nearly a fifth of the goods and services produced are traded each year. This trade is valued at something like $15 trillion a year in exports and imports. Of this over two-thirds is in business-to-business value-added activities.

Throughout the book we will use the US definition of both a billion = a thousand million and a trillion = a thousand billion. These measures have now become common parlance across the world. Both UK and US measures of currency will be used despite the fact that the euro may well be in place across the EU by the time the book is published.

Example 1.5 ## China joins the World Trade Organisation

The European Commission has agreed to settle trade differences with China following the US–China breakthrough agreement over the weekend. This agreement has allowed China accession to the World Trade Organisation this year. China, the world's biggest trading nation outside the WTO, and the United States finally settled outstanding trading issues on Saturday making their entry now a certainty after 15 years of haggling. This should open up China's vast market of almost 1.3 billion consumers to the rest of the world.

Role of governments

We cannot discuss industry growth and business-to-business marketing and not be aware of the political dimensions involved. Politics is about the use (and misuse) of power in the governance of a country. In democratic countries politicians are elected to run a country for the benefit of all and will thus concern themselves with social, legal and economic matters in attempting to create the best possible environment for all to flourish. Areas of political and government involvement can have far-reaching, enormous effects on both industries and individual businesses and many of these areas will surface again and again and will be discussed in this and later chapters. In the UK, business organisations have to be aware of political intentions at national, European and international levels, as decisions made in all arenas can cause great change in both home and international markets that will have an effect on business activities.

Government ministers and business people working together

Prime ministers, presidents and department ministers will often consult with industry senior directors about both short-term and long-term economic matters. Ministers will also use the power of a particular industry regulator to try to force regulated companies to act in one way rather than another. It is not unusual for high-flying business people to be seconded to top political positions or to take part in government committees that need practical business experience.

Probably the most important decision that politicians can make is deciding on the type of economic system that would be most effective in achieving long-term peace, stability and increasing wealth for all, and the arguments for different macro-economic approaches are rehearsed below.

Example 1.6 During the UK petrol blockade in 2000 by transport owners angry at high petrol prices, many press reports appeared about Prime Minister Blair in consultation with the CEOs of the big oil companies looking for ways together to resolve the crisis. Similarly there were reports about President-elect George Bush spending time with powerful captains of US industry including the heads of General Motors, General Electric and Wal-Mart to discuss the US economy before taking office.

National governments working together

National governments now come together on a regular basis through groups like the Organisation for Economic Cooperation and Development (OECD) to work to break down barriers and increase trade with one another. Trading blocs such as the European Union (EU) and the North American Free Trade Agreement (NAFTA) have been formed to facilitate and increase business activity. Large multinational companies meet through world bodies such as the World Trade Organisation (WTO) in the hope of persuading countries around the world to ease import and export restrictions and so encourage more and more trade.

Example 1.7 **Macro-economic control**

Interest rates are one of the major ways in which a government attempts to control economic development and gain national competitive advantage. In the UK the setting of interest rates has been taken away from the politicians and given to a committee headed by the governor of the Bank of England, bringing the UK in line with the USA. In this way it is hoped that decisions here will be made on sound market economic judgements rather than political expediency. Across the European Union national currencies have, in most member countries, been made redundant and a single currency, the euro, installed. Monetary and interest rate measures on the euro are now decided by the European bank, again (hopefully) according to market needs and not because of political exigencies. At the time of writing all interest rates are low around the world and this helps business investment and encourages retail spending. However, at the time of writing interest rates are comparatively high in the UK. This and a healthy economy means that the pound is highly valued compared with other currencies, making exports high and imports low.

Anti-competitive legislation

Governments and supra-governments are bringing forth legislation at a continuous rate to restrain and eliminate anti-competitive behaviour on the part of big business and to beef up the workings of the free market economy. They are also improving and building up the ability of the customer to be the final arbiter on what constitutes product value and what products and services should and should not be produced.

The whole thrust of national, international and global political, social and economic action is geared towards ever more economic growth and B2B marketing operates within this world paradigm. All the issues identified above will be discussed in more detail as we move through the chapter.

Example 1.8   ## International trade

UK

Population: 60,094,648 (2003 est.)

GDP: Purchasing power parity – $1.52 trillion (2002 est.)

GDP – per capita: Purchasing power parity – $25,300 (2002 est.)

GDP – composition by sector: Agriculture 1.7 per cent producing 60 per cent of need; industry 25.3 per cent; services 73 per cent (2000)

Exports: $286 billion (FOB 2002). Exports – commodities: manufactured goods, fuels, chemicals, food, beverages, tobacco

Export partners: EU 58 per cent (Germany 12 per cent, France 10 per cent, Netherlands 8 per cent), USA 13 per cent (2002)

Imports: $330 billion (FOB 2002). Imports – commodities: manufactured goods, machinery, fuels, foodstuffs

Import partners: EU 53 per cent (Germany 13 per cent, France 9 per cent, Netherlands 7 per cent, Italy 5 per cent), USA 14 per cent (1998)

USA

Population: 290,342,554 (2003 est.)

GDP: Purchasing power parity – $10.4 trillion (2000 est.)

GDP – per capita: Purchasing power parity – $37,600 (2002 est.)

GDP – composition by sector: Agriculture 2 per cent; industry 18 per cent; services 80 per cent (2002)

Exports: $687 billion (FOB 2002 est.). Exports – commodities: capital goods, automobiles, industrial supplies and raw materials, consumer goods, agricultural products (7.5 per cent of GDP)

Exports – partners: Canada 23 per cent, Mexico 12 per cent, Japan 8 per cent, UK 6 per cent, Germany 4 per cent, France 3 per cent, Netherlands 3 per cent (2002)

Imports: $1.165 trillion (FOB 2002 est.). Imports – commodities: crude oil and refined petroleum products, machinery, automobiles, consumer goods, industrial raw materials, food and beverages (11.3 per cent of GDP)

Imports – partners: Canada 19 per cent, Japan 13 per cent, Mexico 10 per cent, China 8 per cent, Germany 5 per cent, UK 4 per cent, Taiwan 4 per cent (2002)

China

Population: 1,286,975,468 (2003 est.)

GDP: Purchasing power parity – $5.7 trillion (2002 est.)

GDP – per capita: Purchasing power parity – $4,400 (2002 est.)

GDP – composition by sector: Agriculture 15 per cent; industry 51 per cent; services 33.6 per cent (2001)

Exports: $325.6 billion (FOB 2002 est.). Exports – commodities: machinery and equipment, textiles and clothing, footwear, toys and sporting goods, mineral fuels, chemicals

Exports – partners: USA 22 per cent, Hong Kong 19 per cent, Japan 17 per cent, Germany, South Korea, Netherlands, UK, Singapore, Taiwan (2001)

Imports: $295 billion (FOB 2002 est.). Imports – commodities: machinery and equipment, plastics, chemicals, iron and steel, mineral fuels

Imports – partners: Japan 20 per cent, USA 12 per cent, Taiwan 12 per cent, South Korea 10 per cent, Germany, Hong Kong, Russia, Singapore (2001).

Source: CIA Factbook with permission

The pace of technology

One of the greatest challenges facing industrial organisations is the pace of new technological development. Because it seems to grow at an exponential rate it is difficult for companies to keep abreast of current usage as well as attempting to speculate what technology might and might not be crucial to maintain future competitive advantage. Mistakes now could well lead to loss of market share in later years. A huge problem facing senior managers in the modern world, that perhaps others didn't have to face to such a degree in the past, is the difficulty they might have in understanding much of the new technology. This means that they must put themselves into the hands of others (the so-called 'knowledge workers') to come up with solutions to problems. This can cause more problems as the consultants used might not understand client needs and/or might (unscrupulously?) sell unsuitable systems.

The rush into building intricate computer systems in the early 1990s, with many subsequent failures (some identified below), was repeated in early 2000 by the so-called dot.com failures. A host of businesses rapidly embraced the internet, pouring money into both their own sites and the sites of others, many without having clear, researched objectives. The list of lay-offs, liquidations and asset write-downs is now growing ever longer at the time of writing. These include Boo.com, eToys.com, Letsallbuyit.com, listen.com and beenz.com. It is reported by Webmaster.com that at least 210 large dot.com companies folded in 2000. An important lesson for marketers constantly to remember is that just because the technology is available does not mean that it will be embraced wholeheartedly by business buyers or end consumers. Going back to marketing basics, 'first ask and re-ask the customer if they would like a product or service that will incorporate the new technology'. Despite this catalogue of disasters, the need to embrace new technology in both internal and external operations in a meaningful way is paramount if competitive advantage is to be maintained.

> The role and importance of technology in B2B marketing will permeate every chapter throughout the book.

Example 1.9 ## Technology gone wrong

In 1992 the London Ambulance Service installed new systems to speed response times which failed to work and 999 callers found themselves listening to an answering machine; millions of pounds were lost. The Department of Health lost up to £100 million on a plan to computerise hospitals and the Wessex Regional Health Authority lost up to £63m on its own computer plans. The UK public spending watchdog, the National Audit Office (www.nao.gov.uk), concluded in 1996 that expenditure of £106 million on the Hospital Information Support Systems initiative (Hiss) had yielded savings of just £3.3 million, less than the £3.7 million cost of administering the scheme.

The Ministry of Defence lost about £800 million when computers for the Nimrod air defence early warning aircraft could not tell a Ferrari from a Russian MiG fighter. At the Department of Social Security, a project to computerise the handling and

Example 1.9 continued

payment of welfare benefits was nearly four times over budget and ended up cost-ing £2.6 billion. Recently large sums were lost because of a failure of a £25 million Analytical Services Statistical Information System (Assist).

It is little different in the private sector. Problems with British Gas's new £150 million billing system led to thousands of customers receiving threatening final demands before they had been sent their bills. The company's switchboards were jammed with complaints. In 1993 the Stock Exchange abandoned Taurus, its pro-posed paperless settlement system, after spending £75 million on development. The wider cost to the City may have been as much as £400 million. Book distri-bution specialist Tiptree lost its position as the British Book Awards Distributor of the Year in 1992 after installing a new warehousing system that was supposed to improve services but didn't. The Performing Rights Society, which collects royalties on behalf of publishers, record producers and bands such as Dire Straits and U2, lost more than £5 million when a new system, which was designed to save admin-istrative costs, was aborted.

It is not just UK organisations that are accident prone. In the USA $81 billion was lost in 1993 alone on failed computer schemes, according to market researchers the Standish Group. The Department of Defense, for example, introduced a faulty accounting system that sent out billions of dollars to suppliers by mistake. The department would not have known of the problem but for the fact that the bewil-dered recipients returned most of the money.

Technology adoption

However, despite the failures and the difficulties involved, both business-to-business and business-to-consumer marketing companies have adopted new technology and now use it in so many successful ways. In fact it would be impos-sible to compete at any level without the use of many of the technological innovations that have come to the market over the last decade. It is important that organisations in both B2B and B2C are very clear about the objectives of new technology adoption. All employees that might be affected in some way should discuss strategic needs. Objectives can then be agreed and suppliers approached. If there is lack of knowledge and understanding on the part of the buyer, inde-pendent expert consultants can be used to discuss with both supplier and buyer the problems that exist and the benefit solutions that are wanted. In this way, hopefully the buyer will not end up with expensive technology that seems unable to fulfil wanted needs. (The difference in usage of new technology between B2B and B2C markets is discussed in detail in the final chapter.)

New technology adoption strengths and weaknesses

The adoption of new technology can help organisations in the following ways:

☐ Improve both internal and external company performance

☐ Give added value across the whole distribution chain

☐ Reduce costs and increase profits

☐ Maintain or enhance competitive advantage

☐ Offer greater customer satisfaction.

It can fail to fulfil its promise because of the following:

☐ No clear objectives

☐ The danger of adoption without full understanding

☐ Technology seems unable to fulfil solutions wanted

☐ No clear cost/benefit analysis; little or no added value

☐ Failure to coordinate and to communicate benefits

☐ Technological potential put before customer needs.

Part 2 Characteristics of business markets

Business-to-business markets are characterised by the imperative to break down trade barriers, open all markets in the modern world to the full force of unfettered competition and by this free market paradigm increase productivity for all. At the same time there is the wish, held more strongly by some decision formers than others, that justice and environmental concerns are an inviolate part of the process. All this is happening, albeit at a slower pace than many politicians and business people would like, not only in western economies but also around the world. There is no doubt, however, that the political will is there to see that this happens, despite the backsliding by some organisations and some countries. Laws have been passed, alliances instigated and organisations formed (with more to come) at both a national and an international level, to facilitate this national, international and world vision. This is now discussed below.

☐ Harmonisation of laws in business markets

Whatever the level of government control of the economy, there will always be laws and regulations, as well as accepted codes of conduct, that companies will be expected to obey when interacting with one another. By the very nature of environmental change, laws will also alter and adapt to meet changing circumstances. To complicate matters much further companies must now be aware of laws and acceptable ways of behaving at national (UK), supranational (EU) and global level (the world). In fact the movement on a world platform is to try to standardise trading laws so that all companies work from the same legal agenda. Although it still has a long way to go, the advent of the internet, which crosses all national boundaries, has caused participants to focus on the urgency of the problem.

There is also a move across the EU, across other trading blocs and, in a more limited way, across the world to harmonise laws. The reasons here are twofold: first, because of humanitarian reasons; second, so that one country will not gain advantage by such things as longer working hours, no minimum wage level, no paternity leave, and so on. Below we can see a shortened version of the European Charter of Fundamental Human Rights now incorporated into UK law.

Example 1.10   **European Charter of Fundamental Human Rights**

The European Charter of Fundamental Human Rights seeks to give every worker the right to working conditions which respect his or her health, safety and dignity. 'Every worker has the right to limitation of maximum working hours, to daily and weekly rest periods and to an annual period of paid leave', it adds. It guarantees workers and their representatives 'information and consultation' in accordance with EU law and national law, especially worker consultation over redundancies and factory closures. The law also says that gay weddings might have to be recognised. Article 21, which bans discrimination on religious grounds, among others, is seen as a potential threat to religious schools. The Charter also prohibits reproductive cloning of human beings and making the human body and its parts a source of financial gain after an attempt to make it binding on EU member states.

National business laws

Although in many cases European law takes precedence over national law, there are far more national laws that business organisations have to operate within. Generally accepted national laws are also more likely to be tested in light of cases that have succeeded under EU law. Similarly cases might be settled in the UK courts because of the threat of long, drawn-out and expensive cases being taken to the European Courts. All the areas of law identified below will impose expensive resource implications on both B2C and B2B organisations and it is of the highest importance that managers are aware of what is happening under the legislation both at the present time and into the future. Legislation will affect every member along the supply chain, sometimes immediately and sometimes vicariously as cost and other resource implications of particular law judgements reverberate backwards and forwards from retailer to original supplier and back again. It is also important for both organisation and industry representatives to participate, in some way or other, when new legislation is being discussed or implemented. In this way they will be able to have input into the framing of new laws and so prevent or encourage aspects of the law that will have a good or bad effect on the business. The growth in laws and rules and regulations has been enormous, leading constantly to complaints by businesses about bureaucratic restrictions and red tape that have to be overcome in order to successfully run the business. It is argued that it can add highly to costs in terms of time, effort and product alterations and limitations, leading to competitive advantage being lost. Categories of the law that affect the running of the business in both B2B and B2C can all be seen in detail on the *B2B Marketing* website at www.booksites.net/wright.

European law

Individual member countries, industries and companies now have to accept not only national laws but European law as well. In many cases the EU will override UK law and may even become the last court of appeal in many industrial and other disputes. It seems inevitable that national law will merge ever closer to EU law as more and more individuals, groups and trade unions take cases to the European Court.

The European Economic Community (EEC) originally came into being in 1950 on the idea of creating a marketplace where member countries could trade with one another on a free and equal basis. This would be a market free from trade barriers such as government subsidies, different employee conditions, different trading methods, large amounts of bureaucratic red tape and so on. It was thus agreed that many national trading laws, regulations and market conditions should be harmonised so as to create 'a level playing field' where all businesses could compete on purely product and service advantages. With the development of time, more countries have joined, more difficulties have arisen and more problems have been exposed demanding more political and legal interference. This has caused much controversy within the now renamed European Union (EU), with some politicians (notably in the UK) fearful that a market federation is turning into a political 'European superstate' giving European judges more scope to intervene in British law with the subsequent loss of national sovereignty. European law associated bodies include:

☐ **European Parliament** – our elected representatives meet here; it seems not to have great power yet (http://www.europarl.eu.int)

☐ **Council of the European Union** – 15 prime ministers meet to decide strategic direction (http://ue.eu.int/en/summ.htm)

☐ **European Commission** – this is where the real power lies; 20 commissioners decide the detail of EU law (http://europa.eu.int/comm)

☐ **European Court of Justice** – this court is in Luxembourg with 15 judges upholding European Community law (http://curia.eu.int/eu/index.htm)

☐ **European Court of Human Rights** – this court is in Strasbourg. Signed in Rome on 4 November 1950, the European Convention protects the individual rights of 800 million people in 41 countries. Anyone residing in a Council of Europe member state can appeal to the European Court of Human Rights (1959) if fundamental rights are violated (http://www.echr.coe.int).

World law

There is the hope that eventually there will be political and trading law at an international level that all countries will be prepared to abide by. This is difficult enough at trading bloc level and in some cases it becomes seemingly impossible at the world level. Both politicians and practitioners alike argue that unless nations are prepared to create mutually advantageous trading arrangements, break down barriers and honour trade agreements, realistic movement will not be possible. Until countries refuse to allow irresponsible ways of working, respect patents and licences, stop piracy of all kinds and standardise ways of working together, global B2B growth will be curtailed. It is also argued that there is a moral dimension that includes treating workers in a humane way, not employing child labour and respecting the environment in the ways of working. Some commentators argue that this will never happen because when necessity demands countries will always put national interest before world interest. For whatever reasons some countries, notably the USA and China, have refused to sign up to international protocols such as the Kyoto agreements on environmental and pollution reductions and until all large influential countries agree progress will be stalled.

World law associated bodies

Most international organisations set up to help with international trading laws have been created through the offices of the United Nations (UN). The UN has its head office in New York and is concerned with world political, social, environmental and economic issues. It has representatives from 191 countries and is the only major international body that has any widespread power. Many feel that this so-called 'power' is limited and eventually contingent on the goodwill of each country occasionally to subsume individual benefits to the benefits of others. Others argue that the UN has made a real difference and countries will abide by international legislation the more the benefits become apparent.

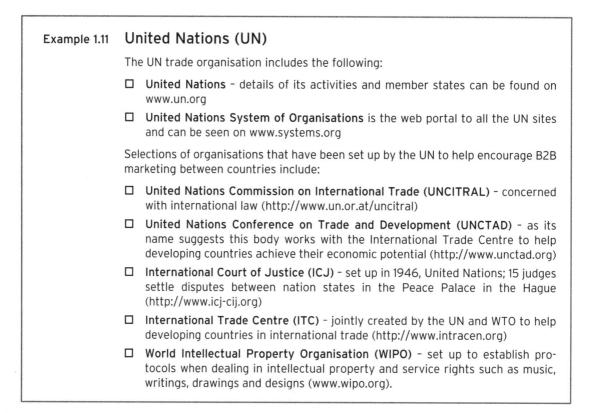

Example 1.11   **United Nations (UN)**

The UN trade organisation includes the following:

☐ **United Nations** – details of its activities and member states can be found on www.un.org

☐ **United Nations System of Organisations** is the web portal to all the UN sites and can be seen on www.systems.org

Selections of organisations that have been set up by the UN to help encourage B2B marketing between countries include:

☐ **United Nations Commission on International Trade (UNCITRAL)** – concerned with international law (http://www.un.or.at/uncitral)

☐ **United Nations Conference on Trade and Development (UNCTAD)** – as its name suggests this body works with the International Trade Centre to help developing countries achieve their economic potential (http://www.unctad.org)

☐ **International Court of Justice (ICJ)** – set up in 1946, United Nations; 15 judges settle disputes between nation states in the Peace Palace in the Hague (http://www.icj-cij.org)

☐ **International Trade Centre (ITC)** – jointly created by the UN and WTO to help developing countries in international trade (http://www.intracen.org)

☐ **World Intellectual Property Organisation (WIPO)** – set up to establish protocols when dealing in intellectual property and service rights such as music, writings, drawings and designs (www.wipo.org).

Other world trade bodies

Other important world trade bodies that have been set up to encourage free trade around the world include the following.

World Trade Organisation (WTO)

Formerly known as the General Agreement on Tariffs and Trade (GATT), the World Trade Organisation (WTO) is the global international organisation dealing with the rules and procedures of trade between nations. WTO agreements are negotiated and agreed by the majority of the world's trading nations and ratified in their parliaments. Its aims are to encourage member countries to reduce and eliminate both formal and informal barriers to trade and to help producers of goods and services, exporters and importers conduct and improve their business. At the end of 2002 it had 146 member countries that meet and negotiate on a regular basis, the last 'round' being in Cancun in Mexico in 2003 (it ended in acrimony and disagreement). Website: www.wto.org.

Organisation for Economic Cooperation and Development (OECD)

Involving the richest countries in the world, the OECD brings together 29 countries sharing the principles of the market economy, pluralist democracy and respect for human rights. The original 20 members are located in western countries of Europe and North America. Next came Japan, Australia, New Zealand and Finland. More recently, Mexico, the Czech Republic, Hungary, Poland and Korea have joined. The OECD vocation has been to build strong economies in its member countries, improve efficiency, hone market systems, expand free trade and contribute to development in industrialised as well as developing countries. After more than three decades, the OECD is moving beyond a focus on its own countries and setting its analytical sights on those countries that embrace the market economy across the whole globe. Website: www.oecd.org.

Pressure group dissenters

Both the OECD and the WTO have their pressure group dissenters who argue that these types of organisations are manipulative and exploitative of both poor people and the environment. In the past, pressure groups such as Friends of the Earth and Greenpeace have severely disrupted negotiating meetings. Interested readers can see the arguments for and against its objectives on related websites including that of the WTO.

Example 1.12   **EU and US in trade dispute**

Europe and the USA have settled their long-running dispute over banana imports, lifting the threat of sanctions against a wide range of European luxury goods including Scottish cashmere.

Pascal Lamy, the European Union trade commissioner, said yesterday that Washington had accepted a compromise formula to end the acrimonious tit-for-tat trade argument. 'After many years and many difficulties, we struck a balance between all parties', he said. The EU has been in a weak position on the issue since the World Trade Organisation ruled in 1999 that Brussels was discriminating against the United States fruit companies operating in Latin America by giving favoured treatment to banana producers in Europe's old colonies in Africa, the Caribbean, and the Pacific. The WTO ruling allowed Washington to impose retaliatory tariffs of £140 million a year on luxury goods imported from Europe. Washington threatened to hit a range of products from Scottish cashmere to lead batteries and French fashion handbags under a 'carousel' system aimed at causing maximum uncertainty and political pressure. Under the deal, the sanctions will be dropped on 1 July.

The G7-G8 group of countries

G7 started as an informal forum for leaders of the world's leading industrial democracies to discuss major economic issues. It does not have a constitution, a founding charter, a treaty or even a headquarters. It is more of a private members' club than other international bodies. Members may join only by invitation and must be a democracies and reliable major powers with a global perspective. They include the UK, France, Germany, Italy, Japan, Canada and the USA. Since 1994, Russia has been allowed to sit at the table for political discussions, thus making G8. The key difference between the G8 and other international bodies is that it is relatively small and informal. Together the G8 countries make up more than half of the world's economy, but the group is still small enough to make quick decisions. During the past decade the G7 led the transformation of Russia into a market-oriented democracy, pushed to complete the Uruguay round of multilateral trade liberalisation and create the WTO. It also made proposals to alleviate the debt of the poorest nations and has helped broker the major international conventions on climate change, biodiversity and high seas overfishing.

The G16 and G22

Set up in 2000, the G22 is a new summit of finance ministers of the G7 plus 15 other Asian, African, eastern European and Latin American nations. The G16 is the group of 16 developing countries that was set up in 1990 to build stronger links between developing countries and to address imbalances in international trade. (These types of groups are constantly evolving to meet changing global demands.)

International Monetary Fund (IMF)

The International Monetary Fund (IMF) has members from over 182 countries. Its purpose is to facilitate international trade and it is involved with exchange rates. It issues so-called special drawing rights (SDR) to help countries with balance of payment problems. It offers a wealth of information and reports about economic activity from around the world. Website: www.imf.org.

World Bank Group

The World Bank Group has members from over 180 countries. It was set up in 1945 to help distressed countries and lends capital for projects in developing countries. Website: www.worldbank.org.

☐ Barriers to trade

Barriers to trade between nations can take many forms and most are now seen as a brake on the successful growth of market economies. The political will across the modern world is to work together to improve market access for industry through the breaking down of these barriers to trade and facilitation of international trade so that markets can operate more effectively and efficiently. Tariff and non-tariff barriers include the following:

☐ Import quotas, restrictive licensing systems, export and domestic production subsidies, e.g. a country supporting its own aircraft industry with heavy subsidies. Different tax amounts, e.g. VAT and excise duties, causing products to be cheaper in one country rather than another, e.g. alcohol and cigarettes.

☐ Employee protection, e.g. it is easier for a firm to make employees redundant in the UK than in Germany.

☐ Exchange rates, e.g. fluctuating exchange rates, often because of speculation motives, can make trading between companies problematic. The euro has now replaced 12 EU currencies and more will follow.

☐ Bureaucracy and red tape, e.g. France forcing all video-recorder imports to be channelled through one town in France causing deliberate hold-ups; cultural custom and practice, e.g. refusing to buy from organisations that are not part of a known network; varying technical regulations and industrial standards, e.g. clean air car emission regulations different in Japan; fraud and corruption – standardising EU criminal law.

Example 1.13   **Trade agreements to break down barriers**

Recent trade agreements – notably the 1993 North American Free Trade Agreement (NAFTA) with Canada and Mexico, and the 1994 World Trade Organisation-Uruguay Round (WTO-UR) multilateral agreements – include commitments by member countries to eliminate or reduce their barriers to trade in agricultural and other goods. Trade barriers include tariffs (taxes on imported products), as well as many non-tariff measures that can restrict trade, including import quotas, restrictive licensing systems, export and domestic production subsidies. Prior to the NAFTA and WTO-UR agreements, these types of tariff and non-tariff barriers (NTBs) were at the centre of major disputes between countries regarding access to each other's market.

International standardisation

There is a worldwide move to attempt to standardise the ways that B2B organisations operate with one another and with governments so as to improve the activity. Different levels of technology, economic development, cultural traits, market environments and industrial policies in nations have led to disparities and inconsistencies in the development of standards. Thus, we frequently witness varying standards in different countries for the same product. Having too many different standards makes life difficult for producers and exporters. The existence of these non-harmonised standards can contribute to the so-called 'technical barriers to trade' which can partially impede the international trade flows. Therefore, there is a pressing need for the world community to agree upon the same world standards in order to help facilitate the international trading process.

Agreements on Technical Barriers to Trade tries to ensure that regulations, standards, testing and certification procedures are not used as an excuse for protectionism and do not create unnecessary obstacles. With industrial products representing an increasingly larger share of the world's total export volume, quality control to meet international standards has become a critical issue. As more developing countries are integrated into the world market, their success will depend on their ability to conform to the standards under the multilateral disciplines and internationally recognised measurement system.

International standards bodies

The International Organisation for Standardisation (ISO) (www.iso.ch) is a non-governmental organisation founded in 1947 to promote the development of standardisation in business activities. The ISO is a worldwide federation of national standards bodies with representatives from 130 countries. Its mission is 'to promote the development of standardisation and related activities in the world with a view to facilitating the international exchange of goods and services, and to developing cooperation in the spheres of intellectual, scientific, technological and economic activity'.

Standards are documented agreements containing technical specifications or other precise criteria to be used consistently as rules, guidelines, or definitions of characteristics, to ensure that materials, products, processes and services are fit for their purpose. For example, the format of the credit cards, phone cards and 'smart' cards that have become commonplace is derived from an ISO international standard. Adhering to the standard, which defines such features as an optimal thickness (0.76 mm), means that the cards can be used around the world. International standards thus contribute to making life simpler and to increasing the reliability and effectiveness of the goods and services we use. More details can be seen on the ISO website.

Trading blocs and the European Union

Trading blocs, groups of countries coming together to form mutually beneficial economic trading partnerships, have come into being around the world. Non-membership of a trading bloc will harm a country's development because membership infers beneficial trading conditions. The European Union has 15 member countries with a total market of over 370 million people. Of all UK imports and exports 60 per cent are now channelled through the EU and for UK organisations its existence is a fact of everyday life. For many B2B businesses the challenges associated with membership of the European Union now hold greatest sway. This is especially so if a company imports and exports with any of the present 15 member countries (projected to increase to 24 member countries over the next decade). Difficulties for the UK associated with membership are manifold and political argument is never out of the media. Problems include, among others, whether the UK would be better off, economically, trading as a non-member outside the EU; the loss of sovereignty over UK law-making and policy decisions; and whether to banish the pound and take on the euro (at the time of writing already adopted by 12 countries as the national currency).

Example 1.14   **European Union**

The EU was set up with the ultimate idea of having a single set of trade rules, a single tariff, and a single set of administrative procedures that would apply across one single market.

Present members: Austria, Belgium, Denmark, Finland, France, Germany, Greece, Ireland, Italy, Luxembourg, the Netherlands, Portugal, Spain, Sweden, UK

Population: 375.9 million (1999)

Example 1.14 continued

GDP: $8458.3 billion (1999)
World trade as a percentage of GDP: Imports 9.7 per cent. Exports 9.5 per cent (1999)
Imports: $818.9 billion, 18.2 per cent. Exports $804.0 billion, 19.2 per cent

EU enlargement
In March 1998 the EU formally launched the process that will make enlargement possible. It embraces the following 13 applicant countries: Bulgaria, Cyprus, Czech Republic, Estonia, Hungary, Latvia, Lithuania, Malta, Poland, Romania, Slovak Republic, Slovenia, Turkey. This will increase the population by 105 million as well as creating a need to incorporate a wealth of different histories and cultures. They are expected to be members by 2006.

European legislation

Membership of a trading bloc imposes an obligation to accept EU law and this will on occasion override national law. The laws passed will reflect both the mission of the EU to break down barriers to trade and increase economic activity and also laws that improve social and moral well-being.

B2B advantages and disadvantages of EU membership

Membership of a trading bloc can be controversial with some organisations for and some against. Some of the pros and cons are outlined below.

Advantages

- One single market with over 370 million customers
- Possibilities for scale, learning and experience economies
- The removal of both formal and informal barriers to trade
- Flexibility and free movement for goods, services, people and businesses across the whole EU
- A single currency (the euro) allowing easy cost and price comparisons to be made and payment transfers to be economically expedited.

Disadvantages

- Loss of national sovereignty over political, legal, economic and social issues
- Macro-economic decisions such as interest rate movements made centrally, not allowing individual country circumstances to be taken into account
- Restriction on trade with countries outside the EU such as the USA
- A single EU currency will not be able to reflect national needs
- Individual countries have economic and social needs that require different governmental approaches.

☐ Economic systems

All countries use resources to produce products and services for ultimate consumption by their citizens in both the private and the public sector. Economists, however, recognise that these resources are finite while citizen consumption of these resources tends to be infinite. This has lead to extreme political differences with regard to the best possible method for a country effectively and efficiently to allocate its resources in the interest of all. These differences are described below:

1. Planned economies

2. Market economies

3. Mixed economies.

Planned economy

With a planned economic approach there is some form of governmental control where macro-economic resource allocation and decisions about the products and services to produce are decided by centralised bodies. It tends to be associated with the writings of Karl Marx, the growth of Communism and authoritarian political regimes. Predictions about future supply and demand for both business and consumer products and services are translated into forward planning covering periods of five to ten years. Politicians and civil servants will attempt to forecast the country's future need for both industrial products and services (e.g. capital equipment, energy, communication services) and consumer products and services (e.g. food, automobiles, TVs) over a set period and then organise and coordinate organisations to work together to achieve forecasted targets.

Empirical evidence from around the world, however, seems to demonstrate that this planned, centralised macro-economic approach lacks the effectiveness and efficiency associated with a market economic approach where the ultimate demand and supply of products is decided by the end consumer. When the Berlin Wall was broken down and western Germany (market economy) reunited with eastern Germany (planned economy) the west German economy was shown to be ten times more productive than the east.

It can be argued that business-to-business marketing is unnecessary in a planned economy as the demand and supply of products and services is not ultimately decided by the customer (although their views might very well be taken into account) but by the decisions of the political class. Although industrial productivity might be demanded for a business to succeed, it must ultimately ingratiate itself with powerful political decision makers. Since the fall of the Russian empire at the end of the 1980s, enthusiasm for total centralised economic planning has declined and is practised by fewer and fewer countries. So we see former eastern bloc countries such as Poland, Czech Republic, Hungary, Slovenia, Estonia, Latvia, etc. rejecting planned economics and turning towards the system adopted by the so-called 'free world'. Even China, the last and most powerful of the old Communist countries, has successfully adopted free market economics in many areas of this vast and populous country, e.g. especially in Shenzhen province.

Example 1.15 **China gives private sector its blessing**

China, where private business was once illegal and even fatal, has given its constitutional blessing to the private sector, calling it 'an important component' of the socialist market economy. The constitution previously permitted the private sector to exist only as 'a complement to the socialist public economy'. From the mid-1950s until the reform process begun 20 years ago by Chinese Prime Minister Deng, capitalism was essentially illegal. Even after private businesses began to reappear in the late 1970s, entrepreneurs risked being jailed as 'profiteers' for some years. As with many reforms, businesses developed not so much because they were officially encouraged, but because they ceased to be forbidden. Until constitutional amendment in 1988, employing more than eight people was seen as criminal exploitation. The private sector has grown rapidly and now contributes 15 per cent of the gross domestic product, according to government statistics. Allowing for China's vast black and grey economies, the true figure is probably very much higher.

Planned economy pros and cons

- ☐ Allows for a balanced approach to the needs of all parts of the economy including such areas as industry, retail, health and social welfare.
- ☐ Market economies are not always effective at catering for population social needs.
- ☐ Political expediency can cause decisions to be made for short-term political gains.
- ☐ Can allow bribery and corruption to fester as contracts can be decided not on need but on the decision of a bureaucratic functionary.
- ☐ Government department bureaucracy and red tape can lead to delays.
- ☐ Economy is unable to react quickly to demand and supply alterations.
- ☐ Demand forecasting, by its very nature, can be unreliable causing unwanted products and services to be produced.

Market economy

Supporters of a market economic approach argue that a planned economic approach leads to too much national and local government interference and decisions are often made for political, bureaucratic and corrupt reasons rather than public need. Decisions about what should and should not be produced are made on long-term demand forecasts which (because forecasting is looking into an uncertain future) are often unreliable in their outcomes, causing shortages of some goods and an overabundance of others. They insist that markets will operate more effectively and efficiently if left to businesses and managers operating in the private sector and where there are many competing companies. The interplay between the demand and supply of products and services (known as the laws of supply and demand) are dictated by the needs of the consumer in a free populous marketplace where there is little or no government public sector interference (see Adam Smith, *The Wealth of Nations*, www.adamsmith.org).

So if enough consumers want digital televisions and are prepared to pay, private companies wanting to make a profit will supply at a competitive price. Conversely, if consumer demand falls for digital televisions then the market will dry up and the TV companies will either have to switch production to new researched customer needs and wants or go out of business. Similarly the same logic will apply across the production of all goods and services with end consumer needs and wants being the final arbiter on which products and services (brands) will be produced. In this way there is little waste and only goods that are needed will ultimately be produced. The theory of the free market underpins the need for marketing at all levels in business-to-business operations.

Example 1.16

The dominant concept

'Capitalism' and the idea of 'free markets' now dominates economic thinking across all developed economies. Organisations such as the G7, the World Trade Organisation (WTO) and the Organisation for Economic Cooperation and Development (OECD) now meet on a regular basis to bring down market barriers and to encourage unfettered trade between member countries.

Market economy pros and cons

☐ Allows supply and demand to be decided by end consumer needs and wants.

☐ Encourages competition to act as the driving force for efficiency, productivity and choice.

☐ Minimises economic waste, drives down costs and prices and stimulates mass demand.

☐ Business must react quickly to changing consumer needs if sales and profits are to be achieved.

☐ Short-term organisational needs can cause long-term environmental problems.

☐ It can marginalise the poor, the needy, the infirm and the less able lacking the money to purchase basic products.

☐ Goods and services can be produced for short-term customer demand and not for long-term wider social needs.

☐ A 'laissez-faire' approach (leaving well alone) can allow bribery, corruption and other self-seeking anti-competitive and anti-customer activities to flourish.

Mixed economies

In practice all market economies are mixed economies and have a combination of both planned and market driven components and in reality the differences between a planned and market economy are not as stark as described above. Government involvement in the market economy, through laws, regulations and codes of practice, has been found necessary:

1. To restrict the seemingly natural capitalistic monopoly tendency of organisations in a free market to grow ever larger by organic growth and mergers and acquisitions and in doing so lose the productivity associated with competition.

2. To protect consumers from unfair exploitation from powerful and better informed business organisations.

Mixed economy pros and cons

☐ Has the advantages inherent in a market economy whilst allowing for its excesses to be controlled by government legislation.

☐ There might be temptation for too much political interference leading to market inefficiencies.

Government involvement

The amount and level of government involvement in the free running of the market economy will vary from country to country usually depending on political considerations. Many countries now have less and less say in economic matters as they become members of large economic trading unions such as the EU, NAFTA and ASEAN and accept some form of centralised planning.

Example 1.17 **Public asset sell-off**

Prior to 1979, the UK possessed one of the largest public enterprise sectors in Europe. The Conservative government then undertook an extensive privatisation programme. Between 1979 and 1995 over £50 billion of state assets, companies in the public market sector, were sold off to the private sector because, it was argued, they would function more productively under private ownership. Organisations included British Airways, British Telecom, British Steel, Electricity, Water and Gas utilities and British Railways, as well as many administration functions. The share of employment accounted for by publicly owned industries fell from 7.2 per cent to under 2 per cent. Even goods and services in the public non-market sector such as health care, prisons, etc. could be considered marketable even if they are not at present marketed to any large extent.

Governments will also be involved, to a lesser or greater extent, in regulating the framework of the economy so that unfair advantage is not given to one over another because of some form of monopolistic situation or to ensure that customers are not manipulated or exploited. Many government and quasi-government bodies (known as quangos) such as the Competition Commission (www.competition-commission.org.uk) and the Office of Fair Trading (www.oft.org.uk) exist to regulate and oversee fair play in the marketplace. (Some of these bodies can be seen in more detail below.)

Governments also involve themselves in market activity through the amount of money they spend on such things as social welfare, health, defence, police, highways and waste management. So we see the approximate levels of government spend as a percentage of GDP at an average of 45 per cent throughout the developed countries. However, this spend can be as high as approximately 55 per cent of GDP in Sweden, 40 per cent in the UK and as low as 33 per cent in the USA. (With a projected GDP of over £900 billion in the year 2002 in the UK this amounts to approximately £360 billion.) Over the last 20 years the movement has been downward with less and less government involvement. We will discuss later in the book the importance of governments as customers as much of their spending is on purchasing business-to-business products and services.

Free market regulatory bodies

Most countries now understand the need to have regulations and have set up statutory bodies to monitor and control the interplay of supply and demand to make certain (as far as possible) that markets function in the most effective and efficient way. Below are examples of UK, EU and US statutory bodies.

Competition Commission

The Competition Commission (www.competition-commission.org.uk) is an independent public body established by the Competition Act 1998. The Commission replaced the Monopolies and Mergers Commission (MMC) on 1 April 1999. It has two basic roles:

1. It carries out inquiries into matters referred to it by the other UK competition authorities (OFT and Department of Trade and Industry) concerning monopolies, mergers and the economic regulation of utility companies. It has the power to stop activity it considers to be anti-competitive and/or abuse of a dominant marketplace position and issue fines and/or imprisonment.

2. It also has an Appeals Tribunal that hears appeals against decisions of the Director General of Fair Trading and the regulators of utilities in respect of infringements of the prohibitions contained in the Act concerning anti-competitive agreements and abuse of a dominant position.

Example 1.18 | **Interbrew – Competition Commission at work**

Interbrew, the Belgian brewer of Stella Artois, lost a quarter of its value on the European exchanges yesterday after the government blocked its unconditional £2.3 billion acquisition of the Bass brewing business. Upholding the findings of the Competition Commission, Stephen Byers, the trade secretary, ruled that the merger with Bass Brewers 'may be expected to operate against the public interest'. The Commission said the merger gives Interbrew 'between 33pc and 38pc' of the market, making it Britain's biggest brewer, leading to 'an effective duopoly' with Scottish & Newcastle.

The government said Interbrew, which argued that its market share was 32pc, must now sell Bass Brewers 'to a buyer approved by the Director General of Fair Trading [John Vickers]'. The shares, trading at Eu37.30 before the decision, immediately fell more than 20pc to Eu29, below the Eu33 float price. Most analysts believe that Mr Powell will be forced to sell, possibly at a substantial loss. One said: 'They're unlikely to get more than £1.8 billion for it. Hugo Powell has basically blown £500m and a lot of management credibility within a month of this float.'

Office of Fair Trading (OFT)

The OFT (www.oft.org.uk) exists to encourage competition, protect consumers and promote their interests. Anybody can apply direct to the OFT if they feel that an organisation is acting against the law. Its activities cover the following:

☐ Monitoring markets and offering advice

☐ Consumer information, raising standards of consumer care, unfair terms in consumer contracts

☐ Consumer credit, credit licensing

☐ Estate agents, misleading advertisements, problem traders

☐ International representation, monopolies, mergers, anti-competitive practices, resale price maintenance, restrictive trading agreements

☐ Consulting on new competition legislation, European competition law and other international liaison

☐ Other competition responsibilities as they might arise.

Example 1.19 **OFT in action**

A Scottish newspaper group has been fined more than £1.3m by the Office of Fair Trading (OFT) for trying to force a rival newspaper out of business. The OFT said Aberdeen Journals, which publishes the Press & Journal and Evening Express newspapers, deliberately incurred losses on advertising rates in an attempt to force the Aberdeen & District Independent from the market. It upheld a complaint from the Aberdeen and District Independent free newspaper that Aberdeen Journals had 'engaged in a persistent campaign of predatory conduct'.

Federal Trade Commission (FTC)

The Federal Trade Commission (FTC) (www.ftc.gov) is the US equivalent of the UK Competition Commission. It says it is working for 'consumer protection and a competitive marketplace' and again it has similar responsibilities to UK bodies with the power to fine and imprison for illegal transgressions. The FTC is fierce in its protection of free trade and in the prosecution of wrongdoers. There are, however, commentators that argue that it is selective in its judgements and has failed at times to stop violation of the competition law.

Example 1.20 **FTC powers**

The Federal Trade Commission has voted unanimously in favour of a merger between Phillips Petroleum and Conoco. The planned merger worth $15.1bn (£9.8bn) will create the third largest oil and gas company in the US. However, the approval from the US regulator was granted on condition that the two energy giants would sell refineries in Utah and Colorado and some of their operations in Missouri, Illinois, New Mexico, Texas and Washington state.

The US Federal Trade Commission (FTC) is reported to be looking into price fixing allegations made against the world's two largest commercial plane manufacturers,

Example 1.20 continued

Boeing and Airbus. Suspicion was aroused when both increased prices at the same time and by similar amounts. Large fines could result if the case is proven.

The US Federal Trade Commission has decided to prosecute the world's largest computer chip manufacturer, Intel, for allegedly abusing its microprocessor mono-poly. Intel makes the microprocessors that power four out of five PCs. It has been accused of, on the one hand, forcing its suppliers and its customers into sharing technical information and, on the other hand, withholding other technical informa-tion that might affect its monopoly market position. The company is one of two dominant companies on the PC market. The other is Microsoft, which is already facing charges of anti-competitive behaviour.

European Competition Commission

The competition law of the European Union applies within the UK although there has to be a potential effect on trade between member states before EC competition rules apply. The European Commission has primary responsibility for enforcing competition rules at this level, although private parties can rely on European law in legal proceedings in the courts in this country.

Other UK market regulatory bodies

☐ **Financial Services Authority (formerly the SIB)** (www.fsa.org.uk) – this authority will eventually be the only overall regulator of the financial ser-vices markets, absorbing all others (including IMRO, PIA and SFA).

☐ **Food Standards Agency (UK)** – an independent quango set up in 2000 to protect the consumer and to make certain that food offered for sale is of the highest standard (www.foodstandards.gov.uk).

☐ **Data Protection UK** – individuals have rights on which information can and cannot be stored in both 'hard' and 'soft' forms and all organisations must abide by legislation relating to both usage and the rights to public access (www.dataprotection.gov.uk).

☐ **National Audit Office** – the public spending watchdog that monitors all UK government body spending (www.nao.gov.uk).

Government regulators

The privatisation of former large public sector utilities and other organisations has often meant privatisation moving natural monopolies such as electricity, water, gas, telecommunications, etc. from the public to the private sector. In many cases governments will still be giving large amounts of money in the form of subsidies to these companies. In an attempt to prevent abuse of this monopoly power and avoid customer price exploitation and to bring competition into these markets, governments set up powerful regulatory bodies to oversee all relevant industries. The regulating bodies have, among other things, the power to control many areas of business activity. Examples are dictating the amount of a price increase (in some cases they can insist on price decreases), insisting on multiple company usage of distribution assets such as pipelines and cables (thus allowing companies such as Dixons and Sainsbury's to sell gas and electricity), and restricting access to certain markets. In many cases effective implementation has not been easy as these now privately owned PLCs fight to maintain market power.

Many argue, however, that this now puts too much regulatory power into the hands of too few people and there should be more political involvement.

Regulatory bodies

In the UK these bodies include the following:

- **OFTEL** is the regulator or 'watchdog' for the UK telecoms industry. It is also responsible for broadcast transmission. Its stated aim is 'for customers to get the best possible deal in terms of quality, choice and value for money'. OFTEL is a government department but independent of ministerial control. It is headed by the Director General of Telecommunications, who is appointed by the Secretary of State for Trade and Industry (www.oftel.org).

- **OFGEM** is the Office of the Gas and Electricity Markets, regulating the gas and electricity industries in Great Britain. OFGEM's stated aim is 'to bring choice and value to all gas and electricity customers by promoting competition and regulating monopolies' (www.ofgem.gov.uk).

- **OFWAT** regulates the water and sewage industry, overseeing quality, protecting customers' interests and proscribing the rate of return on capital invested by the industry companies (www.ofwat.gov.uk).

- **ORR** is the Office of the Rail Regulator (ORR), the independent government department responsible for the regulation of the railways in Great Britain (www.rail-reg.gov.uk).

- **Postcomm** – The Post Office Commissioner (www.postcomm.gov.uk).

- **OFCOM** is a new body that now regulates UK TV and radio, the Office of Communications. The five organisations that have merged to form OFCOM are OFTEL, the Radiocommunications Agency, the Radio Authority, the Independent Television Commission and the Broadcasting Standards Commission (www.ofcom.org.uk).

Example 1.21 **Powerful new government regulator**

There is a powerful new regulator on the block. The new Office of Communications, OFCOM, has been set up to replace five existing regulators, including the Independent Television Commission, the Broadcasting Standards Commission and the telecoms watchdog OFTEL. It has the enormous task of regulating broadcasting, telecoms and the internet in the UK. Questions are being asked as to whether the task is too large for one body and whether its regulatory powers will really be strong enough to control such a diverse and powerful industry.

The strengths and weaknesses of the role of the regulator will include the following:

Strengths

☐ Stops company abuse of a monopoly market position

☐ Protects the consumer

☐ Controls price and quality

☐ Limits excessive profits.

Weaknesses

☐ Reacts to short-term political and populist pressure

☐ Will not allow managers to manage according to market principles

☐ Restricts profit being ploughed back into longer term capital investment.

Ombudsman

As well as regulators many countries have a so-called Ombudsman given the power to investigate grievances that individuals and groups might have with government bodies. An example is the UK Parliamentary and Health Service Ombudsman (www.ombudsman.org.uk) who will investigate complaints free of charge with the power to award compensation where there is justification.

(All the websites identified above can be explored further for more detailed explanation on the role of the regulator and current activity.)

Part 3 Market classification

It seems that the whole world is now a potential market in which to buy and sell business products and services. The accelerated demand for industrial products and services is coming from every corner of the globe, fuelled by the increased needs of the developed, the developing, and the underdeveloped nations, the determination of governments to open up markets and the technological know-how to make it happen. Actual and potential markets have moved from regional to national and now to global markets at a rapidly increasing pace. All business-to-business companies, regardless of size, must now consider sources of supply, customers, markets and competition on a worldwide scale or risk losing competitive advantage.

For ease of understanding it is possible to classify markets by size and geographical area and this categorisation is attempted below. This process is probably more useful in B2C rather than B2B markets because it more readily reflects demographic spread and customer segments and is a useful way for retailers to break down and attack markets. In B2B, however, market boundaries are more likely to be seen as artificial by the competing participants because buyers and suppliers in a particular industry (often small in number and widely dispersed) will buy and sell one-off or repeat orders for products and services from any organisation they deem appropriate, wherever it might be. The growth in technology is enabling this to happen with increased regularity. There are differences in markets, however, and these are discussed below under the following headings: regional markets; national markets; global markets.

☐ Regional markets for industrial goods and services

Regional markets are markets that are localised within particular areas. This can be classified in terms of particular towns, counties, states, areas or regions. Small companies might only market products in regional markets, sometimes selling to only one customer. Larger companies might market products and services in regional markets as well as national or international markets. Regional markets will have particular characteristics that must be considered if business-to-business marketing is to be successful.

☐ Regional markets within countries and from country to country might well differ from one another with regard to culture and business needs, although with more uniformity these differences tend to diminish. So we find that a business in the north of England demands a different approach from one in the south.

☐ Industries sometimes have a tendency to cluster into area zones, such as shoes in Northampton, cars in Luton, electronics in Silicon Valley, etc.

☐ Government and supra-government grants, subsidies, tax breaks, etc. are sometimes available to encourage industry movements to particular areas.

☐ National markets for industrial goods and services

Most organisations start their businesses within national boundaries and as they grow and spread many expand into international and global markets. The successful company going abroad is the company that has a strong market position in the home market. This can give it associated strengths to compete when moving outside national boundaries. In the past many industries tended to stay within national boundaries because markets were more accessible and more understood, language, culture and methods of purchasing behaviour were commonplace (allowing for regional differences) and logistically problems were relatively easy to overcome.

☐ Global markets for industrial goods and services

In many cases B2B organisations have to learn to compete on the world stage if they are to gain the scale advantages associated with size and the experiences that come through competing with the best in the market. There is no doubt that the most significant trend over the last 15 to 20 years has been the development of a truly global economy. The desire of one country to trade with others has increased apace over the last five years with the realisation of the added value that this brings to national economies. There is a now a political commitment by most national governments to the encouragement of free markets and international trade encapsulated by the work of such international bodies as the World Trade Organisation, the Organisation for Economic Cooperation and Development and the World Bank (discussed above under Market Economy). Most of the top Fortune 500 world companies (www.fortune.com/fortune/fortune500) indulge in some form of international trade, either exporting products or importing and sourcing from abroad.

Global markets and trading blocs

Trading blocs were briefly touched on above when we discussed the EU. Groups of countries have found it advantageous for economic growth to come together, form an economic union and dramatically increase the size of the overall market. Within the EU trade barriers are gradually reduced, scale savings made and the law of comparative advantage used to increase productivity for all members. We have discussed the EU in some detail above but other trading blocs exist and these are identified below.

North American Free Trade Agreement (NAFTA)

NAFTA was set up in December 1994 to create a Free Trade Area of the Americas (FTAA) by the year 2005, bringing down trade barriers, bureaucracy and red tape and encouraging the free movement of goods and services between member countries. These comprise, the USA, Canada and Mexico. It will create a total market of over 400 million consumers. There is, however, some imbalance in the power relationship between members with the USA dominating with a population of 275.56 million and a GDP of some $9.255 trillion (1999). In comparison Canada has a population of 31.28 million and a GDP of $722 million (1999) and Mexico has a population of 100.35 million and a GDP of $865.5 million (1999).

Association of Southeast Asian Nations (ASEAN)

The founders of ASEAN were Indonesia, Malaysia, the Philippines, Singapore and Thailand. They came together in 1967 with the aim of cooperating in 'securing the region's peace, stability and development'. The overarching objectives were eventually to eliminate barriers between one another and encourage trade. By the year 2000 ASEAN encompassed all ten countries of Southeast Asia including Brunei Darussalam (1984), Vietnam (1995), Laos and Myanmar (1997) and Cambodia (1999).

The Asia-Pacific Economic Cooperation (APEC)

Since its inception in November 1989, the Asia-Pacific Economic Cooperation (APEC) forum has grown from an informal dialogue of 12 Pacific Rim economies to become a major regional institution that coordinates and facilitates the growing interdependence of the Asia-Pacific region. It now works to sustain and improve economic growth and the general overall well-being of the area. Today, APEC has 21 members: Australia, Brunei Darussalam, Canada, Chile, China, Hong Kong, Indonesia, Japan, Republic of Korea, Malaysia, Mexico, New Zealand, Papua New Guinea, Peru, Philippines, Russia, Singapore, Chinese Taipei, Thailand, USA and Vietnam. Annual meetings of ministers have taken place since 1989 in Canberra, Singapore, Seoul, Bangkok, Seattle, Jakarta, Osaka, Manila, Vancouver, Kuala Lumpur and Auckland.

☐ Marketing trading types

Business markets can be further classified under the type of market trading conditions:

1. Monopolies or monopsonies
2. Controlled monopoly/monopsony markets
3. Oligopoly or oligopsony markets
4. Free competition
5. Adulterated competition.

1. Market monopoly or monopsony

A market can be seen as monopolistic where one organisation in either the public or private sector dominates buying and/or selling of products and services because of market share. In the UK the definition of a market monopoly is where one company has more than 25 per cent of a particular market (a monopsony is where there is one dominant buyer). A true monopoly is where an organisation has total control of the whole market usually because of the following reasons.

Government legislation

In some cases, legislation allows no other organisation to enter, e.g. the UK public sector Post Office (www.royalmail.co.uk) is the only company allowed to distribute letters below a certain weight across Great Britain (although at the time of writing there is a lobby attempting to get this altered).

Patents, copyright, intellectual property rights

Governments will grant patents and copyright to encourage research and development and the marketing of innovative products/services/processes. This is usually for a set period of time, e.g. 20 years, to allow development costs to be recuperated. During this period no other company can copy or use the patented or copyright concept (see UK Patent Office on www.ukpats.org.uk). In some circumstances the patent owner will have built up such an enormous market share that even when others can enter the market they will be uncompetitive because of factors associated with the idea of market size, discussed below.

Example 1.22 **Microsoft accused of running a monopoly**

The US Federal Trade Commission (www.ftc.org) is fighting to break up Microsoft (the biggest computer software company in the world) as it now holds over 90 per cent of the world market in patented computer software. This is considered to be anti-competitive and against the interests of the consumer.

Access to restricted or limited supplies

There might be occasions where the supply of a particular product or service is limited because of a skill shortage, e.g. computer programmers, or the needed raw material, component or service is unobtainable, e.g. uranium or computer chips. One of the main reasons given for why the Ionica Group, a British tele-communications company, went out of business in 1999 with a loss of hundreds of millions of pounds was its inability to receive scarce component supplies for its portable telephones.

Access or control of limited distribution channels

In some cases distribution channels in markets are dominated by large companies (in both the public and private sectors) that are able to dictate which products will have market access and which will not. Large supermarkets will often only stock the number one or number two brand in the market as well as their own label. As the top five supermarkets account for over 70 per cent of the UK grocery market this policy can severely restrict manufacturer access to widespread distribution.

Market size

Large organisations with large market share are able to gain economies of scale advantages such that no other company can possibly compete on cost and price. Learning and experience curve advantages will also increase as time passes, making the situation even more impossible. If left unchecked this can encourage horizontal integration through mergers and acquisitions leading eventually to one dominant market player, no competition, a rise in prices and an eventual falling off of overall productivity (a central Marxist argument for communism and the inevitable downfall of capitalism). To prevent this situation happening governments set up such bodies as the Competition Commission and the Federal Trade Commission with the power to deny mergers and acquisitions or to demand a company break-up.

Cartels

Although now illegal in many countries and trading groups under international trading law, organisations will still collude to create monopoly (or monopsony) market conditions by restricting supply, raising prices or channelling all products through one source. In 1998 the European Competition Commission fined four British sugar companies 50 million ecu (£35.8 million) for attempting to fix sugar prices during the late 1980s. Probably the most infamous example of a cartel is the Organisation of Petroleum Exporting Countries (OPEC), so powerful that it can cause great disruption in national and world economies (www.opec.org).

Example 1.23 **OPEC**

OPEC states that it is 'an intergovernmental organisation dedicated to the stability and prosperity of the petroleum market'. There are 11 member countries currently selling more than 40 per cent of the world's oil and they possess about 78 per cent of the world's total proven crude oil reserves. This gives them the ability to restrict oil supplies or to increase prices at any given moment and in doing so severely influence world economies.

The natural monopoly model

A natural monopoly exists in an industry where a single firm can produce output such as to supply the market at a lower per unit cost than can two or more firms. The telephone industry, electricity and water supply are often cited as examples of natural monopolies. These industries face relatively high fixed cost structures. The costs necessary to produce even a small amount are high. In turn, once the initial investment has been made, the average costs decline with every unit produced. Competition in these industries is deemed socially undesirable because the existence of a large number of firms would result in needless duplication of capital equipment. The classic example might be that of two separate companies providing local water supplies, each constructing its own underground pipelines.

Theory of natural monopoly

In undergraduate textbooks you will most likely find the natural monopoly condition linked to the issue of economies of scale. Traditionally, natural monopoly is often described as a situation where one firm may realise such economies of scale that it can produce the market's desired output at an average cost which is lower than that of two firms operating smaller-scale processes.

---

2. Controlled monopoly/monopsony markets

As discussed above, many erstwhile state utilities in western countries have now been privatised but many are still in some form of monopolistic market position. In an attempt to limit this monopoly power governments set up overseeing regulators, in many cases with enormous power, to cause these companies to restrict price rises and improve quality with the ability to impose fines for poor or inadequate performance. These companies argue that they will not abuse monopoly power and that the regulator has too much power – basing pricing and product decisions on short-term, often populist, demands. UK examples were discussed above under OFTEL, OFWAT, OFGEM, ORR and Postcomm.

Vertical integration (or vertical marketing systems)

Some organisations attempt to control their markets across the whole distribution chain, from raw resource producer to end consumer presentation. In this way they hope to guarantee continuity and speed of supply, product and service quality, freely available distribution channels, economies of scale and their own customer franchise. Critics argue that this movement into disparate industries can expose management diseconomies of scale due to skill inadequacies. In many cases vertical integration might not cause the authorities anti-competitive concerns if the overall result is a distribution chain that adds real economic and customer value. But if it is felt that a monopoly situation is developing, it might well investigate. Examples of vertically integrated industries include Q8 owning oilfields, refineries, distribution and retail forecourts, and Thomson's Holiday Travel (now part of Preussag.com) owning travel agents, Lunn Poly, Britannia Airways and the Holiday Cottage Group (among many others). Thomson's has been investigated by the old Monopolies and Mergers Commission and given a clean bill of health.

3. Oligopoly or oligopsony markets

Oligopoly markets exist where two or more companies dominate the market for particular products (an oligopsony is where there are a few large buyers). This lack of widespread competition can cause the advantages and disadvantages discussed above under the heading of monopoly market share. Oligopoly strength will concern the competition authorities and they will investigate wherever necessary. It is however very difficult to prove collusion as many market practices, such as buying or selling at the same price, demanding the same credit terms, etc. come about through an unspoken sense of mutual self-advantage. In the past few years in the UK there have been investigations into brewing and pubs, oil and petrol distribution, music and CDs, supermarkets and the car industry (under the emotive heading 'Rip-off Britain'). Brewers were made to sell off either the manufacturing or the distribution side of their business and the jury is still out on the car industry. All others were given a clean bill of health.

Example 1.24 | **Monopoly and oligopoly practices – the ice cream market**

Birds Eye Wall's was last night fighting to keep its hold on the ice cream market after the Government announced measures to stop it freezing out competition. Stephen Byers, the Trade and Industry Secretary, yesterday unveiled proposals to end what he believes is the unfair grip which the company has on the £600 million market for 'impulse' ice creams – those purchased for immediate consumption. He has told Birds Eye Wall's to stop demanding shops sell only its products and to stop supplying specially designated freezer cabinets from which all rival ice creams are banned. He has also promised to clamp down on the bonus discount system and

Example 1.24 continued

sophisticated distribution network the company uses to stave off competition. Birds Eye Wall's, Mars and Nestlé comprise 86 per cent of the market and Mr Byers believes they are using their strength to crowd out independent competition. He has banned all three from negotiating new deals which prevent retailers from selling rival brands. Existing agreements would not be affected. Mr Byers said: 'These types of agreement tie the retailer to a manufacturer and restrict competition and consumer choice.' Birds Eye Wall's controls around two-thirds of the market in wrapped impulse ice cream, selling 18 of the 20 brand leaders and 45 per cent of the tub and cone market.

The commission had recommended that Birds Eye Wall's be banned from distributing impulse ice creams to all but its major national accounts, such as supermarkets. This would mean that the company would not be able to use its Wall's Direct network of telesales operators and delivery vans to distribute ice creams to retailers. Direct distribution currently accounts for around a third of Wall's sales. Critics claim that Wall's Direct is trying to kill off independent distributors and make it more difficult for rival companies to get their products to the shops. Mr Byers has also acted to end Birds Eye Wall's practice of giving discounts and bonuses and has also ordered the company to supply independent wholesalers on terms that offer a minimum discount of no less that 22.5 per cent of the retail sales value of the order.

(Daily Telegraph, October 1999)

4. Free competition

In economic terms perfect or free competition is the market situation where there are hundreds of small companies, all producing products and services that are identical or very similar and all able to leave and enter the market at will. Customers have perfect information and are able to move from company to company seeking the best value for money. In this way no one company is able to dominate, profits are minimal, and prices and terms and conditions are set by the interplay of supply and demand.

5. Adulterated or imperfect competition

Of course, in reality perfect competition will only exist (if at all) in a small amount of minority markets or for a short amount of time. Companies will always be continually looking for ways of increasing market share and company profits associated with organic growth, mergers and acquisitions, vertical integration and corporate and product differentiation (by branding, for example) and productivity efficiencies. Successful companies will always be looking to improve performance by minimising competition and they will use every possible acceptable method (and some not so acceptable) to achieve market control (often with state backing). It is the realisation that markets will not remain competitive on their own that motivates national and supranational organisations such as the Competition Commission and World Trade Organisation to attempt to regulate and negotiate to keep national and global markets open and free from stultifying anti-competitive encumbrances.

☐ B2B trading forms: organisational types

We classify organisations into different category types so as to help in understanding both the different benefits wanted and the marketing approach demanded. Six general types in three basic sectors can be identified. The differing marketing approaches will be discussed in more detail later in the book.

1. Commercial enterprises or the private sector
   ☐ Overseer regulated industry (ORI)
2. National and local government
   ☐ Quasi-autonomous, non-governmental organisations (quangos)
3. Not-for-profit organisations (NFP)
   ☐ Non-governmental agencies (NGA).

1. Commercial enterprises or the private sector

Different kinds of organisations exist in the private sector. They include public liability companies (PLCs), private companies, partnerships and single owners. It is not the intention to go into the legal definition of the different types but just to outline the basic differences between the organisations.

Public liability company (PLC)

Both business groups and individual shareholders can own public liability companies and they are set up in order to give a return to the shareholders on the capital they have invested. Shareholders are able to buy and sell their ownership shares on stock exchanges around the world. Senior managers, the chairperson or president of the company, the chief executive officer and the board of directors are employed on behalf of the shareholders to run the company in order to earn the shareholders an acceptable return on the money they have invested. In most cases they will be concerned with low costs, an acceptable profit and an acceptable return on investment for the shareholders.

Example 1.25 **World stock exchanges**

Stocks and shares in PLCs are bought and sold by institutions, commercial organisations and individuals on stock markets around the world. The hope is that in doing this money can be made. Poor performing companies will find that as their shares are sold, the price will fall, confidence will evaporate and they might find that a competitor will purchase or they might even go out of business. The following are some stock markets around the world:

☐ London Stock Exchange (www.londonstockex.co.uk)
☐ Alternative Investment Market, AIM, a global market for young and growing companies from all over the world (www.stockex.co.uk/aim)
☐ New York Stock Exchange (www.nyse.com)
☐ Japanese Stock Exchange (www.tse.or.jp/english)
☐ German Stock Exchange (www.exchange.de/) Gruppe Deutscher Borse.

Private company

A private company is similar to a PLC, as it has shareholders that put money into the company and expect some kind of financial reward in return. The main difference is that the private company's shares will not be available for sale on the stock exchange and can only be bought directly from individual or group shareholders.

Partnership

A partnership is a business in which two or more individuals carry on a continuing business for profit as co-owners. Legally, a partnership is regarded as a group of individuals rather than a single entity, although each of the partners shows their share of the profits on their individual tax returns.

A limited partnership is a partnership that is a business arrangement whereby the operation is administered by one or more general partners and funded by limited or silent partners who are legally responsible for losses based only on the amount of their investment.

The Sole trader

The Sole Trader is the simplest business form consisting of just the owner of the business. There are very few legal formalities, obligations or constraints attached to this type of ownership and only the tax man and contributions agency be notified when trading starts.

Overseer regulated industry (ORI)

Many public sector industries around the world have been privatised and sold into the private sector over the last 20 years. These include steel, water, electricity, gas, coal, airlines, railways, telecommunications, and many more. In theory they can buy and sell products in the market free from government interference. In reality this is not always the case. In most of the industries identified above an office of an independent regulator was set up at the same time as privatisation with the power to influence strategic management and marketing purchasing decisions in certain areas and at certain times.

This power to intervene varies from industry to industry depending on the terms and conditions set down at the time of inception. In many cases the regulator has the power to prevent price rises or to limit price increases within set limits. In a few cases they have the power to limit market expansion into particular business areas and/or to force the sales of strategic business units (SBU) so as to restrict and reduce monopoly power and to encourage the growth of competition. As well as statutory power the regulator can also use (and they do) both political pressure and the power of the media to get these types of companies to conduct their business activities in ways that conform. Regulating bodies were identified earlier.

Selling into the commercial sector

The overt and ultimate reason for all companies operating in the commercial B2B market is to make money for the owners of the business. This has to be the over-riding concern and will affect most purchasing decisions. Buying and selling decisions in the commercial market will be based ultimately on making both short- and long-term acceptable returns for the owners and the shareholders in the business. Increasing sales and making a profit are an obvious contribution to this happening and most commercial organisations set corporate and mar-keting objectives in these terms. This means that organisations will be buying products and services that enable them effectively, efficiently and economically to produce the products and services that will make this happen. So the driving force behind selling in this sector is the need eventually to satisfy customers with products and services that offer better solutions to problems than do the many competitors which will undoubtedly exist, the level depending on the particular market type.

Thus relationships between buyer and seller can take many forms (discussed in greater detail later), but the overriding concern will normally be eventually to make a profit and please the owners of the business. To effect this aim, commer-cial companies will want the following kinds of benefits from their suppliers:

☐ Solution benefits to identified problems

☐ Continuous knowledge and help on the right products and services

☐ Advice on future product and service developments

☐ Quickness of service

☐ Continuity of service

☐ Loyalty of service

☐ Flexibility of service

☐ After-sales service

☐ Guarantee of quality

☐ Price/cost/value.

It should also be recognised that more and more organisations want to operate within a moral and socially acceptable framework. This will usually be made apparent by the company vision/mission statement. It should therefore go without saying that the supplier must be aware of these conditions and not risk buyer wrath and cancellation of orders and contracts by, say, using child labour, paying so-called 'slave wages', or working in countries that could embarrass the business customer.

Selling into overseer regulated markets (ORM)

In theory commercial businesses operating in these markets (former public utilit-ies, railways, etc.) have the same freedom to buy and sell products as other non-overseer regulated businesses. However, in some cases purchase decisions might have to take into account the same factors which sometimes face government departments in areas that might involve political pressure, regulator pressure, media pressure and public pressure. As with all B2B marketing activity, knowledge and understanding of the customer buying and selling environment is paramount if relationships are to be successful. In this case there must be seller sensitivity to this aspect of the business on top of normal commercial pressures.

Example 1.26   **Railtrack**

The Strategic Rail Authority (SRA, www.opraf.gov.uk) document outlines plans for a safer, more punctual service and a 50 per cent increase in passengers. But the commercial company Railtrack is not capable of managing the necessary investment and should stick to the day-to-day running of the rail network, it says. The authority also calls for a more streamlined rail structure with fewer than the current 25 train operating franchises. The government has since forced Railtrack into administration and there is a debate on whether it should be returned to the private sector or run as a not-for-profit organisation.

---

2. National and local government

Governments purchase enormous amounts of B2B goods and services around the world and are usually the single biggest buyer. This will be at local, regional and national levels. The amount of spending can range from as little as 25 per cent of GDP to as much as 55 per cent of GDP depending on the country and its government policies. In monetary terms this could run into trillions of dollars depending on the level of GDP. For example, in the USA with an estimated GDP in 2000 of nearly $10 trillion, 30 per cent, nearly $3.4 trillion, is spent by the government. In the UK, with an estimated GDP in 2000 of $1.36 trillion, approximately 40 per cent, over $500 billion, is spent by the government.

Example 1.27   **Purchasing power parity**

There are difficulties when trying to compare the wealth and standard of living between one country and another. Exchange rates may seem to be the obvious and the simplest method but problems arise with currency demand and currency speculation. The simplest way to calculate purchasing power parity between two countries is to compare the price of a 'standard' good that is in fact identical across countries. Every year *The Economist* magazine publishes a lighthearted version of PPP: its 'Hamburger Index' compares the price of a McDonald's hamburger around the world and the number of hours that a person might have to work to achieve that hamburger. More sophisticated versions of PPP look at a large number of goods and services. One of the key problems is that people in different countries consume very different sets of goods and services, making it difficult to compare the purchasing power between countries.

At national level governments buy B2B goods and services for defence, social welfare, administration, education, hospitals, transport and so on. At the local level they purchase goods and services for police, ambulance and fire services, waste management, schools, road maintenance and so on according to the national/local responsibility mix. Unlike the PLC these organisations are not in business to make a profit but to provide a service to the general public.

Quasi-autonomous, non-governmental organisations (quangos)

The word quango was coined to describe quasi-autonomous, non-governmental organisations. Quangos spend taxpayers' money, are ultimately responsible to central government and are unelected. They can be local or national bodies, advisory bodies or responsible for delivering services. They operate at arm's length from government and are therefore more independent of central government than, for example, civil servants. They will still have some sort of public function but remain at arm's length from any political interference. Their purpose is to perform a non-profit-making public task with a certain level of independence.

Depending on how you define the term, quangos might include the National Consumer Council, NHS trusts, some 'Next Steps' agencies such as the Benefit Agency and Child Support Agency, or even grant maintained schools. The regulators identified above fall into this category. Spending by quangos in the UK could be as high as £50 billion depending on the definition used.

Selling into national and local government

All governments, by their very nature, have dozens of stakeholders interested in the state buying process. This will include people and organisations that use government services as well as companies that buy and sell them products and services. Government departments face different problems and different challenges from companies operating in the commercial sector, which affect the purchasing function.

National government

All government organisations and departments, whether at local, regional or national level, are under pressure from many stakeholders to behave in particular ways. Any government money spent on goods and services must be seen to be spent efficiently and effectively. At the national level ministers can (though not always) be held responsible for the action of civil servants in their department. In the UK, the minister in charge of the health service would be questioned if hospitals were buying products and/or services from a country or a company that had some sort of unpleasant reputation. Similarly, if millions of pounds were seen to be wasted by the Ministry of Defence on computer consultants, then politicians might well be in for a roasting. There can also be a temptation for politicians to interfere with purchasing decisions for political and personal benefit. It is important for suppliers to be aware that government policy might change with one political party leaving and another coming to power.

Example 1.28   ## Governments make huge purchases

The Indian government says it has agreed a price for the purchase of 66 Hawk trainer jets from Britain in a controversial deal that's believed to be worth $1.5b. A defence ministry official confirmed to the BBC that a price negotiating committee has now completed its work and that the matter will soon go before a Cabinet committee for final approval. There had been suggestions that India was considering buying a less costly Czech-built warplane. Britain has the largest trade in armaments after the USA and sells around the world (sometimes under a great deal of controversy). The UK will interfere if it feels that principles are at stake.

Government at local level

Revenue needed to run local government services is obtained both from national government revenue and through local taxation. Amounts given from the national coffers are subject to parliamentary departmental rules and pressure at local level will come from the national government passing laws and issuing orders that buying activity be performed under well-defined terms and conditions. This will include what goods and services they are allowed to buy, under which terms and conditions and from which suppliers. Suppliers might have to apply to be put on an acceptable supplier approval list before being allowed to bid for contracts. Standardised procedures are often set down covering product quality, delivery, prices and costs. In some cases a government department will define for its many buying agencies what products and services can be bought and in what numbers, and which cannot. An example here would be the health service where doctors are told what drugs they can prescribe to patients and those outside buying limits (usually branded drugs considered too expensive).

Example 1.29   ## Local government buying online

A Scottish council believes it will become the first local authority in Europe to buy all of its goods and services online. Highland Council said its education service would pioneer a new internet procurement system which will eventually be rolled out to the entire authority. Officials predict that all council goods and services will be bought electronically by 2005.

Bidding for contracts in the public sector

There are many factors to consider when bidding for contracts in the public sector. Public money is at stake and when this is the case many stakeholders have to be considered. This imposes the need for extreme vigilance on the bidding process, manifesting itself through strict rules and procedures that in most circumstances must be open to full pubic scrutiny.

Corruption

There have been examples of corruption and collusion in the giving and pricing of contracts in the public sector and the temptation will always be there when a buyer has thousands or millions of pounds to spend on government contracts. The problem of corruption is greater in some countries than in others but the move in the UK over the last 20 years has been to make the process as transparent as possible.

Example 1.30 **South African corruption case**

BAE Systems, the UK's largest defence contractor, has become the focus of allegations of bribery and corruption at a South African public inquiry into arms deals worth £3.9bn ($5.5bn). BAE is among a number of firms caught up in an inquiry into claims that senior officials in the South African government siphoned off millions of pounds from a £1.5 billion deal to supply planes to the country's airforce. The company maintains it abides by the law in whatever country it does business.

Optimum buying value

Many buying functions have been moved from an internal government function to some sort of outside agency. This might be an agency still under public ownership but given the freedom to act in an independent and autonomous manner (known as a non-governmental agency, NGA), or an agency that is sold off to private ownership. Both types of agency will have financial objectives and operate in more or less the way described above when commercial behaviour was discussed (with the NGA it will depend on the amount of autonomy given).

Another option becoming as popular with government departments as with the commercial sector is to outsource particular buying functions to organisations with specialised skills in specific areas. The argument for moving many purchasing functions to agencies outside government is to gain management skills that are developed in the commercial sector but are not developed in the public sector. It also removes politicians from having to be involved in embarrassing situations if problems arise with purchasing decisions that could affect their integrity or political position.

Compulsory competitive tendering

To overcome many of the problems identified above, pricing for UK government contracts is now mainly by compulsory competitive tendering. Every government request for products and services has to be offered to a list of preferred supplier bidders on a contracted basis. In some cases internal departments can bid against commercial contenders, but only on the same terms. The bids are usually sealed bids from suppliers setting out benefit offerings in reply to the standards set down by the civil services department. The best value for money will win the contract, often but not always the lowest price.

Private-public partnership (PPP) or private finance initiative (PFI)

In the UK over the last few years there has been the controversial (in political terms) development of the private–public partnership. This government policy invites private companies in to bid, involving anything from the building of roads, bridges and tunnels to hospitals, prisons and schools. Private suppliers put up some or all of the money and in return get the contract to run the capital project. They are either allowed to charge money for public use of the project, e.g. a tunnel or bridge toll, and/or the government pays them back as they would with a conventional loan. This could become an enormous source of work for the B2B market.

Example 1.31 **Private finance initiative (PFI)**

Two arguments are typically put forward in favour of the PFI: first, that it is a good way of financing expensive projects that might otherwise not be undertaken; second, that it offers better value for money than purely publicly funded endeavours. The theory is that private money brings with it better management plus greater incentives to finish projects on time and within budget. Some also argue that it is well worth it to bring capital into public projects which otherwise might not be available because of constraints on the public purse. However, others dispute that logic, arguing that it is just an accounting device. The government asks the private sector to put up the money and then pays it back through annual charges. The taxpayer still pays the bill and the government could borrow the money more cheaply on private capital markets itself.

Public–private partnerships take many forms:

☐ *Design build finance (DBF)* – a company will design and pay for a project such as a hospital or prison, but not run it.

☐ *Design build finance operate (DBFO)* – the most common form of PPP in which a private company will design and finance the project and be involved in the day-to-day running of the completed project.

☐ *Design build guarantee operate (DBGO)* – PFI model in which a financial institution will guarantee the completion of a project on time and to budget.

☐ *Local strategic partnership (LSP)* – a single body that brings together public and private bodies to tackle local issues such as housing, crime or education.

Political policies

All political parties have an agenda with some parts that are similar to and others different from those of other political parties. This will then affect economic policies and legal considerations when one government is voted out of office and another voted in, which in turn percolates down and eventually has an effect on both national and local government departmental purchasing policies. So in the extreme a company may have a large government contract one moment only to find that it is not to be renewed the next. In some cases this can mean the end of the selling company, depending on the contribution of the contract to its revenue.

Social policies

Governments also have social policies that will affect services such as health and social security. Again, any change in policy for whatever reason can have catastrophic effects on the level and source of purchases. Governments also often insist that suppliers operate and behave in socially acceptable ways if they are deemed fit to do business with. This will cover the supplier's internal and external ways of behaving in the production of products and services. The issues might concern internal organisational areas such as health and safety, pay levels and hygiene and external concerns such as how the supplier treats the physical environment and interacts with the local community. These ways of behaving will be set out in some kind of guidelines and regulations that the supplier has to sign up to when applying for supplier status.

Example 1.32   ## Government stakeholders influencing the buying process

There will always be stakeholder groups with more influence than others and the power to influence purchasing decisions will be based on this level of power. Stakeholders include the following: politicians, pressure groups, service providers, general public, policymakers, interest groups, financiers, trade unions, administrators or civil servants, service users, and media.

Departmental and administrative policies

Because of all the stakeholders with an interest in how government purchasing departments do business they tend to operate in very formal and bureaucratic ways, following clear, rigorous codes of conduct and rules of business. This is because they must be seen to be effective and efficient and not be open to any charge of wasting public money. Political and social pressures will always affect the purchase of goods and services by government departments and this might well vary from department to department. So there might be one policy and procedure in the defence department and another in social security. Individual buyers might well interpret the policies differently, which puts the onus on the supplier to learn and understand the thinking behind all purchase decisions in the public sector.

Example 1.33   ## A matter of policy

French chickenburgers were withdrawn from school meals in a local education authority. Devon County Council took the chickenburgers off the menu until representatives could meet local farmers to discuss the council's purchasing policy. The decision follows a demonstration by local farmers in Exeter against the importation of French meats and their use by the local authority in school meals. 'We want all government and local authority food tendering applications to specify that production techniques meet British standards before the supplier is even considered, no matter how competitive the price,' said the deputy chairman of the National Farmers' Union in Devon.

B2B marketing in the government sector

Marketing and selling in the government sector are similar to those in the commercial sector in that they have to be more professional than they were in the past. Apart from this, civil service buying activities are different in many ways including the following:

☐ There are many stakeholders able to influence the buying decisions.

☐ Openness and accountability for all to see and comment on decisions.

☐ The need for purchasing decisions to be seen to be scrupulously fair, with no hint of corruption.

☐ There should be meritocratic systems for internal employee and external buyer appointment and performance evaluation.

☐ Governance and functional structures in ministries and agencies constantly reviewed by the Public Audit office as well as other independent bodies.

☐ Complex decision-making unit.

☐ There are often bureaucratic processes and procedures to overcome.

☐ Policies and procedures can alter with change of government policies and laws or change of government.

☐ Some functions now decentralised, quasi-autonomous or put into the private sector.

☐ Must first become a preferred buyer.

☐ Supplier must be able to demonstrate integrity in the way it undertakes its business.

☐ Products and services offered should have laid-down quality standards.

☐ Usually involves a sealed bidding process.

3. Not-for-profit organisations (NFP)

Not-for-profit (NFP) organisations are, as the term suggests, in business for reasons other than making a profit. Of course that will not mean that they cannot garner a return on investments but as the NFP organisation does not have any shareholders, this will not be returned to shareholders as a dividend but used to reinvest or spent to achieve its not-for-profit goals.

Example 1.34 **Not-for-profit**

Most not-for-profit organisations, provident and mutual groups, associations, foundations and trusts, schools, medical centres, etc. will register for charitable status if they can. In the UK at the end of the year 2000 there were over 160,000 main charities registered with the Charity Commission with a total annual income of £24.5 billion. Two-thirds of registered charities have an income of under £10,000, less than 2 per cent of the total, whilst the largest 5 per cent have 90 per cent of the income. The largest 336 charities (only 0.21 per cent of those on the register) attract approximately 42 per cent of the total annual income. Any organisation can register for charitable status (and they do at the rate of a thousand a month) as long as its objectives are not to make a profit for shareholders or owners but to plough resources into work considered to benefit the community, or some section of it, through: 'the relief of poverty or sickness or the needs of the aged, the advancement of education, the advancement of religion, or other purposes beneficial to the community' (UK Charities Act 1993).

Organisations register for charitable status because of the tax benefits available on income earned and monies spent. Organisations involved in social, cultural, environmental, animal welfare, religious, artistic, sporting, education, health, youth and community activities are all examples of registered charities. NFP organisation classifications include:

☐ Charities, most NFP organisations can apply

☐ Member associations such as trade unions

☐ Member trade associations such as Institute of Practitioners in Advertising (IPA)

☐ Single issue representative pressure groups such as Greenpeace

☐ Interest groups such as NCPCC and RSPCA

☐ Mutual societies such as Nationwide Building Society

☐ Trusts and foundations such as BUPA and Welcome.

Non-government agencies (NGA)

Increasingly we have seen the use of the 'non-governmental agency' or NGA to describe a certain kind of not-for-profit organisation. The World Bank defines non-government organisations (NGOs) as 'private organisations that pursue activities to relieve suffering, promote the interests of the poor, protect the environment, provide basic social services, or undertake community development'. In wider usage, the term NGO can be applied to any non-profit organisation which is independent from government. NGOs are typically value-based organisations that depend, in whole or in part, on charitable donations and voluntary service. Although the NGO sector has become increasingly professionalised over the last two decades, principles of altruism and voluntarism remain key defining characteristics.

It is now estimated that over 15 per cent of total overseas development aid is channelled through NGOs. While statistics about global numbers of NGOs are notoriously incomplete, it is currently estimated that there are somewhere between 6000 and 30,000 national NGOs in developing countries.

Building relationships

The B2B sector is also characterised by organisations cooperatively working together, especially when marketing internationally. Alliances, joint ventures and short-term working agreements share the risks and benefit all contributing members. Commercial companies work with other commercial companies back and forth along the supply chain. The private sector works in harness with the public sector, and not-for-profit organisations work with profit organisations, all finding that this symbiotic relationship adds value to their operations. Similarly B2B suppliers and buyers are more liable to build long-term interactive back and forth relationships than the B2C seller and end consumer. All these different relationships will be discussed in much more detail as we move through the chapters.

☐ B2B selling in the not-for-profit sector

The not-for-profit (NFP) sector is huge around the world and includes charitable, educational, quasi-governmental and volunteer organisations. There are over 185,000 registered charities in England and Wales alone. But charities are only part of a much wider not-for-profit sector, which includes hundreds of thousands of community organisations pursuing social objectives, such as sports and recreational clubs, and mutual bodies concerned with the interests of their members, such as self-help groups, friendly societies and cooperatives. Overall, there is a demand for businesslike management of non-profit organisations. At the same time there is resistance to equating non-profit operations with business and applying business procedures to non-profit organisations. Financial gain is not the object of charitable, educational, volunteer or even governmental agencies, and this will affect the approach taken to the buying of business goods and services.

Influences on buying behaviour in NFP

NFP organisations do not all have the same objectives but they do have the one overriding factor in common in that they are not being run to make a profit, for either the shareholders or the individual owners. They do differ, however, in that some are operated to attempt to bring in as much revenue as they can, which they then use to help good causes, while others come into being to provide help in some kind of meaningful way. They buy both services and products in the B2B market and there is a move to contract and outsource many of the functions that were once performed in-house. The real difficulty for the B2B supplying into this market is in understanding the mission and objectives of the particular NFP segment they wish to be working with. As with all marketing relationships, if the seller fails to appreciate the business of the buyer and fails to see the pressure it experiences from its customers and stakeholders, then it will find it is at a disadvantage in the competitive marketplace.

Example 1.35 | **The UK's first not-for-profit bank**

The UK's first not-for-profit bank, which will use savers' money to offer affordable loans to charities, is set to be launched later this year. The Charity Bank, instigated by the Charities Aid Foundation (www.cafonline.org), opened in September 2002. The new bank is both a registered charity and will also be regulated as a bank by the Financial Services Authority (www.fsa.gov.uk), the UK's financial regulator.

Diverse range of organisations

Such a diverse range of organisations highlights the difficulties when marketing in these sectors. Buying pressures and needs in a school will not necessarily be the same as the buying pressures and needs in a children's protection association.

Similarly an interest group like the National Society for the Prevention of Cruelty to Children (NCPCC) will have different priorities from the Royal Society for the Prevention of Cruelty to Animals (RSPCA). Member associations such as trade unions and the Automobile Association will be run on dissimilar lines to the BUPA health foundation and so on. It is therefore crucial for the supplier to have a clear idea of its target market segment and the needs and objectives that drive that segment.

Influences on buying behaviour in NFP sector

As with the government sector, NFP organisations have a range of stakeholders interested and reporting on the effective operation of the business. Many now work with partners such as the Royal Bank of Scotland and Royal National Lifeboat Institution, Co-operative Bank, Save the Children and Frizzell Bank and the Cancer Research Campaign. If stakeholders become disillusioned or upset with NFP buying behaviour they can and do switch allegiances. The competition in this sector is almost as fierce as it is in the commercial sector.

Transparent operating procedures

There are growing public demands for greater openness and accountability. In addition, the fact that many voluntary organisations receive public subsidies in one form or another such as tax relief and grants makes it all the more important that they operate in a transparent manner. NFP are not only expected to help good causes in some sort of way, but are also expected to be seen to do it without wasting money given to them by donations, contributions, grants and other revenue-raising activities. This has caused problems in the past where a charity has been condemned by sections of the public for wasting money given by volunteers by hiring a marketing consultant at a high price to increase its revenue. It seems to matter not that the exercise was shown to be a cost effective means of raising more money than would otherwise have been the case. Like government departments, NFPs must also be seen as 'whiter than white' in their dealings with suppliers, only buying from companies that have a good track record in areas such as employee safety, product development and environmental protection. It would not go down well with clients if an animal welfare foundation were seen to be working with a company involved with testing products on animals.

NFP stakeholders affecting the buying process include:

☐ Charity Commission (www.charity-commission.com)
☐ Government and other regulatory bodies
☐ Local and national government grants
☐ Grant-giving bodies like the National Lottery
☐ Marketing and promotional partners in the commercial sector
☐ Members
☐ Volunteers, collectors and carers

- ☐ Legacy and deed of covenant givers
- ☐ Corporate, group and individual revenue givers
- ☐ Other charities
- ☐ Associated pressure groups
- ☐ The media.

B2B marketing in the not-for-profit sector

B2B marketers in the NFP sector will encounter some of the problems endured by buyers in both the commercial sector and governmental markets. For example, there is the need for a level of red tape and bureaucracy perhaps being the condition of grant giving, but it will not be of the same magnitude as in the government market. Likewise a charity will be allowed to make a 'profit' (i.e. a level of revenue over costs), but will be criticised if it attacks the process as aggressively as do those in the profit-making market. Overall marketing factors to be considered will take in the following:

- ☐ The not-for-profit organisation type, its mission and its objectives
- ☐ An understanding of the differences between NFP and commercial markets
- ☐ The range of products and services offered by the NFP
- ☐ The NFP stakeholders' needs and concerns
- ☐ The pressure on the NFP to behave and work in proscribed ways
- ☐ Supplier credentials to be within acceptable limits.

Products and services bought in the NFP markets include:

- ☐ Fundraising products
- ☐ Promotional products
- ☐ Event management products
- ☐ Marketing and advertising consultancy
- ☐ Recruitment advertising
- ☐ Direct marketing/direct response
- ☐ Telemarketing/telefundraising.

> Whatever kind of market an organisation may operate in, failure to meet customer needs better than the competitors will eventually result in sales decline and failure. The centrality of the customer is as relevant in the B2B market as it is in the consumer goods market.

☐ The need to understand the behaviour of organisations

Organisational theory is based on the concept that there are many organisational forms and this will cause differing purchase behaviours in the marketplace. In many situations B2B companies will not operate like B2C companies and private companies will not operate like public companies. Similarly large, medium and small companies all have particular ways of functioning when buying B2B and B2C products and services. Understanding the way that organisations are structured and operate is much more important in B2B markets than in B2C, as all activities will involve marketing and selling to other businesses. However, B2C operations are aimed at consumers and, although the initial sale will probably be to a retailer, priority will be given to an understanding of the customer segments and the end consumer. The successful business supplier needs to understand what is going on if sales and relationships are to be initiated, grow and then be maintained on a continuous profitable basis. Every organisation, whether buying or selling, will also need to know how to use an understanding of organisational behaviour so as to maintain and improve efficiency, effectiveness and economy in all activities if competitive advantage is to be maintained. Although more problematic, this 'need to know and understand' will apply across the whole of the supply chain, especially as strategic alliances become more the norm and an important part of the business.

Understanding why people and groups do things in organisations will not change the fact that they do them, but it may enable how to understand and react in a way that modifies the behaviour. The behavioural sciences have not yet reached the predictive level of the physical sciences. However, with the help of many theories developed over the last century, we can now understand many aspects of organisational behaviour and very often explain what is happening, change what is happening and control events to the level of practical need.

> Understanding the way that organisations are structured and operate is much more important in B2B markets than in B2C as all activities will involve marketing and selling to other businesses rather than the end consumer.

 An overview of these theories can be found on the *B2B Marketing* website www.booksites.net/wright.chapter 11.

Understanding organisation behaviour

An understanding of the development of organisational buyer behaviour can lead to the following advantages:

Internally

☐ Helps predict how individuals and groups might behave.

☐ Helps senior executives and managers get the best out of people.

☐ Saves time and energy by demonstrating logically what might and might not work.

☐   Alternative approaches can be evaluated and implemented.

☐   Helps to improve internal efficiency and productivity.

Externally

☐   Allows different business cultures, at both a national and international level, to talk to one another.

☐   Enhances relationships along the whole supply chain.

☐   Enables suppliers and supply sales staff to develop customised approaches to buyers that have differing ways of behaving and operating.

☐   Encourages an all-round more professional approach to understanding internal and external environments.

☐ Summary

In this introductory chapter we discussed what is meant by business-to-business markets and and the part that they play in the economy at both national and international level, and gave definitions of both marketing and business-to-business marketing. The growth of B2B markets around the world was equated with businesses and governments working together to create circumstances that lead to the breaking down of trade barriers and the promotion of free trade among nations. The part that politicians and political issues have to play in the process was recognised, including the passing of supportive laws at national and supranational level, and the creation of the right terms and conditions and the attempt to create a 'level playing field' through standardisation.

National, supranational and world bodies were identified and the part they have to play evaluated. The growth in trading unions – European Union, North American Free Trade Agreement, and Association of Southeast Asian Nations – was examined and their functions outlined. The differences between planned, free and mixed economies were scrutinised and evaluated, leading to the conclusion that the mixed market model had been adopted by all modern economies. Market types, monopolies, oligopolies and free competition were discussed and their existence across all markets recognised. It was also recognised that markets have to be policed to ensure that organisations do not distort the free interplay of supply and demand so crucial in the success of the economy. Bodies that undertake this overseeing role were described. Finally the three industry types, commercial, public sector and not-for-profit, were identified and the basic differences highlighted.

Discussion questions

1.   Outline the differences between a business-to-business market and a business-to-consumer market. What might be the reason for the growth in B2B markets over the last 25 years?

2. Discuss why you think there is a need for government to be involved in the running of the economy. What forms do you think that this might take?

3. Discuss the main global challenges facing companies that operate in B2B markets as we move into the third millennium.

4. Discuss the relative merits of a planned market economy and a free market economy. Which methods do you think work the most effectively? Why do you think the concept of a market economy holds supreme?

5. Why might governments be forced to intervene in the running of so-called 'free markets'? Give contemporary examples of this happening.

6. Identify and discuss the different market types. Give real-life examples of each and explain why you think this is so.

7. Discuss the premise that 'marketing is less useful in B2B markets than in B2C markets'.

8. Identify the roles of the following:

   (a) The World Trade Organisation, WTO (www.wto.org)

   (b) The UK Competition Commission (www.competition-commission.org)

   (c) OFGEM, Office of the Gas and Electricity Markets (www.ofgem.gov.uk).

9. Identify the major trading blocs across the world. What is their purpose and what are the implications for B2B companies?

10. Give examples of how new technology has enabled B2B organisations to become more productive.

11. Identify the different category types of organisation that exist in the B2B market and outline the different major approaches demanded by each when selling in business-to-business products.

12. Discuss how B2B marketing might differ around the world. Give examples where problems have arisen because of the wrong approach taken.

 Visit the *B2B Marketing* website at www.booksites.net/wright for a Case Study, Questions, and an Internet Exercise for this chapter. Chapter 11 on understanding organisational behavioural theory can also be found there.

☐ Bibliography

Books

Brierty, E.G., Eckles, R.W. and Reeder, R.R. (1998) *Business Marketing*, 3rd edn. New Jersey: Simon and Schuster.

Brooks, I. and Weatherston, J. (2000) *The Business Environment – Challenges and Changes*, 2nd edn, Harlow: Pearson Education.

Chisnall, P.M. (1995) *Strategic Business Marketing*, 3rd edn. Harlow: Prentice Hall.

Ferguson, P.R. and Ferguson, G.J. (2000) *Organisations – A Strategic Perspective*. London: Macmillan.

Ford, D. (ed.) (1999) *Understanding Business Markets*. London: Academic Press.

Gross, A.C. and Banting, P.M. (1993) *Business Marketing*. Boston: Houghton Mifflin.

Gross, A.C., Banting, P.M., Meredith, L.N. and Ford, I.D. (1993) *Business Marketing*. London: Dryden Press.

Hutt, M.D. and Speh, T.W. (1998) *Business Marketing Management*, 6th edn. London: Dryden Press.

Lindgreen, L. (1996) *The World of B2B Marketing*. Harmondsworth: Penguin.

Mankiw, N.G. (1998) *Principles of Economics*. London: Dryden Press.

Moller, K. and Wilson, D. (eds) (1995) *Business Marketing: An Interaction and Network Perspective*. Boston: Kluwer. pp. 10–11.

Sloman, J. and Sutcliffe, M. (1998) *Economics for Business*. Harlow: Prentice Hall.

Turnball, P.W. (1986) *Strategies for International Industrial Marketing*. Buckingham: Croom Helm.

Wilson, D. (1999) *Organizational Marketing*. London: Thomson.

Wright, R. (2001) *Marketing: Origins, Concepts, Environment*. London: Thomson.

Journals

Appiah-Adu, K. and Blankson, C. (1998) 'Business strategy, organisational culture and market orientation', *Thunderbird International Review*, 40: 235–57.

Day, G.S. (1998) 'What does it mean to be market-driven?', *Business Strategy Review*, 9: 155–64.

Deng, G.S. and Dart, J. (1999) 'The market orientation of Chinese enterprises during a time of transition', *European Journal of Marketing*, 33: 631–55.

Deshpande, R. and Farley, J.U. (1999) 'Corporate culture and market orientation: comparing Indian and Japanese firms', *Journal of International Marketing*, 7: 111–27.

European Journal of Marketing, MCB Press, Bradford, England (www.mcb.co.uk/ejm.htm).

Industrial Marketing Management, Elsevier Science (www.elsevier.nl/homepage).

Mullich, J. and Welch, M. (1995) 'Government's buying power remains strong', *Business Marketing* July, 21–2.

 Visit www.booksites.net/wright for the Internet references for this chapter.

02

Understanding environment influences affecting organisational behaviour and markets

We are continually faced by great opportunities brilliantly disguised as insoluble problems.

(Anon.)

Aims and objectives

By the end of this chapter the student should be able to:

1. Identify and examine the wider external factors that might affect the management of the B2B organisation including the political, economic, cultural and technical factors.

2. Identify, examine and evaluate the more immediate influences on the running of a B2B organisation.

3. Examine and evaluate the nature of demand for business products and services on both a national and a global level.

Part 1   Macro-environmental factors influencing B2B organisational behaviour

☐ Introduction

All buying and selling behaviour, whether in consumer or in business-to-business markets, will be affected by environmental forces. We only have to turn on the TV or open the newspaper to see stories about environmental factors that have caused people and organisations to alter their buying and selling patterns in some way or other. Whether these be changes in the law that now make something or other illegal that had been legal in the past, or a company hit by falling share prices, all will shape and alter the way that customers and buyers act in the marketplace. We looked at the background of B2B markets in the preceding chapter and we now explore in detail more of these forces that affect the B2B market.

□ Wider environmental forces

Political influences

In the first chapter we outlined the role that political theory and politicians play in shaping the economic market structure. In modern economies the overriding paradigm is to free up markets and give the interplay between supplies and demand ever greater freedom. Company bosses now expect government policy makers to create favourable business frameworks that will allow them the freedom to run their businesses, with little or no government interference, in the most efficient and productive way, arguing with some justification that their success underpins the success of the whole economy. On the other hand small businesses and end consumer champions recognise that large global businesses have many unfair advantages because of superior power and argue for rules and regulations to redress this imbalance. Politicians at national and international level have the task of creating a framework that tries to balance out the demands of competing forces in a way that is best suited for the economic well-being of all citizens.

The growth in the European Community

We saw in Chapter 1 that a growing amount of this political control of the economy has moved from the UK to the bodies that govern and control the European Union (EU), the European Parliament, Council of Ministers and European Commission. It can be argued that more influence over the economy from EU agencies is inevitable if the stated objectives of a free trade area and a level playing field for all businesses across all countries is to be achieved. Many more challenges and opportunities will be presented to all business sectors with the expected growth in the number of countries eventually doubling the size of the 380 million market.

The growth in world bodies

Political intervention in the economy now operates at a world level as well as at a national and supranational level, through both formal and informal discussion at the highest level and modern communication methods which allow instant contact to be maintained. Although there is not yet a world parliament overseeing a world economy, the leaders of the G7 group of the world's richest countries meet on a regular basis to discuss and argue over the best ways to improve world trade and the world economy. The United Nations has agencies such as the UN Commission on International Trading Laws (UNCITRAL) that are concerned with the proper working of trade and industry. An international court for the protection of human rights was set up under the auspices of the UN, which is beginning to consider abuses by companies of human rights as part of its remit. The World Trade Organisation (WTO) meets on a regular basis to vet new membership applications (at the time of writing Vietnam is under consideration) and to discuss ways of improving world trade. As well as world bodies identified earlier, there are myriad other governmental, quasi-governmental and private groups that meet on an ad hoc and regular basis which B2B companies are able to access.

Example 2.1 **International Criminal Court**

The USA, Russia, China and Israel have refused to recognise the International Criminal Court, despite the fact that it has been ratified by 69 countries. The USA argues that it could be used against them in their role of international peacekeepers.

Laws, rules and regulations

Political control of the economy becomes apparent through formal laws and formal rules and regulations identified in Chapter 1. These spell out what organisations can and cannot do in the pursuit of revenue and profit. This will apply to organisations in both the public and private sectors. Areas discussed earlier include taxes to be paid, subsidies on offer, environmental protection demanded, employee and consumer safeguards and, recently taken into UK law, basic human rights. Companies that fall foul of the law can now expect to be tried in any number of courts at national, European and possibly world level. The real problem that businesses still face, however, is the different interpretations that still exist around the world. So what might be illegal in Sweden will still be legal in Saudi Arabia; an infringement in Thailand could be considered of small concern while the same infringement in the USA could be seen as extremely serious. The internet has compounded the problem as different countries' law courts seem able to pass judgements that could affect enterprises on the other side of the world.

Example 2.2 **Libel ruling could affect free speech**

Australia's High Court has ruled that the financial publishers Dow Jones can be sued in the Australian state of Victoria over an article that appeared on their website in the USA. Media organisations fear the ruling could unleash a flood of litigation around the world and will force them to review the content of their internet sites.

Example 2.3 **Breach of international law**

The refusal of the Court of Appeal to act on a European ruling that the Guinness Four's convictions were unfair puts the UK in breach of international law, law lords have heard. Lawyers acting for the men convicted of the Guinness shares fraud said that if the House of Lords fails to act a complaint will be made to the European Court of Human Rights. Ernest Saunders, Gerald Ronson, Anthony Parnes and Jack Lyons were convicted in 1990 of illegally boosting the price of Guinness shares four years earlier.

Political intervention

Politicians will always be tempted to intervene in the running of the economy for short-term political reasons, rather than for long-term economic success, especially at election times. So interest rates are moved up and down, taxes increased and decreased and there is more or less public spending. This can cause violent fluctuations in the economy, leading to the economic condition known as boom and bust. Economic uncertainty can cause real difficulties for businesses, creating the call for more independent agencies to take control of some of the important levers in the economy.

Independent controlling agencies

There is a realisation by many independent observers that politicians should stand back from some of these decisions and allow independent or quasi-independent agencies the right to take on responsibilities for controlling some of the factors that can influence the proper running of the economy. It is felt that certain decisions can be taken away from government and so be made for sound, long-term economic reasons rather than for short-term political gain. The Bank of England and the US Federal Reserve Bank are examples of these types of agencies that, working through a committee of experts, have the power to make decisions on interest rate changes and monetary and inflation rate control. Increasingly, the European Bank is expected to take on similar responsibilities across the EU. This is especially so since the adoption by many countries within the EU of the European currency, the euro, and the ending of own-country currencies. At the time of writing it is still uncertain whether the UK parliament will take up the euro and do away with the pound.

Example 2.4 **One of the most powerful men in the world**

Alan Greenspan, head of the US central bank the Federal Reserve which sets US interest rates, is considered by many to be one of the most powerful men in the world. His decisions impact on the biggest marketplace in the world, the New York Stock Exchange. This then reverberates around the world affecting every other stock exchange in whatever country it might be.

Pressure and interest groups

Pressure and interest group growth is the predictable result of having so many different political and administration agencies with the power to affect the well-being of so many organisations operating in the business-to-business market. Trade associations are created to take on the role of pressure groups to promote the wishes and the welfare of their members, seeking to persuade policymakers to act in ways that will be beneficial to their particular industry. Other pressure groups have come into being to counter the power of big business and in many cases they are prepared to take their protest onto the streets. They may disseminate bad publicity and encourage widespread boycotts of firms and products they consider harmful to the environment in some way. These groups can also cause pressure to be brought to companies that buy from or sell to organisations under attack.

| Example 2.5 | **Pressure group protest** |

Pressure groups, including Greenpeace, Oxfam, Friends of the Earth and the World Wildlife Fund, have condemned the world summit in Johannesburg on sustainable development as a failure that will do little for the environment or the world's poor. Protest action is planned against organisations that continue to exploit these problems in some way or other.

Trade unions

The power of the trade union movement varies from industry to industry and from country to country, but there is no doubt that in the UK membership and power have diminished over the last 25 years (from over a half to less than a third of the workforce). As economic well-being increases, so trade union membership tends to decrease as workers feel that they have less need for group protection against employer and business exploitation. Many free trade supporters argue that strong trade union membership can act as a restraint on industry and company flexibility to react to changing economic and market circumstances. Many governments have enacted trade union legislation restricting what they can and cannot do. On the other hand, where workers are in vulnerable situations, laws have been introduced to give individuals and trade unions more rights in how they might behave. In many countries around the world ethically questionable methods are still used to prevent or discourage workers banding together to present a stronger unified front.

| Example 2.6 | **Trade union repression** |

Although some countries had done more to protect workers' rights, trade union members around the world continue to be harassed, sacked or even murdered, according to a report by the International Confederation of Free Trade Unions. Below are just a few of the cases identified in the 233-page report in 2002.

☐ There were 223 cases of murdered or 'disappeared' trade unionists in 2001, 201 of them in Colombia.

☐ In China, any attempt to create a free trade union can be rewarded with huge prison sentences and even life imprisonment.

☐ In Zimbabwe, striking trade unionists were shot at. Three steelworkers were killed.

☐ In Malawi, unionists appeared to be singled out for the sack, with the state apparently unable to intervene.

☐ In Costa Rica, workers were dismissed if they tried to form a union.

☐ In the USA, it was estimated that 80 per cent of employers used consultants in anti-union campaigning.

☐ In South Korea, riot police using helicopters and bulldozers attacked strikers.

☐ In Oman, Qatar and the United Arab Emirates, all trade unions remained banned.

Business trade associations

Governments and business associations also work together to develop economic policy, sitting on joint committees and taking part in economic forums. Ministers often meet the leaders of business trade associations such as the Confederation of British Industry, CBI (www.cbi.org.uk), the Institute of Directors, IOD (www.iod.co.uk) and the International Chamber of Commerce, ICC (www.iccwbo.org) to consult on business policies. The power of business trade associations varies according to their level of political and economic influence and many now employ PR and lobbying consultants to maximise this influence. This is discussed in more detail below.

Example 2.7 **Investment guidance will reach more poor countries**

A working partnership between business and the United Nations Conference on Trade and Development to promote foreign direct investment in the world's poorest countries is to be extended after successfully completing its first stage. The first least developed countries (LDCs) to benefit from a joint ICC-UNCTAD programme are Bangladesh, Ethiopia, Mali, Mozambique and Uganda. Eight more countries are now being selected for the programme's second phase, over three years.

Investment guides to the five countries were backed by workshops in their respective capitals at which business and government experts make critical examinations of investment policy and potential. Private brainstorming sessions between business executives and government officials form part of the programme. The investment guides are directed at potential investors while the workshops are designed to increase the capacity of LDCs to bring in investors and provide them with the right conditions in which to operate. (International Chamber of Commerce website, www.iccwbo.org)

International Chamber of Commerce (ICC)

ICC is the world business organisation, the only representative body that speaks with authority on behalf of enterprises from all sectors in every part of the world. Because its member companies and associations are themselves engaged in international business, ICC has unrivalled authority in making rules that govern the conduct of business across borders. Although these rules are voluntary, they are observed in countless thousands of transactions every day and have become part of the fabric of international trade. Business leaders and experts drawn from the ICC membership establish the business stance on broad issues of trade and investment policy as well as on vital technical and sectoral subjects. These include financial services, information technologies, telecommunications, marketing ethics, the environment, transportation, competition law and intellectual property, among others.

Lobbying

The lobbying business has grown in leaps and bounds as organisations and trade associations realise how serious is the need to have people and organisations that will represent company and industry interests, either in positions of power or able to have some influence on people in positions of power. This has caused something of a stir in the UK where members of parliament and government ministers have been accused of a conflict of interests, on the one hand by representing constituents and on the other by being paid ambassadors for an industry or company.

Many specialised lobbying consultants exist to help in the process of lobbying and for a fee they will advise industries and/or companies about the best methods to use in achieving beneficial results. All trade associations and individual businesses will want to be involved when politicians and civil servants are developing new industrial laws and policies if there is the possibility that their industry, company or markets might be affected in some way. In many cases this involvement will be welcome as industry knowledge and possible reaction to new legislation could aid the process.

Increased need for lobbying

For many companies and trade associations, membership of the European Union (EU) has increased the need for lobbying because of the reams of new legislation emanating from both Strasbourg and Brussels. The Council of Ministers, the European Parliament and the European Commission all have powers to initiate, legislate or implement new laws, rules, regulations and codes of practice for businesses. There are hundreds of industry and other pressure group lobbyists permanently based in Strasbourg and Brussels making certain that their or their clients' interests are protected.

Example 2.8 ## EU legislation and the role of the lobbyist

Lobbying is especially active in Brussels where the European Commission sets down detail of any legislation and to coin a phrase, the 'devil could well be in the detail'. Without lobbying, companies might find themselves stuck with laws that might cause loss of competitive advantage. In 1999 after three years of lobbying, Cadbury's avoided having to call its milk chocolate 'Vegelate Milk' because of the high content of non-cocoa butter vegetable fats. It will now have to bear the name 'family chocolate' or 'household chocolate' when sold on the continent. Brewers managed to keep beer in pints despite all other retailers being forced to go metric. Similarly we have an official size of the condom (minimum length is to be 170 mm and the width should be 44-56 mm). 'Curly-Wurly' bars, 'Mini Eggs' and 'Strollers' were all banned from export by the EU because of gelatine content and the risk of a link between BSE and CJD.

Example 2.9 ## Role of the Association of Electrical Producers (AEP)

The association's main tasks are lobbying, responding to consultations, publicising issues, identifying problems, pursuing solutions and taking steps to increase its members' business. The funding comes from members' annual subscriptions. The

Example 2.9 continued

> AEP involves itself in parliamentary and industry organisations that take an interest in energy issues, including, for example, the Parliamentary Group for Renewable and Sustainable Energy (PRASEG). When government, opposition parties or the industry regulator are considering policy changes, they usually consult the association. Where appropriate, of course, the association initiates proposals of its own. Either way, this means there is more chance that members' interests will be taken into account by decision makers. (www.oepuk.com)

Example 2.10   ## APCO Public Relations Consultants

> APCO (www.apco.co.uk) monitors issues and develops and implements strategic lobbying campaigns that effectively influence policymakers. Armed with knowledge and in-depth experience with government institutions, it builds support for a client's cause inside the halls of Congress, parliaments, the EU, or any other governing entity. Similarly, it represents governments around the world by strategic counselling and public relations assistance.

Economic influences

The economy

Although political parties and government ministers have enormous power when running the economy of a country and dictating what moves might be good or bad for economic health, some commentators complain that too much of this power has shifted to international market speculators, global companies and supra-governmental bodies such as the EU, making total control by national government increasingly problematic. It is argued by political pundits that this is the most important area of government policy and success or failure here can decide whether people will vote for the ruling party the next time around. This can lead to short-term economic management and unhelpful periods of growth and decline as politicians manipulate the economy to try to ensure election.

The state of the economy also plays the biggest part in the success or failure of business-to-business companies and most would like to have a stable and growing economy with low inflation, low interest rates and constant exchange rates. Attempts to plan ahead when these factors are uncertain can be fraught with difficulty and at times almost impossible. Although economic growth will fluctuate by quite large amounts from country to country, on average economies (measured by GDP growth) have increased by 2 to 3 per cent a year over the last 50 years due mainly to productivity improvements and the continuous growth in new technology.

Example 2.11   ## Economic problems hit UK manufacturing

British manufacturing output registered its most serious slump since the Winter of Discontent in 1979 when figures issued by the Office for National Statistics showed that manufacturing output in June 2002 dropped 5.3 per cent compared to May 2002. Though partly explained by the World Cup and the Queen's Jubilee weekend, when many factories were shut, many economists said the underlying problem was deeper. The UK Trade and Industry Secretary admitted that the government was wrong to court dot.com companies during its first term of office and ignore the producers. She went on to say that manufacturing, as well as the new economy, should be treated as an integral part of the future if economic stability is to be maintained.

Interest rates and inflation

Imagine trying to purchase or sell products up to a year ahead when interest rates and inflation are moving in one direction or another at very high rates. In the 1980s house prices were increasing at up to 15 per cent a year and then at the end of the 1980s they plummeted, in some cases by as much as 25 per cent. Many companies went from being very successful to bankruptcy almost overnight. Even a mild recession will cut deeply into some industries, while leaving others virtually untouched. In 2003 house price inflation is once again on the move although overall price deflation could be the order of the day.

Example 2.12   ## The menace of deflation

Central banks are facing a new economic menace – deflation or constant falling prices. Although it sounds like great news for consumers, there are dangers for the economy. It has arrived in Japan, where the price of goods and services has fallen 0.8 per cent a year since 1994. When prices keep falling then income will fall and less money will be available to pay debts. The debts remain the same so extra income will be needed to pay off the debt and will not therefore be spent on consumer goods, causing a downturn in the economy.

Exchange rates

For companies that buy and sell in Europe and the rest of the world, rising or falling exchange rates can make the difference between eventual success and failure. In the UK, a strong pound will help companies that import goods and services but will be crippling for those needing to export. Similarly, a weak pound will cause the converse effect with cheaper prices for exports but more expensive imports. Although there are financial tools and techniques that enable companies to insure against heavy fluctuations in currency movements and inflation, they tend to be expensive and are only worthwhile for large companies able to buy ahead at lower rates, or companies that work on a large mark-up profit. Some B2B companies get round the problem by guaranteeing price rates for the term of the contract or by reciprocal trading and barter. Many businesses in Europe now see the solution to the problem with the coming of the single currency, with prices now being quoted in the euro rather than 15 different currencies. However the introduction of a single currency, with the loss of the home currency, still causes political problems in some countries, particularly the UK.

Example 2.13   **Exchange rate fluctuations**

Joining the euro would be strongly against Britain's economic interests, a thinktank said yesterday. While joining the currency would eliminate exchange rate fluctuations between the pound and the euro, fluctuations between the euro and the dollar could be considerable. As a global trading country, Britain carries out more than 50 per cent of its trade in the dollar area. The effect on output, employment and prices in response to exchange rate shocks could be immense. Others argue that costs of being outside the euro in terms of constant price volatility and exchange rate costs would be worse.

External cultural influences

Successful companies selling in consumer markets have long ago recognised that consumers in various parts of the world have dissimilar preferences and likes and dislikes because of social and cultural differences. They might manufacture, brand, package and promote products and services differently in Malaysia from how they would in Australia. Similarly, retailers in one country might present their merchandise in a different way from similar retailers in another because of consumer expectations.

Cultural conformity in B2C markets

Many social commentators now argue that cultural differences across the world are becoming blurred and even decreasing in some countries, especially among the young. This seems to have come about because of widespread communications, entertainment, the sale of universal products and brands, and retailers moving abroad. TV, videos, films and the internet all project common cultures and values (often western and American), common ways of behaving, living, dressing, eating and listening to the same sorts of music. You can now go to any major city in the world and order a 'Big Mac' in McDonald's, and get the same product and eat it in more or less the same ambience.

Although the degree of cultural diversity has never been so important in B2B markets as in B2C, it has nevertheless still been a necessary concern. The business world is no different and to a certain extent is even more vulnerable to pressure on conformity and standardisation. English is now accepted as a common means of business communication in many markets, as are western ways of dressing and behaving. The moves to standardise and internationalise all ways of undertaking B2B relationships, including common efficiency systems, international contract law, supply chain management, shared use of information through EDI, the internet and so on, all add to the seemingly irreversible thrust for business sameness in world marketplaces. As companies expand by joint ventures, mergers and acquisitions of foreign companies, they bring universal ways of working as well as giving employees the opportunities to live and work in company divisions elsewhere in the world. Perhaps one day there will be one general way of running a business that has been proven to be the most effective, efficient and economic and this way (with a few minor adjustments) is accepted by all businesses operating in the global market economy.

Cultural differences

Many academics and practitioners argue that cultural differences in the B2B market still exist and are important when serving different markets. For marketing managers to use their own cultural values and priorities as a frame of reference can lead to misunderstandings, confusion and lost contracts. A good example is that of Japan. As the second largest economy in the world after the USA, it is a market that many companies have wanted to enter but they have been thwarted by, among other things, the Japanese business culture.

Example 2.14 **Japanese culture**

Many Japanese cultural ways of behaving have entered the lexicon of the business world. Kaisen or 'continuous improvement', nemawashi or 'behind the scenes consensus-building' and kaban or 'producing to order, not capacity' are rooted in Zen and social and cultural ways of living inculcated since birth. Still today, Japanese people work harder and spend more hours on the job because they identify more closely with their companies than they do with their own families or themselves. They have been conditioned from ancient times to believe that being self-centred and individualistic is one of the worst of all sins, which in the west is praised as a sign of strength. They tend to act more slowly through group decision and 'nemawashi'. Foreign businessmen and politicians are often frustrated because they do not and cannot get 'straight answers', not understanding that Japanese communications operate in ways that are subtly different.

Example 2.15 **Chinese culture**

China, the biggest potential market in the world with nearly 1.3 billion people, has a culture still largely unknown to most western business people. The majority of the population speaks Mandarin, making it the most spoken language in the world. In Chinese business culture, the communist, collectivist way of thinking still prevails, even in sectors experimenting with free enterprise. Presentation materials of any kind should be only in black and white. Colours are attributed special meanings in this culture, many of them negative. Smiling is not as noticeable in China, since there is a heavy emphasis on repressing emotion. A person's reputation and social standing rests on the concept of 'saving face'. Causing embarrassment or loss of composure, even unintentionally, can be disastrous for business negotiations.

The Chinese, especially those who are older and in positions of authority, dislike being touched by strangers. Chinese will assume that the first foreigner to enter the room is head of the delegation. In Chinese business culture, humility is a virtue. Exaggerated claims are regarded with suspicion and, in most instances, will be investigated.

B2B cultural differences around the world

In Malaysia businesswomen should be sensitive to Muslim and Hindu beliefs. Consequently they should wear blouses that cover at least their upper arms with skirts that are knee length or longer. They should avoid wearing yellow because it is the colour reserved for Malaysian royalty.

South Americans generally converse in closer proximity than North Americans and the English, and it may be taken personally if you back away from someone.

In India wearing leather (including items such as belts and purses) may be considered offensive, particularly in temples. Hindus revere cows and do not use leather products. When refreshments are offered, it is customary to refuse the first offer, but to accept the second or third. To refuse any beverage will only be perceived as insult.

In Russia do not expect Russians to work after hours at weekends or during vacation periods.

Arabic is a language of hyperbole; for example, when an Egyptian says yes he may actually mean possibly.

In Thai business culture, the present is often considered more important than the distant future.

In South Africa time concepts also differ: to whites 'time is money'; to blacks 'time is what's happening'.

Technical influences

The first rule of any technology used in a business is that automation applied to an efficient operation will magnify the efficiency. The second is that automation applied to an inefficient operation will magnify the inefficiency.

(Bill Gates, quoted in Manes and Andrews, 1994)

Nobody can over-emphasise the influence that technology has had on the B2B market and organisational and individual buying behaviour. Improved technologies in telecommunications, information technology, transportation, storage and inventory handling, distribution management and financial services mean that virtually all producers, no matter what size, are now able to consider supply sources from around the world. In fact competitive advantage will be lost if this option is not taken up. Information on choice, availability and where to buy a range of products and services is now readily accessible online at the click of a mouse. In the past buyers might have spent days, weeks and months searching though catalogues, seeing manufacturers' reps, or going to trade shows around the country or around the world and still not been able to see the most suitable products at the best prices. As more information comes onto the internet, less time will need to be spent on these buying tasks. Yet better products and services will be available. Depending on the products needed sellers might now be contacted anywhere in the world. Technological developments are discussed throughout the book and in much more detail in the final chapter.

Example 2.16   ## Cars of the future – the 'Coulomb'

A high-mileage, low-pollution car built by students at the University of California will drive from Germany to Paris between September 22 and 25 as part of a competition run by tyre manufacturer Michelin to promote new technology in automobiles. The vehicle is a Mercury Sable converted to a gas-electric hybrid engine with a continuously variable transmission. An electric motor drives the wheels at lower speeds for city driving. On the highway, a 660cc gas engine provides extra power and also maintains battery charge. The batteries can also be recharged from a domestic power supply. It has an aluminium body to reduce weight with additional streamlining to reduce wind resistance. Coulomb is designed to achieve fuel economy of over 50 miles per gallon and acceleration of zero to 60 miles per hour in 11 seconds while meeting California's Super Ultra Low Emissions Vehicle (SULEV) standards. (www.Globaltechnoscan.com)

IT and closer partnerships

We discussed above how culture is changing and standardising as companies create partnerships and close ways of working together. Much of this has come about through the development of technology. We will see continuously throughout the book how technology is used in so many areas of business activity to improve performance and develop competitive advantage. For example, information technology (IT) can now make 'real time' information instantly available to all companies involved in the supply chain relationships.

The internet has been adapted to become the extranet, a closed and private internet system where all supply chain members are able to have instant access to such things as buyer inventory movements, sales figures and individual product needs. Software security firewalls are created to permit only vetted companies access to the information system, allowing immediate reaction to all types of customer needs and even allowing the seller access to buyer financial accounts so that money can be deducted at source to pay for products purchased. This development of IT has, however, brought its own problems, demanding a heavy strategic resource commitment from channel supply partners through the acquisition of expensive, standardised computer software and hardware, known as electronic data interchange (EDI), as well as standardised processes and systems. In this way the purchase and supply of products and services becomes an almost seamless way of working with little distinction between the boundaries of one company and another.

Example 2.17   ## Supply chain collaborative planning software programs offered

The amount of business and marketing software programs available grows in sophistication year by year. The question that might be asked is whether they have become so sophisticated that employees find difficulty in making them work effectively. Below are examples of program software now offered by companies:

☐ collaborative product introduction

☐ collaborative product change management

Example 2.17 continued

- ☐ collaborative planning forecasting and replenishment (CPFR)
- ☐ collaborative planning and forecasting
- ☐ collaborative promotions and event management
- ☐ collaborative inventory issues management
- ☐ collaborative distribution and transport issues management
- ☐ collaborative product returns management
- ☐ collaborative retail actuals management and planning.

Technology and the negotiating situation

The use of technology has also irreversibly changed the relationship between buyer and seller, making the actual sales procedure and sales presentation much more professional than in the past. Both salesperson and buyer can have instant access, through the use of portable computers, to information needed (past sales trends, costs and profit mark-up, availability of products, competitors' figures and so on) to make the sales negotiations more meaningful. There can be instant communications between head office and the salesperson if advice is needed. The product portfolio presentation can be made more dramatic and exciting through a PowerPoint-type computer display. Sales teams need not physically visit the buyer as e-mail, internet video cameras and video conferencing can all be used to make communications simpler and more cost effective.

Company websites

In some cases the salesperson can even be eliminated by the use of interactive company websites. Only time and the ability to concentrate now limit the amount of information that could be made available to buyers around the world on company webpages. Intricate product portfolio details with pictures can be offered at the click of a button; feature and benefit demonstrations can be given with instant question and answer sessions and purchase, availability and delivery details instantly processed. Product spares catalogues can also be put online, making access to hundreds of thousands of spare parts and spare part numbers easy. The customers can search and browse to their heart's content (universal standardisation will enhance the attraction of the service). This also cuts out the need to employ costly spare parts personnel. Financial terms and conditions, costs, pricing policies, discounts, special offers, payment methods, etc. can all be shown safely behind internet security barriers.

Partnership websites

Many companies have taken advantage of IT by joining together with other like-minded supply chain members. They have set up both B2B and B2C internet sites that act as online marketplaces and exchanges, functioning as intermediaries between buyers and sellers. The first exchanges to be set up were founded in many cases by third parties to facilitate the automation of the purchase process. Using the website as a type of auction platform, buyers would jointly post the types of products wanted and the quantities needed on the site and invite prospective suppliers from around the world to bid for the contract. The problem with auctions of this kind is that they can only really be used for basic commodity products, not for the more strategic. These partnership sites are now beginning to offer many more collaborative services, including product development, product identification, and other supply chain hardware and software tools and techniques that are able to give members and customers the ability to reduce costs and bring efficiencies to their business operations.

Example 2.18 **Covisint**

Covisint (www.covisint.com) is a global, independent e-business exchange providing the automotive industry with leading collaborative product development, procurement and supply chain. Developed by DaimlerChrysler, Ford, General Motors, Nissan, Renault, Commerce One and Oracle, Covisint will create a business community of buyers, sellers, designers, engineers and third parties affiliated with the global automotive industry. Covisint will be different from existing exchanges in that sellers of goods and services will be able to buy goods and services from their own suppliers. What's more, programme managers and logistics specialists will benefit from the tools that Covisint will supply in areas such as asset utilisation, collaborative planning and supply chain management. Marketplaces are beginning to evolve beyond providing singular functionalities. Covisint will integrate the best application services, making new and emerging technology available for all levels of the industry. Current Covisint members include:

- ☐ DaimlerChrysler (www.daimlerchrysler.com)
- ☐ Ford Motor Company (www.ford.com)
- ☐ General Motors (www.gm.com)
- ☐ Nissan (www.nissan-us.com)
- ☐ PSA Peugeot Citroën (www.psa-peugeot-citroen.com)
- ☐ Renault (www.renault.com)
- ☐ AK Steel Corporation (www.aksteel.com)
- ☐ ArvinMeritor (www.arvinmeritor.com)
- ☐ BASF (www.basf.com)
- ☐ BorgWarner (www.bwauto.com)
- ☐ DENSO International America (www.denso-int.com).

Other marketplace exchanges
WorldWide Retail Exchange (www.worldwideretailexchange.com) has over 50 members, including M&S, Dixons, Boots, John Lewis, Auchan, Gap, Kingfisher and Safeway.

Transora (www.transora.com) includes as members P&G, Unilever, Coca-Cola and Heinz.

Other technological influences

External technological advances will have a greater or lesser effect on an organisation depending on many factors, including the size of the company, the operating marketplace, the amount of competition and the types of products and services offered. Three main areas where technology has a significant effect in B2B marketing are:

☐ **Products and services** – product testing, product upgrades, new product development.

☐ **Processes, both internal and external** – productivity improvements, customer relationships, distribution and supply chain relationships.

☐ **Management techniques** – involved with the marketing and administration of the business and internal and external communications.

The effects of technology can be seen across all areas of business activity and its pervasive influences will be discussed time and again throughout the book. No organisation, no matter what its circumstances, can ignore technology. More can be seen on technology in Chapter 10.

Part 2 Immediate environmental factors influencing organisational behaviour

☐ Competitive influences

We discussed earlier the international political and commercial movements across the world concerned with breaking down trade barriers and encouraging the free market global economy. Add to this the growth in technology and we have (in theory and increasingly in practice) a dynamic marketplace allowing the freedom for competitors to enter from almost anywhere in the world. This drives the successful company to build competitive intelligence systems (CIM) and obsessively research its markets so as to offer strategic products and services with the sustainable competitive advantage that is crucial if they are to survive and prosper. The competitive environment in B2B markets includes primarily those firms in the industry that offer the same or similar products and services to one another. The more similar are products and services, the easier will it be for competition to take away customers.

Competitive B2B market structures

Competition in B2B markets will be influenced by a number of factors including the market structures at both national and international level. The broad market types identified in Chapter 1 and shown again here will all determine the level of competition. By definition there will no competition in a monopoly market and a lot of competition in a competitive market. It should be understood, however, that a company might have a monopoly market at home but have a competitive market on a global level. In fact many monopoly companies argue this case when criticised about unfair home market dominance.

Market structures discussed in Chapter 1

☐ Monopolies and monopsonies (one buyer and/or one seller)

☐ Oligopolies and oligopsonies (a few buyers and/or a few sellers)

☐ Full competitive ('infinite' number of small buyers and/or small sellers)

☐ Adulterated/imperfect competitive (many buyers and sellers, some collaboration).

Knowledge of the competitor

It is crucial that any B2B organisation is aware of the strengths and weaknesses of the competition in every market where it has a presence or is likely to have a presence. Information can come from many sources such as public statements, annual reports or professional researchers. In this way the organisation will be in a strong position to predict the response that competitors might make to its marketing strategies. Factors to consider about the competition include:

☐ The nature of the competition, market share, market growth

☐ Existing and potential competitors

☐ Competitors' strengths and weaknesses and likely reaction to competitor activity

☐ Corporate image and longevity, brands and unique selling propositions

☐ Present and future strategic direction

☐ Core competencies, e.g. skilled employees, technology, information, innovation

☐ Access to distribution channels

☐ Learning curve and experience curve scale advantages

☐ Organisational buyer base

☐ Product portfolio, value added and unique selling propositions, patents

☐ Cost and price structures and strategies.

Example 2.19 **Expect competition from unexpected quarters**

The block exemption by the EU that allowed car manufacturers the right to dictate who could and could not sell their cars has now ended. Any company can now enter the market and one of the first is entrepreneur Richard Branson. His company, Virgin Cars, intends to operate via the internet, both in the UK and across Europe, selling vehicles from manufacturers including Ford, Vauxhall and Rover. He has promised big savings to customers, claiming prices will be up to 40 per cent lower than those currently on offer. Both B2B and B2C markets will be affected. The big supermarkets have said that they intend to follow soon so expect to see new vehicles on Tesco and Asda forecourts.

Market leaders and followers, major and minor players

Big fleas have little fleas
Upon their backs to bite them
And little fleas have smaller fleas
And so ad infinitum.

We discuss strategic approaches to markets in more detail when we look at strategic planning in Chapter 9. It is important at this stage, however, to understand that not all suppliers are of the same type. Some will be huge B2B players selling across the whole market and able to dictate price and value, while others will be extremely small suppliers perhaps having only a few customers and selling a very restricted range of products. Some suppliers will sell component parts to larger suppliers and so be dependent on their sales for sales of their own, while other suppliers may specialise in a very small niche area and sell in small amounts to many different buyers. Some companies will take pride in having a reputation for innovative and technological core competence advantages, bringing in a constant flow of new products before any other competitor. Others will wait for the ground to be prepared and enter the market with solid products that are slightly better value than the market innovator.

Other companies will develop skills that will enable them to differentiate and specialise in particular niche areas, often working with other companies on long-term contracts. For example, it would be impossible for Boeing to make every part needed to build the 747 Jumbo. So it concentrates on its core skills of aircraft design, logistics and assembly as well as marketing and selling the plane around the world while outsourcing the hundreds of manufacturing jobs, body, wings, tail construction, engines, electronics, interior design, etc. to many small, medium-sized and large specialist manufacturers around the world. In cases such as these price becomes a secondary consideration to quality and delivery specification.

There are many hundreds of thousands of small, medium-sized and large B2B manufacturers around the world that offer commodity component products at rock-bottom prices to any buyer in the market. Some of these products will be unashamedly me-too copies of branded manufacturers' spare parts such as car fan belts, ball joints, battery earth straps, electronic connectors and gaskets. Other products will have been commissioned by the manufacturer and then sold under the branded name. Depending on the industry and the business, it will be more than likely that any large B2B producer will have hundreds of other small producers 'hanging on to their shirt tails', which in turn will have even smaller firms dependent on them. Some of the smallest operators even end up working from home. When one large manufacturer decides to close down or move its operation abroad (where labour is cheaper), the job loss reverberations can be immense.

Example 2.20   ## Leading through innovation

3M is a $16 billion diversified technology company with leading positions in healthcare, safety, electronics, telecommunications, industrial, consumer and office, and other markets. For nearly a century 3M's culture has fostered creativity and given employees the freedom to take risks and try new ideas. It has a mission statement

> *Example 2.20 continued*
>
> which states that a third of its products will have been new to the market within the preceding five years. 3M has many programmes that encourage employees, including the 15 per cent rule, which allows employees to spend part of their work time exploring experiments. This culture has led to a steady stream of products. With no boundaries to imagination and no barriers to cooperation, one good idea swiftly leads to another. So far there have been more than 50,000 innovative products that help make our world better. (www.3m.com)

Competitive intensity

The competitive intensity of any market segment will depend on both the present levels of demand and whether the market is growing or declining. It will also depend on those factors identified by Porter – ease of entry, power relationships between customers and buyers and the availability of substitute goods and services – and on such things as access to distribution channels. Ultimately, however, firms in most markets need to sell products, make profits and ensure an adequate return for the shareholders on the capital employed in the running of the business. This may not necessarily be for the short term so that companies will move into markets if research shows that there is potential to make money in the long run. They might even stay in low profit markets for tactical reasons associated with product portfolio integration and customer service. Taking all this into account, the overriding concern for business market entry and the competitive intensity of any market will be its attractiveness in sales and profits.

> Example 2.21 **Forcing competition into the public sector**
>
> In the 1980s public sector local authorities were forced to open up in-house services such as administration, road maintenance and waste collection to private competition in an effort to cut costs and improve value for money. It was argued that competition increases the overall management effectiveness and efficiency in the spending of public money. However, it was felt that insisting that many projects had to be offered to outside contractors put too much emphasis on cost cutting at the expense of quality and so this policy has largely been replaced by 'best value'. Although still inviting competition it attempts to balance the need for both cost reductions and value.

Dynamic market conditions

Ease of entry, barriers to trade, power relationships and the availability of substitute products and processes have the possibility of changing as markets develop and change. Life cycles cause industries, markets and products to reach maturity and die out. Technology brings new knowledge, new processes and new ways of working. New products supersede old, patents end, trading agreements finish and new legislation causes old ways of working to become illegal. Some industries,

Figure 2.1
Porter's
Five Forces

Source: Adapted
from Porter,
1998c

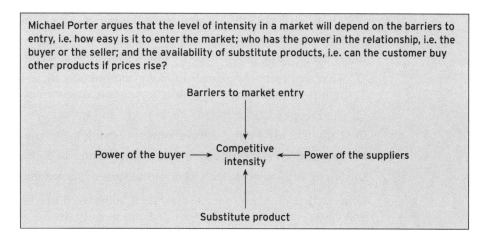

Michael Porter argues that the level of intensity in a market will depend on the barriers to entry, i.e. how easy is it to enter the market; who has the power in the relationship, i.e. the buyer or the seller; and the availability of substitute products, i.e. can the customer buy other products if prices rise?

Barriers to market entry

Power of the buyer → Competitive intensity ← Power of the suppliers

Substitute product

especially those involving new technology, will change more quickly, but no market can have barriers to entry for ever and the advent of more competition is inevitable (Figure 2.1).

Sources of competitive advantage

There are only three basic ways to gain competitive advantage: make your product cheaper, different or of better value.

A business-to-business firm can gain competitive advantage in many different ways by taking advantage of its superior skills, resources and core competencies. Superior skills are the distinct capabilities of staff that make them different from those employed by competing organisations. A company like 3M, identified above, has been able to attract creative people over the years by building a culture and climate where innovation is encouraged, respected and rewarded. Other organisations like Microsoft have been able to attract the brightest and the best IT-driven individuals wanting to work with other like-minded people in the very forefront of computer technology. Other skills result from systems and organisational structures (discussed in Chapter 11, on the *B2B Marketing* website) that enable a company to adapt faster and move more responsively to changing market requirements.

Superior resources (or core competencies) are obviously a source of competitive advantage as long as they are used and managed in the most productive manner. There are many examples, however, of once wealthy and powerful companies squandering superior resource potential through mismanagement and/or lack of business acumen. Superior resources are more tangible than the skills outlined above. Here are just a few examples suggested by Porter and others, with more to follow throughout the book:

☐ Strong and well-respected reputation encompassed in the corporate and product brand.

☐ Strong financial backing allowing expenditure on R&D, marketing research, product and customer development, and promotional and advertising support.

- ☐ Minimising costs by maximising economic, learning and experience curve opportunities.
- ☐ Differentiating product/service offerings with clear segmentation.
- ☐ The latest technology, scale of manufacturing and the ability to flexibly customise and change product offerings as customers demand.
- ☐ Product portfolio matching buyer needs and wants.
- ☐ Large and loyal distribution channels carrying the whole range of products.
- ☐ Experienced and productive sales force reaching all customers.
- ☐ Strong customer base with all buyers identified for contribution to profitability.

Other writers on core competencies which might lead to competitive advantage and give a company the edge over its rivals identify the following problems:

- ☐ Obsessive attention to customers and markets.
- ☐ The speed with which management can adapt, adopt and permeate technology, production skills and other innovations into an overall focused, collective, cooperative approach.
- ☐ The failure of a company to recognise its own core competencies and so be unable to develop and exploit areas of the business that could lead to market growth.
- ☐ Inadequate business processes and capabilities that prevent the flexible responses needed to choose and manage resources and so react to threats and opportunities as they arise.
- ☐ Fear of risk leading to the failure to invest heavily enough in resources that might allow the organisation to take advantage of scale and scope economies.
- ☐ Insufficient capacity to store and disseminate the right kind of information and so achieve an easy flow of information both within and outside the organisation.

Current competitive advantages should not be taken for granted as circumstances might constantly be changing and products and services seen to be offering superior value today could be overtaken by others tomorrow. Benchmarking, constantly comparing and ranking benefit offering with the best in the market, is used to try to prevent this happening and will be discussed in more detail in later chapters.

Global competitiveness influences

The theory of comparative advantage
The idea here is simple and intuitive. If our country can produce some set of goods at lower cost than a foreign country, and if the foreign country can produce some other set of goods at a lower cost than we can produce them, then clearly it would be best for us to trade our relatively cheaper goods for their relatively cheaper goods. In this way both countries may gain from trade and more goods and services will be produced overall.

(Smith, 1991)

When selling goods and services and attempting to compete internationally, some B2B organisations will begin with competitive comparative advantages over those operating from competing countries because of certain favourable factors inherent in the home country. These favourable factors, known as 'factor endowments', will include basic business inputs such as land, natural resources, labour and the size of the local population. Michael Porter argues that a nation can work together with businesses to create new advanced factor endowments such as an educated, skilled and adaptable labour force, a strong technology and knowledge base, government support, and a culture of free enterprise, entrepreneurial spirit and betterment through hard work.

So, according to Porter, the exporting US firm has the tremendous advantage of a strong, large home market (economies of scale to build a solid launch pad), a pliable and supportive government (little interference, few employment restrictions), an able and willing workforce (motivated by the idea of the 'American dream'), the latest technology (driven by mind-boggling amounts of R&D in both the public and private sectors), and access to natural resources (theirs or others). This can be compared to large countries such as Russia and India that do not have anywhere near the same factor endowments. Other erstwhile developing countries such as South Korea and Taiwan have managed to create some if not all of the factor endowments identified above, thus increasing global competitive influence.

Example 2.22 **Illegal factor endowments**

The United States has suffered a bitter blow in a long-running trade dispute with the European Union and could now face sanctions worth more than $4 billion. The World Trade Organisation (WTO) found that massive tax breaks for firms like GE, Boeing and Microsoft amounted to illegal export subsidies. It was the fourth time in five years that the WTO ruled the tax breaks illegal, and it has now paved the way for the EU to impose punitive tariffs on imports from the USA.

A strong home market for global competitiveness includes the following:

☐ Government committed to free markets.

☐ Little government interference.

☐ Powerful pro-competitive, anti-corruption legislation.

☐ A strong, competitive home market for both buyers and suppliers.

☐ Favourable economic circumstances with strong home demand.

☐ The availability of resources and skills.

☐ A flexible motivated labour force.

☐ Adequate quality information.

☐ Firms encouraged, committed and motivated to innovate, invest and grow.

☐ Indoctrination of an entrepreneurial spirit welcoming interfirm rivalry, new challenges and a 'never-say-die' approach.

Government power and competitiveness

The final power in controlling competitive activity will lie with the politicians and government agencies. As Porter argues, they have the power to help create a strong home base, a 'national playing field', for businesses to launch themselves into foreign fields. We have already seen that governments inherently dislike barriers to market entry because they distort trade and create monopolies and oligopolies. This usually ends with overall higher prices and higher costs for the economy as a whole. Organisations such as the UK Competition Commission, European Competition Commission and US Federal Trade Commission have all been set up to break down as far as possible barriers to trade so that as many markets as possible are open to all who might wish to participate.

Government agencies can also encourage companies to raise performance by enforcing codes of practice, stimulating local rivalry and limiting direct government involvement with such things as subsidies and tax breaks that might weaken management ability to grow strong through fighting and building businesses in the cut and thrust of fair competitive markets. The government can also work with industries by ploughing money into R&D, offering grants for creativity and design, and using its tremendous buying power to work with and encourage companies to search for new innovative technological advanced products and services. Overall, governments will need to manage the economy in a manner needed to stimulate demand, encourage the development of an adequately skilled workforce and provide information, help and assistance for businesses wanting to sell abroad.

Example 2.23   ## Price fixing legislation

Company directors who set up price-fixing cartels will face imprisonment under a comprehensive overhaul of competition legislation to be announced today by the UK Chancellor of the Exchequer. It will make engaging in cartels (companies banding together secretly to fix prices) a criminal offence. The new laws will be modelled on the way monopolies and cartels are handled in the United States. He has been frustrated by the lack of painful sanctions for those who seek to fix markets in Britain. Anti-trust legislation in the US led to the break-up of the telephone giant AT&T and more recently an attack on Microsoft. Under the change, rulings on mergers, monopolies and cartels will be left to the commission. It will decide what punishments to impose on companies and sectors – such as supermarkets or the professions – that are found to be engaging in anti-competitive practices. Under the 1998 Competition Act it can levy fines of up to 10 per cent of a company's turnover in three successive years. A government source said: 'The problem with fines is that they get passed on to the shareholder and the consumer. We want to make directors pay the price for criminal activity.'

Competition in B2B and in B2C markets

> Competition brings out the best in products and the worst in people.
>
> (David Sarnoff, www.draytonbird.com)

Competition in most B2B markets is as intense as competition in B2C markets, but because consumers want different benefits from business buyers, it tends to be of a different kind. Competition in B2C markets is just as likely to be on product and service brands as it is on price, while in B2B it is more likely to be on functional benefits offered and after-sales service than on the brand or the price. Although price is important in the B2B market, functionality and reliability can be crucial as a dysfunction in some way could be catastrophic in terms of lost production. There are liable to be more competitors in consumer markets because of the possibility of millions of consumers and millions of different kinds of consumer products. Competition can also come about through alternative, substitute choices, e.g. buying a car or a holiday (known as secondary competition as opposed to primary competition). This is very rarely the case with business markets where the product wanted must match a particular solution sought. In many B2B industries competition will often come from only a few players known by all market players, although it is increasing as world markets shrink.

☐ Customers and markets

Markets and customers in both B2B and B2C are continually changing. Markets grow and expand, reach maturity, decline and die out. One market closes and another market opens up. Regional and national markets are suddenly international and global as organisations find that they are able to import and export with increasing ease. Many B2B customers are discovering that new technology is enabling them to search out and buy products and services from anywhere in the world. This puts added pressure on company buyers to be diligent and professional in examining existing purchases and identifying new sources from which to obtain supplies. Failure to do this will lead to the acquisition of unsatisfactory and non-competitive products and services, leading to the loss of competitive advantage. Large companies will have personnel spending all their time evaluating, benchmarking and seeking out suppliers on a continuous basis. Suppliers need to employ ever more sophisticated customer satisfaction methods to keep ahead of these technological developments.

Market and customer analysis

Questions to be asked about B2B markets and customers would normally include the following:

- ☐ The existing and potential size of the market, growth, maturity or decline
- ☐ The nature of the competition (discussed in detail above)
- ☐ The number of buyers and suppliers in the market and where the power lies
- ☐ The organisational buyer segments, current and possible
- ☐ The types of buying organisations, benefits wanted, buying patterns
- ☐ The availability of distribution channels.

Customer and market types

The major types of markets in B2B are outlined here and we will look in more detail across all these areas as we move through the book. These are producers or manufacturers, intermediaries or resellers, retailers, service suppliers, raw material suppliers, governments and not-for-profit. Influences from each type of market sector are different because organisational objectives tend to be different. This means that the approach used in marketing and selling will have to be shaped and honed to meet the diverse needs across all sectors. Not understanding the fact that government buying departments have to abide by very strict and formalised buying codes and so cannot perhaps be sold to in the same way as the commercial firm will cause a failed sales and marketing programme. Similarly the skills and experiences needed for marketing and selling in the financial services sector are different in many ways from those needed in the mining and aggregates market.

Raw material suppliers

Raw material supplies include everything from agriculture, fishing, energy, forestry and water to aggregates, iron ore, chemicals, rubber and precious metals. Much of this is imported and accounts for only a small amount of the GDP in modern economies.

Example 2.24	**Rise in raw material price**

High oil prices continued to put UK manufacturers under pressure in May, as raw materials are becoming more expensive. The Office for National Statistics (ONS) said on Monday that the cost of raw materials and fuel for manufacturers rose by 2.2 per cent in May, compared with 0.5 per cent last month. The data indicate that manufacturers' profit margins are under pressure because the prices they paid for their raw materials rose more quickly than output prices. Intense competition is stopping them passing on the price rises. (www.statistics.gov)

Service suppliers

Service suppliers are by far the largest customer types in B2B markets and consist of both buyers and sellers. The service industry accounts for nearly 75 per cent of the UK GDP. Retailing, as shown below, is part of this sector.

Producers or manufacturers

Producers buy goods and services to use in the production of other goods and services, hoping to generate a profit. In the UK manufacturing accounts for about 23 per cent of GDP.

Example 2.25 **Manufacturers under pressure**

According to the latest report from the Chartered Institute of Purchasing and Supply (CIPS, www.cips.org) manufacturing output and orders have fallen to two-year lows. This is putting tremendous pressure on producers to reduce costs and make savings as in many cases they are unable to pass on the increases because of competition. Similar manufacturing indices in France, Germany and Italy have also fallen to two-year lows.

Intermediaries or resellers

Resellers are similar to wholesalers and retailers in B2C marketing. They buy goods and services to resell on to other B2B organisations to use in the production of goods and services either for other B2Bs or to B2Cs.

Retailers

Retailers are at the end of the supply chain offering a whole range of goods and services for consumer use. The retail sector in modern economies will account for about a quarter of GDP. Both B2B and B2C suppliers will sell into retailers: B2C finished goods and services to sell on to the consumer and B2B goods and services for the retailer's own use in the running of the business.

Not-for-profit (NFP)

Not-for-profit organisations buy goods and services to help in providing other goods and services based not on making a profit but on providing services that help, aid and advise others with some kind of social need. The NFP organisation will have many stakeholders, all with differing concerns about the way the organisation is run and the types of goods and services bought.

Government

Governments, national, regional and local, are the single largest buyers of B2B, purchasing goods and services for government usage across a range of areas including social security, defence, health, roads and bridges, fire service and ambulance services.

Global markets

It is possible that buyers and sellers of B2B goods can now come from anywhere in the world; it is now truly a global marketplace. Although there is a huge movement towards standardisation, there is still a very long way to go and B2B companies must be aware of the different buying and selling influences and demands in different countries across the world. The World Wide Web is proving invaluable in helping suppliers and buyers to scour the world for the best products and services.

Different types of external environment

Not all market environments will be the same and differences will depend on the industry, products and services sold, geographical location and country and global economic conditions. We have outlined possible categories below, bearing in mind that a B2B company could face differing challenges depending on the type of company and the number of its markets.

Dynamic vs. stable environments

Some markets are stable with very little changing from year to year, while others are dynamic with constant movement and upheaval. Although all markets are more dynamic than they used to be, the following factors designate the type of B2B market.

Stable markets

☐ Monopoly, government, protected markets, legislation

☐ Strong brands, USPs, patents, ownership of distribution channels restricts access

☐ Unaffected by technological development

☐ Relatively unaffected by buyer fashion.

Dynamic markets

☐ Highly competitive, unprotected markets, access from around the world

☐ Many substitute products, technology constantly changing

☐ Little loyalty and customer will change as new and better offerings arise

☐ Information for buyers to change from supply to supply at will

☐ Multiple changes happening at the same time.

Complex vs. simple

Some B2B markets are less sophisticated than others and the following factors apply.

Simple markets

☐ Uncomplicated product

☐ Short distribution chain

☐ Small, easily knowable decision making unit (DMU)

☐ In the home market or exporting on the back of others

☐ Products wanted integrate easily across the product portfolio.

Complex markets

- ☐ Technically complicated product or service with many benefit solutions wanted
- ☐ Diverse customers demand customised benefit solutions
- ☐ Other suppliers/buyers involved
- ☐ Long-term contracts involving after-sales service
- ☐ Long or intricate distribution chain
- ☐ Complex, large DMU, areas of buying responsibility difficult to pin down
- ☐ Foreign remote market with difficult and different cultural factors.

Hostile vs. favourable environments

Opportunities can arise across a range of different markets, some more approachable than others.

Hostile markets

- ☐ Inadequate information available about the country, industry and market
- ☐ A history of political and social upheaval
- ☐ Many competitors withdrawn because of production and marketing difficulties
- ☐ Dictatorial market entry conditions
- ☐ Culturally different from home markets
- ☐ Corruption rife and legal processes suspect
- ☐ Geographically at a distance with long distribution channels.

Favourable markets

- ☐ Politically, economically and socially stable
- ☐ Culturally very similar to home markets
- ☐ Adequate information shows market growth and other encouraging indicators
- ☐ Products and services needed match existing benefit offerings.

Part 3 Demand and supply in the economy

In monitoring and forecasting demand, the business-to-business marketing managers must be constantly aware of the many factors discussed in this and the previous chapter that will affect demand in their particular industry and in industries that are closely related. Demand for most B2B products will depend eventually on the end demand for the product, often the end consumer. In markets that do not have a clear consumer involvement, demand will be affected by a succession of buying points between the supplier and the eventual consuming company.

A downturn in economic activity both at the national and the global level will affect most industries. All B2B companies will be affected in some way or other by what happens to the economy, but it is inevitable that there will some industries and companies that will be hit harder than others depending on many factors.

A recession (or boom) might be worldwide, it might only be in one country, or it might be in one trading bloc and not in another. It might affect one industry rather than another (the collapse of internet stocks at the time of writing immediately comes to mind) or one industry sector rather than many sectors in the same industry (retail sales slowdown in fashion but not in food). A fall-off in demand might be in just a few companies and not in the rest or in just one company and not others.

Example 2.26 **Global economy**

A new report from America's Federal Reserve on 19 September said the American economy remained sluggish even before the terrorist attacks last week. The news came as world stock markets remained nervous, after a stream of corporate profit warnings and job lay-offs in the wake of the attacks. Is a global recession inevitable?

☐ Managing demand

B2B organisations need to be aware of the demand situation across companies, industry sectors, whole industries and national and international markets so that appropriate strategic and tactical action can be taken. The issue might be internal, with problems associated with management, systems or strategic direction. There might be marketing mix difficulties, wrong products, prices, delivery, and so on. Or there might be problems associated with promotion, customers and markets. In some cases the organisation may be able to do very little, but in many cases appropriate action can be taken to safeguard shareholder value. It is important that the nature of demand is understood and this is examined below.

☐ Derived demand

Although organisations in B2B markets will service business markets, there must be a realisation that many business markets are eventually affected by demand further down the supply chain, from the end consumer. Many B2B organisations in the commercial, government and not-for-profit sectors buy goods and services to use to make other goods and services that will eventually be sold to end consumers. This is known as derived demand. Depending on the type of product, the B2B supplier will often be dependent ultimately on the end consumer buying the product from his or her business customer. If we take for example a company

Paint supplier → Sells paint for cars → Car manufacturer → Sells cars to → Retailer → Sells to consumer
B2B   B2C   B2C

Figure 2.2
Derived demand

selling paint to Fords to be used on new cars being produced, then a fall in demand for the cars will result in a fall in demand for more paint (Figure 2.2).

It must therefore be obvious that it would be beneficial for the B2B paint supplier to understand and be able to forecast the eventual derived demand for the end product. Having said this there are many cases where companies have not even known what kind of product their product goes into, let alone who the end consumer is.

Derived demand along the supply chain

Not all derived demand is for the end consumer. As shown in Figure 2.3, derived demand can be happening in many places along the supply chain with ultimate demand in this case coming from a government defence department. Suppliers in this market must be aware of government plans on when to purchase new defence equipment.

Marketing along the whole supply chain

Some B2B associations and organisations not only monitor the level of derived demand but also develop marketing programmes in an attempt to promote and increase this demand, knowing that an increase in consumer market sales will flow back along the supply chain and increase industry and company sales.

> An organisation may need to promote across the whole supply chain including the end consumer.

Industry stimulation of derived demand

Business associations might run TV and newspaper campaigns to increases sales for the industry as a whole and benefiting the supply chain from supplier through to retailer. The Milk Marketing Association will pay for promotional campaigns knowing that the more milk drunk, the more will be wanted at the B2B end of the supply chain. Similarly Intel has managed to develop a brand name known to both business and end-use buyers. In this way it is able both to promote to its B2B computer manufacturer and to stimulate derived demand by promoting to the end consumer.

Figure 2.3
Derived demand along the supply chain

B2B ──→ B2B ──→ B2B ──→ B2B ──→ B2B ──→ Government defence equipment

---

Example 2.27   **Food industry develops logo**

The food production industry has developed its own quality label and it is now on display in around 4000 supermarkets. It has as its logo a red and blue tractor in the shape of an F to remind shoppers of the traditional image of farming. The label will cover meat, poultry, fruit and vegetables and will be used across the whole supply chain.

Example 2.28   **Organisation stimulation of derived demand**

Intel, the computer chip manufacturer, well appreciates the value of knowing and understanding the wants and needs of the end consumer for computers containing its silicon chips. Through researching the derived demand consumer market it discovered that there would be a demand for computers that offered added value benefits through branded components. So the company developed a promotion campaign programme based on both a 'push' and a 'pull' approach. The push approach was used to sell its newly branded Intel product into the computer manufacturers, asking them to put the Intel logo on the machines. The pull approach was to advertise to the end consumer the value of buying a computer containing the branded Intel component.

Measuring derived demand

Information and marketing research should be gathered and the marketing information system used incessantly to scrutinise demand along the whole supply chain. Leading economic indictors might give notice of imminent changes in consumer sales demands. Bought-in consumer secondary research data can identify changes in patterns of demand, and so on. In this way a B2B company can be prepared, anticipate changes before they happen, and so be able to take some form of evasive action. It seems managerially indefensible for a brick manufacturer to be unaware of an expected fall in the sale of houses or an IT components manufacturer in the communications industry to be surprised when the sale of portable telephones declined.

☐ Other demand categories

Horizontal demand

Companies involved in some sort of cooperative alliance such as a joint venture or outsourcing arrangements will have the opportunity of feeding off one another's business activities. An organisation might not export directly but have an arrangement with another company to top up with products when a large order exceeds the exporting company's current stock. Similarly, companies working together might be able to gain economies of scale, reduce costs and so affect the demand for their products by lowering the price (Figure 2.4).

Figure 2.4
Horizontal
demand

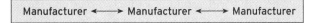

Vertical demand

The vertical dimension is concerned with the demand backwards and forwards vertically along the supply chain. This may include retailers (buying B2C products), manufacturers, component part suppliers, raw material suppliers, and so on. The longer the chain of companies in the supply chain, the more difficult it might be to forecast demand (Figure 2.5).

Figure 2.5
Vertical
demand

Joint demand

This will occur when two or more products are used in the final product, and is linked to the concept of derived demand. So if there is a rise or fall in the demand for bottles, there will be a rise or fall in the demand for glass to make the bottles. Many B2B products are in joint demand in some way so it is important for managers to be aware of the movement of related industries.

Example 2.29

Creating joint demand

Eastman Kodak Company and Sanyo Electric Co. Ltd announced the formation of a global joint venture, the SK Display Corporation, to manufacture organic light-emitting diode (OLED) displays for consumer devices such as cameras, PDAs and portable entertainment machines. They are capitalising on demand for superior displays by combining Kodak technology and intellectual property with Sanyo manufacturing capabilities.

Inelastic demand

The demand for some B2B products, usually components of some kind, is relatively inelastic. This means that an increase or decrease in the price of the product or service will not significantly alter the demand for the product in the short run. This is because the price of a particular component tends to be a small part of the final price further down the supply chain, so price changes are either of a small order or bought under some kind of fixed price contract. It is also a difficult task for producers to make major changes in production operations in the short run (although technology is increasing the speed at which production changes can be made) to take account of cost and price changes and so have to absorb price fluctuations. An example might be Ford not passing on a paint price increase to its customers because it would be a small part of the overall price of the car and market conditions might be too competitive.

Fluctuating demand

Demand for business-to-business products tends to fluctuate more than the demand for consumer products as a small increase or decrease in consumer demand will produce a much larger change in the demand for manufacturing operations needed to produce the additional output. Consumer markets are characterised by millions of customers and a fall-off in sales can take time, be localised and compensated by finding new customers in other areas. On the other hand, B2B markets are characterised by fewer customers, and just a handful (even one!) not buying for some reason or other can have an immediate and disastrous effect. Similarly, a B2C company is more likely to have the protection of a larger and more diverse product portfolio than a B2B company, and is more able to spread the risk if one product area slumps.

> Demand for business-to-business products tends to fluctuate more than the demand for consumer products.

Example 2.30 **Using the web to cope with fluctuating demand**

Increasingly, businesses that want to decrease costs and increase revenues are turning to dynamic pricing applications to pave the way. More and more, businesses are demanding a sophisticated web channel where goods and services are priced instantly, fluctuating in response to supply and demand. The B2B marketplace creates value by aggregating buyers and sellers to create marketplace liquidity (a critical mass of buyers and sellers), reducing transaction costs (search costs, information transfer costs) and delivering standardised liquidation and procurement processes and systems.

Demand for new, improved products and services

There will always be a demand for new or improved products and services in B2B as long as they offer clear benefits of some kind, as discussed above. To reiterate, however, improved B2B products, services and processes that offer increased productivity in terms of speed and timing improvements, better space utilisation and value for money will always be sought after, as will new products, services and processes that offer clear customer advantages over present offerings. With the advent of benchmarking processes across the whole of the supply chain, those organisations that do not keep abreast with new process and marketing mix development will find that competitive advantage is lost.

☐ Trends and shifts in demand

The last 25 years have seen the virtual death of some industries and the creation of others. A small part of this change has been brought about by government policy, but most has happened because of shifts in demand and supply patterns across Europe and worldwide. Heavy industry is a notable example. Shipbuilding, once the cornerstone of the UK manufacturing sector, is now almost non-existent as ship manufacturing has gone to other countries where labour is cheaper and productivity better. Coal, steel manufacturing, clothing and textiles are all examples of industries that have moved from western countries to the Far East because they can be produced at better value. New industries have taken their place, including technology, banking, insurance and business services. These types of shifts have had tremendous implications for the thousands of firms that supplied business goods and services in these areas. As an industry begins to decline, the more prepared organisations will be looking to move into other markets or reinventing themselves to move into new business sectors. The unprepared will go out of business.

Market and industry life cycles

This theory is linked to the concept of the product life cycle. It states that all industries and markets will go through a continuous process of introduction, growth, maturity and decline over a period of time. This is brought about by the introduction of new technology, competition and changing customer demands linked to economic growth and changing economic patterns around the world. The industries highlighted above could be said to have gone through this process. An industry will probably be at different stages of the life cycle in different countries and different markets. Tobacco products are in decline in the west but in the growth stage in the east. The mass market for horse transport products no longer exists and there is a new market for digital entertainment products. It could be argued that in some cases industry and market life cycles take off more quickly and decline and die more quickly.

Business cycles

This is the tendency of economies to move over time through periods of boom and slump. It occurs when real GDP moves away from its usual pattern. Although not every economist is in agreement, it tends to happen every six to eight years. Business cycles are a fact of business life and are brought about by the differences between consumer and business-to-business purchases. They are linked to the concept of the accelerator principle. This theory states that a given change in demand for consumer goods will cause a greater percentage change in demand for capital goods. Conversely, a fall in the demand for consumer goods will cause a greater percentage change in the demand for capital goods. It is this 'gap' between consumer purchases and B2B purchases that causes the peaks and troughs of the business cycle. Different economies around the world can be at different stages of the business cycle at any one time.

Example 2.31   ## Electronic PLCs shorten

The fashion industry has been dealing with it for years, products with long lead times but short life cycles with fickle and unpredictable consumer demand. It is difficult to make money unless your supply chain has hair-trigger responsiveness and flexibility. The semiconductor industry has awakened to a market with a similar scenario. The explosion of applications for electronics means consumers are now in control, not just electronic geeks. So semiconductor marketing managers have to take a cue from the consumer world and realise that when you are trying

Example 2.31 continued

> to sell cellphones to teenagers you can forget about forecast accuracy as life cycles shorten and changes in product demand can happen overnight. Historically, the industry has been driven by technological innovations, not supply chain efficiency, but this must all need to alter if electronics manufacturers want to stay ahead.

Demand in government markets

Demand in government markets is affected not only by the same factors but also by other factors than those that affect demand in commercial markets. As in the private sector, the state of the economy must influence the level of government spending. A reduction in GDP will mean less income (tax, insurance, VAT) and so less money to spend on such things as health, social security, road building programmes and defence. Where this situation happens it might impinge on one industry more than another as money is cut, for example, from the defence budget while the health budget is left alone.

Government spending will also be a function of political and legislative commitments, social priorities and pressure group lobbying. One political party might come to power with the express mandate to reduce the level of government spending as a percentage of GDP, while another party might have promised to increase spending as a percentage of GDP. It might be socially acceptable to cut back in one area but not in another. Pressure group lobbyists will be active at this time, attempting to have spending maintained in their particular markets.

Demand in B2C and B2B markets

Demand in consumer markets is seen as a primary indicator of the state of the economy and alarm bells will ring if it falls below a certain level over a prolonged period. A fall in consumer confidence leading to a fall in consumer demand will act more quickly on business sales than a fall in the demand for B2B products and services. This is because it is direct and linked immediately to the sale of consumer products and services. On the other hand a fall in the demand for B2B products, although often linked eventually to consumer demand, will take longer to filter back to the buying process. A fall in the demand for cars will not immediately affect the demand for, say, paint (short-term investment) because the car manufacturer will not slow down car production straight away, choosing to stockpile cars as the more efficient option. Similarly it will not abandon new capital equipment orders, a long-term investment, unless the demand for its cars continues to fall over a longer period of time (Figure 2.6).

Figure 2.6
Demand in
B2C and B2B
markets

B2C	B2B
Can fluctuate quickly	Longer time to fluctuate
Demand shifts felt immediately	Demand shifts take a while to take effect
Demand movements have a small effect	Demand movement can have a large effect

Example 2.32   **Fall in demand**

Japan's biggest computer maker Fujitsu has cut 9000 jobs and warned that it will continue to make losses. There was more bad news from other electronic and tech companies with Sanyo, Sharp and Mitsubishi Electronic warning of weak demand continuing restructuring costs. The US is Japan's largest export market, but US demand for Japanese IT goods has been weak.

☐ Measuring the level of demand

An organisation will attempt to measure the level of demand for a product or an industry over both the short and long term. If this information is not forthcoming then forward planning becomes very problematic. The level of closeness with the end user also affects demand. The closer the relationship, the easier it is to forecast the level of need. Conversely, the further away the supplier is from the end user, the more difficult it is to identify needs and so the more likely will be the fluctuations in levels of demand. This factor highlights the need for good macro and micro information about sales along the supply chain and the eventual needs of the end consumer. Only then can reliable and realistic forecasts be made.

The economist's view on demand

The economist's view of supply and demand applies in B2B markets in just the same way as in B2C markets. In simple terms the economist will argue that all things being equal (they never are!), the higher the price, the lower will be the demand, and the lower the price, the higher will be the demand. Similarly the higher the price, the more will be supplied, and the lower the price, the less will be supplied. A shortage or glut of products and the availability of substitute products will also have an effect on demand.

Forecasting demand

To be able to garner and allocate resources efficiently, develop and implement strategies and plan ahead, the B2B marketing manager must be able to estimate future growth, sales and profit potential. All estimates of future sales can be fraught with difficulty because forecasting is looking into the future and nobody can ever know with certainty what might or might not happen. Some business markets are more volatile to circumstances than others and changes in single factors can cause a ripple effect across an industry that can put companies out of business, no matter how large.

Example 2.33 **Oil and the effect on demand**

Some possible changes that might happen in the market environment are more predictable than others and so contingency plans for different scenarios can be outlined. A rise in the price of oil instigated by OPEC can push up costs so high that transport companies might at best be forced to cut back on staff and at worse go out of business. This possibility can be allowed for as long as the upward (or downward) movement in oil prices follows expected patterns. The difficulty arises when the change is unexpected and/or of a magnitude not considered.

An example was the 1973 Arab oil embargo, which was the first oil supply disruption to cause major price increases and a worldwide energy crisis. The October of that year brought an oil embargo by members of the Organisation of Petroleum Exporting Countries, cutting the supply of oil and elevating prices to levels previously thought impossible. It seemed to catch politicians and business tycoons alike totally by surprise and there was a global recession causing many organisations to go out of business.

In 1998 oil prices fell to $10 a barrel from a high of $32 because of high oil stocks, but this time companies were more prepared, knowing that OPEC, the oil exporting cartel, would cut production by up to 2 million barrels a day. In the UK, however, there were unexpected ramifications that again caught politicians and business managers by surprise. The subsequent swift rise in petrol prices coincided with an increase in taxation. This led to protests from transport companies who managed to organise a blockade of all petrol distribution depots. For a while the blockade threatened to bring the country to a halt.

The difficulties associated with forecasting demand should not dissuade managers from attempting to make forecasts, but they should give a warning on the limitations involved when trying to look into the future.

☐ Demand potential and analysis

B2B marketing management would be a simple matter if business markets were not in a continual state of change, the pace of which has quickened in recent years. The result of this constant change, however, is that business tasks are becoming more complex and business decisions are becoming more long term in nature. It is increasingly important and necessary for businesses to predict future demand in terms of sales, costs and profits. The value of future sales is crucial as it affects the resources needed as well as both costs and profits, so the prediction of future sales is the logical starting point for all business planning. Understanding market potential, anticipating the needs and wants of the company's customers and their likely purchasing behaviour in both existing and new markets for a period of time to come are the starting points for business forecasting and planning. This concept lies at the very heart of all marketing activity.

Demand analysis across the Ansoff Matrix

A demand analysis might need to be undertaken across all markets depending on the present and future markets. This need can be identified under the Ansoff Matrix. Demand analysis should be undertaken on:

☐ Existing products in existing markets
☐ Existing products in new markets
☐ New products in existing markets
☐ New products in new markets.

☐ Market potential

Market sales potential can be examined from the perspective of a country, a particular industry, a particular market, and a specific organisation. These basic categories are identified below.

1. Country demand potential
2. Industry demand potential
3. Market demand potential
4. Company demand potential.

1. Country demand potential

A B2B organisation wishing to estimate market potential in both existing and new markets will probably begin the process by looking at the markets in its home country. This will involve the undertaking of a macro-environmental analysis of the type used in the auditing and planning process to examine the future growth of the economy, particularly as it might affect its own industry. Relevant levels of government business cooperation, economic growth, rates of inflation, retail sales trends, and so on will all give a good indication of the demand potential at this wider GNP level. The same process will apply, country by country, if wishing to market abroad except that it will probably be more difficult as the needed statistics might be more difficult to come by. At this level government agencies will be only too willing to help with the needed information.

> Country demand potential can be identified as overall level of sales and services that could be achieved across the whole of the economy of a country.

2. Industry demand potential

Overall macro- and micro-environmental activity at both national and global level will have some kind of effect on the level of industry demand and figures. Figures collected in the first stage identified above can now by collated with more specific industry information and the results analysed and evaluated.

More immediately industry demand potential will be affected by overall commercial, not-for-profit and most especially government spending and cutbacks. The pronouncement by the Ministry of Defence to spend more on warplanes, ships or armaments can increase demand potential by billions of pounds. Transport ministry decisions to cut back on road spending, social welfare departments tendering for computer systems, and education ministers declaring that school buildings must be improved will cause fluctuations in industry demand. The intention of a large supermarket to open more outlets, the loss of 5000 jobs announced by a major bank, or the merger of one multinational with another, will all have an effect on B2B industry demand. Government's, trade associations' and market research companies' economic and industry sector statistics should be available, for both national and global markets, to help in building up a picture of industry demand.

> Industry demand potential can be defined as the maximum possible level of sales activity that might be feasible from a given industry (e.g. over a specified time period).

3. Market demand potential

Because of the interconnection, figures identified from the overall industry demand potential can then be used to help inform the various market demand potentials. Industry sectors will consist of many different kinds of markets. The defence industry will contain markets for a whole range of different products from telecommunications, management training and health services to glass, paint and nuts and bolts. Because of technological developments, an industry and its markets can all be at different stages in the product life cycle. Whether the market is a monopoly, an oligopoly, fully competitive, or a combination will have some sort of effect on demand levels. Trade association and research company reports will be of help here.

> Market demand potential can be seen as the maximum possible level of sales in a particular market that can be achieved by all market participants.

4. Organisational demand potential

Existing market conditions and existing market players will dictate the market demand potential for any one company's product and services. If the market is a monopoly, then any industry and market growth can be claimed by the monopolist. If the market is highly competitive, then all must fight to gain a share. The successful company will be continually looking for demand potential from both existing and new market segments. An individual company, unless new to the market, will already have some level of market share. Any increase can only come about if the market is growing or if one company can take sales from another. Organisational sales demand potential can be estimated by using many of the quantitative and qualitative methods discussed below. If the marketing manager is uncertain in which market a particular product or service will operate, then estimated potential demand will be almost impossible.

> Organisational demand potential relates to the level of products that any one company might be able to sell in a market segment (or markets if in more than one segment) over a given time period.

Demand potential by territory, customer and product

The company management will eventually need to break down the company potential demand by sales territory, product category and customer. This will then be used to plan and set targets for its marketing and sales force departments. The demand potential process is as follows:

- ☐ Country demand potential
- ☐ Industry demand potential
- ☐ Market demand potential
- ☐ Organisational demand potential
- ☐ Territory–customer–product potential.

☐ Industry and market life cycles

As well as macro- and micro-environmental factors, demand potential in any one industry will also depend on both business/industry life and market life cycles that can vary around the world according to the particular industry and market. So the level of demand potential might well be in the growth stage in one country, the maturity stage in another, and the decline stage in another. For large multinational companies it is imperative that they are able to identify these differing demand potentials so that they able to take advantage and so forecast and plan the need for future resources. An example might be the cigarette industry that is declining in the west but growing in the east.

Example 2.34 **Innovation or industry life cycle position**

A study by McGahan and Silverman looked at patenting activity in the American economy between 1981 and 1997. Their findings suggest that industry life cycle models based on stages of maturity may not accurately describe innovative activity. Rather, models based on the pace and kind of innovation may be more appropriate. The authors argued that it was much more fruitful to see how open the industry was to absorbing new technologies rather than at what stage the industry stood in the life cycle.

The sales forecast and demand potential

The identification of market potential will not mean that this is the level of sales that a company will achieve as there are other factors that will have to be taken into account. The organisation must have the resources available, or within easy attainment, to take advantage of possible sales potential. This will include elements across the whole marketing mix offering employee skills, technology, product portfolio choice, new product development, necessary channels of distribution and, last but not least, promotional methods. Any demand potential will also be of interest to the competition from both national and international organisations.

> The greater the sales and profit potential, the more intense will be the competition.

The secret for any company wishing to take full advantage of demand potential is to identify markets where it can best use any resource that might give it a sustainable competitive advantage. Ultimately it is from the use of this demand potential process that the B2B organisation will attempt to identify, select and segment markets it might be interested in entering. Broad sales forecasts for each segment will drive the process and from this the eventual markets to be covered can be selected.

More detailed forecasting used in the strategic planning process can then be undertaken. It is crucial that the market segments to be targeted are clearly identified and that products and services are developed with benefits that satisfy the needs of each selected segment. The sales forecast then becomes the overriding budget from which all other budgets will emanate (The process of segmentation selection and targeting is discussed at length in Chapter 4.)

> Assessing the future needs for equipment, services, employees, finance, technology and so on will be very difficult, if not impossible, if the future level of each market segment sales is uncertain or unknown.

 More can be seen on sales forecasting on the *B2B Marketing* website at www. booksites.net/wright Ch 1.

☐ Summary

In this chapter we attempted to build on the background discussion presented in Chapter 1 and began by examining the external environmental influences that will have some kind of effect on B2B organisational buying decisions. The differences between B2B and B2C markets were compared throughout the chapter. External factors discussed included political and legal, economic, cultural and technical. Political factors were considered from both a government and non-government perspective, looking at the role of governments in setting out the legal and moral frameworks of B2B markets at the national and transnational level as well as the role of non-governmental organisations such as lobbyists and trade associations.

The importance of the economy to the well-being of organisations was then discussed, highlighting among other things such concerns as levels of demand, employment levels and exchange rates. The importance of cultural factors was highlighted and examples of different business practices from around the world were compared and discussed in trying to decide whether this importance was stable or declining. Technology was shown to be pervasive and examples were given where B2B organisations can both gain and lose competitive advantage if its importance is not recognised and evaluated. We made it known that all these areas would be revisited constantly as we move through the book.

We then examined the more immediate influences that will confront all organisations both at home and abroad, concentrating first on competition and then on customers and markets. The need for continuous information on the competition was the first area identified and examples were given on the type of questions that a B2B company should be asking. We then moved on to discuss competitive intensity, the existence of market leaders, followers, major and minor players, sources of competitive advantage and the importance of having a strong base to act as a springboard when marketing abroad.

Customers and markets were then brought up and we briefly looked at general customer and market type differences across all markets.

Finally, we went on to examine the concept of supply and demand in the economy and how it will affect the B2B market. Different types of demand were identified, including derived, horizontal and vertical demand, and the marketing implications discussed. The process of investigating demand potential was broken down by country, industry, market and company groups so that it might be inspected more readily.

Discussion questions

1. Identify political and economic factors that will affect the B2B marketing process. Give examples for each area.

2. How important is it for governments to set the legal, social and moral framework for the interplay of supply and demand in free markets? Do you think that governments are doing too much or too little?

3. How much influence might culture have on business buyer behaviour around the world? Give examples and discuss whether you think culture is getting more or less influential.

4. How might business organisations combat the growth of more competition from around the world? Do you think that this is a good or bad thing? Give reasons and examples.

5. Technology seems to permeate every area of business activity. Give examples of its development and speculate on future developments.

6. Discuss the proposition posited by Michael Porter that a strong home market is crucial for a strong global presence. Try to identify examples of real global organisations to illustrate your comments.

7. Organisational corruption and cronyism are problems around the world and some commentators argue that they cannot be stopped. What might your opinion be on this problem?

8. Discuss the importance of understanding demand potential. How might it be successfully undertaken by an organisation across all markets?

9. Identify and discuss the factors that influence the level of sales demand in any one market.

10. Discuss the concept of horizontal and vertical demand. Why has it taken on added importance over the last decade?

11. Many B2B organisations ignore the process of derived demand. Why might this be foolish? Identify and evaluate sales demand forecasting methods.

Visit the *B2B Marketing* website at www.booksites.net/wright for a Case Study, Questions, and an Internet exercise for this chapter.

☐ Bibliography

Books

Aaker, A. (2001) *Strategic Marketing Management*. Chichester: Wiley.

Bartol, K.M. and Martin, D.C. (1991) *Management*. New York: McGraw-Hill.

Bayliss, J. (1985) *Industrial Marketing: Case Histories of UK Practice*. Birmingham: University of Aston.

Brooks, I. and Weatherston, J. (2000) *The Business Environment – Challenges and Changes*, 2nd edn. Harlow: Pearson Education.

Buchanan, D. and Badham, R. (1999) *Power, Politics and Organisational Change*. London: Sage.

Burnes, B. (1996) *Managing Change: A Strategic Approach to Organisational Dynamics*. London: Pearson Education.

Cateora, P.R. and Graham, J.L. (2000) *International Marketing*. New York: McGraw-Hill.

Catt, S.E. and Miller, D.S. (1989) *Human Relations: A Contemporary Approach*. Homewood, IL: Richard D. Irwin.

Daffy, C. (1999) *Once a Customer, Always a Customer*, 2nd edn. Dublin: Oak Tree Press.

Dwyer, R.F. and Tanner, J.F. (1999) *Business Marketing*. New York: McGraw-Hill.

Eckles, R.W. (1990) *Business Marketing Management, Marketing of Business Products and Services*. Harlow: Prentice Hall.

Ford, D. (1997) *Understanding Business Markets*, 2nd edn. London: Dryden Press.

Foss, B. and Stone, M. (2001) *Successful Customer Relationship Marketing: New Thinking, New Strategies, New Tools for Getting Closer to your Customers*. London: Kogan Page.

Heller, R. (1998) *Communicate Clearly*. New York: DK Publishing.

Hill, R. and Hillier, T. (1977) *Organisational Buying Behaviour*. London: Macmillan.

Hunt, J.G., Osborn, R.N. and Schermerhorn, J.R. Jr. (2000) *Organizational Behaviour*. New York: Wiley.

Ingham, B. (1995) *Economics and Development*. Maidenhead: McGraw-Hill.

Lambin, J.J. (2000) *Market-driven Management: Strategic and Operational Marketing*. London: Macmillan.

Lewis, J.D. (1995) *The Connected Corporation: Customer–Supplier Alliances*. New York: Free Press.

Lovelock, C. and Weinberg, C. (1984) *Marketing for Public and Non-profit Managers*. New York: Wiley.

Manse, S. and Andrews, P. (1994) *How Microsoft's Mogul Reinvented an Industry – And Made Himself the Richest Man in America*. Touchstone Books, USA.

Porter, M.E. (1998a) *The Competitive Advantage of Nations*. New York: Free Press.

Porter, M.E. (1998b) *Competitive Strategy: Techniques for Analyzing Industries and Competitors*. New York: Free Press.

Porter, M.E. (1998c) *Competitive Advantage: Creating and Sustaining Superior Performance*. New York: Free Press.

Senior, B. (1997) *Organisational Change*. London: Pearson Education.

Sloman, J. and Sutcliffe, M. (1998) *Economics for Business*. Harlow: Prentice Hall.

Smith, A. ([1776] 1991) *An Inquiry into the Nature and Causes of the Wealth of Nations*. London: Prometheus.

Weber, M. (1947) *The Theory of Social and Economic Organization*. New York: Free Press.

Wright, R. (2001) *Marketing: Origins, Concepts, Environment*. London: Thomson.

Journals

Hunt, S. and Morgan, R. (1995) 'The comparative advantage theory of competition', *Journal of Marketing*, 59: 1–15.

Wilson, I. (2000) 'The new rules: ethics, social responsibility and strategy', *Strategy and Leadership*, 28: 12–16.

 Visit www.booksites.net/wright for the Internet references for this chapter.

03

Understanding business marketing environments

Errors using inadequate data are much less than those using no data at all.

Aims and objectives

By the end of this chapter the student should be able to:

1. Be aware of the importance of information about the business-to-business market environment as a crucial aid in the management decision-making process. This will be at both national and global level.

2. Appreciate the types of data needed and be able to analyse and evaluate the importance of the information gathered when looking at and comparing marketing in B2B and B2C markets.

3. Identify and evaluate both formal and informal organisational gathering processes including the uses of the Marketing Information Process.

Part 1 Information for understanding strategic and tactical decision making

☐ Introduction

In the preceding chapters we looked at the background to B2B marketing, examining the different areas that influence the running of the business and identifying factors in the external environment. In this chapter we examine the role that information gathering plays in the whole process. No important decision should be made without first trying to obtain adequate information. It is true that sometimes there is not enough available and when this is the case the manager will have to move on the level of information available coupled with experience, knowledge and intuition. In a sense it is ironic that the more important decisions that could make or break organisations, seeking out market information and choosing and planning strategies, have to anticipate future direction and have to be made with the knowledge that the further we look into the future the more uncertain and unreliable might be the information. Nevertheless this should not stop marketing managers from trying. There are many agencies, commercial companies and experts that can be consulted to help lessen the risk, but ultimately senior management executives are paid large amounts of money (too much in many stakeholders' eyes) to make important strategic decisions that could sink or save the organisation.

☐ Information is power

> *Knowledge in the form of an informational commodity indispensable to productive power is already, and will continue to be, a major - perhaps the major - stake in the worldwide competition for power. It is conceivable that the nation-states will one day fight for the control of information, just as they battled in the past for control over territory, and afterwards for control over access to and exploitation of raw materials and cheap labour.*

(Lyotard, 1984)

All politicians recognise the importance of having control over the dissemination of information. To be able to decide what should and should not be known and to be able to control the flow of this information has been at the heart of political power for centuries. The democratic process itself depends on the population having access to the right information so that both sides of the argument can be weighed and votes cast accordingly. Similarly, the B2B organisation that has the ability to gather the most realistic, up-to-date environmental information on a continuous basis, and then to exploit and use this advantage wisely, is more likely to be the one that has the most success.

Much has been written about consumer behaviour and new and updated information is constantly coming into the public arena. Just as important for many organisations is the need to have an understanding of how industries and organisations might behave under differing marketing and environmental circumstances, although less information seems available. Anticipating buyer and group and individual reactions, from both a theoretical and practical standpoint, will enhance the supplier competitive marketing approach taken, as will an understanding that there will most likely be differences from country to country. From a wider perspective there must be the need for successful marketing managers to have an overall understanding of human nature if they are to motivate and get the best out of their staff, as well as diplomatically communicating and interacting with staff across other company functions. They will most likely be working with management and staff within other partnership companies where relationships can be more fraught and the same imperative must apply.

Information and competitive advantage

The most successful working person is likely to be the one who is most knowledgeable and has the most information about the industry they have chosen as a career. When we meet someone who truly seems to know the business they are working in and can readily supply information requested, the results are impressive. In consumer markets there are often salespeople who seem to know very little about the products and services offered. This may engender frustration and disappointment and encourage the prospective customer to go elsewhere. This may not cause an immediate problem in B2C markets as there might be hundreds of other potential customers looking for new or replacement products. On the other hand the same outcome between seller and buyer has the potential for creating a huge problem in the B2B sector. The busy business buyer might only offer a supplier's sales representative a small amount of time to put over the benefits of working with his or her company. The B2B salesperson who can talk about all aspects of a particular industry, offering a customer help and advice about relevant products and services, who can discuss competitors in an objective comparative manner and really demonstrate an understanding of the industry, will be highly respected and has every chance of being invited back time and time again.

Example 3.1 **Knowledge is power**

The B2B organisation, the marketing and sales managers and sales staff (as well as all other customer-facing employees) that have more current information about present and future markets and needs than anybody else, know the opposition as well as their own company, and can use this information in a professional manner will have the foundation for an unbeatable competitive advantage over all others. The imperative is to know more about your markets than the competition and know more about the competition than they know about you.

Evolutionary markets require detailed information

In the past there was the need to have information about markets and environments, but not in the detail and degree demanded in the present climate. B2C and B2B marketing in mass markets required participants to garner environmental and industry knowledge and a broad understanding of consumer (in the case of B2C) and industry (in the case of B2B) cultural needs and wants. This might still be the situation when selling into developing markets such as China or Indonesia. With the marketing evolution into broad segmentation, more information was needed about targeted group needs: socio-economic, behaviour and lifestyle in the case of consumer markets; public or private, industry sector and type of organisation in the case of business markets.

The insatiable consumer appetite for ever more choice and the needs (driven by competing business buyers) for state-of-the-art optimising benefits have almost inevitably led to the development of products and services that more readily meet the needs and wants of each individual customer, whether in the B2B or B2C sector. Mass customisation, one-to-one marketing, customer relationship management, marketing relationship management, and so on are all current examples of projects that now reflect the thinking of both marketing academics and business practitioners (and no doubt more will follow in the same vein). The right sorts of information are now needed, interactively if possible, at every stage of the buying process – before, during and after the sale (often along the whole supply chain) – hopefully driving greater long-term mutually beneficial exchange processes for both customer and seller (Figure 3.1).

> Far better an approximate answer to the right question, which is often vague, than an exact answer to the wrong question, which can always be made precise.

Figure 3.1
Level and degree of market information needed

Information for decision making is now of such importance in an ever more competitive environment that the information collecting process must be implemented, directed and supported at the highest strategic level. Without senior management continuous support, information gathering can be seen from a narrow departmental perspective, causing the wrong information to be collected, dissemination restricted and/or the information to be offered in an unusable form. History is replete with examples of expensive information systems that have been constructed with software that does not work and/or are manned by people who are not market and customer orientated. Information gathering has to be customer and client driven and must always be presented in a client-friendly manner, and the process must have feedback monitoring and control systems built in. In this way the management and other users, at all levels in the company, can be encouraged to comment constantly on the quality, reliabilite and relevance of the data collected. If it is not helpful it should be dumped.

Information gathering in B2B markets will be carried out by both seller and buyer organisations all along the supply chain and, depending on the partnerships and working practices in place, shared so that ultimate customer satisfaction is constantly assured. The quality and quantity of information is more important to some organisations than others depending on organisational type, products and services sold and markets served. A supplier making own-label products under contract solely to one of the big supermarkets will not need as much information as the company selling direct to many manufacturers in the continually changing electronics market. Here are a few examples of strategic information needed in B2B markets:

☐ Which market segments are the greatest in terms of sales, growth and profit?

☐ Which segments are growing, declining or static?

☐ Who are the major competitors in each segment and what are their strengths and weaknesses?

☐ Should the company outsource any of its logistic activities, warehousing, transportation and inventory management, or has the trend proved to be short term?

☐ How threatening is the growth in strategic alliances and will it continue?

Information at the tactical level

It must be remembered that information is also needed for tactical decisions and programme implementation. There has been a danger in the past that strategy has become divorced from the tactical implementation with the two processes seen as almost separate in some ways. While successful B2B organisations recognise the need for long-term thinking, they will not neglect the information needed in putting the idea of customer satisfaction into operation. Examples of information needed at the tactical level include:

- Product benefits and level of service needed by each organisation
- Responsibilities allocated
- Performance indicators agreed
- Budgets agreed
- Number of sales calls needed and sales targets
- Support resources needed
- CRM systems in place and working
- Monitoring and control systems.

Why research industrial markets?

There is a need to research all markets whether B2B or B2C. In B2C the major concern is making products and services to match the ever-changing consumer demands. In B2B the pressure to get industrial products with the right benefits to market ahead of the competition is the main concern. In both markets research helps reduce the risk (which can never be completely eliminated) of promoting the wrong benefits with existing products and services and of bringing the wrong benefit packages to new markets. It can also forewarn organisations about impending happenings in both the macro and the micro environments, allowing the necessary strategic and tactical actions to be taken. It should be remembered ultimately that all decisions must be made by managers based on knowledge and experience and using research as an aid to the decision-making process, not as a substitute.

Lack of information about the B2B sector

Some commentators have criticised marketing academics and others on the lack of information available on the B2B industrial sector, at both the academic and pragmatic levels. When searching for inspiration about this important side of business, there appears to be a paucity of relevant material. It could be argued that it has been sadly neglected and very little studied as a business subject. There are those who argue that there are some aspects of academic marketing theory, the use of models and so on, which seem to have little relevance to what goes on in the real world and so are of small use to marketing practitioners.

Information about the B2C sector

Much has been written over the last 50 years about marketing, its origins, concepts and practices, but most of it tends to be focused on the B2C and especially retail fast-moving consumer goods (FMCG). In a way this is understandable because both basic marketing theory and marketing practice lend themselves more readily to the idea of marketing to the domestic consumer, either in segmented groups or as individuals. Empirical examples are everywhere. We are all consumers and most of us are involved in seeking out, purchasing and using many different products and services on a daily basis. Consumer marketing is all around us constantly. Market researchers stop us on the street to ask questions about behaviour. Outdoor billboards, retail outlets, corporate images, point-of-purchase material and stock displays attempt to seduce us into spending our money and adverts hit us every time we watch TV, listen to the radio or go to the cinema. In many cases human behaviour, sociology, psychology, decision making, purchasing processes, branding and advertising have more interest to the researcher in consumer markets than in business-to-business markets and, importantly, examples are readily available.

Information on the B2B sector

Conditions are different in B2B markets. Although individuals or groups are involved, the purchase is being made for the well-being of the organisation. The area of study is organisational behaviour rather than consumer behaviour and, to many, not nearly so exciting. Decisions are made for rational rather than emotional reasons. Products and services wanted could be considered prosaic and mundane and communication strategies lack the drama and exhilaration of B2C markets. Add to this the difficulty of obtaining the right sorts of information and it can be seen why B2B marketing, despite the major part that it plays in the world economy, might be considered the Cinderella of marketing disciplines.

Information needed when looking at B2B organisational behaviour

☐ History, economics, geography, culture

☐ Organisation structure and design, systems and decision-making process, the management of technology

☐ Motivation, teamwork, stress and conflict, communications, power and politics, leadership and communication, culture and change

☐ Managing change, models of organisational change, the managerial and HR aspects of globalisation, new ways of organising work and new managerial systems and the management of innovation, organisational buying patterns.

Information needed when looking at consumer behaviour

☐ Sociology, social anthropology, social class, culture, subculture, personal characteristics, group interaction, group buying patterns

☐ Perception, learning, attitude, motivation, individual and group psychology, social/cognitive/dynamic/physiological psychology, personality, lifestyle.

Scarcity of information on B2B services

Another area of marketing literature that might be considered to be underrepresented in the amount of information available is that of services. Although services have an important part to play in B2C markets, they might be considered even more so in B2B marketing where so many benefits need critically to incorporate a high level of service. A failure of after-sales service in the B2C sector can result in the loss of one customer and perhaps some bad publicity. In the B2B markets, however, it can be catastrophic, both for the buyer in terms of lost production and/or loss of sales and for the seller in terms of the wrath and loss of a major global customer.

Example 3.2   ## Expensive after-sales problems

Continental, the German tyre company, has recalled 600,000 tyres fitted on Ford Expedition and Lincoln Navigator sport utility vehicles in the USA because some tyres have been losing their threads. Continental's recall is the largest since the 2000 recall of 6.5 million tyres by its competitor Bridgestone/Firestone after a series of fatal accidents involving the Ford Explorer sport utility vehicle. Recalls of all kinds have increased tenfold with 1.5 million taken back this year because of faults of some kind. Both manufacturer and suppliers have been accused of bad service practice of some kind.

Research should be used as an aid to the decision-making process, not as a substitute.

Information overload

One of the unhelpful side-effects of the information revolution has been the increase in pressure on employees through different forms of information overload. It should be recognised that just because the organisation, has the capability for almost unlimited information collection and classification that is no reason for gathering and hoarding data that will not be of use in the foreseeable future. The availability of too much information can cause prospective users to be so overcome by the quantity of information available that they cannot distinguish the good from the bad and the relevant from the not so relevant. At best this can cause frustration and withdrawal and at worst it can cause illness and time off work. The answer must be some type of assistance and built-in filtering system and/or skills training that helps the user to judge what is and is not usable data.

Example 3.3   ## Information overload

The Institute of Management and PPP Healthcare have just published a report that shows that keeping up with hundreds of e-mails a day is one of the major causes of workplace stress for managers. Office e-mail systems, leading to information overload, also contributed to the top two sources of workplace stress – constant interruptions and deadline pressures – which can damage performance at work as well as putting personal lives at risk. A report by the Department of Trade and Industry found that workers take an average of 49 minutes a day to sort out their inboxes and many employees found that keeping up with office e-mails had become a logistical nightmare. According to the DTI, sick days as a result of stress cost business £7.11 million a week in the UK.

☐ Information-gathering process

The information-gathering process can be formal, informal or a mixture of the two and will vary between organisations, depending on size, wealth, style, management inclination and the industry itself. It will also depend on the operating climate. The more turbulent the environment and the more open to change and competition the product or service, the greater will be the need for a continuous stream of relevant up-to-date information.

Informal research

Much information gathering is done on an informal basis and tends not to be seen as marketing research, but its value cannot be underestimated. It was argued above that the successful person is the knowledgeable person who has an inquisitive and enquiring mind, always asking questions about customers and markets, competition and products and storing the data in their long-term memory for later use. The wise B2B manager is the one who generates this sort of culture, encouraging employees to seek out and report back any relevant information that might have an influence on and be beneficial to the running of the business. Using the whole workforce constantly to look at what is happening locally, nationally and around the world will motivate all to feel that they are part of the company set-up and, more importantly, provide marketing strategists with a valuable source of informational supply. This process can be semi-formalised by building in some sort of reward system for information that proves to be the most useful. It does not make sense if a supplier is unaware that a competitor is researching a new product range, talking to buyers about partnerships, or thinking about moving out of a particular market segment when a salesperson might have picked up useful information but found little management interest.

Formal research

As well as informal information gathering, most modern companies recognise how strategically important it is to have some type of formal, consistent and constant information-gathering system based upon the need for clear business outcomes. This formal information-gathering, classification and analysis system can be identified under many different headings according to the academic or business practitioner followed. It might be called a management information system (MIS), business information system (BIS), marketing information system, and so on. Many large organisations will develop subsystems to help the different departmental functions. There could well be a 'competitive analysis system', a 'financial information-gathering system', a 'social auditing system', and so on. This should not cause any concern for the user as long as all agree on its usage and title and the information system works. For the purpose here we will adopt the term Marketing Information System (MkIS). This could well be seen as a subset of the management or business information system.

For B2B marketing to function properly it needs constant information about all areas in the internal and external environment. This will cover information on such things as the size, depth, trends of markets, customers changing buying needs, competitor movements and relevant political, economic, social and technical (PEST) factors.

☐ Marketing information system

Most CEOs still believe that it's the chief information officer's job to identify the information he requires. This is, of course, a fallacy. The information officer is a toolmaker; the CEO is the tool user.

(Drucker, 1986)

As discussed above, eventually the information-gathering process will need to be viewed from a strategic perspective and put on a formal footing. This will help communicate to all employees the importance that the company places on using good information when making important decisions about customers and markets. With the advent and development of information technology, any organisation, whatever its size and financial situation, can now afford to have access to information technology, data storage and analysis equipment and services either by purchase or alternatively through leasing, rental, outsourcing and sharing. If the latter options are chosen there is usually an option to buy in on either a continuous or an ad hoc basis.

A strategic approach in setting up the MkIS

Whatever the approach taken, its long-term strategic importance to the well-being of the organisation should be recognised and direction and support should emanate from the very top, at director level. It should involve all potential users (not only in the marketing department but also across all departments) in its design and be tested and retested to make certain that information both in and out is relevant to employee needs. Monitoring, feedback and control mechanisms must be instituted to see that what needs to happen actually happens. The monitoring process should be such that if user access is difficult, if the information collected is of the wrong kind or if the data analysis is unhelpful, the process must be changed. Marketing information systems must, in true marketing fashion, be driven by the needs of the internal customers and not by the agenda and objectives of the designers and operators.

Using outside consultants to set up the MkIS

In many cases, organisations will use outside commercial consultants to set up a marketing information system. This will probably be because the company feels it lacks the skills and resources to set up the process in-house. This will undoubtedly be expensive, sometimes costing tens of millions of pounds. A cost benefit analysis will therefore need to be carried out. It is crucial that the system operates in the desired way. In most cases if the difficulties experienced by the buyer are only small then after-sales service can soon rectify the problems. However, organisations can sometimes experience horrendous difficulties once the system has been installed and taken over by the business users. Complaints usually centre around problems such as computer systems not operating in the functional manner wanted, or the information analysis being more simplistic than was originally discussed, and so on. The faults can be laid at the door of both the consultants and the buying managers. As with all customised and complex systems, the sales consultant will rely on the needs and wants as given by the customer when putting together the product. But if too many people are involved, as is often the case, confusion can arise on prioritising what is and is not wanted. Similarly the client may have a problem in articulating precisely what processes are wanted and so fail to communicate this to the programme designers. It can also be the case that the consultant sales team, wanting to earn lots of money, will promise much more than the marketing information system is capable of achieving for the money the customer wants to pay. Whatever the reasons, buying organisations must take time to discuss objectives among themselves so that they are in no doubt about their needs. These needs should then be clearly communicated to the supplying consultant. If there are any doubts, because of the huge amount of resources that might be involved, independent experts should be called in to advise on the whole project.

Example 3.4   **Expensive computer failures**

Trials on a new multimillion pound computer system for the Child Support Agency have discovered that it will not yet provide the long-awaited reforms it was originally designed to introduce. The new set-up was needed to help speed up the calculation of payments as well as collection times but has been found not to work. Critics have said that it is a classic example of how not to run an IT project, buying an expensive new computer to run old processes. The contract to provide the new technology was awarded to the Texas-based company EDS under a private finance initiative (PFI), but it now looks as if the taxpayer will have to pay. This follows similar computer systems disasters in the Inland Revenue, hospital trusts, Ambulance Service, Stock Exchange and Air Traffic Control. The list seems endless.

☐ The MkIS process

The B2B formal information-gathering process, the MkIS, can be broken down into the following four areas:

1. Internal information.
2. Marketing intelligence system.
3. Marketing research.
4. Information storage and analysis.

1. Internal information

An organisation will have a whole range of internal quantitative and qualitative performance indicators within its many functions. This information is essential to both the B2B and the B2C marketing managers (and others) in the successful performance of their jobs. It is surprising how often this source of information is not utilised as effectively as it should be. There are examples of marketing managers seemingly unaware that certain markets are declining and others are increasing, or uncertain about the financial contribution of one product over another. There cannot be any excuse for not having this information at hand.

Types of information obtained internally

The financial department can supply figures on sales, costs and profitability across the whole product/service portfolio, as well as figures on cash flow, accounts receivable and accounts payable. They can supply costs on which customers are the most profitable and which the most expensive, who is the highest risk and who isn't, which combination of products/services is the most profitable and which the most expensive, and so on (the type of information invaluable to activity based costing).

Production can supply figures on optimum production runs, inventory positions and future needs. Indispensable to the system are the sales force reports coming into the company. The salesperson is in the unique position of being the eyes and the ears of the company out in the marketplace. The information they are able to collect on the customer, competition, suppliers, etc. must be given the recognition it deserves. This is the major reason why the salesperson's report should never be used as a method of policing and control. All employee contributions to the information-gathering process should be encouraged by the use of some form of recognition and reward system.

Information needed on buyers and suppliers

The following are examples of information that can be obtained internally which will help in maximising the relationships with buyers and suppliers.

Internal information on buyers

- ☐ Overall sales and profit figures
- ☐ Numbers of customers, who buys the most and the least
- ☐ Which customers buy across the whole range and which buy selectively and why
- ☐ Which buyers make the company the most and the least amounts of profit
- ☐ Which customers offer the best and the least potential
- ☐ Which competitors buyers are using and why.

Internal information on suppliers

- ☐ Which suppliers deliver on time and which are often late
- ☐ Which suppliers are in or out of stock most often

☐ How supplier prices vary with value

☐ Which suppliers are the most cost effective

☐ Which suppliers also sell to the competitors and why.

The Pareto 80/20 rule tells us that 80 per cent of our business comes from 20 per cent of our customers or 80 per cent of our profits are made from 20 per cent of our customers, and so on.

Information coordination

The marketing department will need to set up a system for collecting and analysing reports from all the different internal areas. Yearly and monthly trends can be monitored so as to identify how the markets are performing and how they might perform into the future. Sales and pricing can be compared with the competition and comparisons made between outlets and distribution channels. Qualitative observations and suggestions should also be encouraged and rewarded if this is thought to be necessary.

Consultation across departments and divisions

Organisations wishing to set up an internal report system should interview the various managers to ascertain their information needs. This can then be converted into a formal system of internal reporting. Like the laying down of any system, it is essential that clear objectives are set. It should then be monitored and controlled to make certain that it is working and there is a flow of the right information to the marketing department. Of course the flow should not just be one way. Marketing information should be available through a well thought out communications system to which every department should have access.

The value of internal information cannot be over-emphasised and it should be formalised, monitored and controlled.

---

2. Marketing intelligence system

It was stated earlier that for an individual or a company to be a success, information about the relevant industry must be collected in a systematic way. It was argued that the superior performer would know more about markets than any other participant. The marketing intelligence system is that part of the MkIS where the environment is monitored on a 24/7/365 *continuous basis* for any information that might have some bearing, present or future, on the company's marketing performance.

Intelligence unit

The size of the intelligence unit collecting information is relatively important and will depend on the size of the organisation. It may be a whole department or just one person working part time. What is important is the motivating thrust. There should be an almost obsessional need to unearth and classify any snippet of information, no matter how small, that might relate to the company's particular industry and can be used immediately or stored for future use. As well as those who work directly for the intelligence unit, all staff will need to be motivated and trained in intelligence-gathering techniques so that it becomes an essential part of the company culture. Because of the seemingly infinite amount of information available, skills needed will include the ability to sort the wheat from the chaff.

In a large organisation, whole departments will spend their time scouring magazines, newspapers, trade press, the web and other relevant sources, pulling out articles that might supply a vital insight into the workings of both the industry and the business, so helping to improve performance. Trends in the marketplace can be analysed and compared over the months and years, looking for significant changes that could affect environments and competitive advantage. Working in this way, a database of information can be built up and then used to analyse and forecast movements in the immediate and wider environment.

External information gathering agencies

There exist commercial companies willing to offer a specific intelligence-gathering service for most if not all B2B industries and businesses (for a price, of course). This might be in the form of an article collecting service and/or a continuous research programme that looks at markets, customers and competition in a particular industry. Much of this can be downloaded to the customer by the agency on a daily basis.

Example 3.5 ## Datamonitor helps with intelligence research

Datamonitor plc is a premium business information company specialising in industry analysis. It helps 5000 of the world's leading companies, to address complex strategic issues. Through their proprietary databases and wealth of expertise, they provide clients with unbiased expert analysis and in-depth forecasts for six industry sectors: Automotive, Consumer Markets, Energy, Financial Services, Healthcare and Technology. Datamonitor maintains its headquarters in London and has regional offices in New York, Frankfurt and Hong Kong.

Datamonitor's reports provide a consummate mix of market data, market intelligence and insightful analysis. Based on exclusive quantitative and qualitative research, Datamonitor's market reports combine insight derived from over ten years of experience in all its key markets. Clients will immediately benefit from Datamonitor's unrivalled perception that comes from blending a thorough understanding of current and future market issues with genuine industry expertise. The result is strategic market intelligence that is vital to market sizing, forecasting and business decision making. (www.datamonitor.com)

3. Marketing research

The difference between marketing research and intelligence gathering is one of degree and should not give the reader cause to insist that a method should be in one category rather than another. The difference between marketing research and intelligence gathering is that marketing research is done for a special purpose while marketing intelligence gathering is something that goes on all the time. Marketing research will be used where some kind of specific information seems to be unavailable from marketing intelligence sources. Care will be taken in setting up this kind or research because the costs can be extremely high. Depending on both the scale and the objectives of the marketing research, it can be undertaken in-house or, as is much more likely, contracted out to one of the large marketing research companies such as BMRB or Mori that operate on both a national and global scale.

Example 3.6 **Pharmaceutical research**

UK drugs companies are investing £8 million a day in research, according to new figures. More than 560 medicines are in development, including new approaches to treating cancer and heart disease. The pharmaceutical industry is footing the bill for two-thirds of the research. The remaining funds come from medical charities, academia and the government.

Benchmarking research for superior performance

Information will be needed so that the organisation can benchmark its processes and systems with the best in the business so that optimum value is added as resources are moved from purchase through the organisation and out to the business customer. Many organisations will also want to implement the same processes within their suppliers, aware that the whole supply chain must operate effectively if competitive advantage is to be maintained. Information for benchmarking can be obtained cooperatively from other companies not in direct competition, from trade associations, governments and agencies that specialise in supplying inter-firm comparison information.

So marketing research will be adopted if information is needed for a new product development or launch or a new promotional campaign, if sales of a particular product are falling, or if a company is thinking of expanding into another country. In all probability one of the hundreds of marketing research agencies would be hired for the purpose. Information from marketing research might be used for any the following purposes:

☐ Analysing new market segments at home and around the world

☐ Identifying new markets and/or customers

☐ Researching the existing market for a new product/service launch

☐ Talking to buying organisations about future wants and needs.

4. Information, storage and analysis

To err is human, but to really foul things up requires a computer.

(Anon.)

Information from all the sources identified above needs to be classified, stored, analysed and, where necessary, cross-referenced for ease of use. In the distant past this task would have been undertaken manually (probably through use of a carded classification system), but now even the smallest of companies can have access to more sophisticated information technology (IT) methods.

Information technology and the use of computers enable large amounts of information to be stored in an information database, retrieved in moments, cross-informational comparisons made, cross-fertilisation exercises undertaken and statistical and computer models used to examine and test the scientific validity of research undertaken or assumptions formulated. One database can be compared with another so organisational spend might be evaluated against promotional activity or buyer behaviour compared with level of personal contact made. Networking and the internet allow this to be done on both a national and an international scale.

Database marketing

The increasing number of uses for IT have led to the development of so-called database marketing. The amount of data now available has allowed organisations to build huge computer databases on their existing and potential customers and markets, full of detailed information that can then be used accurately to market products and services directly and personally to all B2B customers as and when needed. A whole range of customer characteristics can be entered into the database: size of potential order, buying cycle, benefits wanted, and so on, and then cross-referenced so that individual company and buyer profile can be developed. This will enable the seller to offer customised products and services when and where needed that exactly match customer needs.

Relationship marketing

The enhanced capability offered by database marketing enables the producer to develop an ever closer interactive relationship with existing or past customers on a *long-term continuous* basis. Most B2B marketing relationships used to be based on individual transactions, each meeting between salesperson and buyer being a negotiated exercise where the seller would want the highest price and the buyer the lowest. This is still the case in some industries. However, research has shown that it is much more expensive and time consuming to gain new customers than it is to hold on to the existing ones. The development of IT capabilities has enabled constant, personalised, interactive contact to be built. In B2B, one customer can account for a large proportion of the seller's turnover and their loss to a competitor can at best blow a large hole in company sales and at worst put

Figure 3.2
B2B relationship and transaction marketing

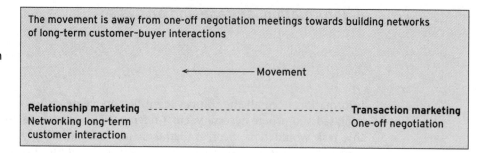

The movement is away from one-off negotiation meetings towards building networks of long-term customer–buyer interactions

←——————— Movement

Relationship marketing - **Transaction marketing**
Networking long-term   One-off negotiation
customer interaction

the company out of business. So B2B buyers like Ford or GKN will be contacted on a regular basis, either personally or by letter, e-mail, magazines, etc., with information and advice about such things as new and existing products, special offers or problems that might be happening. The concept underpinning this form of 'relationship marketing' is the hope that the customer will be so satisfied they are won and held for life (Figure 3.2).

Customer relationship management

Relationship marketing has spawned the development of so-called 'customer relationship management' (CRM) programmes. These programmes might take slightly different forms but the underpinning concept is the building of computer-aided systems that promote good and continuous relationships across every customer contact point. CRM programmes will be discussed in greater detail in later chapters. If they work as hoped, a business can gain the following advantages. At the strategic level:

- Understand and predict customer needs
- Build valued and long-term customer relationships
- Identify heavy and light users and manage customer profitability
- Improve branding and customer loyalty
- Market and sell across the whole product portfolio
- Contain delivery costs.

At the tactical level:

- Provide better customer service
- Make call centres more efficient
- Cross-sell products more effectively
- Help sales staff close deals faster
- Simplify marketing and sales processes
- Discover new customers
- Increase customer revenues.

Example 3.7 **How much does CRM cost?**

A survey (2001) of more than 1600 business and IT professionals conducted by the Data Warehousing Institute found that close to 50 per cent had CRM project budgets of less than $500,000. That would appear to indicate that CRM doesn't have to be a budget-buster. However, the same survey showed a handful of respondents with CRM project budgets of over $10 million. Industries leading the way in CRM implementations include most leading-edge technology implementations, the financial services and telecommunications industries. Other industries on the CRM bandwagon include consumer goods makers and retailers and high-tech firms. Manufacturers seem to be falling far behind.

CRM in B2C markets compared to B2B

We must all be aware of the growth in loyalty programmes and customer relationship programmes in the B2C markets. The challenge is different in B2C than in B2B. In the B2B sector, buyers and buying contact points are restricted and, because of continuous consolidation, are becoming more limited. Sellers tend to know the buyers, often from a personal perspective, and so circumstances are more propitious to building interactive relationships. This is not the case in the B2C sector. Retailers attempt to build CRM programmes with end consumers, but with limited appeal. There are millions of individual shoppers and so contact cannot be personal. Loyalty, if it exists in a meaningful way, is arguably superficial and easily dissipated. Most consumers are now promiscuous shoppers. They might hold many loyalty cards and will shop at different locations and different stores as the mood dictates. The big retailers are aware of this and constantly upgrade benefit offers and methods of contact. They might hold on to certain customer segments for longer than others but, because of competition, choice, and continuous product benefit upgrades, the loyalty demands will always be one-way, from store to consumer, impersonal and under threat.

Figure 3.3
The B2B
marketing
information
system (MkIS)

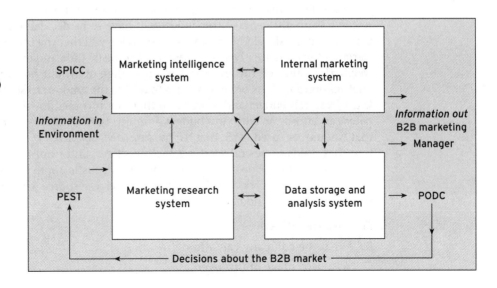

Part 2 The B2B marketing research process

Copying an idea from an author is plagiarism. Copying many ideas from many authors is research.

(Anon.)

We will now look in more detail specifically at the marketing research process. As identified above, marketing research is undertaken for a special purpose and the following factors need to be considered when using it to gather information.

☐ Clear marketing objectives

The beginning of the marketing research process, and arguably the most import-ant stage, is to clearly identify what information is needed. This may sound sim-ple but often this part of the process is the most difficult, frequently characterised by confusion and ambiguity. If the real problem is not identified at the very beginning, the whole process will be distorted. So the problem holder should seek, in discussion with others, to be crystal clear about the marketing research objectives. This will probably mean knowing the answers wanted before the results programme begins.

Marketing researchers, whether working for their own organisation or for an outside agency, must develop skills in getting to the heart of the problem. This will involve talking to the client, going away and analysing the information and then returning with the 'brief' that sets out the client's needs as the researcher understands them. This process will be repeated, back and forth if necessary, until no one is in any doubt about the purpose of the marketing research.

The marketing research budget

All marketing projects will include some form of financial cost. Marketing research is no different, so the budget will have to be decided upon. First, a cost benefit analysis should be undertaken to decide whether the information needed warrants the costs involved. Obviously if the costs, time and effort involved out-weigh the value of the expected returns, then it would be better to choose another option. There are many ways to decide the amount to spend on the mar-keting research budget and more often than not it comes down to what the com-pany can afford. As with any budget amount, there is ideally only one method that should be used and that is by *task and objective*. Decide the informa-tion that needs to be collected, set the objectives, and from this work out what the costs might be. However, this can be an unrealistic approach as many organ-isations have to work within certain financial resource constraints. Budget research setting methods include:

☐ Task and objectives
☐ What the company can afford
☐ As a percentage of turnover

- ☐ Market average
- ☐ The same as the year before.

> If the costs, time and effort involved in undertaking marketing research outweigh the value of the expected returns, then it would be better to choose another option.

Secondary and primary research

There are two distinct types of research: secondary and primary research. The marketing practitioner will probable use a combination of both. Secondary research is probably used more, and primary research used less, in B2B marketing when compared with B2C. This is because the B2B manager is concerned with such things as long-term economic trends, industry norms and market growth and decline, while the B2C manager, although concerned about these issues, will also need detailed primary information about the changing attitudes, lifestyle and behaviour of millions of consumers. We will look at each in turn, beginning with secondary research.

The collection of information can be costly and time consuming, especially if it means calling in an outside agency. Therefore it is important to appreciate that there is a great deal of information that can be collected, at relatively little cost, without the marketer ever leaving the office desk (hence it is sometimes called 'desk research').

☐ Secondary research (desk research)

Because of the nature of the markets, B2B organisations are heavily dependent on quantitative secondary research on which to base planning activity. Business confidence and business purchasing activity are based upon particular economic and industrial trends that will probably affect all in the industry. Market size, growth and potential tend to be the overriding concern, rather than the consumer psychology associated with the B2C. So a variation in interest rates and high value of the pound will affect everybody in manufacturing.

Companies that export products and services will suffer because prices will be more expensive and so could be uncompetitive. Conversely, companies that import will find that these goods and services are less expensive. Similarly a change of market circumstances, e.g. a rise in the price of oil, an increase in the minimum wage or higher steel prices, will probably affect all in the same industry. This effect will probably be felt within a very short time as an increase in B2B costs can often be passed on with the minimum of delay. This is especially so if there are only a few buyers and sellers in the market.

These sorts of changes will impinge on the B2C market, but their effect will probably be diluted, as the affected costs and prices will be spread across millions of customers, possibly across several target markets. It also takes longer to filter price increases through the supply chain to the end consumer, that is supposing the lack of competition will allow this to happen.

Secondary research in B2B Markets

- ☐ B2B industries are more heavily dependent on secondary research than B2C.

- ☐ B2B industries are less dependent on primary research than B2C.

- ☐ More secondary macro information is available about B2B markets nationally and around the world.

- ☐ Governments collect macro information for their own use and this then becomes available to organisations.

- ☐ B2B organisations are likely to respond, often immediately, to macro environmental trends.

- ☐ Fewer buyers in B2B markets make secondary information often directly applicable.

- ☐ Industries and organisations are likely to behave in ways identified by secondary research.

Secondary research in B2C markets

- ☐ B2C markets are more dependent on primary than on secondary research.

- ☐ Hundreds of millions of consumers make secondary information not immediately applicable.

- ☐ Individuals' motives are difficult to ascertain from secondary segmentation information.

- ☐ Individuals and groups can take a long time to respond to changes in the macro environment.

Information technology and the development of the World Wide Web

There has been an explosion in the amount of secondary information now available to businesses at the touch of a keyboard. This is especially so since the advent of the World Wide Web and internet. In fact there could be a case to argue that there is too much information potentially available, creating the 'not being able to see the wood from the trees' syndrome. This said, there is no doubt that the development of IT and the internet have created a revolution in the almost instantaneous availability of limitless data from around the world. A desk and a computer modem linked to the internet now allow the B2B practitioner to seek relevant information from every corner of the globe. Some of the information is free and some has to be paid for. Some information is available to trade association members and some available to all and sundry.

Industry and market reports from organisations around the world can now be either directly downloaded from a website or sent by e-mail rather than having to send a hard copy through the post or by fax machine. This has sped up and in some cases reduced the costs of the whole information giving and receiving process. Research organisations such as Mintel Information Services (www.mintel.co.uk)

make hundreds of industry and market research reports available online that can be downloaded at the click of a button.

Other information collecting tools also include the telephone, fax and services such as Prestel, Ceefax and Oracle that are delivered through the TV set or computer modem. Information is now available online, or on CD-ROM, DVD and magnetic tape.

B2B secondary information sources

Secondary research concerns B2B information that has already been collected by others (hence it is also sometimes known as 'secondhand' research). It is available from many sources and in a variety of forms as long as the marketer knows where to look.

Internal sources

The first place to go for information will be within the organisation itself. This might be from one company or, if global, from many divisions around the world. If there is an MkIS, then it is here that the first approach should be made. There might well be an intranet (internal internet) or an extranet (external private internet available only to a selected group of companies) online system in operation. Again this resource should be the first port of call. The task for internal providers is to make the right information immediately available when wanted in a form that matches the requirements of the internal customer. This task has sometimes turned out to be a problem because of the lack of presentation skills shown by the computer technicians who put together the computer programs.

There should be a systematic approach to the collection, classification and dissemination of information based on the clearly agreed and identified needs of the various internal and partnering information consumers with feedback, monitoring, control and evaluation factors built in.

External sources of information

1. Government
2. Professional/trade associations
3. Commercial information gatherers and consultants.

1. Government sources

All countries operating in modern industrial markets will offer organisations access to information about the workings of government departments, as well as access to specially collected information that might help the individual company in the more effective running of its business. This will include information on political, social and economic matters on a national and global level, at both macro and micro level. As discussed in Chapter 1, most power brokers are now committed to the economic paradigm of the free market and politicians generally accept the need for easy access to all types of information if businesses are to compete successfully in world markets.

Example 3.8 ## Government research spending

The Taiwan government has revealed plans to spend $1.43 billion in fresh loans to help R&D projects in a bid to double the industrial output of key sectors. These industrial development loans would benefit Taiwan's hi-tech industries in particular and would aid the development of products such as computer chips and TV screens, as well as of digital content and of biotechnology. In all, 17 of Taiwan's industries stand to benefit. The government is predicting that colour displays and semiconductor sales are set to soar. Communication technologies, including broadband and wireless, would also benefit. There would also be money available for industries producing precision instruments and for the hi-tech textile sector. Companies working on the production of electric cars and aircraft would also be eligible for support.

Open access to government information

Some of the information is made available because of legal obligation, but increasingly over the last decade many departments have been encouraged to make more available, both as a commercial exercise (to bring in revenue) and as an aid to business effectiveness and efficiency, especially as markets become more competitive. There has also been political pressure on government to become more open in its activities and thus make more information available to the public as a matter of course and as a right in a democratic society. The same demands have been aimed at pan-European information. Whether in reality this is happening is still open to conjecture, with some arguing that, because of vested interests, it will never happen, while others maintain it is only a matter of time. At present some countries allow more public access to information than others, either through legislation or by general consent.

The growth of the internet has hastened the process and the amount of government and quasi-government documents on the web seems to increase exponentially every month. Government information sources which can be seen on the government information website (www.open.gov.uk) include the following areas.

Office of National Statistics (ONS)

The ONS is a so-called *next-steps executive agency*, an independent government department in its own right (supposedly free of government interference). It is accountable directly to the Chancellor of the Exchequer. The ONS works in partnership with statistical staff in other government departments, attempting to give a rounded picture on the state and development of the UK economy as well as an overview of international economies.

The amount of data produced by the ONS is enormous, covering many areas of social, economic and business activity at both a macro and micro level:

☐ Economic data

☐ Product data

☐ General business statistics

- ☐ Labour markets, employment and unemployment statistics
- ☐ Gross domestic product (GDP) estimates on the movement of goods and services in the UK
- ☐ Retail sales statistics
- ☐ General household statistics
- ☐ Retail Price Index (RPI), the measure of inflation used to indicate movements and changes in consumer prices
- ☐ Social and lifestyle changes
- ☐ Demographic changes, movements, births, deaths, marriages
- ☐ The National Census which is carried out every 10 years, making public demographic information available about all residents of the UK.

Government Statistical Service (GSS)
The Government Statistical Service (GSS) is the main publisher of official business statistics in the UK. Most industrialised countries have similar services and, as discussed in Chapter 1, there is movement to standardise procedures and publications across all government statistics so that methods can be harmonised and realistic comparisons made. The GSS publishes information in books, reports and leaflets, as well as on audiotape and disk. In 1997 the Integrated Database (ID) division of the ONS was formed with the task of setting up and maintaining a central database of major economic, social and business statistics produced to common classifications, definitions and standards. In its Digest Series it publishes the *Annual Abstract of Statistics*, *Monthly Digest of Statistics* and *Financial Statistics*.

UK Official Publications (UKOP)
The UK Official Publications (UKOP) is the complete catalogue of all official publications. Many can be viewed both on CD-ROM and on the ONS website. UK Online now contains records for over 360,000 official publications and is updated and expanded on a monthly basis. As well as cataloguing and publishing UK parliamentary, departmental and agency publications, it also publishes works from supranational bodies such as the EU, UN and WHO.

The Stationery Office/National Publishing Group
Formerly HMSO, the Stationery Office/National Publishing Group is the key distributor of government publications and is now a private company, having been denationalised in 1996.

Other government information providers
All government departments will provide information on request, including pamphlets, leaflets, circulars, brochures, books, videos, CDs, DVDs, maps, posters, statistics, codes of practice, consultation documents and press releases. Much information is free, while other information is marketed commercially and has to be paid for. This might be either through the relevant department or through the Stationery Office. The following departments offer information that is covered by Crown copyright:

- ☐ HM Customs & Excise: mainly customs tariffs and value added tax guidance.
- ☐ Ministry of Agriculture, Fisheries and Food (MAFF): food data and food advice.

☐ Defence Department: defence standards, expenditure plans and statistics, manpower reviews.

☐ Education: expenditure, staffing levels, expected educational standards.

☐ Employment: numbers in and out of employment, skill levels.

☐ Environment, Transport and the Regions.

☐ Health Department: expenditure, annual reports, state of the nation's health, advice.

☐ Home Office: police, prison, crime statistics.

☐ HM Land Registry: ownership, applications, consultation documents.

☐ Government Actuary's Department.

☐ Inland Revenue: corporate and consumer tax levels.

☐ National Audit Office: monitors income and expenditure figures for most government departments.

☐ National Savings: savings statistics and trends.

☐ Office of National Lottery.

☐ Office of Fair Trading: press notices, leaflets and annual reports on possible consumer abuse.

☐ Social Security: social income/expenditure, explanatory and legal documents, discussion papers.

☐ Department of Trade and Industry: company, country searches, exports, imports.

☐ Treasury: national income, national expenditure (GDP, GNP).

Most can be found on the UK government website (www.open.gov.uk).

Companies House
Companies House works under the auspices of the Department of Trade and Industry (DTI) and is responsible for legal matters including the registration of new companies, insolvency and deregistration of old companies, enforcing legislation compliance, and supplying company information to the public. It holds information on 1.4 million companies in the UK which is now available on CD-ROM and soon to be available online. Official organisations that publish documents not covered by Crown copyright include the following:

☐ Competition Commission: consultation and investigation documents on possible mergers, alliances and take-overs.

☐ Bank of England: official monetary policy, financial markets, regulations and codes of conduct (www.bankofengland.co.uk).

☐ British Tourist Authority: tourism, leisure, eating out.

☐ Civil Aviation Authority: airports, air transport, regulations.

☐ Gaming Board of Great Britain: gambling statistics, licensing.

☐ Sports Council: sports, leisure, fitness data.

Government electronic business gathering, storage, analysis and presentation
The UK government is committed to putting more information processes in electronic form on the internet. It is particularly concerned about small and medium

sized enterprises (SMEs) as they do not always have the resources to gain access to information in the same way as larger companies.

In 1998 the UK government launched the Enterprise Zone website (www.enterprisezone.org.uk) as an internet portal to monitoring the quality of other business information sites and recommending the best.

Data protection

Many countries have now enforced certain legal obligations with regard to the holding of information on individuals. This means that all business organisations must now follow a strict code of conduct with regard to the collecting, storing, analysing and disclosing of information. Failure to conform can lead to prosecution and compensation awards. Example 3.9 contains the UK rules with regard to data protection, taken from the UK government website.

Example 3.9 ## Data Protection Act 1998, UK, came into force March 2000

The rules

Anyone processing personal data must comply with the eight enforceable principles of good practice. They say that data must be fairly and lawfully processed, processed for limited purposes, adequate, relevant and not excessive, accurate, not kept longer than necessary, processed in accordance with the data subject's rights, secure, and not transferred to countries without adequate protection.

Personal data covers both facts and opinions about the individual. It also includes information regarding the intentions of the data controller towards the individual, although in some limited circumstances exemptions will apply. With processing, the definition is far wider than before. For example, it incorporates the concepts of 'obtaining', holding' and 'disclosing'. Failure to conform can lead to court compensation awards to the injured party. (www.dataprotection.gov.uk)

Information Commissioner (UK)

The Information Commissioner enforces and oversees the Data Protection Act 1998 and the Freedom of Information Act 2000. The Commissioner is a UK independent supervisory authority reporting directly to the UK parliament and has an international role as well as a national one. In the UK, the Commissioner has a range of duties including the promotion of good information handling and the encouragement of codes of practice for data controllers, that is anyone who decides how and why personal data (information about identifiable, living individuals) is processed.

Statistics Commissioner (UK)

The Statistics Commission was set up in response to concerns expressed by some about the independence and use of government statistics, especially by politicians. The independent Statistics Commissioner will have the responsibility of advising on the quality, quality assurance and priority setting for national statistics, and on the procedures designed to deliver statistical integrity, to help ensure national statistics are trustworthy and responsive to public needs. The Statistics Commission is independent of both ministers and the producers of national statistics.

Figure 3.4
Standard
Industry
Classification
(SIC) codes

Standard Industry Classification (SIC) codes	Group A - Agriculture, Hunting and Forestry	
Group A Agriculture, Hunting & Forestry	0111	Grow cereals & other crops
Group B Fishing	0112	Grow vegetables & nursery products
Group C Mining & Quarrying	0113	Grow fruit, nuts, beverage & spice crops
Group D Manufacturing		
Group E Electricity, Gas & Water Supply	0121	Farming of cattle, dairy farming
Group F Construction	0122	Farming sheep, goats, horses, etc.
Group G Wholesale, Retail; Certain Repairs	0123	Farming of swine
Group H Hotels, Restaurants, Bars, Catering	0124	Farming of poultry
Group I Transport, Storage & Communication	0125	Other farming of animals
	0130	Crops combined with animals, mixed farms
Group J Financial Intermediation	0141	Agricultural service activities
Group K Real Estate, Renting & Business	0142	Animal husbandry services, not vets
Group L Public Administration & Defence	0150	Hunting & game rearing inc. services
Group M Education		
Group N Health & Social Work	0201	Forestry & logging
Group O Other Social & Personal Services	0202	Forestry & logging related services
Group P Private Households with Employees		

International official bodies

Organisations also have access to a wealth of information (now much more accessible because of the development of IT) from national and supranational, official and semi-official, 'umbrella' bodies. These bodies have many departments offering information on a whole raft of business, government, NFP, group and individual areas:

☐ The European Union: information, regulations, discussion documents, etc., on all EU member countries.

☐ International Trade Centre: set up to help companies to trade; information, reports, import/export statistics.

☐ United Nations (UN).

☐ Organisation for Economic Cooperation and Development (OECD).

☐ International Monetary Fund (IMF): 182 members; facilitates international trade; exchange rates; issues SDR (special drawing rates) to help countries with balance of payments problems.

☐ World Bank: economic and industrial development data, country by country.

☐ World Trade Organisation (WTO): 134 member countries; set up in 1995; facilitates world trade (GATT), etc.; a mass of information, reports and links on world trade.

There have been moves across the UK, EU and the rest of the world to both classify and standardise information so that red tape can be reduced, business activities more easily undertaken and information made easier to collect and understand. Figure 3.4 shows the standard industry classification codes (SIC) for the UK. The US (NAICS) and EU methods are different, but there are moves afoot to bring all in line with one another.

2. Professional trade associations

There are more than 200 trade associations in the UK and thousands around the world. Some are more important than others and so have more power, often consulting on a regular basis with national and transnational governments, collecting information, offering advice and lobbying on behalf of members. Trade association member opportunities include:

☐ Access to information about the industry and markets.

☐ Legal advice.

☐ Networking opportunities with other members.

☐ Access to government departments and ministers.

☐ Lobbying on behalf of members on a national and transnational level.

☐ A meeting place where members can come on a regular basis to discuss problems of general interest, gather information on current issues, speculate about future scenarios and listen to invited experts in relevant business areas.

☐ Library facilities both online and offline.

☐ Exhibitions and conferences.

3. Commercial information gatherers and consultants

There are also many hundreds of independent research companies working around the world offering an enormous amount of information on every possible aspect of marketing. Example 3.10 presents just a small selection.

Example 3.10 **The top five marketing research companies in the world (both B2B and B2C)**

1. ACNielsen Worldwide (US). Media research, monitors spending of advertisers in main media, addresses worldwide; now owns Multi-Media Services MMS (www.acnielsen.com).

2. IMS Health (US). Health research (www.imshealth.com).

3. Kantar Group (UK). Owns Research International, Millward Brown, BMRB, Goldfarb, Kantar Media Research, IMRB (India). Part of WPP advertising group (www.kantar.com).

4. TN (Taylor Nelson) Sofres (UK). Has quantitative research contract with BARB (4425 modems on TVs in UK households) (www.tnsofres.com).

5. NFO Worldwide. Part of Interpublic Group (www.nfow.com).

☐ B2B primary research

Despite the amount of secondary research information available, there will always be circumstances where information needed is not available. When this is the case the company will have to instigate primary research. Primary research is new research undertaken by an organisation to help solve a problem that existing information cannot solve. It should never be undertaken lightly because of the possible high cost involved. B2B primary research can be broken down into three basic types:

1. Experimental research
2. Observation
3. Surveys.

1. Experimental research

In experimental research the researcher controls and manipulates elements of the research environment to measure the impact of each variable. For example, a group of test subjects might be shown several television commercials (in B2C markets) or video presentations (in B2B markets). After each one the group is asked questions designed to measure the likelihood that they will purchase the product advertised. This tends to be used more in B2C than B2B markets. It might be used to test the following in B2B markets:

- ☐ Effectiveness of new trade advertising, or competitors' trade advertising
- ☐ Effect of various prices on sales of a product, service, or bundles of benefits
- ☐ Buyer acceptance of new products in trial and repeat purchase levels
- ☐ Effect of different package designs on product, protection and on sales.

2. Observation

Observational research is attractive because it is low in cost and can be carried out by people or machines. In simple terms it involves observing some phenomena and counting and recording so as to identify similarities and differences.

Non-human methods of observational research

Non-human, mechanical or computer methods are used for counting the number of vehicles on a particular highway or bridge, traffic on websites or use of electronic point-of-sale (EPOS) computer equipment. For example, transport information is crucial for organisations in the road, bridge and tunnel construction industries. It is especially important for construction companies that are paid according to the amount of traffic using a particular road, bridge or tunnel under the government's Public–Private Finance Initiative (PPFI).

EPOS will identify all the products by name and price and, linked to the customer loyalty card, will provide purchasing information on the customer. Video cameras and electronic eyes are used to watch movement around the store that can then be used to inform product and display layouts. This information is vital in B2C retail markets where its uses are widespread and indispensable. It is also useful for companies that market retail related products and services such as computer systems, cameras, loyalty card technology, retail shelving, and so on. A similar system is used in B2B markets where information can be kept on B2B products and services bought along the supply chain.

B2B organisations can also monitor business website visits more easily than consumer visits. This is because large businesses often have their own dedicated server so that name can easily be trapped and visits monitored. This is not the case with the non-business visitors as they tend to access through a large national or international web server, making their visits more anonymous.

Human observation

Human methods of observational research will have people doing just that. Competitors can be watched, both directly and by news and information emanating from company documents and trade and popular media, to see what moves they might make, what resources are being used and what new methods might be used to gain better customer satisfaction. Salespeople should be able to observe the competitors in action to see which suppliers, inventory holding, channel of distribution and transport system is in use, as well as the competitive advantage being gained overall. They can also look for new customers by observing the addresses on sides of lorries, on display boards at industrial and business sites, etc. Competitors' products can be obtained and stripped down in a form of reverse engineering, and information gleaned on innovation and design advancements.

Some suppliers have even found it profitable to wait outside an existing or potential customer so as to observe which suppliers it does and does not use. In some cases employees from one firm will spend days, weeks or even months working with employees in another. In this way it is hoped that a real and meaningful understanding and insight into both supplier and buyer needs can thus be obtained. Informal observation can be important for many industries and management and staff are encouraged to keep a lookout for activity in the environment that could be a possible source of new business. This might be building taking place, new offices opening or factories changing industry usage.

3. Surveys

The use of the B2C survey is probably the method most recognised by the professional and layperson alike. The image of the person in the high street holding a clipboard and stopping passers-by is ubiquitous. Surveys are used in B2B but not to the same extent as in B2C. Surveys in B2C are widespread and used on a grand scale with interviews involving hundreds of thousands of individuals taking place continuously. Both governments and commercial organisations seek to get information on such things as living standards, leisure pursuits, health, buying intentions, and so on. Because sellers want to know about such things as buying intentions and satisfaction levels from organisation personnel, surveys in B2B, although still ongoing, are on a lesser scale than those carried in the consumer market.

Surveys in B2B markets

As with consumer markets there comes a time when the secondary information available about an industry or a particular market is outdated or not relevant or its integrity is suspect. Under these circumstances the company might have to undertake some primary research in the form of a survey. This is much easier and usually much less expensive than in B2C markets as it is possible to obtain the information needed from relatively few people, as long as they are the right people. This is because in B2B markets a few people can be responsible for extremely large and important purchasing decisions.

Survey methods in B2B primary research

As with B2C there are different ways that surveys can be conducted in B2B markets. These can be carried out by:

☐ Post

☐ Telephone

☐ Internet

☐ Person-to-person.

Post

Postal research is often used to try to obtain information from business decision-makers. It is quick, reasonably inexpensive and can be conducted over a wide area. It is crucial that the right person is contacted by the correct name and title, if at all possible. As with all postal questionnaires, response rates tend to be low but are usually better in business than in consumer markets (they can be as low as 1 per cent in consumer markets and as high as 50 per cent in business markets). This is because named contacts can be used. The questions asked should be industry relevant with the respondent answering for the company rather than himself. Response rates can be greatly increased if respondents are offered some type of incentive and/or the letter is preceded or followed up with a phone call or e-mail. Mail-outs can be used successfully with B2B and B2C respondents.

Direct mailing lists

Up-to-date business names and addresses can be obtained from specialist list brokers, either to purchase or to rent. It is crucial that the information is current and correct so the names, job positions and addresses should all have been recently checked to make certain this is the case. In this way there is every chance that the letter will be opened. A letter sent to a buyer who has retired or died five years ago is an unprofessional introduction to a company wanted as a long-term customer. Ideally the direct mailing list should have been audited by an outside independent body such as the Audited Bureau of Circulation (ABC).

Telephone

This is one of the most favoured ways of contacting business decision-makers. It is inexpensive, quick and, providing one can develop techniques to get past the gatekeeper and voice-mail, a relatively successful way to talk to managers in authority. It can be used successfully in conjunction with other methods such as a follow-up letter or an e-mail, and in both B2B and B2C markets.

E-mail, websites, videoconferencing

There has been an exponential growth in the use of e-mail for marketing research but its success or otherwise is still open to investigation. There is no doubt that it is an easy (for both sender and respondent) and inexpensive way to get information on customers if they are prepared to take the time to answer. As with the other types of research methods discussed above, there is more likelihood of a favoured response if personal contact is made beforehand or if the respondent and sender are already known to one another.

If the respondent can be encouraged to the website, perhaps by a promotional offer of some kind, then a simple questionnaire might be offered. The same research process might be used with regular users of the website if they can be persuaded about the mutual benefits involved.

In some cases companies have persuaded business opinion leaders to take part in online and/or videoconferencing focus group research. All these methods have been used in both B2B and B2C markets although success rates have yet to be realistically measured.

Permission marketing

The growth in e-mail has seen the development of so-called permission marketing. The idea behind this concept is that buyers are asked if they would mind suppliers and researchers contacting them on a regular basis with information on new products and services as well as to ask research questions that would be of value to both supplier and industry. In this way buyers are not offended and there is every chance that the missives will be opened and read.

Person-to-person

This is a very expensive method to use in B2C markets where the need personally to interview thousands of individual end consumers can be extremely costly. Although potentially expensive, it is probably the most effective method for research in B2B markets. If undertaken correctly, costs can be kept to a minimum according to sample size, geographical spread and research objectives. Using salespeople can be attractive as questions can be asked in the course of the sales interview and presentation, but their lack of skill and focus may detract from achieving quality results. The ability to ask questions face to face, to gauge reactions and to help explain difficult questions is a powerful technique to use in seeking out information on future intentions.

A combination

Many organisations use a combination of two or more of the above methods, each reinforcing the other. Because sample sizes needed to get at the relevant information in B2B are so much smaller than in B2C, survey research can be less costly and much less time-consuming. It is possible to obtain valuable information from samples as small as four or five. As with all forms of research, it is crucial, however, that the sample interviewed is representative of the whole wanted target market.

Omnibus edition

A relatively inexpensive way of getting a small amount of primary research is to commission questions on a commercial agency's omnibus research programme. A general research survey covering a particular industry is set up and company or trade association contributors are invited to purchase a number of questions to be asked. These can be undertaken on both a national and international scale.

B2B survey methods

- ☐ Secondary research is more popular than primary research.
- ☐ All survey methods can be used successfully.
- ☐ Telephone, post and e-mail can be directly targeted to known and named respondents.
- ☐ It is easy and straightforward to check integrity of business lists.
- ☐ Forewarning can be given that a survey will arrive, making response more likely.
- ☐ Relatively few business respondents need to be contacted to make the survey worthwhile.
- ☐ Personal interviewing is relatively inexpensive because of the number of people involved.
- ☐ Known contacts vouch for the integrity of the sample and veracity of the answers.
- ☐ Answers are based on rationale nearer the wanted truth.

B2C survey methods

- ☐ Primary research is more popular than secondary research.
- ☐ All survey methods can be used successfully.
- ☐ Telephone, post and e-mail cannot be targeted in a meaningful way at known respondents.
- ☐ Respondent lists are often poor and lack integrity because of the number of addresses involved.
- ☐ Tens of thousands of individuals must be contacted to make the survey worthwhile.
- ☐ Poor response rates and uncertainty about the person responding.
- ☐ Personal interviewing is very expensive because of sample size.
- ☐ There are problems with bias, uncertainty about the veracity of the sample and arguments over the interpretation.
- ☐ Answers often based on emotion can sometimes lead to misunderstandings and a flawed research survey.

Quantitative and qualitative methods of research

It is possible to distinguish two distinct types of primary research methods:

1. Quantitative research
2. Qualitative research.

1. Quantitative research

Most questionnaire surveys use structured questions that have been rigorously tested before use, and with answers that can be quantified into clearly defined, coded compartments. This facilitates the collection, classification and analysis of the data and allows computer and statistical techniques to be used. All questions on the questionnaire are arranged so that any answer given can be coded and recorded in mathematical form. Questions asked need to be 'closed end', 'yes–no' or 'running choice' type questions. This allows the statistics to be presented in terms of percentages so that trends across all areas and past years can be compared.

The quantitative method is attractive because it allows researcher bias and subjectivity to be minimised and the process to be undertaken in a quasi-scientific manner, with results presented in a detached and objective statistical form. Most government economic and trade statistics are collected and presented in this way. Although all organisations carry out quantitative research, B2B companies use it more than B2C companies because small numbers of answers based on rational opinions can translate into reliable statistics which can then be measured alongside the quantitative data.

> Quantitative research is used more in B2B than in B2C.

2. Qualitative research

There are disadvantages and limitations with quantitative research which are felt more in consumer markets than in business markets. Understanding customers also involves seeking out opinions, emotions, gut feelings and latent or subconscious thoughts. To overcome the problem marketers have worked with sociologists and psychologists to develop a group of techniques known collectively as the 'qualitative approach'. Through the use of these techniques, researchers hope to get at customers' innermost thoughts and feelings, often unobtainable in other ways. Because end consumers buy products more for emotional reasons, while businesses buy for rational reasons, qualitative research is used more in B2C than in B2B. Qualitative research will lack the objectivity of quantitative research and so great care should be taken in the interpretation of results. This is usually left to the skills of an expert in this field because of this difficulty.

> Qualitative research is used more in B2C than in B2B.

Having said this, however, there are times when sellers want this kind of information from business buyers and so this type of research might well be used. Qualitative techniques include the following:

- ☐ Panel, focus or discussion groups
- ☐ In-depth interviews
- ☐ Shadowing
- ☐ Psychoanalytical techniques.

Panel, focus or discussion groups

With this method, groups of industry managers, workers, experts, etc. are brought together to discuss particular problems. A recording in sound or video is taken and analysed afterwards by a skilled interpreter. Exercises like these can be difficult in setting up because of the time involved in bringing very busy people together. It will make a difference if all participants feel that they might gain valuable information from the process. Videoconferencing and internet 'chat room' type exercises can also be set up and the same procedure performed and recorded. These can be more attractive as less time and travel will be involved. So-called 'quality circles' are used throughout factories to get internal customers to talk to one another in order to improve quality and effectiveness in business process methods.

Example 3.11   ## Videoconferencing focus groups

While most market research professionals will agree that watching focus groups via videoconferencing is not as effective an experience as observing from behind a one-way mirror, it is far better than listening to audio or videotapes after the event. Videoconferencing does enable the client personnel to observe the proceedings in real time, and therefore have the opportunity to provide input to the moderator. However, there are problems that should be considered. The authority role of the moderator is one of the most important reasons why traditional focus groups are so important. It is virtually impossible to establish authority from behind a computer screen. A good focus group also utilises interaction and body language to explore topics in more detail, show stimuli and draw out the feelings of each of the participants based on their reactions to what others in the room have said. It is also impossible to address these issues with an online focus group.

In-depth interviews

In-depth interviews can be structured (as in quantitative research), semi-structured or unstructured. These have the advantage in that industry-experienced and knowledgeable people can be interrogated in a sympathetic one-to-one situation. Qualitative interviews can also be conducted by telephone, internet and videoconferencing with varying levels of depth information acquired. In contrast to B2C, a great deal of information can be obtained from a small number of interviews in the B2B market because even one 'captain' of industry will be able (if he or she wishes) to divulge an enormous amount of relevant and important information.

Shadowing

In some circumstances a company researcher from a business partner or commercial agency will spend time – days, weeks or even months – with a partner (or potential partner) business, following managers and workers around (shadowing) and collecting information about working practices. This information can then be used in adding value and developing the buyer–seller relationship.

> Because this kind of research lacks the objectivity of quantitative research, care should be taken in its interpretation.

Quantitative and qualitative methods combined

A research programme will often include both quantitative and qualitative research methods. A discussion panel, in-depth interview or shadowing exercise might throw up a consistent factor needing more information, which can then be best tested by a more extensive quantitative survey. The survey content can be matched against known secondary information either before the project has finished, so as to identify questions that might need to be asked, or afterwards, to consolidate or develop the findings.

Quantitative and qualitative research in B2B

- ☐ Quantitative research is used extensively in B2B.
- ☐ Small sample sizes are needed and questions easily tested.
- ☐ Representative samples are easy to obtain.
- ☐ Individual named contacts can be reached.
- ☐ Answers are needed and given based on rational assumptions as people are buying for the company and not for themselves.
- ☐ Very little qualitative research is done, as this is used to get at underlying emotional wants and desires.
- ☐ Qualitative research is used to get at the feelings of employees when these might be based on emotion rather than rationality.

Quantitative and qualitative research in B2C

- ☐ Quantitative research is used but large sample sizes are needed.
- ☐ Quantitative sampling can be a problem because of the need for large samples.
- ☐ Quantitative research answers based on large group averages and individual beliefs can get lost at the margins.
- ☐ In quantitative research the tightness of the questions forces respondents into boxes based on rationality, despite the fact that emotional reactions dominate.

☐ Qualitative research is popular and growing because of the need for researchers to get at emotional feelings and opinions sometimes repressed below the surface.

☐ Qualitative research has developed many methods to get at the many different individual feelings that consumers have when buying products and brands.

Use of information technology in marketing research

The growth in information technology has given the marketing research department or agency a powerful weapon in collecting, classifying, analysing, holding and presenting marketing information in both B2C and B2B. A laptop computer can now store and use more effectively the same amount of information that 25 years ago would have need a computer the size of a small room. They can also be used in research to collect buyer information that can be almost immediately downloaded to head office for classification and analysis. This potential is multiplied an almost infinite amount of times through connection to the internet, intranet and extranet. This information can be made available to company sales representatives as a sales aid at the moment of presentation, allowing for a knowledgeable and more professional approach.

Companies now have access to billions of items of data about markets, competitors and availability of products and services from around the world. The speed of information access is increasing with mind-numbing persistency and organisations can have access to company and customer information often instantaneously from around the world. Even smaller companies can buy in, rent or lease information storage and retrieval facilities on large-scale global networks. E-mail, website and videoconferencing (and text messaging) are all now used as research methods and these were discussed above.

Overall differences in researching B2B and B2C markets

B2B research

☐ Demand is more concentrated in B2B.

☐ Secondary research is used more in B2B than in B2C.

☐ Buying for rational reasons rather than symbolic and emotional.

☐ Market size and potential rather than psychology.

☐ Smaller samples.

☐ Complex industrial buying centres can make decision-makers difficult to locate.

☐ More quantitative than qualitative research.

☐ Markets change more slowly than consumer markets.

☐ A small number of buyers changing demand can have a large effect on purchase.

☐ Research programmes can be relatively inexpensive.

B2C research

☐ Demand can be spread across many millions of individual consumers.

☐ Demand can be spread geographically wide, regionally, nationally and internationally.

☐ Samples often need to be large.

☐ Decision-making unit more easily identified compared with B2B.

☐ Buying more for symbolic and emotional rather than rational reasons.

☐ Qualitative research is as important as quantitative research.

☐ Markets, styles and fashion can change quickly.

☐ A small number of customers changing demand will have a small effect on purchase.

☐ Research programmes are usually expensive.

☐ High degree of consumer data protection laws.

Working with a B2B research agency

B2B research agencies will help organisations collect primary and secondary information both for research projects such as new product development and for all the sales forecasting information identified above. The B2B organisation will have the choice of undertaking the research in-house, contracting out or out-sourcing through an outside research agency. This decision will ultimately rest on whether the B2B organisation can afford to pay the asking price for the information wanted. A full-scale research programme can be prohibitively expensive, especially if primary research is involved. An agency might offer all the research services needed at both local and global levels, or it might choose to specialise by task or by country. The smaller firm may buy services on an ad-hoc basis, with a market report perhaps costing as little as £500. The research contract agreed with the agency may be continuous, lasting over many years, or it may be an agreement for a one-off marketing research programme.

Example 3.12	**Commercial research organisations**

☐ **BMRB** commercial site. Lists and good descriptions of services offered; owns Target Group Index (TGI), part of the Kantar group (www.bmrb.co.uk)

☐ **CACI, Marketing Systems Databases.** ACORN (classification of residential neighbourhoods); range of technological business solutions particularly on customers and markets (www.caci.com)

☐ **Dun & Bradstreet (UK).** UK business failures and expectations; credit ratings; excellent free database of 1.8 million UK companies' names and addresses, etc. (www.dunandbrad.co.uk).

☐ **Euroquest; European Research Co.** Pan-European marketing and social research (www.euroquestmrb.com).

☐ **Forrester Research.** Internet research (www.forrester.com).

☐ **Geodemographic information systems.** Computer-generated maps offered for anywhere in the UK (www.geoweb.co.uk).

Many more can be seen on www.studentshout.com

Syndicated and customised research

Research organisations will offer clients the option of buying in customised research or taking part in a syndicated programme. Customised research will be research tailored to meet the exact needs agreed between agency staff and the B2B organisation. The B2B company might also choose to join with others needing the same or similar research information. This type of syndicated research will involve much less cost than customised research, but it will not offer personalised, detailed information at the same level.

Specialist research agencies

As with all types of business agencies, some are multipurpose and offer every conceivable service and others specialise in a particular type of research. There are companies that offer both B2B and B2C, while others concentrate in one area rather than the another. Some agencies specialise in B2B in the public sector and others in B2B in charities. One agency might concentrate on retail research and another on manufacturing. One might have skills linked to financial services, another skills in telecommunications. An agency might undertake most of its work on quantitative survey research, while another might work mainly using more individual and group qualitative research. The choice to be made will depend on the problem in hand and resources available.

Example 3.13 **B2B research specialities**

Automotives
Taylor Nelson's position as a leading global supplier of automotive research is based on more than three decades of industry experience. Today operating with a team of over 100 skilled automotive research professionals based in 26 countries, TNS Automotive specialises in both syndicated and customised research to address the complex information needs of major automotive manufacturers and component suppliers.

Healthcare
Taylor Nelson Sofres Healthcare is one of the world's foremost specialists in most aspects of healthcare research. With a large team of experienced executives in offices throughout Europe, the US and Asia, TNS Healthcare service suits clients' needs at both an international and a local level. Most of the leading companies marketing ethical and OTC products are included among its clients.

Telecoms
Taylor Nelson Sofres Telecoms is a global provider of a comprehensive range of strategic and tactical business analysis and information for telecoms service providers, equipment manufacturers and government regulators. Its range of syndicated solutions and custom capabilities allows TNS Telecoms to meet most telecoms business information or marketing research challenges. (www.tnsofres.com)

☐ B2B research in international markets

Research can be difficult enough in the home country with problems associated with accuracy, cost, timings, security, sampling and so on, but such problems are magnified when needing to research abroad. Secondary research may be non-existent, scant or just untrustworthy or inaccurate. Information, if in existence, may be difficult to find and difficult to get at. Primary research can cause even greater problems. The wanted target respondent sample might be impossible to put together because of language and cultural problems, as might be the actual questionnaire. Implementation might be fraught with unforeseen, on-the-ground troubles, culminating in end results that are unconvincing and suspect. In these circumstances it would sensible to use a research agency of some kind and, as identified above, many exist. The options open for consideration would include the following:

☐ An international research company with offices and wholly owned subsidiaries around the world. Customer client contact would be centralised and the whole research programme, including objective setting and presentation of results, administered from the home country.

☐ A research company resident in the home country with links to international agency networks and research partners around the world. Work would be subcontracted to agencies belonging to these networks on the basis of their relative merit for a specific project. In this way the clients could be offered the most appropriate and cost-effective international research solution.

☐ Contacting a research company totally resident in the country of investigation. Agencies can be hired that will undertake the selection task.

Costs will vary according to the agency chosen, the research objectives and the scale of the project. Other factors to consider will be the experience and local insight, understanding of cultural and linguistic issues, and experience on working in the particular country from where information is needed.

Choosing a research agency

Whether to choose a large agency, small agency, all-purpose or specialist, will depend on many factors, including research objectives and task to be undertaken, costs, in-house skills and the present level of management knowledge. If the research needs to be undertaken in a foreign country, a choice will have to be made between a global research company with offices around the world or a research company resident in the country under consideration. There are pros and cons between choosing either the larger or the smaller organisation, including such things as scale economies available versus a more personal service and global market experience versus local knowledge.

Having decided which type of B2B agency is needed, there is the problem of deciding which particular agency to choose. Matters to be taken into consideration would include the following:

☐ Senior management inclination

☐ Recommendations from others

☐ Examples of past and present work programmes

☐ Any specialist skills or knowledge that match company needs

☐ Experience of working in the region or country of choice

☐ A large or a small organisation

☐ Costs and perceived value.

There are organisations in existence with the sole purpose of helping companies choose research agencies. They will interview the buying organisation, identify needs and then draw up a shortlist of likely B2B research companies. The buyer can then meet those selected and through presentation, discussion and negotiation choose the most appropriate candidate. We will return in more detail to this subject when we examine the role of marketing and advertising agencies in Chapter 8.

Evaluating the B2B research agency

All reputable research agencies will build feedback monitoring and control mechanisms into the research programme to make certain that objectives are not only met, but also seen to be met. Payment is sometimes linked into performance outcomes in some way to motivate a quality programme.

Management consultants as competitors

Both marketing research and marketing agencies are now threatened by the management consultancy agency entering their market. Management consultants offer a range of services at both strategic and tactical levels, covering areas at corporate, divisional and departmental level. Help offered by the consultant will be much more wide ranging than the B2B research agency, giving advice on how information gathered can be analysed to inform the strategic planning and control process. Business information offered will include information to help organisational direction on both internal and external areas. This will include, among other things, information to help with corporate and marketing planning and objective setting, strategic option discussion and choice, implementation, monitoring and control.

Example 3.14 | **Management consultants**

Management consultants offer a range of professional consultant business services in both the private and public sector, including the following: e-business; corporate strategy financial and administration systems; production and services management; information, communication and technology; human resources; marketing and corporate communications; project and programme management; and economic and environmental studies. Some of the largest are identified below:

☐ **PriceWaterhouseCoopers** (www.pwcglobal.com/uk)

☐ **Andersen Consulting** (www.arthurandersen.com)

Example 3.14 continued

- □ **Accenture.** 75,000 people in 47 countries with extensive experience in 18 industry groups in key business areas, including customer relationship management, supply chain management, business strategy, technology and outsourcing (www.accenture.com).
- □ **Deloitte, Touche & Tomatsu.** 95,000 people around the world. A leading global professional services organisation, delivering world-class assurance and advisory, tax, and consulting services through its national practices (www.deloitte.com).
- □ **KPMG Consultants** (KPMG.com)
- □ **Management Consultancies Association.** The UK trade association for business consultants (www.mca.org.uk).

□ Strategic concerns with marketing research

Information networks straddle the world. Nothing remains concealed. But the sheer volume of information dissolves the information. We are unable to take it all in.

(Gunter Grass, quoted in Preece, 2000)

Information and the use of marketing research should be viewed from a strategic perspective because of the overall importance in B2B markets at both national and global level. To plan with inadequate or wrong information is a recipe for disaster and eventual failure and, because of the amount and quality of information available, an unnecessary factor when attempting to manage a business. The strategic factors to consider when looking at B2B research will include the following.

Objectives

Managers must be clear about the information needed, why they need it and what it will be used for. Possible objectives for the research should then be discussed with the agency, back and forth, until both agency and client are absolutely clear on the purpose of the research programme. If objectives are confused, the wrong information will be collected and all managers will suffer.

Costs

Research programmes can be extremely costly, perhaps running into millions of pounds. Managers must undertake a cost benefit analysis so that the value of the information wanted can be shown to be more than the cost of its collection – otherwise it should not be done.

Time

The collection of information can be a very drawn-out process. If the time taken to collect the desired information is going to be so long that the market has moved on, then it may be necessary at some time to make decisions with less information. Technology can, however, improve the situation and in certain situations information can be collected much more quickly than in the past. In fact using the concept of 'permission marketing' research can be built into the agency and respondent relationship.

Security

An organisation must always be aware that the competition will be watching its every move and will no doubt know that research is underway. If a competing company gains access to the reasons for the research and even the results, then it can put spoiling plans into action.

Accuracy

The big worry with all kinds of research is its accuracy. If the methods used are flawed and the wrong information is collected, decisions made might well end in disaster. To this end a constant vigil must be kept so that evaluation, feedback, monitoring and control mechanisms are forever in place and if errors are suspected positive action can be taken.

☐ Forecasting in B2B marketing

Looking into the future implies some forecasting of impending conditions. In the context of business management, forecasts can be used to support long-term strategic decisions, operational decisions or short-term tactical decisions. Marketing management requires forecasting information when making a wide range of decisions. The sales forecast is particularly important as it is the foundation, the major budget, upon which all company plans are built in terms of markets and revenue. Virtually every manufacturing or service company needs to generate forecasts of their short to medium term sales. Once budgets and forecasts have been made, it is important to be able to track actual performance against the plan. Many companies now use computer software for immediate variance analysis (the difference between predicted performance and actual performance) and outcome reporting. Decisions can then be made about any alterations that might be needed.

 Sales forecasting in B2B markets can be found in more detail on the *B2B Marketing* website at www.booksites.net/wright.

☐ Summary

Marketing information is vital to the B2B marketing manager in making strategic and operational decisions. Too often, such information is not available, comes too late or is unreliable. Evidence that information gathering is happening in a coordinated and systematic way in a company is the existence of a marketing information system (MkIS). This can operate in a formal or informal way depending on the size and the wealth of the company. It was argued that more information is needed in B2B markets.

The marketing information system consists of four parts: internal information, marketing intelligence, marketing research, and storage and analysis. All four parts coordinate so as to provide a constant supply of relevant up-to-date information about the organisation's markets to the interested managers.

We looked at the information process in some depth, including the differences between secondary and primary research. The many sources of secondary research were identified, including governments, trade associations and commercial agencies. The problems associated with choosing and evaluating the research agency were discussed. The use of primary research in B2B was examined and then both methods were compared with usage in the B2C market.

Discussion questions

1. Discuss the value of information to the B2B decision-making process. What are the problems associated with information overload?

2. Describe the marketing information system. What are its many uses?

3. How might competitive advantage be gained by the use of marketing intelligence?

4. What information in B2B markets might qualitative research obtain that quantitative research might not? Give examples.

5. What do you consider the value of secondary research to be? Why is so much now available and what are the many sources?

6. How might a culture of information seeking be instilled into an organisation? What problems might be encountered?

7. Discuss the proposition that the 'research must be used as an aid to decision making and not a substitute'. What are the criticisms levelled by many at the value or otherwise of research information?

8. Identify and analyse the differences and similarities with information gathering between B2B and B2C. Give examples.

9. Describe and evaluate the differences between quantitative and qualitative forecasting. Discuss the different methods used in each category.

10. Discuss the differences between top-down and bottom-up ways of sales forecasting. Do you think that sales forecasting can ever be accurate taking into account the problems associated with looking into the future?

To answer questions 9 and 10 go to the *B2B Marketing* website at www.booksites.net/wright. You will also find a Case Study, Questions, and an Internet Exercise for this chapter.

☐ Bibliography

Books

Aaker, D.A., Kumar, V. and Day, G.S. (2001) *Marketing Research*, 7th edn. Chichester: Wiley.

Baker, M.J. (2000) *Marketing Theory: A Student Text*. London: Thomson.

Curwin, J. and Slater, R. (2000) *Quantitative Methods for Business Decisions*, 4th edn. London: Thomson.

Drucker, P. (1986) *The Practice of Management*. New York: Harper.

Kent, R. (1999) *Marketing Research: Measurement, Method and Application*. London: Thomson.

Kumar, V. (2000) *International Marketing Research*. New York: Prentice-Hall.

Lyotard, J.-F. (1984) *The Postmodern Condition*. Manchester: Manchester University Press.

Peters, G. (1997) *Beyond the Next Wave with Scenario Planning: Imagining the Next Generation of Customers*. New York: Prentice-Hall.

Preece, J. (2000) *Gunter Grass: His Life and Work*. London: Palgrave.

West, C. (2000) *Marketing Research*. Basingstoke: Palgrave.

Wright, R. (1999) *Marketing: Origins, Concepts, Environment*. London: Thomson.

Journals

Bunn, M.D. (1993) 'Information search in industrial purchase decisions', *Journal of Business to Business Marketing*, 1 (2): 67–102.

Ghingold, M. and Wilson, D. (1998) 'Buying centre research and business marketing practice: meeting the challenge of dynamic marketing', *Journal of Business and Industrial Marketing*, 13: 96–108.

Naude, P., Holland, C. and Sudbury, M. (2000) 'The benefits of IT-based supply chains – strategic or operational?', *Journal of Business-to-Business Marketing*, 7 (1): 45–67.

Visit www.booksites.net/wright for the Internet references for this chapter.

04

Decision making and segmenting business markets

The man who is denied the opportunity of taking decisions of importance begins to regard as important the decisions he is allowed to take.

(C. Northcote Parkinson, author and historian, 1909-1993)

Aims and objectives

By the end of this chapter the student should be able to:

1. Identify and analyse all the factors involved in the process of decision-making, including the decision-making unit, the decision-making process and the decision-making difficulty.

2. Define business-to-business market segmentation and be able to evaluate the reasons behind this need for selling companies to analyse and classify organisations and markets.

3. Identify and evaluate the ways in which business markets can be segmented and be able to describe why methods used are different from those in consumer markets.

4. Examine the reasons behind segment selection and describe how products and services can be positioned and targeted to meet identified segment selection criteria.

Part 1 Decision making in B2B organisations

☐ Introduction

The purchase function

The purchasing process will be different in different types of B2B organisations and in different markets and it can and usually will involve one or more persons. It can take days, months or years, depending on the size, value and scope of the products/services that are needed. For example, obtaining an order for nuts and bolts might take one visit by a van salesperson while an order for a new computer system worth many millions of pounds might take years. It may involve one person or very many people across the whole company. Finding the person or persons that make the decision on whether to purchase or not can be straightforward and simple or mind-boggling and complex. It must be remembered that the competition will be vigorously burrowing away at the same task and to be successful the supplier and its sales force must take time to understand the process involved.

Cultural influences on the buying process

Cultural concerns were discussed in Chapter 2 and ingrained ways of behaving can have a profound effect on how buying decisions are made. Socio-cultural patterns, customs and practices, attitudes and beliefs will all have a pervasive influence when talking and negotiating with buyers and organisations in other countries. Some marketers argue that English is becoming the language of business and business people and buyers around the world now exposed to western business approaches are acting in similar ways. Others argue that cultural differences are still apparent and the supplier will need to adopt different approaches when talking to buyers from Japan, China, South America, and so on.

Buying procedures and policies could be different

It might be the case that formal buying and negotiations are different from country to country. Decisions may take more time in one country than in another. Decisions might be made by groups in Japan and by individuals in the USA. Payments may be 30 days in one market and 90 days in another. A supplier might even be expected to take some goods and services as part payment in one country and the home currency in another. Ethical problems might also arise where 'slush' money is demanded by the buyer, paid into a private account, as commission for giving the supplier the sale. Success in foreign markets might ultimately rest on an understanding of the country's business ways and the buyer's particular needs.

☐ Ethics in business

> *I want to work for a company that contributes to and is part of the community. I want something not just to invest in. I want something to believe in.*
>
> (Anita Roddick, www.anitaroddick.com)

Ethics in business have always bothered some commentators, but revelations at the beginning of the decade forced more opinion leaders to become involved in the debate. Stories about misdemeanours such as balance sheet manipulation, price fixing, bribery and under-the-table payments were rife and news items constantly appear in the media. Some of the largest organisations in the world, Enron, Andersen Consultants, Sotheby's and Christie's, were accused and in some cases condemned for misbehaviour and sharp practices that were reckoned to have cost customers and shareholders billions of dollars in lost values. In fact exposure of corporate fraud in the USA at the beginning of the new millennium was so shocking and unexpected that many investors lost confidence in the stock market and as a result share prices fell. Other organisations have been accused of different unacceptable behaviour such as using under-age labour, paying intolerably low wages, and exploiting sensitive environments.

Example 4.1 **Mining ethics**

Mining companies from around the world met in Toronto, Canada to discuss how the industry can develop an ethical international mining code. On the agenda were the mining, minerals and sustainable development (MMSD) project, which was commissioned by the Global Mining Initiative (GMI). The report looks at the most controversial problems of mining, including its impact on poverty, the environment, protected areas, corruption and the management of mining waste.

Companies often provide hospitals, schools and other facilities for local communities, but they have also realised that environmental awareness makes good business sense.

Moral and legal frameworks

Many politicians, industrialists, journalists, pressure groups and others were so worried that demands were made to increase the power of appointed regulators and decrease the ability of industries and associations to regulate themselves. It used to be thought that in a free market business ethics, acceptable ways of corporate behaving, were better left to companies and trade associations, otherwise legal bureaucracy could stifle entrepreneurial effort. With the realisation that organisations, no matter what the size and no matter the expressed codes of conduct, can act in self-centred ways (just like individuals) which can and do harm the public, governments stepped in and constructed moral and legal operating frameworks. The problem now is to try to get the balance right between too much government interference, leading to accusations of being a 'nanny state', and too little, allowing the weak to be exploited by the powerful. The problem becomes more acute with the growth in supra-governmental bodies such as the European Court and the World Court. As with many business dilemmas, there probably isn't an easy solution and perhaps there never will be an answer that will suit everybody.

Example 4.2 The UK Stock Exchange now has an ethical fund where institutions and individuals can invest in companies that have stated moral policies on how they run the business. Eight major firms have backed a ten-point plan intended to ensure that ethical considerations are taken into account in the pursuit of economic success. In a report entitled *A New Vision for Business*, they call for firms to measure and report regularly on how their activities affect communities and wider society.

Ethics in purchasing

The buying and selling of goods and services has always been a prime area where unhealthy practices can take place. It has often been the custom in the past to offer buyers inducements and gifts of some kind, especially at holiday times. Prizes can also be given to buyers as part of trade sale promotions, for example a raffle linked to the number of units that might be purchased. This practice is now frowned upon and the Institute of Purchase and Supply has codes of conduct setting down what practices and gifts are and are not acceptable. One of the biggest problems facing governments in developing countries has been the instances of bribery where buyers and sellers demand extra payments (backhanders) for placing the order or contract with one company rather than another. In some countries this is so common and widespread that every person involved in the passage of a government contract demands an extra payment of some kind to push the deal through.

Extensive corruption of this kind can weaken economies and stultify growth as money is wasted on the wrong projects and goods and services are overpriced. Experience has shown that it can still be a problem for all companies around the world. Buyers and others involved in price fixing, overcharging or undercharging, unlawfully taking money so as to gain personal pecuniary advantage, must ultimately be to the detriment of the organisations. The problem can be seen as worse when it happens in the public or NFP sector. Because public money is involved in the public sector, fraud of any kind will cause concern among many stakeholders and can even reverberate back to the government minister in charge of the department. The Audit Committee is the regulator put in place to monitor and control all public sector spending. Deceit in the NFP sector can cause almost as much embarrassment for the management committee, again because it is seen as public money being wasted. The Charity Commission is in place to try to prevent bad practices happening.

Example 4.3	**The Institute of Supply Management ethics in purchasing (www.ism.ws)**

The Institute of Supply Management in the US has a strict code on ethics in purchasing and it has numerous references in its Principles and Standards of Purchasing Practice. Below are just two such examples:

☐ 'Avoid the intent and appearance of unethical or compromising practice in relationships, actions, and communications.'

☐ 'Refrain from soliciting or accepting money, loans, credits, or prejudicial discounts, and the acceptance of gifts, entertainment, favours, or services from present or potential suppliers that might influence, or appear to influence, purchasing decisions.'

Similarly the US Ethics in Government Act makes it illegal for a public official to accept or solicit 'anything of value ... either [as] a reward for a past act, or [as] an inducement for a future one'.

☐ Choosing a supplier

There will come a time when organisations want to choose new suppliers for many reasons. For example, it might be because they are starting a new business, they want to buy new products and services, or they are discontented with their present suppliers. Some companies insist that existing suppliers be benchmarked against other suppliers in the industry at least once a year. This is to guard against complacency, buying out of habit and therefore not obtaining the best value for money. Buyers take both formal and informal approaches when looking for new suppliers. Examples are shown below:

☐ *Recommendations* – probably the most successful and safest method, especially if the recommendation comes from a well-respected company.

☐ *Building a shortlist* – managers will shortlist maybe three or four known suppliers and ask them to submit product or service specifications. This can then be measured against weighted values such as benefit solutions, quality, price, service levels, delivery times, exclusivity, and so on.

☐ *Selecting from trade association sources* – trade associations will usually have codes of conduct and will also make recommendations. This will offer some degree of safety.

☐ *Using outside agencies* – as with all business processes, supplier selection can be given over to expert agencies. This is particularly apt when marketing internationally.

☐ *Managers' experience and intuition* – depending on the value of the product or service needed, companies may rely on managers' experience and intuition. In many cases they might have little or no option if help is unavailable in other ways. A list of existing and past clients can be asked for, products examined (if tangible) and supplier presentation made.

New suppliers will usually be given a period of probation during which performance indicators will be set. Unacceptable deviation will result in cancellation of the business. This will of course depend on the amount of competition in the market and the exclusiveness of the wanted products.

Centralised and decentralised buying

National, international and global organisations and centralised and decentralised buying structures might determine the speed and complexity of the buying process. Some organisations might insist all buying takes place at head office; others might negotiate the prices and buying terms centrally and allow localised ordering at these prices; yet others might allow almost total autonomy on prices and products across divisions and companies. There is no point in wasting a salesperson's time by calling on satellite divisions if all buying decisions are made at head office and no consulting takes place. There is a case, however, for continuous detailed checking because, although no ordering takes place, they might be part of the Decision-Making Unit (DMU). In addition situations might change and no power to order today could change into ordering power tomorrow.

Single or multi-source suppliers

The buyer will have the opportunity to source from single or multi-source suppliers and there are advantages and disadvantages with both approaches. Single sourcing occurs when a buyer decides that it will satisfy its needs in one or more areas of the business by buying from only one supplier. The subsequent relationship is bound to be close, whether it is cemented through a formal contract or not. It might be used where supplies wanted need expensive set-up costs and training (such as EDI or capital equipment investment), where supplies might be prone to volatility or scarcity or where products are needed at a moment's notice (maybe as a part of a JIT programme). Single sourcing can be dangerous if the one supplier has problems, such as a strike, and the supplies dry up. This is one of the reasons why a company might decide to multi-source, buying the same supplies from two, three or more different suppliers, as well as introducing a large amount of competition into the equation. A buyer will often choose one or other of the two methods, or a combination of both, depending on the product and market circumstances. Advantages of single sourcing will include the following:

☐ Close, cooperative relationships can be formed, essential for developments such as ECR (efficient consumer response) programmes.

☐ The supplier will offer the buyer the best attention and service.

☐ Useful where supplies are prone to scarcity or volatility.

☐ High set-up costs demand heavy strategic commitment on the part of the supplier.

Advantages of multi-sourcing:

☐ If there are problems with one supplier others can be used.

☐ Introduces competition into the process so that all suppliers work harder.

☐ More opportunities to spot new product developments if using many suppliers.

Knowledge attainment

As with all business processes there is an imperative to understand the market and the needs of the customer. Once customers have been identified, more research will need to be conducted by both the research department and salespersons in an attempt to understand the intricacies of the buyer decision-making process. Although the subtleties of the decision-making process may differ from company to company, there are enough common basic factors involved to make simple classification possible. We can now discuss three major areas:

1. The decision-making unit (DMU)

2. The B2B decision-making process (DMP)

3. The buying decision difficulty (BDD)

☐ 1. The decision-making unit (DMU)

The supplier will need to know who is involved in making the purchase decision, known as the decision making unit (DMU) or the buying centre (TBC), what motivates them and how their products and services are perceived. The DMU or TBC is a way of describing all the people that might or might not be involved in some way in the ultimate decision to buy the product. This could be one person, e.g. a small business owner, or it could be many, e.g. buying for a large organisation. It could be argued that almost all buying decisions, whether large or small, will involve more than one person. Even the autonomous entrepreneur will turn to others, perhaps a solicitor or secretary, for advice when looking to make a purchase of some kind. In organisational buying, several roles can be identified. The different roles can be performed through one person or they can be separate roles performed by many people:

(a) *Suggester*. The suggester or initiator is the person (or persons) who begins the purchasing process by recognising that there is a need for a product or service and makes a suggestion or request. This might be for an existing product or service, a modified version, or something new.

(b) *Purchaser*. The purchaser or buyer is the person who makes the actual purchase. As with many other factors, the role and power of the buyer will vary quite considerably from situation to situation. In some companies the buyer will have little power to initiate new orders and be told what to order and what not to order, and from whom. In other companies buyers have full autonomy to buy at their own discretion. The purchaser may or may not reside in an actual purchasing department and could be played by many of the roles within the DMU. Purchasing managers have had to become much more professional in the way they conduct themselves because of the intensity of the competitive environment. Most will now have access to copious amounts of information to help in supplier and product selection. Computer software enables buyers to calculate almost immediately intricate cost benefit analysis where products and services are under consideration.

(c) *Advisor*. Advisors are those who have been brought in to help the buying company in some way. This might be somebody that works in the buyer organisation or it could be an agency outside the organisation such as a consultant or marketing agency. Specialist advisors will be used if technical products or services are wanted. B2B buyers wanting to purchase complex and highly technical services might use management consultants because of their greater expertise, and also to safeguard their own position because of the difficulties which might arise. Public sector organisations have been criticised in the past for spending too much money on outside consulting agencies, especially in circumstances where the advice given turns out to be both mistaken and costly.

Example 4.4 **PriceWaterhouseCoopers**

Management Consulting Services (MCS) provides a broad range of consulting services to multinational and larger domestic public and private entities. The team works in partnership with clients to help decide their strategic direction, re-engineer business processes, enhance their competitiveness and deliver change that transforms their performance, often through the implementation of information technology systems (www.pwcglobal.com).

(d) *Decision maker.* The decision maker is the person or the committee that has the power to make the actual decision to purchase. This might be one or many in the buying centre depending on the power structure and delegation of responsibility. Where strategic issues are involved, the board of directors, particularly the chief executive officer, will probably be the ultimate decision maker. In other cases it might the buyer or the end user.

(e) *End user.* Somebody and some department within the buying organisation will eventually be the end user of the product or service under review for possible purchase. Whether the user is consulted or not will depend on both the culture and structure of the organisation and the type of service to be purchased, but even if they are not part of the buying centre they will usually influence the decision.

(f) *Gatekeepers.* Gatekeepers control access and information into and out of the buying group. In some cases the gatekeeper can actively influence a buying decision by filtering the kind of information made available. A gatekeeper might be a secretary able to make appointments to see the buyer, an administrator controlling access to a preferred buyer status, a service engineer consulted on all purchases in a specialised area, or the financial controller who will monitor all purchases over a certain amount.

The DMU in B2B markets

- ☐ Complex structure
- ☐ Many people involved
- ☐ Long time to make decisions
- ☐ Buying for the organisation
- ☐ Mainly rational reasons for purchase
- ☐ Seller might know DMU members over a long period
- ☐ DMU members can change
- ☐ High value goods, services, projects
- ☐ End user will probably not be the decision maker.

The DMU in B2C markets

- ☐ Simple structure
- ☐ Few people involved
- ☐ Short time to make decisions
- ☐ Buying for self
- ☐ Mainly emotional reasons for purchase
- ☐ DMU members met at time of purchase
- ☐ DMU members stay the same
- ☐ Relatively low value products
- ☐ End user probably the decision maker.

Factors influencing the DMU or buying centre

The marketer and the salesperson will need to know and understand the power and influence of all the B2B DMU members as well as the priority benefits demanded. Only in this way can the right benefits be built, communicated and offered. It should be understood that in some firms the power to persuade to purchase from one company rather than another can rest in unexpected places and with the most unlikely people. The wise salesperson is able to dig this out, approach the right person, and so gain an advantage over the competition. As with everything in life, nothing stands still, and buying centres are the same. Over time the structure of the DMU will change and alter. Some are informal and others formal. Power bases will shift and priorities will take on other values. In a formal situation, authority to purchase will depend on the technical complexity of the product, its overall costs, its importance to the company and the expert knowledge level of the individual. The process can become fragmented as one person leaves the DMU and another takes his or her place. All relevant information pertaining to the DMU can now be stored and analysed in a computer database and updated on a regular basis so that action can be taken when conditions demand.

Vertical decision making

Buying centres will have both a vertical and a horizontal dimension. The vertical dimension is concerned with how many layers of management are involved in the buying process. In bureaucratic, tall structured organisations such as some government departments, this could involve as many as six, seven or eight layers of management, from director level down to factory floor level, which must be consulted before decisions can be made. In flatter structures there might be only one or two layers of management that need to be consulted and the task might be significantly easier. The more widespread the company, the more problems might arise (Figure 4.1).

Figure 4.1
Vertical
decision making

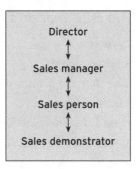

Figure 4.2
Horizontal DMU

Manufacturing ←——→ Purchasing ←——→ Marketing ←——→ Administration ←——→ Outsourcing

Horizontal decision making

The horizontal dimension is concerned with how many other departments might have an interest in the buying process as well as any bodies such as contractors and outsourcing companies. Company type, size and structure will have a bearing here. A company bidding for a long-term road building contract will need to communicate and consult with every department – finance, administration, production, human resource, transport, marketing etc. – and the process will need to be organised and coordinated to perfection if slip-ups are not to occur. Outside contractors will need to be included at an early stage if their input is important (Figure 4.2).

Group influences on decision making

Purchase decisions in B2B will almost inevitably involve more than one person, depending on the factors identified above, in the discussion on the decision-making unit. There might be many people with the ability to influence the buying decision and in some cases purchase decisions come about through a form of group consensus. A committee system can sometimes be used, especially in Government purchasing. Group decisions can be influenced by the following factors:

☐ The power of any one or more members to influence the others

☐ Political differences and jealousies between group members

☐ The inclination to discuss, prevaricate and thus not make a decision

☐ The inclination to compromise and select the least risky option

☐ The inclination to minimise the risk and so go for the more risky option.

Individual influences on decision making

It is argued that end consumers buy products and services for emotional and symbolic reasons while B2B buyers purchase for rational reasons. Research has shown this to be true, but only up to a point. Consumer purchases will be based on a varying element of rational reasons. Similarly a varying element of B2B purchasing will be based on emotional reasons. Organisational buyers are subject to the same personal motives or motivational forces as buyers in the consumer market. However, the buying situation is different and so influences, although similar in some cases, will differ in other ways from those on someone buying products for personal consumption. The power of influence will vary according to the organisation, but the following factors will affect the ability of any one individual to influence the purchase of goods and services:

☐ Management position within the organisation

☐ Whether a prospective user of the product or service

☐ Being the 'official' buyer within the organisation for the category of products

☐ Being seen as an expert in the product/service area

☐ Having access to information not available to others

☐ Being a gatekeeper to the decision maker.

Example 4.5 **The knowledge worker**

In hi-tech markets, senior managers are finding it increasingly difficult (if not impossible) to keep up with current developments and are often not able fully to understand techniques and processes. Thus they become dependent on employees, so-called 'knowledge workers', at a lower level within the organisation who have the right skills and are able to understand the ins and outs of product benefit offerings. Although not necessarily understanding the strategic ramifications, these individuals must therefore be asked to use their superior knowledge and contribute to the decision-making process. In some circumstances this can cause problems, with a compromise between the needs of junior and senior personnel turning out not to be best for overall effectiveness and productivity. Another problem caused by the differences in knowledge attainment between managers is the difficulty of control. If senior managers are unable to understand important tasks performed lower down, there is always the possibility of inappropriate or fraudulent outcomes exemplified by the loss of £800 million by Baring's Bank caused by unfortunate and foolish junior manager activity.

Managing risk

Individuals (and groups) will want to manage the risk involved in buying products. Purchasing the wrong products at the wrong prices could lead, at the very least, to loss of reputation and job change, and at the very worst to loss of the job. This can create a situation where a buyer, fearful of failure, will only use well-known suppliers and will only buy tried and tested products (known as the 'never getting the sack for buying from IBM' syndrome). New innovative products from new companies will not be sampled and then perhaps bought. This could end in the company losing competitive advantage because its marketing mix was dated and unproductive. The sympathetic supplier, aware of this fear, should develop mechanisms to help manage and minimise the difficulty. This might be through the supply of good up-to-date information, expert advice and consultation, free trial of new products/services, supply or return if product performance is substandard, partnership agreements and sharing of the risks, costs spread over a longer period, and so on. Sources of buyer perceived risk include:

☐ *Performance risks* – sale or return if product is substandard in some way, technological upgrades.

☐ *Financial risks* – partnership agreements, sharing the risk, spreading the costs, rental and leasing.

☐ *Informational risks* – supply of good information, expert advice and consulting.

☐ *Social (ego) risks* – reassurance, seller corporate image building, loyalty building measures.

And the trouble is, if you don't risk anything, you risk even more.

(Jong, 1996)

Marketing to buying centres

Buying centres develop in both formal and informal ways. If the culture is one of communication and consultation, then it will come naturally for all interested parties to be asked about product and service preferences. Conversely, if the structure is bureaucratic then maintenance of role power will keep decision making firmly with the individual or within the group. If leadership is weak then subordinates may take over the purchasing role. This might, however, switch back as soon as a stronger manager takes over. The supplier can exploit all these informal states of affairs so long as the situations are recognised.

Formal buying centres can be easier to manage if the supplier is an accepted part of the set-up but will be notoriously difficult if the company is deemed unacceptable because of such things as size, quality or service offered. With the use of IT, suppliers can now clearly identify the type and needs of the buying centre and develop strategies and tactics that will lead to a successful outcome. The following factors should be taken into account when marketing to a buying centre:

☐ Identify the decision-making unit members.

☐ Recognise the different roles that are played out.

☐ Prioritise levels of importance and power to make the final decision.

☐ Appreciate both the group and individual pressures.

☐ Understand individual, group and company needs and wants.

☐ Understand buyer policies and procedures.

☐ Be able to trace product ordering information flows, both back and forth.

☐ Monitor and evaluate changes.

☐ Develop strategies and tactics to manage the whole process.

☐ Build in control mechanisms.

☐ 2. The B2B decision-making process (DMP)

It's better to act too quickly than it is to wait too long.

(Welch, 2001)

Figure 4.3
The decision-
making process

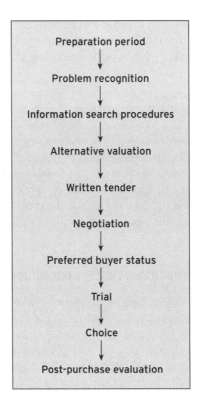

As with consumer buying, most organisational purchases are made in response to a problem or need of some kind. This will then trigger a decision-making buying process, taking the buying centre through to product or service purchase and, hopefully, problem solution (Figure 4.3). Although the basic structure is the same, there will be differences in the way companies approach the process. It will also vary across the world. So sellers will need to work hard at understanding cultural differences in whatever country the suppliers want to sell their products and services in. It is important for the supplier to understand the processes and the influences on them, so that this knowledge can be used in a productive and profitable way. Many B2B decision-making process models exist (practitioners will even develop their own). The following stages represent one such model. For some companies the purchasing process would start before the need arises. This stage could be identified as the preparation period.

The preparation period

For some companies and some classes of product it would seem foolish and unprofessional to start the buying process only when a particular need arises, especially if time, speed, repeat purchase or product complexity are major issues. If issues like these are concerns, then it will be profitable for the buyer to install contingency measures so that the organisation is prepared and can solve the problem easily and quickly. This will include contacting relevant suppliers to discuss quality, value and cost needs, as well as how much stock they are prepared to hold and delivery times. It might be that at this stage prices are negotiated and a contract written up for ordering throughout the year.

Problem recognition

In other circumstances the buying need arises in response to a particular problem. The size and difficulty associated with the problem will be determined by the product/service needed. With simple, inexpensive repeat purchases for goods such as paint, pins or paper, the process will be straightforward, especially if there is a contract already negotiated with the supplier. If the purchase is a modified rebuy or new purchase, then the problem becomes more difficult.

Information search procedures

This stage involves searching around for relevant information. It could be argued that with the introduction and development of the internet the course of action is much easier. Now almost the first stage in looking for information to solve a problem is to go onto the web. Other sources of information will be trade associations, existing dealer contacts, government sources, and so on. Probably the most reliable source, depending on the problem, would be from suppliers already used and recommendation from trusted sources. For B2B suppliers it is crucial that they have information readily available in a customer friendly acceptable form. This might be by inbound or outbound phone call, fax or e-mail request, or on the company or organisational partner website, by pamphlet, booklet or video, or by personal contact.

Companies wanting to sell into government departments will usually have to get onto a preferred supplier list before their products and services will be considered for purchase. This may involve quite detailed procedures (e.g. obtaining certain quality standards) that must be followed if they are to be considered as suppliers.

Alternative valuation

Once the source of the product or services needed has been identified, both the seller and the products on offer will have to be evaluated to measure good value and correctness of fit against wanted benefits. In the case of the products, the buyer will have some kind of criteria in terms of usage, value and price. This might be informal and only exist in the mind of the purchaser or it could be formal, written down and consisting of strict measurement and comparison criteria. The DMU might consider competing products or services from information gathered or, depending on the value of the order, prospective sellers will be invited to demonstrate the goods and be measured against predetermined benchmarks. This process might well be repeated at a given period, for example a year, so that complacency doesn't set in.

Written tender

Again with some organisations, especially government departments, a selection of interested suppliers will be invited to send in a written tender (now possible online) spelling out value and costs. They will then be judged against one another and the best value chosen (usually on price).

Negotiation

It is at this stage that some form of negotiation may take place. This might be on such things as added benefits offered, costs and payment period, and so on. Relationships between buyer and seller may be adversarial or cooperative. Adversarial relationships occur where in negotiation the seller tries to sell at the highest value (price?) and the buyer tries to buy at the lowest value (cost?). This tends to happen with low value products or one-off purchases. Such competition is thought by some to lower the prices while increasing the level of the service and attention paid to the buyer account. Others argue that the level and amount of power held by the two participants will mean that advantage will be taken by one side to the detriment of the other. Cooperative relationships involve agreements to work together over the long term with both buyer and seller concerns taken into consideration. We will discuss this further when we talk about customer relationship management and long-term supplier chain interaction.

Preferred buyer status

In some instances the buyer might have to be elected to 'preferred buyer' status before any order can be given. This will probably mean that certain conditions must be met, for example, achieving investment in people or industry quality standards awards, as part of the process. This tends to be obligatory in some sections of the public sector. Buyers seek to place suppliers on a preferred status basis so as to maximise the benefits that can come from such collaboration. Preferred status relationships are more likely where the products are specialised, high volume and/or of strategic importance or information and training is needed for the buyer staff because of product or service complexity.

Trial

In some cases products or services will be taken on for a trial period to see if they match the benefits promised. This will especially happen if the product is strategically important, a long-term contract, and/or is going to cost a great deal of money. Sellers may not like this arrangement, as it can be costly if the product is not taken up, but they might have to concur depending on the need for the order. It may well be that the buyer will instigate trial from different companies at the same time and it can be an expensive business for organisations whose products and services are not accepted.

Choice

The choice will be eventually made and the order placed or the contract signed. The deal might be for a one-off order, allowing the buyer to measure the level of service before more orders are given, promises of a series of repeat purchases, or a longer term contract of some kind. In some cases a probationary period might be demanded so as to test out the promises of the new supplier.

Post-purchase evaluation

All suppliers will be judged on the promised level of service and some type of post-purchase evaluation will be bound to take place. This might be by comparing actual benefits to those that were promised or measurement against predetermined standards. In the former case salespeople who over-promise on benefits, or benefits that don't match up to expectations, can cause customer loss of faith and no more purchases, thus bringing the company into disrepute. In the latter case, not meeting standards can lead to penalties and fines, depending on the terms and conditions built into the contract. Whatever the situation, loss of a customer can be disastrous in B2B where buyers might be few, whereas in B2C, although unfortunate, the customer will be only one among millions.

DMP in B2B markets

- ☐ Complex and intense
- ☐ Often a long process
- ☐ Detailed multifaceted information needed
- ☐ Rational reasons driving the purchase
- ☐ Formal benchmarking suppliers
- ☐ Trial of the product or service
- ☐ Penalties for product malfunction or shortfall
- ☐ Product/service contracts
- ☐ Negotiations often part of the process
- ☐ Formal preferred supply list.

DMP in B2C markets

- ☐ Simple and straightforward process
- ☐ Emotional and rational benefits wanted
- ☐ Impulsive purchase
- ☐ Product trial the exception
- ☐ Guarantees but no penalty for breakdown
- ☐ Contracts not usual
- ☐ Negotiation not usual
- ☐ Informal preferred retailer/brand.

☐ 3. The buying decision difficulty (BDD)

Once we realize that imperfect understanding is the human condition, there is no shame in being wrong, only in failing to correct our mistakes.

(George Soros, quoted in Kaufman, 2002)

All buying decisions, whether in B2B or B2C, have a certain level of difficulty that will affect the intensity of the decision-making process. Time taken in coming to a decision will vary from instantaneous through to months and even years, depending on the strategic importance of the goods and services that are wanted. Suppliers must be aware of all this and tailor the marketing approach accordingly. The following categories are identified below.

Straightforward rebuy

A straightforward rebuy could be classified as routine problem-solving decision making. The business product or service has been purchased before and all that is required is for the product to be repurchased. Such products include component parts and some services. Because these sorts of products are purchased on a regular basis there is a danger of complacency, staying with the same supplier for years and being unaware that better options exist in the marketplace. Many organisations recognise this problem and implement control systems to make certain that suppliers are regularly checked out for effectiveness and value for money. It is more than likely that very few people will be involved in the DMU reordering, which is sometimes performed automatically by computer. The decision-making process will be more complex if a change of supplier is mooted. An example might be a company wanting to change catering services because of dissatisfaction. Examples in B2C would be habit buying in FMCG markets.

Modified rebuy

At the second level of importance we can identify products and services that need to be purchased with some kind of modification added. This will incorporate a limited amount of problem solving and probably mean more people to be consulted in the DMU. Examples might be the need for chromium-plated bolts instead of steel-plated ones or wanting a technological upgrade on a computer system. The complexity of the decision-making process will depend on the severity of the problem, the risks and cost involved and its importance to maintaining competitive advantage. Suppliers need to be on hand with supporting help and advice. The more progressive supplier will anticipate future buyer needs and be proactive in its support. Examples in B2C markets might be a consumer upgrading a television or a washing machine.

New purchase

Business products and services in this category are those that the company has never purchased before and can cause complex, often extensive, problem solving. In most cases more information will be needed to make a new buy than when making a modified rebuy, and almost no information is needed for a straightforward rebuy. If the bundle of benefits wanted from the purchase is wide ranging, the DMU will be large and may bring together interested people from across the organisation that might not normally be concerned with purchasing. This will include such employees as salespeople, financiers and engineers. The DMP will be complex and intricate and the product/service search and investigation could be wide ranging and intense, according to the level of strategic importance of the decision. Again the supplier must be involved, if possible at the very beginning, helping, advising and suggesting. Supplier–buyer rapport is important and a trusting relationship at this stage could pay dividends when decision time arises. Buyers will sometimes negotiate contracts with trusted suppliers and then rely on their integrity in upgrading to new products because of the difficulties and worries connected with the kind of purchase.

Mixture of decision difficulty

Many buying decisions will fall between the categories discussed above, depending on the industry, market, types of goods and services bought by the organisations and the skills and experience of the DMU. This is especially the case with products and services that are technically complex and continually updated. Even when managers are kept informed and updated, it can seem impossible to keep abreast with what is happening around the world. On some occasions it might be difficult to know how important and how necessary a particular product update will be, even when a cost benefit analysis is undertaken. This may mean relying on the potential suppliers for help and advice, which is a strong argument for forming close 'partnering' relationships. On the downside this reliance on the supplier can cause the wrong product or service to be recommended because of supplier self-interest. Using outside consultants to help with the decision might be a way of solving the problem.

Switching costs

There are costs incurred for a buyer in changing suppliers. Companies will sometimes be reluctant to change for this reason. The more intricate and complex the product, the greater will be the uncertainty associated with change. Costs that might be incurred will include the following:

(a) *Financial costs*. There is always the possibility of financial costs when changing from one supplier to another. These will be costs associated with searching out and evaluating possible alternative suppliers. Of course these extra costs could well be offset by better prices offered by a new supplier.

(b) *Resource costs*. Sometimes there are buyer–seller resource commitments, e.g. training, IT interchange facilities, transport and inventory equipment sharing, and so on.

(c) *Product costs*. In a long-term buyer–seller relationship, product benefits offered will have been well tried and tested over the years. Products from a new supplier will have to be accepted on face value until usage provides a positive or negative outcome.

(d) *Service costs.* The quality of service offered can only be tested out as the relationship develops. If the service offered turns out not to be of the level required, it might be difficult to back out and change supplier.

(e) *Individual risk.* Individual buyers might develop close, often social, working relationships with supplier personnel, building a helpful partnership based on trust and loyalty. They might be loath to jeopardise and risk buying products on the new supplier recommendation and deemed not suitable.

(f) *Supplier risk.* There is always a certain amount of trepidation when deciding to move to and work with another organisation. This is based on the belief that cultures are different, working practice will not be the same and there is always the possibility that the new supplier might develop resource and financial problems. Because of these concerns a buyer might choose the easy way out and stay with existing suppliers.

Suppliers maximising switching costs

In the past B2B buyers would be reluctant to change supplier if a good relationship had been built between supplier salesperson and the company buyer. In the modern marketplace price and value are what count. In the end, buyers want business relationships that are meaningful for their companies, not personal relationships that benefit them as individuals.

It is in the supplier's interest to increase the buyer's switching costs and so be always thinking of ways to help the customer feel more invested in the supplier. Co-location and transport, bundled services, customised products and services, training and software at the company level could make a buyer think twice before switching to another supplier. Switching costs can create a good buffer to competition.

> Because of the strategic commitment in many supply chain relationships, switching costs incurred when moving from one supplier to another tend to be higher in B2B than in B2C.

Example 4.6 **Switching costs in information technology markets**

The most valuable asset in the new information technology economy is not manufacturing prowess or raw materials. It's an installed base of customers, kept loyal by switching costs that deter them from changing brands. Switching costs are more important than ever before because information goods and services work in systems. Hardware requires software, videos require players, browsers require servers and new technology requires learning time investment. Changing a single component often requires changing other components, which can impose large switching costs on users. Installing new software often means retraining employees, upgrading or converting historical data or maintaining incompatible systems. Developers and vendors are acutely aware of these costs and are seeking ways to elevate business buyers' switching costs and thus lock them into the organisation.

BDD in B2B markets

- ☐ Routine purchases increasingly have to be questioned
- ☐ No impulse purchases
- ☐ All purchases questioned and measured by others
- ☐ Supplier contracts often given
- ☐ Heavy risk for wrong purchase
- ☐ Heavy switching costs
- ☐ Experts involved with difficult decisions
- ☐ Little legal protection against supplier duress
- ☐ Preferred suppliers sometimes used
- ☐ The more difficult the decision, the larger the DMU.

BDD in B2C markets

- ☐ Habitual purchasing seldom questioned
- ☐ Impulse purchases
- ☐ Personal disappointment for wrong purchase
- ☐ No switching costs
- ☐ No experts except consumer groups
- ☐ Consumer legal protection against supplier duress
- ☐ Simple DMU.

The buying process in B2C and B2B markets

- ☐ B2C decisions involve thousands or millions of individuals, friends and families buying for their own consumption while B2B decisions involve considerably fewer people buying not for themselves but for the organisation.
- ☐ There are many suppliers and very many buyers in B2C but only relatively few buyers and sellers in B2B.
- ☐ B2B purchases run into large amounts of money, often millions of pounds, while B2C purchases usually involve relatively small amounts of money.
- ☐ B2B decisions can take days, weeks, months or sometimes years to come to fruition. B2C decisions will usually be made much more quickly.
- ☐ One B2B decision can affect the very existence of an organisation, while this will seldom be the case with most B2C decisions.
- ☐ B2B buyers are limited in number and usually clustered in small geographical areas, while B2C customers are widespread and can be found anywhere.
- ☐ B2B buyers are now more professional than ever and a professional supplier approach will be expected. B2C buyers, although more informed than in the past, will generally be at a much lower level of awareness.

☐ B2B decisions tend, in the main, to be made on strictly rational criteria while B2C decisions, although having an element of rationality about them, are made more on symbolic and emotional criteria.

☐ The DMU in B2C markets is likely to consist mainly of individuals, friends, acquaintances and family, although it might include professionals such as solicitors, salespeople and accountants. The DMU in B2B will predominantly consist of groups including directors, managers, knowledge workers, other staff, buyers and professionals such as accountants, marketers, engineers, etc.

Part 2 Business-to-business segmentation

☐ Why segment business markets?

In the preceding chapter we looked in some detail at the many influences that may affect the buying decisions of existing and potential customers. It was argued that these influences will cause organisational customers to want to buy different products and services to satisfy these needs. In this chapter it is argued that only if these concepts are understood by all marketing personnel can clear marketing strategies be planned and developed that will successfully exploit these influences. This will be achieved by developing goods and services that offer precise benefits to meet whatever may be the major driving need of each particular customer.

Of course a company would like to market the same product to every organisation around the world. In that way economies of scale can be made and higher efficiency achieved. However, this option is open to only a few industries and companies. Conversely, the marketing company would like to produce products that meet the special individual need of each and every customer and organisation. In many cases this is possible depending on the type and value of the benefits demanded. In fact some organisations gain competitive advantage by developing strategies of producing customised benefits for each and every customer. This can happen and is happening in consumer markets, but is much more prevalent in business markets. It can also be seen that with the development of modern technology this ability to customise product offerings is becoming more and more possible at both the strategic and tactical levels.

However, with many business products and services it would not be practicable or profitable to alter the benefit offerings to meet the differing needs of each organisation and in many cases it will not even be necessary. Many companies want the same or very similar products and services and the successful company needs to identify these similarities and group them into like-minded clusters. In this way the groups can be closely researched and the products and services offered can more closely match individual and group organisational needs. All customers around the world are prepared to buy products and services from others if these products and services satisfy some kind of need. This is true in both B2B and B2C markets. Market segmentation is dividing the markets into groups, or clusters, of customers based on realistic and meaningful criteria so as to offer clear, targeted benefits to every customer.

Market segmentation

The imperative to divide the market into different segments in order to offer products that match differing needs is at the very heart of both B2B and B2C marketing and is called market segmentation. The strength, width and depth of the segmentation demands will vary from industry to industry and from country to country depending on factors that often change, which will be discussed later in the chapter. Only if the varying and diverse benefits demanded by different industries and organisations are known can products and services be offered with benefits that will satisfy these many disparate needs.

Strategic importance of segmentation

It should be self-evident that if the organisation is uncertain about its customers' differing needs or believes it knows but doesn't bother to keep up with every changing circumstance, then it will not be able to offer products and services that precisely meet those customer needs. If one company is unable to offer desired benefits, then the competition will, and in many industries new technology is making market entry much easier. There are, however, many examples of businesses losing contact with their customer base and market changes and continuing to offer unsuitable or outdated products, even when market signals are sending out warnings, leading inexorably to dissatisfaction and falling sales (e.g. IBM, Xerox, British Steel).

The more forward-thinking marketing managers now realise the long-term strategic importance in having detailed knowledge and understanding of differing customer buying needs and segmentation methods as one of the most important factors in the planning process, affecting the marketing mix and all company resources. This means that strategic support for an understanding of the market and realistic and profitable segmentation must come from the very top of the organisation, with senior managers committed to implementing systems that continually monitor the process with the flexibility to adapt as market circumstances change.

Information, marketing research and segmentation

At the very centre of the process is the need for a continuous supply of good, up-to-date information on all aspects of the marketplace. As discussed in Chapter 3 the marketing information system (MkIS) must be used to collect and analyse meaningful environmental information from all relevant sources to track and monitor customer buying patterns, to find out competitors' strategies and to monitor market developments. The quality and type of information will vary according to the strategic segmentation task to be undertaken. Above all the MkIS must be seen by all as a 'living', important strategic tool that serves the needs of the marketing department (rather than its own needs), which aids the constant update of segmentation factors.

Segmenting existing B2B markets

More will be known about a company's existing markets and customers but complacency must be avoided at all costs. Systems should be in place to gather information about the viability of products and services that are offered to existing segments and customers. Questions should be asked (e.g. What products are being bought? Where are they bought? Why are they bought?) and frequent analysis made on market developments and changing customer needs. One business may take over or merge with another, bringing about a reassessment of suppliers. Business customer goals may change because of a strategic shift of direction. Company buyers move on and new buyers, often with different priorities, move in. Derived demand might shift and change along the supply chain, requiring a different approach from suppliers, and new partnerships might signal the end of old methods of working, and so on. Rich information must be available so that realistic predictions can be made and segmentation strategies altered, often in very subtle ways, earlier rather than later.

Segmenting B2B new markets

When segmenting new markets a company will need to go back to basics – identified in detail later when we discuss the segmentation process. This will entail exploratory, descriptive and causal research used in attempting to really understand the market. It will also involve internal resource and asset analysis and revisiting the mission statement and marketing mix so that matching of products with markets can take place and lead to realistic and profitable segmentation.

Segmenting different B2B markets

Disparate organisations face different changing pressures. Government buying policies often change from the election of one government to another and from the appointment of one minister over another. Similarly in charitable organisations, stakeholder pressure can cause the reassessment of strategies and the subsequent substitution of one strategy for another. All such changes might alter the supplier approach wanted. The successful company is the one that has the information and contingency plans prepared so that the segmentation style can be altered to take account of new purchasing circumstances.

Why segment business-to-business markets?

- ☐ Clearly identify disparate customer needs.
- ☐ Plan strategic and tactical approaches that match each and every customer need.

- ☐ Develop a portfolio of products and services that match customer needs.
- ☐ Focus management and worker attention across every department on customers' needs.
- ☐ Build and maintain competitive advantage.
- ☐ Give continuous superior customer satisfaction.
- ☐ Identify new opportunities in existing markets.
- ☐ Identify new opportunities in non-served markets.
- ☐ Help bring sales, profits and organisational success.
- ☐ Prepare all company members for the likelihood of change.
- ☐ Overall, make the company more competitive.

> Having looked at the benefits of well-thought-through B2B segmentation, it is worth remembering the alternative. If segmentation is not undertaken then clear, focused organisational benefits will not be offered and the customers, demanding a personal service and unhappy about what is on offer, might well decide to go to other suppliers who are more accommodating.

☐ Viability of segmentation

Dig where the gold is . . . unless you just need some exercise.

(Capozzi, 2001)

Not all identified segments will be acceptable as marketing propositions for various different reasons.

Match the objectives of the organisation

All organisations will want to identify markets that match their mission and their marketing objectives. Unless starting from scratch with no product or service direction, they will want to find market segments that match products and service capabilities already at some stage of definition. They might also want to identify markets that fit marketing strengths in such areas as technology, people skills, distribution capabilities, and sales and promotional potency.

Large enough to be profitable

To be attractive to an organisation, the identified market segment must be large enough to be profitable. Market research could well identify a market for 'left-handed' sprockets or for 'ginger hair dye', but this would not be profitable for a large company to manufacture and sell if these markets only consisted of one or two companies. Similarly there may be demand for a product or service but insufficient money available to pay, e.g. computer equipment in an underdeveloped country.

Niche markets

Notwithstanding, it should be mentioned that what might be unprofitable for a large company such as Procter & Gamble or Whirlpool might be profitable for a small company, leading to what has come to be known as a 'niche' market. When Ford stopped producing a soft-top sports car because the market was too small, it left a market niche for companies like Lotus and Morgan to step in. Small new competitors are popping up to take on disgruntled customers who have deserted companies that have been unwilling to change their ways.

Example 4.7 **Targeting the 'pink pound'**

An outspoken gay businessman and political figure made his name and his fortune by identifying a niche market and selling insurance to homosexuals, some of whom were turned down by mainstream insurers due to concerns over HIV and AIDS.

Market measurement

When a company is looking at potential markets it must be able to measure the size of the various customer groups and assess what the possible demand might be in each segment. If it is unable to tell whether there are 1000 or 1,000,000 potential customers, then it will be unable to forecast levels of sales, costs and profits and will not be able to put together a marketing plan.

Resource capabilities

An organisation will also have finite resources depending on its size and asset base. Segment opportunities may be identified but the company be unable to take advantage because of resource limitations. Research may indicate the possible demand for a more luxurious and expensive type of product which the firm cannot produce because it does not have the financial resources to purchase the more sophisticated capital equipment needed for its manufacture.

Ethical and moral perspective

An increasing constraint for many organisations is one that has some form of moral dimension involved. The corporate mission statement or declaration may spell out the manner in which the organisation intends to run its business and so constrain it from expanding into selected areas. The Co-operative Bank ran a series of adverts stating that it will not invest its clients' money in areas that it considers are politically and ethically suspect. The Body Shop undertakes PR, generates publicity and advertising campaigns through its outlets based on similar moral principles. This would include not investing in companies that might cause rainforest destruction or ozone layer damage, as well as countries that they consider have undemocratic regimes.

Example 4.8   **Ethically driven company**

The Co-operative Bank in the UK makes a positive virtue out of its moral stance and is at present running an advertising campaign where it claims that it will offer excellent customer service. It then goes on to say that it will refuse to do business with a company it considers to have morally dubious market and environmental policies. Its copy platform states that it is 'customer driven and ethically guided'.

Legal considerations

Similarly, legal considerations will always preclude market entry into certain defined market segments, although what may be unlawful in one country may be lawful in another (marijuana can be bought legally in the Netherlands, but not in the UK; it can be advertised in neither). Ethical and legal constraints may restrict marketing and advertising in other areas, including selling and advertising alcohol and cigarettes to children and drugs for other than medical or industrial use, selling furniture or clothing that has a high combustibility level, and trading where animals have been used for medical or combustibility purposes. Moving into another market segment may lead to an investigation by the Competition Commission because of fear of a monopoly market being built.

Example 4.9   **A moral dilemma**

The Animal Liberation Front has carried out hundreds of attacks on what it calls 'legitimate targets' since it was founded in 1976. Its methods have become increasingly sophisticated and the violence against people has increased. In 1984 a raid on a Unilever research station destroyed computer equipment and in 1989 a bomb was used against Bristol University after allegations that research animals had been mistreated. In late 1999 the campaign switched to Huntington Life Sciences laboratory, Cambridgeshire and since then there has been a concerted effort to put the company out of business. The company argues that it uses animals for medical experiments which will eventually reduce disease and prolong human life. The ALF is not convinced and over 500 protestors have continued to demonstrate outside the building, names and addresses of employees have been published on the internet, cars firebombed, and senior laboratory personnel have been personally attacked. More menacingly, financial backers and customers of HLS have been targeted, causing a downturn in business and numerous profit warnings. This has forced the government to take supportive action and the unprecedented step of setting up an account for the company at the Bank of England.

Basis for segmentation

There is no single way to segment the business-to-business market and the methods available are diverse and many. Through the use of research, the marketing manager will try to identify how, where and why products and services are purchased and base the segmentation on the method most likely to produce the best results. This basis for segmentation will undoubtedly vary from industry to industry, from product type to product type and from customer to customer. With an ever-increasing demand by the organisation for choice, coupled with growth in the ability of competing companies to provide more personalised offerings to satisfy this choice, the basis for segmentation is continually fragmenting and changing into ever more categories. Market fragmentation, however, is never likely to reach the same level of intensity as consumer markets for reasons discussed below. Twenty years ago the market for financial services was divided into three or four simple segments; now we can identify over 100.

More than one variable used

With very basic commodity-type products only one method will be used as the basis for the segmentation. An example might be the business-to-business market for coffee beans or raw rubber, which will probably be segmented by geographical location, e.g. London, New York or Paris. A company manufacturing nothing but industrial clothing such as donkey jackets or dungarees might segment only by size, but companies are more likely to use other methods such as the type of industry (e.g. the building trade, the car industry) and whether in the private or public sector.

The more sophisticated the product, the market and the customer, the more likely that two, three, four or more variables will be used in the segmentation process. Depending on the business sector and the customer, one variable will probably be more important than another. Using as an example the motor industry, the market might well be segmented in the following ways: the industry (service or manufacturing); the type of product (high or low value); and the level of service demanded (a sales call once a week or once a month).

Example 4.10 Volvo

Volvo segments the B2B market in the following way: international fleet sales – tourist, diplomatic, armoured, emergency, executive, police, service, taxi, ambulance, hearse, limousine, and 'special edition'/'limited edition' variants tailor-made to meet individual customer requirements. (www.volvocars.com)

Segmenting in B2B and B2C

The concept of segmenting a B2B market differs quite radically from consumer markets. B2B products tend to be categorised according to their use while B2C are categorised on how they are purchased.

Although there are some superficial similarities, the basic reasons and methods for segmenting in B2B markets will usually differ quite significantly from those of consumer markets and this is explored below.

Segmentation in consumer markets

Consumer markets consist of many millions of individual customers around the world buying goods and services for domestic use either for personal consumption or for consumption by relatives, friends or acquaintances. The consumer product marketer is therefore concerned about first identifying the wants and needs of all these individuals and dividing the served markets into profitable and manageable segments and groups that reflect these needs. Research has shown that over 70 per cent of the population buy products and brands mainly for emotional and symbolic reasons rather than for functional reasons.

These differences make segmenting consumer markets quite different from segmenting the business market in terms of the kind of research used, segmentation categories used and products and brands produced. Consumer markets can be segmented under the following categories:

☐ *Geographic* – where people live.

☐ *Demographic* – the make-up and movement of the population.

☐ *Socio-economic* – age, sex, religion, social class, occupation, family life cycle, etc.

☐ *Behavioural* – heavy users, brand switchers, past users, role-play users, etc.

☐ *Psychographic* – introverts/extroverts, power seekers, high/low achievers, etc.

☐ *Lifestyle* – grouping attitudes, interests and activities into life-style grouping.

Example 4.11 **Volvo segmenting in the consumer market**

Volvo offers the following models all aimed at different market segments in terms of age, gender, income and lifestyle: S40, S60, S80, V40, V70, XC70, XC90, C70 convertible. Many hundreds of variations are offered across all the range.

Segmentation in B2B markets

B2B marketers market and sell products and services to organisations and organisational buyers for business use and are interested in segmenting the markets in terms of these needs and wants. It is true that individuals make the buying decisions and are sometimes swayed by emotional reasons to buy one product rather than another (e.g. they like the salesperson), but unlike the consumer market most decisions to buy are made on objective professional needs. Many more differences exist (some shown in previous chapters) and more will be identified as we move through the book and discuss the unique nature of B2B marketing.

We now examine ways to segment B2B markets. Unlike B2C markets, B2B markets will not usually be segmented in terms of individual or group needs and wants. They are more likely to be segmented by industry and individual company need.

Part 3 Segmentation methods in business-to-business markets

Below we discuss the many different ways that B2B markets can be segmented so as to achieve optimum effectiveness. Methods chosen will ultimately reflect company objectives, company resources and market opportunities. Ways of evaluating the segmentation methods looked at here will be discussed later in the chapter.

☐ Macro and micro segmentation

Organisations tend to segment B2B markets according to macro and micro market factors. *Macro segmentation* uses factors that distinguish one sector from another, one industry from another and one type of organisation from another. *Micro segmentation* looks at the process involved with the purchasing decision and the behaviour of those involved in making these decisions. The overriding driving force when choosing across both approaches must be its use in providing the supplier with added value to offer the business customer.

☐ Macro segmentation

It makes sense to identify the macro methods of market segmentation and once the broader markets have been broken down, examined and high potential areas selected, then to move into the micro, smaller areas. We begin by looking at the macro environment. The macro segmentation process is as follows:

1. Industrial and/or consumer markets
2. Geographic segmentation
3. Manufacturing, service or agricultural industries
4. Segmenting by public, private or not-for-profit sector
5. Segmenting by small, medium or large company
6. Segmenting by products and services offered.

1. Industrial and/or consumer markets

Almost the first decision that has to be made is whether the organisation wants to operate in both the consumer and business sectors. As we saw above, the markets are quite different and so demand different strategies and different resources. Some companies operate in both markets while others choose to market in one or the other. For example, IBM make computer systems for both B2B and retail; Dulux markets paint for the building trade and to sell on to the end consumer. When both markets are served the company will often keep each division separate and organise the business to take account of the needs of both B2B and B2C markets. Care has to be taken to minimise any rivalry that might arise between the customers served and so avoid harmful inter-channel conflict.

Standard industrial classifications

As discussed in Chapter 1, all countries with modern economies now classify industries under a standard classification code to enable ease of identification and understanding. This enables governments to undertake research and so build a database of information on how different industries are managing and whether they are growing or declining, under the direction of government economic and social policy. It can look at past and present trends in specific industries and then try to predict what might happen in future. There is an attempt now to stand-ardise these classification codes across the world so that meaningful comparison can be made between industries across different countries.

This information is invaluable to suppliers and with more information brought from the private sector it helps them in segment selection and building the right segmentation strategies for the future. Many companies specialise in particular industries, for example construction, and would find it very difficult to move to other industries if and when times are difficult. Other industries, e.g. computer services, would be more easily able to move from one industry to another when opportunities become apparent.

Example 4.12 | **North American Industrial Classification System**

11	Agriculture, Forestry, Fishing, and Hunting
21	Mining
22	Utilities
23	Construction
31-33	Manufacturing
42	Wholesale Trade
44-45	Retail Trade
48-49	Transportation and Warehousing
51	Information
52	Finance and Insurance
53	Real Estate and Rental and Leasing
54	Professional, Scientific and Technical Services
55	Management of Companies and Enterprises
56	Administrative and Support and Waste Management and Remediation Services
61	Educational Services
62	Health Care and Social Assistance
71	Arts, Entertainment and Recreation
72	Accommodation and Food Services
81	Other Services (except Public Administration)

---

2. Geographic segmentation

Geographic areas to serve will be discussed by senior marketing managers very early in the segmentation process. In some cases the decision will be self-evident where industries are concentrated in certain areas, e.g. Silicon Valley in California or the car industry in Sunderland. Also whether the supplier has to be near the customer will also depend on product logistics difficulties such as costs, fragility or time. The size of the company will also have a bearing on the issue as a small company will usually have a smaller market, perhaps regionally localised, than a larger company with a world market.

Geographical segments

B2B suppliers might segment the market geographically in the following ways:

- Region (e.g. the North)
- Town or city (e.g. Manchester)
- International or global (e.g. working from home and selling abroad or setting up operations abroad)
- Country (e.g. Japan)
- Trading bloc (e.g. European Union)
- Trading area (e.g. Pacific Rim) or continent (e.g. Africa)
- Developed or developing nations (e.g. Germany or Vietnam).

Size, industry sector and industry type will all influence geographical markets to be chosen, as will company objectives and strategies, and economic and market conditions. Of course, as with all methods of segmentation, a thorough environmental audit would be necessary before choices can be made.

Density

Companies in the same industry often cluster together in a geographic area for many reasons:

- The infrastructure favours the movement of goods and services; an example is companies clustering around the M25 London ring road.
- A large company moves in and smaller companies follow, symbiotically feeding off one another or buying and selling relevant goods and services made easier because of the close proximity.
- Potential buyers will know where to look when wanting to buy in expertise and particular types of products. The more companies cluster together, the greater tendency there is to 'niche' and provide a unique product or service to large multinational neighbours.

Example 4.13 **Silicon Valley**

In the 1990s, Silicon Valley, the nickname for the high-tech heartland of the US economy, located between San Francisco and San Jose, California, was booming as companies such as Apple, Intel, Oracle and Hewlett-Packard expanded rapidly. But in 2001 Silicon Valley lost an estimated 25,000 jobs, the first net job loss in nine years. In 2001, 537 internet companies folded, more than twice as many as in 2000. However, with the development of new technologies the density of businesses is expected to increase once more.

Geographical segmentation in B2B and B2C markets

Both B2B and B2C organisations will segment markets, but there will be differences according to the following factors. B2C markets have millions of customers spread across the whole of the nation. Segmentation would usually be by demographic breakdown and population spread according to the target market and products sold. This will therefore take into account town, city and region population concentrations. B2B markets have far fewer customers and so segmentation will be by industry density, individual company location and customer contact point. The same differences will apply when marketing abroad.

3. Manufacturing, service or agricultural industries

There are some products and services wanted by both the manufacturing and service sectors alike and some suppliers are able to offer customised products to both sectors. There will, however, be many more organisations that will want different offerings and many goods and services are produced specifically for manufacturing or specifically for the service industries. For example, large amounts of steel and primary metals, copper, wiring, rubber, glass, transistors, electrical machinery, machine tools, food processing, radio and television receivers, communication equipment, and so on are produced by suppliers and so they would naturally need to sell into the manufacturing sector. Similarly, there are organisations that produce such things as retail display shelving, retail lighting, sports and leisure apparatus, restaurant products, alcohol-related equipment and so on which are geared up to market into the service industries.

In both manufacturing and services, supplier skills, resources, product portfolio, identified market opportunities, etc. will dictate which segments are eventually chosen.

Segmenting by the service industries

Over 75 per cent of UK GDP comes from activity in the service industries and it is increasing every year. In the USA over 80 per cent of GDP comes from activities in the service sector. Despite much manufacturing moving from the developed to the developing world, the services sector is still increasing its percentage of GDP when compared with manufacturing, albeit at times from a very low base (China 35 per cent, Thailand 31 per cent, Mexico 56 per cent). As the service industry has grown and manufacturing has declined, more and more organisations now specialise in offering B2B products and services in the service sector. Below are most of the main service sectors:

- ☐ Financial services
- ☐ Leisure services
- ☐ Legal services
- ☐ Travel services
- ☐ Communication services
- ☐ Entertainment services
- ☐ Hotels, restaurants, bars, catering services

- ☐ Electricity, gas and water services
- ☐ Real estate, renting and business
- ☐ Education services
- ☐ Consultants' services
- ☐ Other social and personal services
- ☐ Transport and storage
- ☐ Repairs
- ☐ Public administration and defence
- ☐ Wholesale and retail
- ☐ Health and social work.

A supplier may sell in all, some, or just one of these sectors. Many organisations specialise in any one of the above, perhaps in education, leisure and tourism, transport, and so on. The marketing approach taken by the supplier will usually vary according to the adopted sector.

Segmenting by the manufacturing industries

Although declining in comparison with the services, in 2001 UK manufacturing still accounted for about 20 per cent of Britain's economy (60 per cent of this is exported to the EU) with about four million people employed in the sector. In the USA the difference is even wider with only 18 per cent in manufacturing and 80 per cent in services. In Japan, however, there is still a strong manufacturing sector, 35 per cent compared with 63 per cent in services. There are many suppliers that produce products and services specifically related to manufacturing and would automatically segment into these markets. As with services, there are suppliers that are able to sell products in either sector and there are those that specialise in any one.

Manufacturing industries can be identified under the following SIC codes:

Manufacturing (SIC Code 20-39)
- ☐ Food and Kindred Products
- ☐ Tobacco Manufacturing
- ☐ Textile Mill Products
- ☐ Apparel and Other Textile Products
- ☐ Lumber and Wood Products
- ☐ Furniture and Fixtures
- ☐ Paper and Allied Products
- ☐ Printing and Publishing
- ☐ Chemicals and Allied Products
- ☐ Petroleum and Coal Products
- ☐ Rubber/Miscellaneous Plastic Products
- ☐ Leather and Leather Products
- ☐ Stone, Clay, Glass and Concrete Products

- ☐ Primary Metal Industries
- ☐ Fabricated
- ☐ Metal Products
- ☐ Industrial and Commercial Machinery and Computer Equipment
- ☐ Electrical Equipment and Components
- ☐ Transportation Equipment Measurement.

As with B2B marketing in the services, different marketing approaches might well be used according to the particular manufacturing industry selected.

Agriculture

Business in the agricultural sector in most developed countries is tiny in comparison with the two major sectors identified above. In the UK it is 1 per cent, in the USA 2 per cent in Japan 2 per cent. In some countries, again developing nations, it is much larger. In China 50 per cent of the population still work in agriculture, although it only accounts for 15 per cent of GDP. In India 67 per cent (25 per cent of GDP) of the population work in agriculture and 18 per cent in services (1995 estimate).

Changes in industrial sectors

The last 50 years have seen a tremendous shift in working habits of people in developed nations, moving from agriculture and manufacturing into the service sector. In the USA 80 per cent of the population now works in the service sector. In the UK it is nearly 70 per cent and the trend is set to continue. This has had enormous implications for B2B suppliers over the years. Companies have had to shift benefits offered or go out of business (allowing new firms to enter) as manufacturing has declined and services increased.

4. Segmenting by public, private or not-for-profit sectors

Some organisations supply goods and services across all business sectors selling into the commercial, not-for-profit, institutional and government sectors. Others specialise in only one area, perhaps selling medical equipment to hospitals or consultant services to charities. Because organisational objectives, purchasing polices and product benefits are often different across the public and private sectors, the approach taken by the buyer will have to be tailored to meet these differing needs.

As it is public money that is being spent in the public sector, buying processes and procedures will almost always be more detailed, convoluted and bureaucratic than in the private sector as there are many stakeholders and probity must be transparent in all business activities. This can be the source of much supplier frustration and anguish at the seemingly unlimited red tape that has to be surmounted if sales are to be made. The same difficulties might also arise in the not-for-profit sector because revenue donors hate to see monies given 'wasted' on supplier services superficially seen as unnecessary.

In some countries there has been an increasing trend for organisations in the public and private sectors to work in partnership with one another.

Segmenting by sector

☐ *Public* – government, institutions, departments, non-governmental agencies.

☐ *Private* – small, medium and large companies; PLCs, partnerships, sole traders.

☐ *Not-for-profit* – charities, associations, mutual societies.

> The marketer will need to understand the buying pressure and motives in the private, public and not-for-profit sectors as they will often be different.

Example 4.14 **Public sector purchasing**

Extra nurses, soldiers and council workers in the UK are to become Vodafone users after the telecoms giant completed a deal to supply mobile phones to the government. The government announced that it had signed its first strategic partnership agreement, which could see more than 100,000 public sector workers equipped with Vodafone phones. The deal is the first in a series of strategic partnership agreements to be announced by the Office of Government Commerce.

---

5. Segmenting by small, medium or large company

There is no real definition of what we might mean by a small, medium or large firm and this will vary from industry to industry and from business to business. What might seem to be a large organisation to one supplier might be a small one to another. Similarly how size might be measured will vary from the number of employees and the number of skilled staff in a particular area to the amount of sales volume, sales revenue and level of profit made. It could also be based on the amount of purchases that the company might make over the year, the amount of purchases made in particular product categories, or perhaps the average order size. Ninety per cent of Britain's businesses fall into the small and medium category (SME, small and medium enterprises), but over 90 per cent of total business turnover comes from the 10 per cent largest companies (Figures 4.4 and 4.5). Size can be measured in the following ways.

Figure 4.4
EU definition of micro, small, medium and large organisations

	Micro	Small	Medium	Large
No. of employees	<10	10-50	51-250	>250
Turnover		Up to 7m euros	7-40m euros	>40m euros

Figure 4.5
Top ten
companies in
the world by
revenues and
number of
employees

		$ millions	Employees
1.	Exxon Mobil	210,392	123,000
2.	Wal-Mart Stores	193,295	1,244,000
3.	General Motors	184,632	386,000
4.	Ford Motors	180,598	345,991
5.	Daimler Chrysler	152,446	416,500
6.	Royal Dutch/Shell Group	149,146	90,000
7.	General Electric	129,417	313,000
8.	Mitsubishi	124,283	n/a
9.	Itochu	109,068	n/a
10.	Toyota Motors	106,952	214,630

- ☐ Small, medium, large organisations
- ☐ Number of employees, skill level of employees
- ☐ Sales volume, sales revenue, profit
- ☐ Balance sheet total
- ☐ Annual purchase
- ☐ Average order size, average order size in specific categories
- ☐ Value added by manufacturing
- ☐ Value added in services.

To be classed by the EU definition as an SME or a micro-enterprise, a company has to satisfy the criteria for number of employees and one of two financial criteria, i.e. either turnover total or balance sheet total. In addition, it must be independent, which means that less than 25 per cent may be owned by one enterprise (or jointly by several enterprises) falling outside the definition of an SME or a micro-enterprise, whichever may apply. The thresholds for the turnover and balance sheet totals are adjusted regularly to take account of changing economic circumstances in Europe (normally every four years).

6. Segmenting by products and services offered

The commercial business can be further divided into three categories: users, original equipment manufactures, and dealers and distributors.

Users

User customers in the business or consumer market purchase such products as automated manufacturing systems, computer systems, photocopiers, and so on.

Original equipment manufacturers

Original equipment manufacturers purchase industrial products to incorporate into their products that are then sold on to business or consumer markets. In this way Ford will purchase windscreens from Pilkington Glass, or light fittings from Lucas.

Dealers or distributors

Dealers or distributors purchase industrial goods to sell on to users and OEM, adding little or nothing to the basic product in the process. The distributor will buy from all around the world, holding stock, assuming title, offering choice and delivering to the place of business.

Types of supplier goods required

Having classified and segmented the customers that constitute the business market, we must now ask what types of goods they require and how each type is marketed.

Raw materials and manufactured material and parts

Raw materials and manufactured material and parts are those goods that become part of the finished product. Raw materials might be coffee beans, peas, potatoes, strawberries, apples, if a food manufacturer, or steel, rubber, leather, if in the car industry. Manufactured material and parts might be tin cans, glass jars and printed labels for the food industry, and batteries, nuts and bolts and brake pads in the car industry.

Capital goods

Capital goods include the long-term investment items that support the manufacturing process such as factories, office buildings, fixed equipment and transport. The value of these goods will be depreciated against production cost at the end of the year.

Supplies and services

Supplies and services are goods that are purchased to support organisational operations. These will include such items as photocopier paper, administration forms, maintenance and repair items such as paint and cleaning materials. They also include the use of energy services such as heating and lighting, as well as services such as computer support, logistics, payroll processing and food operations. In the drive for greater efficiency and cost reduction, more and more companies are now outsourcing many services once performed in-house.

Organisations in B2B and B2C segment markets according to products and services sold.

The practice of macro segmentation

We discussed above how it is impossible for all but a very few large organisations to serve all sectors and all organisations in any one market. Therefore markets must be segmented and choices made. So how will an organisation, when first coming into a market, choose the organisation that it should first approach? To begin with, a supplier will have resources, finance, skills, technology, products and services that it already produces, unless it is starting from scratch. It will also have corporate and marketing objectives that it must achieve. These will circumscribe the markets that it can consider for its B2B marketing operations. Of course this should not inhibit a company from continually seeking out markets for future strategic direction because if opportunities can be spotted then resources can usually be obtained to take advantage of these opportunities, as long as time is allowed for strategic planning.

Within these limitations, an organisation can look towards segmenting the market according to the stages identified above. At each stage information will need to be collected, market analysis undertaken and an attempt made to identify demand potential. The earlier the stage, the broader will be the investigation and analysis. It will also be less expensive in terms of costs associated with the type of information gathering. This was discussed in some detail in the preceding chapter on forecasting demand.

☐ Micro segmentation

Once the macro segments have been identified, then the groups can be further subdivided into smaller micro segments based upon organisation, group and individual behaviour. The organisation might choose to micro segment at the strategic level or leave it to the sales manager and sales team at the tactical level. The decision will need to be based on the importance to the company of the customer factors under consideration. What might be unimportant to one customer might be of great importance and value to another.

Segmenting B2B by organisation buying behaviour

All organisations exhibit distinct ways of behaving and these will be discussed in more detail in later chapters. Below are some of the major forms of business behaviour that could have an important impact on the buying situation and the needs of benefit segmentation:

1. Present, past, or non-user
2. Heavy, medium, or light user
3. Centralised or decentralised buying
4. Single source or multiple source user
5. National accounts
6. Partnering and non-partnering relationships
7. Reciprocal relationships

8. Product benefits
9. One-off buyer
10. Repeat purchaser
11. Payment record.

Present, past or non-user

As well as customers in existing markets, there will always be businesses that might have used products or services in the past but now no longer purchase. There will also be those that, for one reason or another, have never purchased. This can be a lucrative source for new segments and information systems and software should be installed within the MIS to throw up instances when past users might be in the market for products and services and targeted marketing promotions might lead to sales.

Heavy, medium or light user

Most businesses will have heavy users (the Pareto 80/20 rule, i.e. 80 per cent of the business comes from 20 per cent of the customers). It should be obvious that loyal and large spending customers should be targeted through the use of some form of customer relationship management scheme. Data mining should identify which customers are the most profitable and which the most costly.

Centralised or decentralised buying

Whether a customer has a centralised or decentralised approach to purchasing will also dictate segmentation strategy. If it has a policy of centralised buying then all sales approaches will have to be through head office. Conversely, if the policy is one of decentralised buying then separate sales approaches will need to be made to all purchasing divisions.

Single source or multiple source user

As matter of policy some firms will buy from more than one company while others might only buy from one. A supplier will want to persuade the multiple source customer always to buy from his or her organisation (by exemplary service?), while the single source customer should be rewarded for continuous loyalty.

National accounts

Many large companies buy for the whole company through a centralised head office buying location. This might be for overall order placing or for price negotiations and individual divisions ordering the products as and when needed. Either way the buying business will expect national account status and

interaction with a senior marketing manager (often the sales or marketing director depending on value).

Partnering and non-partnering relationships

Many associations along the supply chain revolve around cooperative relationships. This may be by formal partnerships, joint ventures and strategic alliances
or through more informal verbal agreements based on nothing more than a
handshake. Many vertical supply partnership relationships are taking on heavy
strategic resource commitments involving joint management schemes such as
'efficient consumer response' and 'electronic data interchange'. This will bring
added pressure to the segmentation process depending on the strategic importance and the power of the relationship.

Reciprocal relationships

Unlike consumer markets, businesses are often both sellers as well as buyers of
products and services. This leads to the reciprocal arrangements where one company will buy from another on the understanding that the seller will then buy its
products. In some cases these can infringe competition law and be illegal.

One-off buyer

One-off buyers will usually purchase infrequently and each transaction will ter-
minate and only reactivate if a future need arises. This might be because a supplier is only used when the main supplier is unable to supply or if the product or
service is seldom used. Again exemplary service might encourage more frequent
usage.

Repeat purchaser

While not necessarily on a contract, repeat purchasers will buy the same products
and services on a regular basis. Many companies buy out of habit and there is
always the danger of complacency setting in on the part of both supplier and
buyer. The danger for the supplier is that standards could fall and the business be
lost if the supplier suddenly instigates a supplier quality audit.

Payment record

Organisations will sometimes have different payment reputations, including
those that pay within the standard allocated time for the industry, e.g. 30 days,
those that demand extra payment time as part of the deal, those that are slow
payers whatever the deal, and those that never pay. Of course the last option can
cause a supplier to go out of business, especially if the amount is a major part of
the company's revenue. Trade organisations exist to credit rate business organisations by a payment risk element.

Example 4.15 **Late payment is still the norm**

Companies are still taking longer to pay their bills three years after legislation to speed up payment was introduced.

☐ Three years after the government brought in legislation to reduce late payment of invoices, the average payment period in the UK is 60.3 days.

☐ It takes companies on average two days longer to pay their bills than when the legislation was introduced.

☐ Large companies take 77.9 days, medium-sized companies 59.3 days, and small companies 50.1 days on average to pay their suppliers.

☐ Large gas companies take 95 days to pay their suppliers, 20 days longer than in November 2000.

☐ Large oil companies are taking 88 days to pay their suppliers, nine days longer than in November 2000. (www.experian.com)

Segmenting by group and individual buying behaviour

We talk about organisational buying patterns, but it must be remembered that ultimately buying decisions are made by individuals and groups with similar sorts of human problems as are suffered by customers in consumer markets. We can divide the process under the following headings:

1. Characteristics of purchasing situation

2. Group buyer characteristics

3. Individual buyer characteristics.

1. Characteristics of purchasing situation

Problem solving degree of difficulty

The level of difficulty the buyer might have with the purchase is associated with the type of purchase being made. It might be a new purchase, i.e. the risk associated with a product never bought before; a modified repurchase, i.e. price, quality or service changes wanted; or a simple repurchase, i.e. reordering products already in use. The seller, being aware of the difficulties involved, can then offer benefits to overcome them.

Purchasing stage in the decision-making process

Many buying situations can take a very long time before a decision is made and the contract signed. The process can take months and sometimes years. Purchasing agreements might also be renegotiable every so often, perhaps every year, so the seller will need to be aware when circumstances are ripe.

Purchasing importance

Linked to the degree of difficulty associated with the purchase stage will be the importance of the product or service being purchased. This will vary from company to company and from situation to situation. Some sellers specialise in market segments where risk minimisation, in terms of delivery time or quality guarantee, is offered as a central benefit.

Purchasing policies

All companies will have buying policies related to such areas as leasing, rental, price setting, price negotiation and method of payment.

Purchasing criteria

Many organisations, particularly in the public sector, will have purchasing criteria based on supplier reputation, product quality, product availability (often insisting on a quality mark such as ISO 9000), and full service benefits. In some cases purchases will not even be considered until a qualifying process puts the seller onto an approved vendor list.

Inventory requirements

Inventory requirements comprise the add-on services required, delivery and storage demands, and whether part of an overall materials management scheme includes such things as 'electronic data interchange' and 'just-in-time' processes. This can lead to a heavy resource commitment, which can be a real problem if the buyer is unprepared to commit to a long-term relationship.

Value in use

Some organisations are more concerned about added 'value in use' in the form of after-sales service, technical support and supply continuity.

Buying centre structure

Some companies involve many people within the organisation in the purchasing decisions, depending on the level of importance. Identification of the roles played by the various members in the buying centre, those with the most influence and the primary decision-makers, must be part of the segmentation and sales process (also known as the decision making unit).

Organisational politics

Politics is about the level and distribution of power and all organisations will have some form of power culture to a lesser or greater degree. The display of power can manifest itself in many different ways according to the type of organisation, internal structure, products and services bought and sold, and the importance of the decision to be made.

2. Group buyer characteristics

The importance of the decision making unit (DMU) in B2B decision making was discussed in the preceding chapter. Here we look further at the need for suppliers, sales managers and sales representative to identify group buyer characteristics.

All groups exhibit many types of buying behaviour according to group make-up, organisational demands and the type of buying decision to be made. How group decisions are made can vary from the authoritarian, where one person dominates, to the democratic, where all group members are involved in the final decision. Other group factors that can influence decision making will include the make-up of the group and who the members are, the role and position of each member within the organisation, who has the power to make decisions, and so on. This can be a problem when groups of people come together for a one-off project and when this is finished move off to another. Some companies will build individual and group member profiles, attempting to answer some of these questions and create the right kind of marketing and personal approach. Many theories exist on the role of groups, how they operate and how they come to make purchasing decisions (see examples).

Example 4.16 **Belbin and group roles**

Dr R. Meredith Belbin describes patterns of group behaviour, attempting to show how team members adopt roles to interact with one another. He identifies nine useful types (roles) of contribution (www.Belbin.com).

1. *Plant* – very creative, the ideas person.

2. *Resource Investigator* – extrovert, good at making outside contacts and developing ideas.

3. *Monitor Evaluator* – shrewd and prudent, analytical.

4. *Shaper* – dynamic and challenging.

5. *Co-ordinator* – respected, mature and good at ensuring that talents are used effectively.

6. *Implementer* – practical, loyal and task orientated.

7. *Completer Finisher* – meticulous and with attention to detail, also full of nervous energy.

8. *Team Worker* – caring and very person orientated.

9. *Specialist* – high technical skill and professional, as opposed to organisational prime loyalties.

Example 4.17   **Group think**

Irving Janis in his book *Victims of Group Think* describes his observation on group dynamics that he came to call 'group think'. He goes on to describe seven symptoms of so-called 'group think' which organisations should fight against:

1. *An illusion of invulnerability.* The group feels that it and the organisation they work for could do no wrong. They feel invincible.

2. *Stereotyping outsiders.* The group will frequently justify its needs and position by stereotyping others they see as enemies or rivals. This might be other departments and even expert advisors who interfere in some way with their decision making.

3. *Bounded rationality.* Members fall under the impression that they are right even when the evidence is telling them otherwise. Members reassure one another that their interpretations and perspectives are correct and they believe what they want to believe without challenging old assumptions.

4. *Belief inherent morality.* They believe that all that they do is right, that the others are wrong and that their cause is morally underpinned.

5. *Self-censorship.* All members tend to conform to the opinion and decisions of the majority, not wanting to stand out as different.

6. *Direct pressure on dissenters.* Anybody that speaks out against the general view is pressurised or discredited. This leads to uncritical thinking, acquiescence and conformity in decisions.

7. *Mindguards.* Members shield the leader from dissenters, giving the impression of unanimity.

3. Individual buyer characteristics

It is difficult at times to take into account personal buyer behavioural and personality patterns because buyers can change quite frequently. However, there is no doubt that, despite increased professionalism, individual personality and attitude of the buyer can have an effect on the eventual outcome, especially if he or she does not like the supplier company, its products or the salesperson.

Despite the standardisation of organisational systems, processes and procedures, buyers will almost inevitably bring their own style and ways of working to the purchasing process. This will vary according to many factors such as age, whether they are new to the job, confidence, the need to impress their bosses, and so on. The importance of these differences cannot be ignored and there are many examples of a company losing all its business when a new buyer moves in and the old one departs. These differences are identified in more detail below.

Individual buyer characteristics take on a higher level of importance in the small business where the buyer is also the owner. Most seller organisations will be dealing with this type of company at some time or other. When selling into these companies the decision to purchase or not is often at the whim and possible eccentricities of one man. In these situations an understanding of human nature and the motives driving the purchasing situation are critical and should only be left to astute salespeople. It should be noted, however, that this level of individual behaviour and personality involvement in the B2B market is nowhere as high as in the B2C market.

Good salespeople have always segmented individual buyers by personality and attitude, many doing it instinctively as they moved from organisation to organisation. Years ago, when a card system was used to record the different buying patterns of each company, a salesperson might write on each card the personal details about the buyer's temperament, hobbies or family. This can now be done more effectively with the help of laptop computers.

Individual buyer factors

The following individual buyer factors might need to be considered by the B2B supplier marketing department and the sales team at the micro level:

- ☐ *Ambition* – high, medium, low, politically (in the business sense) active.
- ☐ *Personality* – sense of humour, aggressive, non-assertive, moody.
- ☐ *Experience* – new to the job, been in the business for years, technophobe/technophile.
- ☐ *Attitudes* – towards own company and supplier: like, dislike, indifferent.
- ☐ *Lifestyle* – gregarious, outward-going, bookish, conservative, work driven.
- ☐ *Self-image* – confident, at ease, insecure, unsettled, need to impress.
- ☐ *Risk tolerance* – high, medium, low.
- ☐ *Decision-making style* – consistent, conservative, aggressive, slow, quick.
- ☐ *Cognitive style* – knowledgeable, quick thinker, slow thinker, interactive.
- ☐ *Job responsibility* – high, medium, low levels of decision-making responsibility.

Intellectual, emotional and instinctive influences on B2B markets

Public commentators as long ago as the Greek philosopher Plato have considered the different ways that people have of 'thinking' about their needs, wants and desires. This is because people do not seem to think in the same way when coming to decisions. Some take their time and ponder long and hard before deciding. Others take no time at all and act almost on impulse. As with other influences, marketers are interested in the thinking process because they want to try to understand what is going on so that benefits can be offered that take these processes into account.

In a simple and very general way the concerns discussed here can be condensed into a theory that people 'think' at three different levels when making decisions (see Figure 4.6):

1. *Intellectual and rational thought*: thinking with the use of the brain, which might be considered to be the highest level of thought.
2. *Emotional thought*: 'thinking' with the heart, which might be considered mid-level thought.
3. *Instinctive thought*: 'thinking' with the gut, which might be considered the lowest level of thought.

Figure 4.6
The three levels of thought

Source: Wright, 2001

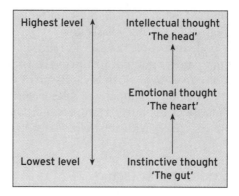

People think at different levels

It can be argued that individuals think and act using varying degrees of intellect, emotion and instinct. Some people think and act more at the highest level, some at the mid-level, while others think and act at the lowest level. This will be the case in both B2B and B2C markets. The level of thought employed will depend on genetic, environmental and situational factors.

Intellectual, emotive and instinctive influences and B2B marketing

We would all like to think that we make decisions based on pure rational analysis, but research shows this not to be the case. In B2C marketing, product branding becomes crucial as research shows that over 70 per cent of consumer decisions are made for symbolic and emotional reasons. In B2B, as buyers purchase for the company and not themselves, purchases tend to be (though not always) for rational reasons.

☐ Changing importance of segmentation factors

The importance of all the various segmentation factors discussed above will quite possibly change from market to market and country to country. A factor that may be important in the UK might be relatively unimportant if segmenting the Japanese market.

Criteria for market segmentation

There are many factors to consider when segmenting B2B markets and the importance of each will depend on different criteria:

☐ Environmental factors

☐ Corporate mission

☐ Corporate objectives and corporate strategies

- ☐ Marketing objectives and marketing strategies
- ☐ Target markets: national, international, global
- ☐ Present structure of the marketplace
- ☐ Level of competition
- ☐ Internal resources and assets
- ☐ Product portfolio
- ☐ B2B market segmentation process
- ☐ Market coverage wanted
- ☐ Products and services sold
- ☐ Direct or indirect
- ☐ Channel structure.

Conjoint analysis

Conjoint analysis is a sophisticated tool for implementing market segmentation strategies. It was developed primarily for use in consumer markets but is now being developed for use in B2B. It tries to measure the various benefit trade-offs that customers are willing to make when they use one supplier over another and when they buy a product or service. This will include benefit areas such as corporate and product brand, price, quality, service, delivery, warranty, timing, speed, and so on. Its primary uses are in developing new products, repositioning old products and deciding prices. The central idea of conjoint analysis is that products and services can be described by a set of attribute levels. Purchasers then attach different values to the levels of different benefit attributes, e.g. on a score of 1 to 10 they may put the speed of delivery at 9, the price at 3 and the service at 7. They then choose the offering that has the highest total value, adding up all the related, weighted benefits. Business buyers have different values, so their trade-offs vary and research should be used to identify these differences. These can be placed on a grid and analysed.

Once we work through the models we find ourselves with various outputs: profiles of companies, products and services, along with expected returns to each company; and a description of each buyer who chooses a particular product profile from the array of choices. The strength of conjoint analysis is that it goes beyond simply telling us what a buyer likes about a particular company, product or service. It also helps us to understand why the consumer might choose one product or or service supplier over another. Once a company gathers information on buyer needs, it must then assess both how potential purchasers are likely to react in the market-place to any changes and, of equal importance, how competitors are likely to react.

The first step in creating a successful conjoint analysis is to examine the competitive marketplace and develop a set of corporate/product/service attributes and levels. Personal interviews and in-house expertise can define these. Conjoint analysis can use statistical design techniques to select a small set of possible profiles from which the user can predict results for thousands of combinations not actually tested.

Part 4   Market segmentation process

This process involves six stages:

1. Identify the basis for market segmentation.
2. Determine the important characteristics of each segment.
3. Evaluate the market attractiveness of each segment.
4. Segment selection.
5. B2B corporate/product positioning.
6. Develop a marketing mix strategy for each targeted segment.

☐ Identify the basis for market segmentation

The first step in segmenting a market is to identify on what basis the segmentation is to be made. We discussed above the many methods and approaches that can be used and it is from these that choices will need to be made. Of course the segmentation process will never take place in isolation from the whole planning process because there are many other factors that will need to be taken into account before reaching this stage. The internal and external environmental auditing process will have identified the opportunities and threats facing the company and its own internal strengths and weakness. Strategic market option analysis should then have clearly described and evaluated the markets that the company should now be considering and the products and services that need to be developed to serve these markets. It is from this analysis that the basis for segmentation strategies can be chosen.

Unless the company is starting from scratch, certain segmentation methods will already be in use, although complacency in spotting new opportunities must always be avoided. The basis for identifying the most likely macro segments will include the following, depending on the strategies to be chosen:

☐   Markets already being served
☐   New markets for new products
☐   New markets for existing products
☐   Size and growth of the markets
☐   Level of competition in these markets
☐   General characteristics of buying companies in the market
☐   Competitive advantage enjoyed by existing players in the market
☐   Market structures
☐   Products and services currently in the product portfolio
☐   Company objectives and strategies
☐   Company skills and resources.

An example of a starting point might be an initial decision on whether to stay within national boundaries or to move abroad. If the decision is to move abroad then the most likely countries must be identified. The segmentation analysis

Figure 4.7
Identifying the
basis for
segmentation

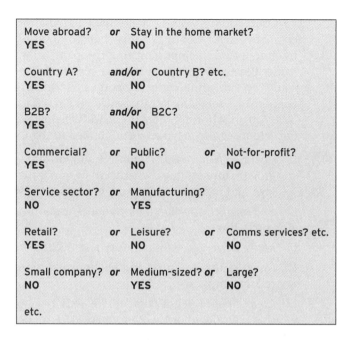

Move abroad?	*or*	Stay in the home market?		
YES		NO		
Country A?	*and/or*	Country B? etc.		
YES		NO		
B2B?	*and/or*	B2C?		
YES		NO		
Commercial?	*or*	Public?	*or*	Not-for-profit?
YES		NO		NO
Service sector?	*or*	Manufacturing?		
NO		YES		
Retail?	*or*	Leisure?	*or*	Comms services? etc.
YES		NO		NO
Small company?	*or*	Medium-sized? *or*	Large?	
NO		YES	NO	
etc.				

process might move on to see whether the market under consideration has both
B2B and B2C markets. An example might be the automobile market, serving both
the car fleet market (B2B) and the car retailer (B2C), or the finance services market with both small business and domestic lenders. Any of the segmentation
methods discussed earlier in the chapter might then come into consideration,
depending on the basis factors highlighted above.

At the end of this first stage the marketing managers should be able to identify the segments that most closely match the future direction wanted for the
organisation. For example, if the company manufactures steel tubing it will not
be interested in selling to the end consumer. Similarly it might not want to go
abroad. Both these macro segmentation methods can thus be eliminated. Likewise it might be geared up to operate in the private sector and not have the skills
and resources necessary to operate in the public sector. Figure 4.7 is a simple decision tree model that might be used.

☐ Determine the important characteristics of each segment

Once the basis for segmentation has been established, each of the possible macro
market segments identified can now be examined in more detail for important
factors that might fit the needs of the organisation. Information about the country of choice should already have been collected and analysed within a SWOT
analysis as part of the overall auditing process. This information can now be
further used as part of the segmentation process. All areas identified above and
considered to be the basis for the segments can be examined and evaluated to
determine the important characteristics of each and how it might fit the resources of the entering supplier.

It is important to understand that what might be considered important to one company might not be so important to another. For example, country infrastructure would be important to a company selling fresh produce to small companies because of the need to make regular deliveries, while not important for a company marketing computer software. Similarly, supply chain structures and relationships might already be sealed and in place, making it very difficult for any other organisation to enter the market. Below we outline some of the possible important segment characteristics linked to the model in Figure 4.7.

☐ *Country characteristics*: political support for a market economy, economic growth, interest rates, whether in or out of the euro, infrastructure, industrial laws and regulations, pressure group activity, etc.

☐ *B2B market structures*: monopolies/monopsonies, oligopolies/oligopsonies, competitive.

☐ *Market sector*: growth, maturity and decline, forecast demand levels.

☐ *Supply chain*: structures and relationships along the supply chain, horizontal relationships.

☐ *Competition*: level of competitive activity across all relative markets, market share, product portfolio, products.

☐ *Size of buying organisations*: small, medium and large, classifications and numbers.

☐ *Number of buying organisations*: buying patterns, buying needs, products and services purchased.

☐ *Business competition*: numbers, sizes, market share in the small business market.

So if size is important then customer buying levels and patterns in a particular market segment will need to be examined, as will the balance between light and heavy users of a particular product or service. In the same way the play-off between quality, service and price might be an important consideration and will need to be highlighted as another important segment characteristic.

Market analysis at this stage will be fairly broad and based on macro statistical information. Little expense will be incurred up to this stage. B2C markets would be examined more for consumer numbers and group and individual buying patterns and buying motives.

☐ Evaluate the market attractiveness of each segment

Once possible market segment contenders have been identified, the market attractiveness of each segment can then be evaluated. This consists of a more detailed examination in terms of market attractiveness and organisational strength. A variety of approaches may be used for conducting market segment attractiveness. The model used is not particularly important as long as it results in a viable marketing segmentation strategy.

Below we look at each segment and important characteristic identified above and compare with the business marketing strength and ability to compete in each particular segment. The factors chosen will be those considered important enough to have been identified and discussed in stages 1 and 2 above. The factors used may well vary from segment to segment, from situation to situation, and from organisation to organisation. A particular factor considered important enough to be selected by one company might not be considered important by another. Similarly a factor deemed to be important at one moment in time might not be considered important at another.

Factor scoring

Each factor in the market attractiveness table is given a score between 1 and 10, 1 being low and 10 being high, measuring its attractiveness to the organisation as a possible market segment. It will also be given a weighting factor between say 1 and 2 depending on its importance when compared with the other factors being assessed. So if the ability to make a profit is considered more important than the size of the market, a weighting of 1.5 might be given. This means that the 1 to 10 points allocation needs to be multiplied by 1.5. The same process will be applied to the factors shown in the marketing strength table. This approach should then be taken with every segment under consideration, so eventually each option can be compared one with the other.

Market segment attractiveness

- ☐ Government regulations
- ☐ Economic stability
- ☐ Size of the market segment
- ☐ Growth
- ☐ Profitability
- ☐ Barriers to entry
- ☐ Competitive intensity
- ☐ Channel structures
- ☐ Number of buying organisations
- ☐ Number of selling organisations
- ☐ Price levels and profitability potential.

Marketing strength (ability to compete in the segment)

- ☐ Marketing research databases
- ☐ Products and service attractiveness
- ☐ Overall portfolio fit
- ☐ Product portfolio selection on offer
- ☐ Costs
- ☐ Distribution contract opportunities

Figure 4.8
Evaluating market attractiveness and company strength using a 3×3 matrix

Company strength

		High	Medium	Low
Market attractiveness	High	Product A		
	Medium		Product B	
	Low			Product C

Product A is more attractive than Product B, which is more attractive than Product C

- ☐ Extensive, selective or concentrated distribution opportunities
- ☐ Concentrated distribution
- ☐ Management skills
- ☐ Technical skills
- ☐ Marketing and sales skills
- ☐ Promotion experiences
- ☐ Ability to control.

Plot scores on a 3 × 3 matrix

The importance of this kind of exercise is not really in the end result achieved but in the management participation process. As with the overall planning process, getting marketing managers to discuss, argue, dispute and disagree over the various factors chosen and the points and weightings allocated concentrates the mind and helps all interested parties gain insight into the most important issues. It is probably helpful for participating personnel to decamp to some type of management centre away from the hustle and the bustle of the company premises. Human resource experts argue that this sort of environment is more conducive to success in this kind of strategic management exercise. Putting the results onto a grid as in Figure 4.8 helps in gaining an overview of all the options available and, through this comparison, hopefully the choice of the right options.

> Market analysis at this stage will be more detailed, based on both macro and micro quantitative statistical analysis. Unlike B2C information gathering, very little qualitative research will be used in the B2B process.

☐ Segment selection

Segment selection in B2B markets must be treated with the utmost care because, depending on products and markets, the relationships between buyers and sellers may well entail long-term strategic commitment with a heavy resource liability making it very expensive to withdraw. However, once the evaluation process has been completed, the segments that are most attractive in terms of market opportunity and organisation match can be selected so long as they fit into the overall corporate strategic plans. More research would now be needed to gain a deeper insight into the needs and wants of the selected segments. This information would be concerned with the more detailed need for micro segmentation. From this information company and buyer profiles can be constructed.

Market segment company profile

A market profile can now be constructed for each adopted segment, giving more detail about the types of organisations in that particular segment and the product benefits wanted. The more detail known about buying patterns, benefits needed and relationships wanted, the easier will be the task of product benefit development, product positioning and customer communication and promotion. The customer profile might include the following characteristics:

- ☐ Average size of the organisations in the segment in terms of sales volume and number of employees.
- ☐ Location of all companies in the market segment.
- ☐ Range of products and services sold, range of products and services bought.
- ☐ Value in use wanted. The relative importance of benefits such as price, quality, delivery and after-sales service.
- ☐ Range of products and services bought in that are produced by the selling company.
- ☐ Buying patterns, buying group membership.
- ☐ Competitors currently used.
- ☐ Existing relationships with current suppliers.

> B2B customer profiling will be based on industry and organisation, unlike B2C customer profiling which will be based more on target segment group and individual customer.

Competition profile

A detailed competition profile will also be instigated, identifying every relevant factor that might be of interest. This will cover such things as competitor market share, product portfolio and benefits offered, costs, prices charged and profits made, as well as supply chains used and supply chain relationships. Competitor sales force activity and promotional spend will also be examined and evaluated.

Demand forecasting

Both quantitative and qualitative demand forecasting (discussed in some detail in the preceding chapter and also on the *B2B Marketing* website) will be used to identify sales and profit potential.

Detailed market, customer and competitor analysis, using both secondary and primary research, might now be used. Expenses will increase the more detailed the investigation and the more committed the supplier to identified markets.

Discussion with the buying organisation

In some cases, before segment selection takes place, the supplier might need to talk to the buying companies to ascertain whether future sales are a possibility. This will be especially necessary if there are only a few customers in a particular attractive segment. It will be a waste of time and money if a particular segment is selected and resources expended only to find that, because of some immovable barrier such as supplier/buyer contract, any new business is impossible.

☐ B2B corporate/product positioning

Identify where the company/product will be positioned in the market so as to gain competitive advantage.

The selling company must now look towards its company and product position in the market within the chosen target segments. Positioning is placing the corporate brand, product or service in the marketplace with distinctive benefit characteristics that distinguish it, in the minds of the customer, from those offered by the competitors. It is self-evident that, if the product service benefits being offered are inferior or even the same as those competitive products already in the market, there will be absolutely no reason why the customer should change. Of course if the market is new and no competitors exist, this problem will not arise, but benefit reasons will still need to be offered to prospective customers if they are to purchase. An example might be the different corporate brand positions between Mercedes and Ford.

In B2B markets all the benefits associated with corporate branding are more important than those associated with product branding. In B2C markets the opposite is more often the case.

Gaining competitive advantage

The product's position in the market should be decided through a combination of the customer benefit needs identified in the adopted market segments, benefits already being offered by the competition, and the ability of the company to add superior value to its product offerings. Ideally the benefits the company decides

Figure 4.9
Product
position map

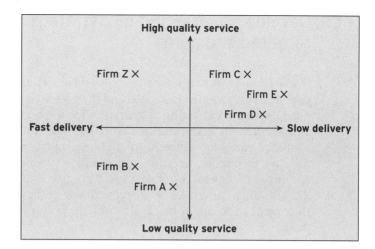

to offer will be benefits that are in some way better than those being offered by any of the competitors. Benefits to be offered could be said to fall into three generic categories:

☐ Making the product better than those of the competition.

☐ Making the product cheaper than those of the competition.

☐ Making the product different from those already on the market.

It is important that the benefits and added value which the company decides to major on must give sustainable competitive advantage and value added. This is discussed in the next chapter. Suffice here to say that the competitive advantage can be more important in some markets than in others depending on buyer demands and the level of the competition. Nevertheless in all markets the customer will mostly be comparing one company with another and one product with another. This task has been made infinitely easier with the growth and the development of the internet. In the past, strange as it may seem, buyers could not always seek out the most attractive suppliers and had to rely on trade magazines, journals, exhibitions and word of mouth. Now it is just a matter of using a search engine on the web to seek out supplier options from around the world.

From the supplier perspective, complacency must be avoided, customers continually researched and new and improved benefit offerings developed before the many sources of competition can position themselves as superior suppliers (Figure 4.9). Product positioning maps are often used as a marketing tool to try to identify 'benefit' gaps in the market that can be filled by a company and/or product in a particular market segment. We can see from the product positioning map in Figure 4.8 that there is a gap in the market for firm Z to offer a high quality service and fast delivery not offered by any other company at the moment.

> Positioning is placing the corporate brand, product or service in a targeted marketplace with distinctive benefit characteristics that distinguish it, in the mind of the customer, from the benefits offered by the competitors.

☐ Develop a marketing mix strategy for each targeted segment

Once the most promising segments have been identified, thoroughly examined, sales demand potential evaluated and then selected, the B2B marketing managers must develop a marketing mix strategy for the organisation and/or its products and services in each market. Working with the researched needs of each identified customer segment, the B2B marketing and other managers will meet together to discuss, examine and evaluate product/service, price, distribution and promotional strategies that meet the needs of each identified segment. In B2B this might also mean working with the actual buyer managers, especially if the organisation might be capable of large orders and/or forming some kind of partnership.

Power of the buyer and supplier in marketing mix strategy selection

The input that the buyer might have in the supplier marketing mix strategy will depend to a large extent on the power relationship between the two companies. One large buyer in the market will be able to dictate product benefit offering, pricing and profit levels and distribution methods to a smaller dependent supplier. Many large companies now form strategic alliances and partnerships with supply chain members and all will be involved in marketing mix strategy at every level of the process.

> In B2B segmentation a different marketing mix strategy might have to be developed for each individual company as well as each separate industrial sector.

Implementing a segmentation strategy

Developing a segmentation strategy will be part of the overall marketing planning and control process discussed in Chapter 10. This will include setting clear objectives, identifying and profiling market and customer segments and developing the right 'bundle of benefits' offering for each individual customer. It could be argued that the most difficult part of the segmentation strategy is its implementation. If products and services sold do not match customer expectations in every part of the process, then so demanding are business customers now that financial penalties can be incurred and business lost. Unlike B2C markets with millions of customers, business lost here can be in terms of a large percentage of supplier revenue. To ensure that this does not happen, it is vital that responsibilities for each task are clearly allocated, performance indicators set, and feedback, monitoring and control mechanisms are in place to cover every possible contingency (Figure 4.10).

Figure 4.10
Segmentation
process

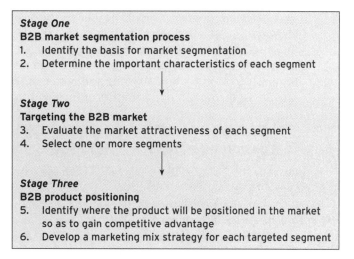

Stage One
B2B market segmentation process
1.   Identify the basis for market segmentation
2.   Determine the important characteristics of each segment

Stage Two
Targeting the B2B market
3.   Evaluate the market attractiveness of each segment
4.   Select one or more segments

Stage Three
B2B product positioning
5.   Identify where the product will be positioned in the market
     so as to gain competitive advantage
6.   Develop a marketing mix strategy for each targeted segment

Unlike B2C markets with millions of customers, business lost from even one B2B customer can be in terms of a large percentage of supplier revenue.

☐ Summary

The decision-making process was examined under the categories of the decision-making unit (DMU) or buying centre, the decision-making process (DMP) and the level of buying decision difficulty (BDD). The complexity of the DMU was compared with the relative simplicity of the DMU in consumer markets. Marketing approaches were evaluated and recommendations given. The stages in the DMP were identified and examples given of how buyers and buying groups might perform at the various stages. We then went on to look at the role of the level of difficulty in the process, examining the problems associated with a straightforward rebuy, a modified rebuy and a new purchase. Finally, the overall differences between buying in B2B and B2C were identified and highlighted.

Segmentation is a crucial element in the business-to-business market planning process. It involves classifying existing and potential buying organisations into homogeneous groups that have similar strategic needs. This enables the supplier to shape and hone the product and service benefit offerings in a way that will meet these needs as closely as possible. Marketing research is an important part of the process, investigating both existing and potential markets to describe and evaluate factors that will contribute to successful segmentation.

Many ways to segment business markets can be identified at both the macro and micro level, including by geographical location, industry sector, type of industry, organisation size, products and services sold, the buying situation and culture of the company. Group and individual differences were identified and reasons given for when and how this information should be used in the segmentation process. It is highly probable that more than one way to segment a market will be used, perhaps using geographical location, industry sector, organisational size and types of products marketed.

A systematic approach should be used by the business marketing manager when identifying and selecting particular target segments, weighing and evaluating the costs and benefits of each segment both in isolation and in contributing to the well-being of the company as whole. Systems should be put in place continuously to monitor both existing and potential segments for change that might provide segmentation opportunities or incipient market and competitive threats.

Discussion questions

1. Describe the DMU, the DMP and the BDD and evaluate the differences between consumer and business markets.

2. Discuss the overall differences between the consumer buying process and the organisational buying process. Give examples.

3. Identify and evaluate the major differences between segmenting B2B markets and B2C markets.

4. How might marketing research be most profitably used in segmenting B2B markets? What differences might there be between research carried out in B2B markets and research in B2C markets?

5. Explain why entry into a particular market segment by an industrial company might require a longer strategic commitment than a comparable decision made by a fast moving consumer goods manufacturer like Sara Lee.

6. How might the concept of B2B segmentation be applied to a charity such as Oxfam in the not-for-profit sector? What are the particular factors that would have to be considered?

7. Discuss the B2B factors that would need to be evaluated in segmenting the following markets:
   ☐ Entering another country
   ☐ Moving an existing product into a new market
   ☐ Moving from one industry to another.

8. Identify the benefits and possible dangers involved with B2B segmentation. Give live examples of companies that have (a) benefited from successful segmentation and (b) suffered from unsuccessful segmentation.

9. Identify and discuss the systematic approach that will be needed when segmenting B2B markets.

10. Identify and evaluate all the different ways in which the B2B market can be segmented.

 Visit the *B2B Marketing* website at www.booksites.net/wright for a Case Study, Questions, and an Internet Exercise for this chapter.

☐ Bibliography

Books

Capozzi, J.M. (2001) *If You Want the Rainbow, You Gotta Put Up With the Rain: 500 Secrets of Success in Business*. New York: JMC Industries.

Dunbar, I. and MacDonald, M. (1998) *Market Segmentation – How To Do It, How To Profit From It.* Basingstoke: Macmillan.

Gross, A.C. and Banting, P.M. (1993) *Business Marketing.* Boston: Houghton Mifflin.

Hill, R. and Hillier, T. (1977) *Organisational Buying Behaviour.* Basingstoke: Macmillan.

Hutt, M.D. and Speh, T.W. (1998) *Business Marketing Management: A Strategic View of Industrial and Organisational Markets.* London: Dryden Press.

Janis, I. (1982) *Groupthink: Psychological Studies of Policy Decision.* New York: Free Press.

Jong, E. (1996) *Fear of Flying.* New York: Signet.

Kaufman, M.T. (2002) *Soros: The Life and Times of a Messianic Billionaire.* New York: Knopf.

Kotler, P. (2000) *Marketing Management.* Englewood Cliffs, NJ: Prentice-Hall.

Minett, S. (2002) *B2B Marketing: A Radically Different Approach for Business-to-Business Marketers.* Harlow: Pearson Education.

Morris, M.H., Pitt, L.F. and Honeycutt Jr, E.D. (2001) *Business-to-Business Marketing: A Strategic Approach*, 3rd edn. London: Sage.

Welch, J. with Byrne, J.A. (2001) *Straight from the Gut.* New York: Warner.

Wright, R. (2001) *Marketing: Origins, Concepts, Environment.* London: Thomson.

Articles and journals

Bunn, M.D. (1993) 'Information search in industrial purchase decisions', *Journal of Business to Business Marketing*, 1 (2): 67–102.

Freytag, P.V. and Clarke, A.H. (2001) 'Business-to-business market segmentation', *Industrial Marketing Management*, 30: 473–86.

Ghingold, M. and Wilson, D. (1998) 'Buying centre research and business marketing practice: meeting the challenge of dynamic marketing', *Journal of Business and Industrial Marketing*, 13: 96–108.

Henthorpe, T.L., La Tour, M.S. and Williams, A.J. (1993) 'How organisational buyers reduce risk', *Industrial Marketing Management*, 22: 41–8.

Hutt, M. (2000) 'Simplifying web segmentation', *McKinsey Quarterly*, 2.

Marino, S. (2000) 'Consumer, business buyers aren't that different', *Industry Week*, 249 (6): 21.

Pettigrew, A. (1975) 'The industrial purchasing decision as a political process', *European Journal of Marketing*, 9 (1): 4–19.

Ridnour, A. (1995) 'Profile of a purchasing professional', *Purchasing*, 13 July: 56–72.

Thomas, R.J. (1989) 'Industrial market segmentation on buying centre purchase responsibilities', *Journal of the Academy of Marketing Science*, 17 (3): 243–52.

Trent, R.J. and Monczack, R.M. (1994) 'Effective cross-functional sourcing teams: critical success factors', *International Journal of Purchasing and Materials Management*, November: 30–1.

Visit www.booksites.net/wright for the Internet references for this chapter.

Managing business products/ services for strategic advantage in business-to-business markets

Profit in business comes from repeat customers, customers that boast about your project or service, and then bring friends with them.

Aims and objectives

By the end of this chapter the student should be able to:

1. Identify the different types of B2B products and services and recognise why organisations need to analyse and classify to gain strategic competitive advantage.

2. Outline the major differences between B2B and B2C products and services.

3. Identify and evaluate the different ways in which an organisation can brand and present its products and services.

Part 1 Organisations, products and services

☐ Introduction

It might be said that the product or service the organisation offers for sale is the very reason for its existence. Without a product or a service there is no company. As marketing puts the customer at the very heart of its business, the product and/or service must be developed and offered in conjunction with both the customer's and the market's needs. It is difficult clearly to identify the value of the B2B industry in any modern economy because many offerings eventually end up in retail products. B2B products cover the whole range of goods and services produced by business organisations over any one period (usually measured over one year) and can account for as much as one-third to one-half of a country's GNP, depending on how the output is measured.

B2B products are defined as goods and services sold by one organisation to another for its own use or sold on to other organisations for their own use. They will not include goods and services sold by the retailer to end consumers, although these products will include B2B goods and services in their make-up. B2B products and services tend to have a lower profile than B2C goods and services because they may be less glamorous than consumer products and sold in a less obvious arena. Nevertheless this should not diminish their importance both to the national economy and to the part that they play in producing consumer products. In this chapter I will attempt to outline the essential differences between B2B and B2C products and services.

Example 5.1 **Vacuum company moves to Asia**

Because of much lower manufacturing costs, as well as the prospect of being much closer both to suppliers and to new markets, Dyson, the UK company which pioneered the 'bagless' vacuum cleaner, moved the manufacturing of its cleaner to Malaysia in 2002, with the loss of many hundreds of jobs. Businesses are about products, not people, and unproductive product would lead to ultimate company collapse.

☐ B2B product definition

Taking a wide definition, a marketing definition of product might be the following: a product can be anything that satisfies customer needs or wants in exchange for some form of payment (where the payment may sometimes be some benefit other than money).

B2B product definition

A B2B product can be anything that satisfies a need or want in exchange for some form of payment offered to the organisational customer for its own use or to be sold on to another organisation for its own use.

Again taking the wider definition, a B2B product can be any of the following:

1. *A product or service or combination of both*. It can be a product, e.g. cement, paint, nuts and bolts, a road bridge; a service, e.g. financial advice, factory insurance, office cleaning, bad debt collection; or a combination of both.
2. *An idea or concept*. It can be an idea or concept, e.g. genetically engineered food, embryo cloning, plasma TV screens, management advice, public health messages.
3. *A process*. It can be a process, e.g. running a marketing information system, wages payment systems, telecommunications systems.
4. *A person or place*. It can be a person or place, e.g. a politician, company owner (Bill Gates), Manchester United, New York, Sellafield nuclear complex, royal palaces.
5. *Written, sung, played or performed*. It can be a book, song, tune, or play.
6. *A smell, a taste, a shape*. Perfume, a unique recipe (KFC?), Nescafé's diamond-shaped bottle.

7. *The whole organisation and/or its products.* The product can be seen as the whole organisation, e.g. Microsoft, BT, NTL, and/or the products marketed such as computer software, mobile phones, entertainment.

Many of these product types will have been patented and this will be discussed in some detail later in the book.

☐ Types of business goods and services

Definitions and classifications

Products are classified into groups by both academics and practitioners alike according to the function they perform for both the company and the consumer. It is important to understand this because different product types will need to be marketed in different ways, which will vary according to the type of product and the market at which it is aimed. Marketing capital equipment worth many millions of pounds will demand a different approach than supplying a basic commodity product such as nuts and bolts. Initially we can categorise B2B products into tangible products and intangible services.

Tangible products

Of course, all products have a level of service attached and increasing expectations make this an ever greater customer demand. Products, however, can be classified as tangible products where the benefits offered can predominantly be seen or touched by the customer. This aids presentation as all members of the buying centre can observe and try out the product before purchase. Features and benefits can be easily demonstrated, good design and quality can be seen and value for money compared with the competition. In some cases, organisations can be encouraged to use the product on trial over a period of time. If, for example, a company is thinking about acquiring a new forklift truck, one can be left for the staff to try out over an agreed period of time, working on the certainty of acceptance if benefit identification has been correctly undertaken.

Intangible services

Services are intangible in that they cannot be seen or touched before purchase. Services are now of such importance to B2B marketing that we discuss them in much greater detail below and on the B2B Marketing website.

☐ Major product/service categories

In general B2B goods and services can be further categorised into the following three main areas. The classifications named below are not mutually exclusive and many products will appear in more than one category. They will also be applicable in both the private and public sectors and vary from industry to industry.

1. Capital goods
2. Materials and parts
3. Supplies and running services
4. Other B2B product classifications

1. Capital goods

Capital goods are major strategic items purchased both at the initial business start-up and at other important times as the business grows and expands. They include the major long-term investment items that are the foundation of the business and the equipment that underpins the manufacturing and service processes. They will inevitably involve large amounts of money. If the company makes the wrong decision at this stage, any hope of maintaining competitive advantage will be lost. Capital goods can be divided into foundation goods and capital equipment.

Foundation goods

Foundation goods will include all those things that need to be purchased before the organisation can begin to operate. They would often be seen as fixed assets on an organisational balance sheet. They will include such permanent items as land, buildings, factories, offices, and so on. Important considerations here will include such things as location, ease of access and costs.

Capital equipment

Capital equipment, also called installations, is the large equipment needed for the production process. It will include such things as industrial robotics, power presses, large computer systems, IT, office equipment, transport, and so on.

Example 5.2   **Goods categories**

The major categories of goods imported and exported in the US in the year 2002 can be identified under the following headings:

☐ Capital goods (aircraft, semiconductors, computer accessories, machinery, engines)

☐ Vehicle parts and engines

☐ Industrial materials and supplies (metals, energy, plastics, textiles, lumber)

☐ Consumer goods (pharmaceuticals, apparel, toys, TV/VCRs, furniture, gemstones)

☐ Food, feed, and beverages.

Automobiles (7 per cent), semiconductors (5 per cent), computers and accessories (5 per cent), aircraft (5 per cent) and telecommunications equipment (3 per cent) are the largest components of US exports. Among imports, automobiles (14 per cent), crude oil (6 per cent), computer accessories (6 per cent), and apparel (4 per cent) are the most significant goods categories. (www.econedlink.org)

B2B marketing of capital goods

The purchase of capital goods will usually involve a large financial commitment on the part of the buyer and many people will inevitably be involved in the buying and selling process, often over a protracted period, making the decision-making unit complex and often difficult to penetrate. The decision on which capital equipment to purchase is usually of strategic paramount importance as it may be in use for many years. The continuous improvement in technological innovation leading to greater choices puts an ever greater stress on the organisation to purchase the right product. Get this wrong and sustainable competitive advantage could be lost for many years to come.

The B2B marketer must take this into account when working in this area and the approach needed will be discussed in more detail later in the book.

Leasing and renting

Capital goods are often leased or rented rather than purchased outright. This means that they never own outright the capital goods but pay rent over a set period of time. At the end of the time period, the contract will be renegotiated (usually at a higher rent), or in some cases offered to buy the product outright at a negotiated price. The company leasing out the property will be responsible for the upkeep of the capital goods to a level dependent on the terms and conditions of the contract. Some organisations even sell off property and then lease it back so as to gain financial capital to expand. This will have an effect on the level of importance given to the decision-making process and the number of people who might be involved. Capital goods rented over short periods will involve less strategic decision making.

Example 5.3 **Leasing**

Leases for the New Delhi, Bombay, Calcutta and Madras airports are expected to be awarded by the end of March 2003. Indian ministers called expressions of interest from the private sector to run the country's four largest airports in a bid to bring them up to international standards.

Licensing

Goods and services are often contracted out to others for use under a negotiated licence. This allows one organisation to use the products and processes owned by another under negotiated conditions. This can be in almost any industry – manufacturing, service, public or private. An example might be Coca-Cola that has licensing agreements with companies around the world to produce, bottle and distribute its coke.

Example 5.4 **Du Pont licensing technology**

DuPont has a Technology Bank where it offers others the right to use its technology systems for a price that is usually far less than the cost of creating technology
from scratch. Once accessible exclusively to DuPont researchers and businesses,
this vast inventory of DuPont technologies is now available for licensing to other
companies through the DuPont Technology Bank. DuPont has active licensing
programmes with hundreds of licensees worldwide across most industries. They
license from a portfolio that ranges from world-scale polyester design packages to
lab-scale analytical devices to micro-medical devices. They provide operational
know-how, patent licences, yield enhancing process improvements, and safer operating techniques. (www.dupont.com)

Government capital expenditure

It is worth noting here that governments around the world are some of the
biggest purchasers of capital goods (sometimes the only purchaser), either
directly or through public–private partnerships (PPP). These types of goods would
be used in such areas as road, bridge, dam and tunnel construction, hospital,
housing and office building. They would include defence equipment, for the
army, navy and airforce. Products purchased and sold for government consumption would cover such things as planes, boats, tanks, weapons, clothing and communication equipment.

Example 5.5 **Government expenditure**

Beijing's victory in the battle to host the 2008 Olympic Games is worth a lot of
money to western businesses. The Beijing and Chinese governments will spend
more than $20 billion to get the city ready for the games. Contracts on offer will be
to build an Olympic Park, five new metro lines and 125 miles of new roads, and to
clean up Beijing's polluted air and water. Bombardier and SNC-Lavalin have won a
$1.5 billion contract to dig tunnels for five new subway lines which is awaiting the
go-ahead. The tender for the main Olympic stadium is said to be worth in the region
of $250 million.

---

2. Materials and parts, or entering goods

Materials and parts are all those goods that a company will purchase for use in
producing the end product. This category can be identified by the stage in the
value adding process and consists of raw materials, manufactured materials,
accessory goods and component parts. It is as well here to make the point that
the categories discussed in this part are not all mutually exclusive and there is
bound to be some overlapping.

Marketing of B2B materials and parts

Businesses need a constant supply of raw materials, manufactured goods and component parts. In some industries, e.g. cars and domestic appliances, failure of supply could lead to product line shutdown with the subsequent loss of production and sales revenue. In extreme cases, where substitute supplies are unavailable, this could drive the company out of business. This will encourage buyer dual sourcing and/or negotiating long-term contracts with suppliers, depending on the importance of the material and goods. These and other options are discussed in some detail in the next chapter Managing business marketing channels.

The growth in just-in-time sourcing and other collaborative projects has had tremendous implications for suppliers in these types of industries, forcing them constantly to reexamine product benefit offerings, delivery methods and costs. The supply chain can also be long and include many intermediaries, starting perhaps in one part of the market (raw materials) and ending up on the opposite side of the world with component parts. Relationships can be adversarial, cooperative, contractual, and so on. Having just discussed capital equipment, it should be remembered that all the categories discussed here are often interdependent and interconnected and so manufactured materials and component parts will often end up in capital equipment, and services identified below will assist in the running of capital equipment manufacturers. This all makes for enormous challenges, as well as dangers, for marketing in supplier companies across the globe.

Raw materials

Raw materials are marketed at the first stage in the supply process and can be identified by commodity materials processed only to a level for easy distribution, e.g. iron ore into iron rods, coffee beans picked and harvested into sacks, trees cut, trimmed and delivered, chemicals refined, etc. There is little added value at this stage and raw material products are usually sold on prices that will vary according to supply and demand and perhaps seasonal variations.

Example 5.6 **Oil price fluctuations**

Oil company Royal Dutch Shell warned that the market for crude oil prices remained uncertain as it reported a 17 per cent fall in profits. The results were just above forecasts but highlighted the continuing problems in the sector, including a possible attack on Iraq which could disrupt oil supply and the constant demands of OPEC, the oil price cartel.

Manufactured materials

Manufactured materials are raw materials that are further processed for ease of use, e.g. iron into steel sheets cut to size, coffee beans into packaged ground coffee, wood cut into usable size and into paper and pulp, cotton and chemicals into textiles, rubber into moulded forms, chemicals mixed into usable form, and so on.

Component parts

Component parts are materials assembled into some type of finished product to be used in the making of the final product, e.g. steel into nuts and bolts, ground coffee into cocoa, wood into house roof supports. In the car industry, for example, materials will include rubber, steel, paint, nuts and bolts, electrical wiring and terminals, glass for the windows, tyres, seat coverings, engine parts, and so on. In the food industry they would include raw and manufactured material and component parts such as potatoes, vegetables, fruit, flour, vitamins, colouring, preservatives, packaging, and so on.

The method of marketing and type of seller/buyer contract will depend on the value, level of production and complexity of the product/service. Entering goods can be purchased customised to meet the buyer needs or offered in a standardised form and bought on a day-to-day basis or on a short, medium or long-term contract. All things being equal, as with all products and services, the more the added value, the higher would be the price the buyer will be prepared to pay.

Example 5.7   **Technology and component parts**

The task of collecting and maintaining information regarding the millions of products, parts, components and materials available in the market is a huge undertaking. Commercial B2B organisations have sprung up that now offer content solutions to the largest manufacturing organisations in the world. Reference databases today span tens of millions of items from thousands of suppliers, ranging from the items used to build manufactured products, to the goods and services used to support and maintain plants, facilities and corporate offices. Subscribing customers can have continuous access with part numbers updated daily – a truly amazing development. They can also have access to business-to-business exchanges and portals that connect many buyers with many suppliers.

---

3. B2B supplies and services, or facilitating goods

Supplies and services are all those products and services that will be used by the organisation in the day-to-day, month-by-month running of the business. The categories identified below are fairly arbitrary, not mutually exclusive, and could vary from company to company depending on the history, customer and practice and the predilections. The range of supplies and services in both the B2B and B2C markets is vast and constantly increasing. It is worth repeating that the industries and markets covered by all of these product and service areas are extremely varied and the marketing factors and priorities involved are often quite different. Imagine the differences that there will be in marketing and selling B2B on the one hand oil and gas for heating of some kind and on the other insurance and legal aid. Many of these services are now outsourced, franchised or operated under licence. Below we offer just a selection of examples.

Energy and waste management services

☐ Energy for lighting, heating and operating the equipment, e.g. gas, electricity, oil, coal, water.

☐ Waste management, including both industrial and office waste.

☐ Recycling services, ever more important as countries increase legislation and rules and regulations.

☐ Cleaning services, including industrial and office cleaning services.

Transport, distribution and storage services

In some industries this is often the most expensive service of them all, with the added pressure of knowing that the problems might only get worse. Transport, distribution and storage services (or logistics management services) are discussed in more detail in Chapter 6 but this has become one of the major areas where companies have saved large amounts of money by more effective transport management. Again, as with all other services, this can be contracted out in a number of ways.

Administrative services

Administrative products and services are needed to run the organisation on a day-to-day basis. They could include tangible products such as paper, files, pens, inks, batteries and computer disks, as well as services such as catering.

Management services

There is an ever-increasing range of services now available to help management in the running of the business and the categories grow year by year. They include the following:

☐ Management consultants, marketing and advertising agencies, research agencies, PR, franchising agencies, innovation and new product development agencies, telemarketing companies, computer and software agencies.

☐ Insurance and legal services.

☐ Recruitment, training and coaching services.

☐ Financial services, including accountancy, cost, factoring and bad debt management, payroll, asset management.

Intermediaries are often used in this market, especially where many small firms are involved.

Maintenance services

All organisations, whether manufacturing or services, will need a degree of maintenance servicing. This might be the constant maintenance of capital equipment, transport, office equipment, energy, waste and cleaning – in fact anything that needs monitoring and care and attention to make certain that costly breakdowns do not occur. This might be on an ad hoc basis or more likely under contract of some kind. Cleaning and waste management services might well be identified here.

Accessory goods

These are goods supporting the production process. Examples might be light equipment, forklift trucks, diggers, bulldozers, filing cabinets, office equipment, computer equipment, and so on. As in many others areas, there will be options to buy, hire or lease.

Marketing of services and facilitating goods

The marketing of intangible services can be noticeably different from the marketing of tangible products and this is examined in detail when we identify the nature of services. Suffice to say here that buyers now want to contract out the types of services shown above in both the private and public sectors. Contracts can be as short as a year and as long as ten years, with bonus and penalty clauses built in for good and bad performance. More and more organisations, from schools and hospitals to government departments and multinationals, now outsource the whole service area programme. It has been a lucrative picking for B2B service companies over the last 20 years with markets expected to increase.

☐ Other B2B product categories

As with the B2C market, B2B products can also be categorised into meaningful groups so that market approach opportunities can be identified.

Commodity goods

As discussed above, commodity products and services are B2B offerings that have little or no obvious added value. If this turns out to be the case then a low price tends to be the overriding benefit demanded. Products that fall into this category might be raw materials such as oil, cleaning fluids, nuts and bolts, basic vegetables, and so on. This type of product will be purchased from companies with low costs and/or access to economies of scale, anywhere around the world wherever the price might be the cheapest. This type of product can be bought either by some kind of forward contract or on a current market known as the 'spot' market.

Example 5.8 **B2B auction sites**

Internet marketplaces or B2B 'hubs' have now been set up where large companies are able to join together so as to purchase commodity products by auction, the contract going to the bidder with the lowest price. WorldWide Retail Exchange, with over 50 members including M&S, Dixons, Boots, John Lewis, Auchan, Gap, Kingfisher and Safeway, is an example of this type of buying organisation.

It can be argued that a company can add value to so-called 'commodity products' in a number of ways. These might include the following:

☐ Location

☐ Delivery time

☐ Delivery speed

☐ Pricing policies

☐ Quality guarantees, and so on.

Added value is discussed in more detail on the *B2B Marketing* website at www.booksites.net/wright.

Convenience goods

There will always be room for the buying and selling of products that are needed immediately or as a one-off order. The ability to offer service can give the smaller selling organisation a clear competitive advantage and enable it to sell to the largest of companies. Although probably a niche market, it is with this type of product that the efficient wholesaler can gain market share. In most cases, because of the relatively small orders involved, the seller will approach the buyer and must be able to show product/service professionalism if it expects a large buyer to purchase. Unlike the B2C convenience market, in most situations the B2B customer expect product delivery, often on the same day, and selling organisations have fleets of vehicles circulating on a regular basis. Added value here will be:

☐ Choice and availability of the needed parts (sometimes on a 24-hour basis)

☐ Instant response and quick delivery

☐ Product quality

☐ Back-up service.

Search-out goods

More complex goods and services will involve an organisation looking around to obtain the exact benefits wanted. Some search-out goods and services will have only a few suppliers and buyers so companies in these markets will be aware of one another. Representatives will be employed to keep in continuous contact. Other search-out goods will be bought and sold by many organisations and contacts will need to be continuously sought by both buyer and seller so that the best products can be obtained. This need is of greater importance because of the advent of increased competition from around the world. The internet and the availability of supplier and buyer websites will make the task much easier. Added value here will be:

☐ Information on products and services made readily available

☐ Personal salespeople and experts always on call

- ☐ Bundle of benefits on offer matching buyer needs
- ☐ Innovation and design
- ☐ Quality and product service value
- ☐ Comprehensive after-sales service.

Integrated solutions

It is worth identifying integrated solutions as a type of product category. In many instances B2B buyers are looking for solutions to whole problems rather than buying separate products and benefits. It can be more cost effective for a B2B organisation to buy in the whole solution to a problem from an expert supplier rather than to atomise and seek out the individual products and services needed to solve the problem themselves. This need has led to the development of a huge outsourcing industry. This is discussed in more detail in other parts of the book. Sources of added value here will include all those identified above as well as:

- ☐ The ability to offer customised integrated 'bundles' of benefits that match a problem need.
- ☐ The skills available to advise on the most relevant customised products.
- ☐ Help and advice always available for as long as is needed.

Example 5.9 **Integrated electronic invoice presentment and payment (EIPP) system**

The new version of the company's end-to-end system for B2B e-billing now lets users resolve invoice disputes online, handles billing in multiple languages and currencies, and streamlines payments via automated buyer controlled rules. It is also claimed to be the first EIPP system to deliver interim messaging, which automatically ensures that a supplier's enterprise resource planning (ERP) or customer relationship management (CRM) system acknowledges the results of an online payment dispute.

Different marketing approaches

As we outlined above, in most cases a different marketing contact strategy will be needed when selling the different products and services categorised above. This might be both entering and foundation types of goods and services. The market for the product categories identified above could be of a very low value or worth billions of pounds. It could a one-off purchase or a long-term contract over many years. It could be a standard benefit offering available 'off the shelf' or every sale could be customised to meet the exact need of each customer. As a rule of thumb, the more senior personnel involved, the more experts involved, the larger the DMU and the more personalised will be the seller–buyer contact when buying and selling products and services according to the following factors.

Different buying sectors

Marketing products and services in different B2B buying sectors (and different organisations) will often demand different marketing approaches, as will selling around the world in different countries. Products and services marketed in the private and/or public sector will inevitably demand a different approach.

Public sector

As we identified above, there are some goods and services that are only purchased by governments. These will include such things as tanks, guns, warplanes, land mines, naval frigates, submarines, etc. Other goods and services such as materials and components for roads, railways, hospitals, schools, public buildings, etc. might be bought by the public or private sector, or a combination of both, according to the political structure of the country. In the past, for political reasons, these contracts might have gone to the home country. However, because of freer markets and trading bloc regulations, contracts are increasingly offered around the world for selective tendering. There will always be more political influence on product type when compared with the private sector. Contract tender specification in this sector will usually be extremely tight with little room for manoeuvre and many disparate people and groups (the decision-making unit) may have some level of input into the final product or service requirement.

Example 5.10 **Government purchase**

The Chilean government says it will go ahead with purchasing ten F-16 fighter jets from the USA. The decision to buy the planes - made by Lockheed Martin - comes after some five years of deliberations. The deal, to modernise the country's airforce, is worth $660 million.

Private sector

B2B products in the private sector will be purchased mainly for functionality, value, service and price. In the past politicians might have tried to influence what products should be bought in the private sector, especially if large amounts of money were involved and jobs and industry survival were at stake. However, with the adoption of free market economics this type of government interference is happening less and less. Different industrial sectors demand different types of B2B products and a different marketing approach. The construction industry will want products and services for roads, bridges and buildings. Manufacturing will want capital equipment and component parts associated with a particular industry such as electrical appliances or car manufacturing. Hotels, restaurants and catering will want food associated services. Different industries will have different priorities and different ways of working, which are discussed below.

> ### Example 5.11 Public to the private sector
>
> In the UK, and increasingly around the world, once publicly owned organisations are now run by private companies. British Airways and the British Airports Authority were among the first major transport businesses to be sold off in 1987. British Telecom, buses and ferries went the same way, as did gas, water, telephones and electricity. Bridges, tunnels and railway lines are now built and paid for by the private sector and then leased back to governments in some way or another.

☐ Importance of product/service purchase to buying company

Some purchases are more important to the well-being of the organisation than others at both the strategic and tactical levels. Buying a property in the right location, having the most technical up-to-date machinery and bringing in the most effective computer service consultants could be absolutely critical for long-term success. In the same way signing a long-term contract for raw material supplies that turn out to be of the wrong kind or the wrong quality could jeopardise company profitability.

Cost of product or service

The same will apply according to the cost of the product or service demanded. The purchase of products costing small amounts of money will probably be left to the buyer in the purchasing department and, as long as desired product specifications are met, little discussion will take place. However, if the amount involved in the purchase is likely to run into millions of pounds then more senior managers will be involved.

Length and complexity of contract under negotiation

Similarly the product buying strategy to be adopted will depend on the length and complexity of the contract under negotiation. To sign up to the wrong contract could involve expensive opt-out penalties, or lead to supply shortages that could severely dent an organisation's competitive advantage. Contracts will often commit both buyer and seller to a heavy financial commitment. These interactions are discussed in more detail when we look at relationships along the supply chain. Buyer contact method will also depend on whether the products and services needed are standardised or customised.

> ### Example 5.12 Negotiate for the long term
>
> E-commerce, both B2C and B2B, is a growing industry in Japan. According to a MITI (Ministry of International Trade and Industry) study, B2C e-commerce transactions

Example 5.12 *continued*

are expected to balloon from $650 million to $31 billion between 1998 and 2003, and B2B from $86 billion to $680 billion in the same period. With such dynamic growth potential, e-commerce would appear to offer numerous new market entry opportunities for foreign companies. There is no doubt that Japan is a huge market, but it requires a long-term perspective for the full realisation of its potential. Japanese customers want localised services and new entrants into the market must be prepared to invest heavily and negotiate for the long term if they intend establishing a strong presence there.

A standardised product

If the product is standard then the strategic approach adopted by the seller will be relatively simple. This will include making available advice and literature on the current range of products, the pricing structure and the benefits available. Trade media advertising tends to be used to reach mass audiences via direct response, e.g. direct mail and telephone. The salesperson will usually act as the coordinator between the selling and the buying company. The level of contact and the advice and information needed by the seller will depend on the complexity of the product on offer, whether the buyer is a first-time buyer or not and the intensity of the competition. Standardised products across the categories identified above might be purchased on a one-off basis or in quantities on a regular contractual basis. As with all products and services there is always a trade-off between the importance of price and the importance of added-value benefits.

Commodity products used on a regular basis might include manufacturing products such as metal staples, wiring connections, nuts and bolts and oil whilst more expensive, added-value products might include medical equipment, metal pressers and transport vehicles. Standardised products are easier for the competition to replicate. Strategic factors to be considered when attempting to gain competitive advantage with standardised product offerings would be price structure, delivery, quality, reliability and support services.

A customised product

Many products will need to be customised to meet the specific need of each different customer. This is particularly so with capital goods. Although the initial customer introduction might be made through trade advertising and direct response, the predominant method of communication when dealing with customised products and services will be by personal contact. This may well involve technical as well as sales staff, particularly if the benefits needed are complex. It is also more likely that the contact will be direct between buyer and seller organisation, although there are occasions when a skilled intermediary might be used.

Example 5.13 **Customised stationery**

'Choose customised stationery for the ultimate in choice and flexibility. You can specify not only your company details and relevant logos, but also colours, type-faces, layout, number of parts and paper colour. You can even choose a ghosted image that gives your stationery a completely unique look and feel.'

- ☐ Your company details in any colour
- ☐ Your company logo in full colour
- ☐ Choose any typeface from our range
- ☐ Design, with us, the layout to suit your company needs
- ☐ Select the colours that reflect your business
- ☐ Use tints for greater clarity
- ☐ Add the logos of trade associations you belong to
- ☐ Add as many business logos as you want
- ☐ Use your logo or another image as a background
- ☐ Choose the size of paper you want
- ☐ Specify the number of parts (laser or continuous)

(Sage Accounting Stationery, www.cadsnet.co.uk)

Customer benefits demanded

Benefits demanded by B2B organisations will be different in many ways from products and services sold in the B2C market. In B2C markets, customers purchase for personal reasons and will often buy for symbolic reasons rather than functional. Though price is important, other emotional factors, characterised by the importance of product branding, come into play. Well-known brands such as Persil, Mars, Windows, etc. have a high level of importance to consumers. This is shown by the value given by the markets to brands such as these. On the other hand B2B products and services are purchased not for personal reasons but for use in the organisation. Although there might occasionally be an element of emotion attached (e.g. buying from a company because of flattery from an attractive sales representative), most B2B products are bought predominantly for logical and functional reasons. These reasons will vary from industry to industry and according to products, markets and organisational and buyer preferences.

Criteria for the importance of B2B products and services

- ☐ Whether of small or large importance to the well-being of the organisation.
- ☐ Small amounts or worth many millions of pounds.
- ☐ A one-off purchase or a contract over many years.
- ☐ A standard or customised offering.
- ☐ Always a trade-off between price and added value.

- ☐ Marketed direct or through a wholesaler, distributor or agent.
- ☐ Trade advertising, followed by direct response and personal selling used for standardised products.
- ☐ Personal selling, followed by direct response and exhibitions for customised products.
- ☐ Government and public sector products.

Strategic differences between goods and services

Products are often categorised as either 'tangible' products or 'intangible' services. It should be noted, however, that increasingly most tangible products have some form of service attached. This level of service might just concern the initial transaction and be limited to delivery times or, at the other extreme, it might involve some type of continuous product top-up system. Whatever the level of service offered, high quality standards are set, controlled and maintained. This is especially important with the advent of buyer quality programmes such as 'continuous replenishment' or 'just in time', as well as the ever-increasing demand for better levels of service brought about by increased competition from around the world.

Other benefit offerings will be almost entirely to do with services offered. There is no doubt that services are different in character from tangible products. These differences must be identified so that the correct marketing approach can be taken. The growth of outsourcing by more and more B2B organisations has also put the need for levels of service quality high on the agenda. It seems that there is no service activity across the whole supply chain that cannot now be undertaken by an outsourcing organisation.

As with all areas of business when marketing B2B products and services the whole relationship between seller and buyer must be strategically thought through, planned and managed in a professional and customer-satisfying manner by the selling organisation. Support must come from the very top and filtered down and discussed throughout the whole organisation. Coaching and training should be given so that nobody is in any doubt about the importance of the relationship between the total customer needs and wants, and the product/service benefits offered.

Services grow in importance

In most developed economies, services have grown as a percentage of gross national product (GNP) when compared with manufacturing and can account for anything from 65 per cent to 80 per cent, with more growth expected. All demand particular B2B marketing skills and many organisations develop specialisms to help in gaining market superiority. Service industries cover every sector, public, private and not-for-profit, and take in the following:

- ☐ Retail services
- ☐ Communications services
- ☐ Information services

- ☐ Consultancy services
- ☐ Outsourcing services
- ☐ Entertainment services
- ☐ Financial services
- ☐ Medical services
- ☐ Energy services
- ☐ Education services
- ☐ Cleaning services
- ☐ Waste management services
- ☐ Catering and food services.

Example 5.14 **Manufacturing sector continues to decline**

According to the UK labour force survey, while there has been growth in sectors such as business services, public administration and retail, this has not been enough to outweigh the decline in manufacturing and mining. A key monthly report by the Chartered Institute of Purchasing and Supply (CIPS) is indicating that Britain's manufacturers are still deep in recession, output having fallen three months in a row, while services still remain relatively strong. Manufacturing accounts for about 20 per cent of Britain's economy, with about 4 million people employed, the other 80 per cent coming almost exclusively from the service sector.

Example 5.15 **Service grows and manufacturing sector falls**

The gap between the UK's service and manufacturing sectors has widened, throwing the spotlight once again on Britain's two-speed economy. The Chartered Institute of Purchasing and Supply's (www.cips.org) closely watched monthly services index climbed to 56.7 in May from 54.5 in April, outstripping the 55.2 score forecast by analysts. A score above 50 on the CIPS index denotes expansion, while a reading below 50 signals a contraction. The figures confirmed that the services sector is once again moving in the opposite direction to the manufacturing sector, which fell to 52.9 in May from 53.2 in April.

 A more detailed discussion of the differences between B2B goods and services can be found on the *B2B Marketing* website at www.booksites.net/wright.

A balanced product portfolio

The number of products in the portfolio of B2B organisations tends to be less than in B2C organisations as business demand polarises around functional specialised products rather than brands and brand extensions. Procter & Gamble offer many different cleaning products and brands for its different consumer segment needs based on emotional as well as functional needs. On the other hand the need for industrial cleaning products will be based almost solely on effectiveness at solving a practical problem and so the range of products wanted will be less. It is still essential, however, that the range of products at all stages in the portfolio matches the needs of the target segments both at present and into the foreseeable future. What constitutes a balanced product/service portfolio will vary from industry to industry, but the need to have new products onstream and coming through the system as older products weary and decline along the product life cycle should be self-evident.

 A more detailed description of the Boston Consultancy Group portfolio matrix applied to B2B marketing, as well as a complete section on adding value to products and new product development, can be found on the *B2B Marketing* website at www.booksites.net/wright.

☐ Market research

As with all types of marketing success will ultimately depend on having the right products and services that can offer relevant benefits that clearly satisfy identified target market segments. Continuous research into both local and international markets around the world is crucial to the process. Markets grow, reach maturity and decline, business customer needs and wants change as their markets change and the supplier must anticipate and be aware of these changing demands almost before they are happening. Information gathering on product development and customer needs from around the world should be fed into the marketing information system so that changing benefit needs can be identified and products and services developed to meet these needs. Research was discussed in detail in chapter three.

Quality signals

It must be understood that when buying services, because of the difficulties identified above, a purchaser will look for signs of quality, reliability and value that will give some indication about the selling organisation. If the company has been used previously these signs will apparent in such areas as: ease of contact, delivery times, service outputs and so on. The most reliable quality signal is, of course, word of mouth. With first time purchases judgements about the seller will be more problematic and will be based on a whole range of value indicators used as a surrogate way of selecting acceptable companies to deal with.

The whole process

From the first initial contact with the client, answering the telephone, dealing with enquires, sending out brochures, the sales presentation, through to benefit service offering, the follow-up and subsequent after sales service, a quality and focussed response must be seen to be the norm. Company literature should be relevant, informative and of a high standard, all contact staff should be vetted for suitability before recruitment and trained to the highest possible level, benefit programmes should be examined and upgraded in line with customer needs. A plethora of customer relationship management (CRM) software programmes are now available to build in systems that will oversee, monitor and control and aid the whole process.

Build in systems

Quality systems should be discussed, tested and then built in for almost every customer serving system so that all within the organisation (and along the supply chain) are aware of standards to be met. The level of detail that might be needed for each system will vary from service contract to service contract.

Benchmarking

The whole B2B service process should be benchmarked to make certain that the level of service will never fall below a determined level. Monitoring and control mechanism should be put in place to make certain that the same standard of customer service is offered every time whatever the company department and where ever it might be in the world. The customer should be continually consulted as to the level of satisfaction and adjustment made whenever performance falls below acceptable levels.

Example 5.16 **Balanced Scorecard**

The Balanced Scorecard concept, developed by Professor Robert Kaplan of the Harvard Business School and David Norton, has been embraced by a rapidly growing number of large corporations as a vehicle to help effectively manage corporate performance and strategy. By studying other organisations' approach to performance measurement and strategy deployment through the use of Balanced Scorecards, companies can better understand how to design, refine and effectively use a diverse Scorecard of Performance Measures to help them meet their strategic business objectives.

Expected performance indicators

Many buying organisations now demand adherence to tightly agreed performance indicators across all bought-in services. Bonuses might be paid for better than expected performance and money deducted for worse than expected performance. Ultimately contracts will be lost if performances do not meet the agreed set criteria. So it can be very expensive for the selling organisation if the services offered do not live up to expectations. This can be disastrous in B2B markets where customer buying contact points are few and the amount of revenue large.

Customer management relationship programmes

Many companies now realise the strategic importance attached to marketing customer services and develop Customer Relationship Management Programmes (CRMP) along the whole of the supply chain.

Planning, monitoring and feedback

As with all marketing programmes it is crucial that objectives are set and monitoring, feedback and control mechanisms are implemented. There is no point in having detailed customer systems in place along the whole process if there are insufficient monitoring and control mechanisms in place to oversee performance. Most customer care systems break down, not because of insufficient planning, but because nobody seems to bother about systematically checking to see that what should be happening happens.

Product/Service Checklist

- ☐ Strategically planned and instigated
- ☐ Top management support
- ☐ Balanced product/service portfolio
- ☐ Continuous research
- ☐ Building and innovative culture
- ☐ Quality signals awareness
- ☐ The whole process considered
- ☐ Build in quality systems
- ☐ Benchmark against the best
- ☐ Performance indicators set and adhered to
- ☐ Customer management programmes across the whole supple chain
- ☐ Monitoring, feedback and control mechanisms implemented

The demands in Marketing B2B services

Because of the factors identified above the following factors might be considered crucial in marketing and selling B2B services

Personal Selling

The more intricate and complex the product or service the more the need to have personal contact between buyer and seller. This will enable trusting relationships to be formed and description and explanation to take place. This tends to be the most used form of supplier to buyer contact and we discuss this in detail in chapter eight when promotions and sales management are shown.

Direct marketing

This is often used to make contact with buyers because, as there are less buyers in the B2B market than in B2C, named and sometimes known buyers can be clearly targeted. Frequently used with personal selling. A telephone call, a letter or email is sent asking to make an appointment or, if the relationship is sympathetic needs discuss by one of these types of direct response methods.

Other methods of communication contact and these are also discussed in detail in chapter 8.

Part 2 Adding value to the products

B2B organisations buy products and services because they hope that the benefits gained from the transaction will satisfy some organisational need, that is to solve a business problem, either in the present or some time into the future. Another way to look at the product or service is as a 'bundle of needs' put together by the producer in the hope that it will be able to satisfy this need. As the customer becomes more professional in they way the business operates more intricate and complex solutions are demanded. To maintain competitive advantage the seller must continually look toward offering ever more sophisticated benefits sometimes on a long-term contractual basis.

Therefore marketing and selling in products and services in the modern, global market can be seen as a process of continually adding value in response to the ever-changing demands of the targeted organisation. This task must be undertaken in a world where competition is increasing and every company looks to gain market share, by adding value in some way or another, at the expense of all others.

There are many different ways that a B2B organisation can add customer value to it products and services both before and after purchase. It is through this added value process that a company can gain competitive advantage and the more progressive company will always be looking for more innovative and creative ways.

☐ Basic Benefits demanded in B2C and B2B markets

In B2C markets added value can be categorised under two general headings corresponding to the types of benefits demanded by the customer. These two areas can be identified as the functional and the symbolic. Most of us would argue that the main reason we want to purchase a product is because of its functional properties. This is the overt purpose of the product and the reason for purchase seems self-evident. So we buy a car to get from A to B, a watch to tell the time and clothes to keep us warm. However in-depth research undertaken over the decades has shown that the main reason for the purchase of many products is symbolic. By symbolic we mean that the purchase is a representation of some other deeper and less transparent, emotional or instinctive need. So we buy the car to make us attractive to the opposite sex, a gold watch to display our wealth and clothes to show how street wise we might be.

In B2B markets this is not usually the case and, because the product or service is not for personal use but for use by the organisation, purchase tends to be mainly for functional and practical reasons. Emotions will come into the buying process but not to the same degree as in B2C. An organisational buyer will purchase from a company because of a personal likeness for the sales representative or because they feel flattered by individual attention. They might purchase from a large, well-known organisation because they feel safe with the purchase. In extreme cases they might purchase because of some kind of personal gain such as money or gifts. As companies and the competition become more professional and effective, however, buyers who purchase products or services for emotional reasons that turn out to be sub-optimal will be exposed as inefficient as the company loses productive advantage.

> In B2B markets products and services are purchased for functional and practical reasons rather than symbolic and emotional

☐ The value added process

The idea behind the concept of value added is that there is a basic core to all products and services around which benefits are then added in response to buyer demand. The process can be examined under the following simple headings

1. the core product
2. primary added value
3. supplementary added value

1. The core product

All products and services have some basic form or core and this is the starting point for the value-added process. This core might also identified under the classification of commodity products earlier in the chapter. Many of these products are still traded in the city on what is known as 'commodities markets'. For our purpose we want to define the B2B core product or service as the product offered in a basic form (without getting into intricate detail about how 'basic' is a basic form) with the minimum level of benefits. In the context discussed here core products will also include core services such as waste disposal, cleaning, catering, education, communications and so on.

2. Primary added value

In response to customer demand and to the benefits offered by the competition trying to gain market share organisations must add more benefits to the product or services in response to customer demands.

Primary added value we want to define as the benefits that are added to the product or service *before* purchase whilst supplementary added value we want to define as the benefits that are added to the product or service *after* purchase. Primary B2B added value benefits would include the following;

- ☐ Creativity, innovation and design
- ☐ New product/service development
- ☐ Choice of product, customised, standardised or integrated product
- ☐ Features and benefits
- ☐ Help, advice and skill level
- ☐ Guaranteed quality
- ☐ Price, payment terms, leasing and value for money
- ☐ Location and point of purchase
- ☐ Promotions, communications and corporate reputation
- ☐ Branding
- ☐ Packaging

These benefits have been listed in an arbitrary order of priority but whether price is more important than quality or choice more important than an innovative approach will depend on the company, the industry, the customer and the products marketed.

Example 5.17 **Added value in many different ways**

Bitrex is the brand name of the most bitter substance yet discovered. It is inert and odourless, but a few parts per million are enough to make products unpalatable. Evolution has given human beings a strong aversion to the bitterness that often marks out harmful plant or animal material. Studies have shown that children are particularly sensitive to these bitter tastes. By adding minute quantities of Bitrex to certain products we can help ensure that no-one, especially children, ingests potentially harmful substances. And by adding the logo to the packaging, customers will see manufacturer care about the products they sell and the people who use them. That's why Bitrex is such a powerful deterrent to accidental swallowing. First used in denaturing alcohol – making it legally unfit for consumption – it is now added to a wide range of household cleaners, pesticides, and DIY and automotive products. (Bitrex.com)

---

3. Supplementary added value

Selling organisations realise that in most cases responsibility will not end with the initial purchase. Customers now want and expect so much more after the purchase. This level of after purchase involvement will, of course, vary tremendously according to the product and service sold and the type of relationship that had been entered in to. Supplementary added value (value added after purchase) benefits would include the following:

Figure 5.1
The B2B Value
added process

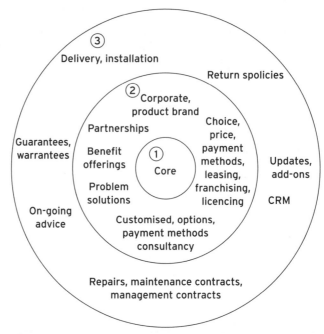

① Core product – little or no added value

② Primary product – added value before delivery

③ Supplementary product – added value after delivery

☐ Strategic relationship commitment

☐ Customer relationship policies

☐ Help, advice, and skill level

☐ Access to information

☐ Management and consultancy services

☐ Service contracts, quality and performance levels

☐ Guarantees and warranties

☐ Delivery and installations

☐ Returns policies

☐ Access to add-on products and services

☐ Security

Prioritising added value

We have looked at the many ways that the organisation can add value to its products and services in response to customer and market ever changing demands and most of the factors outlined above are examined in more detail throughout the book. The B2B marketing manager can build competitive advantage for the company by adding any number of these factors identified under the concept of primary and supplementary added value to the core product or service. Which of these added factors should be prioritised in developing a competitive product portfolio will depend on industry and market conditions and organisational core competencies and strengths. It might be product quality for some companies and after sales service in others. Inherent in the concept of good marketing is the realisation that the correct areas must be identified and the relevant benefits offered.

☐ Unique Selling Proposition (USP)

The idea of a Unique Selling Proposition (USP) was first introduced by Rosser Reves in the USA. Reves argued that all organisations, if they wanted to be successful, should offer the customer some form of unique benefit not offered by the competition. It should be based on an organisational core strength, it should be sustainable over a strategic period, and it should give a positive competitive advantage. A USP can be based on any of the primary and supplementary added value factors discussed above. A USP is particularly important when introducing a new product to the market, especially if there is heavy competition. If the new product or service has nothing to differentiate itself from existing products there is no reason why the customer should switch.

Example 5.18   **Unique Selling Proposition and you**

There is a marketing term that should be thought about when looking for a job and putting together the initial job application form, it's called the Unique Selling Proposition, or USP. When companies are trying to determine how to market a product, they focus on the Unique Selling Proposition, the one thing that makes one product different than any other. It's the one reason they think customers will buy the product even though it may seem no different from many others just like it. It may be that the product has a lower price or more convenient packaging, or it may taste or smell better, or last longer. When preparing to write a job application letter, you may find it helpful to think about your Unique Selling Proposition. What is the one thing that makes you unique? What makes you better than other candidates applying for a similar position with this company? What can you offer that no other applicant can? What is the one reason the employer should want to hire you above all other candidates? If you can determine your Unique Selling Proposition and build it into a dynamic paragraph, you will have a real advantage in creating a dynamic cover letter.

Product/service strategy and the USP

Probably the term USP is probably a bit of a misnomer. The benefit (or benefits) offered would probably not be unique in that no company would have marketed a product or service offering a particular benefit before. It will be unique in the sense that no other company has marketed a product or service benefit in a different way or as well in the past. So the USP might be that the quality is of a guaranteed level not offered in the past, or the service is more strategically comprehensive than promoted by any other company or it might be that delivery is quicker and so on.

In can be argued that there are three simple strategic approaches in developing a B2B product USP and the organisation should chose one or more if they are to successfully market their products. The three approaches are outlined below.

1. Make the product/service cheaper
2. Make the product/service better
3. Make the product/service different

If the organisation cannot adopt one of the above approaches to its product offering there might be little reason why a company would want to purchase.

1. Make the product cheaper

If an organisation decides to use price (with no frills) as the product USP in a highly competitive market it would have to be a price lower than the competition. It could only achieve this in two ways, either working on a lower profit margin or producing the product more cheaply. It could only adopt the former method in the short term because the competition could always respond and a price war may well develop. To maintain price leadership in the long term the organisation would have lower costs than the competition in the long term (in the short term it could achieve this by greater productivity but companies soon catch up). This would probably mean it had achieved market leadership, because only by selling more products than anyone else can greater economies of scale be achieved and a lower price offered.

A smaller company could use low price as its product strategy if it has a monopoly, is in a niche market or it has a contract to manufacture own label products for a larger company. The larger company would guarantee a certain level of orders and carry all of the marketing costs.

2. Make the product/service better

Many companies gain competitive advantage by making the product/service better than the competition in some significant way. This might be offering a better content, higher quality, superior service or in any of the other ways discussed above. This is probably the most successful way that the smaller B2B seller can achieve market share against the might of the larger organisation.

3. Make the product/service different

Other B2B organisations look for a market advantage by adopting a USP that offers the customer something different to that being offered by the competition. The way that a company may chose to differentiate its products and services may take many forms. It might be through have a unique innovative (preferably patented) product or service not marketed by anyone else. Or it could be by having a leasing plan not seen before in a particular industry. Service could be offered on a twenty-four hour basis, delivery guaranteed within a certain time or product taken back if satisfaction not achieved. What is important is that the benefit solutions offered match the continuously researched needs of each target segment served.

Product service strategies in B2C

Because end consumers have different needs than B2B customer the bundle of benefits wanted in B2C tend to of a different order. Such things as quality, after sales service and price, are, of course important, but we find that emotional factors such as advertising, branding and merchandising play a much more important part and this is discussed later in the chapter when we look at branding.

☐ New Product Development in B2B marketing

Creativity is allowing yourself to make mistakes. Art is knowing which ones to keep.

(Scott Adams)

The world's knowledge base doubles every few years with a consequent increase in buyer sophistication and demands .New product development is crucial in B2B product development if the organisation is to maintain competitive advantage in a market characterised by increasing global competition and it is one of the most important ways that a company can add value and so gain competitive advantage.

In B2C markets customers want new and better products that are designed well, work better, look better and offer more value for money. End consumers become easily bored and will look for evermore choice in the things that they purchase, they will seek out products that make them feel better, that satisfy an emotional need, as well as products that function more effectively.

On the other hand the B2B buyer will want new innovative products and services that will enable his or her company to produce and market better products and services that offer their customers better benefits and solutions. This will in turn enable their customers to sell better products and services all along the supply chain finally to the end consumer. There are potentially many more opportunities for B2B organisations to become involved in exciting new developments in IT, Nanotechnology, biotechnology and so on at every stage of the process. In B2C they will manufacture and sell the end product for consumer consumption but the B2B supplier can work at many levels in research and development, in raw materials, component parts, software development, testing and experimentation working with governments and multinationals around the world.

Definition of a new product or service

It is important to spell out what we mean by a new product or service in the B2B market as this will affect the way that it will eventually need to be marketed.

> A new product or service can be, a change or replacement to an existing benefit offering, an existing market concept but new to the organisation, or a totally new concept.

The newer the product or service to both the selling and the buying organisation the more difficult and complex might be the marketing task. Difficulties involved with different types of decision making were examined in some detail in the chapter on organisational buying behaviour.

New product development for internal and external customers

New product development in B2B marketing covers both internal and external customers and factors.

Internal customers

Internal customers will involve all organisational employees involved in the customer value-adding process. Purchasing and managing raw resources, production techniques, marketing and delivery etc. all stages offer new product/service opportunities. An employee becomes the customer of the previous employee as the products and services move through the system. If a company's internal value chain is to compete with the best in the business it must be as good, if not better, than the most successful competitor in the market. So systems, structures, management ways of working, staff training all offer new product opportunities for new and more efficient ways of working with one another. It will embrace such concepts as internal marketing, total quality management, activity based costing, employee empowerment and so on.

Example 5.19 **Best practices**

Today's high-performance companies are developing their knowledge management skills by creating a culture of sharing across departments and business units. They're motivated by the belief that some of the best ideas may be right in their own backyard. Below are some examples of the internal steps to successfully implement a knowledge management/internal best practices program organisations have taken.

☐ Connect best practices to strategy fulfilment.

☐ Identify best practices.

☐ Develop best practices recognition systems

☐ Communicate best practices.

☐ Create best practices knowledge sharing systems.

☐ Nurture best practices on an ongoing basis.

External customers

Ideas shape the course of history.

(John Maynard Keynes)

B2B External customer will always be searching out better ways of running their business, looking to buy products and services that, in turn enable them to sell more attractive products and services all the way along the supply chain to the end consumer. Suppliers must be continuously working and researching to upgrade products and services, to innovate and bring in the latest technology, to offer advice on the very latest methods, in line with customer wants, if they are not to be overcome by a more progressive competitor.

Developing a new product development culture

The world is made up of 1 percent of the population who think, 9 per cent who think they think and 90 percent who wouldn't be caught dead thinking.

(Anon)

Depending on the industry many organisations attempt to develop a new product development culture both in an informal and formal way. Informally staff members are encouraged to discuss new ideas with one another, with suppliers and with customers. Formal systems, with support from the very top, are also set up in some companies. These will include the following.

☐ Company management and worker groups and teams meeting on a regular basis to discuss current practice and suggest how improvements might be made

☐ Creating communication channels through which to funnel new ideas

☐ Suggestion schemes rewarded by a payment of some kind

☐ New product 'shops' set up where ideas can be taken for discussion and appraisal.

☐ Senior managers, new product 'champions', are assigned to new ideas to safeguard progress through the company

☐ Setting up a research and development department

☐ Regular customer testing research programmes

Generating new ideas

All companies, no matter the size, can constantly look for B2B new product/ service idea opportunities for both within and outside of the organisation that might give them a competitive advantage in the market place. The might include using some of the following methods;

Idea generation methods

Organisations such as Sony or 3ms where NPD is crucial will try to simulate new ways of thinking by taking relevant employees away from the conventional place of work to a new setting (a hotel in the country) for a period of time, perhaps a weekend, for a session of idea generation. Many idea generation methods exist and outside consultants will often be used to undertake the process. The belief behind such techniques is that right-side brain creative ways of thinking (the holistic, creative side) need stimulating overriding the natural tendency for most manager to think with the left-hand side of the brain (lateral, numerical and logical). Many hundreds of methods exist and here are just a few.

- ☐ *Brainstorming* – uncritically producing as many ideas (outrageous accepted) as possible for discussion.
- ☐ *Assumption squashing* – taking basic assumptions and arguing ferociously against
- ☐ *DOIT* – The pattern of the DO IT process emphasises the need to Define problems, Open yourself to many possible solutions, Identify the best solution and then Transform it into action effectively.
- ☐ *Innovative Problem Solving* – methods that combine rigorous problem definition, pattern-breaking generation of ideas, and action planning that could result in new, unique, and unexpected solutions.

Constantly comparing and benchmarking products and services with the competition

This will include such a things as the design i.e. functionality, construction, time-to-market and looks as well as the 'fit' between benefit solutions wanted and the ability of the product or service to produce these benefits. Reverse engineering involves obtaining the competitor's products, then breaking them down piece-by-piece to see how they are constructed and then attempting to build better, different of cheaper. At a minimum, companies should compare the competitive strengths of their products against those of their direct and indirect competitors' products at least once a year. Previous product innovations can also be revisited so that knowledge can be captured for re-use.

Constantly talking to the customer and end user

Talking and listening constantly to the needs and wants of the customer, discussing problems, identifying solutions, analysing any complaints will pay dividends in identifying product improvement needs and new product ideas. Somebody should also be liasing with the end users of the product, especially if they have little contact with those that actually buy the product. It is using the product that problems will arise that could well be the source of new ideas. There are many examples of employees complaining about supplier product limitations that few bother to listen to.

Staying close to the sales force

The sales force should be seen as the eyes and the ears of the organisation. They are the people continuously out in the marketplace talking to customers, competitors and industry participants and are often the closest to the latest technology, materials, ingredients, international advances, and competitive improvements.

Formal and informal marketing research

Larger companies will periodically conduct usage and attitude studies, diary panel studies, product perception mapping studies, and other product development monitoring devices. They may also employ research companies to scan patents and new product technology publication sources and talk with consultants, research firms, and industry/trade experts to keep tabs on target customer needs and wants. Smaller companies can still use research companies relatively cheaply or undertake informal research by incessantly asking customers, salespeople, suppliers, employees etc. questions about needs and wants.

Market research during the NPD process

Concept testing

Market research will probably need to be used at other time in the NPD process by suppliers to inexpensively test out new product concepts before committing time and money on ideas that might never be adopted (it's a pity that many business didn't adopt this part of the process instead of throwing huge amounts of money at website construction based on wishful ideas that had never been tested in this way). Methods used will include talking to individual buyers, buyer groups or buyer associations so as to gauge reactions to the ideas behind the new concept B2B products. Asking for example whether they like the idea and would be prepared to use the product if it came onto the market. It is at this stage that partners might also be approached to ascertain their reactions to the concept.

Business market analysis

More formal research will probably be used once a new product idea concept seems to have 'legs', to first to help outline a simple business/market feasibility study, where something like 80 per cent of the costs might be determined. This will include such things as design and production costs, employee costs, promotion and sales costs, distribution costs, service costs (if applicable) as well as the new product fit with products in the existing portfolio. Those involved in these kinds of projects might include technical, electrical and mechanical engineers, stylist and designers, those in procurement, manufacturing, marketing, sales, finance, maintenance as well as suppliers, outsourcers and other partners. All might need to be consulted. It will also involve talking to buyers and others backward and forward along the supply chain to try and estimate overall industry demand and individual company future sales potential.

Market testing

Depending on the product the market might be approached once a prototype had been built to test out the product out in the field. In the case of a consumer product this would be quite an extensive exercise covering a large demographic area. In B2B the process would be much more contained with perhaps just a few buyer organisations involved. At this stage the decision to go with the product would probably already have been made and the market testing be used to discover any customer benefits unexpectedly not catered for and/or faults not picked up by supplier experts. There has to be a considerable amount of trust between buyer and supplier at all of these stages discussed here because if competitors are warned then spoiling tactics might well be used. We discuss market research in much more detail in chapter four on the importance of information gathering.

Research and development (R&D)

Many of the larger companies will have well-funded research and development departments where scientists and researchers are paid to undertake either focussed direct research into specifically defined areas or 'blue-sky' research where they are allowed time to follow new product development research pathways where ever their inclination might take them. Other organisations might utilise the same service from Universities and management schools, forming partnerships with others to share the costs or working without specialist outside product innovation research agencies. According to recent research by the DTI's 'Futures and innovation's group' there is a evidence of a direct link between R&D investment, sales growth and stock market value. They go on to say that cost cutting exercises only result in short term gains and the answer to long-term success is to manage intellectual and application global assets more effectively and to be constantly producing highly desirable category killer products and services.

Collaborative working on innovation

Innovation and design has for many decades often been a collaborative project with organisations working together (for examples universities and innovation agencies) working with industry to bring new products to market because of the costs and skills involved. The growth in competition and customer demands coupled with technological developments and the growth in IT capabilities is fuelling these partnerships. Collaborative Product Innovation (CP) inter and intra-enterprise cross-functional teams are now working together using the power of the Internet to improve project team working and information sharing across the distributed supplier network ensuring that products meet or exceed market requirements as well as costs and time-to-market imperatives. Such a vast amount of expertise in a wide variety of areas is now needed to bring innovative products to market, particularly in heavily segmented and highly technical sectors such as the car industry, that more and more R&D and innovation and design projects are now outsourced to specialist companies (reputably as much as 70 per cent with one car manufacturer).

Why there is a need to develop new products and services

A B2B organisation might have a NPD programme for the following reasons:

☐ Maintain market position and reputation as an innovating organisation
☐ Defend market share
☐ Be in the forefront in the development of new markets gaining market share before others
☐ Take advantage of new technology
☐ Optimise resources, including production and supply chain management so as to gain competitive advantages

☐ To offer greater customer value and satisfaction

☐ To attract the best possible staff and expertise

 More can be seen on the size and scope of new product development on the B2B marketing website at www.booksites.net/wright

Part 3 Branding

The concept of the brand is now firmly entrenched in business and marketing philosophy. Most of the largest and most profitable companies in the world have achieved their success through effective marketing and promotion of a brand name. Business Superbrands Ltd identified 50 of the world's top B2B corporate brands and in a poll conducted with NOP in 2002 found that in general brands were considered more dynamic and accessible than a host of national organisations, ranging from the police service to the National Health Service. Such is its power that for many national and global companies the brand name and all the values associated with it come to be worth more than all the other tangible and intangible assets combined. In 2001 the Microsoft brand was said to be worth $65 billion. New technologies, particularly the internet, now enable companies to build brands faster than ever before by providing customers with highly customised information and services (whether these 'upstart' brands will be endurable only time will tell).

☐ What is a brand?

A brand is a combination of several elements including the actual product/ service, a name, a symbol or logo of some kind, particular colours, and specific shapes and sizes. It is also a set of attributes, associations, expectations, perceptions and promises about some benefit or other coming together to form an overall image of the company or brand in the mind of the beholder.

Example 5.20 **What is your brand?**

If you need to extend market share, build barriers to competition, motivate your workforce, ensure greater performance and profit, or attract and recruit top talent, you must first develop your brand and align it with business strategy. Before advertising, before marketing, before communications, and before company or product launches, your brand is a catalyst to your business goals and the connective tissue for your organisation. Your brand is ultimately your reputation. It begins with the promise you make and therefore the promise you must keep. Much more than a visual face or public identity, the brand is about human nature and success behaviour. It lives in every member of an organisation, advancing your common vision and mission. The brand is a performance measured and recorded in every encounter with your constituents, including customers, investors, employees, business partners and media.

> A brand is a combination of functional and emotional characteristics that define a certain image or personality about a company and/or its products in the mind of the customer. The strength or otherwise of this image will determine the likelihood to purchase.

Some brand terms

- □ *Brand.* The name, term, sign, symbol or design, e.g. for Coca-Cola, the name, the bottle shape and the white slash.

- □ *Corporate brand.* The company itself can be seen as a brand (very important in B2B). BT is the brand name and the company will spend millions redesigning and keeping it up to date. It also has the symbol of the prancing trumpet player, instantly recognisable and symbolically representing the organisation. BP has recently spent a fortune modernising the BP brand and altering the logo to something that looks like a yellow and green sunflower, reinforcing its commitment to the environment.

- □ *Brand name.* The name can be spoken.

- □ *Brand mark.* The brand can be seen.

- □ *Trade mark.* The trade mark gives legal protection (seen as TM beside the ownership mark). Under an addition to the UK Trade Mark Act 1994, businesses can now register three-dimensional shapes as well as sounds and smells for protection under the law, as well as brand names and marks.

- □ *Copyright.* The right, given to the creator, for a fixed number of years, to reproduce books or documents etc., or to perform music or plays etc., and to authorize (or refuse) permission for others to do the same.

- □ *Brand equity.* This is the value of the brand in terms of both customer loyalty and estimated money worth. Consultant companies such as InterBrand.com will try to value the brand by methods such as comparing the sales of the brand to the nearest generic substitute; for example, the operating margin for Tetra Pak might be 22 per cent and that of the nearest substitute 10 per cent. Multiply the difference in the margins (12 per cent) by the level of the sales involved and you begin to have some idea of the value of the brand.

- □ *Brand awareness.* This is the percentage of customers who express awareness of a brand as revealed by market research.

- □ *Brand stripping.* This concerns the acquisition of a company for its brands, e.g. Ford bought Jaguar for the brand name and paid over three times the market share value.

Example 5.21 **Brand piracy**

Chinese authorities are moving to convince the owners of one of the world's best-known brand names, the International Olympic Committee, that the country doesn't deserve the reputation it has as a world leader in intellectual and copyright infringements and the sale of illegal branded pirated goods. The Olympic Games is to be held in Beijing in 2008 and the committee and potential sponsors are worried about the blatant rip-off by businesses using the Olympic logo and other company products on unlicensed goods. Despite the purported crackdown in the area, many

Example 5.21 continued

foreign businesses are still not convinced about the Chinese authorities' commitment. Many foreign firms are threatening to pull out of China because the administrative and criminal sanctions are either too weak or too hard to enforce.

☐ Corporate and product branding strategies

The brand and all that it represents may be attached to the company and/or its products and services. These can be identified under the following strategic approaches:

1. Corporate branding
2. Corporate family branding
3. Product and service branding
4. Own or private label products.

1. Corporate branding

The corporate brand is all the brand factors identified above that are associated with the name of the company. The products and services sold by an organisation, the markets in which it operates, the way it treats its customers, how it runs its business and how it respects the environment will all build into creating a corporate brand image. The development of a corporate brand can be both planned and unplanned: planned through the use of public relations and promotional activity; unplanned in that everything a high profile company does will have some sort of effect on its corporate image.

Example 5.22 **Brands in China**

In China, brands were unknown in the decades following the Communist revolution in 1949. Most products were indistinguishable commodities, so the Chinese had few strong feelings about particular products or their manufacturers. China's unprecedented and rapid transformation from a planned economy to a market-driven society has confronted businesses and consumers alike with an explosion of choices unparalleled in the country's history. From the business-to-business perspective the absence of globally known brands has severely restricted China's ability to market around the world on added value, having to rely purely on low labour cost advantage to sell its products either as commodities or as brands engineered under the names of foreign companies. However, things are changing and spending in this direction has increased apace, particularly since China's membership of the WTO. Companies that have succeeded in building strong brands include such well-established multinationals as IBM, Amway and Carrefour, as well as local companies Sina.com, Yili Dairy Products, AsiaInfo and UT Starcom. Their success stems largely from a strategic focus on maximising the effectiveness of their distribution channels and on building goodwill among key constituencies such as government officials and financial analysts. This movement can only but continue.

2. Corporate family branding

Some organisations will house a group of companies either organically developed but more than likely acquired by purchase or merger. The holding company may choose to keep these companies under separate corporate family brand names rather than bring them under the one umbrella corporate name. In this way values associated with the different brands by different market segments will be maintained. Aerospace Systems, Airspace Safety Analysis Corporation, Continental Graphics, Jeppesen Sanderson, Preston Group and SBS International are all subsidiaries of the giant Boeing Corporation, offering products and services to many different segments.

What makes a corporate super-brand

An NOP poll in 2002 identified 50 of the top brands around the world, giving the following reasons why they might be considered 'superbrands':

- ☐ Delivery of consistent value and quality
- ☐ A strong and distinctive reputation
- ☐ Financial security and stability
- ☐ Innovative products and services
- ☐ Strong research and development credentials
- ☐ High levels of awareness
- ☐ International presence
- ☐ Known only to recruit the best employees
- ☐ High standing with the local community.

Example 5.23   **Prontaprint - superbrand**

Prontaprint (www.prontaprint.co.uk), the largest and best known brand within the print-on-demand market within Europe, has been granted superbrand status by the independent council of marketing and branding experts, the Superbrands Council (www.superbrands.com). This ultimate accolade in brand recognition was bestowed on the company after being identified as one of the exceptional business brands around the world. As a result, Prontaprint will now appear in the Superbrands book dedicated to business-to-business (B2B) branding, which identifies over 50 of the strongest B2B brands in Britain today. It was selected for its innovation, reliability and technical expertise, as well as its reputation for fulfilling its promises, delivering on time and to specification. One of the most significant reasons for being selected, however, was its ability and focus on building long-term relationships among business clients, current and potential franchisees.

---

3. Product and service branding

Branding under separate product or product group names is much more popular in B2C than in B2B markets, really because of the plethora of segmentation methods and the emotional appeal of the brand. Kotex, Huggies, Pull-ups, Kleenex, Andrex and Fiesta are all FMCG brand names belonging to Kimberly-Clark, appealing to different individual consumers. Individual product names are less used in B2B because the buyer tends not to be seduced by the emotion surrounding a particular brand. A toilet roll bought for industrial purposes will not need the same symbolic attachments as a toilet roll bought by mum for the family, nor will cars bought for company use compare with cars bought for own use. However, where a B2B organisation sells many hundreds of different products, the different brand names can be patented to protect the manufacturer and used by the buyer to identify the benefits offered by each separate product.

Example 5.24   **Du Pont**

Chemical giant Du Pont has a range of B2B and B2C chemical-based brands used across a bewildering range of products including materials, paints, plastics, carpets, furniture, curtains, luggage, foods, lawns, gardens and agriculture in both business and consumer markets. Some brand names are known by the consumer and will appear in the products of others and some will be unknown by the consumer but known to the B2B buyer: Cordura durable fabrics, Dacron polyester filament yarn, Delrin acetal resin, Micromatic fire blankets, Smartpaint products, Tynex tapered paintbrushes, Solae soy protein, Supro, Scairfilm food wrappings, Teflon non-stick coating, Freon refrigerants, and many, many more. (www.dupont.com)

---

4. Own or private label products

Some manufacturers choose to produce goods and services that are branded under the name, of another company, e.g. Northern Foods producing under the Tesco name, or under a product brand name such as Nova for Sainsbury. Although more often than not the products are FMCG, the practice of making own label products for others falls firmly into the B2B industry.

Example 5.25   **Growth potential for B2B private label manufacture**

At present there is a major concern in the global retail world on the positioning of branded products versus private labels and who will eventually dominate in the marketplace. In Europe the growth of private labels, non-branded products manufactured by business-to-business suppliers for the retailer, has reached on average 45 per cent of all products sold. The overall feeling is that in the supermarket industry in western Europe the private label market has now matured and little growth will be seen. But in eastern Europe, especially Poland, Czech Republic, Slovenia, Russia and Turkey, there will be huge growth in this market sector. Similarly this might also apply to the USA with only 25 per cent private label products.

Branding in B2C and B2B markets

There is still uncertainty and disagreement about the real value of branding in the B2B market. There is now no doubt about its worth in consumer markets because of the large amount of research conducted over the years, but the same cannot be said in the business market. In the B2C packaged goods markets research has shown that as much as 75 per cent of consumer purchases are made for emotional and psychological reasons linked to the brand name. Names such as Nike, Coca-Cola, Mercedes, Microsoft, McDonald's and Disney are legendary in the attraction they have for the consumer and the worth they bring to their shareholders.

Unlike consumers, B2B buyers will be loath to purchase branded products for the emotional attraction of the brand. Because the purchase is for the company rather than for own use, the value offered in the product must be seen to be real rather than abstract and symbolic. B2B buyers will not generally be prepared to pay a premium for branded products in the same way that consumers will. In this respect it must also be remembered that a large part of the cost in B2C branding is in the promotion and advertising. This will not be at the same level in B2B markets. It must be remembered, however, that not all benefits associated with the brand name are emotional. There are real, functional, practical benefits such as quality, service and long-term value when dealing with a well-respected organisation such as Bosch, Northern Foods, IBM and GKN. In this sense the corporate name offers the B2B buyer many of the benefits and will be taken advantage of as long as customer expectations are met.

☐ Advantages associated with branding

B2B markets

There are many benefits in dealing with a well-known organisation when buying and selling B2B products. As choices rapidly grow from around the world brand appeal is an increasingly important criterion for buyers to apply. Unlike B2C markets, purchase in B2B markets is mainly for rational reasons that are thought through and evaluated. Listed below are some of the factors associated with good corporate and product branding in B2B markets.

From the B2B buyer perspective

☐ Reduces the risk – the 'nobody ever got the sack for buying an IBM computer' syndrome.
☐ Saves time when searching out new products.
☐ Known functional performance matching benefit needs.
☐ Known value, quality, consistency, service.
☐ Safety and peace of mind.

From the B2B seller perspective

☐ Builds a reputation that can be used when launching new products, especially around the world.
☐ Helps segment the market.

- ☐ Strong brand values can protect a product from intensifying price competition.
- ☐ Can serve as a bulwark against substitute products.
- ☐ Holds price levels and prevents the product being seen as a commodity product.
- ☐ Employees want to work for strong branded corporations.
- ☐ Engenders loyalty and pride if linked to adequate recognition and reward system.
- ☐ Can be used when moving into other product/market areas.
- ☐ Extra income can be earned from extra benefits.

B2C markets

The appeal of brands in B2C markets tends to be centred around emotional appeal for the end consumer and rational appeal for the retailer.

From the consumer perspective

- ☐ Brand association satisfies a host of emotional needs such as status, recognition, safety, security, companionship, belonging, sex appeal, and so on.
- ☐ Recognised quality, value and service encourages repeat purchases.
- ☐ Consistent quality guaranteed wherever the product might be purchased.
- ☐ Saves time in not having to seek out and test unknown quality levels.
- ☐ Provides information about both the company and its products.

From the retailer perspective

- ☐ Able to purchase products promoted and advertised by the manufacturer and guaranteed to sell.
- ☐ Avoids confusion when ordering across an enormous range of products.
- ☐ Attracts consumers to the store where more profitable own label products might be bought.
- ☐ Status can rise by being associated with the name of a respected manufacturer's brand, e.g. Mercedes, Givenchy.
- ☐ Helps strategic sales planning as pattern of sales of known brands more reliable than unknown products.

From the seller perspective

- ☐ Builds power with the retailer needing to stock market leaders.
- ☐ Fights against the power of retailer own label.
- ☐ Number one and number two brands in the market virtually guarantee shelf space.
- ☐ Helps segment markets.

Brand extension

Brand extension consists of using the brand name across related products. An example might be an Aga cooker manufacturer producing fridge freezers and Aga cookware. The advantage is that the name and the values attached to the name are readily perceived by the buyer, saving time and money needed to create awareness from nothing and an almost immediate acceptance of new products that are brought to the market. However, there is a downside. Where brands are stretched across a number of products or services, brand failure in one area can taint perceptions of the brand in other areas. An obvious example is in the convergence between banks and insurance companies, where poor claims service in the insurance part of the business might damage customer perceptions of the banking part of the business.

Brand stretching

Unlike brand extension, brand stretching consists of using the brand across many unrelated markets. The obvious advantages are the same as those identified under brand extensions. However, there are dangers associated with this product strategy. Values associated with a brand can be diluted and become weakened if used across too many different industries. It can also be dangerous when the brand is taken beyond its natural boundaries. The brand then loses its power.

Example 5.26 **Branson stretches the brand**

Since Richard Branson launched his own record company, Virgin, at the age of 19, he has defied convention by stretching the brand and moving into an inconceivable range of businesses. In 1984 he went into aircraft, Virgin Atlantic. Hotels and a holiday company soon followed. Now he is trying to tackle the European short-haul airline market. In 1985 he floated his company on the stock market, but he bought it back in 1988 for £248 million following the stock market crash. In 1991 he sold his Virgin Music business to EMI for $1 billion. In 1994 he launched Virgin Cola and challenged Coca-Cola's marketing practices. He acquired MGM's cinemas in the UK and refurbished them as Virgin cinemas.

He then acquired a train business, the West Coast Main Line, and took a stake in Eurostar, the cross-channel service to Paris and Brussels. In 1996 he moved into financial services, launching pensions, insurance, and stock market PEPs that were marketed as Virgin Direct, which has taken £1 billion in funds. He has licensing agreements with Virgin Vodka and even wedding service outlets.

Not all the above have been successful and many critics including specialist brand agency Wolf Olins argue that bad publicity in one area (train failures) will impinge on Virgin's reputation in other areas.

Brand consolidation

There has been a move by organisations to reduce the number of brands in the company product portfolio. In this way more energy can be focused towards building fewer but stronger brands that become market leaders in their particular markets.

As value is concentrated in fewer brands, however, the threat posed by risks to these brands will correspondingly grow in severity. To take one obvious example, the recall of a product accounting for 30 per cent of a company's profits will be more damaging than the recall of a product accounting for 10 per cent of profits.

Example 5.27   **Brand evaluation**

Global advertising agency Ogilvy PR evaluates brands on the basis of six core properties:

1. *Visual*. Does the brand project a clear, consistent visual identity?
2. *Image*. Is the image of the brand engaging and strong?
3. *Goodwill*. Has the brand earned the goodwill of influencers in the communities where the company operates?
4. *Product*. How does a product's performance support the brand?
5. *Channel*. Is the brand adequately leveraged in its distribution channels?
6. *Customer*. Is there an existing brand franchise among a firm's customers? (www.olgilvypr.com)

Brand relationship building

By teaming up with other well-respected companies, a company can sometimes enhance its brand equity in the eyes of customers. An example is the OneWorld airline alliance, currently comprising six major airlines. Brand alliances, however, can expose companies to the risk that their partner's performance may fail to meet business customer expectations, thus damaging the brands of the other alliance members. For example, airline alliances make each participating airline vulnerable to poor service standards on the part of its alliance partner.

☐ Packaging

Packaging in both B2B and B2C markets has become an essential and integral part of the product. This is especially so in B2C markets where it is often seen emotively by the end consumer as part of the brand offering, a quintessential ingredient in all that a particular brand, such as Persil or Budweiser, means to the end user. Package ownership, and through this the brand, brings such things as reassurance, feelings of status, pleasant associations, and so on.

Because the overwhelming reason for purchase in B2B markets is rational and for the firm rather than oneself, packing has different connotations. Where the business purchase is for use by the buyer, product protection in delivery, storage and usage are probably the most important factors as well as cost and ease of use. Recent legislation insisting that all packaging must be recyclable and/or biodegradable has added another imperative to the business buying process. It should be remembered, however, that there are many companies of all sizes from around the globe involved in the retail packing process, making for manufacturers supplying products into the retail trade. These are products and brands that will end up being bought by end consumers for the emotive reasons identified above. In these cases, although the buyer is another business and the initial reason for purchase will be rational, i.e. cost, speed of delivery, etc., the supplier will need to be aware of the emotive factors that the buyer will want to be invested in the packaging. So these factors and skills become B2B product benefit offerings wanted by the business buyer.

Packaging in B2C

Packaging is particularly important in B2C markets, especially in the FMCG industry. Sometimes known as the 'silent salesman', its many functions in consumer markets include attracting attention, enhancing the product, giving out information, offering sales promotions, and so on. In fact it has become such an integral part of the product that in many cases it would be impossible to divorce the two without totally devaluing the product and the brand, reducing the offering practically to a commodity offering. Imagine KitKat without its familiar red and white packing, Coca-Cola without the world-renowned tin or bottle, or Kellogg's Cornflakes without the cockerel on the constantly busy box full of information, free gifts and things for the children to do. Such is the importance of packaging in B2C that many innovations, shapes, colours and designs will often constitute the USP and will now be patented.

Packaging is just as important in the B2B market, but in many different ways when compared with B2C. The consumer will be concerned about the packing mainly for a harmonious and value-added visual perspective. This will include the shape, design, colours and material used related to the overall attractiveness of the product. Higher value packaging reflects the higher value product. There will be some concern about the protection given, but this will only come into effect if the consumer receives a product that is damaged in some way.

Example 5.28 **Packaging makes the first sale, the product the second**

Research has confirmed that an estimated one to three seconds is all the time that a company will get to sell its product as the consumer browses the retail marketplace. So the packaging can mean the difference between success and failure in business. With this in mind, Fortune 500 companies will commonly spend 60 per cent to 80 per cent of the total item cost on B2C packaging, knowing this limited attention of a passing shopper.

Packaging in B2B

Packaging in B2B has many more dimensions and spawns a multi-billion pound industry. The supply chain in B2B packaging can be long and diverse and involve the design, engineering, computer, chemical, biological, paper, metals, adhesives and sealants, glass, crates, printing and labelling, plastics and capital equipment industries, randomly to name a few. Packaging additives and finished products in the B2B sector can be manufactured for other businesses for their own use or they can end up being sold by retailers to the end consumer. Organisations involved might be driven by the buyer's need for delivery protection, consistency and speed, health and safety, security, recyclability and waste disposal. The imperative might be for the packaging to load efficiently into lorries and containers, to fit efficiently onto delivery pallets or to sit comfortably and attractively on the retail shelf. The overriding issue might be one of ease of use causing designers, engineers and computer experts to work together on new ways to open, use and dispose of cans, bags, bottles, boxes, cartons and crates. It might be the constant need for creativity, design, printing, colour combinations and exciting promotions to hold the interest of the consumer in an ever-changing, ever more demanding market environment.

Packaging companies might be working with wood, sealants, steel, paper, aluminium, glass, rubber, polystyrene or chemical products. One B2B organisation might be involved with raw materials, another with component parts, and another with the capital equipment. B2B packaging employs many millions of people from around the world with extremely high and very low levels of skills. A highly paid computer expert might be designing and engineering packaging in Silicon Valley in the west and a very low paid labourer might be putting together paper products in the east.

Example 5.29 | **Campbell's fresh tasting soups in a glass container**

Innovation and function come together in Campbell Soup Company's new line of quality soups. This product line was the first introduction of soups in glass jars on a national scale. Glass was the perfect choice for Campbell's to highlight the quality of their product. Consumers loved the convenience afforded by the resealable glass jars. Bringing back a bygone era, this package shows a venerable idea in a new light. The glass container supplier was Owens-Brockway Glass Containers. (Glass Packaging Institute, www.gpi.org)

New technology and packing

As with all areas of marketing, new technology development is always present, on the one hand offering sellers and buyers wonderful opportunities to gain both productivity efficiencies and competitive advantage, and on the other hand continuously throwing up new threats and challenges. A few examples of new technology in packaging include:

☐ Reducing paper waste within the printing process.

☐ New packaging machinery and constant upgrades to improve efficiency of existing machinery operation as well as changeover times, user interface reliability, maintenance requirements, flexibility and customised uses.

☐ Increasing shelf life of fresh products as well as such things as sell-by-date packaging changing colour as the end date approaches.

☐ Shower products to aid in a non-slip surface, skin care packaging, and a variety of health and beauty aid products.

☐ High-speed 'no-drop' packer for the dairy industry and a brewery machine for packing cans into plastic cases.

- ☐ Computer-aided design (CAD) technology allows designers and engineers to use computers for their design work. Early programs enabled two-dimensional (2-D) design. Current programs allow designers to work in three dimensions (3-D) and in either wire or solid models.
- ☐ Computer-enhanced creativity uses specially designed computer software that aids in the process of recording, recalling and reconstructing ideas to speed up the new product development process.
- ☐ Bar code technology, standardisation, smart computer (radio) chips built into packaging storing unlimited information.
- ☐ Thermal transfer printing technology.
- ☐ Using packaging materials that are stronger, lighter, longer lasting, more environmentally friendly, recyclable and biodegradable yet less expensive.

Areas involved with packaging

These include the following: packing machinery; automatic sealing machines; blister packs, bubble wraps, shrink wrapping, film and foil linings; blowing and injection moulds; commercial and industrial packing machinery cases; custom manufactured skin or blister packaging; food and pharmaceutical industries machinery; films for chemical packaging; labels and labelling systems; inflatable polythene bags; Jiffy and Jiffy Lite delivery envelopes; moulds; polystyrene; sealed air packaging; straps and strapping machines; thermoforming machines; vacuum packaging machinery; crating, boxes, cartons, containers and drums; filling and dispensing; corrugated board and paperboard; bottles, jars and cans; wrapping, sealing and shrinking; chemical coating for health and longevity.

It will also involve the following industries: logistics and transport; trade shows and exhibitions; purchasing; innovations, creativity and design; health and safety; security; point of purchase display; environmental agencies; waste disposal and recycling; engineering; computer software; food technologists and food processing; pharmaceutical engineering; material handling; powder technology; agriculture and seeds; printing and publishing; health and hygiene; metallurgy; chemicals; forestry; rubber; paper; steel; coal; oil. The list is endless.

B2C packaging

B2C markets have the following requirements:

- ☐ Attractive packaging enhances display and encourages purchase, e.g. boxed chocolates, perfumes, jewellery.
- ☐ Packing shapes and designs can be branded and patented for protection against competitors, instant consumer recognition and as a USP, e.g. Jif lemon squeezer, Coca-Cola bottle, Maxwell House coffee jar.
- ☐ Packing shapes and designs can be aimed at ease of use, home storage, reusability and disposability, e.g. wine in a box, toothpaste in a pump-action tube, beer in a ring pull, widget driven, easily disposable aluminium can.
- ☐ Packaging gives the customer information on content, instructions for use, promotions, etc.
- ☐ Legal, health and environmental requirements have to be met.

B2B packaging

B2B markets want:

- ☐ Constant discussions and advice on packaging requirement, especially with customised needs or for B2B products that will eventually end up in retail outlets (where all the above will apply).
- ☐ One-off or long-term contracts executed speedily and within the needed time periods.
- ☐ Product protection and preservation during transportation, storage and usage.
- ☐ Ease of use meeting all logistic requirements.
- ☐ All legal requirements to have been met.
- ☐ Materials that are stronger, lighter, longer lasting, more environmentally friendly, recyclable and biodegradable yet less expensive.

Example 5.30 **National packaging exhibition**

With the diversity and quality of our exhibitors, you will be able to meet face-to-face with the vendors, manufacturers and packagers that can fulfil all of your outsourcing, packaging product or service needs, as well as your equipment or machinery needs in one unique venue. You will meet the vendors you know and some you don't, all with the ability to offer the same or better quality of goods or services with competitive or better pricing than you are presently finding. Meet distributors and reps for lines of packaging machinery and equipment.

Example 5.31 **Packaging challenge**

Faced with the new labelling requirements demanding more space to convey drug information, companies are challenged to develop packaging that will still grab consumer's attention in this ever-competitive marketplace. They understand the need to employ graphic elements that will give their products more shelf impact to stand apart from the competition. One such design features a foldout panel that is normally fastened to the carton exterior to promote brand identity and preserve billboard space, but can be easily opened by consumers to reveal compliance information. A second design incorporates a pull-tab panel that extends to reveal additional drug information or even promotional content such as coupons or brand cross-marketing. (Diamond Packaging)

☐ Summary

In this chapter we looked at how and why business-to-business products and services were categorised, attempting to highlight the basic different marketing approaches that might be needed. Particular attention was paid to the importance of distinguishing between products and services as well as the differences between B2B and B2C products and services. Products and services were initially identified under the categories of capital goods, materials and parts, and supplies and running services. We then looked at other ways in which products an services might be categorised under convenience goods, search-out goods and integrated solutions, recognising that there was much overlap and none of the areas were mutually exclusive. The differences between the first three areas and the additional categorisation methods were outlined and the alternative marketing approaches that could be used were investigated.

Importance levels and risk associated with the purchase of products and services in B2B compared with B2C were examined, highlighting how much higher the risk could be for a business purchaser. The problems and opportunities associated with the need to both customise and/or standardise the products and services were talked about and the pros and cons of each area were identified, recognising that ultimately it must be the customer that should be the deciding factor.

We then looked at the whole process of adding value to the basic B2B commodity good so as to gain sustainable competitive advantage. This looked at the many value added methods that can be used both before purchase, primary added value, and after purchase, supplementary added value. It was recognised that adding value to the product is at the heart of marketing and should be driven by the needs of the target customer. Three basic strategies, making the product different, better or cheaper were shown to be the generic strategies all companies should consider in attempting to position itself in the marketplace and so gain sustainable competitive advantage. In the same vein the need to have a product portfolio of products so as to address the needs of the different market segments was brought up and examined using the model of the Boston Consultancy Group Matrix.

Branding and new product development were selected for special consideration and comparisons made between B2B and B2C because of their differing importance to both markets. Inculcating a new product culture, encouraging employees to be constantly aware of opportunities and developing both formal and informal NPD processes were seen to be crucial to constant success, especially as technology and competition grows and threatens the complacent organisation. Corporate branding was argued to be more important in B2B markets and product branding more important in B2C markets. The advantages of having a strong brand were discussed and reasons given as to why this was so. Finally the role and importance of packaging in both B2B and B2C markets was talked over with the different roles that it plays in the two areas examined and evaluated.

Discussion questions

1. Discuss the different marketing approaches that might be needed for the different categories of products. Will this differ between the public and the private sector? Give live examples.

2. Discuss the concept behind 'added value' in B2B markets. How might a company build on this idea and will it differ in B2B when compared to B2C?

3. How will marketing of B2B products and services differ from the marketing of B2C products and services? Give examples.

4. Discuss the ways in which an organisation might add value to its benefit offerings. Take an industry and give examples. How important is branding in B2B markets compared with branding in B2C?

5. Will B2B products and services demanded be any different in the public sector when compared with the commercial sector? Give examples and discuss how the marketing approach might have to vary.

6. 'Continuous new product development is crucial in B2C but not so important in B2B.' Discuss.

7. How important is the idea of a mixed product portfolio of products in B2B marketing? What drives the concept and how will marketing on a global perspective affect the process?

8. Identify and evaluate the different roles that packaging might have in B2C when compared with B2B. Give live examples to illustrate the points that you might want to make.

9. Identify new technological developments in packing for use in both B2B and B2C. What are the major drivers and where do you think the future might take us in this area?

10. How might the global demand for B2B products and services alter over the next decade and what might be the emerging issues affecting productivity and overall success for an industry and any one company?

 Visit the *B2B Marketing* website at www.booksites.net/wright for a Case Study, Questions, and an Internet Exercise for this chapter.

☐ Bibliography

Books

Bacon, F.R. and Butler, T.W. (1998) *Achieving Planned Innovation: A Proven System for Creating Successful New Products and Services*. Collingdale, PA: Diane.

Baker, M. (1998) *The Marketing Book*, 4th edn. Oxford: Butterworth-Heinemann.

Butte, F. (1996) *Relationship Marketing: Theory and Practice*. London: Paul Chapman.

De Chernatony, L. (1998) *Brand Management*. Aldershot: Dartmouth.

Fifield, P. and Gillian, C. (1998) *Strategic Marketing Management*. Oxford: Butterworth-Heinemann.

Hart, N. (1994) *Effective Industrial Marketing – Business-to-Business Marketing of Goods and Services*. London: Kogan Page.

Hutt, M.D. and Hett, T.W. (1998) *Business Marketing Management*, 6th edn. London: Dryden Press.

Ind, N. (1997) *The Corporate Brand*. London: Macmillan.

Kaplan, R.S. and Norton, D.P. (1996) *The Strategy Focuses Organisation: How Balanced Scorecard Companies Thrive in the New Business Environment*. Cambridge MA: Harvard Business School Press.

Knobil, M. (2002) *Business Superbrands: An Insight into the World's Strongest B2B Brands*. London: Brand Council.

Lury, G. (1998) *Brand Watching: Lifting the Lid on the Phenomenon of Branding*. Dublin: Blackhall.

McNeill, D. and Freiburger, P. (1993) *Fuzzy Logic – The Revolutionary Computer Technology that is Changing the World*. New York: Simon & Schuster.

Mentzer, J. and Bienstock, C. (1998) *Sales Forecasting Management: Understanding the Techniques, Systems, and Management of the Sales Forecasting Process*. London: Sage.

Olson, R.W. (1980) *The Art of Creative Thinking*. London: HarperCollins.

Rogers, M. (1995) *Diffusion of Innovation*. New York: Free Press.

Stern, C.W. and Stalk, G. (1998) *Perspectives on Strategy from the Boston Consultancy Group*. New York: Wiley.

Williams, R.H. and Stockmeyer, J. (1987) *Unleashing the Right Side of the Brain*. Brattleboro, VT: Stephen Green Press.

Wright, R. (2001) *Marketing: Origins, Concepts, Environment*. London: Thomson.

Zeithaml, V.A., Parasuraman, A. and Berry, L.L. (1990) *Delivering Quality Service – Balancing Customer Perceptions and Expectations*. New York: Free Press.

Journals

Berry, L.L., Parasuraman, A. and Zeithaml, V.A. (1988) 'The service–quality puzzle', *Business Horizons*, September–October: 35–43.

Berry, L.L., Zeithaml, V.A. and Parasuraman, A. (1990) 'Five imperatives for improving service quality', *Sloan Management Review*, Summer: 29–38.

Cooper, R.G. (1984) 'New product strategies: what distinguishes top performers?', *Journal of Product Innovation Management*, September: 151–64.

Cooper, R.G. and Kleinschmidt, E.J. (1987) 'Success factors in product innovation', *Industrial Marketing Management*, 16: 215–23.

Day, G.S. (1977) 'Diagnosing the product portfolio', *Journal of Marketing*, April: 29–38.

Devlin, S.J., Dong, H.K. and Brown, M. (1993) 'Measuring customer expectations', *Marketing Research*, 5 (3).

Dickson, P.R. and Ginter, J.L. (1987) 'Market segmentation, product differentiation, and marketing strategy', *Journal of Marketing*, 51: 1–10.

Drucker, P.F. (1985) 'The discipline of innovation', *Harvard Business Review*, September–October: 67–72.

Eagle, L. and Kitchen, B. (2000) 'IMC, brand communications and corporate culture', *European Journal of Marketing*, 34: 667–86.

Levitt, T. (1960) 'Marketing myopia', *Harvard Business Review*, July–August: 46–56.

Millson, M., Raj, S.P. and Wilemon, D. (1992) 'A survey of major approaches for accelerating new product development', *Journal of Product Innovation Management*, 9: 53–69.

Parasuraman, A. (1998) 'Customer service in business-to-business markets: an agenda for research', *Journal of Business and Industrial Marketing*, 13 (4/5): 309–21.

Parasuraman, V.A., Zeithaml, A. and Berry, L.L. (1985) 'A conceptual model of service quality and its implications for future research', *Journal of Marketing*, Fall: 41–50.

Smith, W.R. (1956) 'Product differentiation and market segmentation as alternative marketing strategies', *Journal of Marketing*, July: 3–8.

Van Waterschool, W. and Van den Bulte, C. (1992) 'The 4P classification of marketing mix revisited', *Journal of Marketing*, 56: 83–93.

Workman, J.P. (1993) 'Marketing's limited role in new product development', *Journal of Marketing Research*, November: 405–21.

 Visit www.booksites.net/wright for the Internet references for this chapter.

06

Managing business marketing channels

In theory there is no difference between theory and practice. In practice there is.

Aims and objectives

By the end of this chapter the student should be able to:

1. Identify and evaluate both direct and indirect methods of distribution.

2. Discuss and evaluate the strategic factors that need to be taken into account when choosing a channel of distribution.

3. Identify the supply chain relationships and analyse the importance and the reasons for the different types.

Part 1 Evaluating strategic channel alternatives

☐ Introduction

B2B and B2C channels of distribution are the ways that an organisation makes products and services available to the buying organisation or the end consumer. The choices available are many and the decision on which method or methods to choose is of crucial strategic importance. Opt for the wrong or inferior method and valuable resources can be wasted, customers upset and competitive advantages lost. Well-researched, customer value-added products and service benefits can be wasted if the buyer is confronted by a distribution system that is in some way flawed and inadequate. In the case of B2C this might only be a small percentage, but in B2B this could be a buyer representing a company such as GE worth untold millions in terms of buying power. In some extreme cases the difficulty for a supplier to obtain distribution, perhaps because of a monopolistic market condition or partnership, can make it impossible for a particular market to be entered.

Example 6.1 **Distribution monopoly**

Many retailers can only supply ice cream from one manufacturer. They had been given free freezers for ice cream on the condition that they did not stock rival products. It is a system small manufacturers said discriminated against them. The UK government moved to end the stranglehold of Birds Eye Wall's, Nestlé and Mars on the sale of ice cream in January after a Competition Commission report which found that outlet and freezer exclusivity restricts competition between manufacturers and retailers. Birds Eye Wall's has two-thirds of the market and Mars and Nestlé freezer deals were seen as crucial to helping them compete.

Distribution can be broken down into 'channels of distribution' and 'physical distribution'. We will look at channels of distribution first.

> Channels of distribution are the ways that an organisation makes its products and services available to its selected market segments.

☐ Channels of distribution in B2B markets

To restate in simple terms, the channel of distribution is the way that the B2B supplier makes the products and services available to the organisational buyer. This can be broken down into two major channels, direct and indirect. The distinction is illustrated in Figure 6.1 where it can be seen that distributing direct makes the product or service available without any intervening organisation in between. Marketing indirect, on the other hand, involves channelling the products through an intervening organisation who will then make the product available to the customer. A producer can choose to sell direct, indirect or via a combination of both depending on certain criteria that will be identified and discussed as we move through the chapter. On the other hand the market supply structure might already be in place and the channel of distribution an established fact. In this case the supplier will have to fit in with existing circumstances unless a new method of distribution can be found that will give a competitive advantage.

B2B and B2C channels of distribution

B2B and B2C channels of distribution can both be direct to the customer or indirect through some type of intermediary. Companies will choose one or the other

Figure 6.1
Direct and indirect distribution

Direct distribution

Producer - → Customer

Indirect distribution

Producer - - - - - - - → Intervening organisation - - - - - - - → Customer or, in some cases, use a selection of both methods. In B2C, although products are sold direct to the end consumer, the most popular method is to sell through retail intermediaries such as supermarkets, department stores, chain stores and independent retailers. Depending on the product or service to be offered to the market, wholesalers might also be used. Direct methods, such as selling door-to-door, house parties, product catalogues, direct mail, the internet and TV, are used, but comprise a small percentage of the whole. In contrast, although some products and services can be bought indirectly, most B2B products and services tend to be channelled direct to the buyer. The reason for the use of a different method in the two different sectors is now discussed.

☐ Direct channels of distribution

Most B2B suppliers choose to market the products directly to the buying organisation without the use of an intervening organisation, known alternatively as an intermediary or middleman, and they will do so for a variety of reasons.

B2B buyer/customer expectations

In many cases the customer will expect to see and discuss product and service needs direct with each supplier and will not entertain going through a middleman. If the benefit offering need is of strategic importance, complex or costly, then the buying company may only be interested in talking directly with the supplier to discuss detailed needs. The largest companies will often insist on dealing only with senior managers, often at boardroom level.

Building customer relations

Dealing direct with the buyer can be seen as an intricate part in the process of communicating and building long-term close relationships with buying companies. This will be particularly apt if repeat orders are seen as part of the process. It will also apply if some kind of contract is involved and the buying and selling organisations need to meet continuously to discuss such things as quality, delivery and service. This close relationship, unfettered by intervening organisations, can facilitate greater continuous and long-term satisfaction, supported by the use of market research and database analysis (relationship marketing).

Focused specialised attention

A company selling direct can present its products and services in a concentrated and focused way to the customer unhindered by immediate competitors' products. Product benefits can be matched to customer needs using the specialised knowledge and experience that only comes from selling one's own company's products. This is especially relevant when selling complex and high valued products such as financial services, computer systems and capital equipment. A middleman, on the other hand, will usually be offering a whole range of products from many different companies with only a general knowledge of the whole and limited knowledge of each individual product range.

Marketing of services

In most cases services will need to be delivered direct rather than by an intermediary although service supplies, e.g. food, cleaning materials and administration materials, would probably have come from other suppliers. Because of the personal skills involved, for example in consultancy, it would be difficult though not impossible to operate through an intervening organisation.

Guaranteed outlet

Selling direct should ensure a guaranteed outlet for the company's products (as long as the customer wants to buy) since there are no intervening bodies between the organisation and its customers refusing to take stock or taking stock from elsewhere and so restricting supply. This can be important because of growing competition.

Maintaining control

The major advantage in marketing direct is that full control can be maintained over all elements of the marketing mix. This is the way that the B2B product or service is presented to the buyer, where the product/service is offered for sale and how the product/service is promoted and sold. A carefully crafted benefit offering, tightly targeted to meet a buyer solution, might need special nurturing and care. A supplier might feel that this could not be left to the uncertainties of an intermediary salesperson offering this product as just one among many others.

Building a customer database

Crucial to the insight into business-to-business customers and markets is the need to build a marketing information system (MkIS) and create a database of businesses and buyers. Essential to this is the need to gather information from customers. Dealing direct allows marketing managers and supplier salespeople to observe and ask questions and so collect data that can then be processed through the MkIS and used to dig out valuable information to create more customer value. This would be lost if acting through an intermediary.

Costs

Whether there is a cost saving in marketing directly rather than indirectly will depend on product/customer and market circumstances. Superficially there may seem to be a saving as selling direct eliminates the need to pay a percentage amount, in terms of a reduction on the expected selling price, to the intermediary for undertaking some of the marketing tasks. The amount the supplier will have to discount from the expected selling price will differ according to the type of product and industry but it can vary from as low as 5–10 per cent to over 100 per cent. It really depends on the value the buyer might be able to add before passing on to the next customer. However, this possible saving must be weighed against the cost to the supplier of having to undertake all the marketing mix tasks that would have been borne by the intermediary, for example advertising, selling, delivery, installation and after-sales service.

Example 6.2 **UK farmers sell direct**

With falling farming incomes and distribution networks constantly demanding lower prices and more punitive terms and conditions, an increasing number of farmers have been forced to bypass wholesalers and supermarkets and are now selling direct to the public at better prices. The Policy Commission on the Future of Farming and Food, published this week, encourages such practices. Farmers' markets began to take off about three years ago and there are now more than 200 across the UK with many more expected in the future.

Preferred supplier list

Some organisations, particularly in the public sector, might insist that they would only deal with companies direct and so put these types of suppliers on their preferred supplier roster. The major reason for choosing to develop and have preferred suppliers is the extent to which they can provide the customer with a competitive advantage in the marketplace. In this context 'competitive advantage' means the ability to provide the customer with a unique product or service, or a degree of quality and value that is otherwise not available to the customer's competitors, or not available from other suppliers.

Example 6.3 **Radius and Avis**

Radius, the global travel company, and Avis Rent a Car System have entered into a preferred supplier agreement to provide car rental services at negotiated rates to Radius agencies and their clients. Avis is recognised as one of the world's top brands for customer loyalty. It is felt that this will be a win-win situation for both companies.

Hidden suppliers

Some supplier products will end up in other supplier products and in that sense a buyer might feel they were dealing direct when in fact they were buying products indirectly from a host of upstream suppliers.

☐ Methods used in direct channels of distribution

There are many different ways that the supplier can make its products and services directly available to the customer. The company will have the choice of including the following:

1. Direct sales force
2. Trade exhibitions
3. Mail order
4. The internet
5. Other media.

1. Direct sales force

The most common form of direct distribution in B2B markets is through the use of the company's own sales force and its importance cannot be over-emphasised. This is particularly so where products are complex and benefits multifaceted. The role and responsibility of the salesperson will vary according to the industry, market and type of organisation. In some firms selling very basic products such as motor spares the salesman or saleswoman might be little more than a delivery person topping up customers with such things as nuts and bolts and electrical connections as and when wanted. Wages will be low and probably based on commission. At the other end of the spectrum the salesperson (or manufacturer's representatives, commercial agents, sales executive, sales director, or account director) may be highly skilled in specialised technical areas, working with large companies on contracts worth millions of pounds. In a case like this remuneration, wages, bonuses, commission, etc. could be extremely high and it is not unusual for a good salesperson to be one of the highest earners in the organisation.

The salesperson role

Salespeople are able to meet buyers in person, discuss needs and wants, overcome objections and offer customised solutions to intricate problems. They are able to develop professional, cordial relationships with buyers over the long term and build such an atmosphere of trust that the buyer will not want to consider a rival company. This can even spill over into the buyer ordering large amounts of product, or ordering complementary products, just on the recommendation of the supplier salesperson. Of course this trust would soon evaporate if the suggested product turned out to be of the wrong kind or quality. With products and services involving high value and/or long-term contracts, the supplier will often have a team of representatives including experts as well as salespeople talking to the team of buyers (the DMU). This process might go on for weeks, months or even years if the sale was for something like a large construction project or a long-term office cleaning contract. The supplier must support the salespeople at all times with training and coaching, current information and administration back-up. Nothing can destroy a relationship quicker than such things as a customer wrongly invoiced, low quality products offered, poor delivery or bad after-sales service. In return the salesperson can supply the company with continuous feedback on customer and market developments.

CRM and the salesperson

The best kind of salespeople have always seen the building of good long-term customer relationships as an essential part of the job. Almost intuitively, anybody with any sense will soon see that if the buyer is constantly given excellent service, treated in a helpful, friendly and professional manner and never let down on promises, trust will be built and sales success should follow. Of course there are some types of products that might be bought so infrequently that the salesperson would only need to see a buyer once in his or her career. In this case the buyer–seller relationship will be relatively unimportant, although reputation and word of mouth could well bring in extra sales. Where purchase is frequent or has the potential to be very large, this relationship building is crucial and will soon sort out the good from the bad. The idea of customer relationship management (CRM) that has come to the fore over the last decade is discussed throughout the book. The salesperson has become a crucial part of the process. CRM attempts to take the job of the salesperson and the sales team and integrate their role into an interconnected, formalised company approach to long-term customer care at the strategic level. We will look more at the role of the sales team when we discuss promotion in Chapter 8.

Example 6.4	**Use the face-to-face encounter to sell more in the concrete industry**

Continuously let your customers know of the services you offer. If you do waterproofing for a customer, make sure they know that you also do foundation repair. It is amazing how many times even a regular customer won't know you are also capable of doing something else for them. Offer complementary products and/or services that are natural companion purchases for your customer. Make it one-stop shopping for your customer and you will be providing a valuable service. Share your customer base with another business. This strategy allows you to gain access to another business's customers to whom you can market your business's products and/or services. Target the existing customers of a competitor by making the competitor's customers aware of your business. (With thanks to concretenetwork.com)

---

2. Trade exhibitions

Trade exhibitions (Figure 6.2) are temporary marketplaces where suppliers can meet buyers. In some industries, e.g. armaments, they might be almost the only place where this opportunity might arise, although the internet is opening up many more opportunities for the exchange process to take place. While trade exhibitions are seen predominantly as a marketplace where people can be meet, sales can be and are made, either at the time or later as a result of a sales lead. Again this will be discussed in Chapter 8.

Figure 6.2
Examples
of trade
exhibitions

The Toy Fair (Trade), ExCel Centre, London
Amusement Trade Parks & Attractions, Amusement Trades Exhibitions, Earls Court, London
Hospitality & Foodservice, National Exhibition Centre, Birmingham
Furniture Trade Exhibition, Royal Highland Centre, Edinburgh
British Franchise Exhibition, G-MEX Centre, Manchester
Recycling & Waste Management Exhibition, NEC, Birmingham
Royal International Agricultural Show, Stoneleigh, Coventry
Professional Finisher Trade Show, NEC, Birmingham
SPATEX, Swimming Pool Industry Show, Hilton Metropole, Brighton
Medical Device Technology (MDT 2003), NEC, Birmingham

3. Mail order

B2B products and services are sold through trade magazines, trade journals and mail order and for some organisations this is the most lucrative method. Smaller items can be advertised and sold direct while other products and services might be advertised inviting an enquiry and then followed up with a phone call or personal visit. There are thousands of trade magazines covering every industry from catering and healthcare through to recruitment and road haulage and as fast as one closes another two open.

4. The internet

Still relatively in its infancy, the internet is opening up wonderful opportunities for B2B organisations to buy and sell products and services around the world. Smaller products can be despatched by post or a delivery service to every corner of the globe in response to an electronic order online. Other products and services, information, catalogues and music can be paid for and sent downline immediately. As with direct response, an internet enquiry can initiate a phone call, a video talk line or a personal visit. In the first chapter we discussed the development of auction type websites (e.g. Covisint.com for the car industry) where suppliers from around the world can be invited to bid for large orders from a conglomerate of business buyers. These and similar sites are set to grow in number.

Example 6.5 **Growth in B2B e-commerce**

Until now most UK e-businesses have been relatively small business-to-consumer (B2C) undertakings. However, if e-commerce is to make a substantial impact on the UK economy, the country must move quickly into the rapidly expanding international B2B market. B2B is flourishing because it is a highly effective way to find new markets and to make existing channels more efficient. Analysts project that B2B sales will reach $7 trillion by 2005. To put this figure into perspective, it is no less than the amount of the entire US gross national product as recently as 1993.

---

5. Other media

To a lesser extent B2B suppliers will use other media such as TV and radio to sell products direct but this is limited to a very small market, for example Fisons selling fertiliser to farmers in the UK Anglia region.

☐ Indirect B2B channels of distribution

For some organisations it suits them to market their products and services through one or many intermediaries. An intermediary or middleman is an organisation that acts as a conduit for products and services between the supplier and buyer. In B2B markets indirect distribution is less favoured than direct distribution, but the method chosen will depend on company objectives and the product or service to be sold. Companies starting up will often use an intermediary until knowledge of the industry is gained and contacts made. This is especially so when marketing abroad where local knowledge can be so important.

> In B2B markets direct distribution is used more than indirect distribution but it will vary from industry to industry and from product to product.

Long and short B2B distribution or supply chains

There can be one or more intermediaries in the supply chain from any one producer through to the business customer. Each firm may purchase the goods either for resale in more or less the same form or by adding value in some way and then passing it on to the next business buyer. In some industries the supply chain can include many intervening companies before it reaches its final destination. The end customer may be a B2B customer or a B2C retailer passing it finally on to the end consumer.

In Figure 6.3 the supplier sells the product, e.g. component parts, on to a wholesaler or distributor who then sells it on to the end buyer. The supply chain is very short. In Figure 6.4 there are many companies involved in the process. This might be because the product is bought in bulk initially and gradually broken down into smaller amounts, or it could be because amounts of value are added as it moves downstream along the supply chain. It can be argued that the longer the supply chain, the greater the loss of control over the elements of the marketing mix as the end customer becomes detached from the supplier. This will be more relevant to some products and services than others, but channel length is particularly important where elements such as quality, product knowledge and after-sales service play an important part in the product or service. It is not so important with basic commodity type products such as nuts and bolts or chemicals to go into foodstuffs.

Figure 6.3
A short supply chain

Supplier ⟶ Buyer/Supplier ⟶ Buyer

Figure 6.4
A long supply chain

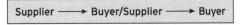

Supplier ⟶ Buyer/Supplier ⟶ Buyer/Supplier ⟶ Buyer/Supplier ⟶ B2B Customer

Methods used in indirect distribution chains

The intermediaries in the distribution chain might include one or more of the following.

Supplier

One supplier may sell on to another supplier either to break down into smaller numbers or to put into another product to resell. It is possible to have many suppliers in one distribution chain. The supplier might be a manufacturer, broker, agent, distributor or wholesaler.

Brokers

There are different definitions of a broker often according to the country of use and the industry chosen. The generally accepted one is the idea of a company (or even an individual) that buys and sells goods, usually upstream and very early in the supply chain, without taking title of these goods. In fact the broker might not even see the goods but acts to put the seller and buyer of goods and services in touch with one another, earning a mark-up on the price difference or being paid a commission on the services. When trading in some countries it seems to be obligatory to work through a broker of some kind and this has at times generated accusations of sleaze, corruption and contracts being given to the wrong companies. Brokers' services will include:

- Bringing buyer and seller together
- Networking and influential contacts
- Help and advice in unknown circumstances.

Agents

Unlike distributors, agents will not take title of (purchase) supplier products but will sell on commission in a defined region or country. Agents might sell only one supplier's products or work for many different companies. This can affect the focus of the approach taken by the agent to any one company's products (they could in many cases be seen as selling direct depending on the control level operated by the supplier). This throws up an interesting problem in terms of the law and the responsibility for products and services that could cause difficulties for all types of intermediaries around the world. If an agent sells products for a manufacturer to another business and there are problems, where will the ultimate responsibility lie, with the manufacturer or the agent?

Distributors

Suppliers might sometimes use distributors to sell products and services for them. A distributor is different from an agent in that they actually take title to the products (purchase them) and then promote, sell, distribute and even offer after-sales service across a designated sales area. As with agents, they can be given sole rights to market a supplier's products in a region, country or continent. A distributor might stock only one company's products or it might stock many. Contracts between producer and distributor will normally vary between three and five years after which the contract can be renegotiated. The contract could be terminated earlier according to such things as target sales not reached, selling other suppliers' products, or a change of control of the distributor.

Example 6.6 **Method of payment**

Methods of payment between the manufacturer and a distributor will vary around the world according to customer and practice, trust and the amount involved. In B2B a few bad debts could drive a supplier out of business. Methods include letters of credit, cash on delivery and an open account with the number of days for payment stated in the initial agreement. Different currencies will cause extra problems and care will have to be taken by both parties to make certain that fluctuations will not bring unnecessary hardship to either party. We discuss this further in Chapter 7 on price.

Agents and distributors will often be used because they are able to offer a network of contacts and local knowledge on such things as business culture, buying needs and channel infrastructure.

Wholesalers

Although few in number compared with 30 years ago, B2B wholesalers will buy products in bulk from many suppliers and then break them down into smaller amounts and sell and deliver to business users. They offer specialist products, continuity of supply and one-off products on a day-to-day basis (Figure 6.5).

Using a wholesaler will usually cost the buyer more money but the convenience in terms of time and effort saved to obtain a needed component will be worthwhile. For the buyer of a company to spend valuable time searching around for a particular product in order to save a small amount of money when a specialist wholesaler might supply immediately would be foolish and not cost

Figure 6.5
Advantages of using a B2B wholesaler

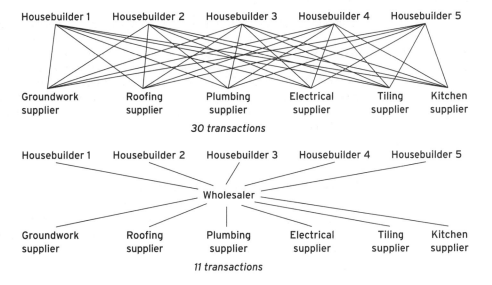

efficient. Imagine a buyer wanting a selection of particular components and having to search around many suppliers before success is achieved when the whole task can be given to one wholesaler operation. Similarly a company might have to buy large amounts of stock, perhaps a year's supply, to get the best price when a wholesaler would deliver on a regular basis at a fraction above this price. Even the largest companies such as Ford will use a wholesaler from time to time when circumstances demand. B2B buyers will use wholesalers for the following reasons:

- ☐ To save time and money
- ☐ A choice of products
- ☐ Convenience and instant delivery
- ☐ One-off urgently needed, or specialist products
- ☐ To save inventory holding space
- ☐ Help, advice, experience and networking contacts
- ☐ Where local knowledge is of importance
- ☐ To sell and distribute to the smaller buyer where it would be uneconomic for the wholesaler to sell and deliver direct.

Full service and specialist service wholesalers

As the name suggests, some B2B wholesalers will attempt to offer a comprehensive service sometimes to business and end consumer trade. An example might be B&Q, the DIY outlet, selling building products and services to both the trade and retail customer. The full service wholesaler will be welcomed by businesses wanting to buy standard products but unhelpful when more specific offerings are needed. In this case a specialist wholesaler will be used. Specialist wholesalers exist in every industry from pets and animals, furniture and soft furnishings to cars, computers and caravans.

Example 6.7 **Wholesalers act as creditors**

Asian and North American suppliers often marvel at the ability of European competitors to garner market share in Latin America, given their relatively high prices. The answer is that credit, not price, is king in Latin America. The region's banks are weak, timid and expensive, leaving importers with little support at home to finance their inventories. Wholesalers, a dying breed in the US economy, function in Latin America as quasi-bankers. They stand between the manufacturer, which cannot evaluate the credit risks for thousands of customers, and dealer/distributors, which cannot operate without credit. (Infoamericas.com)

Voluntary B2B wholesaler trading groups

In the same way as the retail trade, wholesalers will sometimes join together into cooperatives or voluntary buying groups. The nature of this arrangement will vary according to the needs of the member wholesalers, but basically it is the coming together of the smaller wholesalers into groups so as to strengthen their purchasing power and gain economies of scale.

Imagine the differences in financial, time and opportunity costs between the first and second type of wholesaler interaction.

Relationships between a supplier and intermediary

The nature of the relationship between all the above intermediary types – broker, agent, distributor, wholesaler – and the supplier will vary according to the agreed terms of that relationship. There is no one contract type and it is up to the participants (there can be more than two) to talk through the needs of each and come to an eventual agreement that will satisfy all. It can be purely a transactional relationship based on the short-term needs of both parties or it could be a much closer relationship involving a binding contract with terms and conditions covering such things as:

- ☐ Allocated trading areas
- ☐ Product portfolio range stocking and/or selling agreements
- ☐ The restriction on working with competitors
- ☐ Price, trade discounts
- ☐ Responsibilities, etc.

Supply chain relationships have become an increasingly important area in B2B marketing, which will be discussed in much more detail later in the chapter.

Indirect method of distribution favoured in B2C markets (Retailers)

- ☐ Consumers want to see and be able to choose between a range of products.
- ☐ In many cases producers are unable or unwilling to sell direct to every individual consumer.
- ☐ It would not be economic for producers to sell direct to millions of individual consumers.
- ☐ Retailers will offer product advice to the consumer.
- ☐ Retailers will promote product and services.
- ☐ Retailers will deliver, install and offer after-sales service.
- ☐ Retailers will buy and pay for the products, often before the sale is made, offering a form of credit to the producer.

Direct method of distribution favoured in B2B markets

- ☐ Fewer customers and larger orders mean it is economical to sell direct.
- ☐ Having fewer customers allows the supplier to talk, persuade and interact directly with every customer.
- ☐ Buyers often want advice and help directly from the supplier and are unhappy if this is watered down by funnelling through an intermediary.

- ☐ The B2B buyer will want to deal direct as this gives an element of control over the process.

- ☐ Margins can be very tight and competitive advantage might be lost if an intermediary is used.

- ☐ Many of the marketing mix functions offered by the retailer – merchandising, choice of product, promotion, etc. – are unnecessary in B2B markets.

- ☐ The need for close supply chain relationships demands some kind of partnership directly between supplier and buyer.

☐ Disintermediation

Intermediaries survive by adding value. They deliver the product, handle returns and have a place for customer service. If changes in the marketplace make an intermediary's role less valuable, then the intermediary must adapt. If not, the old intermediary will likely be replaced by a new, more valuable intermediary or be cut out altogether. Disintermediation is the inelegant term for the elimination of intermediaries in the supply chain, also referred to as 'cutting out the middleman'. Examples include General Motors bypassing dealerships to sell cars directly to consumers and insurance companies skirting their own agents to sell products and services direct. At times an organisation may try to use both direct and indirect channels with the danger of channel conflict.

Channel conflicts

Channel conflicts arise when a new venue for selling products, such as the web, threatens to cannibalise one or more existing conduits, such as a wholesaler or distributor already used for selling goods. Relationships between organisations along the supply chain can be very fragile and the buyer of products and services from a supplier might well be upset if it is discovered that the same supplier is dealing direct with the same end business customer. In a similar vein a buyer will get upset if one buyer discovers that another is getting better terms or is favoured in the allocation of stock that is in short supply.

Other problems might arise because of different objectives. For example, the wholesaler will want to sell a range of products but the supplier will want a concentrated sales effort on his or her products. There could also be disagreement about the degrees of responsibility over such things as delivery and installation, warranties, the return of damaged stock, and so on. Many of these difficulties can also come about when selling direct. Managing channel partners – distributors, resellers, retailers and dealers – is a tricky business.

Channel relationships are complex and vary greatly from industry to industry. When well-known manufacturers, big distributors and even giant retailers are all trying to agree on a single strategic approach, the problems can at times seem insurmountable as all parties have their own sphere of influence and are used to controlling it. Trust, transparency and cooperation between both buyers and sellers is an essential remedy to these kinds of problems, although it would not be cynical to suggest that ultimately all companies will consider their own welfare before the welfare of others if a cost benefit analysis pointed in this direction. Channel conflict can arise for the following reasons:

- ☐ Supplier using more than one channel to the market.
- ☐ Buyer buying from more than one channel.
- ☐ Different corporate and marketing objectives and tactical focus.
- ☐ Disagreement over strategic issues.
- ☐ Disagreement over levels, degrees and interpretation of product policy.
- ☐ Pricing levels, quickness and amount of payment.

Example 6.8 **Channel conflict**

Facing a roomful of his ten largest distributors at a meeting last march, Simon Elmes confidently revealed his company's latest e-commerce plan. Raynet Electric, a manufacturer of welding equipment, wanted to shift from indirect to direct selling, handling sales leads generated from its website itself while making its distributors responsible for delivering the goods. The reaction was remarkably swift and overwhelmingly negative. 'It didn't go over well at all,' complained Elmes, electronic communications manager at Raynet Electric. By owning the sales transaction, distributors argued, Raynet Electric would be able to set prices and eventually cut the channel out completely. Not wanting to offend its distribution channel, Raynet Electric conceded defeat and quickly drafted a new plan.

☐ The internet in the supply chain

The network economy was initially hailed by many as a way to eliminate intermediaries, enabling a direct path from producer to consumer. This might have been a misjudgement of the nature of intermediaries and networks. Thanks to the near ubiquity of the internet, just about any company that wants to can sell its products and services directly to consumers and businesses online. Many do so because cutting out intermediaries, disintermediation, can mean bigger profits and greater access to valuable customer information. But cutting out the middleman can also mean new kinds of problems, such as obtaining and managing the customer base, figuring out how to fulfil complex orders from consumers, introducing new products and services, setting up new customer service centres, and dealing with backlash from retailers and other spurned channel partners.

Reintermediation

Many suppliers rushed headlong into direct methods of marketing and underestimated the problems associated with disintermediation. Reintermediation refers to using the internet to reassemble buyers, sellers and other partners in a traditional supply chain in new ways. Examples include New York based e-Steel Corp. and Philadelphia based PetroChemNet Inc. bringing together producers, traders, distributors and buyers of steel and chemicals respectively in web-based marketplaces.

Example 6.9   **Reintermediation (bringing back the middleman)**

Using the web to cut out the middleman isn't turning out to be all it was cracked up to be, according to a spokesperson at Gartner Group (www.gartner.com). They predict that more than half of all companies now building or maintaining direct-to-customer websites will abandon them over the next three years. Instead, they will rely on, among other things, new web-based intermediaries that bring buyers and sellers together in new ways. In the business-to-business arena, these include the ever-increasing number of industry specific digital marketplaces, such as PaperExchange.com and e-Steel.com. Another example is Minneapolis-based 3M Co. which, rather than compete with resellers, is working with them to create web-based, co-branded showrooms for its line of ergonomic products and accessories. The online showrooms allow 3M to control how its products are portrayed and to gather valuable data about users of its products.

☐ Combination of direct and indirect distribution

There are some forms of distribution that might arguably be seen as a combination of both direct and indirect distribution, depending on the terms and conditions of the relationship. These will include the following:

1. Agents
2. Franchise
3. Licensing.

1. Agents

We discussed the role of the agent above. The type of contract and level of control negotiated could be said to dictate the character of the relationship. Sometimes an agent can be contracted to work solely for one company, earning commission on the products and services sold. In this way he or she becomes almost an employee of the supplier and could be said to be working direct. On the other hand the contract and the level of control could be weak. The agent could work for many companies and he or she could be said to be working indirect.

2. Franchise

Almost the best way that the supplier can maintain control over the marketing mix, yet still get many of the advantages gained by using an intermediary, is to use a form of franchising. There are many different forms of franchising in both B2B and B2C (some of them now illegal under anti-competition legislation), but the basic concepts are the same. The supplier of the goods and services will set up the franchisee (the intermediary) in business. In return for an agreed sum of money, a percentage of the sales take and an obligation to buy, the supplier will give corporate identity, help and support and allow the franchisee to market the said supplier's goods and services.

Example 6.10 **B2B franchising**

The International Franchise Association's directory lists over 50 franchise compan- ies under its 'business aids and services' category. There is a broad mix of every- thing from printing companies to executive office suites; from sales consultants to shipping and handling stores; from legal documentation services to companies that sell logo-imprinted pencils, coffee cups, and T-shirts. (www.franchise.org)

3. Licensing

Another form of B2B distribution is for one party, the licensor, to grant permis- sion for another, the licensee, the right to manufacture, produce or market goods, services, patents, etc. belonging to the licensor. One company owning a patent allows another company to manufacture or produce under strict guidelines in return for a royalty payment of some kind. Examples of licensing agreements include part manufacture and bottling as with Coca-Cola and Cadbury Schweppes. Microsoft has more than 1000 companies that license access to the Windows source code. A company might want to license its products or processes for many reasons including the following:

□ No capital outlay in set-up and running costs.

□ It allows speed of coverage, perhaps before the competition can come in.

□ In some countries it might be the only acceptable or viable way to enter the market because of entry restrictions and the necessity of local knowledge.

□ The licensee may have an existing dealer/market network in place.

□ The competition might monopolise the market in some way, leaving little or no room for a new player except by this form of joint partnership.

Example 6.11 **IBM, Ariba and i2 in cross-licensing agreement**

Computer giant IBM announced that it will form an alliance with Ariba (Nasdaq, ARBA) and i2 Technologies (Nasdaq, ITWO) to provide what it calls an 'end-to-end solution for business-to-business (B2B) e-commerce and collaboration', saying the alliance will offer seamless integration of IBM's hardware, software and marketing clout with Ariba's and i2's B2B e-commerce platforms and business support services. While Ariba offers trading and procurement software, i2 provides supply chain management software focused around decision support, forecasting and sup- ply chain management. The financial terms were not disclosed. The agreement also calls for Ariba and i2 to enter into patent cross-licensing agreements with IBM.

Reciprocity

Business buyers will often practise reciprocity. Suppliers are selected on the con- dition that they agree to buy the buyer's products in return, e.g. a paper company might buy chemicals from a chemical company that in turn buys the company's paper. The arrangements can be formal or informal. With formal arrangements the mutual exchange process is built into the contract. Both companies would have to be careful about arrangements of this sort as there can be legal restrictions, under anti-competitive practice legislation, leading to the possibility of heavy fines. Informal arrangements are more common and more difficult to prove. Informal reciprocity might take place because the seller feels it prudent to ingratiate the company with a good customer and so buy needed products in return and/or the products/services are cheaper because of the reciprocal arrangements. Counter-trading, although undertaken by companies, tends to be used when the same practice is applied between countries. This is a common practice, especially when dealing with developing or underdeveloped countries. In some cases reciprocity between companies will be encouraged as a way of increasing international trade. In others it might be considered anti-competitive and therefore illegal.

Bartering

Bartering is a form of reciprocity trading in that there is a direct exchange of merchandise and/or services between two different businesses. One company sells another company computers and instead of taking money in exchange accepts a period of business consultant service. The same problems can arise with bartering products and services as with other reciprocity agreements, discussed above.

Example 6.12 **Bartering on the increase**

While many modern companies struggle in the tough global economic climate, a more primitive form of trade seems to be gaining popularity. The ancient business practice of barter appears to be benefiting from the global slowdown. In some parts of the world many people have no choice and are simply forced to use this form of commerce. The International Reciprocal Trade Association (www.irta.com) says barter companies around the world traded nearly $8 billion of goods and services last year and that figure is expected to grow by 20 per cent this year.

☐ Strategic channel selection

The chosen method of channel selection is usually of strategic importance and should be discussed and agreed at board room level. It will inevitably call for the long-term commitment and coordination of expensive resources and failure to get it right could cause the company unrecoverable pain. There will be many options open, which were discussed above, but unless the company is starting from scratch it will already have methods in use working with accepted industry norms.

Channel selection method

There is no one channel selection method that can be said to be better than another. The method that might be better in one industry will not be so successful in another. Some organisations in the same industry might use different methods. Some might use multiple channel methods to reach their end business customers, while others will use only one. Different buyers might prefer different methods and different methods might be traditionally used in disparate industries. Channel methods might also change from country to country, with one method acceptable in Japan (the greater use of wholesalers) but not in the USA or UK.

> It should be remembered that as environments and markets change marketing mix elements, including channels of distribution, should be strategically examined and evaluated on a regular basis to see if competitive advantage might be gained by offering more customer orientated ways of bringing goods and services to market.

Channel selection in B2C and B2B

Reasons for channel selection in B2B and B2C will be similar in that the end objective is to make the products and services available for the customer in the most effective, efficient and economical way possible. There will, however, be some relative differences and these will include the following:

B2C channels

- ☐ The type of outlet is important in retail marketing as the end consumer likes to see the brand value of the product or service being bought reflected by the quality of the purchasing conditions.
- ☐ The end consumer will usually visit the retail supplier.
- ☐ Tens of thousands of outlets are needed to serve millions of customers.
- ☐ Supplier location and ease of access is important in many instances.
- ☐ Buying ambience and choice of outlet are important.
- ☐ Wholesalers are used.

B2B channels

- ☐ The quality of the selling outlet is not so important in B2B as concern is for functionality and not so much for symbolism.
- ☐ The B2B supplier will usually call on the customer.
- ☐ Relatively few outlets are needed to supply relatively few customers.
- ☐ Location is relatively less important as the supplier will visit the buyer.
- ☐ Buying ambience and choice of outlet are unimportant.
- ☐ Wholesalers are used to a lesser extent.

The differences between selling direct and indirect between B2B and B2C were discussed above.

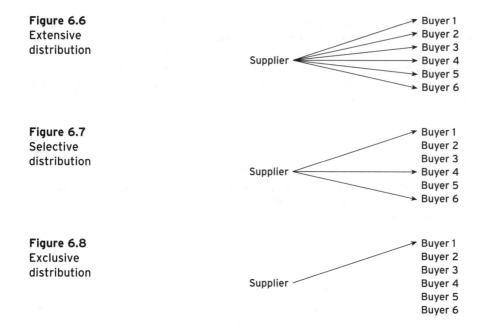

Figure 6.6
Extensive
distribution

Figure 6.7
Selective
distribution

Figure 6.8
Exclusive
distribution

Extensive, selective or exclusive coverage

The supplier channel distribution strategies selected will depend to a certain extent on the market coverage wanted. Depending on company size and products and services produced, extensive, selective or exclusive market coverage might be the channel strategy wanted.

Extensive market coverage

Extensive market coverage as a strategy looks towards securing product sales to every possible buyer type in the market. This could be at national and international level. To make this happen would probably mean using a multi-channel approach. B2B products that might warrant extensive market penetration would include such things as computer software (Figure 6.6).

Selective coverage strategy

Selective coverage strategy is marketing products/services only to selected buyers (Figure 6.7).

Exclusive coverage

Exclusive market coverage consists of distributing to or through only one or a very small number of buyers. This might be because of exclusivity contracts being agreed or because there are only a few buyers in the market for the supplier product or service (Figure 6.8).

☐ Strategic channel selection factors

As we have seen above, there are many ways of reaching the customer by both direct and indirect distribution. What is important to the supplier is to choose the channel method(s) that will be the most cost effective way of achieving customer satisfaction and gaining and maintaining competitive advantage. There is an enormous long-term commitment when choosing a new channel of distribution and to get it wrong can be costly in time, money and opportunity cost. Factors to consider by B2B suppliers when evaluating and selecting the type of distribution channel structure are now discussed.

Buyer product/service needs

Different buyers and segments might want to be approached in different ways depending on the products and services produced. As with most B2B marketing decisions it is important that buyer needs are taken into account. It might be the case that a buyer insists on having selective or exclusive distribution so that the supplier products are unavailable to the competition. A large company might want personal service and a direct approach and/or a range of back-up services that will then dictate the channel method. The fact is that, through complacency and risk avoidance, some organisations would rather stay with existing suppliers than change to others.

Organisational mission and objectives

An organisation will have goals and objectives and these will influence the ultimate choice of a channel. If the marketing objective is for extensive coverage then intermediaries might be used. If speed of coverage, both at a national and international level, is required then a form of franchising might be the most effective. If the buyers are few and scattered then a direct approach by the salesperson might be in order.

Industry structure

No industry will be new to methods of distribution and there will be supply structures and ways of doing things, perhaps going back decades, already in existence. Supplier buyer structures and acceptable ways of working with one another will already be in place and the new entrant might find this very difficult to change and will thus have to abide by these practices. This can be a real dilemma if the distribution arrangements are inclusive and work to shut out newcomers. Cultural factors could add to the problem, especially if wanting to supply to organisations abroad. Many politicians at all levels are now committed to breaking down industry structure barriers, both formal and informal, that operate to restrict new trade in this way.

Role of the competition

When choosing a channel option the amount and role of the competition will need to be considered as all companies will react when another company attempts to move into the market. The competing supplier could develop contracts with major buyers in return for limiting supplies to others. They could load the customer with goods and thus prevent the purchase of the new item. They could lower the prices or offer extra services when news of a possible new entrant surfaces.

One channel method, e.g. sales reps, may be dominated by a well-entrenched competitor forcing other companies to try different channel methods, e.g. taking on an agent.

Example 6.13	**Oligopoly markets**

The wave of mergers in the oil industry has come under close scrutiny from the European Commission. EU competition authorities have launched an in-depth investigation of the planned merger of BP Amoco with Atlantic Richfield Co., better known as Arco. The European Commission appears to be particularly worried that the mergers will create an oligopoly in the oil sector, where just a few players dominate the market for crude oil exploration. The US Federal Trade Commission seems less concerned than its regulatory counterpart in Europe.

Evaluation of current channels and new channels

Unless it is completely new to the market, a company will already be using a channel of distribution. So it will need to examine whether it might continue to use this method, adopt a new method or run both old and new in a multi-channel operation. It will need to undertake a strategic cost benefit analysis taking into account such things as customer, market and product needs, channel advantages and disadvantages, competitive activity and internal resource capabilities.

Products and services offered

There is almost an unlimited amount of different goods and services in the many B2B categories discussed in Chapter 1. The very nature of the benefit offering will almost self-select the channel method. Some B2B services, such as business consultants or advertising agencies, leave very little option but to be delivered direct while others such as cleaning or waste management can take place through intermediaries. One product type, component parts, can be offered on the internet, while another type, capital equipment, would demand direct person-to-person discussion and negotiation. These conditions will apply to very many goods and services.

Type of supply relationship wanted or demanded

Although one-off transactional relationships still exist, there is a movement now for relationship marketing and a closer cooperation between B2B suppliers and buyers involved in any one supply chain. If the dominant player in an industry feels that these closer relationships bring higher benefits, then suppliers will have no choice but to accept the channel of distribution that will comply with this demand. Similarly some suppliers only exist because they supply all or most of their products to one major buyer. Under these developing circumstances many suppliers have lost the ability to choose the channel of supply and must accept the situation given.

Internal resources, skills and competitive strengths

Internal resource capabilities, core skills and competencies will also influence and limit channel choices. However, organisations have discovered ways of creatively using existing competencies to exploit new channel methods and thus gain competitive advantage. It can be argued, however, that if the opportunity is promising enough finance might be made available for additional resources to be brought in. Similarly, as with other business processes, the whole operation might be outsourced to a specialist organisation. Strategic channel design involves the following stages:

- ☐ Specify marketing objectives.
- ☐ Identify and research new buyer needs.
- ☐ Identify existing methods used by the competition.
- ☐ Evaluate current and other channel options.
- ☐ Undertake a cost/benefit analysis.
- ☐ Discuss possible options with the buyer.
- ☐ Select and implement the chosen channel.
- ☐ Monitor and control performance.

Part 2   Managing the supply chain relationship

☐ B2B supply chain structures

There are various forms of B2B channel structures and channel relationships that are adopted for different reasons by participating organisations. The prevalence of one structure will change to accommodate changing environmental circumstances. As competition from all corners of the world has become more intense, B2B organisations are merging with one company acquiring another, strategic and tactical alliances and partnerships are being forged and joint ventures undertaken. In this way companies hope to protect themselves from competition, gain long-term competitive advantage and offer better marketing solutions to solve customer problems all along the supply chain. We can begin by identifying many of the marketing and business structures that companies have adopted, rejected and readopted over the years.

Marketing structures

The following examples of B2B structural types are examined below:

1. Vertical integration
2. Horizontal integration
3. Conglomerate integration
4. Contractual integration
5. Voluntary integration
6. Administered integration
7. Hegemony integration.

1. Vertical integration

This will take two different forms – backward integration and forward integration.

Backward integration
An organisation looks back along the supply chain (upstream) and seeks in some way to control its suppliers. This is usually by acquisition or merger but it can be by some form of coercion. In this way it might hope to achieve one or more of the following:

- ☐ Guarantee supply, crucial in times of shortage or limited supply.
- ☐ Control the quality, input amount and times of supply.
- ☐ Save costs.
- ☐ Offer the opportunity to diversify if business in one of the areas takes a downturn.

Forward integration
Forward integration is where a company looks forward (downstream) along the distribution change and acquires the purchaser of its products. The advantages are similar to backward integration:

- ☐ Guaranteed outlet for its products.
- ☐ Control of the marketing mix and the selling-on process.
- ☐ Opportunity for diversification and profit.
- ☐ Access to more customers.

Some companies will seek both backward and forward integration and so control the whole distribution chain from raw material supplier through to manufacturing and retail.

Disadvantages of vertical integration structures
There are major disadvantages as well as advantages with both backward and forward integration and these will include the following:

☐ Different management skills are needed to run one type of company rather than another. Manufacturing raw material development, wholesaling and retailing all need different skills and success in one area will not guarantee success in another.

☐ There could be a lack of knowledge and experience about the different markets.

☐ Vertical integration could lead to a dilution of company resources.

☐ It can lead to higher prices because of higher levels of single control.

Vertical integration works better in some industries than others but tends to follow a business fashion. When the economy is buoyant and business is good, optimism reigns and mergers take place. The reverse happens when the optimism subsides. Alternatives are to form partnerships and alliances. These options will be discussed in more detail later.

Example 6.14 Gasoline supply

A study of the US petrol industry (Gilbert and Hastings, 2001) looked at the merger of Tosco and Unocal in 1997 that changed the vertical and horizontal structure of a large part of the wholesale and retail market. The data sets showed that an increase in the degree of vertical integration was associated with higher wholesale prices.

---

2. Horizontal integration

Horizontal integration is where one B2B firm will merge in some way with another B2B firm supplying or manufacturing the same or similar products or services on the equivalent channel level. For example, a rubber plantation will take over another rubber plantation; a glass manufacturer will merge with another glass manufacturer; a wholesaler will amalgamate with another wholesaler.

In this way competition can be reduced, economies of scale improved, market share increased and new segments and new customers obtained. This is especially important if the new customer is a market leader and has access to other supply chain customers that are unapproachable in any other way. It can lead, however, to an overstretching of resources, management diseconomies of scale and loss of control and increased bureaucracy associated with large organisations.

Example 6.15 Horizontal integration builds the market

French aluminium producer Pechiney agreed to pay £543 million to steel group Corus for two main aluminium businesses. The sale includes plants in Germany and Belgium as well as interests in joint ventures in Canada and China. The businesses convert aluminium ingots into products such as rods and sheets which are used in the aerospace, car and construction industries. The transaction provides Pechiney with a unique opportunity to develop in the aluminium conversion business, especially in two key markets, aerospace and automotive, now making it a major player.

3. Conglomerate integration

With conglomerate integration a powerful business will buy up a less powerful business at any channel level in often seemingly unrelated markets. So any one company (often a so-called 'holding company') might own a cigarette manufacturer, a brick company, wheat-growing farms, a diamond mine, an insurance company, and so on. There are possible strategic reasons for buying disparate organisations, for example buying at a low price, breaking it up and selling in parts at a combined higher price; or because they were all cash cows capable of making lots of cash with the right skill in strategic management. Conglomerate integration tends also to follow business fashion for reasons similar to those identified when talking about vertical integration.

4. Contractual integration

This is a similar relationship to backward and forward integration except that the relationship between channel members is not ownership but agreed contract. A buyer will not take over a supplier but will negotiate working contracts. The contract may be verbal or written, may be backed up by the force of the law, or based solely on mutual trust. The form of contract (price, terms and conditions, delivery schedule, quality demand, etc.) will depend on the power relationship between the participating members.

Example 6.16 **Less need for B2B vertical integration**

Over the last five or six decades, economists have been explaining why firms become vertically integrated in terms of imperfect information and a desire to reduce transaction costs. These explanations are particularly good for complex manufactured products such as planes, cars, electrical appliances and computers, where numerous component parts can either be manufactured by the firm itself or purchased from outside suppliers. In noting that components could probably be purchased cheaper on the open market, it was realised that firms would have to spend considerable time and money to discover what is available and in negotiating orders. In short, good information is hard to come by and transaction costs are high. This tends to make firms choose to manufacture many components themselves and seek vertical integration. But what happens when circumstances change so that the cost of gathering information and undertaking transactions with suppliers and manufacturers is dramatically lowered? We are alluding of course to the growth and use of the internet in B2B marketing. Opportunities offered in supply chain management could now make it more effective to develop a partnership of some kind and so less necessary or even unprofitable to do everything in-house.

---

5. Voluntary integration

A voluntary integration system can be vertical or horizontal and is a voluntary coming together of channel members who agree to work together for mutual common interest. This relationship might be between firms at a local, national or even global level. They might choose to come together occasionally, perhaps to purchase or supply specific products, or the relationship could encompass many more activities and span a longer time period. Voluntary integration could be informal, with company heads agreeing to undertake particular business activities, or it could be set on a more formal footing with agreed policies put into place and a relationship business structure set up.

6. Administered integration

If the relationship is broader and over a longer time period one member organisation might agree to run and administer the whole business process. For example, a wholesaler might agree to work cooperatively with a group of suppliers to build group market share and economies of scale.

7. Hegemony integration

Hegemony – having power over others – is a type of integration where small companies are tied to larger companies because of the trade that takes place between them. The relationship will not be based on a written contract or, in many instances, even a verbal contract. Many small suppliers will spring up around a B2B buyer, building their trade on the orders they receive, sometimes on an ad hoc basis, from the much larger organisation. They are totally dependent on the one major buyer and can stay in business only as long as the buyer chooses to purchase supplies.

The power in the relationship is one way and the smaller companies have no choice but to accept the status quo. If the purchasing manager decides to buy from other suppliers abroad then some companies would close down overnight.

Large, medium and small organisational structures

There has been an inexorable movement around the world for commercial organisations to grow bigger and bigger. In this manner companies hope to gain economies of scale, access to new customers and markets, and take on competition from around the world. This is happening in both B2B and B2C markets. In fact the three largest organisations in the world cover retailing, manufacturing and raw material supplies: retailer Walmart (turnover nearly $200 billion), car manufacturer General Motors ($185 billion) and oil giant Exxon Mobil ($210 billion). This can cause problems for suppliers as the buyer contacts become less and their power to dominate negotiations increases.

Governments and legal bodies (like the Competition Commission) will step in when the process seems to be getting out of hand and either refuse to let one company merge with another or cause leviathan companies to break into smaller units. Governments have also attempted to break down large public sector utilities when they move from the public to the private sector. As a business grows larger, however, it can allow smaller, more flexible companies to move profitably into niche markets (unattractive to their larger brothers). They can then use these markets as a launch pad to take on larger markets.

☐ The B2B supply chain

Any one supply chain will include all the companies involved in some way in eventually getting a finished product or service from the beginning of the process through to the end business customer or end consumer. If any organisation is unable continually to upgrade its overall productivity in benefit offerings across the entire supply chain, it must eventually become non-competitive, resulting in loss of customers, loss of sales and shrinking profits. As markets become more competitive, customers must be offered ever better value for money in terms of quality, service and price. Today, executives have come to realise their customers' satisfaction or dissatisfaction is linked to the performance of the entire supply chain. To view the supply or distribution chain as a strategic value added process from beginning to end and back again is the challenge that now faces all marketing and business managers, no matter the industry.

☐ The value chain

The value chain is a model that highlights the importance to the organisation of effectively and efficiently managing the whole internal and external supply chain. Internal controls range from raw materials input, operations and output through to business customer usage. The external distribution chain is used to include all the suppliers and buyers that might exist in any one supply chain over a period of time. The analysis focuses on supply chains defined by their product or market characteristics. It takes into account the different storage and transport requirements as well as differences in cost factors, regulations and the general market environment. The model can be broken down into two categories:

1. Internal value chain
2. External value chain.

1. The B2B internal value chain

The internal value chain considers the entire movement of resources through an organisation from inputs and operations through to output, after-sales service and eventual customer satisfaction. Therefore every stage of the process must be thoroughly examined to ensure that it is being carried out in the most effective, efficient and economic way possible. This task can be demonstrated by the use of Porter's internal value chain model (Figure 6.9).

In value chain development each stage of the process should be clearly identified, evaluated and monitored to make certain that it is being performed in the most effective way possible. This can best be undertaken by comparing all value added activity, at every stage of the process, against the most successful organisations in both the same and other industries. A process known as benchmarking best achieves this (discussed in further detail below).

Using the model shown in Figure 6.9, we would expect such things as purchasing, inventory holding, operations methods, marketing, delivery methods, after-sales services and support services to be continually examined and evaluated to make certain that every part was operating in the best possible way. The

Figure 6.9
Internal value
chain

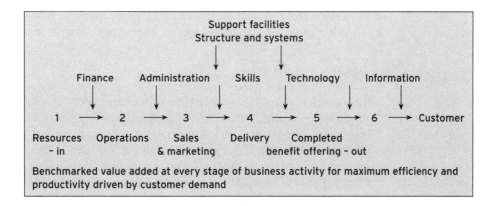

Support facilities
Structure and systems

Finance   Administration   Skills   Technology   Information

1 → 2 → 3 → 4 → 5 → 6 → Customer

Resources   Operations   Sales   Delivery   Completed
 – in   & marketing   benefit offering – out

Benchmarked value added at every stage of business activity for maximum efficiency and
productivity driven by customer demand

overall approach should then be monitored to make certain that it was coming together to achieve optimum business synergy and customer satisfaction. Only in this way can competitive advantage be maintained.

Benchmarking

The continuous, systematic search for, and implementation of, best practices which lead to superior performance.

(The Benchmarking Centre, www.benchmarking.com)

A benchmark is a reference or measurement standard for comparison recognised as the standard of excellence for a specific business process. It can be a financial or non-financial measure. Benchmarking is the process of identifying, learning and adapting outstanding practices and processes from any organisation, in the same or a different industry, adjusted to reflect an individual business situation and then used to help another organisation improve its performance. Information is available from many sources – government, trade associations, commercial businesses – to help an organisation perform benchmarking.

Benchmarking forces organisations to examine present processes, which often leads to improvement and can significantly reduce waste, rework and duplication. World-class benchmarking is looking for best performance in a process, product or service independent of industry, function or location. It is crucial for multinational companies that see themselves as world players. Benchmarking is:

☐ An ongoing management process for continuous improvement along the whole supply chain.

☐ Identifying and examining areas where internal improvement would make the most significant difference to the bottom line, to key areas of the business and to customer relationships.

☐ Providing external focus by setting standards and credible targets according to the 'best' practice that can be found.

☐ Adapting and applying lessons learned from those approaches and ideas to meet and exceed those standards.

☐ Establishing what makes a difference in the customers' eyes between an ordinary supplier and an excellent one. (www.benchmarking.com)

The benchmarking gap

The benchmarking gap is the difference in performance between the benchmark for a particular activity and that of other companies in the comparison or the measured leadership advantage of the benchmark organisation over other organisations. If a company has the resources, benchmarking can be undertaken anywhere in the world. There need to be regular updates of the benchmarking data and feedback of the individual company performance. Tracking the performance relative to the competition over time can be helped by information stored online.

Internal and external benchmarking

Internal benchmarking is performed within an organisation by comparing similar business units or processes, while external benchmarking compares its business units or processes with those of outside organisations.

Strategic benchmarking

This is a systematic business process for evaluating alternatives, implementing strategies and improving performance by understanding and adapting successful strategies from external partners who participate in an ongoing strategic alliance.

Different types of value chains

All organisations, whatever the economic, industrial or business sector, have systems and processes that can be measured, monitored and compared with the 'best in the business'. Taking into account the constraints imposed by different planning needs, value chain development and analysis can be applied to the public sector, not-for-profit and commercial sectors. Hospitals, schools, civil service departments, charities, trade associations, retailers and manufacturers can all profitably learn from undertaking this process so as to achieve greater efficiency in their operations. In B2B markets both suppliers and buyers can gain by the process, which is now examined in more detail.

2. The external value chain

We have discussed the value chain as it relates internally to the individual organisation. However, B2B companies will be involved with other organisations in moving the goods and services from suppliers and producers through to business customers and often on to the end consumer. In many cases, if these relationships up and down the distribution chain are to be mutually productive there must be concern about the efficiency of every member involved in the process. It does not make sense for the buyer to be competitive in every part of the business process only to be let down by a supplier partner who has outdated methods in any part of the activity. This leads us to the realisation that the concept of 'value added analysis' must be applied to every member who might be part of one particular supply chain.

Managing the supply chain

To make this happen partnerships and alliances are sometimes formed between channel members, which we will look at in some detail later. Whether alliances are formed or not, it will often be the case that one member will have more power than others and so dominate and ultimately dictate overall supply chain policy. In many cases this might be the only way the supply chain can be managed in an effective manner. Getting suppliers and manufacturers to trust each other and share sensitive information would be one of the biggest obstacles. Inventory pile-ups and rapid turnover with an effective delivery mechanism become high priority. A good example could be a PC manufacturer: the motherboard may come from Korea, the CD player from Mexico, yet another component from Taiwan. This makes the whole manufacturing process and supply chain very complex. Ultimately, value being added and cost savings will depend on suppliers, distributors, customers and manufacturers working together and giving each other direct access to the entire process.

Example 6.17	**Working together along the value chain**
	Family-owned Yeo Valley has been producing yoghurt for many years, mainly for other companies. It wanted to develop more products using organic milk but a consistent supply seemed difficult to come by. So the company approached a group of farmers and helped them to set up the Organic Milk Suppliers Co-operative, which now has 200 members. Respecting the need for reasonable profits on both sides they gave the farmers long-term contracts so that the market could grow with confidence. The organic market is now worth almost £1 billion a year and growing at 15 per cent a year.

Development of the external value chain

If we take as an example a simple distribution chain (Figure 6.10), it can be seen that there are four organisations involved in the process: two suppliers, a producer and a retailer. Each member will go through the same benchmarking process outlined when we looked at the internal value chain.

The dominant partner in Figure 6.10 might be the retail supermarket chain with a large market share but still in a very competitive market. Having a highly efficient operation and being aware of the pressures to stay ahead, the supermarket management will need to agree benchmark standards and continually monitor performance back along the supply chain so that all members meet the same business standards. In this way the whole operation, including every supplier and

Figure 6.10
External value chain

> Value chain $\longrightarrow$ Value chain $\longrightarrow$ Value chain $\longrightarrow$ Value chain
>
> B2B Supplier $\longrightarrow$ B2B Supplier $\longrightarrow$ B2B Producer $\longrightarrow$ Retailer $\longrightarrow$ End customer
>
> Value benchmarked individually with every supply chain member so the supply chain as a whole operates at maximum effectiveness

producer, will contribute so that the end consumer has products and services second to none.

> This leads us to the realisation that in many modern markets competition is not between one company value chain and another but between one supply value chain and another.

Value chain techniques

Value chain analysis uses every possible relevant tool and technique to improve the way the business is run. This will include the latest technology, communication methods, financial performance measuring techniques and inventory holding and delivery processes. It also means being prepared to adopt proven modern ways of B2B marketing and business management and persuading others in the business relationship about the profitability, for both supplier and customer, in adopting these changes. The measures employed are used to help managerial decision making across the supply chain, at the strategic, tactical and operational levels. They should also enable the identification of drivers for future value creation through improvements in the supply chain.

The heart of the concept is that more value can be achieved by supply chain members working in harmony with one another rather than as isolated business units.

Demand and supply chains

It could be argued that viewing the distribution chain as a 'supply' chain looks at the problem from the point of view of the supplier rather than the customer, which could be considered the wrong approach. If the right approach is managing the distribution chain so that value is added for the customer, then distribution effectiveness and value chain analysis should be addressed from the perspective of customer satisfaction and seen as a demand chain rather than a supply chain.

Efficient consumer response

Efficient consumer response (ECR) looks at the retail distribution chain from end consumer needs, working back upstream to the retailer, then to the manufacturer, supplier and raw material producer (Figure 6.11). It is a form of external value chain implementation initiated by large grocery retailers across the western world.

Figure 6.11
Demand chain – customer driven

Value benefits wanted ⟶

The demand chain – customer driven:
End consumer ⟶ Retailer ⟶ Manufacturer ⟶ Supplier ⟶ Raw material producer

The supply chain – business organisation driven (dominated by the most powerful):
Raw material producer ⟶ Supplier ⟶ Manufacturer ⟶ Retailer ⟶ Customer

Beset by continuous pressures on margins because of consumer demand for more choice and better value, they looked to remove costs from along the whole of the supply chain. At the heart of ECR was a business environment characterised by dramatic advances in information technology, shifts in consumer demand, and the increasing movement of goods across international borders aided by the internal European market. This new reality required a fundamental reconsideration of the most effective way of delivering the right products to consumers at the right price. Non-standardised operational practices and rigid separation of the traditional roles of manufacturer and retailer threatened to block the supply chain unnecessarily and failed to exploit the synergies that came from powerful new information technologies and planning tools. To better serve the consumer, ECR set out to invert the traditional model and break down non-productive barriers. The impacts were extensive and continue to resonate across industry.

Traditionally the fast moving consumer goods (FMCG) supply chain was fragmented into separate competing companies, with interface costs arising between supplier and supplier, producer and supplier, and supplier and retailer. Each link in the supply chain controlled and knew about only a small proportion of total stock in that chain. It was shown that by working together, sharing information and building compatible systems, companies could integrate the supply chain, remove inefficiencies and thus offer the customer better value.

The important concept here was that improvements came about, not by looking at the needs of channel members, but by looking at the whole system from the point of view of ultimate and continuous customer satisfaction. So starting with the needs and wants of the end consumer, both at the present time and predicting into the future, the process was moved back upstream with participants looking at whatever improvements could be made.

Example 6.18 **ECR Europe**

In 1995, the ECR initiative was launched in Europe by the ECR Europe Executive Board. The board includes representatives from Tesco along with other major European grocery manufacturing and retailing companies, as well as service providers such as GE Information Services. ECR initiatives now exist in the USA, Africa, Australia and Asia. (ECR Europe, www.ecrnet.org)

Methods used in internal and external value chain development

Many methods have now been adopted in both ECR and wider value chain development. Existing methods are being constantly updated and new initiatives explored. Many of these value chain component parts are identified below.

Collaborative planning, forecasting and replenishment (CPFR)

Collaborative planning, forecasting and replenishment (CPFR) is one of the important programmes to be developed from Efficient Consumer Response (ECR).

It has consequences for all members along the supply chain. The concept requires retailers, manufacturers and suppliers to agree on sales forecasts for a given period based on sales history, promotion plans and other significant data in order to establish pre-set order amounts. CPFR is supposed to level traditional supply peaks and valleys and reduce out-of-stock situations at the retail level, show comparisons between different trade-offs in the supply chain, for example between stock levels and transport frequency, and thus increase sales and reduce costs. By relating operational supply chain measures to cost structures and financial indicators, comparisons of the financial impact on both operational efficiency and the overall competitiveness of the supply chain can be analysed and evaluated.

Electronic data interchange (EDI)

Electronic data interchange (EDI) is a computer-to-computer exchange of business documents between trading partners using acceptable standards via communication links. These standards are predetermined formats (EDI standards) developed by industry experts and approved by overseeing EU and US standards bodies. EDI requires all supply chain members to use compatible IT hardware and software so business partners can talk easily to one another in the same language. EDI has been shifting the way companies do business for a long time and there are now thousands of companies using it on a daily basis electronically to process business documents between each other. This will include order and acknowledgement documents, processing and delivery documents, and invoicing and payment received documents. It can also be used for marketing research and selling products. Cost effectiveness, accelerated turnaround time, improved customer service and the development of a just-in-time inventory programme are just a few of the benefits that can be associated with the advantages of setting up an EDI programme.

Use of the extranet

Linked to EDI, the extranet, a private internet system, refers to an intranet that is partially accessible to authorised outsiders. Whereas an intranet is protected by firewalls and is accessible only to employees of the same company or organisation, an extranet provides various levels of accessibility to outsiders. Right of entry is given to business supply chain partner organisations (through a password) so all are able to have access and exchange information online. This gives suppliers an immediate insight to such business areas as sales figures as well as stock movements and stock needs.

Just in time (JIT)

Just-in-time systems (JIT) consist of production and inventory control systems designed to produce small lots of goods and services and to produce the right items in the quantities needed by subsequent production processes at the right time. This will be discussed in more detail under physical distribution.

JIT will incorporate processes such as continuous replenishment programmes (CRP).

Activity based costing (ABC)

Activity based costing (ABC) builds a structure for the business that attempts to show how costs and profits are generated for each product and customer. It is a financial method that, more realistically than in the past, attempts to pinpoint the cost, revenue generator and profit from each and every activity. It should identify processes that are efficient and those that are not; products that produce good revenue and those that do not; customers along the supply chain that yield a profit and customers that seem always to generate costs (even sometimes the heavy users of a product or service).

Activity based management (ABM) is the application of activity based costing to improve business performance.

Total quality management (TQM)

TQM is a customer-focused management philosophy and management strategy that seeks continuous improvement in business processes using analytical tools and teamwork that encompass the participation of all employees along both the internal and external value chains.

A collaborative culture

More idealistic, but nevertheless a goal to be sought, is the need to construct a collaborative culture across the whole supply chain. While difficult to implement within an organisation, it is an even bigger task across the whole external supply chain. It can be characterised by a shared vision, shared leadership, empowered and motivated workers, cooperation among organisational units as they work to improve processes, a high degree of openness to feedback and data, and optimisation of the organisational whole versus its many parts. For it to happen support must come from the very top and it must be seen from a strategic perspective. All staff must be included in discussions, information made readily available and individual objectives agreed.

Category management

Category management is the management of product categories as strategic business units. The practice empowers a category manager with full responsibility for the assortment decisions, inventory levels, shelf space allocation, promotions and buying. With this authority and responsibility, the category manager is able to judge more accurately the consumer buying patterns, product sales and market trends of that category. It has implications for B2B as well as B2C because all suppliers along the supply chain will be expected to develop programmes that adhere to this overriding imperative.

Other value chain resources

Manufacturing resource planning (MRP) is a process for determining material, labour and machine requirements in a manufacturing environment.

MRPII is the consolidation of material requirements planning (MRP), capacity requirements planning (CRP) and master production scheduling (MPS).

MRP was originally designed for materials planning only. When labour and machine (resources) planning were incorporated it became known as MRPII.

There are myriad other software packages to meet ever more demanding value chain needs, including customer relationship management (CRM), manufacturing execution systems (MES), advanced planning and scheduling (APS), warehouse management systems (WMS) and transportation management systems (TMS).

Advantages from building supply/demand chain relationships

Such relationships can lead to more effective and efficient ways of working together and produce cost and time savings by the following:

☐ The whole supply chains is coordinated and organised centrally, rather than by each individual member adding value and then connecting to the whole.

☐ Competitors' supply chains can be benchmarked and compared across the whole business process rather than by each individual element.

☐ Helping to set up a collaborative and motivating culture.

☐ Minimising or eliminating overlapping work practices.

☐ Standardising processes, products and services.

☐ Sharing valuable resources including access to skills, knowledge and technology.

☐ Sharing information sources in real time.

☐ Shared monitoring, feedback and control mechanisms.

☐ Allowing for customer satisfaction and service to drive the whole supply chain process.

Disadvantages from building supply/demand chain relationships

As with all good ideas there tend to be some that gain more than others in the process, and supply chain relationships are no different. The following might be considered as disadvantages:

☐ Supply chain cost savings are gained by the more powerful members forcing price cuts on weaker members.

☐ Strategic objectives set by the stronger members may be at the expense of the weaker.

☐ All members are forced to purchase and use standardised resources such as IT hardware and software that can be an expensive outlay, especially if contracts are lost.

☐ Entrepreneurial spirit can be dampened by the need to conform to supply chain conditions.

☐ Employees can be demotivated by feeling lost among the greater number of people involved.

☐ Outsourcing

Although an organisation may feel responsible for every link in the external supply chain, it will find that it cannot do everything itself even if it is totally vertically integrated. We have seen above that it must be able to work with other organisations and we identified many different marketing and supply structures it might use to be able to optimise its overall effectiveness. In some cases it may find that it can even achieve better business results by involving outside organisations in some of the value added processes that take place within the company along the internal supply chain. A business process known as outsourcing is the way that this can be achieved.

B2B business process outsourcing and information technology outsourcing

Outsourcing is the purchasing of a function or functions once administered in-house from another business – an independent contractor – and usually applies to a complete business process. In business process outsourcing (BPO) a third party will be given the opportunity to manage the entire business process, such as accounting, procurement, logistics, marketing and customer services, human resources and even manufacturing.

Concomitant with the expansion in information technology is the growth in IT outsourcing (ITO). With ITO organisations are contracted to manage a particular application, including all related servers, networks and software upgrades. They can be located anywhere in the world and, because of savings in labour and other costs, countries like India now host B2B and B2C customer call centres for enquiries, information, sales and transactions coming from EU countries on the other side of the world. In fact there seems to be nothing that cannot now be outsourced, leading to the concept of the 'virtual' company where only senior entrepreneurial management remains in place overseeing and organising every outsourcing business process.

Example 6.19

Industry analysts predict growth in outsourcing of customer care by utilities in 2002

Research analysts are heralding the outsourcing of services like billing and customer care as a critical path to profitability in today's uncertain utility market. Outsourcing offers a cost-effective alternative to customer care and business process management operations that can improve cash flow, customer satisfaction, and earnings per share for electric, gas and water companies. Using the latest customer care and billing management services, technology processes allow utilities to deliver world-class customer service while controlling costs.

B2B outsourcing and job/batch contract work

Outsourcing is different from job and batch contract work. With job and batch contract work companies are invited in and given instructions on a part of the process. This might be on a one-off or contract basis. They will not be given responsibility for the whole business process. Outsourcing is dissimilar in that the person contracting for the services will have the right to control or direct only the result of the work and not the means and methods of accomplishing the result. In other words, they contract for certain work to be done, but do not tell you when, where or how to do the work. It implies responsibility and a high degree of managerial control and risk on the part of the service provider.

Performance based pricing (PBP) contractual pricing mechanisms can be used that link outsourcer compensation to the meeting of discussed and agreed specific performance objectives. Performance objectives met can trigger bonuses while the opposite can trigger penalty payments. Gainsharing is a contract structure where both the customer and provider share financially in the value created through the relationship. One example is when a service provider receives a share of the savings it generates for its client. Outsourcing should not be confused with mergers, acquisitions, and strategic alliances, which are discussed below.

Outsourcing in the public sector

In many countries outsourcing in the public sector has become mandatory as government ministers seek to inject commercial pressures into many national and local government services. It was argued that in-house public sector departments needed the spur of competition to improve management and service effectiveness and efficiency. The inception of Compulsory Competitive Tendering (CCT) forced national and local government departments to allow outside commercial companies to tender for services such as waste disposal, catering and road maintenance as well as administration activities to do with the running of the public sector. In some instances the running of schools, prisons and even parts of the policing service have also been contracted to outsourcing companies. Bidding and tendering terms and conditions are very strict in this sector and even to be considered for participation can be time consuming and frustrating. Outsourcing in this sector can be controversial and always open to public scrutiny because public money is being spent and public services are under consideration. There are many examples of bad publicity because employees are paid less and services are worse under a new, commercial, regime.

Example 6.20	**Reluctance to bid for outsourcing contracts**

Share price weakness has affected controversial government plans to outsource more public service contracts. Many UK services firms have seen their share prices fall steeply this week, in a sign that investors are losing confidence in the complex 'public-private partnership' deals used to encourage private sector companies to bid for government contracts.

Why outsource?

Companies outsource for both strategic and tactical reasons. Strategic outsourcing is used to achieve a better return on investment and accelerated growth by using outside organisations that can offer specialist, leading edge knowledge and skills in specific business areas. The effects – redirection of the organisation's resources towards its highest value creating activities and core competencies – can happen quickly and with the minimum of capital investment. Senior executives can stand back and look objectively at all business process areas, decide which to keep in-house and which to outsource, set clear and measurable benchmarked performance indicators, and then monitor and control the whole operation from a corporate and marketing perspective. Built-in success and penalty clauses and frequent contract cost benefit analysis should ensure that customer driven performances are maintained on a continuous basis.

Transformational outsourcing can be used to take advantage of innovation and new business models and is approached as a way to reposition the organisation for competitive advantage.

Tactical outsourcing, on the other hand, is seen as a way to achieve operational efficiencies and is sometimes used to create competition between existing internal operations and outside service providers, in this way improving overall value for money.

Nevertheless there are examples of organisations bringing business processes back in-house because of disappointing outcomes. This might be because of performances not reaching the desired and needed level or the difficulties of creating a holistic approach to customers and markets because processes are atomised across different independent companies. It can be that outsourcing companies have several contracts and so cannot give complete focused attention to any one company. Other problems have arisen, especially across areas of IT, where the clients' needs are not fully understood and unworkable solutions are promised to obtain the contract, resulting in expensive failure all round.

Marketing the B2B outsourcing process

Outsourcing is a very competitive process and those companies taking part will need to market and sell their competencies in competition with others wanting to obtain the contract in more or less the same way as any other B2B strategic solution-solving service. The client buying process will often be long and complex because of the importance of the strategic issues. This means that all the factors discussed under B2B decision making in Chapter 4, including the decision making unit (DMU), decision making process (DMP) and buying decision difficulty (BDD), must be considered when the outsourcer is in talks with a client. Terms and conditions demanded by the buyer will vary in line with strategic needs and some are more stringent and bureaucratic than others. This is especially so in the public sector where public money is being spent and the political fallout from failure can be immense. As with all long-term contracts, to put together an intricate bid and not obtain the sale can be very expensive and time wasting for the unsuccessful participant.

Advantages of outsourcing

☐ Obtain the benefits from organisations with highly trained and experienced staff.

☐ Gain a focused approach from companies specialising in different business areas.

☐ Set, monitor and adjust performance indicators.

☐ Pay and set penalties according to these performance indicators.

☐ Able to stand back and objectively assess business processes in isolation.

☐ No cost of ownership.

☐ No need to obtain approval for capital spending.

☐ Costs can be budgeted as a monthly expense.

☐ Predictable costs only pay for what is needed.

☐ Fast and simple implementation.

Disadvantages of outsourcing

☐ Loss of customer ownership and customer information.

☐ Loss of skills and knowledge in business outsourcing areas.

☐ Innovation gains go to outsourcing company.

☐ Lack of focused attention if outsourcing company has many clients.

☐ Difficult to back source if anything goes wrong.

☐ Loss of synergy.

☐ Performances not reaching desired level.

☐ Misunderstanding on the specific needs of the client company.

☐ Unrealistic solutions promised.

☐ In the public sector always open to public scrutiny.

☐ Leasing

Some organisations choose to lease business assets such as land, property, equipment, transport, computers, etc. rather than buying. A lease is a contract in which the legal owner of the property or other asset agrees to another person using that property or asset in return for a regular specified payment (known as rent) over a set term. In addition to buildings, other items such as cars and computers are often leased in order to avoid capital costs in the running of a business. In some leasing contracts the lessee is able to buy the goods at the end of the contract. Leasing is used in B2C markets, but to a very small extent when compared with B2B.

Sell and lease-back

A sell and lease-back is a situation whereby a property is sold by its owner to another person or company on condition that the purchaser leases the property back to the original owner for an agreed rent over a set term. This enables the original owner to raise capital that can be used for other purposes. It also lowers the amount of capital employed in running the business, with the possibility then of improving the corporate return on capital employed (ROCE) ratio.

☐ Other business relationship forms

We can now identify other relationships used by organisations to gain business success and maintain competitive advantage.

Mergers

Mergers are a full joining together of two previously separate corporations. A true merger in the legal sense occurs when both businesses dissolve and fold their assets and liabilities into a newly created third entity. This entails the creation of a new corporation. The term merger is frequently used in conjunction with the term acquisition, as in mergers and acquisitions. Mergers occur if both particip-ants see the new company as a way of adding business strength and gaining added shareholder value.

As with all types of relationships, however, the result will frequently favour one company more than another, depending on the position of strength brought to the negotiations. If company A merges with company B, the resulting com-pany might then be called company AB. An agreed merger is where both com-panies want to merge. A hostile attempted takeover is where one company objects. To avoid a hostile takeover the target company may seek a 'white knight', another company with which it would prefer to merge.

Acquisitions

In business parlance an acquisition means taking possession of another business or another business division. This can be by consent of both parties or by a so-called hostile takeover where the company under threat fights to prevent its pur-chase. Fierce battles between both sets of senior managers can occur when this happens (sometimes fought out in combative press campaigns) as shareholders are persuaded either to sell or not to sell their shares. The big pension fund man-agers who control large blocks of shares in companies more often than not decide the outcome. The acquisition can be by vertical, horizontal or, less often, con-glomerate integration for the business reasons discussed under these headings. As with mergers, if it is to be considered successful the final outcome should add value in such areas as customers served, market share gained and eventual share-holder return.

The Competition Commission will investigate large acquisitions and mergers if the resulting company might seem to break anti-monopoly rules.

Example 6.21 | ## Mergers and acquisitions

In 2001 and 2002 US computer giant Hewlett-Packard merged with Compaq computers in an $18.6 billion tie-up. Northrop Grumman, the US defence company, merged with US weapons maker TRW for the equivalent of $7.8 billion. Ameritrade, the online brokerage company, agreed to pay $1.3 billion for rival Datek. Distressed Korean car-maker Daewoo Motors was taken over by US auto giant General Motors. The oil giant Chevron's $39 billion acquisition of fellow oil firm Texaco was approved by US regulators.

Joint ventures

Joint ventures involve two or more businesses joining together under a contractual agreement to conduct a specific business enterprise in which both parties share profits and losses. Strictly speaking, a joint venture is for one specific project and should not be confused with a strategic alliance, which is a term used for more of a continuing business relationship.

Example 6.22 | ## Troubled joint venture

Swedish mobile phone firm Ericsson has said it will axe 4000 jobs from its information technology operations. The work currently done by the group's IT employees will be outsourced. The news came soon after a suggestion by the chief executive that Ericsson might pull out of its loss-making phone making joint venture with Sony.

Strategic alliance

A strategic alliance is a partnership in which two or more business organisations combine efforts in a business effort involving anything from getting a better price for goods by buying in bulk together, to seeking new customers and markets, with each providing part of the product. The basic idea behind alliances is to minimise risk while maximising the power and force of each member; for example, BA coming together with United Airlines to share markets, flight routes and landing opportunities; or car manufacturers sharing an internet market portal to invite component bids from suppliers around the world. It might also be the only way for a company to move into a foreign country.

Example 6.23 | ## Association of Strategic Alliance Professionals

The Association of Strategic Alliance Professionals (ASAP) is a professional organisation dedicated to strategic alliances. By providing management resources, sharing best practices and supporting the professional development of those involved in strategic alliances, ASAP is committed to providing the professional and educational support that executives and managers of strategic alliances need to be successful. It offers members the following services:

Example 6.23 continued

   □ sharing information on opportunities for strategic alliances

   □ disseminating best practices in the management of strategic alliances

   □ raising awareness of the unique professional discipline of strategic alliance management and its contribution to both individual companies and the field of management. (www.strategic-alliances.org)

Use of mergers, acquisitions, joint ventures and strategic alliances

Mergers, acquisitions, joint ventures and strategic alliances are used in national, international and global markets and can appear in different forms depending on the objectives and strategies of the participating players. The following might be reasons for building these types of relationships and alliances:

□ Gain economies of scale.

□ Build market share.

□ Shut out the competition.

□ Share mutual distribution systems, customers and markets.

□ Share resources including finance, skills, knowledge, information and technology.

□ Gain access to restricted resources such as patents, licences, customers and markets.

□ Gain access to cultural and political knowledge and influence.

□ Share managerial and entrepreneurial knowledge and skills.

This area will be discussed again in more detail when we look at strategic entry methods and international and global marketing.

Example 6.24 A failed alliance

A decade ago, IBM and Apple launched a much-vaunted strategic alliance, including investments in joint ventures and research. Together they intended to take on Intel and Microsoft. It didn't happen. Eight years later the alliance faded away, leaving unfulfilled hopes, frayed relationships and wasted effort.

Factors to consider in a B2B partnership

1. *Total commitment*. There must be a total commitment from all senior managers to want to make the partnership successful.

2. *Strategic fit*. Objectives and strategies in the chosen area of activity should be complementary.

3. *Cultural fit.* Employees from each company must be able to work with one another.

4. *Risk sharing.* All business ventures will incur risk of some kind and participating organisations must be aware of this when discussing the level and type of commitment.

5. *Resource allocation.* Both sides must allocate sufficient resources.

6. *Knowledge exchange.* Partners will be expected to share knowledge and expertise and a company may be loath fully to disclose important valuable information in case the partnership fails.

Part 3 Management of logistics in B2B markets

Management of logistics is the process that plans, implements and controls the efficient, effective flow and storage of goods, services and related information from the point of origin to the point of consumption in order to meet customers' requirements. It is making sure that raw material, components and products and services are available at every needed stage of the supply chain operation in the right number, at the right time, at the right costs and of the right quality. If any of this fails the whole production activity can at best be non-competitive and at worst can grind to a halt.

☐ Reverse logistics

With reverse logistics the supply chain flows opposite to the traditional process of order acceptance and fulfilment. For example, reverse logistics includes the handling of customer returns, disposal of excess inventory and return journeys of empty trucks and freight cars.

☐ B2B physical distribution

Physical distribution involves the physical movement of goods and services from supplier to producer, from producer to wholesaler and retailer and eventually to the end consumer. It involves planning, implementing and controlling the physical flow of goods from company to company efficiently, effectively and at the lowest possible costs. B2B organisations can be involved in the movement of their own goods; they can have their own goods and services transported by others; or they can be involved in transporting others' goods and services. The function of physical distribution consists of the principal subfunctions of transportation, order processing, warehousing, inventory and inventory control, packing and packaging, and materials handling.

In addition to the subfunctions, distribution managers get involved in many decisions that are related to the distribution process, including product design and the location of fixed facilities. The transportation subfunction often includes the management of a transport subsidiary, as well as purchase of transportation services from lease or hire companies.

Physical distribution management (PDM)

Physical distribution management (PDM) is concerned with ensuring the right product is in the right place at the right time at the right costs. To think of the logistical process merely in terms of transportation is much too narrow a view. PDM is concerned with the flow of goods from the receipt of an order until the goods are delivered to the customer. In addition to transportation, PDM involves close liaison with production planning, purchasing, order processing, material control and warehousing. All these areas must be managed so that they interact efficiently with each other to provide the level of service that the customer demands and at a cost that the company can afford.

> Physical distribution management (PDM) is concerned with ensuring the right product is in the right place at the right time at the right costs.

There are four principal components of PDM:

1. Stock levels or inventory
2. Order processing
3. Warehousing
4. Transportation.

1. Stock levels or inventory

Stock holding is another important area where decisions need to be made with regard to customer satisfaction. There will always be a trade-off between stock levels, stock choice and the costs involved. The seller's sales staff and the buying organisation will always want every item held in stock for immediate delivery while the financial director, ever cost conscious, will want the minimum levels possible. Some kind of inventory control is crucial to maintain the right amount of each item in stock or to maintain the required level of service at the minimum cost. Other factors concerning supplier stock are now considered.

Cost of holding large amounts of goods in stock

Holding large amounts of material and goods in stock can be an enormous drain on cash flow and all organisations have to make the choice between how much to hold for customer satisfaction and the overall cost and space involved. Using a 'just-in-case' (JIC) philosophy, large amounts of inventory were held in company warehouses just in case there was a sudden shortage brought about by such things as increase in demand from existing or new buyers or a shortage brought about by bad weather, labour strikes or transportation problems. A whole range of products might be stocked including unusual and seldom demanded shapes, sizes and designs for the occasion when the odd one might be wanted. B2B organisations holding material and goods in stock across the whole portfolio for the contingencies outlined here can cost billions of pounds in what was considered an unproductive use of company resources, and the idea of 'just in time' (JIT) was developed. Companies now try to resolve the problem by holding as little as possible in stock themselves and being able to call on suppliers for immediate or quick delivery. This means that suppliers and producers have to work extremely closely with one another (the supplier even basing itself within the buyer complex) as a breakdown in supplies could lead to a loss of sales.

Just-in-time stockholding

JIT is a Japanese management philosophy which has been applied in practice since the early 1970s in many Japanese manufacturing organisations and subsequently adopted by the industries in the west. It was developed and perfected within the Toyota manufacturing plants by Taiichi Ohno as a means of meeting consumer demands with minimum delays.

The alternative to JIT, 'just in case' (JIC), meant that an organisation would hold large amounts of stock (sometimes for weeks or months) just in case there was a shortage or increase in demand. This could be very costly and would be reflected in the sell-on costs. The advantages of JIT for the buyer are that non value-added tasks involved with buying, warehousing and moving the large amounts of stock around are avoided. It is a process developed for buying in stock from suppliers only at the very moment of use. It encompasses such processes as lot to lot (LTL), a rule defined on inventory items wherein a certain amount of product or material is reordered so there is just enough to cover the next time period in the demand schedule. A so-called 'reorder point' is a low-water mark on inventory levels that triggers a reorder notification.

JIT saves costs by cutting down inventory levels, not needing large warehouses holding many months' supply of stock, eliminating delay and requiring near-zero defects and fast set-up times, particularly for repetitive, discrete manufacturing. It lowers insurance costs (as less stock is held) and reduces the opportunity for pilfering and the likelihood of damaged and outdated material and goods. On the other hand it should be remembered that many of the costs associated with these savings will be passed on to the supplier.

The biggest disadvantage of JIT for the buyer is the fear that the right material and goods will not available when wanted. There must be a close professional relationship between buyer and supplier, with highly organised systems for ordering raw materials and component parts to make certain that there are no delays at any stage as shortages of stocks can result in serious delays in production. There can also be higher costs in not holding stock due to economy of scale losses associated with one-off bulk deliveries. In some cases this can be offset by period targets (yearly?) and retrospective discounts given on the amount taken during the given period. Payment might be spread over a longer period matching deliveries. This will be good for the buyer, but less welcomed by the supplier.

Kanban

Kanban is a simple just-in-time (JIT) control system for coordinating the movement of material to feed the production line. The method uses standard containers or lot sizes with a single card attached to each. It is a pull system in which work centres signal with a card that they wish to withdraw parts from feeding operations or vendors. Loosely translated from Japanese, the word kanban literally means 'billboard' or 'sign'.

JIT systems become more complex

Gradually simple just-in-time control systems become more sophisticated as buyers demanded better and better stock control management. As fast as one organisation gained competitive advantage by more planning and cooperating with a supplier, another organisation would fight back and so improve the process. Management consultants moved in and improved the process even more. The rapid growth in IT brought many more options and future possibilities look endless. The following inventory management techniques ensued.

Continuous replenishment

Building on the beliefs underpinning JIT is the concept of continuous replenishment. This is the practice of partnering between supply channel members that changes the traditional replenishment process from distributor-generated purchase orders, based on economic order quantities, to the replenishment of products based on actual and forecasted product demand. This will require even closer contact between supplier and buyer.

Direct procurement

Direct procurement is the purchasing of raw materials and parts needed for the manufacturing of finished goods. Automating direct procurement can enable faster cycle times, making a manufacturer more responsive to the market. Significant savings can be realised by optimising the process of order submission and confirmation, as well as improved vendor collaboration. This results in fewer shortages of essential materials, thus reducing the need for large inventories along the supply chain.

Materials requirement planning (MRP)

Materials requirement planning (MRP) was developed during the 1980s, brought about by the realisation that materials requirements should be planned from forecast demand and purchasing through to inventory control, production scheduling and usage to invoicing and payment. It has since been superseded by enterprise resource planning (ERP).

Enterprise resource planning (ERP)

ERP developed with the realisation that no one part of the business could be seen to act in isolation from all other business processes. Using the power of developing computer software systems, ERP is being positioned as the foundation and integration of enterprise-wide information systems. Such systems will link together all of a company's operations, including human resources, manufacturing, finance, sales, purchasing, inventory management, and distribution, as well as connecting the organisation to its customers and suppliers. These systems usually have extensive set-up options that allow their functionality to be customised to meet specific business needs.

Vendor managed inventory (VMI)

Building on the above techniques and use of the extranet, vendor managed inventory (VMI) is a just-in-time technique whereby a supplier of goods is able to manage the inventory process more comprehensively. The supplier can access the inventory records of a customer to determine whether to make a shipment to that customer. They can look into buyer stock levels and identify shortages and are then able to refill stock automatically without the buyer initiating the order. The customer can be notified electronically when goods are to be sent and their inventory records updated accordingly. The supplier can even enter a selective part of the buyer's bank account and take payment when due. As cost savings were highlighted by these processes, we gradually see an evolutionary building of trust and a more cooperative way of working between buyer and seller, leading to the value chain relationships discussed earlier in the chapter.

Advantages of JIT/ERP and VMI developments

Buyer advantages

- ☐ Close relationship enables continuous discussion leading to more accurate benefits.
- ☐ Keeps stock of raw materials and component parts as low as possible.
- ☐ Saves costs until the stock is needed.
- ☐ Saves on timings and space.
- ☐ Lower security and insurance costs.
- ☐ Less opportunity for pilfering, write-downs and spoilage.
- ☐ For the wholesaler and retailer less storage space and more selling space available.
- ☐ Smaller transport system.

Supplier advantages

- ☐ Guaranteed contract.
- ☐ Learning associated with a close working relationship.
- ☐ Close relationship can build loyalty, trust and long-term contracts.

Disadvantages of JIT/ERP and VMI developments
There could be high set-up costs involved for all members.

Buyer disadvantages

- ☐ Goods not available when wanted.
- ☐ Higher costs in not ordering in bulk delivery.
- ☐ Delivery and transport problems associated with frequent deliveries.

Supplier disadvantages

- ☐ Payment spread over a longer period according to the contract.
- ☐ Possibility of erratic ordering if buyer sales and needs fluctuate.
- ☐ Higher storage and delivery costs.
- ☐ Higher insurance and security costs.

2. Order processing

We can look at order processing in terms of both B2B seller and buyer concerns:

(a) Seller concerns

(b) Buyer concerns.

(a) Seller concerns

Order processing is the business function concerned with following the buyer order from the moment the sale is made through to delivery and payment. It is axiomatic that a sale is not a sale until payment is received and many organisations forget this at their peril. In fact more small companies go out of business because of lack of order payment and cash than for any other reason. The written, verbal or electronically received order must be processed through the organisational system and this can cause all sorts of problems if controls are not of the highest order.

Fulfilment is the process that occurs when an order is received by the supplier or by an intermediary of some kind. Fulfilment processes often include tasks such as customer order management, shipping management, returns and status tracking. When the order is received the following factors need to be considered:

☐ Is the prospective buyer legitimate, do they have a record of bad debt and/or do they have adequate funds for repayment?

☐ Has the salesperson given the right information? Are the needed products, make, size, specification and customisation in accordance with customer specifications in stock or, if not in stock, is a request for manufacture or a supply order sent and the customer notified about any time delay?

☐ A pro-forma invoice is sent to the customer with product description, costs, delivery point and expected payment terms and conditions.

☐ In some cases insurance will be necessary and responsibility for cost must be clear.

☐ Care must be taken if the product is to be shipped over long distances including overseas. It will need to be clear where the delivery responsibility ends and the customer collects. This could be free delivery to the dockside, on board ship, to the embarkation port or all the way to the buyer's premises.

☐ Correct products are allocated and a delivery time confirmed.

☐ Tracking procedures might be necessary if the product has to travel long distances to make certain that movement is happening as planned.

☐ Products are dispatched and received by the customer, shown by a signed delivery note.

☐ A correctly priced invoice is on time and a check carried out to make certain payment is made when it should have been made. Reminders will need to be sent out if necessary.

☐ Product returns policies are adhered to.

Despite the development of sophisticated computerised order-processing systems, many organisations still have inadequate order-processing systems that can cause many problems. These are identified below.

Time and speed in processing

Delays in processing orders and invoices can be costly in terms of the time it takes to get the order from the salesperson into the system and the products delivered. The speed of order delivery is a major way of gaining competitive advantage. Issuing payment invoices late can mean payment delays and cash flow problems. The use of sophisticated complementary IT applications has allowed organisations to become more professional in this area, as discussed below.

Accuracy

Dispatching the wrong stock because of unsound processing systems can cause both customer irritation and excess company costs. Invoices wrongly assessed can also cost money in terms of underpricing when inadequate payments will be received. If products are found to be wrongly priced, then not only will there be extra costs in rectifying the mistakes but customer confidence will begin to be dented.

Information

Customer information must be up-to-date, accurate and clearly reflect the needs of the customer.

Example 6.25   **FedEx – collection, delivery and tracking**

FedEx is the delivery company with a website offering a feature that allows customers to generate their own unique bar-coded shipping labels and summon couriers to pick up shipments. FedEx technology enables customers, couriers and contract delivery personnel to wirelessly access the company's information systems networks anytime, anywhere. FedEx couriers, contract delivery personnel and other team members use wireless data collection devices to scan bar codes on shipments. These 'magic wands' are a key part of what makes it possible for you to find out where your package is in transit, whether on a FedEx Express jet speeding across the Atlantic Ocean or a FedEx Ground tractor-trailer on the Pennsylvania Turnpike. On average, FedEx Express and FedEx Ground packages are scanned at least a dozen times from pick-up to delivery. At pick-up, each package's shipping label bar code is immediately scanned to record the pick-up time, destination and delivery commitment. The scanned information is uploaded to the FedEx mainframe. Bar codes are scanned again at every key step of the shipping process, allowing customers to follow the status of their shipments throughout the journey. (www.fedex.com)

Technology and seller order processing

As with all areas of B2B marketing, technology now permeates every nook and cranny in order processing. Commercial organisations offer ever more sophisticated products to help solve problems. Technology and computer software programming can now be applied across all activities associated with customer ordering in an attempt to ensure effectiveness, continuity and control across the whole process.

Order management systems (OMS)

Customer order management (COM) includes, but is not limited to, customer and customer credit management, sales order processing, pricing, availability checking, transportation, billing, invoicing and accounts receivable processing. Trends that can influence order management include customer relationship management (CRM) systems which amass detailed information about customers and their orders and allow for the application of that information throughout enterprises, such as in sales and marketing or production planning.

Typically, an order management system (OMS) receives customer order information from the host system and an up-to-the-transaction view of inventory availability from the warehouse management system and from trading partners via electronic data interchange (EDI) transmissions. The OMS then groups an enterprise's orders by customer and priority, allocates inventory by warehouse site, and establishes delivery promise dates. In a fully integrated system, order management system (OMS) applications optimise the way orders are presented to the transportation management system (TMS) and the warehouse management system (WMS).

(b) Buyer concerns

Procurement begins with perhaps a request for a quotation – an invitation to suppliers to bid on supplying easily described products or services needed by a company or public agency. Acceptance may follow with the creation and sending of a purchase order, tracking and tracing orders, updating inventory, request for product modifications or new products information and, where necessary, the return of defective or unwanted products. These are all tasks that turn a planned supply chain into a working live entity.

No buyer likes to have problems associated with the procurement of goods and services, delivery and payment of stock. Unfulfilled orders, wrong goods or materials dispatched and late deliveries all cause buyers unnecessary problems in terms of disrupted production lines, extra costs and unhappy customers. Wrongly priced invoices, especially overpriced invoices, can cost companies millions of pounds a year, leading to expensive rectifying actions, buyer anger and eventual change of supplier. Order processing systems should be developed in conjunction with buyers so that all contributors and users are happy and feel that real savings are being made. Information systems and technology need to be compatible so that buyers can talk to suppliers in 'real time' if necessary.

3. Warehousing

All organisations must at some time or another store materials and goods while waiting to use or to sell and deliver on to customers. This storage and delivery function becomes more important in some industries where factors such as product size and space needed, value, security against theft, perishability, amount needed for seasonal demand and so on might play a part in the process. Warehousing is a non-productive process in that the longer paid-for stock is held idle in the warehouse, the more will be the costs to the organisation. This can be a crippling expense, especially for a company working on very small margins.

Research has shown that warehousing and delivery costs can be as much as a third of all costs. The challenge over the last decade has been for managers to search for ways to reduce this cost while at the same time continually increasing customer service. As with most other business process functions warehousing can be outsourced in the manner described in the section on outsourcing.

Buyers and suppliers working closely together

There are many factors to be taken into account when deciding on warehousing policy. As with all marketing decisions, customer needs and wants and continuous customer service must be overriding considerations. This will mean supplying products and services as and when wanted in the most value driven way possible. We have discussed supply chain relationships, the need to work closely with member companies, throughout this chapter and, as with all distribution decisions, adding value for the customer will be the major driving force in warehousing considerations. Factors that need to be considered are now examined.

Distribution strategies and objectives

Warehousing should not be seen in isolation but as an important part of the strategic marketing whole. As with transport and inventory control it should fit into the logistical pattern developed through the planning process. An organisation will have discussed and set distribution and warehousing objectives and strategies in line with the overall marketing plan and this will dictate policy factors looked at here. Strategic issues driving all logistic decisions will cover such things as:

☐ Overall marketing and distribution objectives
☐ Distribution strategies
☐ Buyer–seller relationships, buyer and channel member needs
☐ Buyer/supplier inventory holding strategies
☐ Direct or indirect distribution.
☐ Regional, national and international distribution
☐ Extensive, selective or concentrated coverage.

Location

Depending on the goods and materials produced, location will need to be in a place convenient and effective for both supplier and buyer. This will be in terms of timings, speed and cost of delivery. It might be a centralised or decentralised system or a combination of both. These options will be outlined in more detail below. The availability and cost of suitable premises and the cost and availability of skilled labour must also be examined and evaluated.

Costs

Always a part of the equation in any management decisions, the cost of warehousing will impinge on the price of the goods when sold on to the buyer. If the supplier is in the more powerful position, these costs will be passed on to the buyer, but if competition is rife, the supplier will have to bear this imposition. Costs that will need to be considered will cover the following:

☐ Costs of buying, renting or leasing buildings
☐ Stockholding costs, pilfering, depreciation, spoilage costs
☐ Insurance and security costs
☐ Delivery and returns costs

□ Transport costs

□ Labour costs.

Costs can be offset by:

□ Economies of scale

□ Quickness of delivery

□ Shared buyer/seller warehousing

□ Customer satisfaction.

Choice of warehousing system

Both supplier and buyer organisations will need to decide on the most advantagous situation for warehouse location. Decisions of this magnitude should be seen as strategic and made at the highest level in the organisation. In B2C, end consumer location will be of greatest importance and suppliers will deliver to retail warehouses, retail shops or direct to the consumer. In B2B, suppliers will usually deliver direct to a manufacturing plant or producer warehouse. A B2B supplier will sometimes deliver to a retailer warehouse or retail outlet if the order is for a B2B product, e.g. shelving, refrigeration or administration.

Example 6.26   **Contract out your warehousing**

A full-service company providing international and domestic contract warehousing, transportation and distribution services, Locust Industries offers flexibility and cost-effective operations from modern buildings. New equipment and the latest computerised systems serve your business and meet the needs for inventory control and rapid shipment tracking. Locust's warehousing and distribution operations feature modern and diverse facilities, equipment, and capabilities affording you flexibility in storing your goods. We can also take care of your business needs for transloading, palletising, stretch wrapping, blocking and bracing.

Supplier direct to manufacturer

Small suppliers and those with very few business customers, depending on the material and goods on offer, will not need to warehouse products or will hold and warehouse products at the point of production. These will be shipped direct to the buyer as and when needed either as a continuous flow or in separate batches. The amount of product-holding warehouse space needed by the supplier will depend on levels and timings of production and buyer call-off needs. There is always the danger of shortages brought about by seasonal or erratic demand if too little supplier back-up stock is held, leading to the competitor being invited in. Similarly too much stock held can lead to expensive storage costs.

B2B centralised and decentralised warehousing systems

The strategic issues identified above will drive companies to look for the most effective and efficient way of holding and moving stock both within the organisation and thence on to the buyer. Different warehousing models have been used in this search for competitive advantage and we can look at some of these below.

Centralised system

Some organisations opt for using a centralised system. If selling into a national market the centralised warehouse might be at or near the place of production or in the middle of the organisation's market. If selling internationally the company might have a central warehouse in each of the countries or regions in which it operates. Great amounts of material and component parts can then be delivered to the central distribution depot, by train or large lorries, and then redelivered in smaller loads and smaller lorries to the various business customers. In this way economies of scale can be gained.

Decentralised system

With a decentralised system the supplier will have a series of warehouses located strategically across a region or country, each serving an optimum number of customers. Deliveries from the manufacturing plant will then be made directly to each separate location. In some cases, goods will be delivered to one decentralised warehouse and then delivered on to a number of smaller satellite stockholding points. Stock will then be delivered on from there to the buyer. The greater the number of delivery and holding points, the greater will be the costs and risk of damage and theft.

Strategically coordinating the warehousing process

As with all management processes warehouse management has progressed immensely over the years. Its strategic importance is recognised by forward-thinking companies and it is now approached in a cohesive and professional manner. As with most business decision-making processes, information technology has helped immensely and warehouse management innovation now makes full use of computer programs used in conjunction with customer research, manufacturing, purchasing and inventory control and transportation.

Warehouse management systems

Warehousing and distribution used to be seen as a necessary exercise to hold and move products from supplier through to buyer. It tended to be viewed in isolation from other business activities and past methods were more often than not costly, time consuming and inefficient. Modern practices now demand that it be approached in the same way as all company functions in a professional and integrated fashion. Warehouse management is now seen as a strategic business function incorporating well thought through systems and processes developed as part of the logistical whole. It includes organising existing warehouse locations and the planning of new ones, stock movement process modelling, preparing a description of warehousing functions, and recording the flow of information.

Warehouse management (computer) systems (WMS)

The evolution of warehouse management (computer) systems (WMS) is very similar to the evolution of many other software solutions. It was initially a system to try to integrate mechanical and human activities and to control movement and storage of materials within a warehouse. It has expanded to include transportation management, order management and accounting management, with an information and automated data collection system to manage warehouse business processes and direct warehouse activities effectively. The lines between warehouse management, inventory control, order processing, distribution, and transportation systems are blurring as more warehouse systems handle logistics functions such as incoming delivery schedules, load planning and building, shipment scheduling, and yard management. The WMS can prompt workers to do inventory cycle counts, order picking, packing, shipping, and so on. The use of radio frequency technology in conjunction with bar codes provides the foundation of a WMS talking to both supplier and buyer staff and delivering accurate information in real time.

Cross-docking

Warehouse management will include the concept of 'cross-docking'. In its purest form cross-docking is the action of unloading materials from an incoming transport and immediately loading these materials onto outbound vehicles, thus eliminating the need for warehousing and storage. Products are sorted by destination by the incoming supplier working on the instructions of the buying company. The whole warehousing operation is automated, including unloading, movement round the warehouse and loading onto outgoing vehicles. Minimal warehouse staff are needed and it speeds up the time it takes to move goods from supplier to buyer, minimising costs and increasing overall inventory productivity. In some cases warehouses that used to employ hundreds now employ no more than five or six.

WMS advantages

☐ Reduce inventory

☐ Reduce labour costs

☐ Increase storage capacity

☐ Increase product turnaround

☐ Increase customer service

☐ Increase customer satisfaction

☐ Increase inventory accuracy

☐ Help cement supplier/buyer relationships.

WMS disadvantages

☐ Expensive to set up

☐ Complex to operate

☐ Loss of flexibility.

4. Transport and delivery methods

The other major area where substantial cost savings can be made, and the fourth principal component of PDM, is in the choice of delivery methods used to move goods from one area to another and eventually to the customer. There have been tremendous technological and management strides in this area and huge cost savings have been made.

Multi-modal transportation

The transportation of material goods and services can involve the use of several modes of transportation including, road, rail, water, air, pipelines and telecommunications. Methods chosen will depend on such things as, country infrastructure, types of products, distance from supplier to buyer, the importance of speed and time and costs involved. With some goods and services there will be a combination of more than one method in getting the goods from supplier to buyer. So expensive products (e.g. industrial diamonds) might be transported by plane and then by road, as might products needed quickly (e.g. computer system component parts) or having a short life span (e.g. plants). Bulk commodity products to be moved from one part of the country to another might go by rail (coal), large finished products to be exported from one side of the world to another, by sea (e.g. cars) and liquids such as oil through pipelines. Other products such as music, books, pictures etc. can now be sent electronically. All these methods are used to a lesser or greater extent dependent on the factors identified above but it is not intended to get involved in a discussion about the nature of each method here. By far the most important and widely used method is by road and many of the issues discussed below can be applied equally in a general sense to these other modes of transportation.

Road transport

This is the most widely used and important form of transport. When deciding where to put factories, storage and delivery warehouses and retail outlets a company should look towards the most favourable location so that it can reach its customers quickly, efficiently and at the lowest possible costs. If road transport is the method chosen then it would make sense to be located near a suitable motorway system offering easy access to every part of the company's market.

Technology in transportation

As would be expected, technology has played a big part in the development of road transport, constantly improving productivity, safety and customer satisfaction. Satellite tracking and precise scheduling maintain consistently achievable time-sensitive delivery levels. Drivers can be contacted at all times and in all places. Refrigerated containers allow for product protection across long distances and over increasing time periods. Lorries run more efficiently and effectively as vehicle safety improves and breakdown risks lessen.

Transport options available

Many transport options are now available for a company running its own fleet to outsource the whole process. If a company chooses to buy its own transport fleet, high discounts can be had from vehicle manufacturers. In fact in the UK fleet purchases for both vans and cars now account for over 70 per cent of all sales. Collection and delivery can now be made (and are demanded) 365 days a year throughout the UK and Europe, transporting a diverse range of products from manufacturing to consumer goods, handling every type of consignment and load combination, offering a single or multi-drop option to and from any location. The service can be backed by efficient vehicle planning, and modern communication systems to ensure accurate tracking of vehicles and to maintain time-sensitive delivery schedules.

Example 6.27 **Transport today**

All of the vehicles are equipped with a mobile telephone. This reinforces their commitment to providing the most reliable service possible. All drivers are uniformed and all their vehicles are clean and well maintained. This further emphasises the company's commitment to quality and service for the customer. The haulage company is a specialist in refrigerated transport. They operate locally, regionally and nationwide and will provide both chilled and frozen storage facilities as well as dry goods storage. They are also now branching out into Europe as demand for their specialist services grows. They are a Member of the Freight Transport Association.

Refrigerated transport

Refrigerated transport is operated throughout the UK and Europe using the latest technology to offer customers flexible loading options which are able to create cost and efficiency advantages. State-of-the-art trailers have computerised chill and freeze facilities that allow the driver to monitor the state of the load at any time during the journey. Internal movable bulkheads and decks allow any combination of ambient, chilled and frozen goods to be carried in a single load.

Bulk transport and heavy haulage

Bulk transport encompasses a whole range of goods and manufacturing products, from raw materials to scrap metal. A diverse range of vehicles can be hired which are capable of moving bulk consignments to demanding schedules and which are made cost effective by experience in load combinations and planning. Heavy haulage contractors specialise in the movement of heavy equipment such as machinery and plant for all sectors of industry. Their vehicles can transport up to 65 tonnes and feature specialised loading equipment, including outriggers and heavy-duty winches.

Fleet contract is an attractive option for companies with strong identities and reputations to preserve, and exact requirements can be discussed between contractor and user. In some cases specialist vehicles can be acquired to operate in the customer's livery. This option allows the customer a continuity of image, with expertise in fleet management from the contractor protecting reputation and ensuring a reliable and cost-effective flow of product to customers.

Contract distribution

Contract distribution affords the customer a highly reliable level of service with fixed costs, which in turn bring long-term benefits through the ability to plan effectively. With predetermined volumes and routes assessed, vehicles are assigned from the fleet or often purchased solely to service the contract. External variations in work levels have no effect on a dedicated distribution contract. The ability to analyse customers' requirements in advance allows the contractor to prepare a cost-effective efficient service. On-site contract managers liaise between the customer and a planning team to organise a time-sensitive schedule.

Transport leasing

Transport can be leased in the same way as any other type of product or service. Payment is made on a monthly basis and can include finance and cleaning as well as breakdown recovery and maintenance services. Under a leasing system, transport can be bought at a reduced price when the leasing contract is finished if the user so desires.

Transportation management system (TMS)

As with all the other logistic processes identified above, computer software programs can be purchased to increase the overall functional efficiency and effectiveness. Transportation management system applications determine the most efficient and profitable way to execute the movement of product to its final destination. The TMS receives orders from an order management system (OMS), then confirms shipping dates required to meet delivery promises, checks rates, assigns carriers and establishes pick-up and delivery schedules before releasing orders to the warehouse management system for processing. Once orders have been processed and are ready to be shipped, the TMS manages the delivery and freight payment process. Transportation planning and scheduling (TPS) specifies how, when and where to transport goods. Transportation planning and scheduling applications may provide weight/size restrictions, merge-in-transit, continuous move, mode or carrier selection, and less than truckload (LTL)/full truckload (FTL) planning functionality.

☐ Other transport issues

B2B organisations now have many other issues to consider in choosing and running their whole transport system. Whether they are operating it themselves or using one of the many other systems, managers are continually threatened with a rise in transport costs. It is true that efficiencies connected with use of new technologies work to improve performance and push down running costs, but many other factors outside the control of the organisation work to push costs in the other direction. This will include such issues as rising and/or volatile petrol and diesel prices, road congestion charges and pollution charges. There are also problems and possible legislation and further costs associated with such disparate concerns as stowaways found on board, the transportation of dangerous goods and higher road charges.

Example 6.28 **Cut out CO$_2$ emissions**

Road traffic reduction is one of the government's major issues, yet forecasts predict an increase of 37 per cent on 1990 levels by 2010. Vehicle CO$_2$ emissions are seen as a prime contributor to the greenhouse effect and climate change, issues at the heart of the Kyoto Agreement and LA21. Vehicle leasing and rental are an effective way to cut down on ownership, and promote a specific type of alternative fuel through a large number of vehicles. (www.greenconsumerguide.com)

Transport and marketing

Most organisations now appreciate the importance of a good corporate image in both B2B and B2C markets and will work hard to make certain a consistent approach is taken across all business functions. Only in the last decade was the significant part that transport might play in the process appreciated. Large companies will have hundreds if not thousands of cars, vans and lorries moving around the country by day and night. These are moving communication adverts representing the values of the company, not only by the words, colours and designs on the back and sides, but also by how clean and tidy each vehicle comes onto the road each day. In many cases the company would have to pay hundreds of thousands of pounds a year for the same promotion exposure if contracted through outdoor advertising companies such as Maiden or Moore and Allen. If transport managers are not careful, dirty, rusting and badly kept lorries will be characteristics associated with the company by customers and other stakeholders alike. As well as clean and tidy vehicles, signs are appearing on the backs of vehicles asking the public to phone in if they feel that the lorry is being badly driven – surely an indication that organisations are taking this communication form seriously.

Integration of logistics into all other organisational functions

The need to manage purchasing, transportation and inventory levels has led to an increasingly close relationship between organisations along the supply chain. Over the last decade, through the use of innovation and technology, great strides have been taken in building ever-closer working relationships, superior communications and better mutual understanding between organisations along the supply chain, leading to continuous logistic effectiveness. Purchasing, inventory movement, production, administration, human resources, marketing and finance have all been brought closer together in the planning process so that the organisation and its supply chain operate at both the strategic and tactical levels as an integrated whole rather than in separate parts.

Supply or demand chain management (SCDM, DCDM) is a strategy through which integration can be achieved across the whole supply chain, including all supplier and buyer organisations. The challenge for all organisations in operating their physical distribution systems is to manage the goods and material flow across a carefully planned supply chain effectively and efficiently. The use of information technology gives automated intelligence to a network of vendors, suppliers, manufacturers, distributors, retailers, and a host of other trading partners. The goal is for each player in the supply chain to conduct business with the latest and best information from everyone else, guiding supply and demand into a more perfect balance. Effective management of the supply chain enables a company to move products from the point of origin to that of consumption in the least amount of time at the smallest cost and giving the best possible value to the end customer (B2B or B2C).

☐ Summary

In this chapter we looked at the management of business channels starting with the strategic alternatives available. The major strategic decision facing the senior manager is the choice between going direct or indirect in marketing to the buying organisation. Reasons given for choosing one way rather than another were discussed and advantages and disadvantages of each evaluated. Methods used in direct distribution were identified under the headings of direct salesforce, trader exhibitions, mail order, internet and other media forms. We then went on to look at indirect methods under the categories of supplier, broker, distributor and wholesaler. Again the pros and cons of each were briefly outlined before going on to talk about the relationships between suppliers and intermediaries, disintermediation, channel conflict, reintermediation and the role of the internet in the supply chain. We then went on to identify other methods of distribution seen as a combination of both direct and indirect. Here we examined the role of agents, franchising, licensing and contracting. The many factors that need to be considered with strategic channel selection and the differences in the process between B2B and B2C markets were shown as we moved towards the end of Part 1.

In Part 2 we began by examining the management of the supply chain relationships. It is important to appreciate that B2B managers will operate in different types of marketing structures, sometimes demanding different approaches. To this end many were identified and discussed including vertical and horizontal integration, voluntary, contractual and hegemonic. The business supply chain has taken on enormous importance over the last 20 years and understanding the need to manage in partnership with all members now dominates management thinking. Experience has demonstrated that the supply chain must now be viewed as both an internal and external value chain if improvements are to be made. Starting with the internal value chain, each part of the business process from inputs through to outputs must be benchmarked so that it is as good as, if not better than, the competition in delivering eventual customer satisfaction. This concept must then be applied to the external value chain; that is every other organisation involved in the supply chain, from one end to the other. Only in this way can the competition be beaten or held at bay. Developments that improve this concept were identified under the heading of efficient consumer response (ECR). These included developments known under the acronyms CPFR, EDI, JIT, ABC, TQM, and many others. We then examined the upsides and the downsides of this close cooperation among supply chain members. The growth of outsourcing as an alternative way of operating certain business functions has been phenomenal. This was discussed in some detail before moving on to look at how and why companies merge or acquire other companies or form joint ventures and other types of strategic alliances.

The role of physical distribution and the management of logistics in B2B markets were discussed in Part 3. Organisations have to move goods and services from one point to another in the most effective and economical manner possible. Better management understanding coupled with the growth in new technologies has brought great resource savings across all the major areas that might be categorised under the heading of logistics. We therefore chose to categorise under the headings of stock levels and inventory, order processing, warehousing and transportation. Concepts identified under inventory included cost of holding stock, JIT stockholding, continuous replenishment, direct procurement, materials requirement planning, enterprise resource planning and vendor management inventory. Advantages and disadvantages were then outlined. If order processing takes too long or is flawed in some way, then costs can rise, orders can be lost and customers left dissatisfied. Technology has played a big part here, allowing cost and time savings to be made and both seller and buyer satisfaction levels to rise. Warehousing is yet another area where savings have been made because of greater management understanding and business developments. Different ways of managing transport were then identified before finally discussing the need to integrate logistics into all other organisational functions.

Discussion questions

1. Identify the different channels that B2B organisations can use in getting products and services to their markets. What methods, and why, will best suit the following organisations?

    (a) A company selling paint.
    (b) A business consultant.
    (c) A chemical manufacturer.

2. Identify the differences between marketing direct and indirect in the B2B market. Give real examples of each and explain why companies choose to supply in this way.

3. Discuss and evaluate the methods that might be used in both direct and indirect distribution. Give examples.

4. Describe and analyse the criteria that will be used when selecting a B2B channel to market. How will this differ when compared with channel choice in B2C markets?

5. Discuss the value of the internal and external value chain and identify the major differences in its use between the organisations described here.

    (a) Public sector.
    (b) Not-for-profit sector.
    (c) Manufacturing sector.
    (d) Service sector.

6. Examine the business process of outsourcing. What are its many forms and why do you think there has been such a growth in its use, at both the tactical and strategic levels, over the last few years? What are its major disadvantages?

7. Discuss the development of just-in-time inventory management systems. What part did JIT play in the development of supply chain management?

8. Sixty per cent of strategic supply chain alliances fail over the first three-year period. Discuss why you think this might be.

9. Identify and evaluate the part that technology now plays across the supply both in the running of the supply chain relationships and in physical distribution.

10. The Internet will alter forever methods of distribution in many industries. Discuss.

 Visit the *B2B Marketing* website at www.booksites.net/wright for a Case Study, Questions, and an Internet Exercise for this chapter.

☐ Bibliography

Books

Badaracco, J.L. Jr. (1991) *The Knowledge Link: How Firms Compete Through Strategic Alliances.* Boston: Harvard Business School Press.

Banfield, E. (1999) *Harnessing Value in the Supply Chain: Strategic Sourcing in Action.* Chichester: Wiley.

Bovet, D., Martha, J., Mercer Management Consulting and Slywotsky, A.J. (2000) *Value Nets: Breaking the Supply Chain to Unlock Hidden Profits.* New York: Wiley.

Bradach, J. (1998) *Franchise Organisations.* Boston: Harvard Business School Press.

Chopra, S. and Meindl, P. (1999) *Supply Chain Management: Strategy, Planning and Operations.* New York: Prentice-Hall.

Christopher, M.A. (1999) *Logistics and Supply Chain Management: Strategies for Reducing Cost and Improving Service,* 2nd edn. London: Pearson Education.

Dwyer, F.R. and Tanner, J.F. (2002) *Business Marketing: Connecting Strategy, Relationships and Learning,* 2nd edn. New York: McGraw-Hill.

Foss, B. and Stone, M. (2001) *Successful Customer Relationship Marketing: New Thinking, New Strategies, New Tools for Getting Closer to Your Customers.* London: Kogan Page.

Gilbert, R. and Hastings, J. (2001) *Vertical Integration in Gasoline Supply.* Berkeley: University of California.

Hahin, P.W. (1991) *Business-to-Business Marketing: Strategic Resource Management and Cases.* Needham Heights, MA: Allyn & Bacon.

Handfield, R.B. and Nichols Jr, E.L. (1998) *Introduction to Supply Chain Management.* New York: Prentice-Hall.

Hines, P. (1999) *Value Stream Management: Strategy and Excellence in the Supply Chain.* Harlow: Pearson Education.

Landvater, D. (1997) *World Class Production and Inventory Management.* Chichester: Wiley.

Laseter, T. (1998) *Balance Sourcing: Cooperation and Competition in Supplier Relationships.* London: Jossey-Bass.

Lewis, J.D. (1995) *The Connected Corporation: Customer–Supplier Alliances.* New York: Free Press.

Lynch, R.P. (1989) *The Practical Guide to Joint Ventures and Strategic Alliances.* New York: Wiley.

Minett, S. (2002) *B2B Marketing: A Radically Different Approach for Business-to-Business Marketers.* Harlow: Pearson Education.

Ohmae, K. (1995) *Global Logic of Strategic Alliances.* New York: Free Press.

Randall, G. (1994) *Trade Marketing Strategies: The Partnership between Manufacturers, Brands and Retailers,* 2nd edn. Oxford: Butterworth-Heinemann.

Roos, J. (ed.) (1994) *European Casebook on Cooperative Strategies.* New York: Prentice-Hall.

Shapiro, J.F. (2000) *Modeling the Supply Chain.* New York: Duxbury Press.

Sheth, J. and Parvatiyar, A (2000) *Handbook of Relationship Marketing*. Thousand Oaks, CA: Sage.

Timmers, P. (2000) *Electronic Commerce – Strategies and Models for B2B Trading*. Chichester: Wiley.

Tompkins, J.A. (2000) *No Boundaries: Moving Beyond Supply Chain Management*. Rayleigh, NC: Tompkins Press.

Wheeler, S. and Hirsh, E. (1999) *Channel Champions: How Leading Companies Build New Strategies to Serve Customers*. New York: Jossey-Bass.

Journals

Anand, B.N. and Khanna, T. (2000) 'Do firms learn to create value? The case of alliances', *Strategic Management Journal*, 21: 295–315.

Anderson, E. (1990) 'Two firms, one frontier: on assessing joint venture performance', *Sloan Management Review*, Winter: 19–30.

Bensaou, M. (1999) 'Portfolios of buyer–supplier relationships', *Sloan Management Review*, Summer: 35–44.

Campbell, A.J. and Cooper, R.G. (1999) 'Do customer partnerships improve new product success rates?', *Industrial Marketing Management*, 28: 507–19.

Contractor, F.J. (1981) 'The role of licensing in international strategy', *Columbia Journal of World Business*, Winter: 73–81.

Gomes-Casseres, B. 'Do you really have an alliance strategy?', *Strategy and Leadership*, September–October: 6–11.

Holmström, J. (1998) 'Business process innovation in the supply chain – a case study of implementing vendor managed inventory', *European Journal of Purchasing and Supply Management*, 4(2/3): 127–31.

Porter, M.E. and Fuller, M.B. (1985) 'Coalitions and global strategy', in M. Porter (ed.), *Competition in Global Industries*. Boston: Harvard Business School Press, Chapter 10.

Scannell, T.V., Shawnee, K.V. and Droge, C.L. (2000) 'Upstream supply chain management and competitive performance in the automotive supply industry', *Journal of Business Logistics*, 21(1): 23–48.

Visit www.booksites.net/wright for the Internet references for this chapter.

07

Pricing strategies for business markets

Chapter

The bitterness of poor quality is remembered long after price is forgotten.

Aims and objectives

By the end of this chapter the student should be able to:

1. Recognise and evaluate how price is used in business-to-business marketing and how it interacts with other elements of the marketing mix.

2. Identify and evaluate the factors that must be taken into account when considering price strategies.

3. Identify and evaluate different strategic approaches.

4. Identify and examine the operational factors associated with price.

5. Compare and evaluate the differences in the use of price between B2B and B2C markets.

Part 1   The meaning of price and marketing in business markets

☐ ## Introduction

Price is the element of the marketing mix that seems to be most misunderstood by students and practitioners alike. Many approaches underestimate the all-round contribution that pricing can make to the optimum use of marketing resources. This is not only because of revenue and profit contributions but also because of the many other functions that price can perform in developing successful marketing mix strategies. As in other chapters there is an attempt to constantly highlight the difference between B2B and B2C marketing. So let us start with a definition of price.

> Price is the value (usually measured in monetary terms) at which the seller agrees to sell a product or service to the buyer and the value at which the buyer agrees to purchase.

This exchange transaction can be either:

☐ *Fixed*: the price is given and the buyer either agrees or disagrees.

☐ *Negotiable*: buyer and seller bargain in some way until a mutual price is agreed.

☐ *A variation*: one or more elements may be fixed and other elements negotiable.

Of course price cannot be looked at in isolation and will be linked to many other factors such as added services, delivery and installation, payment method and credit terms, security risk, and product and competition alternatives. Many of these factors will apply to both B2B and B2C markets, but with many differences which will be identified as we move through the chapter.

Setting prices strategically is a matter of knowledge, and not simply a financial decision but a strategic one. Setting price requires an understanding of certain factors: the value of the product to the consumer, the likely competitive response, the costs used in setting the price and the price sensitivity of the market. Many people can be involved with the process, often approaching it from a particular perspective. The management accountant might be concerned with minimising running costs, the financial accountant with obtaining good returns for the shareholder, the sales manager with price concessions to obtain new accounts, and the marketing manager with long-term customer satisfaction. Although disagreements will happen, it is up to senior managers to balance the decisions made on price with good business and marketing practice, leading ultimately to constant customer satisfaction.

☐ The business-to-business pricing process

There is no one set way for setting the price for products and services in the B2B market. As in B2C markets the price to be charged will vary according to a multitude of interconnecting factors. These will include the pricing objectives, costs involved, market structures, demand levels, intensity of the competition and the type of product and level of service to be offered. Ultimately, the price to be charged should ideally be based upon the price the customer wants or is able to pay. This should be identified through constantly talking to customers, using both quantitative and qualitative marketing research. As with B2C goods and services, the pricing mechanism is the only way that the organisation can obtain revenue and profits and too low or too high a price will, sooner or later, tip the company into failure and bankruptcy. As well as too low or too high a price, other problems can arise because of faults related to the pricing process. Prices that are inconsistent across the product portfolio and fail to identify specific related costs, prices that ignore the competition and prices that disregard customers' differential needs can all cause profound problems. These as well as other pricing issues are discussed throughout this chapter.

Pricing and marketing

Price is an integral part of the marketing mix and should be never be discussed and set in isolation. The idea that price can be set according to internal costing needs with little or no regard for other marketing factors could be said to be naive and foolish and only happen where some kind of monopoly position existed. Customers, markets, the type of product, the channel of distribution and methods to be used in promoting the finished offering will all need to be considered when deciding the strategic method of setting the price.

The marketing definition which states that, driven by the need for customer satisfaction, marketing is 'having the right product, at the right price, in the right place and then communicated in the right way' applies as much to B2B markets as to B2C marketing. There is a continuously shifting relationship between the price and all other elements of the marketing mix and this must be addressed when setting prices.

Product positioning

Price will also play a crucial part, with all other elements of the marketing mix, in positioning the product or service in the marketplace. Positioning – how the companies' products are viewed in relationship with the competitors' products – is an essential end objective of the marketing process. For example, high quality, high value, high priced products will be viewed differently from low value, low quality, low priced products. If the products are viewed as high priced but low value products, then the marketing mix application can be said to be faulty. In B2B markets product positioning would be based mainly on rational criteria while positioning in B2C markets is based on emotional criteria and happens within the consumer's mind.

B2B and B2C markets

In some ways pricing in B2C markets is easier than in B2B. In most B2C markets, customers are segmented into like-minded groups with needs and wants (hopefully) identified and, taking into account marketing factors outlined above, products and services are priced accordingly. There will be little personal contact or negotiation with individual customers who will pay the price wanted if the marketing mix components have been correctly identified and integrated. If a price change is needed in B2B markets individual customers may have to be consulted and won over. The customer might refuse the price hike unless the supplier makes a clear, unarguable case.

☐ Price and the B2B marketing mix

The relationship between price and other elements of the marketing mix can now be discussed in more detail under the headings identified below:

1. Price and product

2. Price and distribution

3. Price and promotion.

1. Price and product

The complexities tied up with the concept of product were discussed in more detail in earlier chapters. Research has shown that when customers purchase products and services, in both B2C and B2B markets, they are purchasing a range of added value benefits that will help solve some kind of problem. In B2C markets these 'problems' will probably be personal and encompass both emotional and rational concerns. In B2B markets they will tend to be organisational and rational. Just to reiterate for a moment, these benefits will include such things as innovation, packaging, branding, quality, servicing, and so on. We can now look at the relationship between these added value benefits and the price that buyers are prepared to pay.

Pricing across the product portfolio

Most B2B organisations will have a portfolio of products built up in response to customer demands. When price and costs are being considered on any one product or product line, there is a need to consider the effects that any one decision might have across the whole portfolio mix. Costing ramifications are discussed in the section on costs later in the chapter.

The relationship between price and product value

There will always be a relationship, a trade-off, between price and the product services value offered. Although this will apply to both B2C and B2B markets, the process and outcomes are very different.

Price and product value in B2C markets

In B2C markets there is a continually shifting relationship between the price of the product and the added value elements such as packaging, quality, function and, most importantly, branding. When looking around and comparing different products and services the end customer will be continuously balancing the price and the product to arrive at what they consider best overall value. As a rule of thumb, in times of economic well-being (a high 'feel good' factor) consumer demands might be said to move towards added value factors and away from price. Conversely, during times of economic stringency (low 'feel good' factor) demand moves towards price and away from added value factors.

Unlike B2B markets the interplay between price and value in B2C products and services will mostly take place in an informal manner in the mind of the consumer. It will often be helped by discussion with others, friends, family, salespeople, reading the literature (and the internet), TV and radio programmes, and so on. The eventual choice will be greatly affected by advertising and product branding and will be made according to both emotional and rational factors (the decision-making process was discussed in more detail in Chapter 4). Not all target segments are the same and price will be important to one group and less so with another. Ease of payment methods and low interest rates will also be contributing factors with borrowing on the increase every year (Figure 7.1).

Figure 7.1
Factors that
affect the
interplay
between price
and added
value in B2C
and B2B
decision making

B2C	B2B
☐ Emotional as well as rational needs	☐ Rational and functional needs
☐ Advertising and branding	☐ Delivery
☐ Ease of payment method	☐ Innovation and technical input
☐ Economic circumstances	☐ Importance of product/service to company in optimising market position
☐ Importance of the decision	
☐ Type of product or service	☐ Risk involved
☐ Target segment	☐ Product knowledge and training offered
☐ Convenience	☐ Other benefits such as service and quality
☐ Other benefits such as service, delivery, knowledge, etc.	

Price ◄-------- Continuous movement --------► Added value

Price and product value in B2B markets

He knows the price of everything and the value of nothing.

(Anon.)

In B2B markets, buyers will usually approach the process in much more of a professional, formal and logical fashion, evaluating the cost/benefit trade-offs between price and all other added benefits (Figure 7.1). This will vary between one company and another and between one industry and another, depending on products, customers and markets. Buyers will weight the various benefits by how they might successfully contribute to solving specific problems and give overall competitive advantage. Delivery times may be the overriding consideration in one industry, quality in another, service in another, innovation in another, and so on. The buyer will be able to weight the various benefits offered in line with the efficiency opportunities that particular benefit could contribute to the over-all strategic marketing opportunity. Added value ratings will then be rated along-side the price demanded by competing suppliers and a choice made.

As an example, one company may rate delivery continuity as being worth 8 out of 10, service 5 out of 10, innovation 5 out of 10, and so on. Another company may rate innovation 9 out of 10, service 7 out of 10, and relationships 6 out of 10. Both companies would then rate alongside the price to be paid from suppliers and make some sort of cost benefit judgement. So we can see that it will not always be the lowest price that will be accepted.

2. Price and distribution

The channel of distribution, that is how the product is made available to the cus-tomer, will have a greater or lesser effect on the price depending on the type of product and the methods used. There are two basic strategies available for B2B and B2C organisations: marketing direct (doing it yourself) and/or marketing indirect (operating through an intermediary). It was identified that the B2C company will mostly sell through retailers while the B2B will sell direct. Both methods will incorporate costs of some kind and so have an effect on price to be charged both directly and along the whole distribution channel.

Price and marketing indirect

If the supplier operates through an intermediary, usually a wholesaler or reseller, payment of some kind will be expected for the duties that it will have to perform in selling on to another buyer. Depending on the tasks to perform, this amount could be anywhere between 10 per cent and 100 per cent of the intermediary sell-on price. Industry norms dominate percentages given so that 15 per cent might be common in one industry and 25 per cent in another. Prices to be paid by the wholesaler can be expressed as a mark-up margin on the supplier's selling price or as a mark-down margin on the wholesaler's selling price. Costs will then be passed along the whole distribution chain and so have an effect on the price eventually paid by the end user. It is not uncommon for industry percentage margin norms to vary across the supply chain as different members perform different tasks.

Management tasks performed by B2B intermediaries

Intermediaries will expect payment for undertaking all or some of the following tasks:

☐ Offering an established route to market.

☐ Holding inventory at levels that will satisfy customer demand.

☐ Demonstrating, explaining and selling goods and services.

☐ Handling customer complaints.

☐ Delivering the amount when and how needed – this task can take on added importance with the advent of JIT inventory adoption methods.

☐ Handling damaged stock and returns.

☐ Paying for stock and so offering the supplier a type of early payment.

☐ After-sales service.

An intermediary might perform one or many of the management tasks identified above. As a common rule of thumb, the more tasks to be performed and the more complex those tasks, the higher will be the expected margin. A supplier might offer the reseller such benefits as exclusivity of selling area, customer leads, advertising and promotional help and extra discounts for taking a range across the product portfolio. In return the middleman might offer loyalty, not stocking a rival's products, and willingness to work with lower price margins.

Supplier and middleman arrangements on price would need to satisfy the Office of Fair Trading on competition policy as transgressions could result in heavy fines.

Price and derived demand

Some original suppliers will want to influence price further down the chain as this will have an effect on the price (and amount) at which they are is able to sell in the first place. They might be able to do this by building relationships along the supply chain and/or promoting along the supply chain, and in this way, help maintain a particular price level.

Role of the intermediary in B2C markets

B2C wholesalers selling to retailers might also carry out many of the tasks identified above. The relative differences will include the following.

☐ Less complexity in the products.

☐ Dealing with 'finished' products, often branded, rather than component parts.

☐ Less urgent delivery times.

☐ Less need for product knowledge as this is usually given direct by the producer's representative.

Price and marketing direct

B2B companies that market their products direct will obviously not have to pay a middleman for selling the product. This will not necessarily mean that the price of the product will be any cheaper as the supplier will have to bear the costs of undertaking all the tasks that might have been performed by the intermediary. These will include display, advertising and selling, delivery and installation, and sometimes after-sales service. Some industries and some organisations are more likely to sell direct than others, depending on the type of product, the necessary skills involved and the traditions existing in the industry. Cost per customer purchase is a cost effectiveness measure used in direct marketing based on the cost-per-sale generated.

Managing prices and costs along the supply chain

The importance of pricing and costs along the whole supply chain in maintaining competitive advantage was alluded to in the previous chapter. Modern global market developments have fuelled the need for constant efficiency monitoring along the whole chain. High costs leading to too high prices can mean overpricing and loss of sales at the channel end. Many channels tend to throw up channel 'leaders' that take on the responsibility of controlling costs and prices. Suffice to say that these leaders are the most powerful members, often having the ability to push cost reductions upstream to be borne by the weaker suppliers. The concept of efficient consumer response (ECR) came into being to examine the whole process as a demand chain. Beginning with and based upon the end consumer need, and then looking back vertically along the supply chain, it seeks to make cost savings from suppliers using IT and the latest management methods.

Overall prices must adequately compensate all those that are involved in moving products and services along from supplier to supplier and buyer to buyer. Too high prices at any stage in the process can lead to high costs, loss of sales and/or a movement to a competitor. Conversely, too low a price can mean inadequate compensation, deterioration in quality and service and, at worst, the forced closure of a good supply chain member.

3. Price and promotion

The promotional mix, the different methods used to communicate messages to the target audience once the product or service is available for purchase, will be discussed in great detail in Chapter 8. As with other elements of the marketing mix, a relationship exists between price and promotion and a few of these elements will be examined here.

Advertising and price

Advertising is used in both B2B and B2C. The costs of the advertising will have an effect on the price that is eventually charged. Mass advertising – TV, newspapers and radio – is used mostly in B2C markets because of mass market segments, and much less in B2B because of smaller markets. Its great strength is in promoting brands both nationally and across the world. There is no doubt that the large costs involved must be eventually seen in the price charged, which in the end many consumers are prepared to pay because of the extra (emotional) value associated with these brands (Nike, Levi's, Mercedes, etc.).

Advertising is used to a lesser extent in B2B marketing through specialised B2B journals, directories and magazines rather than mass media, TV and print. There is obviously a cost involved, but it is minute compared with B2C. Although again it must be absorbed into the cost of the product, it is offset in two ways: awareness created should lead to more products being sold; and price information should allow buyer comparisons among competitors' products, leading to lower prices. Many businesses now use the internet to obtain price comparisons from around the world as well as to sell products and services.

Sales promotions and price

Sales, trade and staff price promotions can be used in both B2B and B2C markets as short-term ways of boosting sales or opening new accounts by offering extra value. However, in both markets care should be taken to see that price cuts do not become the norm rather than discretionary, so that customers will only purchase when prices are reduced. Price decreases due to volume and promotional discounts cannot always be planned for. Competitors may react to one another using defensive or offensive promotional campaigns offering discounts to customers for volume purchase and/or to defend market share.

Price and trade promotions in B2B markets

Price will be used in B2B markets to 'push' products and services downstream along the supply chain. In purchasing extra products, the buyer will then take on the responsibility of making certain that the extra stock purchased is used and/or sold on to the next organisation, thus 'pushing' it along the chain. Sales promotion can be used for the following purposes:

☐ As an incentive to open new accounts.
☐ To stock new products.

☐ To encourage a buyer to take extra stock and so keep out the competition.

☐ To help sell on existing stock held by the buyer as well as the seller.

☐ To take on added value and complementary products or services.

☐ To help with cash flow.

☐ Reacting to competitors' promotional activities.

Price and sales promotions in B2C markets

Price and sales promotions are also used heavily in B2C markets as part of a 'pull promotion' campaign. Price cuts directly off the product, by the use of money-off coupons, 'buy now and pay later', added value for the same price, and so on, are aimed directly at the end consumer, encouraging them to visit the retail outlet to search out the reduced price stock. The retailer in turn seeks more from upstream suppliers and so stock is 'pulled' down along the supply chain.

Extra benefits rather than price cuts

In both B2B and B2C sales promotion campaigns, suppliers would rather offer some short-term added benefits as an incentive to buy because direct price cuts send out the wrong messages to buyers. They highlight prices and indicate that the seller might always have room for manoeuvre on price offered, so encouraging price cut expectations. Price cuts also come straight off the bottom line and sales would have to increase by a large amount to make up for a reduction. For example, if a company sells a product at £15 and makes a £5 profit, the mark-up is 50 per cent. A 20 per cent price reduction will come off the selling price, in this case £3. The company is left with a £2 profit. The supplier would have to sell 150 per cent more products to make up the difference. Whether this is possible will depend on demand elasticity.

Using price as a marketing tool

Price can be used as a B2B marketing tool in the same way as all the other elements of the marketing mix – both to enhance the product offering and to be attractive to different segments of the market. Many organisations have developed a USP by adopting and specialising in one or more of the following.

Pricing by behaviour

Many customers will price by customer behaviour in both B2B and B2C markets. So heavy or regular users can be offered better prices, loyalty bonuses and extra discounts. Buyers can be offered better terms to switch from another company, past users persuaded to repurchase, and existing users encouraged to buy other products across the whole portfolio range. Earlier payers can be given extra discounts and companies willing to negotiate long-term contracts offered better overall terms. In B2B markets, pricing by behaviour can be used on a micro level right down to individual companies. In B2C it tends to be used on a mass scale and focuses around customer loyalty schemes.

Pricing by time

Time will always be more of an important factor for some businesses than others, allowing it to be used by suppliers as a way of segmenting the market by offering more value. So a range of prices can be charged for the product or service at different times of the day, week, month or year depending on the customer need. This might be price given on each delivery or based on a year contract with identified deliveries throughout the year. Many businesses are also affected by seasonal trends and demand fluctuations, so if buyers can be encouraged to take in stock, production can be evened out and supplier costs saved. Examples might be an ice cream manufacturer agreeing to take in a constant supply of ingredients throughout the year to be used mainly at holiday time.

Pricing by speed

In some cases a buyer may want products and services quickly and be willing to pay a premium price, as delays will cost money. Some suppliers have set themselves up to offer this type of service. So we see examples of same-day delivery on such things as motor spares, parcels, packages and letters, and specialised component parts.

Pricing by level of service wanted

We have discussed buyer needs for added services and customised products and extra prices can be charged. Extra services can be priced separately or as a complete system. The secret of good business is to be able to offer services that have high value to the customer and low costs to the supplier. In this way profits can be increased and/or supplier gratitude enhanced.

Other price considerations

Most B2B suppliers will offer better prices for cost saving measures, including those listed below.

Pricing by quantity demanded

Most suppliers will offer quantity discounts: the more purchased, the better will be the price. Quantity discount price might be set out in the company product price list or negotiated on a quantity by quantity basis. It is not unusual for small and medium sized companies to purchase together so as to take advantage of quantity discounts. With these so-called voluntary buying groups, the supplier might insist on delivering all member orders to one drop-off point or deliver orders to each company as and when wanted, with the quantity discount worked out retrospectively at the end of the year.

Pricing by payment method

The reason why many small and medium sized organisations go out of business is cash flow problems caused by slow payment or non-payment for goods and services delivered. To help minimise the possibility of this, most companies will offer extra discounts off the price, perhaps 2.5 per cent if payment is received within seven days. All industries have a norm for payment and this will usually be within a 30-, 60- or 90-day period. Research has shown that the largest companies tend to be the worst payers. Cost and benefit analysis can be used to identify the most profitable customers. Invoicing, control and payment can now be exercised electronically, speeding up the process as well as cutting costs.

Pricing by delivery method and distance
In some instances delivery can be by plane, ship, road, pipeline, or electronically. The most costly will affect the end price to be charged. Depending on the distance and speed wanted, high valued products might go by air at a higher price and low value by sea at a lower price. Innovative technology developments have broadened the options and lowered the price for the delivery of certain products and services. An example might be the injection of biochemicals into fruit, vegetables and flowers used with refrigerated containers, making cheaper, slower methods of delivery a reasonable option. Different prices might also be charged if the buyer collects from the supplier factory, from a centralised warehouse or from the docks (if coming by sea) rather than wanting direct delivery.

Part 2 Strategic factors determining price

We will now look in some detail at the factors which determine the final price that customers will pay. Some of these factors will be internal to the organisation and some external. The organisation should be able to control the internal factors while most external factors are market driven and generally outside the control of the organisation:

1. Price objectives and strategies
2. Costs
3. Customers
4. Market structures
5. Level of demand
6. Competitors' prices
7. Legal considerations.

☐ Price objectives and strategies

The price approach adopted by the management will depend ultimately upon what the organisation hopes to achieve through its corporate and marketing objectives. For a publicly quoted company, corporate objectives will usually be set in terms of a certain level of return on the money invested in the organisation needed to satisfy the shareholders in that company. For example, a return on capital employed (ROCE) or a return on investment (ROI) of 15 per cent each year over a three-year period might be the level of return expected on the amount of money invested. This level of return expected will vary from company to company and industry to industry depending on such things as company strength, market conditions and the amount of risk involved. Corporate headquarters will also demand return levels for subcompanies and divisions operating in both national and global markets. The need for a certain return on investment might also apply to the privately joint-owned organisation, partnership or sole trader, but not necessarily with the same level of urgency. The need to link prices to corporate objective will be virtually the same whether in B2B or B2C markets.

It should be recognised that when looking for a certain return on corporate investment, price will be only one of the determinants (albeit very important). Other considerations will include production effectiveness, financial borrowing costs, levels of fixed capital equipment used, and so on.

Marketing objectives

Marketing objectives are usually set in terms of sales or market share and how the marketing department can contribute to the desired return on capital invested. Subpricing objectives can then be added and these will include profit levels, product mix sales, opening new customers and new markets. Marketing objectives will be revisited in more detail when we discuss B2B planning in Chapter 9.

Pricing objectives in the public and NFP sectors

It is not intended to go into any great detail about pricing in the public and the not-for-profit (NFP) sectors as this is a specialist area discussed elsewhere. However, pricing here will not necessarily be linked to the level of expected return on capital invested, although it can and does happen, as this is not usually the purpose of these types of organisations.

In the public sector, the prices set will reflect wider objectives linked to economic, social, political and organisational needs, as many departments are not expected to make a profit in the same way as commercial organisations. For example, a company wanting government collected information on exporting to a foreign country could pay cost or market price for the service if the department is expected to act as a cost or profit centre; or more likely it could pay a subsidised price (or even be given the information free) if the government of the day felt that this would encourage exports and so benefit the well-being of the country.

Similarly products and services sold in public areas such as health, welfare, local government, education and defence will also have set price objectives that reflect society's and political needs rather than commercial effectiveness. It is worth adding here that public sector organisations are expected to operate in an efficient and cost-conscious manner. In the UK, the National Audit Office (www.open.gov.uk/nao/home.htm) is in place to oversee and make certain this happens.

Pricing in the not-for-profit sector

Although selling very little in the B2B sector, charities, trusts and mutual organisations will price according to commercial considerations wherever possible, but there will always be the need to take into account the wishes and demands of the many interested stakeholders.

Price and buying concerns in the NFP sector

In both types of NFP areas, the price that an organisation will be prepared to pay for B2B products and services will also reflect concerns other than those found in the commercial sector. In the health service, for example, political pressure has forced suppliers to supply drugs at a buyer dictated price. It can also force government departments to only buy within predetermined price limits. Similarly, charities will be expected to buy in products and services within strict pricing limits and non-adherence can cause stakeholder disapproval and sometimes some kind of public outcry. Of course this hasn't stopped public sector and NFP organisations paying well over the odds for products and services. This can be because of commercial inexperience and pricing naivety brought about by working in the public sector.

Specific B2B strategic pricing objectives

At the corporate level

☐ To fit with the corporate mission

☐ To obtain a required level of return on the capital invested.

At the marketing level

☐ To reach sales targets

☐ To make a profit

☐ To improve liquidity levels

☐ To open new accounts

☐ To open new markets

☐ To build long-term relationships

☐ To reward loyalty

☐ To offer added-value choices

☐ To meet fixed and variable cost considerations

☐ To sell across the product portfolio mix

☐ To match the competition

☐ To defend or attack against a competitor.

B2B pricing strategies

B2B pricing strategies and objectives might include the following.

Pricing low compared to the market norm

Some organisations will develop strategies based on trying to price as low as possible, sometimes across the whole product portfolio or on selective product lines. The following are reasons why a company might price low.

B2B markets

To achieve and maintain market share

Pricing may be consistently low across all markets so as to achieve and maintain market share. This strategy will tend to be used in commodity markets where competitive advantage might be difficult to achieve in any other way. This approach might only be available to the larger companies because of the need for economies of scale leading to lower costs and therefore lower prices than other market players. However, it can also be practised by the smaller organisations specialising in a particular product or service area. Examples might be a food company manufacturing and selling soups to a large supermarket chain under an own label brand (e.g. Wal-Mart or Tesco) or a small manufacturer specialising in particular types of metal fasteners.

To enter new markets

Pricing may be low when entering new markets so as to gain market share or to gain new customers. This is also known as penetration pricing and can often be the only way that a newcomer can enter into markets already served by others. The hope here is that once the supplier is seen as a worthy company to work with prices can be raised. Whether this wish can be fulfilled will depend on whether the value that might be added to the product or service is sufficient, in the mind of the buyer, to warrant a price rise.

B2C markets

To achieve and maintain market share

Some large retailers will also strategically price at a consistently low level so as to achieve and maintain market share. We see retail pricing strategies such as 'everyday low prices' (EDLP) from the supermarket group Asda and the 'price promise – find it at a lower price elsewhere and we will refund the difference' from electrical retailers Dixons and Comet. However, whether this truly applies to all products across the ranges offered can be difficult for the consumer to discover (unlike B2B) and some commentators argue that price confusion hides the more realistic picture.

To enter new markets

Lower prices and penetration strategies can also be used when companies want to enter new B2C markets, particularly fast-moving consumer goods (FMCG), hoping to gain market share. The hope is that the consumer will be satisfied and so want to repurchase at the higher price. Retailers, however, are just as likely to use advertising to create brand value or offer extra value, e.g. two for the price of one, as a market entry strategy, preferring to keep the consumer's mind off price comparisons.

Building relationships

B2B markets

B2B suppliers will often have large buyers spending large amounts of money. In these cases pricing strategies will be used to build, reinforce and maintain long-term relationships, rewarding loyalty, blocking the competition and encouraging greater supplier use. This can be carried out by up-front lower prices, quantity discounts, retrospective discounts (extra discount given at the end of the year if target purchase levels are met), and so on.

B2C markets

Retailers in B2C markets attempt to use price to form relationships with individual consumers, but the relationship is of a very different kind. Because they are dealing with millions of consumers it tends to be with segmented groups rather than with individuals, superficial rather than deep, and undeniably more valued by the retailer than the end consumer. Consumer loyalty is rewarded by added-value benefits such as loyalty points and money-off coupons on future purchases, rather than directly off the price when products are purchased.

Pricing high compared to the market norm

An organisation might feel that its products and services justify pricing above the market norm. The following are reasons why it might successfully follow this strategy of premium pricing.

B2B markets

Customers in both B2B and B2C markets are prepared to pay more for added value and premium products. The differences are that in B2B the added value must be tangible and meaningful, contributing to market advantage in a clearly defined, pragmatic way. In many product areas of B2B price is less important than added value because the particular component might only be a small part of the overall whole. The equipment offered must compare favourably with offerings currently on the market, ideally last longer, perform more effectively and/or be more economic than products or services already available. In the main premium products will not be purchased for symbolic reasons.

B2C markets

Whilst the functional benefits identified above are important in B2C markets, research has shown time and time again that a premium will be paid for products and services that have an emotional attraction encapsulated in the concept of the brand and are perceived to be of great value. Some consumers will pay more for a product such as Nike because of symbolic associations ('street credibility') and will be relatively unconcerned about such rational concerns as comfort and durability. This is a major reason why the product brand is more important in the B2C market than in the B2B.

Discriminatory and differential pricing

There are circumstances when a company is able to price its products and services differently in different markets. This can be controversial as there are some people that argue that this is an unfair practice based on a dominant market condition.

Example 7.1 **Dual pricing**

The European Competition Commissioner has barred GlaxoSmithKline (GSK) from the dual pricing of wholesale drugs in Spain. The Commission said EU rules barred GSK from charging one price to Spanish wholesalers for drugs they sell domestically and a higher price to the same wholesalers for the same drugs exported to the rest of the EU. It said that pharmaceutical companies, or other companies, cannot put into place distribution arrangements which perpetuate the partitioning of the single market into national markets. Drug companies argued that different health regulations across European countries caused the price variations.

B2B markets

Country and market conditions can, under certain circumstances, allow suppliers to discriminate and charge different prices in different markets. So the same product could cost more in the north of the country than in the south, or more in France than in Sydney. This could be because of such things as the extra delivery costs and different customs and exercise duties and tax laws. It could also be because customers are prepared to pay more in one market than in another so pricing is according to 'what the market will bear'. The opportunities for flexible differential pricing in B2B markets are receding, however, for a number of reasons.

1. *Competition.* An increase in global competition restricts the freedom on the prices a company can charge. Unless justified by added value, too high a price will allow other companies to move in and capture a market or customer.

2. *Small customer base.* Most B2B markets have a relatively small number of buyers and so one customer can know fairly quickly what other customers are being charged. Similarly, one supplier will usually know what other suppliers are charging and knowledgeable market players can easily overcome attempts at price secrecy by working through component costs and/or searching out information from a multitude of sources.

3. *Increased information.* Information technology has given comprehensive access to B2B supplier and buyer information from around the world. Costs and prices can now be compared almost immediately.

4. *International and global companies*. There has been an increase in mergers of organisations on both a national and global scale, so that in many cases a supplier might be selling to the same buyer in many parts of the world.

5. *Power*. As buyers become more powerful, they can insist on price parity.

6. *Legislation*. Anti-competition bodies, such as the UK Competition Commission, have increased power to search out and prosecute organisations that price products and services unjustly, especially if some buyers are deemed to be at an unfair advantage.

B2C markets

Discriminatory pricing could be said to be more prevalent in B2C markets than in B2B. There are opportunities for discriminatory pricing in B2C markets for the following reasons:

1. *Competition*. The competition tends to be contained and localised. Although multinationals exist in retail, many operate competitively on a local basis. The Tesco supermarket group might well charge different prices for its products in London compared to the provinces.

2. *Large customer base*. Although segmented into groups, most retail markets consist of many millions of customers and one individual/group will often be unaware of the prices that other individuals/groups are paying.

3. *Many different product offerings*. Many millions of products and product types exist in these markets and, unlike B2B, it can be very difficult to compare like with like.

4. *Increased information*. Similar to B2B markets, more information is now available through the internet and also through pressure groups such as the Consumers' Association and TV programmes such as 'Watchdog' on the BBC. However, because of the many different product offerings available, perfect information can be difficult to obtain.

5. *Power*. Consumers have relatively little power individually and it is only when they come together in groups that they can lobby effectively for price parity.

6. *Legislation*. Consumer legislation is channelled through bodies such as the UK Office of Fair Trading and the EU Competition Commission that seek to root out unfair discriminatory pricing policies, both nationally and across national boundaries. How successful this tends to be is continuously discussed, with some arguing that the power of the large producers and retailers will block any meaningful change.

Flexible and dynamic pricing strategies

Flexible pricing

Flexible pricing, as defined here, includes both differential pricing – in which different buyers may receive different prices based on expected benefits – and dynamic pricing mechanisms such as auctions, where prices and conditions are based on bids by market participants. Depending on the product or service, buyers will always be prepared to pay for extra benefits offered that are tailored to meet exact needs. Although this is true in both B2B and B2C, it is much more prevalent and individualistic in B2B markets where suppliers are invited in to customise solutions to particular problems and then price accordingly. In these circumstances the supplier must have a flexible pricing policy so that every possible contingency is catered for. This puts a great onus on supplier sales and backroom staff involved to make certain that the price eventually asked is enough to make a profit, takes into account competitor pricing, and covers the buyer benefits wanted.

Systems pricing

A variation of flexible pricing, systems pricing is an approach where prices are not given for the individual items or services that go to make up the whole product or service. All the benefits wanted are brought together and one overall price is given. For example, a computer system might include hardware, software, furniture, installation, staff training and servicing. This can make it very difficult for a buyer to compare one supplier with another. This should cause the buyer to insist that clear, detailed benefits are agreed and written into a systems contract so that arguments do not arise at a later time. All employees contributing to the costing and pricing process must have the skills and knowledge to prevent loss-making contracts, sometimes worth millions of pounds, being entered into over a long period. Systems pricing is used extensively in B2B markets but less in B2C. Areas in B2C might be buying fitted kitchens (furniture, fitting, electrical work, plumbing, and so on) or fitted bedroom furniture.

Dynamic pricing

Dynamic pricing allows for the increased use of auctions as a way of both buying and selling goods and services. The use of the internet as a way of buying and selling products and services has spearheaded this growth and many companies have developed flexible pricing policies to cope with this new market form. Only in special circumstances will B2C products be sold in this manner.

Competitive harmony pricing

Although active price collusion between companies is illegal (and the overseeing anti-competition bodies in the EU can fine guilty companies up to 10 per cent of their turnover), competitive harmony pricing or passive shadowing, that is charging the same price as the competitor, is not illegal. If market structures are favourable, for example oligopolistic, then tacit, unspoken agreements to compete on added value, e.g. quality, service, delivery and not price, may evolve between suppliers and retailers. This practice occurs in both B2B and B2C markets, but is probably easier to spot in the latter because of the many interest bodies concerned for the well-being of the consumer. Encouraging competition into these markets wherever possible helps to eradicate this practice.

Figure 7.2
Pricing across
the product life
cycle

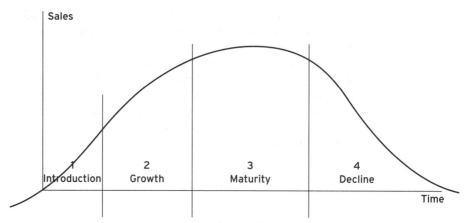

1. *Introduction*: Low price for market penetration; high price for premium product before
   competition comes in.
2. *Growth*:   Maintain price as market grows, increase profit through economies of scale.
   Lower price/add value in line with competition.
3. *Maturity*:   Lower price constantly increases value to defend market share.
   Offer special price contracts to existing or new outlets.
4. *Decline*:   Lower price to phase product out. Reposition product in new segment.
   Sell off at bargain price to specialised buyer(s).

Pricing across the product life cycle

As products move through the product life cycle (PLC), they might need to
change to take account of changing circumstances. With some products and services these changing needs could well have been strategically planned from
introduction and growth through to maturity and decline. With other goods and
services this might not have been possible because of market uncertainties over
the long term. Innovation has shortened the life cycle of many products, especially in the B2B market where functionality and effectiveness are at a premium.
For example, IT hardware and software have shorter and shorter life cycles and it
can take as little as 12 months for products to become outdated. So we see introductory high pricing decreasing significantly over a six- to twelve-month period.

Managing the price over the PLC (Figure 7.2) will need to take into account
other marketing mix functions as well as market activity. There are many strategic approaches and an example will include a high introductory price gradually
reducing as growth begins to move into maturity, and finally lowering even further as the product moves into decline and liquidation. Of course such things as
advertising and distribution would have to be examined as part of the process.
More strategic approaches will be discussed when we look at planning and control in Chapter 9.

Strategic pricing of new products

The pricing of new products in B2B will depend on the type of product, market
conditions and company objectives. Market research should have been used to

ascertain the customer segment reaction to products launched at different prices. New product objectives will determine whether the company wants to gain market share, claw back costs as quickly as possible, dominate a premium niche market, and so on. If the objective is to gain market share as quickly as possible and so restrict the movement of the competition, then penetration pricing will be used. If the objective is to make as much profit as possible before the competition comes in, then price skimming will be the strategy. This would entail charging an initial high price and then gradually reducing it as competitors entered the market. If the product is of high value, to be positioned in a niche market, then a premium price will be charged and constantly justified by customer communications. When in doubt, price higher (if possible) as it is easier to lower prices than to raise them.

Strategic and tactical pricing

There is a difference between long-term or strategic pricing objectives and short-term or tactical pricing objectives.

Long-term or strategic pricing objectives

As we outlined above ultimately the price objectives that the organisation sets and the strategies it adopts to achieve these objectives for its products and services must link back through agreed marketing and sales and profit objectives to the overall corporate objectives and corporate mission. Strategic pricing objectives must be established with care because they outline the approach that the organisation will adopt for the long term and involve a coordinated effort from all company departments. 'Long term' is relative and will vary from industry to industry. It might be one, two or three years in one area where dynamic change is inherent, e.g. technology, and five or ten years in another where relative market stability is more the norm, e.g. cars. Pricing policy must also integrate with all other elements of the marketing mix so that, for example, a premium price will reflect a premium service offered, or a low price the level of market share wanted.

Contrasting the pricing strategies of Federal Express and Blue Circle Cement illustrates the importance of a unified corporate marketing approach. FedEx (www.fedex.com) offers express packing and information transportation across the world within a guaranteed one to two business days – a premium service at a premium price and high profit margin. The strategy of Blue Circle Cement (www.bluecirclecement.co.uk, now part of the Lafarge Group) focuses on low-margin commodity products being priced low to build and maintain market share.

Significant company coordinated investment will be put into the strategic pricing approach to be adopted so the policy must be well thought through and rigorously implemented. To change the pricing strategy from premium pricing to low cost pricing would have serious resource and market implications and could well cause serious damage to the company's markets.

Short-term or tactical pricing objectives

Despite the long-term strategic objectives for the price, there will be many occasions when a need will arise for a company to react in the short term, tactically, to market and environmental circumstances. These might include the following:

☐ Loss of market share

☐ Defence against increased competition

☐ Cash flow difficulties

☐ Guaranteed pricing because of inflation

☐ Discount pricing as a form of trade promotional incentive, e.g. taking extra stock or pushing slow moving lines.

In theory the company would revert back to its original pricing strategy when the particular circumstance had changed back to normal. There is an academic argument about when the objective is strategic and when it is tactical (survival could be seen as both a strategic and tactical pricing objective). It could be argued that there is no right or wrong answer to this as whether an objective is strategic or tactical will depend on market circumstance, products offered, individual organisations and personal predilections.

☐ Costs

In both B2B and B2C markets the costs involved in producing goods and services must play a major part in determining the final price charged. Any fool can manufacture a product and sell below cost. However, to do this would very quickly lead to the company going out of business. So costs must be covered and a percentage amount added to allow for a reasonable profit. There are two ways that the company can increase its profitability: increasing the price and/or reducing its costs. In highly competitive markets it is impossible to do the former, so the latter becomes a major consideration when looking at the pricing of goods and services.

Customer demand for better products and lower prices forces suppliers continuously to examine and benchmark cost drivers so that the wasteful practices can be eliminated and efficiencies optimised in order that customer products and services are supplied at the best possible value. It is a truism that if a company isn't incessantly undertaking this process, the competition will, and so competitive advantage will be lost.

Because cost plays such an important part in deciding the final price (and determining the profit to be made), it is important that organisations are aware of all types of costs, where they arise and how they might be minimised in the most effective way.

Marketing and costs

As with all other departments, marketing can look towards its own costs and accountability structures, eliminate waste, set clear performance indicators, allocate levels of responsibility and implement value for money programmes. There should be a constant search for new and innovative ways of using the marketing tools and techniques to achieve optimum customer satisfaction.

Different sorts of costs

Marketing and financial managers must know which costs are linked to pricing decisions and how these will impinge on the efficiency and effectiveness of the business. To begin with we will look in simple terms at fixed and variable costs and their relationship with the product portfolio mix, volume of sales and levels of profits.

1. *Fixed costs*. These are the costs incurred whether the company produces goods and services or not. They include expenditure such as rent, rates, loan interest payments, administration, wages for permanent employees and any form of long-term contract such as a three-year sponsorship deal.

2. *Variable costs*. These are costs incurred only when products are produced, so they will be linked directly to the product or service itself.

3. *Mixed costs*. These are costs with both fixed and variable elements.

Fixed costs, variable costs and volume

The relationship between fixed costs, variable costs and volume sold across the whole product portfolio must be understood if the optimum cost savings are to be made. As fixed costs must be paid whatever the production, it is to the benefit of the organisation to spread these as widely as possible so all resource capability is used to its optimum level. All products in the portfolio need constant scrutiny to assess overall cost demands and revenue contribution. It is sometimes in the interest of a company to market low profit items because of the contribution to overall costs. A food manufacturer producing its own branded products for sale to retailers (B2C) might decide to make own label goods for the supermarket Tesco (B2B) to take up spare capacity and so spread the fixed costs.

It is important to remember that fixed costs are 'fixed' across a range of activities over a certain period of time and can change when this period ends. Wages, rent and interest payments could all increase at the end of the year. This possibility must therefore be examined when identifying the relationship between cost, volume and profit.

Identifying where costs arise

B2B marketing managers must be aware of where and how costs arise if they are going to be able to influence them in a meaningful way. They must also attempt to understand which activity within the business will benefit from the expenditure and who should be held responsible. Only in this way can clear objectives be set and the results monitored, controlled and improved. This is not always as easy as it may seem. Some costs, predominantly variable, can usually be attributed to the actual activity, e.g. the amount of paint on the car. Fixed costs are more difficult and have to be allocated, e.g. heating and lighting or administration costs. Direct and indirect costs are identified below.

Direct costs

Direct costs, both fixed and variable, are expenses that can be directly attributed to a particular project, activity, product, customer, or sales territory. They can be directly assigned to that project or activity with a high degree of accuracy.

Indirect costs

Indirect costs are expenses that cannot be specifically identified with a particular project or activity. Sometimes called 'overhead' or 'facilities and administrative' (F&A) costs, these are the costs of buildings, utilities, wages, marketing, and the many other expenses necessary for the operation of the business. These have to be allocated across all activities in as accurate a manner as possible. This can prove to be very difficult in practice as it can be nigh impossible at times to know which business area benefits from a given resource and by what amount. An example might be the cost of a long-term advertising campaign costing millions of pounds. Should the full cost be borne by the advertising department or spread among product development, manufacturing, sales, and so on? Similarly who should be responsible for damaged product returns – sales, distribution, or production? There might also be political problems involved as managers seek to gain advantage by pushing more costs onto others in order to appear to have a more efficient operation. The use of cost and profit centres and activity based costing are ways that managers try to overcome some of these problems. Cost factors to consider when pricing include:

- ☐ Costs of goods sold
- ☐ Marketing spend
- ☐ Overheads
- ☐ Sales commissions
- ☐ Intermediary mark-ups
- ☐ Shipping costs to distributors
- ☐ Possible returns
- ☐ Profit objectives.

Cost and profit centres

One way around the problem is to set up cost and profit centres. The business is divided into different 'centres' where costs and/or profits will arise. These can be in almost any form that the company wishes and include strategic business units, departments, sections, operations, processes and part processes of a business. Marketing will be concerned with the products, distribution, promotion mix, sales and customers, and so on. There is then an attempt to allocate the exact costs (and profits in the case of a profit centre) as they arise to each and every centre identified for usage. This will organise the business, help achieve financial control, motivate and give realistic responsibility for cost improvements to all employees involved.

Activity based costing (ABC)

Activity based costing is an accounting methodology that assigns costs to activities rather than products or services. This enables resource and overhead costs to be more accurately assigned to the products and services that consume these costs. It should operate to show clearly how costs flow into activities and what activities are involved for each marketing area, e.g. product and customer. Traditional accounting systems are often arbitrary and inaccurate in the way that they allocate costs so any particular activity can falsely show costs that are higher or lower than the actual case. ABC allows the manager to model more realistically the way that costs behave, and so manage processes for better results.

How ABC can be used with the customer

Organisations also need to know the costs involved with each and every customer as well as sales if a realistic profit figure is to be reached. Used with the marketing information system, ABC can provide managers with the information they need regarding the contribution each customer makes. If correctly applied and utilised, ABC can rank the customers in terms of costs and profits made. Studies have shown that 20 per cent of customers provide virtually all the profits of a company. Another 60 per cent break even and the remaining 20 per cent actually cost the company money. To determine how much a customer costs, every activity relating to each customer must first be identified, separated into individual cost drivers and then a total cost given. Cost drivers might include, but not be limited to, inside/outside sales, order processing, credit, delivery, telephone expenses, training and product returns. In this way all customer interactions can be measured and valued. Strategies can be adopted that maximise the relationship with the better customers, while minimising or even eliminating the more wasteful (Figure 7.3).

Activity based management (ABM)

ABM is a term for the management process that uses ABC information to improve performance as the key to better outcomes. It incorporates modern management techniques such as quality assurance, process re-engineering, benchmarking, best practice and Balanced Scorecard in attempts to constantly improve cost/benefit ratios.

Figure 7.3
Cost of a particular customer call

Traditional		ABC	
Salaries	£100	Obtain customer appointment	£40
Equipment	£80	Call on customer	£75
Supplies	£20	Order processing the customer	£75
Overhead	£45	Admin. for the customer	£55
TOTAL	£245	TOTAL	£245

The learning and experience effect on costs

The marketing strategist must also be aware of the changes in costs over time. Learning curve theory reflects the concept that we learn to do things quicker and more efficiently the more we undertake a particular task. Similarly, experience curve theory argues that as well as learning to do things more efficiently, experience should enable us to identify ways (e.g. new technology) to undertake the task more effectively. So a combination of learning skills, leading to task improvement, and experience and knowledge attainment should bring about an overall reduction in costs. As costs fall then prices will come down and sales will increase, leading to more cost savings through greater economies of scale. Learning and experience curves can be measured with a fall in costs seen as a function of the increase in turnover.

Selling at or below costs

Having just said that selling below costs will eventually lead to a company going out of business, there are circumstances when it might be propitious to allow this to happen.

As a loss leader

Selling at or below costs is practised in both B2C and B2B markets. In B2C a supermarket might sell a staple product such as bread, milk or petrol at a loss to encourage traffic flow and the sale of other more profitable goods. BSkyB offered its modems and dishes at low prices or even free of charge knowing that the consumer must then purchase its entertainment services on a regular basis. Likewise the B2B supplier will also offer goods at cost price to encourage the sale of other goods. This might be selling or leasing office equipment on the expectation of selling accessories and supplies, or heating equipment knowing that the continuous sales of running materials and servicing would then be locked in.

As a way of breaking into new markets and new customers

We outlined above how a seller might offer a particular product or service below cost as a means of obtaining initial entry into a buying organisation. Many large buying organisations such as Ford or Unilever will have some kind of relationship with existing suppliers and might be disinclined to try others because of the switching costs involved. Selling below costs can be used tactically as an initial sop to encourage trial and so, hopefully, encourage further orders. Of course there must be buyer potential to make this exercise worthwhile.

Spare capacity

If there is spare capacity, increased sales can absorb this slack and so contribute and spread the overall fixed costs.

To gain overall economies of scale

Similarly selling one type of product at cost or below can greatly increase the overall purchasing power of a supplier – enabling scale gains to be made in other areas that more than compensate.

Predatory pricing

Although difficult to prove, predatory pricing is illegal and stiff fines can make the perpetrator repent at leisure. The product is priced below cost so as to drive out the competition. Once they have gone the prices are raised.

Bad debts and costs

Some commentators might want to argue that the selling of goods and services is the easier part while the collection of the money is the hard part. It is a truism that a sale is not a sale until the goods and services have been paid for. This can be a real problem for some small (and not so small) suppliers serving just a few large buyers. The deferral of large payments can mean that urgent bills cannot be paid, leading to a downward circle of debt and eventually supplier closure. The small or medium sized supplier can find itself between a rock and a hard place: to refuse to serve the large buyer or to prosecute for late payment can lead to loss of sales so large that collapse would be on the cards. All the supplier can do under these circumstances is to talk to buyers, appeal to their sense of fairness, and hope that this will have the desired effect. There have been calls by trade associations, politicians and government departments for legislation to force companies to pay more quickly but up to now to no avail.

Debt factoring

It is possible for a creditor to sell off the debt to a third party, that is debt factoring, in return for an early payment at a lower price (perhaps 10 to 15 per cent off). It is then up to the debt factoring company to collect the money from the supplier.

☐ Customers and prices

Ultimately the price charged must be attractive to the customer. If a product or service is considered not to be of value then it will not be purchased. We know that B2B markets are segmented by industry and individual customer. It is crucial that communications are continuous so that changing benefit solutions are identified and relevant problem-solving products offered (Figure 7.4).

Pricing for different segments

In B2B markets different customer segments will derive different benefits from the products and services on offer. This will often happen with individual organisations

Figure 7.4
Forces shaping
the customer's
perception of
value

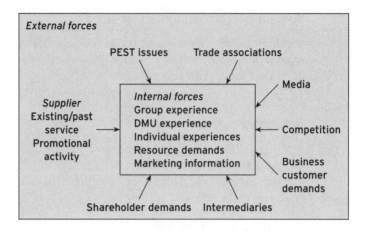

within customer segments, which will allow the supplier to charge varying prices depending on the added-value wanted. Marketing research should be used to identify benefits wanted and price expectations. Costs on the overall package can be made and the prices developed. The importance of price will vary from customer to customer and from segment to segment. Offering the customer the exact benefits wanted will shift the emphasis away from price, and the concomitant commoditisation of the product. Generally price in B2B is less important than in B2C.

B2B markets

In B2B markets customer product and service benefits wanted can often vary from country to country, from industry to industry and even from company to company. A single business product can be used in many different ways according to requirements. The costs and price to be charged will need to reflect both this and the importance it might have in its eventual usage. It is usual in the markets for buyers to indulge in meticulous price analysis and price comparisons. The sellers will need to have the relevant information at their fingertips, otherwise the level of professionalism will be questioned.

B2C markets

Needs and wants in B2C markets are also a major consideration and customers will be often be charged differing prices according to the quality and level of service offered. However, it will mostly be according to large segmented groups rather than individual customers. The differences in the product and the subsequent price variations charged will also be much less than in the B2B market where discussion on service benefits needed can be on a one-to-one basis. Customers in both markets will be prepared to pay a higher price for convenience, time and risk reducing factors. Some organisations will develop niche markets to take advantage of these types of benefits wanted. Although price will be of relative importance, customers do not indulge in such intricate price comparison as in B2B markets.

Customers in the public sector market

As with many other aspects of B2B marketing, buyers in the public sector and to a lesser extent in the NFP sector will have to justify the prices paid to many stakeholders as the money spent will ultimately come from the taxpayer. This will probably mean that prices and costs have to be detailed, transparent and available for public inspection. The Public Accounts Committee is the UK overseeing body that monitors all public spending.

☐ Market structures and price

Market structures were discussed in detail in Chapter 1 and each structure identified will have an effect on the prices that can be charged. The price effect and some of these structures are now discussed:

☐ Monopoly
☐ Controlled monopoly
☐ Oligopoly
☐ Monopolistic competition
☐ Free competition
☐ Adulterated competition.

Price and monopoly markets

Because of government commitment to competition we see fewer examples of monopoly markets. Where monopolies exist, perhaps through having a patent or access to new technology (Microsoft), the organisation can either control the price or control the level of demand. Setting a high price will cause demand to fall, and setting a low price will cause demand to rise. Public indignation leading to a general outcry and bad public relations are about the only protection from overpricing in monopoly situations. An example might be pharmaceutical companies being persuaded to reduce the price of AIDS treatment to Third World countries through international condemnation. There can be markets where there might be only one buyer, known as a monopsony market. This market will operate under similar circumstances to monopoly markets but with roles between buyer and seller reversed.

Price and controlled monopoly markets

We know that many erstwhile public monopolies were sold into the private sector under the control of an independent regulator. In many cases the regulating bodies (OFWAT, OFGAS, OFCOM) are able to restrict price increases to within preset boundaries.

Price and oligopolies

Oligopolies are characterised by only a few sellers all offering very similar products and services. Oligopolies find it unhelpful to compete on price because the lowering of price by one of the players will only encourage the others to follow suit. This might trigger a price war with the end result being lower prices and lower profits for all, with no one firm gaining any advantage. This situation encourages a tacit acceptance of price levels while attempting to gain differential advantage through non-price added value competitive activities such as corporate image enhancement, innovations and customer relationship service.

In B2C markets product brand and sales promotions are more likely to be used to gain this differentiation. Where there are only a few large market players, the temptation to collude on maintaining price levels is always an option. Although difficult to prove, this practice is against UK and EU competition law and transgressors can be very heavily fined if it is shown to be happening. On an international scale it is more difficult to prevent and probably the most striking example is the OPEC cartel set up by a number of countries to keep oil prices and oil production within agreed limits. There are occasions when a seller will face just a few major buyers, known as oligopsonies. In such cases as this the seller becomes a price taker as this market will operate in a similar way as an oligopoly market.

Price and monopolistic competition

Monopolistic competition is similar to oligopoly markets in that it is a market dominated by just a few major organisations. It is different, however, in that there are many close substitute products and so demand is elastic – making it reasonably simple for buyers to switch to another seller. Firms try to differentiate their products through non-price competition such as corporate and product branding, location, service, etc. This type of market structure is more prevalent in B2C markets than B2B where supermarket groups such as Tesco, Asda, Sainsbury's and Safeway try to differentiate themselves by value added marketing rather than price. B2B markets can more easily buy from around the world, and are less susceptible to emotion-driven corporate and product branding.

Price and free competition

Like monopoly markets, free or pure B2B competitive markets are rarely observed in practice. Very few industries have many competitors all selling the same or very similar products with no way that the customer can differentiate between them. This might perhaps apply to some commodity markets such as aggregates or basic minerals, but even here companies can differentiate in terms of quality, delivery, location and long-term relationships, which are highly important factors in B2B markets but less so in B2C. Where elements of free competition operate, demand is elastic and buyers can easily substitute and switch from one company to another. Thus all sellers become price takers rather than price setters. Profits will be minimal and the inefficient will be priced out of the market because of too high costs.

Price and adulterated competition

Most markets have elements of all the above, but with differences between industry and industry. Because of company size, financial strength, access to information, location and other circumstances we can find localised elements of monopoly, oligopoly and free competition in many industries and markets.

Price, the public sector and its influence on commercial markets

Pricing objectives in the public sector were discussed earlier in the chapter but it is worth identifying how public body pricing policies can affect B2B commercial markets. Because public bodies are not set up to make a profit, they are not under the same pressures as a commercial company. So in circumstances where the two sectors are in competition or one is buying from the other, the public body is powerful enough to dictate the price level for a whole industry. Similarly when borrowing money on the open market governments will heavily influence money-lending rates in both the long and short term.

☐ Price and levels of demand

Demand was discussed in some detail in a previous chapter. There is no doubt that levels of demand will have an effect on the prices that companies are able to charge for their products and services. Basic economics informs us that heavy demand will push the price up and low demand will push the price down. The difficulty for the marketing strategist is to try to forecast levels of demand at various price points. Revenue objectives depend on both number and price of products sold. Using some form of time value method the marketer must estimate the different levels of sales over a certain time period. This must take into account fluctuation in demand at the various stages of the product cycle as well as the different prices which might have to be charged.

Levels of demand and price changes are more volatile in B2B than in B2C. In some cases in B2B markets price cannot be changed once contracts have been agreed and so demand and supply fluctuation might have to be lived with, at least in the short term. In general, however, demand and price changes for many products and services will feed through pretty quickly in B2B markets. In some cases component parts have little effect on the overall price and a price will not alter greatly the buyer's selling price.

Some B2B have a small product portfolio and little room to absorb price increases, especially if they are working on a small profit mark-up. Commodity prices can also be very volatile so price can alter quite rapidly at the back end of the supply chain. In B2C markets, demand is more stable and it takes time for the need for products and services to decline or increase across large market segments. Often price increases can be absorbed more easily in stages down through the supply chain before they arrive at the retail outlet. Competition, substitute products, publicity and consumer resistance are factors that also make it difficult to pass on price increases to the end consumer. A good pricing strategy will contain guidelines for a response to price increases or decreases by others in the market. Although it is not possible to make allowances for every contingency, at least the organisation can make sure it has some outline plans in abeyance.

☐ Competitor response to pricing

Competitors in B2B markets will inevitably influence the pricing in the market and organisations must have as much information as possible on the price and cost structure and strategic objectives of other players in the market. In this way competitors' reactions to price changes can be predicted. This information can be obtained by one salesperson talking to another, from compliant buyers and from annual reports and public statements. Knowledgeable marketers should also be able to examine and evaluate competitor behaviour and make realistic deductions about pricing, cost strategies and objectives.

Competitor behaviours in the different market structures were discussed earlier and it is safe to assume that in any type of competitive market a price change by one firm will trigger some kind of reaction from another. This reaction will depend on such things as the importance of the segment, direction and magnitude of the price change and the ability and power of the competitor to be able to respond. Market leaders will want to maintain this position and a price attack by others will result in the price change being matched or even bettered. In some situations a company will be prepared to take a loss in order to maintain the status quo.

☐ Price and role of legislation in B2B markets

Although there has been a movement to diminish the amount of legislation, red-tape and bureaucracy that can hinder the free flow of goods and services both at home and across the EU, there has been an increase in the amount of legislation brought in to stop anti-competitive pricing activity.

Anti-competitive pricing legislation

Legislation exists in both B2B and B2C markets to control the movement of prices. In extreme circumstances the Secretary of State for Trade and Industry, the Office of Fair Trading and overseeing regulatory bodies will refer cases to the Competition Commission where it is felt that price movements are suspect and could cause political, social and economic difficulties. Any company that has a problem with price demands in the market can complain to the Office of Fair Trading, which exists in some form in most developed countries. An investigation will take place and if there is evidence of wrongdoing such as price collusion, price fixing, unfair discriminatory pricing, and so on, the matter will be referred to a competition commission that can order the practice to stop, and in extreme cases impose heavy fines.

Companies will look for ways to circumvent the law. With price signalling sophisticated ways are developed by which companies tell one another their pricing strategies without overtly colluding and thus breaking the law; e.g. talking to the press about the need for general price increases will signal intentions to other competitors.

Pricing and incomes policies

There are occasions in times of high inflation when governments have introduced price legislation, restricting the amount that prices (and often incomes) can rise across the board. Such measures seldom work as supply and demand factors have the effect of developing two markets: the official market where prices remain within the government guidelines but cause a product shortage, and the unofficial or 'black' market where prices are higher and products are available.

Subsidies

Some countries will subsidise the price of certain basic commodity products such as bread, rice and milk to make certain that the economically disadvantaged do not suffer. Suppliers are given guaranteed prices and products are then made available at reduced prices. The government makes up the difference. Considered to be anti-competitive except to protect fledgling industries, most governments are attempting to reduce and eventually eliminate subsidies. As you would expect, this is not well accepted by those sections of society that receive the subsidies, but welcomed by those that do not and consider it unfair practice.

Example 7.2   **The Competition Commission (www.competition-commission.org.uk)**

The Commission has two distinct functions: first, carrying out inquiries into matters referred to it by the other UK competition authorities concerning monopolies, mergers and the economic regulation of utility companies; second, the newly established Appeal Tribunals hear appeals against decisions of the Director General of Fair Trading and the regulators of utilities in respect of infringements of the prohibitions contained in the Act concerning anti-competitive agreements and abuse of a dominant market position. It has the power to fine miscreants up to 10 per cent of their turnover.

Example 7.3   **Competition Commission investigation**

In March 2002 the Civil Aviation Authority (CAA) (aircraft business regulator) asked the Competition Commission to investigate and report on the maximum charges that could be levied over the five-year period from 1 April 2003. The charges relate to the three London airports owned by BAA plc, namely Heathrow, Gatwick and Stansted, and cover those levied for landing and parking aircraft, and include passenger-related charges. It also asked for the report to consider whether any of these airports has acted against the public interest in any of their airport-related activities at any time since the last investigation in 1995.

The European Competition Commission operates across the whole of Europe and the Federal Trade Commission operates in the US. Many others operate in individual countries around the world with the same or a similar mandate.

UK National Audit Office

The UK National Audit Office is the independent public spending watchdog. With 750 staff it audits expenditure of over £600 billion on behalf of parliament. It audits the accounts of all government departments and agencies as well as a wide range of other public bodies, and reports to parliament on the economy, efficiency and effectiveness with which government bodies have used public money. It purports to save the taxpayers millions of pounds a year.

Part 3 Other aspects of price in B2B marketing

In Part 3 we will look at many other aspects that have an effect on costs and pricing. These include the following:

1. Price and the concept of elasticity
2. Price negotiations
3. The internet and its effect on pricing
4. Price and global markets
5. Strategic and tactical methods used in determining price.

☐ Price and the concept of elasticity

The concept of product elastic and inelastic demand is important to marketing managers in both B2C and B2B as it will impinge on their ability to move the price of the product either up or down and so increase sales and profit. There is little point in increasing the price of the product by 10 per cent in the hope of making a profit only to find that demand falls by 50 per cent. Similarly the results will be disappointing if the price is reduced by 10 per cent only to find that sales do not increase. In both cases a loss of profit will ensue. However, if the 10 per cent decrease leads to a 50 per cent increase in sales, then profits will increase from both a jump in products sold and the resultant cost savings as greater economies of scale are achieved. So price elasticity of demand refers to the percentage change in quantity demanded caused by the percentage change in price. It may be profitable in some cases to delay price increases if the market segment is price elastic. Although profit margins will decrease this could be offset by a temporary increase in volume and maybe a longer term increase in market share.

Price elasticity in markets

In B2B price elasticity of demand can vary from market segment to market segment and even from customer to customer depending on many factors including the following:

☐ The value that product or service represents to the buyer (commodity or premium?).

- ☐ The importance of the component in the cost structure of the customer's product.
- ☐ Information available on alternative products and prices.
- ☐ The costs involved in switching from one supplier to another.
- ☐ The risks involved in moving supplier.
- ☐ The ability to pass on costs.
- ☐ The amount of competition.
- ☐ The availability of substitute products over both the short and long term.

Price elasticity in B2C markets

The concept of price elasticity of demand is also important in B2C markets. Although there are similarities to B2B markets, there are also subtle differences including the following:

- ☐ The amount of disposable income enjoyed by the consumer.
- ☐ The basic need for the product.
- ☐ The importance of the product to a certain lifestyle and the availability of substitute products, e.g. petrol.
- ☐ The availability of substitute brands; consumers tend to buy from a repertoire of acceptable brands.
- ☐ The strength of brand in building loyalty. Advertising and global branding can create a sense of uniqueness that will appeal to consumer emotions and through this build in more inelasticity.
- ☐ Switching costs are less than in B2B and it is relatively easy for a consumer to move from one retailer to another and from one product to another as long as substitute products are available.

The existence of huge market segments can cause large volume changes with elastic products or higher profits with inelastic products. By lowering its prices and accepting lower profit margins (epitomised by the slogan 'pile it high and sell it cheap'), the Tesco supermarket group was able hugely to increase its sales. Increased sales gave greater buying power because of economies of scale, an increased customer base and swifter product turnover, which all enabled it to grow to be the largest and most profitable grocer in the UK.

☐ Price negotiation

You don't get what you deserve, you get what you negotiate.

(Anon.)

In many markets, especially low value or commodity markets, price will be a continuous process of negotiation and prices will shift back and forth according to levels of supply and demand, extra benefits on offer and power position in the marketplace. In other situations the negotiations on price are for long-term contracts and so could be considered more important because of the commitment involved. Some exchange processes are with existing customers and some are with brand new customers. In all cases the negotiation strategies could be different and personal and interpersonal skills should be honed so as to acquire the most professional approach. Below we have identified two basic approaches: cooperative and adversarial.

Cooperative or adversarial approach

Two distinct approaches to price negotiation between B2B buyer and seller have developed over the ages. In the past the major approach would have been adversarial, with both buyer and seller seeing each other as on opposite sides of a divide and the buyer trying to buy at the lowest price and the seller trying to sell at the highest price. Negotiation would then involve quantity amounts, benefits demanded, delivery terms, and so on. There would bluff and counter-bluff until a price could be agreed. This might be a mutually beneficial arrangement, a win–win situation, or it could be more beneficial to one than the other, a win–lose situation. With the adversarial approach, every encounter is a new round of negotiation and the process starts all over again.

Cooperative strategic pricing

Although some buyers are happy with the adversarial method of negotiation many are now more sensitive to traditional sales techniques, manipulation and tricks and so reject this approach as inefficient, costly and not fully utilising all buyer and seller skills and resources in a synergistic manner. The movement on pricing in many B2B markets is now towards a more cooperative approach with both sides wanting a longer term relationship where price and costs are discussed in parallel with other added value factors focused on competitive advantage and ultimate customer satisfaction.

We have discussed in earlier chapters the growth in the closeness of supply chain relationships with all buyers and suppliers working together to increase the effectiveness of the whole and building extra customer value at every stage. Pricing is a major part of the process and strategic pricing decisions will often need to be discussed and decided by both buyer and seller. It is here that the degree of power in the relationship will often dictate the prices to be charged. The negotiation process might be democratic and balanced, with both sides contributing to the eventual prices to be charged, or it might be a case of one partner, usually a large buyer, autocratically telling the other, a small dependent supplier, the price it will be prepared to pay.

The more understanding and enlightened buyer will appreciate the cost and profit needs of the seller, open this up to sympathetic discussion, and both agree a 'win–win' pricing scenario. Pricing contracts might be agreed for the forthcoming year to be renegotiated at the end of this period. In this way loyalty can be developed, leading to a mutually beneficial association.

Price negotiation in B2B

Although many B2B organisations will have clear pricing policies and catalogues with identified prices across a range of products, others will not and a process of negotiation will decide prices. We have discussed above how price can vary according to benefits demanded, but it can also vary according to factors such as length of the contract (if any), quantity amounts wanted, delivery conditions, payment methods, and power relations and partnership arrangements between the negotiating companies. In fact depending on the B2B products and services offered and market conditions, price might always be open to some degree of negotiation because of the possible large amounts involved and the continuous pressure along the supply chain on costs and efficiency. The more value in the deal being negotiated, the more senior will be the sales managers involved, as no organisation wants to be committed to a long-term unprofitable contract.

Price negotiation in B2C

Pricing in B2C markets tends to be less open to price negotiation. Finished branded products sold to the retailer offer little room for price negotiation as established producers have clear percentage mark-downs, calculated from the estimated selling price, that are offered to the retail buyer based on accumulate costs. Of course that is not to say that there are no occasions when retailers will be offered lower prices, e.g. for extra amounts ordered or on outdated products. Independent retailers often join together into 'voluntary buying groups' so that they can obtain better prices on larger group orders.

Although consumers are consulted about pricing levels in B2C markets through the use of both qualitative and quantitative research, it tends to be on a mass superficial level. In the main, end consumers have very little room for price manoeuvre and have to accept the asking price on most products. Only if they come together can they usually obtain better prices.

☐ The internet and its effect on pricing

For hundreds of years, businesses used negotiation and bartering as a matter of routine. The industrial age saw the emergence of mass production and extended distribution chains, which made face-to-face negotiations with each customer impractical. Fixed prices became necessary to manage the enormous growth in both the volume and variety of products, distributed over larger geographic regions.

The advent of the internet and electronic commerce has greatly affected the way businesses price their goods and services. It has allowed for more flexible pricing based on customer characteristics or is dynamically determined based on supply and demand.

Two trends in electronic commerce are causing this shift from fixed to dynamic pricing. First, the internet has reduced the transaction costs associated with dynamic pricing by eliminating the need for people to be physically present in time and space to participate in a market. The menu costs are also considerably reduced. Whereas in the physical world changing a price incurs huge costs, the same task in electronic commerce is reduced to a database update.

Second, price uncertainty and demand volatility have risen and the internet has increased the number of customers and competitors, and the amount and timeliness of information. In addition, the increased use of flexible pricing leads to increased price uncertainty. Businesses are finding that using a single fixed price in these volatile internet markets is often ineffective and inefficient.

The internet and differential pricing

Electronic markets can reduce customers' costs for obtaining information about prices and product offerings from alternative suppliers. They can also reduce these suppliers' costs for communicating information about prices and product characteristics to customers. This has implications for the efficiency of an economy in terms of the search costs experienced by buyers and their ability to locate appropriate sellers. Electronic catalogues were the first step in this direction. Over the past few years, companies have put their product catalogues on the web in order to make them widely available. Most electronic catalogues are comprised of fixed offers in the form of fixed list prices. Search engines make it easy for customers to compare these offers and so the supplier must be continually updating its pricing on standardised products if it wants to stay ahead of the game. This problem will not be so acute where unique benefits and services are being offered.

Example 7.4 Pricing on the internet

The type of B2B arrangement that raises the most antitrust questions involves cooperative efforts by members of the same industry to buy or sell over the internet. The Federal Trade Commission examined a fledgling cooperative effort among General Motors, Ford, Daimler-Chrysler, Renault and Nissan to provide services to firms in the automotive supply chain. These are, of course, among the largest automobile manufacturers in the world and compete with each other for sales. The entity formed is supposed to facilitate the purchase of supplies. Pricing is the antitrust problem most commonly identified with cooperative B2B arrangements. If each participant can post its own individually established prices and is free to negotiate pricing with particular customers (e.g. 'off-line pricing') then a price fixing problem will probably not arise. Any restrictions on pricing can raise problems, however. For instance, a B2B arrangement involving restraints on participants to alter prices or requiring uniform prices would be almost certain to violate the antitrust laws. In addition, a cooperative B2B arrangement that restricted credit terms or resulted in some members boycotting particular suppliers would also raise serious antitrust issues. Participants in joint B2B arrangements need to realise that under the antitrust laws all members of a 'conspiracy' may be held equally liable, even if they did not actively participate in the particular transactions raising questions.

IT technology, computer software and its effect on pricing

As with all areas of business, technology is now firmly entrenched as an essential part of the pricing process. The marketing information system should be constructed to easily provide information, past, present and future, on customers and markets. Customised software is also available to measure demand elasticity and to model the sales that might be made from various price charges. Software programs will enable users to review price changes quickly and see how changes have affected costs, movement and contribution. Models can be built mirroring the whole market so that all reactions to different price changes can be measured and evaluated. Competitor, customer, overall demand, etc. can be looked at individually and/or as a group and predictions made about the future. Computer simulations allow pricing strategies to be established against competitors in a particular trading zone, while measuring the potential gross profit of the strategy. From this costs, sales and profit targets can be generated that permeate from the top down to the bottom of the organisation.

☐ Price and global markets

International and global suppliers will need to price their goods and services in other countries as well as their own. The question arises as to how this might be done: whether to centralise marketing mix decisions at HQ or to allow all or some of these decisions to be made in individual countries. This is a recurrent problem in both B2B and B2C markets and will be discussed in more detail in the next chapter. If costs and pricing policies are controlled then a clear line of monitoring and control can be established. However, this does not allow marketing managers to take into account localised factors that will impinge on costs and prices across the product portfolio. These factors will include the following:

☐ Standards of living will vary from country to country and a reasonable price in one country will seem exorbitant in another.

☐ If production is in the home country, then the same costs will dictate the price wherever products are sold. This has driven many organisations to outsource production to the lowest cost countries.

☐ By custom and practice prices across the whole market may be higher or lower than in the seller's home market.

☐ Similarly culture may have an effect on the way that prices are negotiated, agreed and then paid for.

☐ If production is in the peripheral country where the products are to be marketed rather than in the home country, costs would probably be lower and so the price can be lower.

☐ Where exchange rates fluctuate, price changes can cause buyer concern and loss of sales if the products become too uncompetitive. Long-term contracts and/or the use of a universal currency such as the euro can help alleviate this.

☐ Transfer pricing by global companies can push the costs and profits to the most propitious and beneficial country.

☐ Although countries are forming large trading blocs moving towards similar market conditions, legislation, tax laws, subsidies and barriers to market entry will still possibly vary from country to country. These factors will all have an effect on the prices that can be charged.

Pricing and power relationships

All relationships to a greater or lesser degree are power relationships and it is no different between buyer and seller in B2B markets. In most situations the large and strong buying organisation will nearly always be able to dictate costs and prices where any type of supplier competition exists. The responsible buying organisation will want to build good relationships with suppliers and so negotiate prices that allow the partnership to grow and blossom, enabling quality goods and services to be supplied. Other organisations are not so responsible and negotiate very low prices, forcing the seller to cut costs to the bone. This has led to notorious examples of producers in developing countries paying very low wages, operating dreadful working conditions and employing child labour. In some cases the moral outcry and subsequent bad publicity have forced buyers to revisit and readjust supplier relationships.

☐ Strategic and tactical methods for determining price

The factors affecting the pricing of the product need to be considered and pricing methods chosen. There are many different methods available, at both the strategic and tactical levels, and the following will be discussed:

☐ Cost-plus pricing

☐ Going rate pricing

☐ Break-even and target revenue/profit pricing

☐ What-the-market-will-bear pricing

☐ Customer-driven pricing.

Tactical or secondary methods will include:

☐ Psychological pricing

☐ Lease pricing

☐ Sealed bid pricing

☐ Open bid pricing

☐ Auction pricing

☐ Bartering

☐ Reciprocal arrangements.

Cost-plus pricing

This method of pricing has an immediate attraction because of its apparent simplicity and it can be used in both B2B and B2C markets. The cost of the strategic business unit (SBU), e.g. the product or service, is worked out by allocating a portion of the fixed costs to each product (using cost and profit centres and ABC costing will help in more accurately achieving this) and then adding it to the variable costs. This will give the total cost of each SBU. The percentage profit wanted is then added to the total cost to give the expected selling price. Although it is crucial for planning and control purposes to know wherever possible the total cost of all designated SBUs, there is a misassumption made here. This is that having established total costs, all the product manager needs to do is add the desired mark-up to obtain the selling price and then offer the product onto the market.

What this does not take into account is the fact that the competition may be offering a similar product at a lower price because of greater productivity or a willingness to work on a lower mark-up. Similarly, the customers may be unwilling to pay the price because they might be willing to go without, buy a substitute product or buy it cheaper from the competition. This method of pricing will only work where there is excess demand or a monopoly or oligopoly type market.

Cost-plus pricing in B2B

Cost-plus pricing can work in B2B under the following circumstances:

☐ Where the benefits offered are specialised and/or complex.

☐ Where there are no substitute products.

☐ In a monopoly or oligopoly market.

☐ Where there is excess demand.

☐ Where costs and pricing policies have been agreed between buyers and sellers.

Going rate pricing

In many industries, in both B2B and B2C, the structure of the market will decide the general level of prices. In an unregulated monopoly market, almost any price can be charged bearing in mind the trade-off between profit and sales. At the other end of the market – perfect competition – the price will be decided by the interplay of supply and demand and be outside the control of the organisation. Most companies, however, will be setting their prices somewhere between these two extremes.

Adopting the going rate pricing, the company will set the price according to price levels that are already used in their particular market. These price levels might have come about through tacit agreement, similar cost and profit needs, customer demands, or by competitive market interaction. A pattern of different price bands tends to develop, each aimed at different target groups. A firm launching a new product will price its products and compete within these price bands (or price plateaus).

The advantage in adopting a going rate pricing policy is that there is little or no effort needed in deciding the price as the market will have set the parameters. This is particularly helpful if the going rate allows for high profit margins due to little competition and/or a concentration on added value rather than price (oligopoly market?). It is in no company's interest to rock the boat by lowering the prices and perhaps causing a price war and a downward spiral.

The disadvantage of going rate pricing is that it can lead to complacency and inefficiency. Almost any market is now open to invasion from competitors around the world prepared to ignore custom and practice and set their prices according to a lower cost base or offer more innovative products at the same prices and so steal market share. This is particularly so in B2B where products and services tend to be aimed at narrow and more specialised markets.

Break-even and target revenue/profit pricing

Some organisations, in both B2B and B2C, will price products to break even (cover both fixed and variable costs) or reach profit targets within a certain period. If a higher price is charged then total costs recovery will be quicker and if a lower price is charged then total costs recovery will be longer. This might be because financial backers impose time demands, in terms of payback period and profit targets, and so the prices charged would need to conform to agreed revenue and profit targets. The flexibility to do this would, of course, depend on the factors identified earlier.

What-the-market-will-bear pricing

Pricing by what the market will bear is to take advantage of market conditions such as shortages, scarcity, or a product's uniqueness at a particular moment in time, and setting the price at the highest figure the customer is prepared to pay.

This may, on the surface, seem to be an attractive method because optimum profits can be achieved. A word of caution, however. There are times when higher prices can be charged and customers have little or no choice but to pay. This will not necessarily cause hardships in B2B markets if the component accounts for a small amount of the finished item. But there will be occasions when illwill might be generated which could have long-term detrimental effects, with the buyer looking elsewhere when the first opportunity arises.

Customer-driven pricing

If we were to take a marketing approach the price should be set at the level the customer is willing and satisfied to pay. This level can be found through the use of marketing research. This price may vary from segment to segment and according to the many benefits that might be added to the product or service. The benefits offered by others, and the overall prices traditionally charged across the whole marketplace, will determine the degree of buyer expectation on what benefits could normally be obtained from any one pricing level (see Figure 7.5).

☐ Tactical or secondary pricing methods

Psychological pricing

Although there are occasions when psychological pricing, for example charging £999.99 instead of £1000, might be attractive in B2B markets, these are rare and much more prevalent in B2C markets. This is because of the many different reasons for purchase between the two markets identified in many places throughout the book.

Figure 7.5
Factors to
consider when
deciding the
final price in
B2B markets

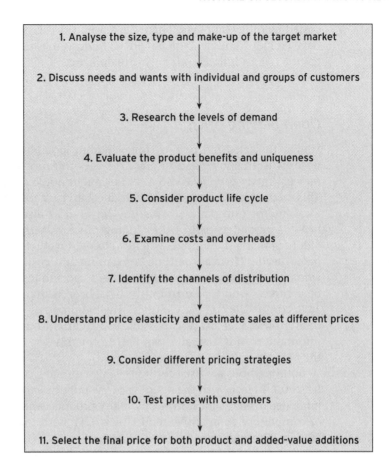

1. Analyse the size, type and make-up of the target market

2. Discuss needs and wants with individual and groups of customers

3. Research the levels of demand

4. Evaluate the product benefits and uniqueness

5. Consider product life cycle

6. Examine costs and overheads

7. Identify the channels of distribution

8. Understand price elasticity and estimate sales at different prices

9. Consider different pricing strategies

10. Test prices with customers

11. Select the final price for both product and added-value additions

Lease pricing

Leasing allows the business to use high value products and services over an extended period rather than making one large purchase investment for immediate ownership. Payments are spread over a negotiated period and can include extras such as maintenance, servicing and repairs. At the end of the lease period the product can be purchased at about the current market price. The use of leasing in B2B markets has increased over the decades and can be used for all B2B products and services. It is beginning to be used in B2C markets, e.g. the purchase of cars, but the occasions are few and far between.

Sealed bid pricing

With sealed bid pricing, suppliers are invited to submit a price and a description of the level of benefits to be offered to a buyer wanting a particular product or service. Usually (though not always) the lowest price will win the contract. Often only a small number of suppliers (e.g. six or seven), previously vetted and placed on an acceptance list, are allowed to tender. The sealed bid tender is usually in writing (or perhaps now on the internet) and each supplier is unaware of the price costed by other suppliers. There have been occasions when competing suppliers have colluded and deliberately priced high so that each one in turn receives the contract at an inflated price. This malpractice, if discovered, will result in a fine and/or imprisonment.

Open bidding pricing

Similar to sealed bid pricing, open bidding pricing allows suppliers to discuss needs with the buyer and to make offers both formally and informally. A buyer may use many suppliers who might or might not know what others are bidding. This method is often used where product/service needs are complex, highly technical and/or uncertain. In this way buyers can discuss problems and possible benefits needed as part of the bidding process. With both sealed bid and open bidding pricing the supplier will need to put together a quote based on identified buyer needs. This can be time consuming and costly, especially if the order is won by another company. On the other hand and just as much of a problem can be contracts won that turn out to have been badly thought through, so ultimately costing the company money. The bid proposal will need to be put together in as professional a way as possible using current buyer, market and competitor information. Bids that fail should be thoroughly scrutinised to help discover why the bid lost.

Both methods are used for high value contracts in both the private and public sector. In fact, with the opening of the public sector to competition, more and more departments must now buy many products and services through a process of compulsory competitive tendering (CCT). Both the above methods are rarely used in B2C markets.

Auctions

Internet growth has seen the increase in website market exchanges as a method to facilitate the use of auction as a way of buying and selling B2B products. Auctions have been used in the past, especially in commodity 'spot' markets. A spot market is where a commodity is purchased 'on the spot' at current market rates for immediate delivery. The following are types of auctions:

☐ *English auction*: buyers start bidding at a low price. The highest bidder wins and pays the last price bid.

☐ *Dutch auction*: the auctioneer starts very high and calls out progressively lower prices. The first buyer to accept the price wins and pays that price.

☐ *Reverse auction*: used to purchase instead of sell. The lowest bid wins. All auction types can be used in reverse.

☐ *Double auction*: both buyers and sellers submit bids and the closest are brought together.

Example 7.5   **WorldWide Retail Exchange (www.worldwideretailexchange.com)**

Online marketplaces or B2B 'hubs' are where large companies join together to purchase products by auction. This one has over 50 members including M&S, Dixons, Boots, John Lewis, Auchan, Gap, Kingfisher and Safeway. Suppliers from around the globe are invited to bid for B2B products wanted and advertised on the website. Lowest supply price wins.

Bartering and other reciprocal arrangements

Some companies agree to 'barter' and exchange or swap goods or services directly without the use of money. Both buyer and seller must be happy with this arrangement for this to happen. Although price isn't used directly, a value of some kind must be negotiated and agreed by both parties if this to happen. Bartering arrangements are sometimes implemented by governments anxious to support their own industries by insisting that goods and services bought from abroad are paid for not by precious foreign exchange, but with home country goods and services. If forced into this arrangement, the initial seller may have to make arrangements to sell the bartered goods on to others if the seller cannot make use of them. Bartering arrangements can fall foul of legislators and tax authorities.

A buyer may sometimes insist on the seller purchasing some of the buyer's own products in return for an order. Of course the seller must use the buyer's products in some way, otherwise the agreements couldn't work. Reciprocal arrangements such as this work well and help to build fruitful relationships if there is a genuine need for each other's products. Care must be taken, however, not to upset the competition authorities who will strike hard if it is felt that the reciprocal arrangements are anti-competitive in some way. Bartering and reciprocity arrangements are rare or non-existent in B2C markets except in very small markets in developing countries.

Example 7.6   **Bartering growing**

The International Reciprocal Trade Association (www.irta.com), the bartering industry's trade body, estimates that $16 billion (£11 billion) worth of products and services were bartered in the USA in 1998. BarterTrust (www.bartertrust.com) is one of the major players and is backed by General Motors Investment Management Corporation, Deutsche Bank, Alex Brown and GE Equity. It has become the largest business barter exchange in North America, with more than 7000 clients and $130 million worth of transactions in its first year of operation. It now claims to have 10,000 businesses on its books producing $150 million worth of transactions through 15 regional exchanges, and to have enjoyed revenues of $10 million last year. Industry experts say that the internet has given bartering a fresh impetus. A US academic has been quoted as saying: 'Business-to-business barter is going to be massive. With the internet it is inherently global. BarterTrust say they are now focusing on the European and Asian markets where the potential is expected to be enormous.'

Table 7.1	B2B	B2C
B2B and B2C pricing differences	Price negotiation possible	Little price negotiation
	Consultation through group qualitative and quantitative research	Individual discussion on price
	Costs as well as price discussed	No discussion on costs
	Price auctions used	Little use of price auctions
	Price bidding used	Little or no price bidding used
	Flexible pricing linked to customised products and services	Little price flexibility
	Individual company pricing	Pricing by group segments
	Large and complex DMU involved	Small, simple DMU
	Pricing to build supplier/buyer relationships	Pricing to build mass loyalty
	Relationships more important than price	Price more important than relationships
	Long-term contracts	No contracts
	High pricing on premium products based on functionality	High pricing on premium products based on brands and emotion
	Elasticity of price quickly filters through to buyer price	Elasticity of price takes longer to affect consumer price
	Cooperative pricing along the supply chain	No cooperative pricing
	Difficult to price discriminate because of small number of customers and easy access to information	Easier to price discriminate because of mass markets and lack of information
	Payment by extended credit	Credit card, debit card or cash

☐ Summary

In this chapter we have examined the role that price and costing play in B2B marketing. A definition of pricing was given and then its place within marketing was discussed. The interaction between price and products and services, distribution and promotion was examined and B2B compared with B2C (Table 7.1). It was argued that price was an underutilised business tool in B2B marketing and so ways that it might be used were identified and evaluated. We then went on to discuss the strategic factors that should be determining the price.

Company objectives, strategies, costs, customer, market structure, levels of demand, competition and legislation were identified and related to the pricing process. It was made clear that the overriding concern was for pricing objectives to meet both the marketing and corporate objectives and examples of different objectives were given. The main pricing strategies used to achieve pricing objectives were identified and reasons given for usage. Again B2B was compared with B2C. New product pricing and pricing across the product life cycle were briefly outlined before moving on to talk about the differences between strategic and tactical pricing.

The importance of costs in the pricing process, their association with marketing and the different types of costs were discussed, emphasising the need constantly to monitor, control and reduce these to maintain competitive advantage. Cost and profit centre and activity based costing were recognised as ways of trying to make certain that this would happen. Monopolies, oligopolies and competitive markets were again examined, but in the context of different pricing needs. Price and levels of demand, price and competitive response and price and legislation were all shown to have an influence on pricing strategies and could not therefore be ignored in the process.

Other influences on pricing were discussed including price elasticity, price negotiations, the effect of the internet on pricing, price and global markets and strategic and tactical methods that could be used in determining the price to be charged. B2B and B2C markets were compared wherever possible.

Discussion questions

1. Identify the factors that need to be examined when pricing in B2B markets. What are the differences when compared with B2C markets?

2. What part will marketing theory and marketing concepts play in B2B marketing? Are there major differences when compared with B2C markets?

3. How might pricing factors differ when comparing the public sector with the commercial sector in B2B marketing? Why do some commentators argue that the movement of an organisation from the public sector to the private sector could be beneficial for cost and pricing efficiency?

4. Discuss the various pricing strategies that might be used by B2B suppliers. Give examples of companies that use the different strategic pricing approaches and examine why this might so.

5. Why might a supplier be able to charge different prices for its products and services in different regions and countries? Are circumstances the same in both B2B and B2C and what forces might work to stop this type of discriminatory pricing?

6. Discuss the proposition that 'there are only two ways that an organisation can increase profits, sell more or reduce costs'. How might a company reduce costs both internally and along the supply chain?

7. Discuss the various pricing methods identified here. How might they be used in practice and what are the advantages and disadvantages of each?

8. Is there an ethical case for paying above the norm prices in Third World countries so that working conditions can be improved? Identify and discuss examples where organisations have attracted bad publicity.

9. Identify the role that governments play in B2B product and service pricing policies. Examine the part that overseeing regulators, both nationally and internationally, have in policing the current pricing legislation.

10. Identify and analyse the steps involved in determining the price of the product.

Visit the *B2B Marketing* website at www.booksites.net/wright for a Case Study, Questions, and an Internet Exercise for this chapter.

☐ Bibliography

Books

Cunningham, M.J. (2001) *Business-to-Business: How to Build a Profitable e-commerce Strategy.* Cambridge: Perseus.

Daly, J.L. (2001) *Pricing for Profitability: Activity-Based Pricing for Competitive Advantage.* Chichester: Wiley.

Dolan, R.J. and Herman, S. (1997) *Power Pricing: How Managing Price Transforms the Bottom Line*. New York: Free Press.

Nagle, T. and Holden, R.K. (1998) *The Strategy and Tactics of Pricing: A Guide to Profitable Decision Making*, 2nd edn. Harlow: Pearson Education.

Seymour, D.T. (ed.) (1989) *The Pricing Decision: A Strategic Planner for Marketing Professionals*. Chicago: Probus.

Spar, D.L. (1994) *The Cooperative Edge: The Internal Politics of International Cartels*. Ithaca: Cornell University Press.

Journals

Dolan, R.J. (1995) 'How do you know when the price is right?' *Harvard Business Review*, September–October.

Sashi, C.M. and O'Leary, B. (2002) 'The role of the internet auctions in the expansion of B2B markets', *Industrial Marketing Management*, 31: 103–10.

Shapiro, B.P. and Jackson, B.B. (1978) 'Industrial pricing to meet customer needs', *Harvard Business Review*, 56 (6): 119–27.

Smith, G. (1995) 'Managerial pricing orientation: the process of making pricing decisions', *Pricing Strategy and Practice*, 3 (3): 28–9.

Woodside, A. (1994) 'Making better pricing decisions in business marketing', in A. Woodside (ed.) *Advances in Business Marketing and Purchasing*. Greenwich, CT: JAI Press.

 Visit www.booksites.net/wright for the Internet references for this chapter.

Business-to-business strategic communications

Aims and objectives

By the end of this chapter the student should be able to:

1. Identify and evaluate the differences between corporate and product communications at the corporate and marketing levels in both B2B and B2C markets, and show how they might be changing around the world, including the use of innovation and technology.

2. Identify, compare and evaluate both 'above' and 'below the line' communications and promotion strategies and demonstrate how they might be used together to reach different target segments.

3. Recognise the importance of selling and sales management to B2B marketing and communications and show how it might be used with all other media forms.

4. Demonstrate how all communications and promotion must be integrated to achieve optimum effectiveness and objective achievement.

Part 1   Corporate and marketing communications

☐   Introduction

The role of communications

All organisations have to talk to their customers, if only to try to sell them benefit offerings. Experience tells us that very few products and services, if any, will ever sell themselves and customers have to be informed about why they should use one company rather than another or buy one product rather than another. Methods used to communicate vary not only between B2B and B2C markets but also from industry to industry and from customer to customer within both these markets. As well as customers, businesses communicate with many other interested stakeholders, in both an informal and a formal way, collecting and providing information on a continuous basis. Communications will be at both corporate and product level, providing information about the company and information about its product portfolio of goods and services.

   The levels of marketing communication range from short-term tactics to a long-term strategic vision. Communications at the corporate level will be concerned with enlightening people about the organisation itself, promoting company values, explaining policies, rectifying misunderstandings and minimising anything that might cause any form of bad feeling. Communications at the product and service level will be about talking, and listening, to customers and telling them how supplier company product benefit offerings could solve problems both now and in the future. They are about creating new customers, building expectations and explaining how one's company's products and services are better value than any of the competition's offerings. In this way it is hoped that customers will be persuaded to purchase the product on a one-off or continuous basis.

In B2C markets the customers are individuals, or groups of individuals, buying for themselves, while in B2B the customers are individuals, or groups of individuals buying for the organisation that employs them. The differences between corporate communications and product communications and between B2B and B2C markets have engendered the growth of many and various communications methods specifically developed to take into account these differences. When communicating, the company will use many of these methods to augment and build the strength of the message. This will be discussed throughout the chapter. We will also discuss the crucial need to bring together all communications into an integrated programme that can be measured and seen to have achieved its objectives.

The changing role of communications

In the distant past communicating would not have been so daunting as it appears to have become over the last 20 or so years. The seller and purchaser would have lived in the same hamlet, village or town so information about product or service availability and/or development could have been communicated, fairly quickly, by word of mouth. Feedback on the retail outlet, the owner, price, value, functionality and competitors' offerings would have been obtained, almost immediately. In many cases this directness of communications is no longer possible in the modern, complex and widespread global marketplace, especially in B2C markets. The seller and many buyers (possibly millions) will probably live many hundreds or thousands of miles apart, never actually seeing one another, and so be reliant on some type of non-personal contact. The same problem exists in B2B markets but not anywhere near to the same extent. Although B2B suppliers and buyers could be anywhere in the world, they are larger and fewer in number, making it more possible to talk individually or in small compact groups.

However, these problems are not the only major factors to be considered when attempting to communicate to select target segments and individual customers. Hundreds (in the case of B2B markets) or thousands (in the case of B2C) of other organisations, advertising agencies, competitors and non-competitors, will also be attempting to talk to the customer at the same time. The successful organisation must make sure that its message is heard rather than the message of another.

Development of different forms of communication

It is impossible in B2C markets for company personnel to talk directly on a face-to-face basis with every separate consumer. Although it is theoretically possible to talk with every buyer in B2B markets, this would not be practical for any but the largest of companies for reasons of costs, time and travel implications. This has led to the development of ever more intricate and sophisticated methods of communication that have been given an immeasurable boost with the unprecedented growth in information technology and particularly the internet. These many options will be discussed and evaluated throughout this chapter under the concept of the communications or promotional mix. It is important to understand that the category is called the promotional 'mix' because it consists of various communication methods available to the marketing manager to inform, educate, interest and persuade the customer eventually to try and/or purchase the product or service.

A selection of promotional techniques or 'tools' is needed because there are different communication and promotional objectives that the marketing strategist and operational manager must achieve in informing and moving the audience through to seeking and buying the product. These can and will be different between the B2B and B2C markets. The promotional objectives to be achieved will include creating awareness, stimulating desire and persuading action of some kind. Feedback between the two markets will also differ in that B2B marketers can usually readily talk to business decision makers, being relatively few in number, but B2C marketers will have many more difficulties because of the large numbers involved.

Communications in B2B markets

- ☐ Relatively few customer to talk to.
- ☐ Person-to-person communications often a possibility.
- ☐ Complex DMU or buying group.
- ☐ Hundreds of others attempting to persuade at the same time.
- ☐ Different techniques from B2C needed.
- ☐ Messages will have a high rational content.
- ☐ Feedback more immediate.
- ☐ Used to build long-term relationships with individual companies.

Communications in B2C markets

- ☐ Mass markets consisting of millions of customers.
- ☐ Methods other than person-to-person must be used.
- ☐ Individual or simple DMU.
- ☐ Thousands attempting to talk at the same time.
- ☐ Different techniques from B2B needed.
- ☐ Messages will have a high emotional content.
- ☐ Feedback complex.
- ☐ Attempt to build long-term relationships with market segments.

☐ Corporate and marketing communications

Although there is an enormous amount of overlap, B2B communications can be profitably examined under two headings: corporate communications and marketing communications. Corporate communications are communications emanating from the organisation itself, and marketing communications will come from the marketing department.

Corporate communications

B2B corporate communications are communications to all corporate stakeholders, usually directed and controlled from head office. Many large organisations now have corporate communications departments (previously called public relations departments) managed by specialist communications people given the task of maintaining good relations with all company stakeholders and creating and maintaining a good image for the overall organisation on a continuous basis. All the factors that go to make up this 'good image' could be said to be represented by the corporate name and logo, the so-called 'corporate brand'.

It is at this level that communications strategies are determined, outlining how the organisation will behave to stakeholders both within and outside it. So these communication strategies will be responsible for both corporate internal image management to employees and shareholders and corporate external management to local communities, local and national government, pressure groups and of course customers. Every contingency should be planned for, not in detail but in broad terms, so that all managers know how to respond, on the one hand to opportunities for organisational advancement, and on the other to mollify and minimise negative criticism (Figure 8.1).

B2B and B2C

There are similarities in corporate communications between B2B and B2C organisations. There are also important differences. B2B will be concerned about how its image is perceived by other companies and not by the end consumer. This implies that it will be judged purely in rational business terms and even with a certain amount of sympathy for bad publicity ('there but for the grace of God go I' syndrome). In contrast, end consumers and the population as a whole will

Figure 8.1
Corporate and marketing communications message flexibility

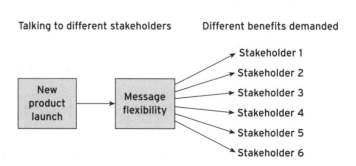

judge B2C organisations on emotional as well as rational considerations (often driven by the popular press) and can often expect little sympathy.

Stakeholders

Corporate communications might have to talk to the following stakeholders.

Internal stakeholders

☐ Managers, workers, workers' families, trade unions
☐ Shareholders.

External stakeholders

☐ Value/distribution chain members; suppliers, producers and intermediaries
☐ Local community
☐ Trade and professional bodies
☐ Local and national government, politicians
☐ Independent legal and regulatory bodies
☐ Pressure groups, environmentalists, moral campaigners
☐ Financiers, the 'City'
☐ Media, newspapers, TV, etc.
☐ Customers, DMU
☐ Competition.

Crisis management

Having outline strategic and operational plans available in manual form so that all responsible managers can respond in an appropriate way is an intrinsic part of corporate communications. An example might be the case of one of the big chemical companies being slated for spilling harmful ingredients into a river and thus causing pollution. Although best not to commit the misdemeanour in the first place, the company will also be judged on its reaction to the public outcry. Crisis management should help by at least giving managers access to well thought out ways of response that might help appease the condemnations.

Example 8.1 **Andersen's faces a crisis**

When Enron collapsed because of fraud, nobody thought it could get any worse. But then WorldCom collapsed. The demise of the telecoms giant has now overtaken the energy trader as the biggest bankruptcy in US history. The crisis has brought chaos to the markets and shaken the foundations of the world financial systems. One name is at the heart of both scandals – Andersen. It signed off the accounts of both WorldCom and Enron, companies whose billion dollar profits were built on lies. And there are a string of other accounting scandals that have Andersen's name attached to them.

Marketing communications

Strictly speaking, the concern of marketing communications is with talking, listening and promoting the company and its brands to customers and markets and attempting to build up long-term relationships. But in many cases there is a very grey area between what should be corporate communications and what should be marketing communications. For example, it is a marketing axiom that many buyers will think twice about buying products from companies that they don't know and/or from companies that they don't like. This homily is particularly applicable for B2B suppliers moving into new countries and new markets. So all activity, whether by the corporate communications department or marketing department, that enhances the image of the corporate brand will be helpful to the sales and marketing effort. Conversely all criticism of a company can rebound in a negative manner on the purchase of goods and services. In some companies and in some instances corporate communications people will be involved in marketing, and marketing people in corporate communications.

B2B and B2C

Marketing communications in B2B and B2C are similar in that both use a mixture of tools and techniques to communicate and persuade customers to buy the product. But the actual process can be very different because of the dissimilar buyers, reasons for purchase and the use that will be made of the bought product or service. So we find that personal selling, for example, will be heavily used in B2B but not in B2C, and main media advertising used in B2C but not in B2B. The reasons will become more apparent as we move forward.

Importance of audience targeting

It is imperative that the target audience is clearly identified and profiled in detail if relevant messages are to be constructed in the correct manner and a medium used that will reach and be understood. We discussed in Chapter 4 the importance of segmentation and targeting, but it should be self-evident that the wrong messages sent in the wrong way will be lost in the ether and be money and opportunity down the drain. Stakeholders will often want different benefits from an organisation and its products and services. This must be taken into consideration when building communication and promotional strategies and responding to events that demand a reaction. Pressure groups will want to hear that the launch of a new product will not harm the environment; government that new jobs will be created; intermediaries that some amount of profit will be made; and the customer that it will offer more innovation and value for money than existing products.

Unintentional and intentional communications in B2B markets

Organisations are always communicating to stakeholders whether they intend to or not. Both intentional and unintentional corporate messages may be generated in the following ways.

1. *Where the company is situated.* This might be the town, region or even country from which the company operates. A bad employer and/or an uncaring environmentalist will create negative messages that will spread and ripple a large distance from the place of operation. The company's treatment of the local community, whether it contributes positively in some way, will be part of building a local and national identity.

2. *The manner and way the company operates.* Companies that always push down price, never pay on time or never reward loyalty will sometimes find that when circumstances change they have very few friends to turn to for help. The customer contact with the organisation can turn off the relationship before it has even begun: telephones not answered or that mechanically force inbound callers to move from one humanless contact point to another; unhelpful, unknowledgeable, or rude staff; how enquiries and complaints are dealt with. All such contacts can build up an unfortunate image with the stakeholders.

3. *Products and services marketed and sold.* The products, services, brands and packaging that the company manufactures, the prices charged, the channels of distribution used, the state of the delivery lorries, returns policies and methods of selling promotion and advertising adopted all contribute to identity formation.

Example 8.2 **Bad behaviour**

Pepsi and Coca-Cola have been fined by India's Supreme Court after painting advertisements on the side of the Himalayan mountains. The two companies were among 12 companies who placed adverts on ecologically sensitive rockfaces on a stretch of highway running through the Himalayan range. Judges fined the two companies 200,000 rupees ($4000) each, while the other companies were ordered to pay 100,000 rupees each towards the cost of repairing the damage.

Strategic communication integration

It is the concern of both corporate and marketing communications senior managers to be aware of the power and extent of business communications and to plan and strategically harness all forms into an integrated whole. In this way unplanned, unhelpful messages can be minimised or eliminated and all communications, both corporate and marketing, be brought together as a positive, image-enhancing force. The integration of communication methods will be discussed in more detail as we move through the chapter.

Communications and relationship marketing

We have argued in earlier chapters that most if not all organisations would like to have close and friendly relationships with customers in both the short and long term. Friendly relationship will hopefully engender loyalty and so create repeat purchases over the customer lifetime. There is also the hope that this loyalty and satisfaction will persuade the customer to recommend others to buy

Figure 8.2
B2B Corporate
Communications
Model – talking
to many
stakeholders

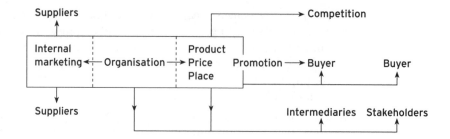

from the same organisation. Communications are an essential part of the process in building this relationship. Of course the benefits offered must live up to or exceed customer expectations, otherwise all the communications will succeed in doing is to dissuade any further purchases. If relationship marketing is going to work then the marketing communications must clearly identify target audiences and send out consistent quality messages in an integrated manner, monitored, controlled and adjusted as benefits need to change. Planning software is available to help guide and focus the programme (Figure 8.2).

Understanding basic communications

Good promotion is all about good communications, that is sending a specific benefit message to clearly identified target audiences, listening to the feedback, readjusting the message if confusion or ambiguity is apparent and finally being certain that the truth and the core of the message are fully understood. This simple concept will apply whether the market is B2B or B2C. No matter how complex the message process becomes, its basic tenet should be rehearsed so as not to be forgotten whenever possible.

With corporate communications this might be to any number of different stakeholders, while product/brand communications will be sending and receiving messages to target markets and specific customers. In B2B markets the target for the message will be another company. In B2C this will be mostly the end consumer. Bearing this in mind it is worth examining the basic communication model (Figure 8.3).

Sender, medium and receiver

The sender, B2B or B2C organisation, must put the message in a form that will be easily understood by the receiver – another business or the end consumer. The medium to be used, face-to-face, direct mail, TV, etc., must be a communications

Figure 8.3
Basic
communication
model

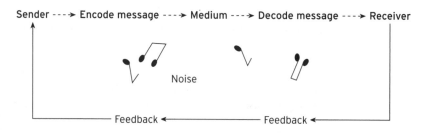

vehicle that will be both seen/heard and understood by the receiver. The receiver, another business or the end consumer, will decode the message so as to make sense of it. Feedback will enable the sender to know whether the message has been understood and, if not, readjust the message until it is understood.

Noise and feedback

By noise we mean all of the many types of interference that can stop the message getting through to the target market and the feedback back to the sender. This is less of a problem in B2B than in B2C. In B2B there can be close contact between supplier and buyer, while in B2C feedback has to be representative and often has to filter back through research companies and their ilk. Below are some of the barriers to communications, in both sending and receiving messages, identified under the two market types.

Noise and feedback in B2C

Feedback can cause enormous difficulty in B2C markets and many of these were discussed when we looked earlier at market research and feedback. Consumer markets can be huge and therefore it is impossible to talk to everybody individually. Messages can be sent at any time (day or night) but care must be taken that they reach the right target group. This forces use of mass communication media such as TV, newspapers and direct mail. Feedback then becomes extremely problematic with research used to talk to representative samples. Emotional messages, favoured in this category, can be notoriously easy to get wrong. Below are just a few of the problems and barriers:

- ☐ Time and costs.
- ☐ Misidentification of target audience.
- ☐ Poor encoding in the message for the target segment perhaps using more or less emotion and rationality.
- ☐ Poor decoding by receiver because of target audience level of understanding and readiness to receive.
- ☐ Messages sent at any time but must be the 'right' time for the target audience.
- ☐ Poor decoding because wrong medium used.
- ☐ A multitude of competitive messages can cause confusion, hostility, cynicism or rejection.
- ☐ Feedback by research and representative sample.

Noise and feedback in B2B

Noise in B2B is not of the same magnitude as in B2C and is of a different kind. Audiences are smaller and can often be quickly researched to check understanding. Messages are in the main functional and should not lead to receiver confusion as homework on the particular segment or buyer has been professionally undertaken. In theory it should be reasonably easy to contact the decision-maker but sometimes it is more difficult in practice because of complexity and work rate of important members.

Feedback can often be direct by personal contact but salespeople are not always encouraged to take this seriously. Below are some of the differences in B2B:

☐ More difficult to misidentify target audience.

☐ DMU complex and it is possible not to 'hit' all members.

☐ Decision-maker too busy to listen.

☐ Messages sent predominantly during work time.

☐ Competition based on use and functionality, not emotion, i.e. the message must offer a real difference.

☐ Feedback by personal contact not taken seriously.

Medium

The way the message is sent can be identified under the concept of the 'medium' and this will be discussed in much more detail later in the chapter. The main categories, however, can be identified under person-to-person and non-human media:

☐ *Person-to-person media*. This will include spoken, written, telephone, body language and facial expressions, including the use of sound, vision, taste, touch and smell.

☐ *Non-human media*. This will include the main media, TV, newspapers, magazines, directories, outdoor billboards, radio, cinema, internet, direct response, and so on.

We have argued that person-to-person media are more important in B2B and non-human media in B2C, although both will use the two forms. All of this will be examined later.

There are a number of factors to consider in choosing a medium. First of all will the chosen medium reach the target audience? That this is vital should be self-evident, but past media activity is replete with examples of adverts being placed in newspapers or magazines, and now on the internet, that were unlikely to be seen, for whatever reason, by a worthwhile number of the target audience. Although more of a problem in consumer markets, it still happens in business markets.

Second, the characteristics of the media are important. Communications media have characteristics that make them more appropriate for one form of message carrying than another. For example, a person selling has advantages for products and services that need detailed question and answer explanations (B2B), while packaging is ideal for content description on the shelf (B2C). TV might be good at introducing simple visual products (B2C), and a magazine for more specialist complex products (B2B).

☐ Internal marketing communications

We outlined above how all employees are able to repel both existing and new customers as well as other stakeholders by bad behaviour and lack of interpersonal skills. Many companies develop processes in the name of efficiency that become anti-customer and anti-stakeholder, which must also be identified and adjusted. Internal communications are about coaching and training staff to try to see that this will not happen. Internal marketing is using marketing concepts internally to make certain that the correct communications are applied to identify where things are going wrong, and then developing programmes to rectify these wrongs. In true marketing style, research should be used to audit and discover the existing needs of employees. Many will be at different stages in terms of knowledge and information attainment, personal and interpersonal skills, human management skills, attitudes and levels of motivation, and so on. As with external markets, personnel can be grouped into different segments based on needs and the relevant programmes developed.

This will include such things as management education on the importance of marketing and ultimate customer satisfaction (including managers from all departments), how to manage staff so that all work towards this satisfaction of needs, and knowledge of all companies' and buyers' needs and how to satisfy them.

Internal marketing communications involves imparting information that will have an effect on the development and coordination of the marketing mix within the B2B organisation. Suffice to say that if the supplier staff, including everybody from the shop floor to the board of directors, are not coordinated and geared towards customer satisfaction, then sales will be lost. If every department from finance and administration through to production and (of course) marketing are not working together for greater and more effective comprehensive buyer service, then competitive advantage will eventually be lost. Internal marketing management, working with human resource management, is an essential, constant process, instigated so as to make certain this will not happen. Internal communications methods include:

- ☐ Open door policies, talking to one another
- ☐ 'Walking the talk'
- ☐ Regular meetings, conferences
- ☐ Training and coaching sessions
- ☐ Company newsletters and magazines
- ☐ Telephone
- ☐ Comment-boxes
- ☐ E-mail
- ☐ Video-conferencing
- ☐ Intranet
- ☐ Access to customer feedback.

Internal marketing in B2B and B2C

Internal marketing and internal communications have to take into account the fact that employees in B2B organisations have to deal with buyer staff while employees in B2C organisations have to deal with retailers and end consumers. We have discussed throughout the book how these two groups often behave differently from one another, want disparate benefits and expect a certain response from the supplier organisation. This will put differing pressures on staff, especially those on the front line.

B2C

In B2C the end consumer walks into a retailer and expects to see a choice of products across a range of suppliers. The salesperson is expected to be knowledgeable about all the makes and able clearly to identify customer needs and wants, both functionally and symbolically, and then to sell the product. Such things as retail outlet image, colour, packaging, brand, delivery, installation and so on are important. Backroom staff will need to be able to deal with queries based around these benefits. To upset one customer (as unwanted as this may be) will not be the end of the world as long as the approach is correct with all others. Similarly the retail buyers will be concerned with things like quantity, prices, quickness of stock turnaround off the shelves, merchandise display, consumer advertising spend, and so on.

B2B

In B2B the buyer will want to know that supplier products and services function in a particular way so as to satisfy their own business needs. A professional and knowledgeable approach will be expected from supplier staff that, most importantly, puts (or at least appears to put) that particular buyer business at the very centre of all supplier activity. Among other things they will expect to be treated as if they were the supplier's only customer. They will expect immediate, relevant information when contact is made and value products that are delivered when wanted and perform as expected. We know that the DMU in B2B markets can be large and complex. Any number of influential people might make contact; upset any one of these in B2B and the amount of business lost could be monumental. So staff must be trained and coached to the appropriate level, in both B2B and B2C.

Barriers to internal marketing communication

☐ Unawareness at the highest level of management of its strategic importance.

☐ Lack of a formal (or informal) strategic approach.

☐ Lack of realistic communications systems.

☐ Bureaucratic, multi-layer structures.

☐ Corporate functions, such as marketing, administration, human resources, finance and production, not talking to one another.

☐ Inward looking, blame-fearing culture.

Part 2 Managing business-to-business marketing communications

☐ Marketing, communications and corporate brand

We have identified and examined many of the factors associated with business communications including the roles that might be performed on the one hand by corporate communications and on the other by marketing communications. It was also suggested that there were areas of overlap. The development of corporate image or the corporate 'brand' is one of these areas. How others, stakeholders, perceive the organisation is important for its overall well-being because of the many reasons identified earlier. It is equally important for the well-being of the marketing department and the achievement of marketing objectives. This happens to be more so in B2B markets than in B2C for reasons that are explained below.

To repeat the adage companies will very seldom purchase from companies they don't know and this seems to apply particularly to B2B markets. Developing corporate awareness is the responsibility of the marketing communications strategy manager but both corporate and marketing communications will work together to establish the name of the company in new markets both at home and around the world.

Corporate brand in B2C

Depending on products and service brand strategies, B2C consumers will sometimes be concerned with corporate image, e.g. Sony or Heinz, and sometimes just with product brand, e.g. Snickers chocolate bar, Persil soap powder. They may not even be aware who the parent company is (Mars and Unilever). In the main, although not always, consumers tend to be more concerned with product brand than with corporate brand. So marketing communications and promotional spend tend to concentrate on the product, and where advertising the corporate brand they do so from an emotional rather than a functional perspective.

Corporate brand in B2B

Communications and corporate image building in B2B marketing are crucial. It has been established elsewhere that buyers in B2B markets are more interested in corporate branding than they are in product branding. So the reputation of the supplier's products is based on the reputation of the parent organisation. A bad company reputation among stakeholders and customers will ultimately percolate down to affect the reputation of the goods and services offered.

Marketing, communications and B2B product and service

A supplier will have developed a range of products and services, through the use of marketing research, in conjunction with small, medium and larger buying organisations. This will include quality levels, service enhancements, packaging, pricing, channels of delivery, and so on. Known collectively (if not simplistically) as the marketing mix it also includes the ways that these benefits must now be communicated to the buyer. As we have seen earlier, it will also include feedback, readjustment of the marketing mix offering when necessary in line with professed needs and a recommunication of these changes. All this must be built into the overall strategic marketing and control process. In this way the market is constantly monitored for changing technology, innovations and customer choices and appropriate steps taken to stay apace or ahead of the market and the competition.

☐ Marketing communication strategies

The organisation has many tools and techniques available to achieve its communication objectives and collectively these can be known as the communication mix. Some of the methods identified below will be used on a continuous basis, as part of a customer relationship management (CRM) programme to build, develop and maintain long-term relationships. Other methods will be used specifically for short-term promotional campaigns to launch new products, open new accounts, move existing stock, sell new features on existing stock and so on. CRM programmes are also developed in B2C markets with both retailers and end consumers and these will be discussed later. To understand the task of communications strategies we must recognise the forces that shape and influence company buying decisions and the target market – the 'audience' – must be the most important factor.

The target audience in B2B

The B2B supplier might have just a few customers localised within easy reach, or many thousands spread around the world. It might sell to both the private and the public sectors. It might be serving many industries in many countries. The product and services may be complex, requiring detailed explanation, or may be simple, needing little or no explanation. The decision-making process may be long and drawn out over many months, or it may be short and immediate. The decision itself may be of high or low importance to the company concerned. All this must be taken into account when putting together communication strategies. There is, however, an extra complication in B2B markets and that is the possible number of people that might have an interest in the purchase. Add to this the strength of the various interests and the communication task can become quite daunting.

Two-level approach

Supplier strategic communication approaches have to be developed at two levels. First, for the industry and the individual companies, this will take into account aspects such as size and number of customers in the market, the industry, benefits wanted, competitor activities and the traditional and acceptable ways of communication. Plans, approaches and benefit messages have to be developed at this level either in-house by the marketing and promotions department or with the help of an outside B2B marketing agency.

At another level will be the need to identify the people who might or might not have a vested interest in the purchase (the DMU). This can be very difficult, especially if the customer is a large company with many divisions at home and around the world. Whether DMU identification, qualification and approach should be left to the salesperson, sales manager, agency, or a combination is for senior managers to investigate and conclude whether the task should be addressed at the strategic or tactical level. The amount that any one buyer will contribute to supplier revenue will, of course, contribute to this particular debate.

The DMU in large organisations

The intricacies of the target audience in B2B, the so-called DMU or the buying centre, have been well examined in earlier chapters, but are worth repeating here in the context of communications. Messages must get through to all people within the buying organisation who might be able to have an influence of some kind on the purchasing process. They must also get through to every separate company on the supplier customer list. The problem of a complex DMU can therefore be multiplied many times over.

Identification of those who are able to influence buying decisions can be a very real problem when the number of people might vary from very few to as many as 20 or 30. Just to find out who they are can take considerable time and ingenuity, even for the best of marketing or sales personnel.

To add more complications, the composition of the DMU, in terms of both function and individuals, might possibly change from product to product. It can be certain that the DMU membership will also be different in different companies and vary from industry to industry. Separate members might also have their own priorities and agendas on types of benefits wanted, suppliers that are favoured, and price and value levels expected. Level of awareness by the buying centre about the supplying company, its market ethos, products, services and long-term view on forming close relationships must all be part of the equation. Only when all this information is known can realistic communications programmes be constructed.

The DMU in smaller organisations

Not all companies are as complicated in how they purchase, and smaller organisations will inevitably have a smaller number of people involved in buying decisions. This should make contact easier and communications programmes simpler to put together. At this level the sales management team will probably be left to identify individual buyer needs.

Characteristics of B2B target audiences

☐ Complex DMU, variable number of members with differing decision-making powers.

☐ Make-up of the DMU can change.

☐ Buying for the organisation so communications on a rational level.

☐ Levels of supplier awareness.

☐ Relatively few company buyers, easy to contact.

☐ Views of the individual important.

☐ Can be localised or spread around the globe.

☐ Advertising corporate rather than product brand.

☐ Depth of product/company awareness high.

Target audience in B2C

Target audiences in consumer markets are probably more researched, more understood, and more promoted to than in B2B despite, or perhaps because of, the large numbers involved. Marketing and research strategies will have segmented potential and existing consumers into relatively large groups of like-minded individuals; sampling would have identified benefits wanted and levels of awareness and readiness to purchase. With this type of information communication strategies can be identified.

Characteristics of B2C target audiences

☐ Segmentation into large groups.

☐ Mass audience, can be difficult to communicate with.

☐ Simple DMU, e.g. husband and wife.

☐ Views of individuals relatively unimportant.

☐ Views of the segment important.

☐ Buying for self so communications on emotional as well as rational level.

☐ Advertising product as well as corporate brand.

☐ Depth of product/company awareness minimal.

☐ Communication and promotional methods

There are many different ways that suppliers are able to talk to buyers. The methods chosen will depend on the communication and promotional objectives to be achieved. They will also depend on such factors as the amount of money available, what needs to be said, activity of the competition, plus all the factors on the target market audience examined above, as well as on other issues specific to B2B marketing communications that will be discussed throughout the chapter. The following strategic communications methods are used in both B2B and B2C marketing communications, but in different ways. They include the following:

☐ Advertising

☐ Sales promotions

- ☐ Merchandising, packaging
- ☐ Direct response
- ☐ Public relations (PR)
- ☐ Publicity
- ☐ Exhibitions
- ☐ Sponsorship
- ☐ Word of mouth
- ☐ Personal selling.

Before moving on to look at these elements in more detail it might be helpful here to explain further why so many methods of communication have been developed.

Different techniques achieve different communication objectives

It is important to realise that there are many different types of communication objectives, as well as different types of audiences, which all demand different approaches. If one communication technique were good at solving all communications problems, there would be no need for such a mixture. If a seller were able to talk personally to all customers then most other methods would be superfluous. Unfortunately circumstances such as distance, location and time make this all but impossible in most cases. In practice, one communication technique tends to be good at solving one type of communications problem while another is good at solving another. Together they can integrate and work together to solve the whole. Very rarely will one method be used in isolation.

In this respect, TV advertising is good at creating mass brand awareness among B2C audiences and not good at getting consumers actually to try the product. Conversely a sales promotion (e.g. two for the price of one) is good at getting the end consumer to try the product but not good at creating mass awareness. In the same vein, mass TV would be wasteful if used in talking to smaller B2B audiences, but a specialist magazine might be known to be read by a company decision maker and so therefore would be the technique to choose.

Example 8.3 **Cost of TV advertising**

The US comedy *Friends* is now the home of the most expensive advertising on US television, according to an influential trade journal. At about $455,700 (£291,399) for a 30-second spot in one of the hit show's advert breaks, *Friends* has now over-taken the US version of reality show *Survivor* and hospital drama *ER*. In *Advertising Age's* advert price survey, *ER* cost $438,514 (£280,403) per 30-second advert, while reality show *Survivor* dropped to third at $418,750 (£267,765) from first place last year. (www.adage.com)

A salesperson can introduce the company and explain product benefits in detail but would be prohibitively expensive if not impossible to use if target markets were

Figure 8.4
AIDA hierarchy
of effects

(Unawareness) ---➤ Awareness ----➤ Interest ----➤ Desire ----➤ Action (trial or purchase)

Awareness is created when the potential buyer is introduced to the company and/or its products
Interest happens if the buyer sees some benefit and wants to learn more
Desire occurs when the buyer recognises that this will be the company to deal with or the product to buy when and if the need arises
Action is obtaining an agreement to buy or try the company or the products

large and widespread. Conversely, newspapers might reach a large audience but a B2B advertisement might be missed or seen not have the same persuasive effect.

AIDA hierarchy of effects model

Hierarchy of effects models can be used when developing communication strategies and many exist. The AIDA model is one of the simplest, developed to aid understanding of the problem of the need to use different techniques to achieve different communications objectives. It is worth noting that the model will be used here purely as an aid to understanding the complexities of the communication process. As with most models it is not necessarily a reflection of reality and its limitations must be continually appreciated.

There are many variations of the model but the concept is simple. The customer is unaware of the company and/or its products (and people 'don't buy products from companies they don't know'). The marketing communications manager must therefore use a mixture of the methods highlighted above to take the customer from this state of unawareness through to awareness, interest, trial and hopefully buying the product. Different techniques are necessary because moving the customer along the process might involve different communication tasks (with different objectives) at different stages of the process (Figure 8.4).

Different customers on different levels of the hierarchy

In markets around the world as well as in any one market, targeted buyers will be at different levels on the AIDA hierarchy. Some customers may be completely unaware of the supplier, others may be aware of the supplier but not of the products it sells, others might be aware, but have little interest, while others may be interested but need more persuasion. Customers can move backwards and forwards along the AIDA process so they could be interested now, but because of inertia or because a decision-maker or influencer leaves, might move back to a lower level of awareness in the future.

Suppliers should make it their business to see that existing customers are always aware and interested in new products and services, perhaps as part of the CRM process. With new or peripheral customers the level of awareness should be researched and the relevant and most appropriate technique used to move the customer into eventual action and purchase.

Simple and complex communications theory

Many argue that the idea of moving an audience up and down a hierarchy from awareness to wanting to purchase the product is too simplistic a theory and in reality the communication process is far more complex. Complex theory sees the communication process as a constant movement back and forth between awareness and forgetting, attention and inattention, interest and uncertainty, decision and indecision and, depending on the intensity of the need, one decision being quickly overtaken by another more pressing. Complex theory, if having any truth, would support the need for the supplier salesperson in some industries to act positively, quickly and decisively ('strike while the iron is hot') in selling the benefits and close the sale before the opportunity is lost.

Setting clear communications objectives

As well as an overall strategic communications objective, clear, measurable objectives must be set for every communication method used (as with all business objectives). Only in this way can success and value for money be gauged. It is an appalling indictment on any business activity to spend money and not know whether it has been spent wisely. So SMART objectives (specific, measurable, achievable and agreed, realistic and time based) must be set for every communication and promotional task undertaken as it attempts to move the customer through the AIDA process. Setting communication objectives for some methods can be difficult, but this must not preclude an attempt being made.

SMART objectives

- ☐ Measurable objectives must be set for the levels of awareness achieved by the advertising.
- ☐ Measurable objectives must be set for the levels and intensity of interest achieved by the trade magazine.
- ☐ Measurable objectives must be set for the depth of the desire created by the direct mail shots and telephone calls.
- ☐ Measurable objectives must be set for the personal selling, the only objective in term of sales volumes. The rest are set in terms of customer behaviour.

Ongoing marketing communications

If there is the need to create a corporate image enhancement communications campaign over say three years, then clear objectives must be set to take corporate awareness from where it is now to where the company would like it to be in three years's time. All media used must have clear objectives that can be measured before, during and after the corporate awareness communication campaign.

A promotional campaign

A promotional campaign will tend to be over a well-defined period of time, usually over the short term. For example, one could use magazine advertising to create the initial awareness, direct mail with more information to create interest, a telephone call to make an appointment and instil the desire and a sales visit to close the sale. Again, all medium forms must have objectives that will be measured before, during and after the promotional period (Figure 8.5).

Figure 8.5
Moving the B2B
buyer through
the AIDA
process

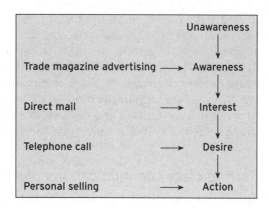

The concept of DAGMAR

It is worth mentioning here the concept of DAGMAR, which was developed by Russell Colley (1961). DAGMAR is an acronym for **D**efining **A**dvertising **G**oals for **M**easured **A**dvertising **R**esponse and is the basis of the AIDA model. Colley advocated the evaluation of advertising goals by communication goals rather than by sales. He argued that separate behavioural objectives should be set for every method used and every part of the process, with one objective building on the other, going backwards when necessary, but culminating in the eventual sale of the product. He proposed that different customers might be at different stages of the process, so advertisers would need to adjust communications campaigns to make allowances for these differences.

B2B communications and promotional techniques

☐ Used to achieve different corporate and product objectives.
☐ Move the audience from unawareness through to action.
☐ All good at different things.
☐ Reach different target audiences.
☐ To suit the amount of budget available.

☐ Advertising

> The first rule of advertising is to get noticed.

The first of the communication and promotional tools to be identified is B2B advertising and the following definition might be used.

> B2B advertising is making it publicly known that an organisation has benefits, usually products and services, it wishes to offer to an identified company or group of companies in return for some other benefit, usually money, in both the short and long term.

Advertising - many objectives

Advertising can be used for many communication purposes, at both corporate and product level, to create awareness and move the customer eventually to purchase from the supplier. It can be used to inform about a new technology a supplier has patented and to educate about its intricacies and how it might work. It can be used to bolster the corporate image and its products and so reinforce buyer loyalty. It can be used to persuade the trade to take in extra stock during a time of plenty. The major forms of advertising, TV and print, tend not to used for selling products but because of their national and international presence they are good at creating corporate and product brand awareness and in this way work well with personal selling. Buyers are usually very busy and will seldom see representatives from unknown companies. If a buyer is aware of a company, however, then the salesperson has at least a chance of an interview; the better known the company, the more likely the chance of getting past the gatekeeper and demonstrating the seller's products and services. In some cases advertising is also good at encouraging buyers to send for information, perhaps a leaflet or catalogue and, if the advertiser is really lucky, to ask for a representative to call. There are, however, some forms of advertising that will be used to sell products and services and these are discussed below:

B2B advertising objectives

☐ Informing
☐ Educating
☐ Persuading
☐ Reinforcing
☐ Selling.

Example 8.4 **Procter & Gamble**

Fast-moving-consumer-goods maker Procter & Gamble invented the soap opera in the 1930s as a way to sell more detergent. Since then, the maker of Bold detergent, Head and Shoulders, Crest toothpaste and Pampers nappies has become the single largest advertising buyer, spending in excess of $1 billion each year on ads spanning media as diverse as radio, television and print. Now the company has signed a $300 million landmark deal with media giant Viacom that would eventually allow P&G to pitch its products across a variety of media platforms, from the internet to billboards, a strategy the ad world sees as the shape of things to come.

The media mix (above the line communications)

The media mix, known as 'above the line communications', consists of the major methods of advertising used by both B2B and B2C advertisers. These are TV, print, outdoor, radio and cinema. The bulk of UK advertising, over 90 per cent, takes place through the TV and print media. The largest part of this is B2C, but B2B still utilises a significant part. They tend to be used together – TV to create the awareness and newspapers and magazines to add more detailed information and encourage the buyer to make further investigation.

TV advertising

TV advertising is probably the most obvious of all the main media because of its all-pervasive nature. Since it is predominantly an entertainment channel it is used mainly in B2C markets because its strength is the creation of mass levels of awareness among very large target markets. Those working in the B2B industry, however, are also TV viewers so it can be used, selectively, to talk to this market. Care would have to be taken to see that money was not wasted by paying for air space to send messages to a non-interested audience. Examples of mass B2B advertising in this way include IBM selling its web and e-mail services for business use or one of the big banks advertising its services specifically for small businesses.

Example 8.5   **BARB**

British Audience Research Board is owned by the BBC and the UK commercial channels. BARB acts as an independent auditor of all UK TV audience figures. Its measurement service provides television audience data on a minute-by-minute basis for channels received within the UK. These data are available for reporting nationally as well as at the ITV and BBC regional level. Viewing estimates are obtained from panels of television owning households, representing the viewing behaviour of the 24+ million households within the UK. The panels are selected to be representative of each ITV and BBC region. (www.barb.co.uk)

There has always been the opportunity to advertise in selective regions where although much of the message will be wasted there is still a large enough number of buyers to justify the spend (e.g. informing farmers in the East Anglia region on fertilisers and insecticides, or talking to caterers and hoteliers on the south coast about catering facilities). Of course there is always the spin-off from consumer advertising for companies that sell in both B2B and B2C. When Renault advertises its cars to its consumer audience it is also building on corporate image among suppliers and fleet car buyers (B2B). Similarly, when British Telecom runs a campaign, because many of its products sell in both markets it is able to impact on the different segments. Six Continents put its Holiday Inn brand on TV in 2002 in a bid to win business travellers away from rivals such as Moat House, Thistle and Best Western, believing TV could build on emotive reasons behind the business person's choice of hotel. The growth in commercial 24-hour news channels such as CNN and Sky News has also opened opportunities to get at business decision-makers, shown by research to watch these channels. The real difficulties here would be attempting to set objectives and monitor, measure and control the advertising spend.

The fragmentation of these media into hundreds of specialist channels has opened up the opportunity to hit the right market and its use is increasing. There are B2B specialist channels and specialist programmes coming on stream for business areas such as finance, horticulture, building and construction, leisure and catering, management education, and many more. The increase in digital technology now enables narrowband TV to be projected directly onto a TV monitor screen on the office desk with interactive capabilities through broadband internet connections.

Example 8.6 **Industrial advertising**

Industry associations will often advertise to both B2B and B2C audiences in a push and pull campaign. Scotland's meat industry is funding a £500,000 advertising campaign to boost consumer confidence following the foot-and-mouth crisis. Quality Meat Scotland, the body which promotes beef, lamb and pork, says the campaign is needed as sales have continued to fall despite the excellent reputation of Scottish meat. However, they have to be careful about the claims that they make. A complaint against the marketing of Scottish beef was upheld by an advertising watchdog, because 5 per cent of the meat actually came from English cattle. Quality Meat Scotland has agreed to change the wording of an advert following the ruling by the Advertising Standards Authority (www.asa.org.uk).

Print

Print is the largest of all the 'above the line' media. Like TV, modern technology has brought about tremendous progress in this medium. Information technology now allows newspapers, magazines, books and directories to be produced and launched more quickly than ever before, with more pages, better quality print and higher definition colours. The print media consist of national and local newspapers (free and paid for), magazines (free and paid for), and journals and directories. Although the B2C market is again the biggest user of print advertising, B2B advertisers will selectively use all three types.

Newspapers

National sales of the major newspapers are over 13 million a day in the UK with a pass-on readership of over 35 million. Most of this readership consists of end consumers who buy tabloid newspapers such as the *Sun, Daily Mirror, Express* and *Daily Mail*. A respectable minority of this readership figure will be the B2B target market buying lower circulation upmarket broadsheets such as the *Daily Telegraph, The Times* and *Financial Times*. All UK national newspapers now offer a website version, as do others from around the world. As with the other main media, all newspapers offer advertisers a detailed readership profile in terms of age, occupation, social class, and so. Knowing that most of their customers will take one of the daily broadsheets, some B2B advertisers will selectively advertise here; an example would be the *Financial Times* as its readership is predominantly business people.

Magazines

Estimates of the total number of UK magazines vary depending on the definition employed and the moment in time chosen, as the numbers starting up and closing down have increased with developments in print technology, making it so much easier for companies to enter and leave the business. BRAD lists nearly 6500 magazines in the UK that take advertising, a large percentage of which are B2B magazines. Some are free (paid for by the advertising) and others invite subscriptions. These are large markets for B2B advertisers and in many cases used as the main media because there are specialist magazines, selling just a few thousand or selling hundreds of thousands, that cover virtually every industry. The opportunity to see (OTS) an advertisement can be large as a weekly or monthly edition might be picked up and read many times. In some cases this may be the only way for a B2B marketer to reach a target audience, especially if some distance away or hard to contact. Many magazines are also now available in web form. Titles include *Architect Today, Autotrader, Catering Update, PC Dealer, Heating and Ventilating News, Marketing*, and so on.

Example 8.7 **Cosmetic advertisements**

A report by the UK parliament Commons Health Select Committee says that cosmetic surgery advertisements should carry health warnings. The MPs say they are 'disturbed' at the claims made about cosmetic surgery in some advertisements featured in magazines and newspapers.

Specialist magazines
Specialist magazines have the added attraction for B2B advertisers in that readers will be more susceptible to ads that run alongside information that is of interest. Magazine owners will be prepared to run advertiser specific articles and editorials in return for advertising space purchased.

Example 8.8 **Research finds B2B magazines essential to business decision-makers**

B2B magazines are an essential medium for business decision-makers, according to a major new study conducted by NFO WorldGroup. The study shows that B2B publications are used regularly by 87 per cent of business decision-makers and that 73 per cent of more than 500 interviewed find that B2B magazines contain advertising that is useful to their jobs. Of respondents 80 per cent went on to say that business magazines were the source normally used when looking for good quality job advertisements. Although B2B magazines remain the dominant medium, the internet is quickly making an impact. Seventy-nine per cent of respondents agreed that the internet and business publications complement each other. More than 500 business decision-makers from the 20 largest industry sectors according to advertising expenditure were interviewed to measure media usage. (Periodical Publishers Association, www.ppa.co.uk)

Journals and directories
There are over 5000 directories and yearbooks published in the UK and they cater for every interest including business, professional, industrial, technical, educational, and leisure. There are also all-purpose directories such as Yellow Pages (yell.com on the web). Directories and yearbooks are very similar and advertisers tend to treat the two as interchangeable. Containing names, addresses and other details on businesses and associations across the UK and Europe, they are an excellent medium for B2B advertisers. Business users consult them on a regular basis so any advertisement will have the opportunity to be seen many times throughout the year.

Example 8.9   ## Directory and database associations

The Directory and Database Publishers Association represents the industry and they say that they are there to protect and promote directories and databases as advertising media and as sources of information. Six per cent of all ad spend comes from this source. More details can be obtained from their website (www.directory-publisher.co.uk). The European Association of Directory & Database Publishers represents the industry across the world and has some 200 members in 37 countries worldwide (www.eadp.be).

Online magazines and directories

Many of the magazines, directories and newspapers have complementary versions on the web, e.g. Yell.com and Yahoo.com. They attempt to persuade business users to use both hard and soft forms in a complementary way. A word of warning is in order here. Owners of the media are all in competition. They need to sell advertising space to stay in business and often have the tendency to inflate the efficacy of their vehicle. All advertising should be monitored and controlled for value for money. If it can't be shown to be working, it should be stopped and the money spent on other proven methods. It is still early days as far as advertising on the net is concerned and caution should be the overriding watchword.

BRAD
British Rate and Data, published by Emap Publications (emap.com), is a business communications monthly directory of UK advertising media. It contains over 11,500 detailed media entries covering regional newspapers, national newspapers, consumer press, business press, new media, television, radio, poster and outdoor. Prices, circulation and audience figures and target markets are included (www.brad.co.uk).

Audit Bureau of Circulation (ABC)
An independent body, paid for by all media owners and users, the Audit Bureau of Circulation (www.abc.org.uk) provides free access to the circulation, distribution and attendance data for ABC-certified magazines, newspapers, exhibitions and directories within the UK and Republic of Ireland. Its main task is to act as an independent auditor of newspaper, magazine and directory circulation figures to make certain no media owner is fixing the figures. It also monitors some website viewing figures.

Example 8.10   ## Official auditor

IPC Media, the UK's biggest consumer magazine publisher, has appointed the Audit Bureau of Circulation (ABC) as the official auditor for all its titles (www.abc.org.uk).

Advantages for B2B advertisers using the print media

1. *Accurate targeting.* Specialist B2B editions exist for both magazines and directories. Even low circulation magazines, e.g. *Sea Container*, can be profitable to advertise in if the 5000 readers all work in the industry.

2. *Figures available.* Detailed target audience, price, circulation, and pass-on readership figures are available from newspaper, magazine and directory owners. Independent audits on these figures can be obtained from the Audit Bureau of Circulation (ABC).

3. *Mass coverage.* All business people will read the national press and a few newspapers, including the *Financial Times* and *Daily Telegraph*, will reach large numbers of B2B buying centre members.

4. *Longevity and high opportunity to see figures.* Unlike TV, the printed word has a certain permanency and so can be read and reread. Some magazines and directories will lie around for months, allowing many opportunities to see (OTS).

5. *More detail.* As opposed to the instant nature of TV, more complex detail with coloured diagrams and pictures can be given about the products and services on the printed page as the reader can take time to imbue.

6. *Coupon, telephone, e-mail response.* As well as more detail, a B2B advert can also include some type of coupon or response box, inviting the reader to send away, ring, e-mail for more information, invite a rep to call, or even purchase the product or service.

7. *Costs.* As with any medium, costs are relative and an effort should be made always to attempt to have systems installed that can measure benefits obtained against the amount of money paid out. Intermedia comparisons can then be compared and benchmarked.

Disadvantages of using print media

1. *Demands active participation.* Printed matter does not have the same dramatic, active impact on the reader that TV has on the viewer as it has to be picked up and deliberately read. It lacks movement and sound and is not so instantly appealing as TV. There will be extra incentive to read, however, if the content is business relevant and can be seen to add value to individual business knowledge and company operations.

2. *Adverts are easily missed.* Adverts can easily be skipped or inadvertently missed, especially if the ad is too small, one of many, has been placed in the wrong position or magazine, or content and presentation fail to attract in some way.

Example 8.11 **Advertising associations**

☐ The **Advertising Association** is a federation of 25 organisations representing the advertising and promotional marketing industries including advertisers, agencies, media and support services. It is the only body that speaks for all sides of an industry that was worth over £16.5 billion in 2001 (www.adassoc.org.uk).

Example 8.11 continued

☐ The **International Advertising Association** is the world body and represents 1000 organisations in 94 countries (www.iaagloba.org).

☐ The **Incorporated Society of British Advertisers** (ISBA) represents the interests of UK advertisers in all areas of marketing communications, including TV advertising, new media, press, radio, outdoor, direct marketing, sponsorship and sales promotion. (www.isba.org.uk)

☐ The **Institute of Practitioners in Advertising (IPA)** represents the advertising and marketing agencies operating in the UK and around the world (www.ipa.co.uk).

Radio

Radio is only used in a very small way by B2B advertising. There are fewer opportunities than TV because of the nature of the medium and it is almost exclusively a B2C medium. There are over 100 local radio stations in the UK and these can be used in the same way as local TV stations, but the specialist radio channels, growing on TV, are not yet available. There are only three national commercial radio stations and only Classic FM might hit a worthwhile number of identifiable business decision-makers. Global radio is really non-existent so the audience reach will not match that of a commercial TV channel. At present digital radio promises much but the uptake is very slow. It is relatively inexpensive to use and is all-pervasive as some listeners, perhaps in a factory or workshop, have the radio on all day, every day. On the downside, it can be seen as vocal 'wallpaper' (a background noise where content is fleeting). There is bound to be lots of advertising 'waste' and measurement is problematic. It also lacks impact and longevity when compared with TV and print respectively. Radio accounts for about 5 per cent of all UK advertising, most of this by B2C advertisers.

Outdoor advertising

Again predominantly a B2C medium although used selectively by B2B advertisers, outdoor sites can be seen everywhere: on the roadside, at retail outlets, shopping centres, airports, railway stations, leisure and sports centres, football grounds, motorway restaurants, hotels, car parks, business parks, conference centres, on every type of transport; in fact anywhere that people congregate. Posters spring up everywhere – from the handle of a petrol pump, on the wall of the toilet, on the side of a hot air balloon – and they can be small (762 mm × 508 mm) or extremely large (3048 mm × 12,138 mm).

Technology has been used to offer an enormous number of beneficial refinements. Outdoor adverts can be backlit, revolving, animated, projected onto the sides of buildings and shown in 3D. With the use of computer technology a 'virtual' ad can be created to appear on the TV screen as if in situ when in reality it isn't.

Outdoor companies such as Maiden Outdoor (www.maiden.co.uk) offer broadcast and narrowcast packages or individual sites. The big advantage for B2B advertisers is that an outdoor advertisement can be selectively placed anywhere the buyer decision-makers might be: at business events, opposite the manufacturer's offices, in the aeroplane business class section, and so on. These adverts can be researched and awareness measured. If outdoor advertising is used it would tend to be as a reinforcement to other forms of communications. Although growing, outdoor advertising accounts for less than 5 per cent of all advertising spend and is a minor media form in both B2B and B2C advertising as a poster can offer only a limited amount of information and there is no guarantee that it will be seen and/or taken in.

Example 8.12	**Best ad of the 20th century**

Abbott Mead Vickers BBDO company has judged the 'Labour isn't working' advert designed by advertising agency Saatchi and Saatchi, and seen by some as playing a key role in the Conservative general election victory of 1979, as the best poster advert of the century. Second place in the competition went to the 1914 poster featuring Lord Kitchener, which urged young men to sign up to fight in World War I.

Communications, the internet and company websites

Because it is such a new media type, advertising via the internet – either on the company's own site or on the sites of others – seems to sit comfortably as either an 'above the line' or 'below the line' media form. Interested participants only have to browse through a selection of these sites to realise that many companies are uncertain about the objectives of the site. This is reflected in poor design, poor content and how people should interact and move around the site.

Website uses

Owning a website has opened up wonderful communication and promotional opportunities for the B2B industry and it is experiencing phenomenal growth. It can be used in B2B markets for data collection, storage, analysis and the passing on of selected information. This will include catalogues on products, services and such things as component parts, as well as advice and help on current and future problems as they arise. It can be used for transactions such as order taking, delivery tracking, invoicing and revenue collection.

It can also be used for marketing, which will include advertising, sponsorship, PR, publicity, exhibitions, sales and auctions, and interactive personal selling; in fact almost any of the media strategies identified. All organisations, buyers and suppliers along the supply chain can share information, transact operations and buy and sell products and services safely within secure 'firewalls' utilising EDI processes.

Example 8.13 | ## Internet web advertising

Yahoo, with a total global audience of over 150 million, is thought to be the world's most visited website. However, it is having trouble getting enough advertisers onto its site. Unlike many of its dot.com competitors, internet portal Yahoo has managed to turn a profit before but is now having problems. It has shaken the industry when it blamed the difficulty in selling advertisements for its profits shortfall.

Spending on internet advertising or sponsorship has matched the amount spent on commercial radio advertising in the past, said a spokesperson from the Institute of Practitioners in Advertising (IPA, www.ipa.co.uk) but there is now uncertainty about the future. (Internet advertising by bureau, www.iab.net)

Measurement and research

As with all the media, feedback measurement and control are crucial if efforts and money are not to be wasted. Because the market is smaller it can be easier to measure effectiveness on B2B websites than B2C. The bigger companies will have own server access so site visits to a supplier can be immediately identified. This is not the case with B2C where millions will come through a multinational server such as Freeserve. Smaller companies can more easily be researched in traditional ways to identify levels of awareness and amounts of usage. Requests for information, sales or a sales call can be recorded directly.

Example 8.14 | ## ABC eReturns system hailed as huge success

The June end returns period saw the Audit Bureau of Circulation (ABC, www.abc.org.uk) successfully issue over 200 certificates to B2B publishers using its new online submissions system, eReturns. eReturns proved extremely popular with publishers with 43 per cent of business-to-business magazine titles due to report this period choosing to use the new system. eReturns was designed to improve ABC's reporting systems by using advanced web-based technology which allows publishers to submit their circulation returns online and automatically receive their ABC certificates via return e-mails. Publishers using the system have benefited from a faster certification service from ABC that has enabled them to bring their new circulation data to market faster.

Integrate website with company media use

Many companies will build and design their own sites and there have to be clear strategic reasons behind their use. As far as communication is concerned, there have to be clear objectives and a clear understanding on how it will integrate and fit in with corporate image and overall corporate and marketing communications. Advantages for B2B communications on the internet include:

☐ Design and content opportunities covering film, colour, sound and movement and interaction.

☐ Information, transaction, marketing and promotional uses.

☐ Sales and sales auctions.

☐ Extranet allows secure interaction of all kinds backwards and forwards along the supply chain.

☐ Intranet allows secure information and transactions to take place within the organisation and its divisions around the world.

☐ Multimedia opportunities, e.g. communications delivered direct to the place of work and through the modem or TV at home.

☐ Almost limitless global reach potential.

☐ One-to-one relationships can be developed.

☐ Competition restricted at the point of contact.

☐ Opportunities abound across the whole range of communications.

Disadvantages for B2B communications on the internet include:

☐ Still many uncertainties about the medium, audience use and reaction.

☐ Measurement methods and value for money uncertain.

☐ Difficulties on how to integrate with conventional communication and promotion methods.

☐ Some concern about safety and security measures.

Below the line and new media methods

All communication methods other than the main media discussed above are collectively known as 'below the line' media.

Direct marketing and direct response

The term direct marketing is used when producers and buyers deal direct with one another rather than through an intermediary. Direct response advertising is when messages are sent direct (rather than through TV or print) to the B2B customer in the hope of creating a direct and interactive line of communication. It can be undertaken by the following methods:

☐ Mail

☐ Magazines

☐ Newspapers

☐ Telemarketing (on the telephone)

☐ Broadcast direct (TV, radio)

☐ The internet, extranet and intranet.

Growth in direct response

The enormous growth in direct response advertising in both B2B and B2C markets has come about because of the need for advertisers to provide ever greater accountability, value for money and waste elimination. Coupled with explosive technological developments that have improved techniques for effective personalised contact to a level undreamed of 20 years ago, this media form is set to grow even more over the next decade. It is used among other things for sending information, obtaining sales leads, selling products and gaining customer feedback.

Direct mail

Direct mail is still the most important and widely used of all the B2B direct response methods, although electronic methods are rapidly catching up. Over 70 per cent of all UK direct mail (both B2B and B2C) takes place through the Post Office (www.royalmail.com). They offer a comprehensive service including buyer list rental or purchase, sales letter creation, catalogue packing, promotions, order taking, order processing, distribution, billing and payment. They also offer special deliveries, international deliveries and person-to-person recorded deliveries. The Post Office monopoly is now under threat from many commercial B2B mail and parcel delivery companies. Well-targeted direct mail sent to a named decision-maker can be a very effective way of making buyer contact. Most people will open letters and packages if they seem relevant and interesting and offer the possibility of benefits. A preparatory or follow-up phone call will utilise the method to its fullest advantage.

Example 8.15   ## Bucking the downturn

While advertising spends shrink around the globe, direct marketing has been booming. UK industry figures show a jump of nearly 10 per cent in the second quarter of this year. That is partly because it can be easier to track direct marketing. With budgets becoming scarcer, every penny has to work, and if it doesn't work you have to know why, a direct agency spokesperson said. Every year the Royal Mail handles five billion direct mail items, a number expected to grow as competition in the postal sector drives prices down.

Direct response in magazines and directories

Many magazines and directories will offer a direct response facility, called off-the-page advertising. Certain suppliers, perhaps selling component parts, will use this to advertise direct to the buyers to sell or elicit a response of some kind. In response to a request, the supplier might post a catalogue or leaflet and then follow up with a phone call. Specialist, small component parts might be dispatched by post, or delivered by road if larger, or a representative will call bringing the product and looking to sell more.

Direct response in broadcasting

TV and radio both have a direct response facility similar to that offered by magazines and directories. Response is invited by telephone, e-mail and letter. It is not used much in B2B except on the specialised TV channels because of the disadvantages of the broadcasting media in B2B advertising.

Telemarketing and direct response

The use of the telephone for direct response is another growth area. It is quick and relatively inexpensive. Many business people are willing to come to the telephone, especially if asked for by name, even where the 'gatekeeper' is adept at blocking communications. Many suppliers will outsource their telephone marketing, sales and advertising operations and many specialised companies now exist. Telemarketing is also used extensively to follow up mail shots, to prepare a customer for a mail shot, to make appointments, or to invite buyers along to supplier events.

Direct response and the internet

Such is the ease of usage that the internet seems to have been built for the direct response industry. The direct mail industry plays down consumer fears that people could be swamped by large numbers of e-mails and text messages. While for some businesses – such as those in IT – e-mails are an ideal marketing tool and make up a large percentage of the marketing mix in general, digital media make up only 5 per cent of the industry.

Junk messages

Unasked for and unwanted mail, telephone calls, faxes and e-mails – so-called 'junk' – are constantly growing problems in both B2B and B2C markets. Suppliers would need to weigh the advantages of extra sales contacts against the amount of damage that could be caused by upset customers. It is argued that junk messages are those which were wrongly directed and if all were targeted correctly there would not be a problem. E-mail seems particularly susceptible to junk downloading. Known as 'spamming', it consists of advertisers using computer programs to target thousands of buyers around the world and sending mass messages in the hope of a small percentage take-up. Even large, reputable companies are guilty of this activity. Software now exists for buyers and internet servers to block unwanted messages.

Example 8.16 **Spamming**

Internet direct marketers are also keen to distance themselves from the spam merchants. But there are clearly still many operating outside its parameters - one-third of the 300 million e-mails sent in the UK each day are reckoned to be spam. When you can buy one million e-mail addresses cheaply, it might only need a 0.01 per cent response to make money. The E-mail Marketing Association has been set up to bring best practice into digital marketing and legislation has gradually given consumers more ways of opting out of mailing lists. Permission marketing is the concept where customers are first asked if they want to receive e-mails on product updates, etc. If permission is given then the chance of that e-mail being read is increased.

Direct response customer lists

At the heart of good direct response advertising practice is the need to have up-to-date, relevant and correctly constructed business names and addresses. Nothing can be more unprofessional in direct response marketing than to send addressed material to a buyer who has left, retired or died. There are many list brokers that rent, lease or sell business lists. These can contain business names and addresses, telephone and fax numbers and e-mail addresses of departments and individual personnel. Some will even offer a brief resumé of the companies' buying habits as well as a description of the decision-making unit members. The better address lists will be regularly updated and cleansed for impurities such as wrong names and addresses and audited by an independent body such as the Audit Bureau of Circulation (ABC) to make certain that everything is above board.

Direct response, relationship and database marketing

The enhanced capability offered by the use of the marketing information system for database marketing enables the supplier to develop an ever-closer relationship with existing customers on a direct response, long-term basis. Research has shown that it is much more expensive to gain new customers than it is to hold on to existing customers. It has also shown that by focusing attention on all customer needs and matching to supplier portfolio benefit offerings, more sales and long-term value can be achieved. Computerised programs allow messages to be customised to meet the needs of each individual customer as and when required. Systems can be programmed so that relevant messages are sent at times when the buyer will be responsive to contact. This will be when the customer might need a product, product services, information, help or advice. The role of B2B direct response includes:

- ☐ Use as part of a customer relationship management programme, communicating and obtaining customer feedback and undertaking continuous marketing research.
- ☐ To send information, leaflets or catalogues or to invite the respondent to send in for a catalogue.
- ☐ To send out invitations to seminars, conferences or product launches.
- ☐ To attempt to make appointments for the sales team and sell products directly.
- ☐ To inform the prospect that a telephone call, letter, fax or e-mail will follow.
- ☐ To open new accounts.

Direct response advantages include:

- ☐ Direct relationship with the customer, bypassing the intermediary, thus allowing relationships to be built.
- ☐ Relatively inexpensive way of making and maintaining customer contact.
- ☐ Solo contact with the customer cutting out the competition.
- ☐ A quick way of contact when speed could be of the essence.
- ☐ Often the only way to make contact with the decision-maker.

Direct response disadvantages include:

- ☐ Intrusive nature can cause buyer annoyance and/or short- or long-term harm.
- ☐ Can be very wasteful, especially if expensive promotional material and catalogues are dumped because of disinterest.
- ☐ Will only work with a certain section of the market and be ignored by the others.

Example 8.17	**Direct marketing associations**

The Direct Marketing Association can be contacted on www.dma.org.uk.

The Direct Selling Association can be contacted on www.dsa.org.uk.

☐ Point-of-purchase and merchandising in B2B

Point-of-purchase (POP) has grown by leaps and bounds in the B2C market with the realisation that many purchase decisions are actually made in the retail outlet at the time of purchase. Creativity, innovation and technology have been expertly exploited so that merchandising, enhancing the consumer experience, is now an art form.

Although much less used for B2B products because they are not considered to need too much 'flowery wrapping', there are times when merchandising – that is making the product look as attractive as possible for customer appreciation – is used to full advantage in B2B. This might be at trade fairs and exhibitions, conferences and seminars, as well as in B2B intermediaries. New product launches can employ the use of 'theatre' where selected dealers are invited to watch some kind of glamour show, perhaps with display stands, flashing lights, funky music and dancers, as a prelude to the showing of the product. Just as important in B2B as in B2C, however, is the availability of sales literature such as booklets, videos and DVDs that will explain benefits and help sell the product. There are many instances where costly display material is thrown away without ever being used. It also includes the use of free give-aways such as putting the company name and/or its products on pens, calculators, desk pads, clocks, and so on. Merchandising material can be very expensive so objectives should be set and results monitored to make certain value for money is achieved. First, these can be in terms of advantageous display; second, in terms of customer attention, interest and take-up of promotional material. The role of merchandising in B2B includes:

☐ Setting the right ambience for the product display.

☐ Enhancing the product and attracting attention.

☐ Supplying its take-away information about product and services.

☐ Generating sales leads.

☐ Disadvantages might be costly promotional material never used.

Exhibitions and trade fairs

Exhibitions or trade fairs are an essential strategic part of B2B communication and promotional activity. They can be seen as a temporary marketplace for the showing of products and services. In many cases they are the only way in which some suppliers are able to meet the buyers in their industry in one place. They can be broadly divided into public fairs in the B2C market (e.g. Ideal Home Exhibition) and trade fairs in the B2B market. Public or general fairs are open to the public and can be either general interest fairs or special interest fairs. General interest fairs are used to exhibit a wide and diverse range of products and services to the general public. These types of exhibitions are widely promoted so as to attract as many people as possible. Special interest fairs are targeted at specific segments of the general public (e.g. leisure pursuits, technology, computer games, and so on).

In B2B markets, trade fairs can be horizontal, vertical, conference bound, or trade mart fairs. Trade fairs in general are open to people working in a certain field of activity or industry. Horizontal trade exhibitions invite people from a single industry. At vertical trade fairs, different industries exhibit their goods and services to one specific target group from one industry: e.g. producers of uniforms, linen, crockery, food samples and office furniture may participate in a trade fair aimed at the hotel industry.

Conference bound exhibitions are usually small and linked to a conference, e.g. a medical conference on heart disease. They have a low but highly selective reach and are able to target with pinpoint accuracy. A trade mart is a hybrid kind of exhibition and will have permanent stands. In some industries trade shows are the only way that suppliers can meet buyers, e.g. selling into the government defence industry or the security business where attendance is strictly by appointment only.

When planning the trade show strategy, clear objectives and policies should be identified about why the supplier is going to attend, who they hope to meet and what might the end objectives be. B2B exhibitions can be very costly in terms of setting up equipment, space rental and staff manning and extremely wasteful if little seems to be achieved. In most cases the objectives will not be set in terms of sales (they will not be refused of course), but more in terms of contacts, appointments made and sales leads taken. As with all media types, objectives must be set in measurable terms and monitored and controlled during and after the event.

Example 8.18 **ABC announces programme of support for the UK exhibition industry**

The Audit Bureau of Circulation (ABC) and the Association of Exhibition Organisers (AEO) have announced a strategic alliance which will see the two parties working together to build the profile and importance of auditing in the exhibition industry to ensure the continued raising of standards.

Example 8.19 **Examples of UK B2B trade exhibitions**

National Franchise Exhibition, NEC Birmingham.
IDMF – International Direct Marketing Fair, Earls Court, London.
Total Marketing Solutions, NEC Birmingham.
Brand Licensing London, Business Design Centre, London.
Retail Interiors, Earls Court, London.
More can be seen on the Trade Fairs and Exhibitions UK website
    (www.exhibitions.co.uk).

Trade fairs and exhibition associations

Trade Fairs and Exhibitions UK is the official website for the UK exhibition industry, sponsored by Trade Partners UK, the new UK government organisation responsible for all trade promotion and development work. (More information can be seen at www.exhibitions.co.uk.) The roles of exhibitions include:

☐ To make new contacts, make appointments and take leads for the sales staff to follow up.

☐ To meet existing customers, reinforce relationships, generate goodwill and improve public relations.

☐ To show off the product range as well as new innovations.

☐ To gather market research, examine competitors' products/services, new technology and innovations.

☐ To sell products and services.

Disadvantages of exhibitions include:

☐ Lack of clear objectives.

☐ Can be time consuming.

☐ Opportunity cost of using sales staff to look after the exhibition stand.

Sales and trade promotions

Sales promotions (known as 'below the line media' as opposed to main media advertising known as 'above the line') are heavily used in B2C and less so in B2B markets. They can take many forms and refer to any short-term incentive (added value) used mainly to encourage and persuade buyers and end consumers to try or buy the seller's product or services. This might be the manufacturer taking in raw material supplies (B2B), the retailer taking packaged brands for resale (B2C), or the end buyer for own consumption (B2C). They are more popular in B2C markets because consumers buying for themselves are more readily emotionally attracted by extra incentives such as 'buy one, get one free', points collection for prizes or competitions. Professional buyers, on the other hand, are buying for the company and effectiveness and efficiency are the most important considerations, not short-term, superficial perks.

Advertising is used to create the awareness and perhaps gain access for the salesperson. Sales promotions are offered to get the buyer at least to try the product. They are also used at such activities as trade fairs, conferences, factory visits and sponsorship events to encourage buyers to make appointments to see sales representatives, or to try or buy products and services.

Sales promotions are also used to encourage and motivate the company sales force to sell more of particular products. In this way products are pushed through the distribution chain through to end users. It is important to realise that the incentive is additional to basic benefits provided and is used to encourage purchase over a designated period. If the additional benefit is adopted on a continuous time basis it will no longer be seen as an additional benefit, but as an integral part of the product.

B2B sales promotions

Offering the buying centre an extra incentive to try a new product or service is a well-established practice in business markets. It is an added weapon in the marketing and sales departments' armoury, allowing the sales manager to offer something special that in some way might lessen the risk for the buyer in trying a new company or product. So a lower price or extra product value might be offered on the first order; it might be a free trial of some sort, or the supplier being willing to take back the products if they do not sell. It might be the offer of extended credit, perhaps 60 days instead of 30 days, or free installation and operating advice or extended warranties. Care should be taken not to use a sales promotion too often as the added incentive will come to be expected rather than discretionary.

In some cases it could be offering the individual buyer some kind of personal incentive such as redeemable points on products that are purchased, entry into a competition or holiday vouchers. Care must be taken with this option as many buyer companies now frown on and actively discourage such practice. This is because they insist that purchases should be made for objective, pragmatic reasons and not because of personal reward. The role of a B2B promotion includes:

☐ To persuade the buyer to make an appointment to see the supplier representative.

☐ To lower buyer risk and encourage trial of a new company, product or service.

☐ To encourage larger purchases and so block out the competition.

☐ To shift stock from the supplier warehouse so more or new can be bought.

☐ To motivate sales staff.

Disadvantages of a B2B promotion include:

☐ Sales tend to increase during the sales promotion and then decrease as soon as it stops.

☐ It can encourage 'cherry picking' – only buying sales promotion stock.

☐ Public relations and publicity

The role of public relations (PR) in an organisation is to create and maintain a favourable image for the company on a continuous basis with regard to both internal and external stakeholders. This will require PR personnel to communicate with all interested parties seeking to build and maintain harmonious relationships. As we discussed at the beginning of the chapter, it is the process of strategically communicating with the people who are important to the business. For package tour operators and packaged goods manufacturers alike, keeping the trade informed is as important as targeting the public. In addition there are whole groups of industry and professional services that have no need to talk to the end consumer but do need to talk to suppliers and customers. As a result B2B publicity is consistently shown to be bigger than consumer publicity.

To support the process, the larger company will have a dedicated PR or corporate communications department as well as working with outside PR agencies. The smaller company, because of the costs involved, might choose to work solely with a PR firm. Some PR will be seen to be the responsibility of the marketing and promotions department while other PR work will be the responsibility of the corporate communications or PR department; of course both will work very closely together. PR, as used as an integral part of the marketing communications mix, will be about rectifying problems that will impinge on how the company and its products are viewed by the suppliers, intermediaries and especially the customers and to build and maintain harmonious customer relationships. The B2B marketing communications managers will use planned publicity to strategically gain free exposure in the media for news stories and articles that portray the company and its products in a good light.

The practice of PR should not be confused with the role of publicity. PR is what you 'do' and publicity is what you 'get'. Some PR is about alleviating problems, e.g. product faults and complaints, that you would not want publicised, while other PR is about publicising events that you do want to publicise, e.g. the use of new technology.

Gaining publicity

To gain publicity the marketing communications department, in both buyer and seller organisations, will attempt to cultivate long-term relationships with B2B and B2C media owners, editors and journalists, talking to them about what information, presented in what particular way, would best suit their readership, viewers or listeners. In this way favourable news stories issued by a supplier would then appear on TV, in the press or on the radio, showing the company in a worthy light. The B2B firm can gain successful publicity from good stories appearing in either the B2B or B2C media. The target customer will be hit directly and in B2C media the target will still be hit or be hit indirectly. The good effects can be the same.

Publicity tools and techniques

There are many tools and techniques that can be used to elicit free publicity. What is important is that the whole publicity-seeking process is planned and integrated in exactly the same way as any other component of the communication mix. As with advertising, sales promotions, merchandising, etc. clear measurable objectives should be set, a budget given and measurement and control mechanisms instigated. Techniques include:

☐ Events and similar activities
☐ Sponsorship
☐ News conferences
☐ Press and broadcast releases
☐ Lobbying.

Magazines, newspapers, TV or internet sites all need to unremittingly fill their pages and programmes with interesting and lively news stories day after day and week after week, sometimes 24 hours a day. A planned and well executed publicity campaign with stories that are orientated towards each particular media audience will be welcomed with open arms by the news-hungry media, and so valuable media exposure will be obtained at little or no cost. As with other communications strategies, it can be difficult if not impossible to set objectives in terms of sales (much as the publicist might like to do this), so other more realistic methods should be used. This will include setting a target, linked to the budget, according to the amount of free exposure achieved in the media and comparing this with the costs if payment had been made (known as media equivalents) and/or trying to measure by research and awareness methods.

Uncontrolled publicity

Much generated publicity can be uncontrollable and so cannot be used in the formation of publicity plans. Unexpected events can cause stories and news items to appear that are beyond the influence of the organisation. This is not a problem if the items are favourable, but can be disastrous if they are not. Unforeseen events can happen to the most well-prepared organisation and the difficulty with even the well-designed, expertly written press release is that the newspaper, magazine, TV or radio journalist ultimately has control over what appears in the media.

Example 8.20 **Publicity**

Procter & Gamble, the global leader in the hair care business, has admitted to spying on its closest rival, Unilever. It is alleged to have searched through the rubbish of Unilever, which owns the Organics and Sunsilk brands of shampoo, to try to discover any information that would help in marketing its own new hair care brands. Press reports say that Unilever is demanding a settlement - potentially running to tens of millions of pounds.

Publicity and word of mouth

There is no doubt that employees in an industry, by talking to one another and passing on their experiences, disseminate good and bad images of organisations and their products. This will be more of a factor in B2B markets than in B2C because of the relatively small number of buyers in business markets compared with consumer markets. People working in a particular industry for many years get to know other suppliers and buyers and will talk with one another at conferences and trade association meetings about the levels of service and value they might have had from one company rather than another. The difficulty is the inability of the communications manager to control the process. The answer must be that if a quality service is offered at all times this will be passed on when one company recommends another. The role of publicity is to communicate good images of the organisation to customers and other relevant stakeholders and to do this through articles and stories appearing free in the media as news, thus being seen as legitimate, third-party endorsement.

One of the disadvantages of publicity is that it can be difficult to control. Although free at the point of issue, there are background costs such as hiring PR and publicity agencies, setting up events and entertaining media staff.

Example 8.21 **Top five UK PR B2B agencies**

	Annual turnovers *£ millions*
1. Weber Shandwick Worldwide	14,862,000
2. Countrywide Porter Novelli	14,659,000
3. Hill & Knowlton PR	9,350,000
4. Euro RSCG Corporate Comms	8,615,000
5. Edleman PR Worldwide	6,589,000

Sponsorship

Sponsorship is used in both B2B and B2C markets and can be seen as 'the giving of some form of support, usually money, to an event, organisation or person in return for some form of association and communications opportunity'. Widely used in B2C, it is applied selectively and in a smaller way in B2B markets. Under certain conditions a supplier will find it profitable to pay to have its name linked and associated with an organisation, event, or happening. This could be on a short promotional campaign or on a more long-term basis.

Example 8.22 **2008 Olympics sponsorship**

China-based multinationals have been lining up to sponsor Beijing's Olympic bid committee overseeing the 2008 Olympics. Procter & Gamble, which sells Lux soap and shampoos in China, is said to have donated $362,000. Telstra, the Australian telecoms giant, has sponsored with equipment and facilities. The brewer of Budweiser, Anheuser-Busch, is expected to be the official sponsor for the Chinese Olympic team for the third year running.

Corporate hospitality

Although used in B2C, corporate hospitality – 'the entertainment of customers and other important stakeholders at staged events in order to reward and encourage loyalty and to seek out new customers' – is used more in B2B markets. It will include inviting selected guests to events such as the Open golf tournament, Wimbledon tennis tournament, Grand National horse racing or Henley regatta, as well as trips to the factory to view new production methods. There might be hospitality tents set up in the grounds and guests given food and drink. It can be a free-standing event or part of a sponsorship arrangement. There is the hope that by invitations such as these profitable relationships can be built and

Figure 8.6
Advertising
value chain

B2B advertiser ---→ Advertising agency ---→ Media owners ---→ Audience

Communicating and building corporate and product brand values

business between buyer and seller increased. There should be a clear attempt to integrate a hospitality event into the overall communications and promotional activities. Results can be difficult to monitor and control but measures must be taken to make certain that value for money is being achieved (Figure 8.6).

Part 3   The strategic role of personal selling in B2B markets

Because of its nature, the role that personal selling plays in B2B and to a lesser extent in B2C marketing cannot be underestimated. Strategic sales planning and selling can be seen as the marketing climax. Without adequate sales the whole of the marketing effort has to be seen as failure. Although some products will sell themselves – packaged, branded products sitting on the retailer's shelf – most products and services need some type of personal selling, whether into another manufacture, into a retailer, or off the shop floor to the end user. Any form of communications or promotions that involves direct interaction between a company salesperson and the customer can be seen as personal selling. It involves strategic and detailed operational planning, skill, knowledge, commitment and hard work. The customer might be another business, an intermediary, a retailer or an end consumer.

In B2B markets the customer will be a manufacturer or producer of some kind, buying for own use. In B2C the customer will be a wholesaler or retailer buying products and services for end consumer use, or selling to the end consumer by direct contact. In many industrial markets using personal selling is the only viable strategy to communicate with the customer because of the complex products, information needed and the possible large size of the order for both initial and long-term purchases.

☐ Differences in personal selling in B2B and B2C markets

Personal selling is the dominant form of communicating and selling goods and services in the B2B market because the number of potential customers is relatively small compared to consumer markets, while the revenue possibilities from each customer can be many times higher. Conversely, personal selling is used to a lesser extent to communicate and persuade purchase in B2C markets. Because of the millions of potential customers, mass advertising makes much more sense. Paradoxically, depending on the definition of personal selling, there will be more people employed in B2C markets if all those employed in retail are included.

In B2B markets the sales representative will be selling products and services to other organisations for their own use or to sell on to other businesses for their own use. In B2C markets the salesperson will be selling consumer branded products and services to consumer wholesalers and retailers or direct to the end consumer. In B2B markets the goods and services might be component parts, capital equipment or services used in the production of these goods and services. In B2C markets the products and services will have been packaged by the supplier into consumer usable benefits and sold either through retail outlets or direct to the end consumer. Salespeople in B2B markets are:

☐ Sales representatives employed to market goods and services to other businesses, in both the public and private sectors, for use in the business.

☐ Sales representatives used by a B2B wholesaler to sell on to other businesses for their own use.

Salespeople in B2C markets are:

☐ Sales representatives used to sell producer branded goods and services to wholesalers or retailers to sell on to the end consumer.

☐ Salespeople used to sell goods and services direct from the producer or manufacturer to the end consumer.

☐ Salespeople used in retail outlets to sell direct to the end consumer.

Strategic and tactical role of the salesperson

The role of salespersons has become increasingly complex and challenging. They will need to be constantly upgrading knowledge and skills to keep apace with new market and customer demands. As buyers become more professional in the way they perform business and make purchases, so must the sales staff, if reputations are to grow and be maintained.

In many cases, the sales manager and sales representatives are the only supplier staff that the buyer will see. The corporate image, ways of running the business and company policy are all conveyed by how the sales staff behave and present themselves. They will be expected to have comprehensive knowledge of each and every customer on their area, as well as knowledge of the market and competition at both macro and micro levels. They will be expected to know the current and past industry's and companies' revenue, cost and profit figures, so that comparisons, calculations and predictions can be made. Laptop computers with access to online information and presentation ability will help in making the process as professional as possible.

Performance of many tasks

The salesperson will often perform a multitude of tasks, both strategic and tactical, for the company. They will include prospecting, that is looking for new customers and making first contact, as well as constantly calling and satisfying existing customers. They will then be expected to build on this, developing and maintaining close contact, discussing the buyer's problems and helping to supply benefit solutions through the use of both existing and new products and services. They should be on hand to offer help, information and advice and deal with customers' dissatisfaction and complaints, both with the immediate buyer and if necessary the buyer's customers. They should also collect and feed back information about general happenings in the marketplace. The sales director, sales manager and sales representative will often all be involved in price negotiations. This might be the sales director and sales manager at board level if negotiating long-term contract pricing with a large organisation or the salesperson if negotiating a one-off transactional price at operational level. The amount and level of responsibility will increase the higher the salesperson is within the organisation.

The buyer's representative with the selling organisation

Meaningful long-term relationships are built on sincerity and trust and the salesman or saleswoman will be central to this process. While never forgetting that they are employed by the supplier, in many cases they should become the buyer's representative within the supplier organisation. In this way they will be able to report back to R&D, production, transport, finance, and so on about additional benefits needed, difficulties with products and services, financial issues and delivery problems. Setting up this kind of circuitous communication process will then become part of a wider customer relationship strategic programme.

Strategic and operational role of selling in B2B marketing

- [ ] Opening new accounts.
- [ ] Monitoring and building existing accounts.
- [ ] Communicating and imparting information and advice.
- [ ] Gathering customer, market and competitor information.
- [ ] Acting in a PR role as the supplier's representative in the marketplace.
- [ ] Dealing with complaints, coming up with solutions and solving problems anywhere relevant along the supply chain.
- [ ] Promoting benefits and persuading the purchase of products and services.
- [ ] Acting as the buyer's representative within the supplier organisation.
- [ ] Negotiating price, terms and conditions in both long-term and transactional negotiations.
- [ ] Working with other functions within the organisation as well as with other channel members.
- [ ] Contributing to the implementation and running of a CRM programme.

Communications working together to build customer relationship programmes

All supplier business functions and processes, both internal and external, must work cohesively together to build customer relationship management (CRM) and customer retention programmes. Driven by the need to build long-term relationships, based on constantly seeking better solutions to customers' problems, the interactive communication relationship becomes a consultative one rather than a straightforward business transaction. CRM takes on added difficulties when the interaction is on a global basis. Whether the market is national or global, the strategic approach taken to customers and the language used must be consistent, standardised and controlled to maintain the highest optimum quality. It will include all members along the supply chain, as well as consultants and outsourcers, collaborating and communicating by the use of electronic data interchange systems. The use of an extranet will allow customers to have the same access to online information as the supplier staff so that there is instant rapport. The intranet will be able to communicate and update the CRM programme to all staff members, sending out market information and updating customer developments.

> *We live in a time when customers are under increasing pressure to cram more into each day. By thinking broadly about the challenges your customer faces, rather than narrowly about what you can sell them, you can always find ways to make their lives easier. That more than anything else will earn their loyalty.*

(*Harvard Business Review*, May 2001)

Building a value-based sales force

The sales force will play a crucial role in any customer relationship management and customer retention management programme. Constant upgrading, coaching and training in human resource management (for sales managers), innovations and new technology, personal and interpersonal skills and motivation methods, as well as knowledge on new developments with customers and markets, will be an essential part of the process. The front-line sales force must be supported by a sales support team supplying up-to-date continuous and ad hoc data from the marketing information system about customers and markets, on both sales and technical problems. An integrated CRM programme should offer backing to the whole sales team, if necessary on both a national and international basis.

Software can be acquired to enhance the sales effort in many different ways. By profiling all customers, identifying benefits and products purchased over a period, complementary products can be cross-sold and future needs predicted. The most profitable and most costly can be analysed, reasons sought for differences and business processes implemented to build on the strengths and minimise weaknesses. New technology and software programmes can automate e-mail and telephony response processes so that both inbound and outbound messages are segmented and customer-centred responses formulated. Sales force communications can be also automated so that customer call times, sales readiness states, current and past purchases, as well as customer needs and problems, can be instantly transmitted to the sales team. It can also encompass monitoring, feedback and control mechanisms. The website can be used to issue informational and pictorial updates on products, services and component parts, as well as on changes and developments in company policies, terms and conditions.

More than one person

Depending on the sales force strategy adopted, there will often be more than one supplier employee visiting the supplier DMU. Because B2B problems can be specialised and technically complex, the supplier sales representative may not have the requisite knowledge and skill to understand the problem and so recommend the correct solution. Technical experts will therefore have to accompany sales staff to spell out what the solution might be. Sometimes other staff members might also need to go along. This may include finance staff if convoluted costs and prices need clarifying, legal staff if a long, detailed contract is in the offing, and production and R&D if a new process might be needed. It is not unusual for supplier staff to spend time, perhaps months, in the buyer organisation working and learning to help solve problems and then supply the right solutions.

Change management

Employees cannot be expected to work efficiently and effectively with new ideas, new technology and new methods without help, advice, coaching and training. A CRM programme will only work if the internal sales team and the external sales force are given solid support from the top down. Internal change management strategies should be integrated in tandem with the internal marketing programmes discussed earlier. As CRM systems and processes are introduced, staff are prepared and motivated, welcoming what is happening and understanding why it is necessary. Tasks should be clearly detailed, responsibilities allocated, control mechanisms implemented and feedback given.

Benefits of CRM strategies

The benefits to be had from a well thought out and implemented strategy will include the following:

1. *Better and stronger customer loyalty*. Close contact and personalised service offerings, while constantly outmanoeuvring the competition, will encourage customer loyalty and increased sales.
2. *Better customer management*. At every point across the changing customer life-cycle, needs and wants can be more effectively identified and managed.
3. *Better focus*. The whole organisation is customer focused.
4. *Improved customer service*. Sales representatives will have up-to-date information on products and services across markets and be able to offer help and advice on both sales and after-sales service problems.
5. *Reduced costs*. Costs are reduced through an optimal mix of channels and streamlined customer service operations.
6. *Increased revenue*. By identifying and taking advantage of cross-selling opportunities based on accurate customer data and comprehensive employee training, the revenue is increased.
7. *Partnership agreements*. Working closely with suppliers, outsourcing companies, consultants and other channel members will allow a cross-fertilisation of information and other resources.
8. *Enhanced profitability*. Detailed customer analysis, coupled with more effective benefit offering, will give better insight into how costs and profits are affected.
9. *Innovation opportunities*. CRM networks should identify opportunities for innovation and new technology from around the world.

Why CRM programmes fail

As with all business initiatives, there is always the possibility of failure. Trying to implement customer value added or customer retention programmes is no different. Failure might come about for many reasons, including the following:

☐ No real strategic commitment from senior managers.

☐ Too many staff entrenched in old ways of working.

☐ Not enough commitment, understanding, knowledge and skill development for the staff.

☐ Internal politics and individual/departmental objectives working against the overall CRM business objectives.

☐ Poor and misunderstood IT processes and systems.

☐ Lack of integration across all involved areas.

☐ Poor implementation, monitoring and control mechanisms.

☐ Different level of readiness for global divisions and countries around the world.

☐ Managing the sales force

People cannot be managed. Inventories can be managed, but people must be led.

(H. Ross Perot)

Managing the business-to-business sales force in an effective and coordinated way is fundamental to the success or otherwise of the company's marketing effort. In the B2B industry the sales force comprises the people that have contact with buyers on a day-to-day basis and can make or break any initiative designed to give absolute customer satisfaction. We have seen that they are an integral part of any CRM programme and failure here would cause failure throughout the system. Large organisations might have a sales director on the board as well as a marketing director. With smaller or less sales-orientated companies the sales function would probably sit within the marketing function. The sales director might then have sales managers covering specific regional or other country areas, depending on size of the market and number of customers. There would then be a team of salespeople working for each sales manager.

Example 8.23 **Selling in financial services**

The door-to-door and B2B financial salesman is fast becoming a thing of the past as consumers turn to the internet for financial services. Thousands of salesmen have lost their jobs as a result of companies saving money by selling online instead – savings they feel can be passed on to the customer. Many companies see online selling as the easiest and quickest method for customers.

The sales manager

The sales manager will be the person with overall responsibility for the management process of planning and forecasting, organising and coordinating, directing (motivating, decision making, communicating, delegating), controlling and evaluating (PODC) the sales effort and the sales staff towards agreed organisational customer satisfaction and sales targets. Sales managers will operate in both B2C and B2B markets. In B2C markets the sales manager will be responsible for selling into retailers, and in B2B for selling into other industrial businesses. Because B2B customer needs are usually more technical and complex than B2C, the organisation of the sales management team and the strategies adopted take on added importance. Sales management strategies will cover the following.

Sales objectives

The sales targets will be set and agreed within the umbrella of the overall marketing objectives and take into account levels of demand and the quantitative and qualitative sales forecasting methods discussed at length in Chapter 2. The sales manager will be responsible for breaking down the sales target into individual targets for the whole sales team. Other sub-objectives will include number of new accounts opened and selling across the product portfolio, as well as communicating and collecting information. As well as yearly targets, the sales force will be an integral part of any short-term promotion campaign and be given separate sales targets to achieve within this period.

Sales strategies

How sales objectives are achieved will determine the sales strategies to be used. This will include whether the sales force is direct or indirect, in-house or using outsourcing, the size of the sales management team and skills required, and the make-up of the sales team needed to visit each customer. A clear identification of the needs of the industry, of the individual buying company and all the members of the buying centre and levels of influence will be necessary. It will also cover the overall approach to be taken, i.e. personal calling, telephone, website, electronic conferencing, or a mixture.

Example 8.24 **Selling the wrong products**

The UK Financial Services Authority (FSA) has announced that the pensions misselling scandal will have cost insurers and financial advisers at least £11.8 billion in compensation payments. More than one million customers who were missold personal pensions and pension top-ups are in the process of receiving pay-outs. Financial services organisations were accused of encouraging their sales force to sell customers the wrong products by paying high switching commission rates. (www.fsa.gov.uk)

Sales force organisation

The way the sales force is organised will depend on factors such as costs, size of the company, type of product, number of customers and geographical spread. Probably the most common method is by geographical spread. This might be by towns, districts, regions, country or even trading bloc. This has the attraction of minimising costs, with the salesperson living in the centre of the region as well as knowing all customers within the designated area. It has the disadvantages of expecting the salesperson to be responsible for all products and services in the range as well as all customers – small, medium or large.

The areas could be organised according to the products and services produced. This is particularly appropriate where the company has a large and/or complex range of products and services requiring specific knowledge, skills and understanding. On the other hand it could be the buyer that has technical and complex needs and this would indicate the necessity to have the sales force arranged according to specific customer needs. This method would also be used where some customers are more valuable than others – major accounts – or there is a customer buying for all the company's divisions spread around the country – known as national accounts. Both these methods can be costly because salespeople will have to cover the length and breadth of the country or continent, with some passing fellow sales employees doing the same thing. In reality sales teams tend to be a mixture of all methods identified.

The sales call rate varies according to the size and value of the customer and can be anything from once every six months to every week. With all the issues discussed under the concept of CRM, successful major and national accounts programmes now adopt a strong relationships marketing perspective, with salespeople constantly on call to solve problems and meet customers' immediate and long-term requirements. The right ambience must therefore be created involving such concepts as job satisfaction, the right rewards and professional levels of support for the sales manager and the team if this is to happen.

Example 8.25 **Gaining superior global sales and marketing IT strategy**

First, planners must align global IT strategy with the needs and goals of the entire company. Second, they must implement excellent processes and tools that support the needs of both internal and external customers. This requires dedicated ongoing efforts to improve IT tools through pilot programmes, training and adaptation of best operating practices. Finally, executives must ensure that they wisely incorporate emerging technologies. These new tools offer great value, but they must be managed to control costs and ensure delivery of promised benefits. (www.benchmarkingreports.com)

Sales force administration

The successful sales management team will required continuous support and back-up involving help in recruitment, selection and induction training, as well as ongoing coaching and management development. Industrial marketing will often need specialist salespeople who are able to talk in highly technical language about macro and micro issues that could affect a particular industry both at home and around the world. This will have to be combined with all the personal and interpersonal skills required to talk to buyer management at all levels from the boardroom to the shop floor. It can be very expensive with regard to recruitment costs and sales lost if the wrong type of person is employed and then found out to be poor in performance. Ongoing coaching and training are crucial for all staff, but never more so for the sales manager and sales team. Backroom support must also be there to supply information, help and advice the moment it is needed – perhaps covering the sales team anywhere in the world. Order processing, invoicing, delivery and after-sales service should be of the highest quality, leaving no room for sales team embarrassment and loss of face. The pace of change happens more and more quickly and buyer contact people must keep ahead of what's happening in the market if they are to retain credibility with the professional buyer and industrial buying centre. The salesperson is the single most costly resource for the supplier and must be cosseted, measured, evaluated and benchmarked at all times to make certain that value for money is achieved.

☐ Personal selling and other elements of the communication mix

Personal selling cannot be viewed in isolation from other elements of the communication mix. Although in many cases the most important method in B2B markets, personal selling will inevitably be used with many other methods, both as part of the communication strategy and as part of a specific promotional campaign. This will be outlined below and discussed in more detail when we look at the need to integrate the whole communications and promotional strategies into a synergistic whole.

Personal selling and advertising

It is possible for the salesperson to work in isolation while selling the company's products and services, unaided by any other elements of communications mix, to move the customer through the decision-making process from unawareness through to desire and purchase of the product. However, even in B2B, where personal selling has such a strong reputation, it is still the exception. Customers will always tend to be wary about buying anything from a salesperson when they are unaware of the company or the brand name. The aphorism that 'people don't buy products from companies they have never heard of' tends to be true. If the salesperson is lucky, it could be that an appointment is gained through word of mouth and a recommendation from another buyer. Usually, however, other communication methods would generally be used to create organisational and product awareness and so support the selling process. Advertising in the trade press or through sponsorship, direct response or appearance at a trade fair might be used to create the initial awareness. Then when a personal visit or telephone call is made the buyer, having heard of the supplier, will be willing to make a sales appointment to discuss the products on offer.

Personal selling, exhibitions, sponsorship

Personal selling will also be used with sponsorship and exhibitions. Sales staff will look after the exhibition stand, talk to buyers, demonstrate existing and new products and services, obtain leads, follow through and try to convert the leads to trial and product sales. If sponsorship is involved, salespeople will be on hand at the event, perhaps in the hospitality tent, to talk, reinforce and build relations with new, existing and old customers.

☐ Marketing communications and promotional campaigns

Having stated at the beginning of the chapter that the concepts of communications and promotions will be used interchangeably, it might be worthwhile to show how the two terms could be used in a slightly different context.

Marketing communications

A B2B company will be using marketing communications to continually talk to its customers. This might be through the media types identified above, direct response, sponsorship, publicity or even advertising, but overwhelmingly by use of the sales force. Salespeople will be out in the sales territory daily, seeing and communicating with small, medium and large customers in both the public and private sectors. Information can be imparted and collected, products presented across the product portfolio, and added features or new products discussed and sales orders obtained. Yearly area sales targets will be agreed with sales managers and broken down for each individual salesperson. Budgets will be set, time points agreed, and monitoring, feedback and control mechanisms agreed.

Promotional campaigns

A promotional campaign, however, is the use of the communications mix to develop and integrate a communications programme over a shorter period and usually for a particular reason. It might be a campaign to increase awareness of the corporate name, launch a new service, try to increase the sales of existing products and services in a new market, or open new customer accounts.

It will take place over a specific period of time, perhaps three to six months. Promotional campaigns will be used in both B2B and B2C markets – the difference being the target audience and the make-up of the promotional mix to be used. Partnership promotions are sometimes used horizontally, where similar suppliers work together to break into a market, or vertically where buyer and supplier share costs to promote to customers along the supply chain.

Responsibilities will be allocated and clear, measurable objectives will be set (SMART). Budgets will be agreed, the promotional mix selected and results monitored before, during and after the promotional period to check that results are as

Figure 8.7
Relative
importance
of the basic
strategic
promotional
elements in
B2B compared
with B2C

Business-to-business		
1	2	3
Personal selling	**Business** advertising	**Sales** promotions

Business-to-consumer		
1	2	3
Advertising	**Sales** promotions	**Personal** selling

intended. It will be very likely that B2B marketing and advertising agencies will be used to run the campaign and a research agency used to monitor and control the process (Figure 8.7).

A promotional mix that works effectively for B2B markets can be different from that for B2C for the following reasons:

☐ Communication more technical in nature.

☐ Relatively small number of potential buyers.

☐ The geographical dispersion of customers.

☐ Complex nature and time length of the buying process.

☐ Decision making often the result of group discussions.

☐ Customers have more knowledge and understanding.

☐ Individual customers more important and more difficult to replace.

☐ Fewer alternative products and services.

☐ Fewer competitors.

☐ Customer and supply chain relationships more important.

Integrated marketing communications (IMC) and promotional campaigns

Integrated planning is at the heart of B2B marketing communications; only if we all know where we are going can correct and adequate resources be integrated and made available and monitoring and measurement controls be implemented so as to ensure a satisfactory outcome.

(Account manager)

All communication programmes and promotional campaigns will inevitably use more than one strategy to achieve the end objectives. It is important that the communication or promotional strategies adopted are well planned and shown to work together harmoniously to achieve overall objectives. In this way synergy can be achieved. This should motivate all departments to work together, but because of different agendas this isn't always the case. Integrated marketing is strategic in that the content and delivery of all messages by all media used are the result of an overall communications or promotional plan. IMC should be based on clearly researched and identified organisational and buying centre needs. Once the target audience has been selected and needs identified, communication objectives can be set. This might be raising corporate awareness over a long time period or the market share wanted from the launch of a new product. Budget will be agreed and the best methods of contact chosen. The company/product positioning statement and message content, style and presentation should be understood by everyone so that all communications, from whichever media, are consistent and market the same identified benefits to all selected target segments.

Because the process may involve taking the audience from unawareness (remember the hierarchy of effects model discussed earlier) through to interest, desire and action – that is buying the product – different strategies will be used: advertising to create awareness; direct mail shot description and benefits to build interest; a sales visit to close the sale. Different strategies might be used because the media forms have attributes that are more likely to be read or seen by one target group rather than another: specialist magazines for detail; the website for interactive communications; telephone for contact, and so on. What is important is that all media forms used must have clear, measurable objectives that can be monitored, controlled and measured to see that objectives are being achieved. All separate media objectives should build and integrate to meet the one overall objective for the programme or campaign.

Measuring communication and promotional performance

> If you can't measure it, you can't manage it!

All organisations would like to measure the value of all money spent, whether production costs, human resource productivity, or transport efficiency. Marketing and promotional communications are no different. Most companies would like to measure the results according to sales and revenue generated, but except for the role of the sales force this is not always possible. However, this should not prevent an attempt being made to put performance indicators on strategies used. Without a measurement of some kind the results achieved cannot be compared with past performances, benchmarked against the competition, and improvements made so as to gain better cost/benefit ratios. Wherever possible, ultimate objectives will be set according to an increase in revenue figure, because this is the most obvious and direct way of judging the success or otherwise of a communications or promotional programme. But in many cases this is not possible so surrogate behavioural objectives such as levels of awareness and interest, as well as intentions to buy, will be used.

Measurement, control and monitoring of objectives should take place before, during and after a communications programme or promotional campaign. The target market can be consulted as the campaign progresses and adjustments made if parts are found not to be working. This can be undertaken by marketing research, talking to a sample of the target market, number of requests for information and catalogues received, sales leads taken or increase in sales. Research agencies will sometimes be used to undertake this type of research. The success or otherwise of any programme will be judged by objectives being achieved.

Budgeting for marketing communications

Budgets should be part of the planning process and this will be discussed in more detail in the following chapter. Too often budgets are set before the communications planning process has been thought through, leading to some projects being underfunded while others are in surplus. Budget allocation should be part of the overall communications integrating process. If budgets are set individually for, say, advertising, sales promotions and exhibitions, when communication strategists attempt to integrate for optimum performance it might be found that there hasn't been enough allocated for exhibitions and too much for sales promotions. Bureaucracy and departmental barriers may then prevent the transfer of monies from one to the other.

Methods of budgeting

Ideally the best method of budgeting in all areas, including communications and promotions, should be by task and objective. The overall integrated objectives and best strategies are identified, costs ascertained and then budgets set. In reality this is not the way it is always done and the following methods may be used:

- By what the company can afford – probably the most popular method.
- The same as last year with or without a percentage increase for inflation.
- As a percentage of current or expected turnover or profit.
- Based on the industry and market norm.

Planning and control in the communications process

There will be little discussion here on the communications planning process as the overall B2B planning process will be examined and evaluated in comprehensive detail in the next chapter, but it might be worthwhile just to outline the factors involved (Figure 8.8).

Use of B2B marketing and advertising agencies

Experience has taught me that advertisers get the best results when they pay their agency a flat fee ... It is too unrealistic to expect your agency to be impartial when its vested interest lies wholly in the direction of increasing your commissionable advertising.

(David Ogilvy)

Many communication campaigns are planned and instigated by working with outside marketing and advertising agencies. The big advantage is the expertise and professionalism that the agency personnel will bring to the project. Agencies will offer general services in both B2C and B2B markets, while others will specialise in one industry or marketing area. The downside is the costs involved as it can be very expensive to employ such organisations. Services offered will include the following:

Figure 8.8
Factors involved in the B2B communication planning process

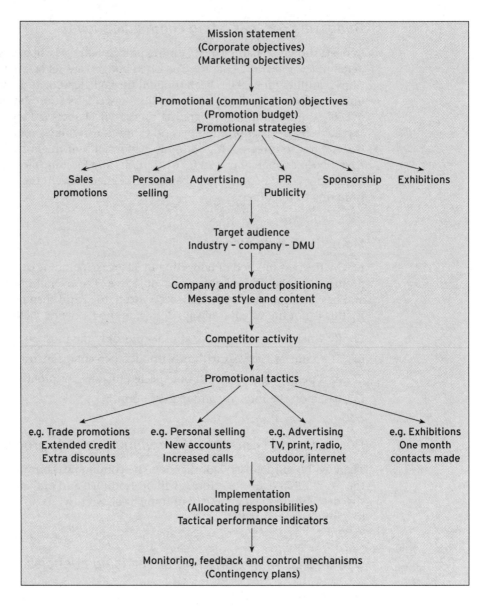

☐ Target identification and benefits wanted
☐ Corporate and product positioning
☐ Strategy choice
☐ Message construction
☐ Media selection
☐ Media payment
☐ Sales support
☐ Research, monitoring and control
☐ Integrating the whole communications effort.

Example 8.26   **The B2B full service agency**

Cross-Border Communications, or CBC, is a full-service, business-to-business advertising agency based in central Copenhagen, Denmark. They say that they specialise in providing marketing communications services to international businesses across four broad areas: corporate branding, product positioning, lead generation and strategic sales support (www.cbc.dk).

Innovation in B2B communications

One of the real difficulties with communications in both B2B and B2C markets is the problem associated with 'clutter' – the term for all the interference between message sender and message receiver that can prevent meaningful contact (identified when we discussed the basic communications model). It is more of a problem in B2C markets because of the need to reach millions of individuals at the same time as thousands of other advertisers, predominately through the use of mass advertising – a one-way medium. Because B2B markets are smaller, we can use personal selling – a two-way medium more favourable to good communications and understanding. We know that there are times, however, when other media methods must be used, often as a complement to personal selling. Innovative communication ideas and processes are used to attempt to break through this clutter and try to make certain that one company's messages are seen above all others.

This will embrace all customer contact material such as advertisements, catalogues, merchandising material, letters, e-mails, faxes and videos where approach, style, content and promotions must be constantly explored, upgraded and measured to try to make certain that they stay fresh and welcoming so that contact is made. Good B2B advertising agency account managers should discuss such issues continuously with supplier marketing staff demonstrating innovative approaches and making recommendations.

Use of technology in B2B communications

There has been an enormous upsurge in the use of technology in B2B marketing communications in an attempt to improve reception and feedback. All forms of electronic conferencing make it possible to have interactive supply chain meetings with people contributing across the whole market. Adverts can be digitised and sent to media agencies instantaneously – again almost anywhere in the world. They can be altered at a moment's notice to incorporate up-to-date information and news. Computer technology can plan, place and track ads using mathematical and statistical theory, undertaking advanced testing, response modelling and performance prediction to maximise the effectiveness of a campaign in all media. This can be used in conjunction with traditional research methods to give an all-round measurement approach.

Advertisements can now be made interactive, with instant feedback obtained through specialised TV and computer modems. LED screens allow TV-type ads to be run on outdoor sites. Computerised virtual ads can appear on TV screens at any event without being actually present. Sales promotions can offer information on DVDs and video and computer chips can be embedded into merchandising gifts and calling cards.

Web ads are being designed with banners that allow users to interact, for example by adjusting the size, shape, colour, etc. of the product to see the effect. Flashing, buzzing and pop-up interactive ads, as well as larger ad formats, are already appearing on popular sites. Another up-and-coming form is the 'super-stitial'. A TV-style ad pops up and plays a 20-second animation or video with a talking head or product demonstration. In the world of technology it now seems that almost anything is possible to enhance the communications process in an attempt to improve the supplier's chance of being noticed and their products eventually purchased. Ultimately, of course, it will depend on the receptiveness of the receiver, perhaps overstimulated by too much information, and the use-fulness of the products on offer.

Example 8.27   **Billboard technology**

High street billboards could soon start talking to people walking past as advertisers look to harness new technology. Poster adverts could be made to speak, play music or produce sound effects when a potential customer is within range. An infra-red sensor clipped to the back of the ad site detects the presence of people and activates a recorded audio message about the product. We already have billboards that are lit, move and rotate. Soon they will send text messages on our mobiles as we pass.

Legal concerns in B2B communications

There are legal aspects and ramifications to consider in all business activities, and communications and promotions are no different. There is always the tempta-tion for salespeople to exaggerate product and service benefits to clinch the sale. This can prove extremely costly if the law considers this to be unfair or even criminal. Salespeople must be seen to be truthful in B2B and B2C markets. Adverts must be seen to be honest, legal, truthful and decent (ASA) and not give offence to any reasonably minded person. Recruitment ads must abide by equal opportunity legislation and be seen to be operating in an ethically acceptable manner. Advertising and promoting on the web have thrown up many legal conundrums, not least where the law should be enforced – at the home base of the advertisers or where the ad is received. Law in this area is still being debated and the jury, as they say, is still out.

Example 8.28   **ITC looks at banned areas**

Groups from escort agencies to hypnotists could be allowed to advertise on tele-vision under plans to relax the strict rules surrounding advertisements. The Independent Television Commission (ITC) is consulting on whether to scrap many of the restrictions which dictate what can and cannot be advertised on television. There are currently 30 categories of goods and services that are banned. (www.itc.org.uk)

Although consumer law is more detailed and comprehensive than in B2B markets, the feeling being that companies are more able to look after themselves than individual consumers, it is still a force to be reckoned with where there is a proven case of deliberate misleading. The ultimate sanction for a supplier (or buyer) is bad publicity and loss of customers. The law will have an effect on all types of communication discussed throughout this chapter, at both UK and EU level, and the movement is towards standardisation across the trading bloc and world markets.

UK broadcast and print regulatory bodies

A new regulatory body for the broadcasting media has now come into force in the UK. Ofcom says it will regulate TV and radio by means of a new framework that will allow flexibility for industry while fully meeting the expectations of viewers and listeners and maintaining high levels of quality and diversity. The five organisations that will merge to form Ofcom are Oftel, the Radio Communications Agency, the Radio Authority, the Independent Television Commission and the Broadcasting Standards Commission (www.ofcom.gov.uk).

The Advertising Standards Authority (ASA, www.asa.org.uk) is the UK body responsible for regulating print advertisers, including newspapers, magazines and directories as well as the sales promotions industry. It issues codes of practice and now publishes its complaints and adjudication reports about accused companies. It is a self-regulating body, however, and some commentators argue that it lacks any power to enforce its judgements. Similar bodies exist in the EU and around the world with varying amounts of power.

EU body

The European Advertising Standards Alliance (EASA) is a non-profit organisation based in Brussels. The alliance says 'it acts on behalf of the European advertising industry, and is the single authoritative voice on advertising self-regulation issues promoting high ethical standards in commercial communications by means of effective self-regulation, while being mindful of national differences of culture, legal and commercial practice' (www.easa-alliance.org). The EU has a European Commission which oversees advertising law and instigates new European legislation.

Example 8.29 **EU and advertising law**

The European Commission has put forward new legislation that would stop cigarette adverts in newspapers, magazines, on the radio and internet. A previous EU law banning advertising was overturned after the tobacco industry challenged it in the European Court of Justice.

☐ Summary

In this chapter we have examined the role of communications at both the corporate and marketing levels, evaluating its users in both areas and outlining how it might be used at different levels. As with all other chapters there was an attempt to differentiate between communications in B2B and B2C markets, with particular reference to both intentional and unintentional marketing communications at both corporate brand and product brand levels. Two communications models, the individual basic and the corporate basic, were highlighted to show how it works and to stress the fact that simplicity in understanding communications should not be forgotten. The importance of market segmentation, research, customer profiling and identification of benefits to the communications process was recognised.

We then went on to talk about how the organisation might manage the communications process, identifying the need to set clear, measurable objectives that match the needs and benefits of each clearly selected industry, company and decision-making unit in the target audience. Communications and promotional strategic methods were discussed and evaluated. These included the use of both 'above the line' and 'below the line' media. Above the line media were recognised as the media mix or main media and include TV, print, radio, outdoor and the internet. Again comparisons were made between B2B and B2C usage. A simple 'hierarchy of effects model' demonstrated how communications might work using a combination of communications strategies.

Below the line methods were then identified and discussed. These include direct response, trade sales promotions, merchandising, PR, publicity, exhibitions and sponsorship. The need to measure, research, monitor and control all individual media as well as the overall communications results was emphasised, arguing that value would be lost if this was not conscientiously performed.

The importance of personal selling in the B2B communications and promotion programmes was recognised and sales and sales management strategies were discussed. This included the absolute priority to build long-term relationships with many buyers, under the umbrella of customer relationship and customer retention management schemes, if value is to be maximised. The different parts that the supplier salesperson could enact for buyer benefit were described before we went on to look at the sales force as a whole and how it might be organised under the supervision of the sales manager. It was recognised that, though of utmost importance in B2B markets, personal selling could not usually work effectively on its own and needed to be incorporated into the whole communications programme. The difference between communications programmes and promotional campaigns was then given, before moving on to discuss the need for the total integration of all the media into one holistic approach to the target audience if synergy is to be achieved.

Finally we looked briefly at budgeting methods, innovation and technology in communications and the legal aspects.

Discussion questions

1. Discuss the full implications of business-to-business communications and examine and evaluate all the factors that have to be taken into consideration when looking at communications planning.

2. Identify the differences between corporate and marketing communications. How might B2B and B2C differ in the use of the two business functions?

3. Discuss communications and the internal marketing process in B2B marketing. How would a company need to set about undertaking such a programme and what might the difficulties be?

4. Identify the major forms of communications and promotion used in both B2B and B2C marketing. Why might the mix be different? Give real live examples whenever possible.

5. What role might B2B marketing research play in promotion and advertising? Discuss the methods that might be used, paying close attention to the advantages and disadvantages.

6. Discuss the part that advertising and sales promotion play in B2B markets. Some commentators would want to argue that they are both sometimes undervalued in the B2B marketing process. How would you address this criticism?

7. How relevant are models such as the AIDA hierarchy of effects model? What are their advantages and disadvantages?

8. Identify all the possible media types and evaluate usage for advertising in the B2B market.

9. The sales function is considered the most important communication strategy in B2B markets and advertising the most important in B2C markets. Why might this be so? Examine and evaluate the role of the sales representative in business markets. Give live examples.

10. Discuss how innovation and technology is affecting all aspects of B2B communications. Give live examples and attempt to speculate on what you think the future will hold.

 Visit the *B2B Marketing* website at www.booksites.net/wright for a Case Study, Questions, and an Internet Exercise for this chapter.

☐ Bibliography

Books

Berry, M. (1998) *The New Integrated Direct Marketing*. Aldershot: Gower.

Bovee, C.L., Thill, J.V., Dovel, G.P. and Wood, M.B. (1995) *Advertising Excellence*. Maidenhead: McGraw-Hill.

Colley, R. (1961) *Defining Advertising Goals for Measured Advertising Response. DAGMAR*. New York: Association of National Advertisers.

Cummins, J. (1993) *Sales Promotions*. London: Kogan Page.

De Chernatony, L. and McDonald, M.H.B. (1994) *Creating Powerful Brands*. Oxford: Butterworth-Heinemann.

De Pelsmacker, M., Geuens, M. and Van der Ber, J. (2001) *Marketing Communication*. London: Pearson Education.

Fill, C. (1999) *Marketing Communications: Context, Contents and Strategies*. Harlow: Pearson Education.

Foxall, G.R. (1994) *Consumer Psychology for Marketing*. London: Routledge.

Haig, M. (2000) *e-PR – The Essential Guide to Public Relations*. London: Kogan Page.

Hart, N. (1998) *Business-to-Business Marketing Communications*, 6th edn. London: Kogan Page.

Jefkins, F. (1988) *Secrets of Direct Response Marketing*. Oxford: Butterworth-Heinemann.

Kent, R. (1994) *Measuring Media Audiences*. London: Routledge.

Shimp, T.A. (1997) *Advertising, Promotion and Supplemental Aspects of Integrated Marketing Communications*, 4th edn. London: Dryden Press.

Smith, P.R. and Taylor, J. (2002) *Marketing Communications: An Integrated Approach*, 3rd edn. London: Kogan Page.

Van Reil, C.B.M. and Blackburn, C. (1995) *Principles of Corporate Communications*. London: Pearson Education.

Wright, R. (2000) *Advertising*. Harlow: Pearson Education.

Wright, R. (2003) *Business and Marketing Dictionary*. Chelmsford: Earlybrave.

Journals

Cox, J. (1996) 'Making a case for trade shows', *Business Marketing*, 81: T4.

Dywer, R. (1987) 'Direct marketing in the quest for competitive advantage', *Journal of Direct Marketing*, 1: 15–22.

Eagle, L. and Kitchen, B. (2000) 'IMC, brand communications and corporate culture', *European Journal of Marketing*, 34: 667–86.

Edmonston, J. (1996) 'Practical tips to measure advertising's performance', *Business Marketing*, June: 14.

Fojt, M. (1995) 'Becoming a customer driven organisation', *Journal of Service Marketing*, 9 (3): 7–8.

Jones, E. (1996) 'Leader behavior, work attitudes and turnover of salespeople: an integrative study', *Journal of Personal Selling and Sales Management*, 16: 13–23.

Kaydo, C. (1996) 'Making a marketing impact', *Sales and Marketing Management*, September: 89–94.

Lohita, R., Johnson, W.J. and Rab, L. (1995) 'Business-to-business advertising: what are the dimensions of an effective print ad?', *Industrial Marketing Management*, 24: 369–78.

Morrill, J.E. (1970) 'Industrial advertising pays off', *Harvard Business Review*, 48: 4–14.

Sashi, C.M. and O'Leary, B. (2002) 'The role of the internet auctions in the expansion of B2B markets', *Industrial Marketing Management*, 31: 103–10.

Shoham, A. (1992) 'Selecting and evaluating trade shows', *Industrial Marketing Management*, 21: 335–41.

Tanner Jr., J.F. and Chonko, L.B. (1996) 'Using trade shows throughout the product life cycle', *Centre for Exhibition Industry Research Report*.

Visit www.booksites.net/wright for the Internet references for this chapter.

09

Formulating business-to-business marketing strategy

Planning is everything - the plan is nothing.

Aims and objectives

By the end of this chapter the student should be able to:

1. Demonstrate an understanding of the importance of strategic thinking to the success of the small, medium and large B2B organisation in the public or private sector.

2. Identify all the factors that make up the strategic planning process and be able to transfer this learning to a real situation.

3. Identify and analyse the problems associated with the tactical implementation of strategic plans.

Part 1 The need for business marketing strategy

☐ Introduction

Not all organisations, whether in the B2B or B2C markets, will look very far into the future in an attempt to ascertain what direction markets might take and what future demand might be. Some managers are so busy 'firefighting' and managing the business from day to day that they don't have the time, energy or wherewithal to look any further than a month or more into the future. This is especially so with small and medium sized businesses but still the case with the occasional larger business. This is not to say that some businesses, usually owned or managed by an entrepreneurial type, cannot succeed in this way, if only in the short term. There are also times when markets are so unstable and unpredictable in some industries that any long-term planning seems to be not worthwhile; any planning becomes just a series of short-term plans as market conditions change almost from month to month. These problems, however, do not mean that formal strategic planning should be abandoned, only that the process and techniques used must be made more flexible, adjusted and constantly reviewed to take into account changing circumstances.

☐ Importance of strategic thinking

Most organisations realise the importance of strategic thinking, looking ahead and attempting to understand how market conditions might change, how the levels of demand might alter and what the reaction of competitors might be. Imaginative and entrepreneurial thinking unguided by a strategic perspective is much more likely to fail than to succeed. Innovation, the use of new technology and new product development are all meaningless if not linked into an idea of future customer wants and needs. For example, attempting to alter employee culture, implementing motivation projects and putting on management coaching and training programmes to improve performance without aligning it all to how the organisation intends to build competitive advantage is a recipe for confusion and mismanagement and just plain unprofessional.

Very few B2B companies, whether in the service industry, manufacturing, retail or electronics, have been able to escape the unremitting competition or the movement in markets coming at them from every corner of the globe. Deregulation, privatisation, anti-competitive legislation, unpredictable stock markets, globalisation and phenomenal technical and innovative changes have attacked industry after industry. The problems that good planning seeks to solve – future needs of buyers, what competitors will do in the future, how the economy will influence events, how to gain and maintain competitive advantage – will never alter.

Example 9.1 **An uncertain world**

The UK stock market notched up the longest losing streak in its history yesterday as fears of an impending war with Iraq triggered an unprecedented ninth successive daily fall in share prices. The FTSE 100 index of leading shares has seen £80 billion wiped off its value since 13 January. Anxiety is growing at the impact of a conflict on already fragile global markets. There are also fears that the price of oil could soar if an invasion of Iraq leads to prolonged turmoil in the Gulf. The wider FTSE All Share index has not experienced such a sustained fall since November 1974, when Britain was struggling towards the end of the previous massive bear market. Many are asking where it will all end.

Changing planning environments

Business and market environments around the world are, to a lesser or greater extent, always in some kind of change process that will have ramifications for the organisational planning process. The change might be environmental, economic or social and affecting all markets at the same time or, as is more likely, the change will affect one part of the world or one country at different times. Global companies might be affected in all markets at the same time, as in a world recession, or only in one trading bloc or country because of relatively localised factors. The changes might be gradual, e.g. brought about by demographic factors, or sudden and unexpected, e.g. OPEC raising the price of oil. Sudden change might also affect one industry more than another, either positively or negatively, e.g. terrorist attacks devastating air traffic but leading to an increase in other types of transport and/or leisure activity. Generally the retail environment and B2C markets will alter less often and more slowly than B2B markets as change factors take longer to filter down through the supply chain, but this will vary according to the B2B industry and market.

Stable and dynamic planning environments

Although most world market environments are more liable to change than in the past, markets in some sectors will be more susceptible than others. In some industrial markets change is constant almost month after month, e.g. information technology, while others barely change from year to year, e.g. pharmaceutical markets with long-term patents. In some industries, such as cars and lorries, the lead time (planning horizon) for producing new products and introducing new processes will be much longer than in other industries such as publishing because of the resource implications involved. Although the pace of technology now makes it easier for most industries to adapt more quickly to market circumstances than in the past, it will always be quicker to change direction in some sectors because of products and services offered, design times, skills training, financial commitment and risk, level of competition, and so on. The size of the company, its structures, systems and scope of its market activities will also have an enormous influence. A company the size of General Electric will take longer to radically adjust than a company employing 50 or 60 people and operating in only one market. Taking all these factors into account will make any form of long-term strategic planning more predictable and so much easier in some areas and some companies than in others. It should also be noted that the longer the strategic planning time period, the more uncertain will be the power of predictability; therefore the less detailed and more problematic the plan will be (Figure 9.1).

Planning in turbulent economic times

Strategic planning is much easier when major economic forces, inflation, interest rates and employment levels are stable and relatively predictable. It is much more difficult when times are turbulent and economic factors fluctuate. Under these circumstances long-term planning has to be constantly revised, perhaps every year, and so becomes a series of shifting short-term plans. Some commentators argue that under conditions of complexity and chaos strategy is developed on the hoof and emerges in the manner discussed below under prescriptive emergent planning (Figure 9.2).

Ability to plan for change

The ability of the organisation strategically to plan for change will depend on the following factors:

☐ Predictability of the change at political, economic and industrial level.

☐ How sudden or gradual the change might be.

☐ Susceptibility of the industry/organisation to changing circumstances.

Figure 9.1
The strategic planning challenge

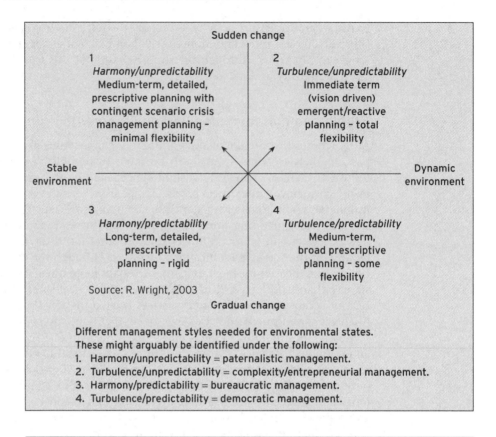

Sudden change

1
Harmony/unpredictability
Medium-term, detailed, prescriptive planning with contingent scenario crisis management planning – minimal flexibility

2
Turbulence/unpredictability
Immediate term (vision driven) emergent/reactive planning – total flexibility

Stable environment ———————————————— Dynamic environment

3
Harmony/predictability
Long-term, detailed, prescriptive planning – rigid

4
Turbulence/predictability
Medium-term, broad prescriptive planning – some flexibility

Source: R. Wright, 2003

Gradual change

Different management styles needed for environmental states.
These might arguably be identified under the following:
1. Harmony/unpredictability = paternalistic management.
2. Turbulence/unpredictability = complexity/entrepreneurial management.
3. Harmony/predictability = bureaucratic management.
4. Turbulence/predictability = democratic management.

Figure 9.2
Strategic planning under uncertain circumstances

☐ Long-term, detailed, prescriptive planning becomes problematic
☐ Short-term, emergent, reactive planning becomes the norm
☐ Decisions made must still link to company mission, goals and values
☐ Constant, up-to-date 'sensing' of information on environments and markets crucial
☐ Knowledge, experience, intuition and a flexible mind become overriding management characteristics
☐ Wherever possible strategic decision making should be decentralised
☐ Responsibilities must be given to managers nearest the problem so that decisions can be made quickly and efficiently
☐ Constant, meaningful communications across all departments and between headquarters and divisions must be embedded into the culture
☐ Regular strategic meetings should be used for continuous planning updates
☐ Monitoring and control mechanisms should be kept to the minimum without threatening overall company viability

☐ Stability of the country or trading bloc served.
☐ Products and services offered.
☐ Markets served.
☐ Strategic horizontal and vertical alliances formed.
☐ Ease of competitive entry.
☐ Size, diversity and geographical spread of the organisation.
☐ Structure, culture and preparedness of the organisation.
☐ Level of understanding about the planning process.

Strategy and implementation gap

Strategic planning should never be seen as something to be discussed and agreed by senior managers at boardroom level, detached from the implementation. Too many rigid, formal plans end up never being acted upon in any meaningful way because the strategists abdicate responsibility once the plan has been formalised at the higher level and never become involved in seeing it through to the tactical and operational level. This has given formal strategic planning a bad name in many quarters, leading to disillusionment and rejection by many practitioners and commentators alike. To be effective, it must be part of an agreed process including the implementation and then judged on both strategy and operation as to whether or not it has been successful.

Example 9.2 **Operational effectiveness and strategy**

According to Michael Porter (1996), operational effectiveness (OE) and strategy are both essential to superior competitive performance but they work in different ways and so should not be confused. Operational effectiveness means performing day-to-day, week-to-week and month-to-month activities more effectively and efficiently than the competitors. Companies must be structured and managed in a flexible way so as to respond rapidly to competitive and market changes as (or before) they happen. They must benchmark continuously and outsource aggressively to achieve best practice and to gain efficiencies. However, he argues that on its own this is not enough as few companies will be able to constantly keep ahead of the competition in this manner because rivals will also have access to the same operational efficiency processes.

On the other hand Porter sees strategy as the creation of a unique and valuable corporate position in the market that unifies and focuses all individual activities into a market and customer approach that is different from or superior to the competition. There must be a continual search for ways to reinforce and build on this selected company position so that the competition finds it impossible to imitate. He goes on to identify three generic ways that this might be achieved by an organisation.

1. Variety-based positioning – producing products or services that are different, better or cheaper than the competition.

2. Needs-based positioning – serving the needs of a particular customer group, for example, a public sector area.

3. Access-based positioning – segmenting customers who are accessible in different ways, perhaps by direct personal contact, through partnerships or by private internet connections.

While operational effectiveness is about achieving excellence in individual activities, strategy is about combining all organisational activities so that a 'fit' exists between positioning strategy and clearly identified industry and customer needs. Porter sees this as fundamental to obtaining and sustaining competitive advantage: 'It is harder for a rival to match an array of interlocked activities than it is merely to imitate a particular sales-force approach, match a process technology, or replicate a set of product features.' Finally he goes on to suggest that an overall fit amongst a company's activities will improve operational effectiveness as transparent interdependency will quickly identify and rectify areas of weakness.

Strategic planning and implementation gap

The strategic planning and implementation gap might come about for the following reasons:

☐ Market positioning strategy not understood, communicated or agreed by all employees.

☐ More kudos given to the strategic planning process than its implementation.

☐ Management and marketing strategists unwilling to be measured by practical implementation performance indicators.

☐ Too harsh a dividing line between strategic and front line managers.

☐ Lack of focused interlinking, interconnected systems.

☐ Lack of consultation and a breakdown in communications between all interested members.

☐ Strategic plans too rigid and thus defying translation into practical forms.

☐ Uncertain levels of responsibility.

☐ Involvement of managers and all company functions

Managers at all levels and across all functions, from the line managers upwards, should be involved in the process of discussion and debate, including marketing and sales managers, production, finance, administration, human resource, R&D, and so on. In this way a sense of ownership and commitment is engendered as everybody can feel a part of the process. Strategic thinking should not be something that occurs rigidly once a year but be part of a continuous ongoing debate where, if necessary, sections of the plan are altered as and when circumstances force this to happen. A good, coordinated plan will translate down to operational detail over the shorter period, be discussed, agreed and acted upon by all participants. Systems should be put in place that invite back comments, suggestions and requests for new information needed so that the strategic plan is constantly updated to meet the needs of the changing environment (Figure 9.3).

Figure 9.3
Good strategic
and tactical
planning

☐ Encourages discussion, argument and debate, among all managers as part of a continuous process
☐ Dissemination of information should give a sense of long-term direction for all involved in the process
☐ Can empower and motivate employees allocated clear responsibilities
☐ Provides leadership
☐ Resources can be garnered, organised, upgraded and coordinated in preparation for change
☐ Monitoring and control mechanisms, at all levels, permit the plan to be managed effectively and efficiently
☐ Encourages the continual monitoring of the internal and external environment
☐ Built-in flexibility allows changes to be adopted as and when environmental and market circumstances demand
☐ Should not become a substitute for good operational management decision making

Size and type of organisation

The size of the organisation will have an effect on the planning process. It should be easier to plan in small companies than in very large companies, especially those with many divisions across the world (although more professional help will be available for the larger organisations). One organisation might have a policy of central planning while another might opt for decentralised planning. One company might have an autocratic planning procedure while another might have the opposite – a democratic planning procedure. Planning in the public sector will usually be more rigid and formal than in the private sector because of the involvement of government and other stakeholders.

Prescriptive planning

Care has to be taken when making assertions about the level of planning that may or may not take place within an organisation. Formal, prescriptive strategic planning – discussing, agreeing and translating a plan into a written document covering perhaps three years – is not the only method applied. In some cases strategic thinking is happening but is not presented in the formal way described above. It is only when we look back at how a company got to its present position that we can see a distinct and logical strategic pattern taking it from whence it came to where it is now. It is as though the entrepreneur running the business has been thinking about the long term and reacting strategically, and often intuitively. In many cases the entrepreneur is able to transmit this to surrounding managers so that all will hopefully be moving in the same direction.

Planning under emergent circumstances

Other strategic thinking and planning takes place in reaction to emergent circumstances rather than to clearly identified objectives. The marketing department will know what it achieved in the previous year and hope to improve on it in the current year. Performance targets will be set at all levels at the beginning of each year with this in mind. A post mortem will be held at the end of each period, but a full audit will not be held at the beginning of the next period. Strategy tends to be changed in reaction to circumstances, either as they happen or a short time before they happen. There may well be an awareness of the possibility of future events but, unless cataclysmic in nature, a reaction will only take place as events appear within the working time frame.

Example 9.3 **Emergent change**

Many practitioners and business commentators argue that the future is unknowable in any real meaningful way and a business can only react to circumstances as they happen. Emergent change is the whole process of developing a strategy where the outcome only emerges as the strategy proceeds. There is no defined list of implementation actions in advance of the strategy emerging, although experience and intuition will hopefully inform senior managers on the best course of action to

---

Example 9.3 continued

take. Emergent corporate/marketing strategy is a strategy where the final objective is unclear and whose elements are developed during the course of its life, as the
strategy proceeds. 'Logical incrementalism' is the process of developing a strategy
by small, incremental and logical steps interacting with circumstances as they
happen.

Prescriptive planning – the future is knowable

- ☐ Past, present and expected situations are audited.
- ☐ Clear short, medium and long-term quantitative objectives set.
- ☐ Long-term strategies discussed and developed to reach long-term objectives.
- ☐ Strategic marketing plans (3–5 years) written up identifying future courses of action.
- ☐ Tactical plans (six months to one year) written up detailing implementation requirements.
- ☐ Whole process is monitored and controlled and alteration made as happenings demand.

Emergent planning – the future is uncertain and basically unknowable

- ☐ Unclear objectives, developed as strategies proceed.
- ☐ No single final objective.
- ☐ Based on assumptions that strategies are not always logical and rational.
- ☐ Tries to take into account the reality of management decision making.
- ☐ Constantly influenced by internal and external factors.
- ☐ Decisions emerge in reaction to circumstances as a system of experiment, negotiation, discussion and small steps forward.
- ☐ Organisational structures and systems must be flexible and able to respond quickly to change.

Practical consequences of planning

Students and practitioners becoming involved with the planning process will
find that they have to adapt to two basic sets of circumstances. First, from a practical perspective all companies probably approach the planning process in different ways. This will not be a problem as long as those involved understand that
this will always be the case whatever the organisation they are involved with.
Having learnt the prescriptive formal approach discussed throughout this chapter, it will be a matter of adjusting and adapting as circumstances demand. This
might mean making adjustments in a minor way, perhaps just according to the
different language used, or it could be in more major ways, perhaps a different
emphasis on certain areas.

Second, the company planning process might take the emergent and more informal form. Again, an understanding of the formal process should be a positive help, almost as an 'ideal type' example which the planner will be able to manipulate and adapt in a flexible and orderly fashion as company and market circumstances demand. For example, long-term measurable objectives may not seem possible but shorter term objectives could be used and changed in instant reaction to changing environments.

Finally, it should be said that planning at whatever level is not easy because it is an attempt to look into the future; no one can know with any certainty what tomorrow might bring, yet alone next year. We only have to go back and look at some of the previous year's predictions by so-called economic and business experts to see how terribly wrong some of them have been. Nevertheless experience has shown it to be better to attempt to minimise the risk by planning and forecasting than just leaving everything to chance. Ultimately, it is crucial to take part in the discussion: *Planning is everything – the plan is nothing.*

☐ Levels of strategic decision making

Both strategic and operational planning take place at all levels and across all functions within the organisation in both B2B and B2C industries and include the following areas now discussed.

Corporate planning

Planning at the corporate level involves all managers from all areas working together so that the whole company functions in a holistic way to meet the overall objectives of the corporate body and to add value for the shareholders. If synergy cannot be achieved in this way then shareholders may sell and so reduce the value of the company. It could also be argued that the organisation should be split up and sold if greater shareholder value could be achieved in this way. Of course this will not apply to NFP or public sector organisations because of ownership differences.

Finance cannot plan if expected marketing and sales are unknown; production cannot invest in new machinery if uncertain about customer benefit wanted from new products; human resources cannot develop people without knowing how many employees might be wanted. The larger the organisation, the more difficult it will be to organise, coordinate and manage the planning process. It is important that all interested parties, at all levels, take part in the debate, and all contributions are valued. In practice this is easier said than done as some managers will have more power than others and so be able to push opinions at the expense of others. This is why wide-open debate should be encouraged and include an amalgam of bottom-up and top-down aspects of planning (Figure 9.4).

Marketing planning

All planning takes place within a larger planning framework. Marketing, finance, production and human resource planning will take place within the wider

Figure 9.4
Corporate
planning

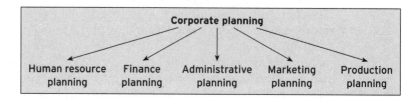

framework of corporate planning. Communications planning will take place within marketing planning and exhibition planning within communications planning, and so on. Most employees will be involved in lower level functional or departmental planning rather than at corporate level. This can mean that by the time participation takes place the corporate and marketing objectives might already be given and planning has to be accepted within this constraint.

Strategic and tactical change at different organisational levels

It can be confusing when strategic and tactical issues are discussed, as at times they may seem interchangeable. What is important to understand is that strategy and tactics can change depending on the organisational level. What might be strategic at one level will be seen as tactical from a higher level and similarly what may be tactical at a higher level will be seen as strategic at a lower level. An example might be advertising. At the boardroom level advertising methods, e.g. TV or magazines, will be seen as tactical, but at the marketing communications department level they will be seen as advertising strategies. Similarly the sales force approach to customers might be seen as strategic at the marketing level, but tactical at the corporate level. There is no one clear definition as to what is tactical and what is strategic. It will depend on the product, the company and the long-term importance of the activity to the well-being of the organisation.

Market-driven management

Although there are different approaches when attempting to prepare an organisation for what might happen in the future, most commentators and practitioners would argue that every company manager should be thinking in a strategic manner. This would include some kind of forward-looking, strategic plan that takes account of both external events and internal situations. Organisational resources can be upgraded and coordinated so that new challenges, new legislation, technological changes, substitute products, etc. can be taken on from a position of strength.

Although some organisations still operate in monopoly or oligopoly markets, we have discussed throughout the book the fact that most industries are opening up to more and more competition. When operating in competitive markets, market-driven management would always consider planning from the perspective of past, current and potential segments and customers. There have been many examples of suppliers becoming complacent about the needs of the customers and finding that innovative products, better channels of distribution or new communication methods have allowed a competitor to steal a customer before defence action can be taken.

Marketing intelligence, marketing research, MIS

Market communications are at the heart of good marketing management; continually talking and listening to knowledgeable and respected market practitioners, both inside and outside the organisation, and market commentators, as well as suppliers, intermediaries and customers. Senior management in the organisation should drive this quest for good information and be involved in all stages of the project so that the focus is on asking the right questions and reporting the data in such a way as to drive performance. Marketing strategy decisions will be made on information gathered in this way and fed through a sophisticated and constantly updated marketing information system (MIS). Marketing intelligence systems should collect information on such things as industry and market trends, current and predicted competitive behaviour, market growth (or contraction), and potential and expected developments in products and services.

A good strategic plan must clearly identify industrial market segments and the individual companies and customers within those segments. There should be a clear statement of what constitutes value in the industry as a whole and for the organisations within that industry. Detailed cost benefit analysis should have been used to identify customers that make the most money and those that make less or even cost money. Many suppliers in B2B markets will have national or multinational customers that are responsible for a large part of company revenue and profits. It is these buyers that have to be treated with the most respect and their needs and wants spelt out quite specifically in the plan. Ultimately the supplier must be able to evaluate business markets and country demand if strategies are to be chosen and implemented successfully. Demand evaluation was discussed in some detail in Chapter 2.

Too much rigidity regarding knowledge leads to the stultification of creativity. Knowledge management thrives in a chaotic environment.

(Begbie and Chudry, 2002)

☐ CRM and customer retention schemes

It is now a generally accepted truism that it costs much more to look for and obtain new customers than it does to keep existing customers. Examples abound where suppliers spend lots of effort and money on wooing new customers and seem to take existing customers for granted until it is too late and they have moved elsewhere. Customers appreciate being valued and they change their suppliers due to a number of small errors rather than one large error.

We have discussed at length the growth in customer relationship management programmes and how important they are in relation to customers. Good market-driven management must therefore have customer retention systems as part of this programme as well as new customer generation systems. Customer loyalty, customer relationship management (CRM), relationship marketing, one-to-one marketing, whichever term you use, all comes down to building successful relationships to promote profitable customer behaviour. A successful customer loyalty programme can have significant commercial impact, delivering increased profitability, improved customer retention, incremental revenue, greater share of customers, lower cost of sale and a medium for more cost-effective marketing.

Understanding the business

Customer loyalty, however, is not a simple isolated issue. It touches every part of the organisation – the boardroom, back office and front office staff, business managers, salespeople and intermediaries through to the customer contact point. It requires skills that cross every corporate function from strategic planning and systems to database marketing and customer service. Too many expensive CRM projects have failed almost inevitably because they have been driven by IT systems at the expense of the overall cultural change required to make them work. Building successful loyalty strategies requires comprehensive analysis and careful planning throughout an organisation to fully understand the business, the company culture and operational issues and how these interact with customer needs and wants. Resources need to be examined and questions asked about the suitability of such things as the current IT infrastructure and its capability to manage the required degree of customer information, the core customer database. Is it sufficiently integrated for efficient collection and effective use of data? What are the limitations on delivery to the customer?

Types of customers

We then look at the customers themselves, profiling the existing base, identifying potential and defining existing patterns against which to track the impact of future activity. There are a number of ways that a supplier can categorise the types of organisations that buy its goods and services and each should choose the best method for them. They might be categorised in terms of the amount and types of products and services purchased over a given time period, and the business potential. Most importantly, customers should be categorised by the importance of benefits expected. For example, speed of delivery may be important for one buyer; for another quality; for another the range of components available, and so on. These 'soft' facts can then be incorporated into a database that will then include a detailed 'commitment' code for each customer. All this information will then have massive implications for database management, marketing and customer relationships that must be comprehensively understood to be implemented and administered successfully.

Example 9.4 ## QCi CRM consultants (www.Qci.co.uk)

QCi has created an audit methodology that scores companies against 400 benchmarks. The Customer Management Assessment Tool (CMAT) is now used around the world by systems consultants and suppliers such as IBM, Axion and BT to analyse the needs of their blue-chip customers. In this way they hope to determine how their treatment of customers impacts on the bottom line, or where improvements need to be made. QCi staff might spend two or three weeks interviewing staff and managers, learning what they do and don't do and scoring their activities. They cover marketing, sales, service, IT and HR, and focus especially on customer-facing departments.

Figure 9.5
The wheel of customer retention programmes

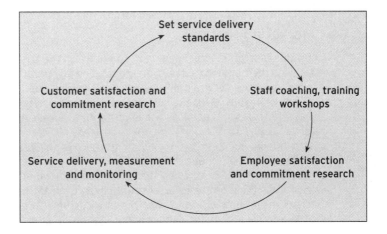

Building the customer retention loyalty proposition

Only after a thorough internal and external quality audit, understanding the market and analysing customers' requirements, buying behaviour, market analysis and segmentation, and customer satisfaction/retention, can strategic loyalty programmes be built (Figure 9.5). These will consist of a set of loyalty initiatives benchmarked to meet a company's objectives, which will fit the specified budget and be workable within a given infrastructure. The customer retention programme will include:

☐ Continuous buyer/DMU focus processes

☐ Management/employee cross-functional involvement

☐ Management/employee ongoing coaching and training

☐ Benchmarking, measurement and control

☐ Continuous service/product improvement.

Managing the implementation

Strategic thinking sets the context for planning but, as we outlined earlier, this is only part of the process. Just as important is the strategic execution. A strategic customer relationship or customer retention programme is useless if it is not implemented or carried out in an ineffective way. Marketing intelligence and research will help identify organisational and individual customers' needs, but knowledgeable, skilful and well-motivated managers and other staff are essential for successful implementation. It is trite but true that good employees are the major asset of the successful business organisation and can make or break the soundest of strategic plans.

Example 9.5 **Marketing tactics**

It's all about constantly keeping in contact with the customer, always being there, knowing their buying cycles, preferences, and any problems they have experienced while using the services. In this way trust can be built. Dealing quickly with complaints while reassuring the customer of their value keeps their trust. Courtesy calls and after-sales and services are important. If there is a large order from any customer, a call to acknowledge their business indicating appreciation and giving acknowledgement can make all the difference to the next order. Customers should be kept informed about the progress of their purchase; for example, whether it needs after-sales care, when the guarantee expires, etc. Call to let the customer know that their products are being delivered on time. In some cases a call just to say 'hello, how are you?' can retain a customer. Remember that in B2B word of mouth plays a major part in either increasing or decreasing loyalty and sales, depending on the quality of service received.

☐ Assessing competitive advantage

Most B2B organisations have core competencies that, if managed properly, are capable of giving the company a competitive advantage in an intensely competitive world. A well-thought-out strategic plan should contain a detailed awareness of what constitutes general competitive advantage in any one industry and a more detailed description of competitive advantage in any one market segment. The switching costs for a buyer to move from one supplier to another may be high, but if a supplier becomes complacent and unfocused about its benefit offering over a prolonged period the buyer might suddenly move to a competitor. If this happens then any attempts to win back the customer can be costly and time consuming with no guarantee of success. What constitutes competitive advantage will also be continuously moving and changing as innovations, technology improvements, management efficiencies and cost savings translate into ever-increasing customer expectations. This must drive an organisation never to stand still and always to be looking to upgrade its goods and services from a standpoint of strength, rather than from a position of weakness with such changes being forced upon it by the competition.

Understand the competitive advantages of competitors

There should be an analysis of both existing and potential competitors so as to understand the strategic competitive advantages they might enjoy at the present time, as well as those they might develop in future (Figure 9.6). Competitive channels are now opening up worldwide and marketing managers must remain aware of possible new entrants into their markets. All competitive advantages are relative and one supplier will be constantly measured against another supplier. Innovation, low costs, good after-sales service, quality products and services do not really make sense in isolation; only when one supplier is compared with another will they make any sense.

Figure 9.6
Broad sources
of competitive
advantage

☐ Lower costs and high efficiency and effectiveness
☐ Portfolio of products across the product life cycle matching customer needs
☐ A strong customer base
☐ Leading edge research and development capacity
☐ Highly qualified people, including entrepreneurs, creators and strong skilful managers
☐ Knowledgeable sources of venture or investment capital
☐ A comprehensive and meaningful management/marketing information system
☐ A culture of innovation, learning and service to the customer
☐ Access to new technology
☐ Knowledge-sharing infrastructure
☐ Channels of distribution and access to markets
☐ Partnerships at many levels, both horizontal and vertically along the value chain
☐ Corporate and product brands, patents, licences and copyrights
☐ Ultimately a clear, comprehensive and integrated corporate position strategy based
upon clearly identified industry and customer needs

Understand the detailed nature and sources of competitive advantage

As well as making broad generalisations about relative strengths and weaknesses and opportunities and strengths (SWOT analysis), managers will want to know in more detail about the sources of competitive advantage, for example: Why does a particular firm possess a culture of innovation? How does it have access to constant technological updates? Why does it have such a broad customer base and a reputation for communications excellence? All sources must be explored, if they are relevant to a particular market.

We have identified costs as a major source of competitive advantage that will allow lower prices, greater sales and bigger profits. This will then enable the lean, efficient and effective organisation to obtain many of the other sources of competitive advantage identified above. An organisation will therefore try to estimate its competitors' cost positions and look at differences in activities in order to understand why and where its competitors' costs differ from its own. An attempt should be made to understand why large differences in profitability are sustained within the same industry and to identify major cost drivers for competitors' value chain activities. If possible, precise measurable figures would need to be obtained so that direct comparisons could be made and the reasons analysed as to why one company is doing better than another so that competitive advantages can be benchmarked and improved.

Those firms that manage to embed the development and exploitation of innovation and intellectual assets deeply within their business may be able to create competencies that cannot be easily copied and these will therefore differentiate them from the competition.

The value chain and competitive advantage

Partnerships and value chain relationships were discussed in Chapter 6 where it was recognised that competitive advantage was enhanced by organisations, both vertical and horizontal, working together. Competitive advantage is gained by business cooperation and so comparison has to be made between the strategic differences in a company's value chain activities and the competitor's value chain activities to find out why one works better than the other.

Detailed analysis

As well as the comparison between one value chain and another, there should also be detailed analysis along the competitor's value chain. This will then be compared with the supplier's own value chain so that sources of competitive advantage or otherwise can be highlighted across the different supply chain member firms. As with an individual company, one value chain can then be benchmarked against another.

Changing sources of competitive advantage

In many cases the broad sources of competitive advantage identified above are no longer enough to maintain that advantage. Incessant competition, improved understanding of the importance of strategic thinking and a greater understanding of all the issues that must be considered in strategic implementation have brought competitors closer together with regard to factors such as cost efficiency, use of new technology and employee motivation. This has encouraged the more enlightened organisations to revisit customers, to discuss in more detail needs and wants, and then to examine their internal resources to identify core competence and look towards more personalised, customised products and services. So factors such as service, innovation, quality products and add-on services are still ways that B2B suppliers can gain competitive advantage, but they are used in ways that tailor the benefit offering more closely to each buying organisational need. This approach is exemplified by the customer relationship and customer retention management schemes talked about earlier.

☐ Strategic role of marketing

There is now no doubt in management circles that marketing, with its emphasis on customer understanding and satisfaction, plays a pivotal role in corporate and marketing planning in both B2B and B2C markets. Time and time again, however, many of the basic truths associated with the concept of the organisation as a customer value creating entity seem to get forgotten. Many organisations initially produce products and services that are wanted by customers, but then seem to become complacent and expect a period of plenty and customer loyalty to last forever. It is as if they revert back to the comfort zone of product orientation and are taken by surprise when the buyers begin to move elsewhere. The relentless pace of change, more and more competition and constantly growing customer demands drive marketing and an obsessive concern with customer satisfaction to the top of the strategic agenda. It is not enough to run 'investment in people' programmes, total quality projects or benchmarking exercises separately from an overall customer and market-driven strategy, where value is defined not by the organisation but by constant customer feedback on satisfaction levels and experiences with the supplying organisation. This concern for customer satisfaction, the need to exceed customer expectations, should permeate every activity and be the measure by which all business initiatives are judged. Successful companies are continuously altering themselves so as to deliver more customer-driven value over the long term. This becomes a business promise that informs every strategic decision and should be revisited time and time again. If at all possible, short-term imperatives will not then be allowed to interfere with this overriding commitment.

Marketing and other company functions

All other company strategic functions, finance, human resources, administration, production, and so on, should be there to support the strategic marketing objectives and policies, with all working together in a coordinated and consistent way to offer benefits that meet the needs and wants of the customers more effectively than the competition. This can be more difficult in practice as day-to-day departmental problems affect employees' attitudes, causing concern for the customer to be pushed into the background. The danger is that this approach becomes so entrenched that it solidifies as part of the company culture. Customer relationship management schemes and employee coaching programmes should have feedback, monitoring and control mechanisms built in at every critical point to make certain that these unwanted developments are avoided.

Example 9.6 **CRM gone wrong**

We have all had experiences of being hooked into a system of telephone calls that moves us from one recorded message to another, often seeming to go on for ages. We are asked to punch in our telephone number and our account number sometimes twice or even three times as we travel around a soulless system. At any time we may be cut off, told that we are in a queue and perhaps it would be better if we phone back, or forced to listen to mindless renditions of Vivaldi or Elton John. When we reach a human voice it is only to be told that the journey hasn't ended and we are entered back into the system. We could be talking to somebody in London, Liverpool or Calcutta. We are told that this endless circle of technical manoeuvring is to our benefit, enabling the supplier to offer a much better service. I don't believe it! I would rather have a phone that rings for ages and at least the possibility of conversing with a human being than go through this mind-boggling, time-wasting, intensely irritating process. It's a product-driven, cost-cutting exercise masquerading as a customer relationship management programme – and it's fooling no one.

Part 2   The B2B marketing planning process

At the beginning of the book we looked at different definitions of marketing and identified a management process that anticipates, identifies and satisfies customers' needs and wants at a profit (or cost effectively). Another definition we touched on was that marketing could be seen as a strategic process 'developing and matching the resources of the organisation to meet the needs of the target market while taking into account the demands of the market environment'. This definition lends itself more readily to the idea of B2B strategic marketing planning and control.

So marketing planning is about taking all the areas of marketing within the organisation and combining these resources in such a way that products and services are offered that meet the current and future needs and demands of the business marketplace better than the competition. This will include such factors as marketing research, understanding organisational behaviour, R&D, innovation and product development, the use of technology, pricing, distribution and channel relationships, promotion, and so on.

To be able to do this successfully the whole marketing process must be rigorously planned, taking into account the state of current organisational resources and the present and future market and environmental direction. This is why marketing planning must begin with an investigation into prevailing company and market circumstances before any decisions can be made about long-term strategic direction. All relevant members of staff should be involved in the discussion process from senior management down. The investigation should begin with the collection, classification and analysis of all information that would be relevant to the company's present (and perhaps past) market position. It would be impossible, for argument's sake, to make decisions about selling existing products into new markets without knowledge of the company's product portfolio mix and present financial situation, or the level of competition and potential sales growth in the selected new market.

☐ Scope of strategic planning

Therefore stage 1 of the planning process consists of asking questions and collecting and analysing as much information about the current situation as is considered both manageable and relevant. This we call the strategic situation analysis or the strategic audit. Once the audit has been conducted we can move on to stages 2 and 3 in which the analysed information is used to decide both the marketing objectives and the strategic methods that must be employed to achieve these objectives.

1. Strategic situation analysis: Where are we now?
   Seeking to understand the organisation's internal and external strategic situation.

2. Strategic choice: Where do we want to go?
   Choosing between the strategic courses of action and setting objectives.

3. Strategic implementation: How are we going to get there?
   Putting the chosen course of action into effect.

We can now look at each of these areas in more detail, beginning with the marketing audit.

☐ Strategic situation analysis: Where are we now?

There exists an infinite amount of information both within an organisation and in the outside world where it operates. The difficulty that faces the B2B marketing manager, business consultant or marketing student is where and how to start this information gathering process: how to decide what information is relevant and should be collected and considered; what information is irrelevant and should be discarded; whether to start the process from outside the company looking in, or from the inside looking out, and so on.

> The job of the audit is to collect, classify and analyse information so that understanding can take place and realistic decisions be made about future organisational direction.

To facilitate understanding, the intention here is to look at the marketing auditing process in two parts:

1. Collection and classification of information from:
   (a) the external environment
   (b) the internal environment.
2. Analysis of the information collected.

1. Collection and classification of information

To help in this part of the auditing process, information collection and classification, we can return to the simple model developed and briefly discussed in Chapter 1.

Factors in the external environment

Under the heading of the external environment we identified two areas for consideration: the wider or macro environment and the immediate or micro environment. Within these two areas, acronyms were developed to guide us.

Wider or macro environment

The factors to be considered here can be identified under the acronym PEST, which stands for:

Political/legal – Economic/demographic – Social/cultural – Technical/physical

Information that might be needed from the wider or macro environment on the B2B market, at both national and global levels, would include the following:

☐ What laws are relevant or could be relevant in the future?

☐ What is the political climate? Is it hostile or appreciative to foreign businesses, and will it change?

☐ How stable is the market region under investigation?

☐ What is the economic level and trend of activity – GDP, per capita income, income spread, disposable income?

☐ What are the interest/exchange/inflation/employment rates?

☐ What are the organisational demographic movements?

☐ How important is social class? Is English spoken?

- ☐ What are the major business cultural norms and mores? Are customs and practices changing?
- ☐ How important is innovation and technology?
- ☐ What infrastructures are in place? How important is the climate? Are global markets changing?

Immediate or micro environment

The factors to be considered here can be identified under the acronym SPICC, which stand for:

Suppliers – Publics – Intermediaries – Competition – Customers and markets

The types of questions that might need to be asked here will have been identified and discussed throughout the book. Below we have identified just a few examples:

- ☐ Who has the power along the supply chain – the producers, the intermediaries or the buyers?
- ☐ How many buyers/suppliers are there? How efficient are they? What are the pricing and delivery policies? How is value added along the supply chain?
- ☐ How active or strong are pressure groups, local communities or the media in any particular industry?
- ☐ What is the structural role of the intermediary? How much control do they have over distribution channels?
- ☐ Who is the competition? Who are the major players and market leaders in the relevant market? What are the competitors' product portfolios and product advantages? How easy is it to enter and leave a particular industry?
- ☐ Who are the customers – size, spending power and how might they be distributed across the country or global market? Is the market growing or declining and are new markets opening up?
- ☐ Which customers are the most/least profitable? Can lifetime customer value be ascertained?

This is just a very small indication of the types of questions that might be asked across the B2B macro and the micro environment. Of course in reality the questions to be asked and the answers to be obtained would need to reflect the particular circumstances of each industry and organisation.

The macro and micro B2B environment

It should be recognised that in reality there is no dividing line between the macro and micro environments, between PEST and SPICC, as both are in the organisation's external environment. The division is artificial and the separation is purely to help understanding.

Factors in the internal environment

We can now look at the business organisation's internal environment. This information was identified using a model that incorporated the acronyms of the eight Ss and the eight Ps.

The eight Ss

It is impossible to look in isolation at the conventional marketing mix (product, price, place and promotion) without consideration for other back-ups such as structures and systems; satisfactory product and service delivery are so dependent on other organisational factors. For example, a good product that is offered through a substandard system is bound to lose competitive advantage. We want to look at these so-called 'back-up' factors under the acronym of the eight Ss, which consist of the following: structures, strategies, systems, staffing, skills, shared values, style, sustainable competitive advantage. A small example of the type of information required will include the following:

☐ What sort of structure does the organisation have? Is it bureaucratic? Is it tall and hierarchical or flat and flexible? Is it centralised or decentralised? Which structure will be more conducive to the company's marketing effort?

☐ What systems and processes (MIS, communications, finance, training, customer complaints, etc.) are in place? Are they adequate and sufficiently customer orientated? What control mechanisms are in place?

☐ Is there evidence of long-term strategic thinking across all marketing areas or is short-term thinking dominant?

☐ Are staffing levels sufficient to meet the needed customer service levels?

☐ What skills, or lack of skills, exist and what training and development programmes are in place and also might be needed?

☐ What is the culture (shared value) of the organisation? Is it customer orientated? Are the staff happy, innovative and enthusiastic?

☐ What is the style adopted by the company? Is it democratic, autocratic or patriarchal? Is it consistent across the whole corporation and how does it affect the corporate image from the customer's standpoint?

☐ What are the core assets of the organisation that might help it build and maintain sustainable competitive advantage: its culture, its people skills, its approach to technology/innovation/service or having access to a valuable customer database or long-term channel relationships and alliances built on trust and loyalty? It might have market leader brands, legally protected patents and low-cost operations, all giving an organisation possible superior advantages.

The job of the audit is to unearth answers to these and very many other questions.

The eight Ps

At the heart of the B2B marketing audit is the marketing mix. This will cover an examination of the use of marketing research, the company's product portfolio (including people, especially if there is a large service input), its supply and distribution channel relationships, pricing policies and the amount and type of communication and promotion carried out. The marketing mix will also be concerned with costs, profit levels and cash flow ratios. We will look a little more closely at the type of information needed, beginning with marketing research and moving on to look at the other factors identified under the acronym of the eight Ps.

The evidence of a marketing information system will give some indication of how important the company considers the need for an up-to-date marketing database. Questions can also be asked about the level/type of quantitative/qualitative marketing research undertaken (if any), how it is used and to what degree it involves the use of information technology.

We have identified the marketing mix under the acronym of the eight Ps. Again it is worth reminding the reader that this is an arbitrary method used as a memory aid and to assist in understanding. The eight Ps model has been developed from the basic four Ps model beloved by marketers down the ages. The types of questions to be answered in each category might include the following:

Products/services

- ☐ What is the organisation's product/brand portfolio? How interrelated are its components and is there synergy? Where are they on the BCG and PLC models?

- ☐ Are the sales levels increasing, decreasing or stable?

- ☐ What are the cost and profit structures?

- ☐ What is the level of new product development/innovation/new technology and how important is all this in this kind of industry?

- ☐ What do customers/suppliers/intermediaries think about the products and services offered and how do they compare with the competition?

Place or the channels of distribution

- ☐ Have any channel relationships/partnerships been developed and what are their value?

- ☐ Is the company getting the quantity and quality coverage it wants? Are the existing channels still relevant? Is there a possibility of opening up new channels without causing channel conflict?

- ☐ What physical distribution techniques are used? Is there centralised or decentralised warehousing? How is information technology being used and what costs are being incurred?

Price

- ☐ What pricing methods are used and are they sufficiently customer orientated?

- ☐ Is there an adequate return on the prices charged on all products and from all buying organisations?

- ☐ What is the relationship between fixed and variable costs and between costs, profit and volumes?

- ☐ How does pricing relate to the other elements of the marketing mix?

Promotion

- ☐ What is the level of promotional spending in relation to the level of sales and to other companies in the industry?

- ☐ How is communications success controlled and measured and does it make sense?

❑ What promotional mix methods are used and are all methods integrated to give a uniform approach? Is an advertising agency used? If so, how long has the same agency been used?

People
Information will be required that covers all the areas which relate to the people who in any way represent the organisation and its products. This is especially important if the service content is significant in the product marketed.

❑ What are the marketing/customer skills of the management/workforce/ marketing department/salesforce/all other departments? Are they adequate and is there training and coaching available to supplement and improve wherever necessary?

❑ Is there a shared company culture/values and is it positive and motivating? Is it geared towards innovation, customer satisfaction and overall marketing orientation? Do all departments work together?

Profit
There are commentators who argue that marketers should disregard profit as a marketing mix factor because it will eventually come about through a customer satisfaction focus. It could be argued that this approach is not realistic and all marketers and salespeople must be aware of 'bottom line' issues.

❑ What are the fixed and variable costs across the product portfolio and how do they relate to total costs and sales volume?

❑ Is the company making an overall profit? On which products and from which customers?

❑ Are there synergies between costs, volumes and profits? What part will price and demand elasticity play?

❑ How do the organisation's financial ratios compare with competitor and industry ratios? Is there heavy company debt and does it have any liquidity problems?

Physical evidence
The P for physical evidence is included here because many buyers will judge a service supplier on some kind of physical attribute, as they will be unable to examine a tangible product.

❑ Do the sales representatives appear to be professional and know what they are talking about? Have they the latest technological aids and access to up-to-date relevant information?

❑ Are the sales literature, brochures and catalogues attractive, informative and presented in a professional manner?

❑ Is the corporate image consistent with the type of service on offer?

Processes
Excellent products and service offerings can be nullified if the back-up processes and systems are substandard. To order a product and then have to wait an unacceptable amount of time is the quickest way to lose a customer.

Figure 9.7
Tools of the
B2B marketing
audit

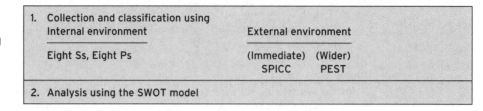

1. Collection and classification using		
Internal environment	External environment	
Eight Ss, Eight Ps	(Immediate)	(Wider)
	SPICC	PEST

2. Analysis using the SWOT model

2. Analysis of the information collected

Once all the relevant information has been collected and classified, it can be discussed, argued over, examined and analysed. Information will continue to be collected as discussions and suggestions throw up more options and open up other areas for investigation. Of course in practice the whole auditing process is very organic, with many things going on at the same time, so there is bound to be a certain amount of analysis taking place at the same time as collection, but definitive judgement should be postponed until an overall picture is obtained (Figure 9.7). Many different models are available to simplify and help in the process of analysis. We look at two: SWOT analysis and force field analysis.

SWOT analysis

Probably the most popular model is SWOT, which stands for **s**trengths, **w**eaknesses, **o**pportunities and **t**hreats. Opportunities and threats are used to analyse the external informational factors collected (PEST and SPICC factors). Strengths and weaknesses are used to analyse the internal factors (the eight Ss and eight Ps).

It is important not to confuse internal and external factors because if this happens it might also confuse both the management approach and decisions eventually taken. The SWOT process can continue as long as the participants feel it is still productive, with the SWOT information being brought forward and refined through argument and discussion. Eventually there should be some form of agreement on which to reject and which to retain so that the final SWOT will contain only the *major* strategic marketing external opportunities and the *major* strategic organisational internal strengths and weakness.

SWOT as a strategic matching process
It should be recognised that the SWOT is a matching process. Ideally the organisation would like to match its strengths to the opportunities in the marketplace (you may remember the strategic marketing definition as a matching process, i.e. matching the resources of the organisation to the demands of the market). However, this is not always immediately possible because of the circumstances pertaining to the organisation and the state of the market environment. Therefore it can be the case that the weaknesses of the company are such that it cannot take advantage of the external opportunities. In this case it might have to seek some form of outside resource investment (e.g. financial investment or even a merger) so that it can take advantage of these opportunities.

The SWOT analysis might show the company to be in the unfortunate position where the threats from the external environment are so large and the weaknesses

Figure 9.8 The SWOT strategic options

SWOT position	Possible strategies
Strengths > Weaknesses Opportunities > Threats	Match strengths to opportunities for success
Weaknesses > Strengths Opportunities > Threats	Seek help to eliminate weaknesses and take advantage of opportunities
Strengths > Weaknesses Threats > Opportunities	Move to new markets where strengths can be optimised and threats eliminated
Weaknesses > Strengths Threats > Opportunities	No hope, divest or liquidate

internally so dire that the only organisational strategy possible might be to divest or liquidate, depending on the seriousness of the situation. Figure 9.8 lists a number of SWOT situations with possible options on how to rectify the position.

As with the whole planning process, the value of the audit process and SWOT exercise is in the 'doing' rather than in the final document that might be arrived at. So practitioners should not be afraid to argue, discuss, adjust and readjust before coming up with the end product. The important thing is that debate takes place and involves all interested parties.

Force field analysis

An example of another model that might be used for discussion, debate and analysis is known as force field analysis. It is a useful technique for trying to understand the pressures for and against change and for looking at all the forces for and against adopting one strategy over another. It is a method of weighing up the pros and cons for making one decision rather than another and is a useful technique for looking at all the forces for and against a plan. It helps participants to weigh the importance of these factors and decide whether a plan is worth implementing. To carry out a force field analysis, follow these steps:

☐ List all forces for change in one column and all forces against change in another column.

☐ Assign a score to each force from 1 (weak) to 5 (strong).

☐ Draw a diagram showing the forces for and against change. Show the size of each force as a number next to it. A simple, rough example is in Figure 9.9.

Once the analysis has been carried out, decisions can be made on whether the project is viable. Where it has been decided to carry out a strategy or project, force field analysis can help managers to work out how to improve the probability of success. Two choices are shown here:

☐ To reduce the strength of the forces opposing a project.

☐ To increase the forces pushing a project.

Figure 9.9
Force field
analysis

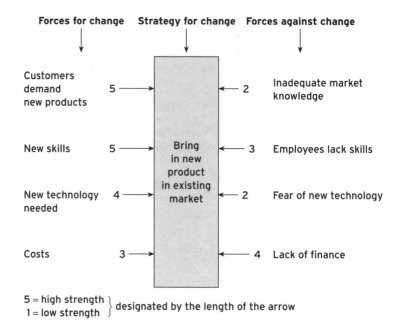

5 = high strength } designated by the length of the arrow
1 = low strength

There are other models that encourage investigation, argument, discussion and debate during the audit analysis; here we have identified just two.

Figure 9.10
The
organisational
audit

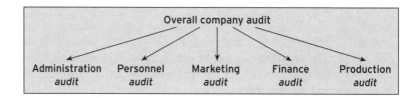

Where the B2B marketing audit sits within the overall company audit

The marketing audit is part of the much wider company or business audit and will only be undertaken in isolation if senior management decides there is a special need in this area. Even if this were the case, it would still demand cross-company consultation. A corporate or business audit should be undertaken by the whole organisation, division by division, function by function, department by department. So personnel, finance, production, administration, marketing, etc. will all collect and analyse information within their departments, working in joint consultation with all other departments. All the information will then be brought together into a corporate management or business audit and SWOT (Figure 9.10). Much smaller audits may be undertaken within the marketing mix such as a product, promotion or sales audit, as and when deemed necessary.

Figure 9.11
Model of
business-to-
business
marketing as
a matching
process

Internal resources		Matching	External environment
Eight Ss	**Marketing mix**	**Micro**	**Macro**
Strategy	Product	Suppliers	Political/legal
Structure	Price	Publics	Economic/demographic
Systems	Place	Intermediaries	Social/cultural
Skills	Promotion	Customers and markets	Technical/physical
Shared values	People	Competition	
Staffing	Processes		
Style	Profit		
Sustainable competitive advantage	Physical evidence		

Auditing in B2B and B2C

The structure of strategic business planning in B2B and B2C markets is virtually the same, the differences being in the manner of the processes involved. The models identified above can be used in both markets, with the difference being in the type of information collected. For example, in B2B the emphasis will be on quantitative secondary macro information about companies and markets, while in B2C it will be qualitative micro information on individual consumers. There are many more differences and these have been highlighted throughout the book.

The 'matching process' involves gathering and analysing information from both the external and internal environment and then identifying, examining and evaluating strategic issues in the light of strengths and weaknesses internally and opportunities and threats externally. The most attractive strategies can then be developed (Figure 9.11).

A strategic definition sees marketing as a 'matching' process: matching the internal resources of the organisation to the external demands of the marketplace.

☐ Strategic choice: Where do we want to go?

A choice now has to be made between the strategic courses of action and setting objectives.

At some point in the B2B planning process the company mission should be clearly defined and overall corporate objectives set. The importance of the B2B organisational mission statement and its corporate objectives must not be forgotten as marketing planning will need to take place within the framework set by both the mission statement and the corporate objectives.

The need for common overall objectives cannot be over-emphasised because experience has shown that disaster can occur when all or some departments within the same organisation ignore, confuse, or seem to be unaware of overall company direction and behavioural policy, preferring instead to implement their own aims and objectives. The end result of this could be each department or area

Figure 9.12
All functional objectives operate under umbrella of corporate objectives and mission statement

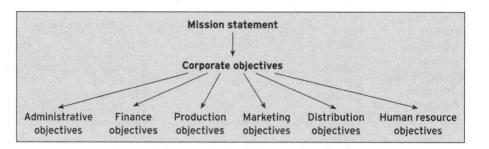

going its own way, causing the company to perform its corporate function in an inefficient and uncoordinated fashion, promising eventual bankruptcy.

The company mission statement

The mission statement (vision statement, corporate values, etc.) should lay down the long-term corporate aims and values and answer the following questions:

1. What business are we in (in broad terms), e.g. entertainment, branded packaged products, road transport, and so on?
2. What constitutes value to our shareholders, e.g. adequate return on capital employed, an acceptable dividend pay-out?
3. Who are our customers, i.e. the relevant target market and organisational profile?
4. How should the company conduct its business with regard to our customers, our employees, all other stakeholders, and the environment?

   ☐ Our customers – offering high quality, technically innovative solutions.

   ☐ Our employees – treating them as we would like to be treated ourselves.

   ☐ All other stakeholders – seeking mutually beneficial long-term relationships with suppliers and intermediaries.

   ☐ The environment – acting as a responsible and caring citizen.

The answers to these questions should be understood by all, hopefully believed by all members of the organisation and should be the overall guiding principle that gives direction and moves the company forward (Figure 9.12). For a mission statement to work, it should be offered in a simplified form, have meaning for all employees and be in use continuously in the day-to-day running of the business. Otherwise it will remain nothing other than a list of esoteric intentions gathering dust at boardroom level (see case study on the B2B Marketing website.)

> The mission statement can be imputed at the beginning or end of the business auditing process depending on the level of organisational change that might be taking place.

Corporate objectives

The corporate objectives are the business objectives for the whole organisation (including production, human resources, administration, finance, marketing, etc.) and should spell out for all stakeholders the exact purpose of the organisation. As with all business objectives, corporate objectives should be quantified over time (SMART) so that results can be monitored and controlled. If the organisation is in the private sector then the corporate objectives will most probably be set in financial terms, this being the return to the owners of the company, the shareholders, for the use of their capital (e.g. ROCE, ROI). This can then be broken down, if necessary, by division. If the organisation is in the not-for-profit or public sector, then the corporate objectives may be set in ways that reflect the guiding principle of the organisation as well as in financial terms: for example, speed and coverage for the fire service; revenue generated for a charity; efficient use of capital for a hospital. All B2B planning will take place under the umbrella of the corporate objectives.

> All business objectives should be SMART - specific, measurable, achievable (agreed), realistic, time-based.

Marketing objectives

The planning process discussed up to now would apply to all functions of the organisation, each making its contribution to the overall corporate objectives. Although discussion will take place across the whole of the company, the B2B marketing role in the planning process really begins with the setting of marketing objectives. The marketing objectives are the overall performance targets for the whole of the marketing function and will tend to be set in terms of sales volumes, units, market share and profit, and should be SMART. The time period will vary depending on the company and industry, but would usually be about three to five years and then broken down to cover short, medium and long term.

Closed and open objectives

It is worth mentioning here that there are closed and open objectives. As stated earlier, all business objectives should be closed, SMART. However, an organisation will sometimes use open or secondary objectives, usually for consumption outside the organisation. These objectives are less defined and not capable of clear measurement: 'to create greater customer satisfaction'; 'to develop more innovative products'; 'to contribute to a safer environment'. Although having meaning to some stakeholders, they would have to be quantified over time to be of use to managers within the company.

Estimating demand and sales forecasting

An important function of the B2B marketing manager is to identify demand and forecast future sales potential and of course marketing objectives cannot be set without this taking place. The importance of reliable predicted sales forecasting cannot be overestimated as it is on this figure that all other budgets are based.

Figure 9.13
Gap analysis

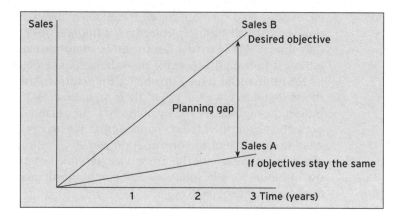

Methods of estimating market demand and qualitative and quantitative methods of sales forecasting were discussed in depth in earlier chapters. Suffice to say that this will take place on a constant basis during the audit, at the setting of overall marketing objectives and again during the discussion on strategic marketing alternatives and the setting of strategic marketing objectives. More detail on sales forecasting can be found on the B2B Marketing website.

Gap analysis

Once the sales forecasting has taken place and marketing objectives have been set, strategies must be developed to show how these objectives are going to be achieved. This introduces us to the model and concept of gap analysis. Gap analysis is a model that can be used for looking at the difference (the gap) between where the company's sales will be in X years' time if present strategies are followed (sales A in Figure 9.13) and where shareholder/corporate board pressure and/or research and forecasting methods demand they should be. Like all models, gap analysis can be used to stimulate discussion and debate on possible strategic directions the organisation will be able to take.

Objective A shows the sales that the company would achieve in three years' time if existing strategies remain unaltered. Objective B (the overall marketing objective) shows where the company would like to be according to demand estimates and sales forecasting. Possible strategies to 'fill' the planning gap are discussed below.

B2B marketing strategies

Strategy is the combination of methods used by the company to obtain its long-term corporate and marketing objectives. Corporate objectives are, hopefully, obtained by corporate strategies involving the integrated use of finance, production, administration, HR, marketing, etc. working together in harmony. Likewise marketing objectives will be achieved through the use of marketing strategies, bringing together all the marketing areas. These will be discussed below. Corporate and marketing strategies should do the following:

Figure 9.14
B2B Ansoff strategic choice matrix

Source: Ansoff, H.I. (1957) 'Strategies for diversification', *Harvard Business Review*, September–October

1. Clearly describe the major ways that the organisation intends to achieve its objectives.

2. Be long term.

3. Act as a coordinating umbrella giving the same direction to relevant functions and departments.

B2B marketing strategic options

Having decided on the overall marketing objectives, the various methods that can be used to achieve these objectives – the strategic marketing alternatives – must now be analysed to find the most fruitful and productive methods. (It is worth mentioning once again that, although identified here, the process will have been discussed throughout the auditing and objective setting stages.) To assist this process, another model known as the Ansoff strategic option matrix can be used.

The Ansoff matrix

Like all models, the Ansoff 4×4 matrix is a method used to encourage argument and debate and to simplify a very complex situation. It should not be judged as an ultimate reflection of reality. In very simple terms, through the use of the Ansoff matrix it can be argued that there are four major strategic alternatives that a marketer could use when looking for ways to fill the planning gap, identified earlier, and so achieve marketing objectives (Figure 9.14). Many different strategic approaches can be used within these four options and these will be discussed in more detail below. The four basic methods are:

1. Existing products in existing markets – market penetration.

2. New products in existing markets – product development.

3. Existing products in new markets – market development.

4. New products in new markets – diversification.

Existing products in existing markets – market penetration

This strategy will only be possible if there is market growth and/or one company is able to take sales from another. It should be noted that the competition would most likely retaliate if an attempt were made to capture more market share. It tends to be more difficult to gain more market share in a B2B market than in a

B2C because of limited buyers, existing loyalties and almost instant information being available on competitive movements.

New products in existing markets – product development
The second alternative is to develop new products/services/benefit solutions for existing customers. B2B buyers will always welcome new solutions as long as they offer more productive ways of running a business. More on new product development and innovation can be found on the B2B Marketing website.

Example 9.7 **New products**

The Japanese motorbike and compact car maker Suzuki Motors has said it will increase output this year thanks to the introduction of many new models. Motor-cycle production is set to be boosted by strong demand from China and the release of a new 50cc scooter called 'Choinori'. Suzuki has also unveiled a new two-seater 'Twin' car, the first minicar to offer a hybrid engine which can run on either petrol or electricity.

Existing products in new markets – market development
The third alternative is to find new markets for existing products. This might be new customers, new usage or new geographical markets. The more ambitious B2B company will have salespeople scouring the world in search of market opportunities. The growth in the internet will have greatly helped this process.

New products in new markets – diversification
The fourth alternative is to develop new product solutions for new markets. This might be considered the most risky because of the 'double' risk involved with developing both new products and new markets at the same time. The risk can be lessened in B2B markets by the development of strategic alliances and partnerships.

'New' and 'existing' definition
Confusion is sometimes caused by the terms 'new' and 'existing'. As with all models, the Ansoff matrix is a marketing tool used to simplify and help managers when examining and evaluating strategic choices. The value is in the discussion and argument. Whether a product/service is new, or an added feature to an existing product, or whether a market is new or not is really only important in terms of customer perception. Whether the buyer considers something to be new or just an added feature will dictate the marketing approach and so is important only with regard to this aspect.

Strategic choice

Having identified the four basic strategic options the B2B company must decide on the marketing strategies it will use to fill the planning gap, the sales and profit it will achieve if nothing is changed, and the sales and profit objectives demand and forecasting analysis have shown could be achieved.

Evaluation in strategic choice

A thorough, ongoing evaluation needs to take place before some strategies are rejected and others are chosen. This will be an organic process coming about through discussion, argument and debate involving employees across the organisation, as well as the possibility of supply chain members. It will be inextricably linked to the audit, the results of the SWOT and demand and sales forecasting analysis.

Criteria for strategic choice

Criteria for strategy rejection and strategy selection based on a form of superior benefit offering will include some the following:

☐ *Company mission/corporate objectives/corporate image.* The chosen strategies must sit comfortably within the scope of the mission statement, corporate objectives and corporate image. To adopt a moral stance to business and then become enmeshed in the armaments industry would not go down well with some stakeholders.

☐ *Results of the audit/demand and forecasting analysis.* Research and information analysis, if used properly, should have identified the more obvious attractive strategic directions.

☐ *Business organisational need.* A real organisational need for the identified solution not offered by others must exist.

☐ *Competitive structure of the industry.* High competitive rivalry and low profits in some markets may preclude some strategic options. Similarly the presence of a market leader with a high market share and high economies of scale will severely limit what can and cannot be done.

☐ *Target markets.* Some markets may be growing and others declining. Some will be more profitable, some more approachable and some match more closely the skills developed within the organisation.

☐ *Strategic alliances.* Strategic alliances may exist between buyers and sellers that could make it difficult, if not impossible, to enter a market.

☐ *Level of risk involved.* Some strategies will be riskier than others and the cost of failure will have to be weighed against the level and certainty of reward.

☐ *Financial implications.* All strategies have financial implications and one project must be compared with another to judge investment and payback levels.

☐ *Opportunity costs.* There will always be opportunity costs involved in going for one strategy rather than another and these will have to be measured.

☐ *Time and speed.* Timing and speed may be important. There could be a need to block others, quickly build market share or support other products.

☐ *Existing marketing mix.* All marketing mix factors must be considered, including the need to maintain and develop portfolio synergy, profit margins, cost advantages, value chain relationships and promotional expertise.

☐ *Creativity, innovation and learning.* These relate to the ability of the organisation and skills of the staff to stay ahead of the competition in information and knowledge attainment, as well as use of new technology.

☐ *Core competencies giving possible competitive advantage.* Customer base and loyalty, supply chain relationships, patents, brands, knowledge and skills, etc. are core competencies to consider.

☐ *Overall company resources.* Ultimately the balance of all company resources and core competencies, physical, financial, human and informational, must be considered when matching to identified strategies.

Weight the strategic choice criteria

Many models exist to help formulate discussion and argument among senior managers when looking towards strategy analysis and choice which can be used in either B2B or B2C markets. Many organisations have customised or built their own versions so as to stimulate debate in an area that relates specifically to their own needs and wants. Basically, strategic choice participators should attempt to put some kind of importance weighted measurement (perhaps on a scale of 1 to 10) on the various internal and external factors that will contribute to the success or failure of a particular strategy. A very brief outline of the models that can be used is given here.

Criteria product and market models

An example of models that have been used will include the following:

☐ BCG 2×2 matrix

☐ General Electric (GE) matrix

☐ Shell matrix

☐ Balanced Scorecard.

BCG 2×2 matrix
The most well known to marketing students and practitioners alike is the BCG 2×2 matrix, which attempts to measure product market share against market growth, comparing one company with the competition.

General Electric (GE) matrix
This is a 3×3 matrix (Figure 9.15) that attempts to put a measure on internal factors, under the heading of 'competitive business strengths', and external factors, under the heading of 'market attractiveness':

☐ Market attractiveness is measured and weighted under criteria such as 'market growth rates', 'market size', 'competitor strength', 'sales and profit opportunities', and so on.

☐ Competitive/business asset strength is measured and weighted under criteria such as 'market share', 'customer base', 'alliances and distribution', 'access to technology', and so on.

Figure 9.15
Example of
a 3×3 matrix

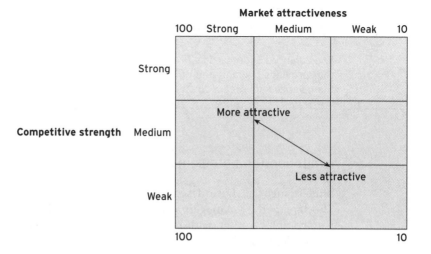

Shell matrix
Very similar to the GE matrix, the Shell matrix adopts the 3×3 matrix but uses 'prospects for sector profitability' on the horizontal axis (instead of market attractiveness) and 'enterprise's competitive capabilities' (instead of competitive/business strength) on the vertical axis.

Balanced scorecard approach
Kaplan and Norton developed the 'balanced scorecard' strategic approach to planning in the early 1990s. Recognising some of the weaknesses and vagueness of previous management approaches, the balanced scorecard suggests that we view the organisation from four perspectives and, to develop metrics, collect data and analyse it relative to each of these perspectives:

1. *Learning and growth perspective.* This highlights the importance and value of employees. An attempt should be made to measure cultural attitudes and employee coaching and training related to both individual and corporate self-improvement. In the current climate of rapid technological change, it is becoming necessary for knowledge workers to be in a continuous learning mode.

2. *Business growth perspective.* This refers to internal business processes. Metrics based on this perspective allow managers to know how well their business is running and whether its products and services conform to customer requirements.

3. *Customer perspective.* If customers are not satisfied they will eventually find other suppliers that will meet their needs. Poor performance from this perspective is thus a leading indicator of future decline, even though the current financial picture may look good.

4. *Financial perspective.* The need for timely and accurate financial data will always be a priority, but it must not be the only business driver and its usage must be 'balanced' with the need to consider the other three perspectives.

Example 9.8 **The Balanced Scorecard Institute**

The Balanced Scorecard Institute is an independent, non-profit, educational institute that provides training and guidance to assist agencies and companies in applying the balanced scorecard to strategic management (www.balancedscorecard.org).

Limitations and problems in using models

Models such as those described above should never be confused with reality. They are used by managers as way of simplifying, describing and analysing often very complex and difficult business situations, stimulating argument and debate and in doing so, hopefully, increasing participants' knowledge and understanding about some problem associated with the need for future development of products and markets. When using models, care should be taken with regard to the following points:

☐ Over-simplification – complex problems can lose meaning.

☐ Confusing the model with reality – a model will always remain a model and should never be seen as a true picture of the world.

☐ Predictive value – models cannot predict, but can only be seen as an aid to understanding. Ultimately managers will have to make decisions about the world based on experience and information from many sources.

☐ Important factors missed – the use of models will not guarantee that all marketing factors are identified and discussed.

☐ Subjective measurements – comparative measurements used, weighted or otherwise, on most business models will be subjective and can be both over- and under-generous.

> When planning, clear succinct reasons should always be given why one particular strategy has been selected and another has been rejected.

Assumption and constraints

Planning and forecasting look into the future so certain assumptions must be made and articulated about major future happenings by marketing planners to indicate awareness. If not, the whole exercise could be called into account by senior managers questioning the relative wisdom of particular strategies. Similarly, there will always be constraints that might prevent a company taking a particular strategic direction and these too should be made known within the marketing plan (Figure 9.16).

Figure 9.16
The B2B
strategic
planning
options

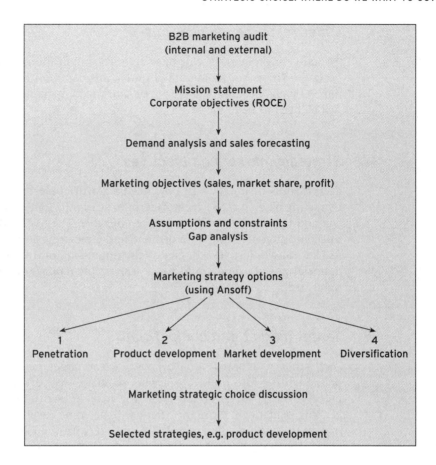

B2B marketing audit
(internal and external)

↓

Mission statement
Corporate objectives (ROCE)

↓

Demand analysis and sales forecasting

↓

Marketing objectives (sales, market share, profit)

↓

Assumptions and constraints
Gap analysis

↓

Marketing strategy options
(using Ansoff)

| 1 | 2 | 3 | 4 |
| Penetration | Product development | Market development | Diversification |

↓

Marketing strategic choice discussion

↓

Selected strategies, e.g. product development

Strategic positioning of the B2B marketing mix

Under each selected strategy, market penetration, new product development, market development and diversification, a little more information is needed about the long-term direction that should be taken with regard to the marketing mix elements (shorthand for the eight Ps). This concerns the coordinated strategy that will be adopted for the product, price, place and promotion, and can be identified as the marketing mix strategic positioning. A marketing mix strategic positioning statement will broadly outline the long-term approach to be taken with regard to the marketing mix elements. Below we have identified, in very simple terms, some of the marketing mix strategic options across the four Ps basic mix.

1. *Products/service strategy options.* Make the product better/different/cheaper.

2. *Price strategy options.* Premium/penetration/discriminatory/niche pricing.

3. *Place.* Indirect/direct/extensive/selective/partnership distribution.

4. *Promotion.* Personal selling/advertising/trade promotions/exhibitions.

All the following (as part of the eight Ps model) will also need consideration at this strategic level: people, profit, processes, physical evidence.

A marketing mix positioning strategy will need to be developed for every marketing strategy adopted by the organisation.

Other resource implications

All marketing planning will have resource implications for other areas of the business. These can be identified under this common heading; for example, if more systems need implementing or skills need upgrading, other business areas will be need to be involved.

Strategic marketing objectives

Each identified strategy will now need a SMART objective known as a strategic marketing objective (SMO) set in term of sales. All strategic marketing objectives will add up to the overall marketing objective. The SMO will need to be monitored and altered if long-term demand and forecasting circumstances dictate. Unrealistic sales objectives will give a false impression of the company's market and financial position and could cause irreversible damage when yearly results are published.

Target market and competition

Each strategy adopted should have a clear target market/organisation/buyer profile written into the strategic plan so that every participant in the planning process will be in no doubt about the make-up of the target market and the benefits demanded. Similarly there will be some level of competition in the market to be attacked and a full description, with the likely response, should be given. The plan should be systematically adjusted as customers and competition develop and change.

Strategic monitoring, feedback and control mechanism

Monitoring, feedback and control mechanisms must be added to all forms of planning, whether at the strategic or tactical levels. This is to make certain that the plan follows the course set down and achieves the desired results. At its simplest, strategic monitoring and control mechanisms would consist of weekly strategic planning meetings where open argument, discussion and debate should take place. It is worth repeating here that the strategic plan should not be seen as set in stone as it is an overall guide to future action and should be regularly adapted and changed whenever the strategic management team think necessary. All marketing environments are subject to constant change: existing markets may begin to lose sales and sales potential and new markets may start to open up. To allow for strategic planning adjustments whenever and wherever necessary, the marketing audit, both internal and external, should be conducted on a regular basis so that opportunities and threats can be anticipated and action taken to exploit the former and defend the latter. The more dynamic the market, the more intense this process will become. We will look in more detail at control mechanisms when we look at planning implementation. It is now possible to identify the whole B2B strategic planning process (Figure 9.17).

Figure 9.17
The B2B
strategic
planning
process

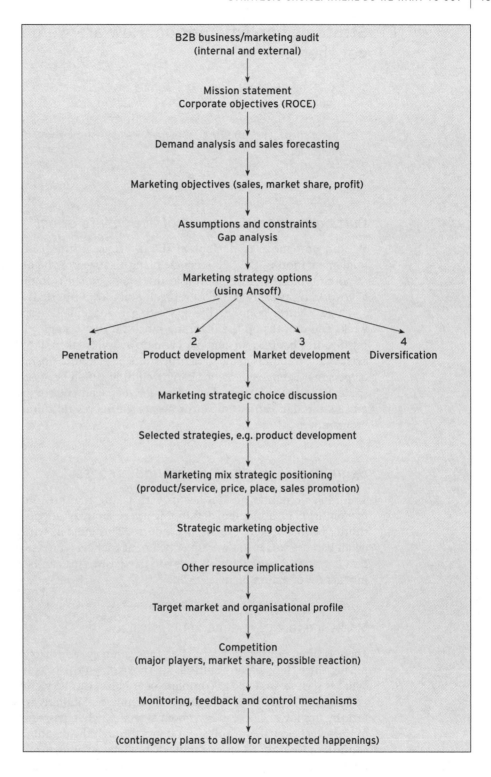

☐ Strategic implementation: How are we going to get there?

I try to keep in touch with the details – you can't keep in touch with them all, but you've got to have a feel for what's going on. I also look at the product daily. That doesn't mean you interfere, but it's important occasionally to show the ability to be involved. It shows you understand what's happening.

(Rupert Murdoch)

Putting the chosen course of action into effect

We can now move on to look at the last stage in the planning process – the implementation of the B2B strategic plan. All stages of the planning process are important, but making certain that the strategic plan is implemented and actually works is probably the most difficult and most important part.

There is little point in the marketing management team spending hours, weeks and months on the planning process if the strategic plan ends up gathering dust in a boardroom cupboard and no action is taken. Problems can still arise even as an attempt is made to put the strategic plan into operation. Departmental or personal agendas, fear of change, cultural differences across functions and strategic partnerships and lack of senior management commitment to see the process through can all impair or negate the successful running of the strategic programmes.

Beginning of the implementation process

The implementation process begins with taking the three- to five-year strategic marketing plan and then developing every strategy adopted in detail over a shorter period, usually the first six months. This must be written out in intricate detail because this is the working document that everybody within the organisation is going to work with on a day-to-day basis. This can be called the marketing tactical or action plan.

Marketing tactics and marketing strategy

There is often confusion about the terms 'strategy' and 'tactics'. This is not surprising since the meaning shifts as we move down the organisational hierarchy. What is seen as strategic at corporate board level can be viewed as tactical when given to the level below for further development. Similarly, what is seen as strategic by this lower level can be viewed as tactical when passed on for development to the level below them, and so on down through the organisation. To add to the confusion, whether a factor is strategic or tactical will depend to a certain extent on management opinion. Basically, the differences between tactics and strategy can be summed up according to the following:

- ☐ Marketing strategy is long term; marketing tactics are short term.
- ☐ Marketing strategy is a broad description of what needs to be done to achieve marketing objectives; marketing tactics show how resources are to be garnered and tailored so as to implement strategy.
- ☐ Marketing strategy gives an organising and coordinating framework providing the same direction for all company functions over the long term; marketing tactics spell out detailed action over the short term.

Difficulties associated with strategic plan implementation

The difficulties involved with the implementation of a B2B marketing plan cannot be over-emphasised. It has to be the most difficult and problematic part of the whole planning process. It is almost certain that problems will arise because of the following:

- ☐ Planning and attempting to look into the future will by its nature have a level of unpredictability.
- ☐ Making certain that all departments and divisions work together can be most difficult because of rivalry, confused and competing objectives, differences in culture and bad communications. This becomes even more of a problem when attempting to work with alliance partners.
- ☐ Poor information dispersion and communication systems.
- ☐ Inadequate skills and confused allocation of responsibilities.
- ☐ Lack of cohesive leadership and disagreements over priorities.
- ☐ Failure to have the right resources available when needed.
- ☐ Lack of adequate monitoring, feedback and control mechanisms.

Example 9.9   ## Bounded rationality

Bounded rationality is the principle that managers reduce tasks, including implementation, to a series of small steps, even though this may grossly oversimplify the situation and not be the optimal way to proceed. In this way 'things' are seen to happen and change becomes much less threatening.

Elements involved with the implementation process

We can now examine the many elements that are involved with the implementation process. It is probably artificial to make the distinction between strategic and tactical because of the interconnectedness of the two areas. Many of the factors identified and discussed here will relate to both the strategic and operational planning but this should not cause a problem as long as this is recognised. The other point to remember is the need to understand the concept of strategic thinking taking place at different levels in the company. So bearing this in mind we can proceed.

Marketing tactical objectives

The overall marketing objectives (e.g. over three years) need to be broken down into the short, medium and long term (perhaps years 1, 2 and 3 sales objectives). The short-term objective, the tactical marketing objective, is then taken and broken down into a detailed description. This is the plan to be used for the implementation and will become the working document for most employees, senior and junior managers, supervisors and individual workers.

Detailed target segment and organisational profile

The target segment will have been outlined in the strategic plan but it is at this level that more detail will be added. This will consist of such facts as the number of organisations, their size, growth rate, product benefits wanted, and even, if relevant, a description of the DMU and buying policies.

Timing

The tactical plan will be broken down into realistic and relevant time periods over the 12 months (e.g. every week) across all programme areas, detailing clearly what needs to be done by whom and by when. Rolling marketing tactics consist of taking each strategy and detailing the plan, rolling it out over the first 12 months, adding on a new month as the old month is completed and in this way moving through the three-year strategic plan.

Allocation of responsibility

Crucial to effectiveness and efficiency of the marketing planning process is the allocation of responsibility. The managers who have to implement the plan must be adequately empowered and will need to have personal and interpersonal skills in organising, garnering and allocating resources, monitoring progress, and communicating and interacting with others, both inside and outside the organisation. Staff should be assigned clear responsibilities so that everybody is aware of who is responsible for every task and no area of possible confusion exists. Coaching and training must be made available to overcome problems associated with personal and interpersonal skill deficiencies, and help and advice must be offered where lack of motivation might hinder implementation. Ideally those responsible for an area of control should play a part in the performance indicator setting and have knowledge of the broader planning picture. Every management control area should have a monitoring back-up system so that checks can be made across important areas. Care should be taken to ensure that monitoring and control structures and systems do not become too bureaucratic and inflexible, thus restricting the smooth running of the marketing programmes. The higher up the organisation, the greater will be the level and importance of the decision-making process. Ultimately there has to be a certain amount of trust if the process is going to work efficiently and effectively.

Detailed marketing mix planning

A detailed marketing mix plan for every strategy is at the heart of the strategic plan and will include the following:

☐ Marketing research plan

☐ Product/service/packaging plan

☐ Price and finance plan

☐ Place (distribution) plan

☐ Personal selling plan

☐ Promotion plan, advertising, trade promotions, exhibitions, sponsorship

☐ Internet plan.

Budgeting

All elements of the planning process, both strategic and tactical, will involve some degree of costs. To a certain extent, the sales forecast figures, the expected revenue for the year, will decide many other budgets as it will determine what needs to be spent to achieve a certain level of sales.

Methods of deciding the budget amounts

Many budget amounts will be more or less decided because of the tasks that need to be undertaken. For example, cost of sales will include such things as the purchase of raw materials, production and distribution costs and be linked directly to the projected year's revenue figure. Other budgets, however, are more speculative and the amount can be decided in different ways. For example, the advertising or marketing research budget will not be linked directly to sales and so will be decided more by managerial discussion combined with prevailing circumstances. The following methods might be used by companies in setting these types of budgets:

☐ Task and objective – ideally the most effective way of allocating budgets

☐ Same as the competitors

☐ Same as last year

☐ Same as last year with an increase for inflation

☐ What the company can afford

☐ As a percentage of sales

☐ As a percentage of profit.

The marketing control process

Monitoring and control, 'making certain that what is expected to happen, happens', are crucial to the successful running of any business, whether in the profit or not-for-profit sectors. To set goals and performance indicator targets, whether for the long or short term, and then not effectively monitor and control them is a recipe for disaster. The daily newspapers are replete with examples of organisations that have lost millions because of projects that have failed or run enormously over budget because of lack of controls. The need to set SMART objectives across the whole of the business marketing process was outlined earlier because numbers of any sort should be easier to track, but this must only be the beginning. The numbers must be constantly monitored from the top of the organisation down through all levels to the very smallest department or activity. Management must find ways of making this happen, even in cases where open and not closed objectives are used.

> We know whether improvements work because we can measure them.

Feedback, monitoring and control at different organisational levels

At the strategic level

The control process can and should be applied at any level within the organisation from the strategic down to the tactical. We discussed earlier the need for frequent evaluation on whether general B2B marketing strategies were working effectively and whether they were still appropriate with regard to market, customer and competitor changing circumstances. At this level senior managers will need to monitor every aspect of the marketing effort to be sure that optimum effort and the most efficient allocation of resources are happening. Anticipation and a certain degree of informed speculation are important at this higher level, as management decisions will have to be made about long-term strategic direction. This will inevitably take time in collecting internal and external environmental information and pulling together more or different resources and changing particular approaches. The faster the change in the market, competition and customer needs, the more that strategy might have to be altered, the greater the flexibility that will have to be built into structures and control systems. It is at this level that benchmarking activity with others can be promoted down through the organisation so that the best standards are built in and maintained. Strategic marketing control will entail feedback from all other departments as well as information from all factions of the marketing department. This will also apply across partnering companies where alliances have been constructed. Regular strategy meetings should be used to ensure discussion and argument from the strategic planning team and in this way keep the plan on course.

At the tactical level

It is just as important to know that all the individual elements in any one marketing strategy are working effectively at all levels down through the organisation. New product development, marketing research and data development, sales training, advertising, sales promotions, and so on must all be monitored and controlled for optimum effectiveness. Management might also want to compare and evaluate scarce resource allocation, say between the use of personal selling and direct response or between direct and indirect distribution.

At the operational level

The B2B tactical plan was described earlier as the breaking down of the strategic plan into intricately detailed programmes, one for each strategy, over a shortened period, perhaps six months to a year. The strategic objectives identified in the strategic plan will have been broken down into smaller performance standards, costs, sales and profit, over the six months. These performance standards become the benchmark against which actual performance is measured. If, for example, we take the forecast sales figure for the six months, this might be broken down month by month and actual sales figures compared with the budgeted sales figure. The sales figures can then be broken down into cost to sales ratios, taking into account such things as cost of materials, administration, distribution, advertising, selling, and so on. Sales analysis is an attempt to determine why actual sales varied from planned sales, then allowing corrective action to be taken. Control mechanisms should be built in at relevant points across the six-month period so that variance checks can be made between actual and planned performance indicators.

Approaches used in control

Control approaches can be broken down into financial and non-financial terms.

Financial controls

Financial controls look at costs and profits across a whole range of indicators comparing the planned budgets with the actual outcome. They will look at such things as cost of goods purchased, stocking and delivery costs, labour costs, administration costs, product and packaging costs, advertising costs, salespeople costs, etc. B2B management should also be concerned with target market and individual buyer organisation sales costs and profits, possibly breaking them down into individual product fixed and variable costs, share of market and profit contribution. Financial ratios should be used to compare efficiency and effectiveness past and present and attempts made to benchmark with the best, not only in the industry of operation but the best in other industries. Use will be made of cost and profit centres and accounting methods such as activity based costing (ABC). These were discussed in some detail in Chapter 7.

Example 9.10 **Examples of financial ratios**

☐ Sales, costs and profits, by market segment, by sales channel, by buyer organisation, by sales team and by individual salespersons.

☐ Sales, costs, contribution per sales call, costs of opening new accounts.

☐ Product portfolio sales, costs, contribution by product line, individual products.

☐ Advertising costs and effectiveness by media, promotion costs.

Non-financial controls

Non-financial controls should be implemented to cover important areas such as production and delivery times, product availability and product returns, customer satisfaction and complaints, competitor activity, and so on. Ongoing use of internal reports, marketing intelligence and marketing research should be made to help in this area.

Control methods

☐ Regular meetings, discussions, interaction, video-conferencing, appointments, feedback.

☐ Feedback deadlines in person, memo, e-mail, intranet, extranet.

☐ Financial/computerised blocking when cost reaches an agreed level.

☐ Internal and external ongoing marketing research.

☐ Clear allocation of responsibilities and person-to-person back-up checking system.

☐ Regular benchmarking.

Contingency plans

Once business marketing strategy is formulated and implemented, the B2B marketing manager must continually evaluate the target segment/individual organisation response in order to ensure that any discrepancy between planned and actual results is kept to a minimum. Of course this is easier to arrange in stable markets than in the more dynamic, but there will always be differences between what is predicted to happen in the market environment and what actually happens. It is better to be prepared than to be taken by surprise. Contingency plans allow resources to be made available to take into account changes in market circumstances. No organisation, however, can really make contingency plans for totally unexpected events such as the September 11 2001 terrorist attacks in New York. This might be where crisis management planning comes into play.

Crisis management planning

Many organisations (usually large) now have a crisis management planning programme in place so that broad management tactics and strategies to major unexpected events can be discussed and put into place. Proactive crisis management activities include forecasting potential crises (often by scenario planning) and planning how to deal with them, not in detail but in general terms. These plans are then translated into document form, outlining areas of responsibility and alternative courses of action in both the short and long term.

Example 9.11 **Perrier's crisis**

Fifteen years ago Perrier immediately withdrew millions of bottles of mineral water from stores around the world when it was revealed that there were traces of benzedrine hidden in its bubbles. This instant action, although costly, showed the company in a responsible and caring light and long-term damage was avoided – an example of crisis management planning.

Tactical planning process

☐ Marketing three years' objectives broken down into the short, medium and long term (perhaps one, two and three years' sales objectives).

☐ Marketing tactical objectives – the short term (perhaps 12 months' sales objectives).

☐ Detailed target segment and organisational profile.

☐ Competition – detailed description of the immediate competitors.

☐ Timings – important measurement milestones across the 12 months (perhaps every week).

☐ Marketing mix plans for marketing research, products and services, price and finance, distribution, sales and communications, etc.

☐ Allocating responsibilities – selecting adequately skilled staff (training where necessary) and describing individual task requirements.

☐ Budgets – allocation of expected cost amounts across the marketing mix and all areas of expenditure.

☐ Monitoring, feedback and control mechanisms – for all performance indicator measurement points at all levels, followed by a planning review.

☐ Contingency plans.

Strategic planning in a changing world

Throughout the book we have identified and discussed the internal and external factors that confront managers when attempting successfully to pilot the B2B organisation through the sometimes murky, troublesome and stormy waters, especially in international and global markets. The greatest challenge facing any organisation is the need to develop a coherent and appropriate strategy that is based on internal resources and able to take advantage of external opportunities, thus building sustainable competitive advantage. Managers have to be able to undertake this task in a series of different markets across the globe which are forever developing and changing as new competition enters, technological possibilities multiply, and customers become more demanding. Despite the fact that environments change, managers must methodically plan at both the strategic and tactical levels so that decisions can be made about future direction and resources allocation based upon sound informed judgements. It must be remembered that one company's opportunity is often another company's threat. Those with established market presence could lose significant share if they do not adjust to changing market conditions.

 To examine in detail the strategic B2B options available to an organisation go to the *B2B Marketing* website at www.booksites.net/wright.

☐ Summary

In this chapter we have taken all the elements of marketing and attempted to pull them together to show how they might be used in the B2B planning process. Marketing planning is about taking a systematic, disciplined approach in deciding the future direction of the organisation. We re-examined the concept of marketing driven management, stressing the critical importance of continual buyer and organisational satisfaction as the driving force behind strategic choice and strategic implementation. In the same vein the need for the B2B supplier constantly to collect information on the competition (both immediate and potential), assess competitive advantages, and work to gain superiority were discussed and examined and recommendations were made. The importance of marketing at both management and strategic levels was identified and an attempt made to show how this becomes the guiding force in the planning process.

We then went on to look at the planning process itself, categorising it into three areas: strategic analysis, strategic choice and strategic implementation. Strategic analysis, or 'where are we now?' is the environmental auditing process, broken down into the internal and the external environment. The external environment was discussed under the acronyms PEST and SPICC and the internal environment under the acronyms of the eight Ss and the eight Ps. The SWOT model was used in the second part of the process to collect and analyse the information for future strategic decision making.

We then moved on to look at the next stage in the planning process – strategic choice. The roles of the corporate mission statement and corporate objectives were briefly outlined and the roles of sales forecasting and gap analysis in the setting of B2B marketing objectives were examined. The Ansoff matrix strategic choice model was used to assist the process of strategic direction analysis and strategic choice. The need to produce clear marketing mix strategic positioning statements, identify target segments and relevant competition and set SMART strategic marketing objectives and control mechanisms for each selected strategy was discussed before moving on to examine the last category in the strategic planning process – strategic implementation.

All the factors that should be considered when looking at the tactical implications and implementing strategic programmes in B2B markets were then scrutinised with the reminder that strategic planning without successful implementation was a waste of time and a recipe for failure. It was shown how tactical objectives arose from short-term strategic objectives. They were broken down in detail with clear performance indicators across a designated time period, 12 months in this case. Finally, all the important areas and stages used in programming and tactical planning were identified and briefly discussed, including target organisations, immediate competition, marketing mix, day-to-day planning requirements, allocation of responsibilities, timings and budgets, and the building in of feedback monitoring and control mechanisms.

Discussion questions

1. Identify in general terms the differences between strategic and tactical planning. What are the advantages and disadvantages of strategic planning and do you think that it is necessary for all successful organisations?

2. Formal planning is said by some to be unrealistic and not the way that business managers actually look to the future. Discuss this premise and identify reasons why it may or may not be true.

3. Discuss the development of customer retention programmes. Identify and critically examine the part that computer programs might play in the process with reference to relevant websites.

4. What do you understand by the concept of market driven management? Give real examples of its use and identify when it might not be feasible.

5. How might a B2B organisation gain competitive advantage? What might be the differences, if any, between B2B and B2C in developing and maintaining competitive advantage?

6. Identify the major factors involved in the process of auditing. What criticisms might you make about the process as identified in this chapter?

7. Discuss the relationship between the company mission statement and the hierarchy of objectives identified in the B2B strategic planning process. Why must business objectives always be quantified over time?

8. Identify all the factors involved in the B2B strategic planning process. What are the differences in strategic planning between B2B and B2C markets?

9. Discuss all the factors involved with tactical planning and tactical implementation.

10. It can be forgotten that the implementation of a plan is a crucial part of the strategic planning process. Why do you think this might be and what are the many problems that might be associated with attempting to make a plan happen?

 Visit the *B2B Marketing* website at www.booksites.net/wright for a Case Study, Questions, and an Internet Exercise for this chapter.

☐ Bibliography

Books

Aaker, A. (2001) *Strategic Marketing Management.* Chichester: Wiley.

Bias, S. and Twitchell, D. (1999) *Marketing Consultancy: A Complete Guide to the Industry.* Chichester: Wiley.

Chaston, I. (1999) *New Marketing Strategies.* London: Sage.

Cunningham, M.J. (2001) *B2B, Business-to-Business: The Next Generation of e-commerce.* London: Perseus.

Dwyer, F.R. and Tanner, J.F. (2002) *Business Marketing: Connecting Strategy, Relationships and Learning,* 2nd edn. New York: McGraw-Hill.

Ferguson, P.R. and Ferguson, G.J. (2000) *Organisations – A Strategic Perspective.* London: Macmillan.

Ford, D. (1990) *Understanding Business Markets: Interaction Relationships and Networks.* London: Academic Press.

Hahin, P.W. (1991) *Business-to-Business Marketing: Strategic Resource Management and Cases.* Needham Heights. MA: Allyn & Bacon.

Haig, M. (2001) *The B2B e-commerce Handbook – How to Transform your Business-to-Business Marketing Strategy.* London: Kogan Page.

Hammer, M. (1995) *The Re-engineering Revolution: The Handbook.* New York: Harperbusiness.

Honeycutt, E., Morris, M.H. and Pitt, L.F. (2001) *Business-to-Business Marketing: A Strategic Approach,* 3rd edn. Thousand Oaks, CA: Sage.

Kaplan, R. and Norton, D. (1996) *The Balanced Scorecard.* Cambridge, MA: Harvard Business School Press.

Lambin, J.J. (2000) *Market-Driven Management: Strategic and Operational Marketing.* London: Macmillan.

Lorents, A.C. and Morgan, J.N. (1998) *Database Systems: Concepts, Management and Applications*. Fort Worth, TX: Dryder Press.

Lynch, R. (2000) *Corporate Strategy*, 2nd edn. Harlow: Pearson.

Minnett, S. (2002) *Business to Business Marketing: A Radically Different Approach for Marketers*. London: Pearson Education.

Mintzberg, H. (1994) *The Rise and Fall of Strategic Planning*. Englewood Cliffs: Prentice-Hall.

Morden, T. (1999) *An Introduction to Business Strategy*, 2nd edn. Maidenhead: McGraw-Hill.

Morris, M.H., Pitt, L.F. and Honeycutt Jr, E.D. (2001) *Business-to-Business Marketing: A Strategic Approach*, 3rd edn. London: Sage.

Peters, T. (1987) *Thriving on Chaos*. New York: Alfred Knopf.

Porter, M.E. (1980) *Competitive Strategy: Techniques for Analysing Industries and Competition*. New York: Free Press.

Powers, P.L. (1991) *Modern Business Marketing: A Strategic Planning Approach to Business and Industrial Markets*. Eagan, MN: West Publishing Company.

Rogers, M. (1983) *Diffusion of Innovation*. New York: Free Press.

Tapp, A. (2001) *Principles of Direct and Database Marketing*. London: Pearson Education.

Turnball, P.W. (1986) *Strategies for International Industrial Marketing*. Buckingham: Croom Helm.

Webster, F.E. and Wind, Y. (1972) *Organisational Buying Behaviour*. Englewood Cliffs: Prentice-Hall.

Webster, F.E. (1991) *Industrial Marketing Strategy*, 3rd edn. New York: Wiley.

Wright, R. (1999) *Marketing: Origins, Concepts, Environment*. London: Thomson.

Yovovich, B.G. (1995) *New Marketing Imperatives: Innovative Strategies for Today's Marketing Challenges*. Harlow: Prentice Hall.

Journals

Begbie, R. and Chudry, F. (2002) 'The intranet chaos matrix: a conceptual framework for designing an effective knowledge management intranet', *Journal of Database Marketing*, 9 (4): 325–38.

Bowman, B.J. (2002) 'Building knowledge management systems', *Information Systems Management*, summer: 32–40.

Donaldson, B. and Wright, G. (2001) 'Sales information systems: are they being used for more than simple mail shots?', *Journal of Database Marketing*, 9 (3): 276–84.

Goddard, J. (1997) 'The architect of core competencies', *Business Strategic Review*, 1 (1): 43–53.

Gummesson, E. (1987) 'The new marketing: developing long-term interactive relationships', *Long Range Planning*, 20 (4): 10–20.

Hitt, M.A. and Ireland, R.D. (1985) 'Corporate distinctive competencies, strategy, industry and performance', *Strategic Management Journal*, 6: 273–93.

Mckim, R. (2002) 'The differences between CRM and database marketing', *Journal of Database Marketing*, 9 (4): 371–5.

Porter, M.E. (1996) 'What is strategy?' *Harvard Business Review*, 74 (6): 61–78.

Sheth, J. (1973) 'A model of industrial buying behaviour', *Journal of Marketing*, 37: 50–6.

Slater, S.F. and Narver, J.C. (1995) 'Market orientation and the learning organisation', *Journal of Marketing*, 59: 63–75.

Webster, F.E. (1963) 'Modelling the industrial buying process', *Journal of Marketing Research*, 2 (3): 251–60.

Webster, F.E. (1992) 'The changing role of marketing in the corporation', *Journal of Marketing*, 56: 1–17.

Visit www.booksites.net/wright for the Internet references for this chapter.

10

Strategic business approaches to different and changing market conditions

The biggest joke about 'business management' is that the majority of people in business don't have business management education, while the majority of people, who have business management education, are not in business!

Aims and objectives

By the end of this chapter the student should be able to:

1. Examine and evaluate the business strengths and weaknesses that will be of importance in the future world of business-to-business marketing.

2. Examine and evaluate the strategic role that new technology and the internet will play in the development of business-to-business marketing, both now and in the future.

 To examine in detail the strategic B2B options available to an organisation go to the *B2B Marketing* website at www.booksites.net/wright.

Part 1   Future of national and international B2B marketing

It can be argued that the world changed irrevocably on September 11 2001 with the terrorist attack on the World Trade Center. Such is the impact that the USA has on world trade that any action or reaction on its part will have an enormous effect on all other markets. The USA has the largest and most technologically powerful economy in the world. With a GNP of over $10 trillion, imports of $1.5 trillion and exports of nearly $800 billion, it accounts for over a quarter of all world trade. 'When the US sneezes the rest of the world gets a cold' is a saying that might accurately reflect its effect on world trade. There is no doubt that any business which engages in international trade, at whatever level, will be affected by what happens in other parts of the world (this especially applies to what happens in the USA). Global events therefore require constant monitoring. Concomitant with this will be the need to build and maintain business strengths, both strategic and tactical, so that market reactions can be both timely and appropriate.

Figure 10.1
Fortune
500 nine
key attributes
of reputation
score industry
rank

Sources:
www.fortune.com,
Fortune, 3 March
2003

The well-respected Fortune 500 US business magazine invites speculation on America's most admired global companies by asking 10,000 of the top executives across many industries. The key attributes identified below are given a score of between 1 and 10 and then the scores are added and averaged to obtain the most admired companies. The key attributes used are interesting and enlightening.

Key attributes	Industry rank out of 10
1. Innovativeness	
2. Employee talent	
3. Use of corporate assets	
4. Social responsibility	
5. Quality of management	
6. Financial soundness	
7. Long-term investment value	
8. Quality of products/services	
9. Globalness	

☐ Business strengths

B2B organisations have to be strong to face up to future global market challenges (Figure 10.1). This applies to their internal capabilities and the suitability of their market entry strategies. The meanings of internal strengths and weaknesses have been discussed throughout the book, but it is crucial for management to appreciate the different challenges to be faced when marketing abroad and in global markets.

Strength in home markets

Research has shown that strength in home markets can be a springboard for moving abroad, as well as providing support to maintain and grow a strong presence. Access to resources of all kinds can then be utilised to enhance strategic direction as required. Problems in the home market can soon percolate into foreign markets and force a company to retrench in some way so as to move resources back into the original base market. Marks & Spencer is an example of a company forced to sell off most of its foreign businesses because it ignored detrimental changes in its home markets.

Example 10.1 | **China's airline industry merges for strength**

China's nine biggest airlines are to merge and shares in Air China, the flagship international carrier, will be listed on international stock markets. The airlines will be consolidated into three major new international players, Air China, China Southern Airlines and China Eastern Airlines. This will give the industry the strength to compete with major airlines around the world. The carriers will control about 80 per cent of the domestic market and almost all international routes flying out from China.

Figure 10.2
Top ten global companies by turnover, 2001

Source:
www.fortune.com

	($million)
1. Wal-Mart Stores	219,812.0
2. Exxon Mobil	191,581.0
3. General Motors	177,260.0
4. BP	174,218.0
5. Ford Motors	162,412.0
6. Enron	138,718.0
7. Daimler Chrysler	136,897.3
8. Royal Dutch/Shell Group	135,211.0
9. General Electric	125,913.0
10. Toyota Motors	120,814.4

(revenue figures reflect sales and purchases in both B2B and B2C markets)

Niche and mass global market strengths

As with home markets, the smaller B2B player will still be able to market specialised goods and services abroad to smaller niche markets. The increased need for effectiveness, efficiency and economy compels buying organisations to become more demanding in the specification of products and services they buy from other organisations. This is forcing business suppliers constantly to upgrade and customise benefit offerings and problem solutions, thus allowing market opportunities to the smaller company able to dedicate itself to innovation and development in one focused area of business. In some cases the very large company can make use of technology to build a mass customised product but there will still be parts of the business where this will not be possible or cost effective.

Mass market strengths

The major players in the global markets are companies such as Exxon Mobil, Ford, Shell and General Electric, each with an annual turnover larger than half the countries of the world (Figure 10.2). Although total earnings in 2001 for Fortune's Global 500 companies were less than half those of 2000 and 297 companies saw profits fall, future global revenue figures are expected to continue to rise long term, with these world behemoths expected to grow ever larger and more dominant. (The terrorist attack in New York on September 11 and a world teetering on the edge of recession, rather than any long-term endemic problem, seem to have caused the downturn.)

A turnover of anything between $10 billion and $200 billion will continue to open up mass market opportunities to these major players in growth markets such as China, Brazil and Indonesia which would not be possible for lesser companies. Enormous spending power, economies of scale, political influence, and so on should enable large companies to build on market growth strategies, as well as opening new markets unavailable to the smaller players.

Partnership for strength

We discussed in an earlier chapter the importance of working with other companies in some sort of partnership across the world to open up markets, build market share and restrict the activities of the competition. This is expected to continue. Even some of the largest companies are finding it advantageous to work with others in sharing risks and resources as well as knowledge and expertise. For the smaller company or niche player it still might be the only way to grow and improve market share. Partnerships are also expected to grow between companies not in direct competition with one another where mutual benefits are apparent. This will cover such areas as purchasing, information sharing, benchmarking, distribution and customer sharing.

Partnership with governments

Although governments have pulled out of direct involvement with many companies, either by privatisation or by reducing and eliminating subsidies to increase competition, it would be naive to believe that under certain circumstances they will not continue to get involved in the future. Although member countries vote to improve internal trading bloc anti-competitive laws, there will always be circumstances where national interests outweigh the interests of the many. On occasions, the government in one country may still provide subsidies to protect industries or large companies against competition which is threatening to overwhelm from another country. Many of the large global companies and industries are now too important to the national well-being in terms of jobs, income and prestige to let them go out of business. So despite the commitment to free trade, governments will continue to subsidise in some sort of way. For example, Airbus Industries, the aeroplane manufacturer, competes against the American giant Boeing for commercial jetliner sales. Airbus was started with capital supplied by several European governments and continues to enjoy financial support. Despite being the bastion of capitalism and free markets, the USA continues to impose import tariffs and quotas on products and services it feels threaten home industries and companies. This will not change in the future.

Example 10.2 **Competition between countries**

President Bush risked provoking a trade war with Europe when he imposed tariffs of up to 30 per cent on steel imports despite a last-minute appeal by the EU not to damage EU and US relationships. He argued that it was to stop the illegal subsidised dumping of steel exports from both the EU and Far East. Outraged by US steel tariffs, which threaten the EU with £1.5 billion annual losses, the European Commission is almost certain to vote for levies on US airlines in Europe and for a restriction of their landing rights. US carriers had benefited from a £10 billion government rescue package since the terrorist attacks on September 11, allowing them to slash fares on transatlantic routes.

Networking for strength

Many companies find it profitable to talk to one another in an informal way, sharing information and knowledge on a networking basis. This interaction is bound to increase as communications become so much easier around the world.

It makes sense for strategic managers in non-competitive industries to talk and share experiences about strategies and systems, helping one another on a reciprocal basis. Many senior managers from the Fortune 500 top companies talk and meet on a regular basis to discuss issues such as benchmarking, value chain relationships and global market change.

☐ Market challenges and future of global and business markets

There are many challenges facing the B2B organisations operating in international markets as we move through the first decade of the twenty-first century. Successful businesses will have to be constantly looking for better and cleaner ways of working, in terms of both offering buyer choice and value and how they conduct their market activity. Many of these challenges have been discussed and alluded to throughout the book and some of the major issues can be highlighted here.

International market growth

Ignoring short-term economic recession, many business home markets are either not growing or only growing at a relatively slow rate. Long-term economic growth in modern western economies is averaging about 2 per cent a year. In many other countries around the world, however, economic growth is much larger and set to grow at higher rates well into the future. Not only are there huge expected growth rates, but the size of the potential market in some of these countries is enormous. Managers know that they must be in these markets if their companies are to remain serious global players.

China has a population of nearly 1.3 billion (ten times that of Japan) and expected growth rates of 8 per cent. Brazil has a population over 270 million with expected growth rates of over 4 per cent. Indonesia has a population of nearly 230 million with expected growth rates of nearly 5 per cent. Of course some exporting industries and companies will be more welcome than others. Global companies such as IBM, Shell, GE and Microsoft are already in and carving out market share. China, to take the most important example, is slowly opening up its markets to imports from around the world and has shown real commitment to the concept of free trade across most industries by joining the WTO in 2001.

European Union growth

The European Union is set for more expansion with applications from 13 countries. Cyprus, Czech Republic, Estonia, Hungary, Latvia, Lithuania, Malta, Poland, Slovakia and Slovenia are expected to become members some time in 2004, with Bulgaria, Romania and Turkey following. There are approximately 376 million people living in the EU member countries, of which Germany has the largest population. Some 170 million people live in the 13 candidate countries. Turkey is the largest with a population of 64 million, and Malta is the smallest with a population of 380,000. Eventually there could be a market of some 446 million people, offering enormous expansion possibilities. There will be hundreds of industries and hundreds of thousands of organisations all competing in one barrier-free market.

Breaking down world trade barriers

Although many countries find new ways to protect their industries against foreign competition with barriers that hinder or exclude sales of products and services, there is no doubt that the spirit of free trade is driving world economic and political agendas. Although the USA may voice concerns about importers selling below cost or receiving subsidies and dumping steel on their markets and the EU threatens retaliation if trade barriers are erected against EU industries, under the auspices of the WTO, the movement for free trade travels inexorably forward. International cooperation and legislation are forcing industries and companies to face up to competition and the need to become increasingly more productive and customer driven.

☐ Environmental concerns

The realisation that economic activity is damaging the earth and its resources has pressurised politicians and governments around the world into taking some kind of action to try to repair and prevent any more damage that could cause suffering to both present and future populations. Legislation has been enacted, with much more to follow, to prevent environmental abuse by business organisations. Huge fines and even imprisonment can be imposed on senior managers who ignore or attempt to circumvent environmental rules and regulations. Consumers are also now aware of these concerns and seem increasingly vociferous in condemning errant organisations, with some even refusing to buy products and services.

Most if not all large corporations now have codes of conduct and ethical values statements that clearly set out how they intend to operate with regard to concern for the environment. The companies state that they have taken this approach because they are responsible corporate citizens, while the more cynical might argue that it is because of fear of bad publicity and boycott actions that customers might take against organisations that fail to conform (Figure 10.3).

Many of the policies being adopted by business organisations could restrict the scope of marketing activity and ways of working, causing higher costs and lower levels of productivity. The creative and innovative company could avoid such negative effects and even gain competitive advantage through improvements in its ways of working. All business functions will be affected including production,

Figure 10.3
Environmental
concern issues

| ☐ Genetic engineering or genetic modification of food |
| ☐ Depletion of ozone layer |
| ☐ Climate change leading to flooding, droughts and unstable weather patterns |
| ☐ Depletion of natural resources on land, sea and air |
| ☐ Damage to ecosystems |
| ☐ Long-term health problems |

processes, distribution, transport, packaging, promotion, advertising, and so on. If all companies conform, however, the playing field will be level and the environment safeguarded.

Example 10.3 **Recycling programme**

All electrical goods sold in Europe after 2005 will have to be recycled at the manufacturer's expense after a vote in the European parliament yesterday. Under the new legislation, householders will not be allowed to throw away unwanted electrical goods but will have to sort them out ready for collection and recycling. The legislation will cover TVs, washing machines, stereos, computers, mobile phones, vacuum cleaners, hairdryers or anything considered electrical or electronic. Legislation requiring old cars and fridges to be recycled already exists. The cost of collection, dismantling and recycling will be borne by manufacturers but they are expected to pass it on to consumers. Authorities say prices for electrical goods are likely to rise by up to 5 per cent. Green groups are delighted with the new rules and believe they will force manufacturers to design more environmentally friendly products.

Pressure group activity

There is no doubt that the growth in information technology and use of the internet have encouraged the activities of many different pressure groups around the world. Individuals are able to talk to one another, disseminate ideas and formulate aggressive strategies against organisations they feel are acting irresponsibly and mistreating both people and the environment. Such is the power of some groups that they are able to muster hundreds of thousands of activists to protest on the streets or outside premises, boycott goods and services, synchronise complaints, stage publicity-seeking events, and so on. Successes in the past, such as Greenpeace forcing Shell to reconsider sinking an oil platform in the North Sea, have made even the largest of the multinationals wary of creating situations that could cause pressure group attention, leading to bad publicity and customer boycott (Figure 10.4).

Figure 10.4
Pressure
groups

> ☐ **Anti-globalisation groups** bring thousands onto the streets to protest at the meetings of the WTO, IMF, World Bank and G7
> ☐ **Human Rights Watch** (HRW) challenges governments worldwide to end abusive practices and support human rights laws (www.hrw.org)
> ☐ **Liberty** works to promote human rights and protect civil liberties through a combination of test case litigation, lobbying, campaigning and research (www.liberty-human-rights.org.uk)
> ☐ **Greenpeace International** fights on environmental issues (www.greenpeace.org)
> ☐ **National Society for Clean Air and Environmental Protection** - self-explanatory (www.nsca.org.uk)
> ☐ **Corporate Watch** is a non-profit organisation which holds the corporate world accountable for its actions from economic and ethical perspectives (www.corporatewatch.org.uk)
> ☐ **Human Genetics Alert** is concerned about the ethical side of this technological revolution (www.hgalert.org)

Global terrorism

Global terrorism continues to pose a clear and present danger to the international community and no business can afford to be complacent about its effects. The effects of the attack on the Twin Towers in New York on September 11 2001 are still reverberating around the world. Any country or company can be considered vulnerable to an attack of some kind leading to possible loss of life, destruction of property and heavy costs. Industries such as travel, tourism and insurance are particularly susceptible and businesses need to have contingency measures in place for any such attack. As well as the loss of revenue, a huge rise in the cost of insurance cover for war and terrorism risks could result in heavy losses and even ruin of some businesses operating in areas such as the airline and tourism industries.

Increased litigation

National and supranational governments are increasingly bringing in new laws, rules and regulations about how organisations must conduct their operations. Individuals, groups and organisations are now much more likely to resort to legislation to overcome a problem they may have with a business. Increased knowledge and easy access to lawyers, often with a 'no pay-out, no fee' clause, encourages all to take this kind of action when a wrongdoing is perceived. Miscreant organisations can now expect customers, communities, employees, regulators and governments around the world to take legal action to recover damages, sometime running into millions of pounds, for actions considered inappropriate or wrong. This might be because of the harmful effect of products and services being sold, the way a company operates in a market or the manner in which employees are treated. Global organisations must be aware of the possible local legislative differences which, coupled with language and geographical barriers, can lead to expensive and protracted problems. Below we have identified some of the key issues, discussed throughout the book, that relate to the future of business markets.

Key issues in the future of business marketing

- ☐ Integrating marketing in all departments, divisions and functions of the organisations with total strategic commitment from the CEO downwards.
- ☐ Training and developing employees at all levels across all divisions to put concern for the business customer, as well as ethically acceptable ways of working, at the very centre of all activity.
- ☐ Making certain that up-to-date, relevant information on customers, markets and environments around the world is readily available to all employees for decision making at both strategic and tactical levels on a continuous basis.
- ☐ Streamline business strategies. Lean strategies provide efficiencies to save costs and increase profits. Take stock of what is measured and why. All measurements should be aligned with business strategies.
- ☐ Constant seeking out of new markets and new customer benefit solutions wanted.

☐ Giving every buyer customised products and services that offer benefit solutions to individual problems across mass markets, with built-in controls that constantly monitor and measure satisfaction levels and new demands.

☐ Optimising the use of technology in an innovative and customer-driven manner in all areas of the business, including manufacturing, communications, delivery, servicing, information collection and dispersion as well as bringing all relevant stakeholders into the process.

☐ Forming mutually beneficial partnerships and alliances across all areas of the business.

Part 2 Use of technology in the growth and maintenance of business strength

Nobody doubts the importance of technology to the success or otherwise of the business organisation, whether in B2B or B2C markets. Although we have talked about the growth of technology and its use across all business activities throughout the book, such has been its dramatic and awesome growth over the last decade that it must have the final word in the discussion on the future of global marketing. No area of the business can fail to benefit from clearly thought out application in researching and building B2B problem-solving products and services and customer satisfaction.

☐ Business-to-business and new technology

Research has shown that the number of organisations in a country that are active in a technology may indicate that country's ability to innovate and its potential for innovative activity. It also associates clusters of innovation with higher rates of innovation, productivity growth, and new business formation. If customers are to be won and held and competitive advantage sustained, senior management must understand and be totally committed to innovation and the application of advanced technology to increase the effectiveness of business relationships between trading partners. This is particularly true in B2B markets where technology must be continually updated to meet the knowledgeable needs of buying organisations. Professional buyers are aware that if their own company, as well as suppliers, cannot upgrade to the latest technology, competitive advantage will be lost along the whole supply chain. Governments and pressure groups are increasingly strident about products and services that use up scarce resources and ways of working that cause harm to the environment. New technology is important across all business operations from ordering, inventory management, innovation, design and production through to warehousing, distribution and customer service. We see its marketing application in factories and offices, management, production, engineering, transport, packing, research, advertising and promotions as well as in innovative products and services.

Example 10.4 **Intelligent product**

Cars already come equipped with navigation systems, but soon they will become smarter in other ways. Computers will diagnose problems with the car and send information about the car's performance back to the factory. Home appliance manufacturers will begin adding intelligence to washers, dryers and refrigerators. It will allow the history of the product to be monitored, faults immediately diagnosed and even let the user call home and make sure that the cooker has been turned off. Radio chips in supermarket products will allow shopping trolleys to be scanned as they move through the checkout without taking the goods out. Pervasive computing means that every device, every appliance, everything we have including the things we wear is going to have computer capability.

Leading edge technologies

New or leading edge technologies (not without controversy in some areas) are emerging across a whole range of industries and offering the innovative company almost unlimited opportunities. The US Bureau of Census has classified the following areas for exporting and importing purposes:

1. *Biotechnology.* The medical and industrial application of advanced genetic research to the creation of drugs, hormones, and other therapeutic items for both agricultural and human uses.

2. *Life science technologies.* The application of non-biological scientific advances to medicine. For example, advances such as nuclear magnetic resonance imaging, echocardiography and novel chemistry, coupled with new drug manufacturing, have led to new products that help control or eradicate disease.

3. *Opto-electronics.* The development of electronics and electronic components that emit or detect light, including optical scanners, optical disk players, solar cells, photosensitive semiconductors and laser printers.

4. *Nanotechnology.* The ability to create materials from building blocks smaller than atoms will unleash unprecedented capabilities. Cars and aeroplanes, chemicals and plastics, computers and chips, cosmetics and drugs – all of these industries and plenty more are facing upheavals that could make the advent of the internet seem like a minor adjustment. Pocket-sized supercomputers, material one hundred times stronger than steel but a sixth of the weight, 1000 miles to a gallon of fuel, car batteries the size of small torch batteries are only some of the opportunities.

5. *Information and communications.* The development of products that process increasing amounts of information in shorter periods of time, including fax machines, telephone switching apparatus, radar apparatus, communications satellites, central processing units and peripheral units such as disk drives, control units, modems, and computer software. We will look in more detail at this area below.

6. *Electronics.* The development of electronic components (other than opto-electronic components), including integrated circuits, multilayer printed circuit boards and surface-mounted components, such as capacitors and

resistors, that result in improved performance and capacity and, in many cases, reduced size.

7. *Flexible manufacturing.* The development of products for industrial automation, including robots, numerically controlled machine tools and automated guided vehicles, that permit greater flexibility in the manufacturing process and reduce human intervention.

8. *Advanced materials.* The development of materials, including semiconductor materials, optical fibre cable and videodisks, that enhance the application of other advanced technologies.

9. *Aerospace.* The development of aircraft technologies such as most new military and civil aeroplanes, helicopters, spacecraft (with the exception of communication satellites), turbojet aircraft engines, flight simulators and automatic pilots.

10. *Weapons.* The development of technologies with military applications, including guided missiles, bombs, torpedoes, mines, missile and rocket launchers, and some firearms.

11. *Nuclear technology.* The development of nuclear production apparatus, including nuclear reactors and parts, isotopic separation equipment and fuel cartridges.

Example 10.5 Hydrogen fuel cells

Honda cars using the highly promising hydrogen fuel cell system will be introduced in Los Angeles later this year as part of a test campaign. Honda is one of the major auto manufacturers currently vying for a mass market commercial launch for the technology in the next two to three years. Five models will initially be used in LA in the year-long trial, with a further 25 to be added at a later stage. The development is a result of the California Fuel Cell Partnership, which brings together manufacturers, fuel suppliers and government authorities. Other companies involved in the scheme include Ford, Nissan, VW, ExxonMobil and the US Environmental Protection Agency. Fuel cells are regarded as zero-emission, and widespread use will reduce inner city air pollution levels. Infrastructure for consumer refuelling is widely seen as the main barrier to a fast-track introduction of the technology, therefore closer relationships with vehicle manufacturers, fuel producers and local authorities. (www.greenconsumerguide.com)

Example 10.6 Human Genome Project

The Human Genome Project has generated huge amounts of information on genes and gene fragments. In 2000, the US Patent and Trademark Office (PTO) issued about 2000 patents on full-length genes for all species. The patentability of genes and gene sequences in the USA is based on the 1980 Supreme Court decision *Diamond* v. *Chakrabarty*, which ruled that genetically engineered living organisms could be patented. This decision was followed by internal actions by PTO in the mid-1980s that extended patentability to plants and non-human animals. (United States Bureau of Census - www.nsf.gov/sbe/srs/)

Managing the technological transfer process

Technology transfer can be defined as the successful advancement of a technology through the development chain from research to commercial application in the home or overseas market. Ultimately the measure of success of any development is its commercial uptake. Technology platforms support product platforms, which in turn support families of new products. All technology development needs to have some market awareness. The market drivers strengthen the closer one gets to the commercial application stage.

High-tech products are developed from technologies, whether internally developed or externally acquired. The responsibility of technology management is to identify opportunities for applying new technologies and to fully develop the technology inputs that will form the foundations of new products. The technology management process thus incorporates technology assessment and selection, technology development and/or acquisition, technology transfer from research to development and from development to manufacturing, and the periodic review and upgrading of key underlying technologies, all of which are vital to effective product development and product life cycle management.

The degree of risk in developing a new product is determined by the riskiest indispensable element. If that element is a piece of core technology, the risk can be enormous. Despite this fact, companies routinely launch product development projects without having all the necessary technological underpinnings in place. Organisations can become so fixated on rushing new products to market, in fact, that they end up trying to fold technology development activities into the product development process, leaving product development teams scavenging for missing pieces of technology or improvising their way around immature technology elements. Formal strategies and processes for selecting, incorporating, and managing the right technologies for a company's product and market ambitions should be discussed, agreed and implemented.

Communications, information and web technology

Nowhere is the technological revolution more apparent and widespread than in the world of information and web technology. Manufacturing and services companies alike are under tremendous pressure to reduce overheads, speed production and improve flexibility. Increasing competition and globalisation of operations continue to fuel this trend. No wonder business organisations throughout Europe have implemented business-to-business systems to enhance business efficiency. Today information technology is being deployed to help manufacturers minimise expenditure on raw materials, match output to orders and deliver on time. Service industries must offer customised benefits at ever-lower costs and both sectors must adapt quickly to changes in customer demand. Perhaps nowhere is the impact so great as in the area of supply chain management. Integration with supplier systems helps ensure that the raw materials are available when needed, which in turn enables manufacturers to meet customer requirements and satisfy demand without ending up with unwanted goods. Even transportation can be managed and controlled more efficiently when integrated with back office and manufacturing production systems. Below are examples of how web technology has revolutionised the working practices of some nationally and internationally known B2B organisations.

Example 10.7 ## Intel and Barclays Bank

Barclays and Intel have worked together to build a web-based enterprise-wide risk management system capable of monitoring credit exposure across all of its accounts worldwide. It now has a system that enables the production of management reports on global risk exposure, analytic simulation of over 30,000 economic scenarios multiple times a day, and the provision of on demand recalculations for 'what if' analysis.

Example 10.8 ## Philips – information technology and manufacturing

Manufacturing companies such as Philips are under tremendous pressure to reduce overhead, speed production, and improve flexibility. Increasing competition and the globalisation of operations continue to fuel this trend. No wonder manufacturers throughout Europe have implemented business-to-business systems to enhance business efficiency. Today, information technology is being deployed to help manufacturers minimise expenditure on raw materials, match output to orders, and adapt quickly to changes in customer demand. Perhaps nowhere is the impact so great as in the area of supply chain management. Integration with supplier systems helps ensure that the raw materials are available when needed, which in turn enables manufacturers to meet customer requirements and satisfy demand without ending up with unwanted goods. Even transportation can be managed and controlled more efficiently when it is integrated with back office and manufacturing production systems. (www.philips.com)

Example 10.9 ## Audi – design development

☐ Virtual car crashes for Audi can be performed using powerful computers enabling an increasing number of more lifelike simulations for increased vehicle safety and reduced costs.

☐ Faster time-to-market with new, safer well-designed cheaper cars lead to increased customer satisfaction and loyalty. (www.audi.com)

Example 10.10 ## Xerox – Supply chain management strategy

Xerox, the office equipment and software manufacturer, has embraced the internet with open arms and now offers a B2B comprehensive internet channel strategy for its markets and different categories of resellers around the world that delivers numerous benefits. It has put its complete product portfolio catalogue on line and its customers can now customise needed benefits, immediately obtain prices, order the finished product and then follow delivery, online, from factory through to buyer premises. It also offers training, promotions and personalised e-mails or faxes regularly to notify resellers of new information and programmes. Payment can be made online. It has a customer web-based follow-up, monitoring and control system reporting and forecasting on such things as customer satisfaction and future sales demand. The one internet site offers the same consistent customised service, whether the buyer is in Hong Kong or New York, all within a safe, secure environment. (www.xerox.com)

☐ Internet uses in both B2B and B2C markets

The world wide web and use of the internet now permeate every corner of every business activity. Even the most fervent technophobe must now be aware of its many uses, if not actually using it in day-today operation of his or her job. It is used extensively in both B2B and B2C markets, with organisations operating through both their own websites and those of others. A successful e-enterprise is an entity that blends the traditional assets of a bricks-and-mortar company with the speed and agility of net commerce. 'Click-and-mortar' enterprises combine net business models to create a new kind of organisation. E-enterprises will also combine business-to-consumer and business-to-business initiatives with a fluidity that defies all past experience. These uses can be discussed under the following headings (TIMES):

1. Transactions
2. Information
3. Marketing
4. Entertainment
5. Selling and buying.

1. Transactions

Both B2B and B2C organisations now use the internet extensively for transactions of all kinds. The ability to talk to others in any part of the world, in 'real' time, has opened up mind-boggling opportunities, especially for B2B businesses of all kinds. Information can be exchanged, product complexity reduced, deals negotiated and finalised, payments and settlements made, views exchanged and advice given. Documents, invoices, contracts, scripts, videos and music can be downloaded in an instant and immediate decisions made. Tax and VAT payments can be discussed with government departments and payments made. Architects, engineers, scientists, accountants, lawyers, marketers and advert creators can discuss projects and swap and build on ideas, saving enormous amounts of time and costs in the process. Surgeons talking and offering advice and using miniature cameras can perform medical operations many thousand miles apart. Overall this should reduce transaction costs. Encryption and decryption software is getting better all the time, building security firewalls to protect sensitive business activity. Private networks allow transactions to be made between partners using such processes as EDI. User detailers can be sent and downloaded and goods and services for delivery around the world can be tracked and monitored every step of the way from source through to arrival by suppliers and buyers alike. A third party processor/agency/outsourcer can be hired to undertake many of the tasks identified here, including sending out bills and collecting payments on behalf of a company using their own e-commerce infrastructure. The buying and selling of goods and services is the biggest area and this is discussed in more detail below.

2. Information

Never has so much information been available to so many at the click of a mouse. In Chapter 3 we examined the many research sources now available. B2B firms can obtain industry and market information from governments, trade associations and commercial companies, either free or for an agreed fee. Access to partner suppliers' and buyers' information systems can be negotiated and information obtained on product component parts, services and finished products as well as new products and processes in the pipeline. Daily, weekly or monthly e-bulletins can be issued to keep all concerned employees and customers up to date. Vast databases can be developed to inform on customer preferences, purchases, costs and profits. Intranets can be used to keep all employees informed about every relative company development. B2B businesses can buy into media services that will customise and send almost anything online, including news, health, travel, legal information, training courses, company and industry information, and so on.

3. Marketing

The internet is used heavily by both B2B and B2C in all the following marketing areas.

Marketing research and market testing

The internet is used for marketing research in B2B and B2C business areas at local, national and international levels. Both quantitative and qualitative research can be undertaken. It is an easy and simple way of obtaining rich information, particularly in B2B where decision-makers can be targeted by name and company. Research seems to indicate that click-through response rates for permission based market research in B2B campaigns are about 5 per cent but can reach as high as 20 per cent. Opt-in, permission-based e-mails are people who have specifically requested information within their area of particular interest.

Advertising

After a healthy start advertising revenues for both business areas have faltered and in some cases fallen because of the uncertainty in measuring results and an economic downturn. Companies can advertise corporate and brand awareness both on their own site and on the sites of others. Although seen in B2B, advertising is mainly used in B2C markets. Internet advertising should be planned and strategically integrated with all forms of traditional communications. Traditional advertising can be used to drive buyers to a website.

Sales promotions

We know that sales promotions offer extra value over a short period and are used in B2B marketing to get potential buyers to respond to e-mails or to get them to delve deeper into a company website. A recent study by Harte-Hanks Technology found that B2B sales promotion e-mails had response rates of between 2 per cent and 10 per cent.

Sponsorship

Sponsorship is often confused with advertising. A sponsoring organisation will want their company or products to be deeply associated with the values of the company it is sponsoring. Perhaps a mention all through the site should be made, including sales promotional tie-ups and merchandising material.

Sales and selling

Sales and selling are discussed in more detail below under a separate heading.

Website and tracking

All marketing on the web should be measured and controlled to judge value for money. Each individual promotional campaign must be tracked to establish response rate. Each target market can be assigned a unique URL for that individual list, category, offering or message. Each 'unique' user entering the site from a targeted campaign will be tracked and analysed to determine the best response rate and return on investment.

4. Entertainment

As would be expected the use of the entertainment medium is heavy in B2C markets and light to non-existent in the B2B. Individual and interactive games, music, films, chat rooms, etc. are growth areas and, because consumers spend large amounts of time on a site, a great way to both advertise and sell products.

5. Selling and buying

The web is heavily used to sell both B2B and B2C products and services. Although early interest centred on the growth of retailing on the internet, forecasts are that B2B revenue will continue to exceed B2C revenue into the future. According to studies published in early 2000, the money volume of B2B already exceeds that of 'e-tailing' by ten to one. Over the next five years B2B is expected to have a compound annual growth of 41 per cent. The Gartner Group estimates B2B revenue worldwide to be $7.29 trillion by 2004.

In B2C conventional retail sites as well as auction sites are growing (and closing down) week by week, selling everything from cars and carpets to alcohol and groceries. Their uses are slowly growing as consumers and business buyers become confident about credit card transactions, and security increases. In theory anything can be bought and sold on a retail site, including groceries, clothes, cars, cosmetics, holidays and transport. B2B markets are similar in choice although products and services can be both bought and sold either in a straightforward manner or by a bidding process. Organisations also join together to reap the benefit of economies of scale. Brokering sites act as an intermediary between someone wanting a product or service and potential providers. Equipment leasing is an example. It has opened the opportunity for even small firms to purchase component parts from around the world, which would have been practically impossible in the past, particularly in specialised areas. The ability to put a whole catalogue of parts online is a real bonus for suppliers and buyers alike, saving both costs and time for all participants. Buyers can be given constant access through virtual private networks (extranet), allowing new product updates to be shown and customised benefits instantly communicated.

Net B2B market

The term 'net markets' is used generically to describe all online marketplaces where buyers and sellers congregate to exchange goods and services for money. One descriptive term that has been widely adopted is butterfly market or butterfly hub. Imagine that one wing of the butterfly is made up of buyers and the other made up of sellers; where they meet – the body of the butterfly – makes up the hub. There are a number of other markets, including the following:

1. *Horizontal markets* cut across many industries, typically providing a common service such as financial services, benefits management and MRO (maintenance, repair and operating) equipment procurement process management. Popular examples are Ariba Network and Commerce One's MarketSite.net.

2. *Vertical markets* concentrate on one specific industry such as agriculture and chemicals and seek to provide all the services needed by that industry. Popular examples are VerticalNet, Chemconnect and Covisint.

3. *Buy-centric markets* exist where a few big buyers join forces to build a marketplace where small fragmented sellers can sell their goods. This is great for buyers since it permits quick and easy price comparison shopping.

4. *Sell-centric markets* are markets where one or a few big sellers work together to build a marketplace for many small fragmented buyers. Typically revenues are derived from ads, commissions on sales, or fees for delivering qualified leads to suppliers. Examples are GlobalFoodExchange.com, E2Open.com and TradeOut.com.

5. *Neutral exchanges* appear where both the sellers and buyers are fragmented. In this environment, a third party creates a neutral exchange and performs the transactions through a bid/ask system. The middleman will receive a cut or transaction fee for each deal.

Web-based enabling technologies

The ability to conduct business-to-business electronically has been around for years, but the industry has recently experienced an explosion of web-based applications and technologies to automate B2B over the internet. Search engines allow customers to find what they are looking for on the site. Streaming media video clips can be used to illustrate content and syndicated content providers can be used to provide interesting and relevant news and stories to ensure that customers return to the site.

Security and encryption software allow secure transactions over the web while virtual private networks or private marketplaces enable approved suppliers to bid on a large buyer's business or permit more cost-effective transactions under negotiated terms. Personalisation and analytics applications remember users, provide personalised experiences, and decrease transaction times. Analytics help site owners analyse past activity on the site in order to uncover crucial aspects of visitors' activities. It is easier on B2B sites than on B2C to identify users as most of the big organisations have their own dedicated servers. On B2C sites, individuals come through one of the major commercial servers such as Freeserve. Wireless logistic mobile commerce (M-commerce) is the next frontier for B2B, building the tools and infrastructure to stay constantly in touch with customers and employees through wireless devices such as cellphones and personal digital assistants. Benefits from using web technology include:

☐ Fully customised products and services.

☐ Creativity, innovation and design.

☐ Instant customer monitoring and feedback.

☐ Shortened buying cycles.

☐ Market research, market sensing, scenario planning.

☐ Economic demand and sales forecasting.

☐ Reduced time from conception through to market.

☐ Online catalogues, design facilities, product service display, ordering, payment and settlement.

☐ Buying, selling, exchange and bartering opportunities.

☐ Procurement including strategy, sourcing, purchasing, inventory control, etc.

☐ Auctions: one seller, many buyers; reverse auctions – many sellers, one buyer.

☐ Promotion campaign management, electronic newsletters and product updates.

☐ Transactions and record keeping.

☐ Workflow tracking on multi-party projects.

☐ Customer and market risk analysis.

☐ Printed material elimination.

☐ Reduced process and delivery costs.

☐ Logistics, distribution, storage, monitoring and control facilities.

☐ Competitive bidding to cut costs.

☐ Up-to-date, relevant information on customers and markets.

☐ Access to world markets.

☐ New ways of supply chain working such as auction sites, EPOS, EDI, co-managed inventory, CADCAM, cross-docking, MRM, CRM, ERP and wireless technology.

☐ Internal and external communications improvements including the intranet/extranet, e-mail, videoconferencing and WAP phones.

☐ Information gathering and dispersion – access to databases around the world.

☐ Coaching and training opportunities.

☐ Home office working, reducing office costs and improving flexibility.

☐ Strategic options on internet applications

Organisations might use the internet for the following strategic applications.

Information only

A company information website can be used to tell people about the company and its products and services, perhaps being seen as a 24-hour mini trade exhibition. Sometimes a company website serves as the entrance to an exclusive extranet available only to customers or registered site users. These may be simple or very complex. Other sources cite the web's use as an information tool by customers who later make purchases in the so-called bricks-and-mortar stores.

Sell products and services

A company might choose to use the web to sell products and services. This might be all products, with detailed selection options, or an appropriate selection.

Customer services

Many B2B products and services require extensive after-sales service in terms of help, advice and add-on products and services. For example, an interactive in-depth informational website could be used to show buyers the component parts needed for service or repair, explicit product or service diagrams, new upgrades and recommendations for changes to current models, as well as the ability to discuss problems online. An extranet (private site over the internet), which allows customers or clients to do transactions electronically that otherwise might require telephone calls or paper transactions, can now be used as a part of the process.

Export

The corporate website can be used as a relatively inexpensive way of exporting products or services, either as a stand-alone business or as a way of inexpensively entering a market. More traditional ways could then be used if demand was seen to be high enough.

Subsume into existing business

The internet can be subsumed into the existing business and be used as an extra option or channel. In this way a greater service can be offered to the customer. Some products might be offered for sale or information might be given on the website and then the buyer invited to visit the supplier or offered a visit by the company's representative.

Set up as a separate business

There is the option to set up the internet as a separate business aimed at a different target market, even using a different corporate brand name. Some companies see this as the best way forward, either setting up a web company from scratch or buying a promising organisation already trading. This may be for the following reasons:

☐ The management feels that the market and/or the buyer is different and so demands a unique strategic approach.

☐ The internet business has the potential to pirate business from the parent company.

On the downside this approach can lead to duplication of infrastructure and investment and thus be very costly. The new company will have to be built up from scratch and not be able to take advantage of the economies of scale associated with an already well-known overall corporate image and a single focused business approach. Since launching in October 1998, Egg has established itself as one of the UK's most recognised names in internet financial services. Its customer base now exceeds one million customers. Egg is owned by the Prudential.

Mixed systems (clicks and mortar)

Many companies are learning to combine the advantages of high-tech e-commerce with traditional service and distribution techniques through an integrated 'clicks and mortar' approach. Companies large and small have used the web in this way and examples include Schwab Investments, Circuit City, Toys 'R' Us and Barnes and Nobel. These are just a few of the retail and service businesses that have entered cyberspace. Even big car-makers are carving out a niche, with both General Motors and Ford forming alliances with Sun Microsystems and Microsoft respectively.

Switch fully onto the web

The best option may be to fully switch to the internet as the method of undertaking the business, but this would of course depend on the particular business and its suitability for this channel of communication. Although the set-up costs could be extremely high, the advantages come through concentrating all resources on the one business strategy. Amazon and Dell computers are examples of companies that market and sell products and services only on a website basis.

Ignore and revitalise the existing business

During the explosion of interest in developing websites during the 1990s many firms were driven to adopt web strategies more through the fear of losing out than in strategically thinking through the whole process. When the furore died down, many companies reassessed, and decided that perhaps this was not the best way to move the company forward. Other companies deliberately chose to ignore the internet, using the threat of this business model to update and revitalise the existing strategic approach to business.

Move offshore

Goods and service producers have used offshore resources for many years because they are able to build the same high quality products or offer better services for less. Because web technology can be utilised in any part of the world, depending on the skills and resources available, many businesses are now transferring part or the whole business process to other countries and either managing it themselves or, as is more usual, outsourcing to a specialist company.

The B2B internet model

The use of web technology as an integrated part of the business is still relatively new and strategic success or otherwise still open to usage, speculation and the movement of time. Some business models have already, quite dramatically failed; others are limping along and others seem for the moment to be successful. Some products, services and types of markets lend themselves to its use while others do not. Similarly some organisations have chosen to adopt one strategic approach while others in the same business have chosen different strategies. Organisations around the world lost many billions of pounds in the headlong rush not to be caught out and miss the boat. Things have now settled down and a more professional, calm and calculated appraisal of the internet's strategic and tactical advantages and disadvantages for B2B activity is now taking place. Senior managers will not and cannot spend money like water on half-baked and ill-thought-through internet ideas because large amounts are no longer available. Having said this, however, the world of marketing will never be the same since the web's inception and to be successful organisations will need to be constantly searching for increasingly innovative ways of using its awesome power.

Example 10.11 **E-commerce**

According to a report released this week by Forrester Research, the vast majority of US corporations will move aggressively to e-commerce in the next two years, drawn by emerging 'e-marketplaces' where goods are sold through auctions, bid systems and exchanges. The study of several reports on business-to-business (B2B) e-commerce issued recently by major US research firms predicts that US B2B sales will reach $2.7 trillion in 2004, as e-commerce evolves from one-on-one transactions to larger marketplaces that facilitate multiple buyers and sellers.

☐ Summary

Under the heading of business strengths we looked at the many areas that might constitute success when operating in foreign markets. This included using strength in the home market as a springboard, niche and mass global market strength, partnerships between other commercial organisations as well as governments and finally networking for strength. We then went on to study the market challenges and the future of global and business markets. International market growth, EU growth, the breaking down of world trade barriers, environmental concerns, pressure group activity, global terrorism and increased litigation were all identified as issues and challenges that business marketers will increasingly have to address.

Because of its enormous importance and quite phenomenal growth, the use of technology in the expansion and maintenance of business strength was deliberately left to the last section. Examples were given of areas of new technology that will increasingly confront many organisations as they attempt to sell their products and services around the world. A brief description was given of the management problems this will cause. Last but by no means least, the role that communications, information and web technology now play in the success of B2B marketing, and will play into the future, was examined. Under the acronym TIMES, its uses in both B2B and B2C were compared and examples given of how some companies are taking advantage of this phenomenally innovative medium to gain competitive advantage. The benefits to be had from web-based enabling technologies were briefly delineated before outlining the options open to B2B organisations when choosing the strategic approach to take when deciding their internet strategy.

Discussion questions (in conjunction with website)

1. Examine the different strategies that might be used by a B2B supplier in its existing markets. Give examples of how each identified strategy might be used.

2. Discuss the different problems that might face a B2C exporter compared to a B2B exporter. How might a direct or indirect approach be taken?

3. Identify and discuss the many B2B strategic methods that might be used for market entry into foreign countries. What might be the best method for a medium-sized company manufacturing specialised computer components?

4. What are the reasons that might force a company to consider selling its products in overseas markets? Evaluate the problems compared with staying in the home market.

5. Discuss the premise 'the downstream activities are more important than upstream activities along the supply chain'. What are the particular problems associated with international value chain management?

6. It has been argued that customers around the world are becoming more homogeneous in their needs. Discuss whether you feel that there is any truth in this assertion. Would your conclusions apply equally to both B2B and B2C markets?

7. Evaluate the differences between an adaptive strategy compared with a standardised strategic approach to every market. Give examples of the use of each strategy.

8. Discuss the assertion that 'there will never be real free trade around the world because ultimately governments are more concerned about national issues than they are about world issues'.

9. How might B2B suppliers deal with unexpected world events? Is it possible to make contingency plans to take into account such things as world economic disasters and terrorist attacks?

10. Discuss global business-to-business marketing and speculate on what you think the future might hold. What part will web technology and the internet play in this development?

 Visit the *B2B Marketing* website at www.booksites.net/wright for a Case Study, Questions, and an Internet Exercise for this chapter.

☐ Bibliography

Books

Badaracco, Joseph L. Jr. (1991) *The Knowledge Link: How Firms Compete Through Strategic Alliances*. Boston: Harvard Business School Press.

Brandenburger, A. and Nalebuff, B. (1996) *Co-opetition*. New York: Currency/Doubleday.

Bresnahan, T.F. (2001) 'Prospects for an information technology-led productivity surge'. Paper presented at the Innovation Policy and the Economy Conference, National Bureau of Economic Research, Washington, DC, 17 April.

Child, J. and Faulkner, D. (1998) *Strategies of Co-operation: Managing Alliances, Networks and Joint Ventures*. New York: Oxford University Press.

European Commission (1994) *The European Report on Science and Technology Indicators 1994*. Brussels: European Commission.

Franko, L.G. (1971) *Joint Venture Survival in Multinational Corporations*. New York: Praeger.

Hamel, G. and Prahalad, C.K. (1994) *Competing for the Future*. Boston: Harvard Business School Press.

Kanter, R.M. (1995) *Thriving Locally in the Global Economy*. New York: Simon & Schuster.

Lindgreen, L. (1996) *The World of B2B Marketing*. Harmondsworth: Penguin.

Lynch, R. (2000) *Corporate Strategy*, 2nd edn. Harlow: Pearson Education.

Minett, S. (2002) *B2B Marketing: A Radically Different Approach for Business-to-Business Marketers*. Harlow: Pearson Education.

Mintzberg, H., Ahlstrund, B. and Lambel, J. (1998) *Strategy Safari*. Harlow: Pearson Education.

Morden, T. (1999) *An Introduction to Business Strategy*, 2nd edn. Maidenhead: McGraw-Hill.

Ohmae, K. (1999) *The Borderless World*. New York: Harper.

Porter, M.E. (1990) *The Competitive Advantage of Nations*. New York: Free Press.

Rangan, V.K., Shapiro, B.P. and Moriarty, R.T. (1995) *Business Marketing Strategy: Concepts and Applications*. Chicago: Irwin.

Roessner, J.D., Porter, A.L., Newman, N. and Xu, H. (1997) *1996 Indicators of Technology-Based Competitiveness of Nations, Summary Report*. Atlanta: Georgia Institute of Technology.

Seybold, P.B. and Marshak, R.T. (1998) *Customer.com. How to Create a Profitable Business for the Internet and Beyond*. New York: Random House.

Tennant, H.R. (2000) *Effective e-Strategies. The Themes and Strategy at Work on the Web.* Dallas: Stanbury Press.

Turnball, P.W. (1986) *Strategies for International Industrial Marketing.* Buckingham: Croom Helm.

World Bank (1996) *World Development Report 1996.* New York: Oxford University Press.

Wright, R. (2001) *Marketing: Origins, Concepts, Environment.* London: Thomson.

Yovovich, B.G. (1995) *New Marketing Imperatives: Innovative Strategies for Today's Marketing Challenges.* Harlow: Pearson Education.

Zeithaml, V.A. and Bitner, M.J. (1996) *Services Marketing.* New York: McGraw-Hill.

Zemke, R. and Schaaf, D. (1989) *The Service Edge: 101 Companies that Profit from Customer Care.* New York: New American Library.

Journals

Achrol, R.S. and Kotler, P. (1999) 'Marketing in the network economy', *Journal of Marketing,* 63 (special issue): 146–63.

Berry, L.L. and Yadav, M.S. (1996) 'Capture and communicate value in the pricing of services', *Sloan Management Review,* 37(4): 41–52.

Dannenberg, M. and Kellner, D. (1998) 'The bank of tomorrow with today's technology', *International Journal of Bank Marketing,* 16(2): 8–16.

Day, G.S. (1981) 'The product life cycle: analysis and application issues', *Journal of Marketing,* 45: 60–70.

Harrigan, K.R. (1988) 'Strategic alliances and partner asymmetrics', in F.J. Contractor and P. Lorange (eds) *Cooperative Strategies in International Business.* Lexington: Lexington Press.

Hasek, G. (1997) 'Missing links: extranets act as bridge for online business relationships', *Industry Week,* 3 March: 57–60.

Hit, M.A. and Ireland, R.D. (1985) 'Corporate distinctive competencies, strategy, industry and performance', *Strategic Management Journal,* 6: 273–93.

Kalafatis, S. (2000) 'Buyer–seller relationships along channels of distribution', *Industrial Marketing Management,* 31: 215–28.

Moriarty, R.W. and Moran, U. (1990) 'Managing hybrid marketing systems', *Harvard Business Review,* November–December: 146–55.

Naude, P., Holland, C. and Sudbury, M. (2000) 'The benefits of IT-based supply chains – strategic or operational?', *Journal of Business-to-Business Marketing,* 7: 45–67.

Pender, L. and Madden, J. (2000) 'Business grapples with how to take a relationship online', *PC Week,* 28 February: 1–2.

Pitt, L., Berthon, P. and Berthon, J. (1999) 'Changing channels: the impact of the internet on distribution strategy', *Business Horizons,* 42(2): 19–34.

Quinn, C. (1999) 'How leading edge companies are marketing, selling and fulfilling over the internet', *Journal of Interactive Marketing,* 13: 39–50.

Stewart, A. (2000) 'Insider track; diverging routes to the on-line buyer's heart', *Financial Times,* 15 March.

Swartz, B. (2000) 'E-Business: new distribution models coming to a site near you', *Transportation and Distribution,* 4(2): 3–4.

Tucker, D. and Jones, L. (2000) 'Leveraging the power of the internet for optimal supplier sourcing', *International Journal of Physical Distribution and Logistics Management,* 30: 255–67.

Visit www.booksites.net/wright for the Internet references for this chapter.

Note: **emboldened** pages indicate major treatments of topics. **Most** references are to *business-to-business marketing*, which is omitted as a qualifier.